PERSUASIVE
COMMUNICATION

PERSUASIVE COMMUNICATION

Fifth Edition

ERWIN P. BETTINGHAUS
Michigan State University

MICHAEL J. CODY
University of Southern California

HARCOURT BRACE COLLEGE PUBLISHERS

*Fort Worth   Philadelphia   San Diego   New York   Orlando   Austin
San Antonio   Toronto   Montreal   London   Sydney   Tokyo*

PUBLISHER	*Ted Buchholz*
ACQUISITIONS EDITOR	*Barbara J. C. Rosenberg*
DEVELOPMENTAL EDITOR	*Cathlynn Richard*
PROJECT EDITOR	*Laura J. Hanna*
PRODUCTION MANAGER	*J. Montgomery Shaw*
ART DIRECTOR	*Nick Welch*
PICTURE DEVELOPMENT EDITOR	*Annette Coolidge*

ADDRESS EDITORIAL CORRESPONDENCE TO:
Harcourt Brace College Publishers, 301 Commerce Street, Suite 3700,
Fort Worth, TX 76102

ADDRESS ORDERS TO:
Harcourt Brace & Company, 6277 Sea Harbor Drive, Orlando, FL 32887
1-800-782-4479, or 1-800-433-0001 (in Florida)

Library of Congress Catalog Card Number: 93-77630

Printed in the United States of America

ISBN: 0-03-055352-0

3456789012 016 987654321

PREFACE

"Read my lips, no new taxes!" "I swear to you that if I am elected your President, I will never lie to you." "The Surgeon General's warning: Cigarette Smoke Contains Carbon Monoxide." "Not only does this car look wonderful and drive well, but it is rated the third safest car in America and ranked No. 1 in resale value for the last three years." These are all persuasive messages. And although there are differences between them, they are all designed to produce some change in the receiver. Some persuasive messages ask us to change what we *believe*, others to change how we *feel* about something, and still others to change how we *behave*. What we eat, what we wear, what music we listen to, and what car we buy are all affected by persuasive communication. Persuasion is so pervasive in daily life that we often fail to recognize it. We tune out commercials and notice them only when something catches our eye or ear, causing advertisers, marketers, and political strategists to use even more sophisticated ways of getting our attention.

Persuasive messages are inescapable. From the video you rented last weekend to the airplanes' aerial advertisements overhead at the beach last Sunday; from appeals at work to donate to United Way and appeals at church to give money to the poor, to the sales pitch by the car salesperson, and the Girl Scouts at the mall, we are bombarded by persuasive messages.

There are many reasons to study persuasive communication. We all want to be successful, to be recognized and promoted, to sell more goods or services, and so forth. To be effective at work and in life, we need to know as much as possible about the persuasion process. How are attitudes formed and changed? What types of receivers are most susceptible to emotional appeals, to image-oriented ads, or to product-quality ads? When is it important to be an expert, a celebrity, a physically attractive speaker, or a "likable" one? How do you use language in order to persuade? How do you use nonverbal communication in order to persuade? What should you do to be effective in bargaining? In an organization? Each of these questions and many others will be addressed in the following chapters.

This book is organized into three major sections: I. Fundamental Theories of Attitude Change; II. Components of Persuasion; and III. Contexts for Persuasion. In Part I, we introduce what is meant by a "theory" of attitude change and talk about how attitudes are learned, reinforced, and/or "conditioned" (Chapter 2). We also discuss "motivational theories"—theories that deal with the *need for consistency* in the beliefs we hold. We do not hold beliefs and attitudes in isolation; when we change some beliefs (or attitudes), other beliefs (or attitudes) also change.

In Chapter 3, two popular theories of attitude change are introduced. "Message Learning Theory," which dates to World War II, deals with making persuasive messages that catch the receiver's *attention* and are easily *comprehended*, that provide incentives for the receiver to yield to the speaker's conclusion, and in which information is easy to retain. The "Elaboration Likelihood Model" argues that receivers listen to and think about messages differently when they are either highly involved with a topic or find the topic personally relevant.

Chapter 4 focuses attention on theories—reasoned action and attribution—that discuss how receivers make decisions. The goal of all three chapters on theory is to illustrate fundamental ways of viewing *why* and *how* people are persuaded by messages. No single theory deals with long-term effects of persuasion. A solid understanding of persuasion requires that the reader know all the theories discussed in Chapters 2 through 4.

Part II contains five chapters, each focusing on a significant aspect of the influence process. Chapter 5, which is concerned with the message makers, presents the various sources persuasion experts study—the expert, the attractive person, those similar to the receiver in some manner, the celebrity, the "opinion leader," the person in a power position, and the charismatic leader. Each type of speaker has an important role in some persuasion setting. Chapters 6 and 7 are devoted to those who receive messages. Chapter 6 deals with personality and Chapter 7 with such demographic variables as age, gender, and ethnicity.

Chapter 8 deals with questions as to how the message is constructed. What language should be used? How should the message be organized? What visual aids should be used? How should photographs be employed? Should the speaker use emotional appeals such as fear, humor, warmth, or nostalgia? Chapter 9 looks at the major issues of nonverbal communication and speaker credibility as well as identification of deception and a number of important topics related to gesturing, communicating emotions, speaking fluently, and the like.

Part III examines the use and effectiveness of persuasive messages in five important areas of everyday life. Chapter 10 discusses the world of "compliance" and reviews the various reasons that receivers agree to donate time, money, and blood, to sign petitions, and so forth. Chapter 11 is devoted to questions dealing with effective bargaining; and Chapter 12 focuses exclusively on persuasion inside the organization—managerial influence, political strategies, and the importance of communication networks, for example. The last two chapters deal with how the media are used, often in conjunction with interpersonal channels, to change "social" behavior. Chapter 13 demonstrates how campaigns work to change and improve health behavior. Chapter 14 discusses the fact that "educational" shows (traditionally the domain of public education channels) are merging with "entertainment" shows to alter the role of women and minorities in society, to encourage safe sex, to encourage organ donations, and to tackle other social problems.

ACKNOWLEDGMENTS

Many of our students and friends have helped us write and rewrite this book over the years. Most importantly, we benefitted tremendously from wonderful teachers and colleagues at Michigan State University over several decades: G. R. Miller, in Communication, and Bill Crano, in Psychology (now at the University of Arizona).

A number of graduate and undergraduate students at the University of Southern California provided suggestions or feedback while the book was underway. Most importantly, Dr. Colleen Keough reworked Chapter 11, Persuasion in Conflict Management; she completely updated the material from our old "Bargaining and Negotiating" chapter, adding considerable new research findings along with journalistic stories about everyday negotiations. Further, Dr. Stephen R.

Phillips, now at the University of Montana, revised our version of Chapter 12, Persuasion in the Formal Organization, and added material on political tactics and other recent advances in organizational behavior. We also want to thank Diane and Jerry Burns, Dr. Lynn Miller, David Braaten (now at the American Graduate School of International Management in Arizona), Bill Brown (now at Regent University in Virginia), Jeff Robinson, Risa Dickson (now at Cal State University-San Bernadino), Valerie Manusov (now at the University of Washington), and Dan Canary (now at Ohio University). We also want to thank Elva Veliz and Dan O'Hair (at Texas Tech University) for comments on chapters. Thanks also go to a number of USC undergraduates for their help: David Tunnel, George Lyons, Jennifer Lively, Joel Miller, Jodi Wolf, Jason Faries, Jeny Esagian, Carrie Mikhar and to Bruce and Simone Friedman. And a special thanks goes to Julia J. Cody for being so patient.

At Michigan State University, we must single out Mrs. Cindy Greenwood for her efforts in preparing the final manuscript. In order to meet all of our deadlines, Cindy frequently had to take work home. Mrs. Barbara Haslem made it possible for Erv Bettinghaus to have time to get this book done. And Cay Bettinghaus deserves a special thanks for being willing to endure the book-writing process so many times over the years.

The following individuals gave us valuable suggestions during various stages of development of the manuscript: Barbara Bearden, Lane Community College; Karen Bacus, Purdue University-Calumet; Terry M. Perkins, Eastern Illinois University; Hal Eitteman, Penn State University; Frank Venturo, Western State College; and Joan E. Aitken, University of Missouri-Kansas City.

Thanks also go to the staff at Harcourt Brace College Publishers: Barbara Rosenberg, acquisitions editor; Cathlynn Richard, developmental editor; Laura Hanna, project editor; Annette Coolidge, picture development editor; Monty Shaw, production manager; and Nick Welch, art director.

CONTENTS

PART
one

FUNDAMENTAL THEORIES OF ATTITUDE CHANGE

CHAPTER 1

PERSUASION AND COMMUNICATION

O U T L I N E

We begin our discussion of persuasion with a basic issue: by defining what, exactly, we mean by the term "persuasion." We will then discuss four fundamental concerns: (1) What are the effects, or consequences, of persuasive communication? (2) How should we conceive the persuasive communication situation? (3) How is the effectiveness of persuasive messages judged? and (4) Why does it sometimes appear that attitudes do not seem to impact on, or to predict, behaviors? We will conclude this chapter with a discussion of a number of concerns dealing with ethics and persuasion.

COMMUNICATION AND PERSUASION

What is Communication? What is "Persuasion"?

Many attempts have been made to define human communication. At the simplest level communication exists whenever one person transmits a message that is received and acted upon by another individual. When a teacher walks into a room and says "Hello!" to a student who looks up and smiles, the teacher is engaging in a simple form of communication. S/he is acting as a source

of communication, using symbols or stimuli that have shared meanings for individuals, as a message to be delivered or passed along some channel, to someone who is a receiver of communication.

These four elements—source, message, channel, and receiver—are present in every communication situation. These are modeled as the basic communication model in Figure 1.1. A source has an idea, puts the idea into words, perhaps organizing visual aids and the like, and transmits that message through a channel (a live presentation, a videotaped presentation, a print message, or a mass media message) to a receiver. Receivers, it is hoped, will react in some positive way. For example, the receiver may nod agreement, laugh or smile, applaud at the end of the speech, and sign a petition or offer assistance in a campaign. Of course, the feedback can be negative if the receivers politely applaud and quickly leave the building, or actually boo or heckle the speaker. However, when using the mass media, feedback to the source may take days, weeks, or months.

As situations become more complicated, the basic elements remain, although we may have more than one source, more than one receiver,

THE SOURCE-MESSAGE-CHANNEL-RECEIVER MODEL

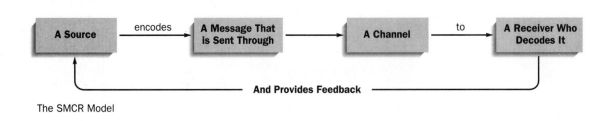

The SMCR Model

many messages spread out over time, and several different channels being used. As communication situations become increasingly complex, the models we must derive to explain those situations also become more complex. Such elaborations have been provided by Berlo,[1] Gerbner,[2] Schramm,[3] Westley and McLean[4] and Shannon and Weaver.[5]

Persuasion always involves communication. To highlight the difference between "a communication situation" and "a persuasive communication situation," let us contrast two situations: The first is the one we used above, where a teacher walks into a room, and says "Hello" to a student. For the second situation, imagine that same teacher walking into a room and saying, "Will you go to the photocopy room for me?" The student in the first situation looks up and smiles. In the second, the student looks up and says, "Of course. How many copies do you need?" In both situations, there is a source of communication and a receiver of communication. In both situations, there is a message being transmitted, and the use of an oral channel to transmit the message. In both situations, the receiver makes a response to the message. The major difference lies in the intent of the source. The first situation is one in which the source does not expect any specific reaction from the receiver. The second, however, is one in which the source hopes that the receiver will respond in a particular way to the message. The intent of the source was to influence a specific behavior of the receiver.

There is general agreement that the concept of intention is what distinguishes persuasive communication from other communication situations. *The Random House Dictionary* states that persuasion implies ". . . influencing someone's thoughts or actions."[6] Over the years, communication scholars have offered a number of different, yet similar, definitions.

Andersen, for example, says that "Persuasion is a communication process in which the communicator seeks to elicit a desired response."[7]

Scheidel, in writing about persuasive speaking, says that it is " . . . that activity in which speaker and listener are conjoined and in which the speaker consciously attempts to influence the behavior of the listener by transmitting audible and visible symbolic cues."[8] Bostrom defines persuasion as " . . . communicative behavior that has as its purpose the changing, modification, or shaping of the responses (attitudes or behavior) of the receivers."[9]

Each of these definitions emphasizes that persuasion involves a conscious effort at influencing the thoughts or actions of a receiver. Any message might have an effect on the behavior of any recipient of the message, whether the effect was intended or not. For example, you might overhear someone saying to another, "That movie is one of the best I've ever seen. It is an absolute must." Although the message was not intended for you, you might well decide to see the movie as a result of hearing the remark. We do not wish to label such situations as persuasive situations, even though the outcome affected your behavior. The argument has sometimes been made that since the effects of persuasive communication are frequently impossible to distinguish from outcomes of other communication situations, the insistence on intent as a necessary condition of persuasion makes little sense. We argue that it is necessary to preserve intent because we wish to include ethics of persuasion as an essential part of the process. Obviously, if we do not include the concept of intent in our definition, then we run the risk of having *every* communication viewed as persuasive communication. Further, if persuasion cannot be distinguished from any other communication events, especially accidental ones, it is impossible to urge would-be persuaders to adopt some standard of ethical behavior in the messages they create.

This book, therefore, is concerned with those situations in which people deliberately produce messages designed to elicit specific attitudes or behaviors on the part of receivers. As a minimal condition, to be labeled as persuasive, a communication situation must involve a conscious attempt by one individual or group to change the attitudes, beliefs, or behavior of another individual or group of individuals through the transmission of some message.

Having adopted this definition, we want to compare it with similar and related terms you will be hearing about: "information campaign," "compliance," "propaganda," and "mass media effects." An "information campaign" seeks to change *beliefs* receivers hold about a topic, but the campaign does not *directly* focus on changing attitudes or behaviors. Sometimes you will pick up a newspaper or a pamphlet and the only purpose of the material you read is to *inform* you. The source of the material doesn't draw any conclusion for you nor does it make a recommendation concerning the course of action you should take. It does not try to change your *feelings* about something.

The Surgeon General started to place cigarette warning labels on packages and print advertisements in the 1960s. The intent was to inform the public of potential negative consequences of smoking. The original message stated that cigarette smoking "may" be a cause of cancer. In the last 10 years, however, the word "may" has been deleted and a number of direct statements are made concerning the negative consequences of smoking (smoking results in low birth weight; smoking is a contributing factor in emphysema; smoke contains carbon monoxide, and so forth). This is a way of disseminating information about the negative effects of smoking. Eventually, people become aware of all the negative consequences associated with smoking. Stronger messages could be used, but stronger messages make the smoker defensive and more resistant. We say more about information campaigns in Chapter 13.

By "compliance" we mean that an individual agrees to change an overt behavior.[10] An individual *complies* to a request when s/he agrees to give us a ride to the airport, agrees to give blood, agrees

to help clean up the beach on Saturday, to give money to a heart fund, or to contribute to an alumni association. A typical compliance request usually involves only asking for a behavioral response, and the request takes only a brief period of time at the mall, on a street corner, at the airport, over the phone, or at work. Rather than change beliefs concerning a number of facts about the heart fund, multiple sclerosis, or the Girl Scouts of America, the compliance request relies on existing beliefs about obligation, feelings of commitment, norms about what others are doing, and so forth, in order to prompt the receiver to say "yes." Chapter 10 is devoted to the topic of gaining compliance from others.

The term "propaganda" is used to refer to an attempt by one individual or agency to change the view of others *in order to further one's own cause or damage an opposing one.*[11] Usually, propaganda promotes a particular ideology. A "liberal press," a "right-wing bias," a "pro-life distortion campaign," a "pro-choice propaganda piece" are some of the attempts to label another group's persuasion campaign as propaganda. Propaganda is used to bias information, withhold information that harms one's own view, teach nonfactual information as true information, or used to make an opinion appear as fact.[12] Propaganda that misleads, misrepresents or attempts to influence others through hidden and indirect methods is unethical (see below).[13]

Finally, sociologists have studied "mass media effects" from television, radio, and movies for years. The number of examples of "modeling" or "imitating" the behavior viewed in the media are endless—from children poking each other in the eyes after watching the Three Stooges, to swinging on ropes after watching Tarzan. How African Americans, women, Hispanic Americans, and others were portrayed in the media over decades certainly influenced attitudes and beliefs, and certainly represents "mass media effects." However, not all "mass media effects" involve "persuasive communication." We have adopted the definition that persuasion is a *conscious attempt to change a receiver's attitudes, beliefs, and behaviors*, and this definition of "conscious attempt" excludes many of the shows and movies geared to primarily *entertain* viewers. However, given our definition, persuasion does occur in films and in television when a company pays a film company money to have their products (that is, sunglasses, beer, cigarettes, chips, guns) visibly shown, with the intention of influencing filmgoers' attitudes and buying behaviors. There has been a growing attempt over the last several years to use entertainment programming in order to promote, *intentionally,* improved images of minorities, equality of the sexes, and the like (See Chapter 14).

The Effects of Persuasion

THE IMPORTANCE OF ATTITUDES AND BELIEFS

The ultimate goal of persuasive communication is to change a receiver's *behavior* (that is, to recycle, rideshare, buy a car, give money). But changing a behavior is usually a very difficult task, more difficult than changing attitudes or beliefs. Some behaviors are *habits*, such as smoking, drinking coffee, and related matters of consumption. Changing behaviors such as these require a number of different messages concerning a wide variety of different beliefs and attitudes.

Other behaviors are routinized, meaning that people buy and do the same thing each week (often without much thought). For example, research claims that our shopping patterns in a store are routine and nearly mindless, as we loyally or routinely buy the same brands of toothpaste, cookies, potato chips, and lunch supplies. To influence routine behaviors the persuader wants to promote brand switching; the proposed product is new, improved, lasts longer, and is better than other products. It is also advisable to link the products to emotions; happiness, fun, enjoyment, satisfaction, nostalgia. For example, after repeatedly showing

that cookies made by the Keebler elves are fun and delicious, a consumer (it is hoped) will switch from his/her usual brand to a new Keebler cookie; that at some future date, the consumer will stand in the cookie aisle and say, "Hey, let's try these Keebler fudge elves! Something different for a change."

Other behaviors are only infrequently engaged in: we buy a car perhaps every four or five years; a new lawnmower every five or six years; a new refrigerator, washer, or dryer every six to nine years. Here, once again, messages focus on both the attitudes and the beliefs of the consumer. For example, the use of mild humor (the snoring Maytag repairperson) or something cute that catches our eye (the beagle asleep on his lap), prompts attention (as opposed to switching channels), but at the same time the series of ads reinforces the important belief: Maytags are well made. Later, when a washer breaks down, consumers may consider shopping for a Maytag.

So, a good deal of persuasion is designed to change a receiver's beliefs and attitudes. *Beliefs* are the information that a person has about other people, objects or issues. Beliefs express the relationships we see between two or more events, or people; or the relationships between events and the characteristics of those events. Everyone possesses a number of beliefs about automobiles, universities, religion, political parties, and so on. Concerning cars, for example, our beliefs link our car to specific characteristics:

—This Chrysler is a reliable car.

—This Chrysler gets a pretty fair gas mileage on the freeway, given how I drive. The gas mileage is better than my old Ford, and about the same as the Volvo.

—The car insurance I pay for this Chrysler is average for what people pay in Los Angeles, far less than what people pay for a Jaguar, BMW, Mercedes, or Honda Accord.

—Statistics indicate that this Chrysler ranks low in the number of cars reported stolen in Los Angeles County.

—The local Chrysler dealership here is dependable and reputable.

—The top on this Chrysler is easy to put up and down.

—The back seat of this Chrysler convertible is larger and roomier than the back seats of other convertibles I've seen.

—I spend less on maintenance for this Chrysler than I did on my Ford or my Volvo.

—The Chrysler Corporation of America mails me letters and questionnaires every several months. No other company did that. I believe they value me as a customer.

Given this list of beliefs (and many others we won't bother to list), it is easy to see that this owner likes the Chrysler.

The term "attitude" means our likes and dislikes. An attitude reflects a predisposition to respond in a certain way—we spend more time with people and things we like and avoid people and things we do not like. Most scholars hold that attitudes are in fact the preeminent concept in persuasion, and that there are several reasons for this.[14] First, attitudes are believed to reflect strong emotions and feelings toward both well-liked objects (such as, french fries, milkshakes, pasta salads, cheesecakes) as well as disliked objects (liver, squid, beef tongue). By "strong emotions and feelings" we mean that the receiver reacts physiologically—showing emotions in the face, heart rate, skin response and in other physiological ways. There is a considerable difference, for example, in intensely held beliefs ("I am 100 percent convinced that this Chrysler convertible offers more overall advantages for the price than any other convertible.") and intensely held attitudes ("I simply love driving home in the evening to my beach community with the top down, with the stars and moon out, the wind and cool breeze blowing overhead."). Strongly held attitudes are more likely to involve physiological aspects of happiness, excitement, and so forth. Such strong emotions are related to behavior.

Attitudes are useful because one's attitude can subsume many beliefs about a topic or issue. As we just saw, a large number of beliefs support and reinforce holding a positive attitude toward the convertible. Our example concerning the convertible is a very "rational" approach. Often, we will first have an attitudinal reaction ("I like that blue Miata over there! That's great!"), and as we continue to search for a car to buy, we can list the benefits about the Miata that would support buying the Miata: it is smaller and would be easy to park; such a car would impress friends; and the power it has is a good feature to have when passing on the freeway. Zajonc and his colleagues,[15] in fact, not only argue that there is "affective primacy" (we like things first, and then give thought about the object), but go so far as to claim that we can have an attitude toward an object without ever thinking about the object. For example, objects we are frequently exposed to become familiar and likable, but we may never stop and think, "I like that painting" (in our grandparents' living room), or "I like that person" (referring to someone you saw in the cafeteria every noon hour for the last six months). While some people debate the question of "Which came first, the attitude or the belief?" few would dispute: (a) the concept of "attitude" is central to our study of persuasion, and (b) the majority of research in persuasion, in politics, in advertising, and in marketing deal with changing both attitudes and beliefs in order to promote a change in overt behavior.

Besides (a) representing our emotional and affective states; (b) reflecting a predisposition toward, or away from, objects; and (c) summarizing many specific beliefs; attitudes are also *socially important*. If a friend attempts to set you up on a blind date, you are likely to ask, "What is s/he like, and what does s/he like to do?" It isn't likely that you'll say, "What are his/her beliefs?" We get to know others and we are known by others on the basis of our attitudes. Suppose you are told s/he likes driving his/her convertible with the top down, s/he likes western movies starring Clint Eastwood, s/he likes science fiction, s/he likes being at the beach, s/he likes pasta, Tex-Mex food, listening to classic rock and roll music, and s/he hates rap music. Given these likes and dislikes, you get an idea of what the stranger is "like"; you can make predictions about other likes and dislikes s/he might have; you might predict the person's weekend behavior; and you would have some knowledge of how you'd interact with her/him—which movie, restaurant, or concert to attend. Note that if we listed all of the person's *beliefs* concerning cars, movies, and such, you would not gain much information that is socially relevant. Communicating only beliefs just isn't the same.

Finally, attitudes also can tell us much about the type of receiver with whom we interact. In a seminal work, Katz[16] argued that attitudes can serve several different needs or *functions* for the individual. First, people hold some attitudes because they serve an *ego-defensive function*. Such attitudes are held and espoused because they help protect the individual from ". . . . unflattering truths about themselves or about others who are important to them."[17] For example, some men may hold intensely negative attitudes toward homosexuals, and they may make a number of very negative statements about homosexuals. Such a negative attitude about homosexuals serves an ego-defensive function because it helps the men to enhance their own perceived self-worth and masculinity by putting down and devaluing others. Others may *defend the self (the ego)* by adopting and espousing negative statements about any group perceived as a threat.

Attitudes may also serve a *value-expressive function* in that a receiver perceives that his/her

attitude also enables him/her to express an important value. There are many examples of persuaders attempting to tap into a "value-expressive function" in persuasion. For example, keeping planet Earth green and environmentally safe is an important value, and attitudes toward the use of diapers, fast-food wrappers, recycling, the use of toxic chemicals in our clothing, the use of "environmentally safe" trash bags, and so forth, link the value to a number of attitudes and behavioral solutions. Indeed, the United Colors of Benetton clothing company has focused considerable attention on a "worldwide" perspective of the environment, human suffering, and, generally, the message that "we are all the same." Other messages that capitalize on energy conservation, ozone-safe products, drought-resistant plants, solar power, and other replenishable energy sources reflect a similar value-expressive function. In the 1992 presidential campaign, the Republican Party linked voting Republican to "family values."

Third, some attitudes serve a *knowledge function*. A receiver needs to give adequate structure to his/her universe, to come to a better organization of perceptions and beliefs that provide a coherent explanation for how the world, or some aspect of it, operates. Examples of attitudes conforming to a knowledge function are often political or deal with social issues. A political example would be the story of Pat, a person who liked President Reagan and voted for Reagan in both elections:

Look, I just don't like the guy anymore. We voted for him because he was going to end deficit spending, but he didn't. We voted for him because he was going to build the Star Wars defense system, but it was cancelled after we spent millions. We voted for him because he advocated traditional values, but his own children weren't welcome at home, and they say unkind things about their family life. He was President of the United States, the strongest country in the world, but he can't remember what happened when he was in power. I really don't like the way the tax laws were changed in the 1980s. President Reagan went to Japan and got paid a million dollars for two speeches, but look at the homeless in our streets! Then I find out that some of the stories he told weren't true, but old movie plots. He couldn't tell the difference between reality and movies. Granted, I liked some things that took place during the Reagan years, but the more I think about it, the more unhappy it all makes me.

As Pat reflects on the 1980s in order to provide an understanding and an explanation for why things occurred as they did, she was led to question liking Reagan, and instead changed the opinion to disliking because, basically, "dislikable people do dislikable things," and the bulk of evidence (to Pat) was that more negative things happened in the 1980s than good things (but see below, because Pat's spouse disagreed).

Box 1.1 is a story about a family that joined the Ku Klux Klan out of an *ego-defensive* need to protect themselves (or so they thought); later, once learning about life in the KKK, what their actions meant, and what the KKK meant to them as a family, the couple experienced a reversal, learning instead to reject the organization and try to persuade others not to join. They experienced a need to understand what was happening to them and why. This restructuring of beliefs and attitudes reflects a movement toward the *knowledge function* of attitudes.

Attitudes can serve a *utilitarian function* in that people are motivated to gain rewards and avoid punishments. Much of the persuasion discussed in this book serves this function. Pat's spouse, for example, simply stated, "All Pat's complaints don't bother me. The President couldn't fight Congress, and anyone would have taken money for speaking in Japan. I still like President Reagan. Our lives are much better because of him." To

focus on the fact that life is better is to focus on the gain in rewards.

Lastly, it is important to realize that different people may hold the same attitude, but do so for different reasons. For example, one group of voters may vote Republican because they perceive that the Republican Party is best able to restore traditional American values (value-expressive function); another group of voters may do so because they perceive the Republican Party as providing the best economic opportunities (utilitarian function), while yet another group does so because they perceive the Republican Party as best able to combat their enemies (homosexuals, minority members, and such) (the ego-defensive function). Each of these groups was obviously exposed to, and influenced by, different messages over the years, and is seeking to satisfy different needs. Of course, changing each group of receivers would require focusing on its underlying needs and the functions that such attitudes serve.

We conclude by saying that while behaviors are often the outcome we want to change, most persuasion focuses on changing attitudes and beliefs. The concept of "attitude" is assigned a special role, and has been the focus of study in persuasion for decades. Now we turn to the question, just what are the outcomes one can expect from persuasive communications?

THE CONSEQUENCES OF PERSUASIVE MESSAGES

Imagine listening to a speaker who advocated raising local taxes in order to build an addition to the high school. Before the speech, a receiver might declare flatly, "No more taxes. I am tired of all these people coming here and asking for more money." The speech is competently crafted and delivered, and the speaker has taken great care to point out how each member of the community will benefit from the proposed new addition. After

BOX 1.1

AN EXAMPLE OF BOTH THE EGO-DEFENSIVE FUNCTION OF ATTITUDES (A FAMILY JOINS AND ACTIVELY PARTICIPATES IN THE KKK), AND THE KNOWLEDGE FUNCTION OF ATTITUDES (THE FAMILY LEARNS WHAT THE KKK IS ALL ABOUT)

STONE MOUNTAIN, Ga. -- Hard times and bitterness made the Ku Klux Klan an appealing choice for Gary and Jan Ralston.

They gave their children no choice at all.

In 1988, the life the couple had begun two decades earlier as 16-year-old high school dropouts was crumbling. Gary lost his job at a radiator shop. Their church rejected them as youth ministers because of their appearance. They had pulled their only daughter out of school at 14 because she said she was hassled by black students for refusing a date with a black youth.

"I had a lot of anger in my heart at that time," Gary said. "The Klan seemed to listen and they seemed to care."

For the next three and a half years, Gary and Jan's fierce loyalty to the Klan drove them to abandon friends and turn on their children. They forced their daughter and a 13-year-old son to join the white supremacist group. An older son who balked was beaten.

Their eldest son, Allan, was thrown out of the house after he refused to join and the family learned he was gay. Gary Ralston now acknowledges brooding with Klan buddies about killing him.

"I just couldn't believe they got into an organization that would make anyone want to kill their own flesh and blood," said Allan, now 22.

Ultimately, his parents could not believe it either. Despite a campaign of anonymous vandalism and threats, the Ralstons now are rebuilding their lives and aggressively trying to steer others from the path they chose.

They take their Klan scrapbook and memorabilia to schools to tell students of the dangers of hate groups. They have appeared on television talk shows and say they are negotiating deals for a book and a movie, although they will not discuss details.

"I'm sorry for what I've done and what I've put people through while I was Klan," said Gary, who bears a "White Power" Klansman tattoo on his shoulder. He said he will have it removed eventually.

Continued

The Ralstons signed up for the Klan during a 1988 membership rally. They chose the militant Southern White Knights chapter and dragged their youngest two children to a nighttime initiation ceremony several weeks later in the north Georgia woods.

Shannon, now 19, and her younger brother, Steve, now 17, were ordered to reject their nonwhite friends and participate in Klan activities.

Steve took down his posters of Michael Jordan and hid his rap music tapes. But he refused to abandon his black friends and invited them over to play basketball when his parents were not home.

"I was always afraid the Klan would see it," he said. "But I just couldn't turn my back to all my friends because my parents went to join the Klan."

Meanwhile, Gary and Jan were appointed officers of their 200-member chapter. They shouted fiery, racist speeches during rallies and spent all holidays with fellow Klansmen.

Gary often received phone calls in the middle of the night, after which he would leave for several hours. He declined to be specific about the outings but said the mission was to terrorize blacks and other Klan targets.

"I never killed no one, I'll put it that way," he said.

When sons Allan and Bill, now 21, returned home from military duty in 1989, neither wanted to join the Klan. Both also brought home explosive news: Bill was engaged to a Latina, and Allan was gay.

The family says Gary beat Bill several times until he agreed to call off the engagement and joined the Klan.

The revelation of Allan's homosexuality prompted Gary to spend a night by the pool, drinking Jack Daniels and telling fellow Klansmen he planned to kill his son. Instead, he and Jan disowned Allan and kicked him out of the house.

The Ralstons' loyalty to the KKK began to wane after Jan and Shannon appeared on a "Sally Jessy Raphael" show about mothers and daughters in the Klan. Producers also invited Allan to appear. The audience cheered him for rejecting the Klan and jeered Jan for embracing it.

When Allan told Jan after the show that he was not returning to Georgia, she feared that she would never see her son again. Jan also was struck by an article she read on the flight home about Paul Michael Glaser, the TV actor whose wife has AIDS (acquired immune deficiency syndrome) and whose child died from it.

"I was reading this and thinking, 'How do I have the audacity to praise God for AIDS?'" she said. "I talked to my husband and said, 'I'm going to come out of the Klan. It's destroying us and it's destroying me to hate.'"

Gary also was having doubts. He said he cringed watching Bill deliver a speech at a Klan rally and seeing the "hateful monster" his son had become.

Jan agreed to do another "Sally Jessy Raphael" show about leaving the KKK, despite Gary's threats of divorce. But Gary stopped balking when fellow Klansmen began calling the house.

"They were threatening my wife while I was still a member," he said. "This was my so-called brotherhood that I would have died for, conspiring against my wife and kids."

Gary never attended another Klan function and denounced the group a few months later in January on "Oprah Winfrey."

Today at the Ralston home, Allan is welcome. Steve has his Michael Jordan posters back on the wall. Jan and Shannon plan to take an exam this fall to obtain high school diplomas.

But life is far from normal. Since they broke with the Klan, the family dog has been fatally poisoned, the windows at Gary's new radiator shop have been shot out twice in one week, and the lining in the back yard pool has been slashed.

Police have not caught the vandals.

"We always get a call a couple of days later and that's how we know it's the Klan," Jan said. "They say stuff like, 'Your dog is dead and y'all are next.'"

The hate mail and threatening phone calls become more frequent after the Ralstons appear on a talk show or grant another interview. Gary has spent nights crouched in his bushes cradling a shotgun.

From the *Los Angeles Times*, Sunday, September 20, 1992. Reprinted by permission of Joan Kirchner Sanchez, Associated Press Writer.

the speech, our receiver says, "I'm still opposed to more taxes, but that speaker was really great."

The speaker did not succeed in getting the receiver's vote with that one speech, but do we want to say that the speech had no effect? Certainly something happened. The outcome was not precisely what was intended, but further speeches might lead our receiver eventually to vote for the proposed school addition. Changes in a receiver's attitudes or behaviors often take place in small, incremental steps, and may be difficult to assess at any particular point in time. It is inaccurate to attempt to make final judgments about the effects of persuasive messages in terms of immediately observable behavior. There are short-term and long-term effects.

Rosenberg and Hovland[18] proposed a general model of persuasive outcomes that is illustrated in Figure 1.2. In persuasive communication situations, persuasive messages directly impact on attitudes via three kinds of changes: (1) changes in cognition, (2) changes in affect, or (3) changes in behavior.

Cognitions include the concepts we have, the beliefs we hold about various objects, the values we place on objects and the perceptions we have of the world around us. Typical changes in cognitions can be identified by the verbal statements

FIGURE **1.2**

THE RELATIONSHIP OF ATTITUDE TO INTERNAL CHANGE AND TO OBSERVABLE EXTERNAL CHANGE

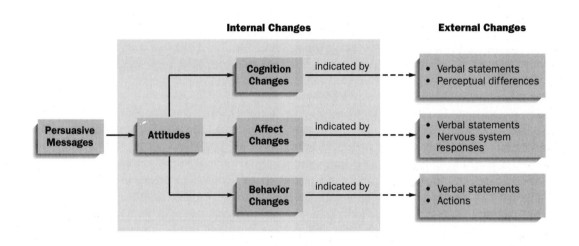

that people make after being exposed to a persuasive message. Cognitive changes can also be indicated by changes in perceptions, that is, the way in which individuals see the world around them. Such indicators of change can be illustrated by a simple example. Imagine looking at a picture containing some "hidden objects." You look intently at the picture but fail to spot any of the objects. Then a friend says, "Look at the upper left-hand corner next to the tree trunk." You do so and find a hidden tennis racket (or hidden rocket launchers). The chances are very good that when you look at the picture again, the previously hidden objects will seem to almost leap out of it. Your perception has been changed as a result of the message telling you where to look.

Perception changes are not limited to such simple examples. Perception changes can influence how we see a number of objects, people, or qualities around us. How we look at teenage run-

aways, the homeless, or the chemically dependent can all be the outcome of a persuasive message we have heard at church, on campus, on PBS or at a movie. In our example above, the voter may now drive around town and actually see more teenagers simply "hanging out" in parking lots; s/he may see that the parks do in fact appear to be too crowded, and that groups of people have to wait in order to get on the basketball courts. Now that the voter perceives a need, s/he will be more motivated to search for a solution.

Of course, cognition changes also include changes in beliefs. Beliefs (and/or belief changes) have already been described concerning anti-smoking campaigns and the ownership of a Chrysler. Belief changes may sound easy, but this is not always true. The French-made Renault automobile was once sold in America at the dealerships of the American Motors Corporation (who built Ramblers and Jeeps). When Chrysler bought the

Jeep/Eagle division, and Ramblers disappeared, Renault was placed in a very poor sales position. Renault hired George C. Scott (who won an Academy Award for the movie *Patton,* and who had a reputation for having high standards) to *promote and improve the image of Renault.* The goal was to alter the perceptions of Renault so that more Americans thought of them like other quality European imports (Volvo, Saab, BMW, and the like). Renault has since pulled out of the competitive American market.

Affect changes are changes in our emotional states, or our mood, and they may be indicated by laughing, crying, having shivers running up and down the spine, and similar bodily events. In some cases, an investigator working in the laboratory can show changes resulting from the presentation of messages through the use of instruments for detecting changes in heart rate, blood pressure, galvanic skin response, and sweating. Outside the laboratory, such instruments are not available, and we must depend on verbal statements from receivers about emotional changes and the extent to which a particular persuasive message produced the change.

Regardless of the difficulties in indexing affect changes, there is ample evidence that these changes can result from persuasive communication. Examples may be noted when someone exclaims, "I cried at the end of that movie," or "That film really upset me and made me worry about neglecting to get a mammogram," or "Boy, that film on AIDS sure scared me, and convinced me not to take any chances." Fund-raisers frequently send persuasive messages attempting to make listeners or viewers feel sorry for the victims that a charity has been set up to help. For years, the Easter Seal campaign has been based on a poster showing a crippled child. The obvious intent is to produce a sympathetic reaction on the part of receivers that will then be translated into donations.

Finally, persuasive messages resulting in behavior changes must be discussed. In one sense, any observable change in behavior, including changes in the nervous system and verbal statements, could be called behavior changes since the individual is doing something, but it is helpful to distinguish between cognitive changes, emotional changes, and other types of overt, easily observable behavior. Getting an individual to agree, cognitively, that recycling plastics is a good idea is far easier than getting the same individual to actually start recycling, and to continue to do so over years.

Cognitive, affective, and behavioral changes are not always easily separated into three distinct and mutually exclusive categories. In almost any situation involving persuasive communication, combinations of effects will be noted. A person may listen to a speech which argues for a constitutional amendment to give voters the right to vote on all tax increases. Following the speech, the man signs a petition to place the amendment on the ballot, and also tells a friend how the speech changed his mind about taxes. He clearly exhibited a behavior change, but his comments also indexed a cognitive change. You can be emotionally stirred by a speech, and also make a contribution to charity. Or you can be emotionally stirred by a speech, but never make a contribution because of financial inadequacy. You can be exposed to a television commercial, laugh at the commercial, but pass up the product when you see it on a store shelf a few days later. The combinations of cognitive changes affect changes, and overt behaviors that can occur as a result of persuasion are complex.

Judging the Effects of Persuasion

Ultimately, persuasive communication must be judged in terms of its effect on the participants. Was it successful? Did it fail to achieve its goal? What if only part of a speaker's goals are realized? Do we conclude that persuasion was successful, or unsuccessful? There are four criteria used to judge the effectiveness of persuasive communication.

First, we can assess the correspondence between the intentions of the source and subsequent behavior of the receiver. In the previous example, a person gave a speech arguing for an increase in taxes in order to pay for an expansion of the high school. The speaker failed to persuade the voters, but was successful in increasing awareness of a problem, and was successful in changing cognitions. Thus, the speech failed to secure the vote the source wanted, but helped create an improved atmosphere for the next vote. This situation is, in fact, quite typical in politics, where a candidate running for office may expect to lose at least the first election. After the politician has established a presence (has high name recognition, has met many people, is known to the media, and so forth), the political novice may have greater success on the second, third, or fourth attempt. A more realistic goal in the first campaign is to create awareness and begin to build a positive image with certain segments of the electorate—not to win it all at once.

A second criterion for judging the success of a persuasive message is the degree of change that is secured. Sales messages are one of the best examples we can use to illustrate this situation. Jane Jones is demonstrating a new food processor in the local department store. A crowd of twenty-five people is watching as she demonstrates the appliance and tries to sell it to the audience. Her chances of getting all twenty-five members of the audience to buy a machine are obviously very small. How many machines does she have to sell before the message can be considered effective? To more than half the people? Less than half? Only one? If no one rushes up to buy one of the processors, do we consider Jane a failure? Should we fire her? The difficulties in making an immediate assessment are obvious. Some members of the audience might go home, think about the demonstration, talk to their friends and neighbors, and finally buy a processor two months later. If the store had fired Jane in the meantime, most of us would agree that an injustice had been done.

Persuasion must be judged in terms of gradations of success. One end of the scale may represent no change at all in any of the participants along any of the dimensions we have discussed. At the other end of the scale, we would find that all of the participants in the situation have changed in ways which reflect their mutual desires to find common ground on which decisions and actions are possible. Most outcomes of persuasive communication fall between these two extremes.

A third criterion that can be used to measure the success of a persuasive campaign is the nature of the opposition to the campaign. We expect that persuasion is going to be more successful if there is no organized opposition. In the United States, there has been a strong campaign opposing the Supreme Court's decision allowing abortion. If one examined only the persuasive messages which oppose abortion, one might expect that most Americans would be demanding the abolishment of abortion in the country. The campaign conducted by those opposed to abortion is intense and anti-abortion messages are presented in many different media. Attitude studies conducted through national polls suggest, however, that there has been relatively little change in the basic attitudes of most Americans toward abortion. People who opposed abortion before the Supreme Court decision by and large still oppose it. People who favored legalizing abortion still favor it.

What has happened? Those opposed to legalizing abortion are not conducting their campaign in a vacuum. There is just as powerful a group of individuals who argue for freedom of choice in matters of abortion as there are people who oppose freedom of choice. The end result is that there is little visible public change in this area. People hold their beliefs more and more strongly, but few are converted. Both sides are trying to attract the uncommitted to their position. The presence or absence of opposition will have significant influence on the success or failure of persuasion.

The final criterion we must use in judging the success or failure of persuasion is the level of difficulty of the task being proposed. Advocating a tax reduction is easier than advocating tax increases. If you are advocating strong efforts to control crime, your task may be easy, since few people are in favor of increased crime. However, if you are in favor of an increase in the state income tax in order to finance increased welfare payments, you are likely to have a very difficult time. The persuasive speaker who advocates stronger measures to control crime may have an easy time and will feel that the audience is with him. That same speaker may be totally rejected when he advocates an increase in the income tax to pay for new prisons. In the one case, we might label the speaker a success. In the other, we might label the same person a failure.

Changing firmly fixed attitudes and habits is more difficult than changing attitudes which are weakly held. The difficulty level of the communicator's task can be assessed by comparing the initial position of a receiver on a particular topic to the position desired by the communicator. If the change in attitude desired is large, successful persuasion will be more difficult to achieve than if the source wants the receiver to change only a small amount from a currently held position.

Four criteria must be considered in judging the effects of persuasive communication. Situations can be assessed in terms of the *nature of the correspondence* between the intentions of the participants, the *degree of correspondence* between the intentions of the source and the subsequent behavior of the receiver, the *nature of the opposition* to be expected to the communicator's position, and the *difficulty level* of the task being engaged in.

The Attitude-Behavior Problem

In the 1930s a professor named LaPiere[19] toured the United States with a young Chinese couple. They visited 251 hotels, restaurants, and other establishments, and *one* of the 251 businesses refused them service. Several months later, LaPiere wrote to each of the businesses and asked "Will you accept members of the Chinese race as guests in your establishment?" Only 128 establishments responded to the letter, and 90 percent said they would not serve members of the "Chinese race."

LaPiere, and others,[20] argued that *attitudes* expressed by the "no" to the letter, and *behaviors* (actually serving the couple) do not correspond with one another—attitudes do not predict behavior. This "attitude-behavior problem" has prompted a good deal of interest over the years. Obviously, it concerns us here; why read an entire book on changing attitudes and beliefs if there will be no corresponding change in behavior?

Actually, the LaPiere study was hopelessly flawed. There is no proof that the managers or owners who answered "no" to LaPiere's letter were the same people who served the three travelers several months earlier. Further, scholars are still puzzled by why LaPiere used the term "members of the Chinese race" in his letter, as opposed to saying "a young Chinese couple." Perhaps LaPiere *wanted* to demonstrate that attitudes do not predict behavior and he wanted to elicit a more racist response from his letter. Also, if LaPiere wanted to show that racist attitudes correspond to behaviors, why select only *one* behavior (the choice of serving or not serving the couple). We would also expect racist business owners to be rude, make the couple wait a long time, place them next to the kitchen in the dining area, and so forth. Racism is reflected in a wide array of behaviors.

Sufficient research has been conducted on this issue to provide insight into when attitudes are more likely to predict behaviors. We will highlight three topics: (1) The prediction of multiple-acts, (2) The problem with general measures of attitudes, (3) The issue of direct experience.

The Prediction of Multiple Acts

A person's attitude toward many general issues, such as the ecology, supporting a strong military, and racism, among others, can be manifested in many different behaviors. It basically is unrealistic to think that an attitude one holds toward, say, the ecology, will *always* correspond with more *pro-ecological behaviors*. For any number of reasons, a person may be pro-ecology, but unable or unwilling to recycle plastics this week, or is not free on a particular Saturday when there is an organized beach clean-up. However, that person's positive attitude can have a bearing on a number of behaviors that do in fact reflect his/her attitude.

Such an outcome was demonstrated by Weigel and Newman.[21] Forty-four individuals in a medium-sized New England town were recruited to participate in a project on attitudes concerning a variety of social problems, and part of the questionnaire dealt with environmental attitudes; specifically, they were asked to agree or disagree with sixteen questions dealing with pollution and conservation. The individuals were not contacted again for three months, and then three different types of pro-ecology opportunities were made available to them. On three occasions they were able to sign petitions concerning limiting offshore oil drilling, limiting the growth in nuclear power plants, and maintaining stringent auto exhaust systems. They were also asked to circulate the petitions to friends. A second type of opportunity occurred when a different person weeks later asked each of the individuals to help in a roadside litter pick-up program that was being organized to clean up certain areas of the town. They were given three different days to select from, and they were asked to recruit a friend to help pick up litter. Two months later, a third person approached each

individual and asked each one to participate in recycling. The recycling involved bundling papers, removing metal rings from bottles, and setting aside all recyclables on pick-up day.

The results are illustrated in Table 1.1. A "yes" means that the people who had indicated a stronger pro-ecology attitude at the beginning of the study did in fact *behave* in a more pro-ecology manner over the course of months. A "no" means that they did not behave in a more pro-ecology manner. Attitude did not have any impact on whether the individual agreed to circulate petitions to friends, did not have an impact on recruiting a friend to pick up litter, and did not have a substantial impact on recycling during weeks five, six, and seven. However, individuals with positive pro-ecology attitudes were in fact more likely to sign each of the three petitions, to pick up litter, and to recycle during weeks one, two, three, four, and eight. Further, when the behavior for each specific act was averaged together, pro-ecology individuals were, on the average, more likely to sign a petition, pick up litter and recycle (see "categories of behavior"). We conclude that attitudes do have a general impact on multiple acts that are related to the attitude, but may not have an impact on any *one* act at one specific point in time.

The Problem With General Measures of Attitude

Sometimes scholars investigating the attitude-behavior relationship use questionnaires that measure the person's "general" attitude toward behaviors, such as cheating, using birth control devices, racism, and so forth. General questions about cheating, for example, ask people to strongly agree or strongly disagree with statements like "Cheating disgusts me." "I am offended by cheating." "Cheating is morally wrong." Do such attitudes predict who does and does not cheat on tax forms? What happens if a close friend begs to let him or her copy a lab assignment because the close friend is failing a class and is desperate to

TABLE	1.1

THE RELATIONSHIP OF ATTITUDE TO SINGLE BEHAVIORS AND TO CATEGORIES OF BEHAVIORS (SUMMING TOGETHER MULTIPLE SINGLE BEHAVIORS)

Behaviors	Did Attitude Predict Behavior?
Petition Signing:	
Offshore Oil Drilling	Yes
Nuclear Power	Yes
Auto Exhaust	Yes
Circulating Petitions to Friends	No
Petition Signing: Averaging together all the above four opportunities	Yes
Litter Pick-up Program	
Individual Participates	Yes
Recruits a friend to participate	No
Litter Program: Averaging together the two above opportunities	Yes
Recycling Program:	
Week 1	Yes
Week 2	Yes
Week 3	Yes
Week 4	Yes
Week 5	No
Week 6	No
Week 7	No
Week 8	Yes
Recycling Program: Averaging together all the above eight opportunities:	Yes

Adapted from: R.H. Weigel and L.S. Newman, "Increasing Attitude-Behavior Correspondence by Broadening the Scope of the Behavioral Measure," *Journal of Personality and Social Psychology*, vol. 33 (1976), pp. 793–802. Reprinted by permission of the authors and the American Psychological Association.

get off scholastic probation? Would the person with an anti-cheating attitude decline the offer of collaboration in cheating?

The more general the measure of attitude, the less likely it is to predict specific behaviors. According to Ajzen and Fishbein,[22] there are four components that must be evaluated when constructing an attitude questionnaire in such a way as to increase its usefulness. First, what is the specific *action* that is involved? The general notion of "cheating" involves many specific acts in different contexts. For example, copying another's answers during an examination, copying another's lab report, buying a term paper, copying whole paragraphs from a friend's paper from the previous year, all incorporate aspects of cheating. You may differ in your attitude toward them (some are more morally objectionable than others), and some are simply easier to commit and less detectable. Second, there are different *targets*, the people or agencies on or to whom the action is committed: the federal government, the state government, the automotive insurance company, the instructors you have in general education courses, the professors and assistants you have in your major (whom you like, whom you don't like), a business rival, a minister, and so forth.

Third, there is a *context* component that involves the physical setting, situational pressures, norms, expectations, and so forth concerning the behavior. Fourth, there is a *time* component related to behaviors; smokers claim they need a cigarette in the morning with the first cup of coffee, or at night after dinner. Every action is located in time, which marketers have always employed in their surveys ("Have you or anyone in your household purchased a frozen TV dinner in the last three weeks?" "Do you anticipate purchasing a freezer within the next three months?").

Persuasion scholars increase the likelihood of detecting a relationship between attitude and behaviors by constructing questionnaires that ask questions about specific actions, targets, and contexts within a time frame. Davidson and Jaccard,[23]

THE ADVERTISING CODE OF AMERICAN BUSINESS

1. *Truth.* Advertising shall tell the truth, and reveal significant facts, the concealment of which would mislead the public.

2. *Responsibility.* Advertising agencies and advertisers shall be willing to provide substantiation of claims made.

3. *Taste and Decency.* Advertising shall be free of statements, illustrations or implications which are offensive to good taste or public decency.

4. *Disparagement.* Advertising shall offer merchandise or service on its merits and refrain from attacking competition unfairly or disparaging their products, services, or methods of doing business.

5. *Bait Advertising.* Advertising shall offer only merchandise or services which are readily available for purchase at the advertised price.

6. *Guarantees and Warranties.* Advertising of guarantees and warranties shall be explicit. Advertising of any guarantee or warranty shall clearly and conspicuously disclose its nature and extent, the manner in which the guarantor or warrantor will perform, and the identity of the guarantor or warrantor.

7. *Price Claims.* Advertising shall avoid price or savings claims which are false or misleading, or which do not offer provable bargains or savings.

8. *Unprovable Claims.* Advertising shall avoid the use of exaggerated or unprovable claims.

9. *Testimonials.* Advertising containing testimonials shall be limited to those of competent witnesses who are reflecting a real and honest choice.

This code was developed by the American Advertising Federation and Association of Better Business Bureaus International and has been endorsed by many trade organizations. Reprinted by permission.

for example, conducted a two-year study on women's attitudes toward both birth control and conception. Questionnaires were constructed that compared (a) general attitudes toward "birth control"; (b) general attitudes toward "birth control *pills*"; (c) the individual's personal attitude toward *using* birth control *pills*"; and (d) the individual's attitude toward *using* birth control *pills* in the *next two years*. Davidson and Jaccard found that as each part of the set of questions became more specific there was a stronger relationship between the attitude expressed in the questionnaire and use of oral contraceptives (during the two years). Similarly, a general attitude toward children was unrelated to birth control or attempted conception over the two year period, but attitude toward *having* children and attitude toward *having* children in the *next two years* were strongly related to birth control/attempted conception over the two-year period.

THE ISSUE OF DIRECT EXPERIENCE

When we have direct experience concerning a topic, such as racism, eating particular foods, smoking, exercising, dieting and studying, our attitudes are more strongly formed, better defined, held more confidently, and possibly held for a longer duration. Fazio and Zanna[24] have conducted a series of studies in this area. It is easy to see that children's attitudes toward behaviors they have not experienced (such as, smoking) can be strongly influenced by a number of messages when they are young, but these attitudes are not very long-lasting. On the other hand, students who have had experience in music lessons, gymnastics, swimming, and so forth, will develop attitudes more strongly predictive of behaviors concerning continued or similar behavior in extracurricular activities, while students who have no previous experience can only *imagine* whether the behaviors would be positive or negative.

THE ETHICS OF PERSUASION

Since persuasion is so pervasive in society and sophisticated tactics can be used so easily to influence others, it should not be surprising that considerable attention has focused on ethical guidelines. Louis A. Day, in *Ethics in Media Communications: Cases and Controversies*, provides an excellent discussion of ethical standards and dilemmas in the communication industry.[25] Day also presents the code of ethics for the Society of Professional Journalists, the American Society of Newspaper Editors, Radio-Television News Directors Association, The Advertising Code of American Business and the Public Relations Society of America. Box 1.2 presents the Advertising Code of American Business, and Box 1.3 presents the Code of Professional Standards for the Practice of Public Relations. Brown and Singhal[26] discuss ethical dilemmas associated with using television to promote prosocial behaviors, beliefs and attitudes around the world (relevant to Chapter 14).

Karen S. Johnson-Cartee and Gary A. Copeland's *Negative Political Advertising: Coming of Age* devotes an entire chapter to "Combating Negative Ads," and devotes another chapter to "Law and Ethics."[27] Box 1.4 presents the Code of Professional Ethics of the American Association of Political Consultants.

Children represent a large group of receivers who can be influenced very easily by advertisements. Since they can be easily exploited, considerable attention has focused on ethical guidelines and children. Box 1.5 presents an edited version of a proposed list of ethical guidelines for children's television programming originally offered by the National Association of Broadcasters. A longer version can be found in Adler, Lesser, Meringoff, Robertson, Rossiter, and Ward's *The Effects of Television Advertising on Children*.[28] The

BOX 1.3

Public Relations Society of America: Code of Professional Standards for the Practice of Public Relations

Declaration of Principles

Members of the Public Relations Society of America base their professional principles on the fundamental value and dignity of the individual, holding that the free exercise of human rights, especially freedom of speech, freedom of assembly, and freedom of the press is essential to the practice of public relations.

In serving the interests of clients and employers, we dedicate ourselves to the goals of better communication, understanding, and cooperation among the diverse individuals, groups, and institutions of society, and of equal opportunity of employment in the public relations profession.

We pledge:

To conduct ourselves professionally, with truth, accuracy, fairness, and responsibility to the public;

To improve our individual competence and advance the knowledge and proficiency of the profession through continuing research and education;

And to adhere to the articles of the Code of Professional Standards for the Practice of Public Relations as adopted by the governing Assembly of the Society.

Code of Professional Standards for the Practice of Public Relations

These articles have been adopted by the Public Relations Society of America to promote and maintain high standards of public service and ethical conduct among its members.

1. A member shall conduct his or her professional life in accord with the public interest.

2. A member shall exemplify high standards of *honesty and integrity* while carrying out dual obligations to a client or employer and to the democratic process.

3. A member shall *deal fairly* with the public, with past or present clients or employers, and with fellow practitioners, giving due respect to the ideal of free inquiry and to the opinions of others.

4. A member shall adhere to the highest standards of *accuracy and truth*, avoiding extravagant claims or unfair comparisons and giving credit for ideas and words borrowed from others.

5.   A member shall not knowingly disseminate *false or misleading information* and shall act promptly to correct erroneous communications for which he or she is responsible.

This code was revised in 1988. Reprinted by permission of the Public Relations Society of America.

guidelines were developed in the 1970s for use among practitioners in the area of children's advertisements. However, the guidelines were never implemented because the Federal Trade Commission and the Federal Communications Commission have jurisdiction in this area, and there was considerable concern over who has authority to implement guidelines and whether there was overlap or any potential inconsistencies between these guidelines and ones that the federal agencies might one day propose.

The FTC and FCC agencies will occasionally implement a rule concerning the protection of children. For example, a rule exists forbidding a cartoon character like Fred Flintstone from endorsing a product *during* a show in which he is featured (that is, "The Flintstones") because it has been determined that younger children have a difficult time realizing when a show breaks for a commercial and when the commercials start and stop. The child, in this situation, is not aware that s/he is being influenced by a commercial, thinking instead Fred Flintstone is eating Flintstones cereal or taking Flintstones vitamins. A fundamental rule of ethics is that the individual being persuaded has a right to know that s/he is being influenced, and must be in a position to resist and possibly say "no" to the attempt. The same rule accounts for why subliminal messages are banned from the public airwaves (radio and television).[29]

The fact that these and many other organizations have devoted so much attention to ethics does not mean receivers are protected from abuse. It is most important to realize that in a democracy such as ours, and in an era of governmental deregulation, it is extremely difficult to enforce guidelines and there are few punishments that one can mete out; a single employee can be blamed for questionable actions, fired, and an unethical practice is then hushed up.

Our own (Bettinghaus's and Cody's) biases would be for ethical standards that have a bite to them, and for imposing those ethical standards for the protection of groups that might otherwise be easily exploited. Children do not understand puffery (defined below) in the same way as adults, nor do they understand comparison ads in the same way. For example, a comparison ad for bicycles might dramatize a young boy beating others in a race, and so the message is that a Rambo bicycle is a faster, better bicycle. We adults can understand this ad, but a child's esteem may be threatened and the ad basically tells him/her, "Your parents should buy you a Rambo bicycle." Should 5-year-olds be subjected to such advertisements? The counterargument to regulating this industry is the claim that parents are obligated to watch television with their child, and to help instruct the child on the nature of advertisements—after all, by the time these children are thirteen or fifteen years old, they should be able to process any

B O X   1 . 4

CODE OF PROFESSIONAL ETHICS, AMERICAN ASSOCIATION OF POLITICAL CONSULTANTS

Code of Professional Ethics

As a member of the American Association of Political Consultants, I believe there are certain standards of practice which I must maintain. I, therefore, pledge to adhere to the following Code of Ethics:

—I shall not indulge in any activity which would corrupt or degrade the practice of political campaigning.

—I shall treat my colleagues and my clients with respect and never intentionally injure their professional or personal reputation.

—I shall respect the confidence of my client and not reveal confidential or private information obtained during our professional relationship.

—I will use no appeal to voters which is based on racism or discrimination and will condemn those who use such practices. In turn, I will work for equal voting rights and privileges for all citizens.

—I will refrain from false and misleading attacks on an opponent or member of his family and shall do everything in my power to prevent others from using such tactics.

—I will document accurately and fully any criticism for an opponent or his record.

—I shall be honest in my relationship with the press and candidly answer questions when I have the authority to do so.

—I shall not support any individual or organization which resorts to practices forbidden in this code.

_____   _____

Signature   Date

Reprinted by permission of the American Association of Political Consultants.

B O X   1 . 5

Formerly Proposed Children's Television Advertising Guidelines

---

Formerly Proposed Children's Television Advertising Guidelines (edited version)

1.   Documentation adequate to support the truthfulness and accuracy of all claims and representations contained in the audio or video of the advertisement must be made available upon request to broadcasters and/or the Code Authority.

2.   Television advertisements shall not include presumptions that a product or service requiring material investment can be had for the asking. Children shall not be directed to purchase or to ask a parent or other adult to buy a product or service for them.

3.   In order to help assure that advertising is non-exploitative in manner, style and tone, such advertising shall avoid using exhortative language. It shall also avoid employing irritating, obtrusive or strident audio techniques or video devices such as cuts of less than one second in length, a series of fast cuts, special effects of a psychedelic nature (for example, flashing colors, flashing lights, flashing supered copy, or other effects which could overglamorize or mislead).

4.   Any representation of a child's concept of himself/herself or of his/her relationship to others must be constructively handled. When self-concept claims are employed, the role of the product/service in affecting such promised benefits as strength, growth, physical prowess and growing up must accurately reflect documented evidence.

5.   Appeals shall not be used which directly or by implication contend that if children have a product they are better than their peers or lacking it will not be accepted by their peers.

6.   Material shall not be used which can reasonably be expected to frighten children or provoke anxiety, nor shall material be used which contains a portrayal of or appeal to violent, dangerous or otherwise anti-social behavior.

7.   The use of real-life authority figures/celebrities as product presenters shall not include their personal testimonials or endorsements.

8.   Persons who are recognized as being identified, specifically or generically, with an advertised product's counterpart in real-life may not be used as spokespeople or endorsers. This prohibition also applies to actors representing such persons.

Continued

9.   Positive exposition of a product's own attributes are acceptable. However, because of their potential to encourage dissatisfaction on a child's part, competitive/comparison/superiority claims or techniques are disallowed.

10.   The original purchase must be clearly disclosed in the body of the commercial. There shall not be any implication that optional extras, additional units or items that are not available with the toy, accompany the toy's original purchase.

11.   Given the importance of sound health and nutritional practices, advertisements for edibles shall be in accord with the commonly accepted principles of good eating and seek to establish the proper role of the advertised product within the framework of a balanced regimen. Any representation of the relationship between an edible and energy must be documented and accurately depicted.

12.   Feature films, other than those appropriate for a general family audience, shall not be advertised in or adjacent to programs initially designed primarily for children under 12 years of age.

The guidelines were proposed as part of the NAB code, which was cancelled in its entirety in 1982. For more details of the proposed guidelines, consult: R.P. Adler, G.S. Lesser; L.K. Meringoff, T.S. Robertson, J.R. Rossiter, and S. Ward, *The Effects of Television Advertising on Children* (Lexinton Mass.: Lexington Books, 1980). Reprinted with permission.

commercial as an adult. We would also voice concern over the use of emotional appeals aimed at older receivers.

All of the guidelines concerning ethics claim that deception, fraud, or manipulation are to be avoided. However, consider two dilemmas for the consumer:

Being Manipulated and Not Knowing You are Being Manipulated

Story A: You go to a clothing store and you try on clothes. In the dressing room another shopper says, "Looks good!" or, "Boy, I love that dress; is that in the Anne Klein II section?" A stranger praised what you are wearing, and the praise from a stranger is more credible than praise from the salesclerk (who you know is trying to influence you). You buy the clothing. Three weeks later you read in the newspaper that an investigator discovered that high school students were being paid hourly wages to change clothes in the dressing rooms and to praise shoppers. You are shocked! You were lied to (the praise was phony) and manipulated (you might not have purchased the clothing otherwise). What do you do?

Story B: You go to buy a used car, after calling about an ad in the newspaper. The seller listed $3,000 as an asking price, and you know that s/he will settle for less with a little haggling. You look over the car, and as you do so, another person comes to look at the car. You don't worry, because you were there first. Then, a second person arrives and looks at the car. The seller and the second arrivee are talking livelily with each other and you suspect that they are talking about a sale price. You go over and say, "I'm sorry, but I was here first and I want the car." You buy the car for $2,900 thinking you saved $100, but you are also confident that you could have bargained better if there weren't competition for the car. Later in the day, as you drive your new car around, you drive by the old owner's house and see all three people having a beer. What happened? Maybe those two other guys weren't really buyers, but friends. Did you pay more for the car than you expected because of this competition (this is called the "scarcity principle" in Chapter 10)?

Story C: You see an ad for a video game on TV. Your child wants it very badly. You say, "Well, if you are a good girl, maybe you'll get it for Christmas." The child fully expects to receive this game for Christmas. You travel to twenty-two toy stores, and they are all sold out of this toy. When you do see one available, it is marked up an extra ten dollars. So, for Christmas you buy your daughter different video games. After Christmas, the desired video game is available everywhere, and your daughter reminds you that you promised to get it. Were you manipulated by a *planned shortage or scarcity* (see Chapter 10) into buying more videos and/or buying the game at a higher price?

Story D: You see a radio advertised for a certain price. You go to the store after work, and the salesclerk sadly tells you that they are out of stock. S/he recommends a different, "slightly" more expensive item. Is this "bait and switch," in which a desired product is advertised, but really isn't available and the customer is directed toward a more expensive product, or an inferior one? You have the right to ask for a rain check at the price that is advertised for this product. If you suspect that this was intentional bait and switch, you should contact the Better Business Bureau.

Story E: You and your spouse are in your fifties and a salesperson sells you a supplemental retirement package. You are led to believe that if you pay into the fund for fifteen years, you will receive $500 a month in supplemental financial assistance after you retire, plus there will be $50,000 in a life-insurance policy that will help pay funeral expenses and debt when either of you die. After you retire, you realize that you cannot have both benefits; you cannot be paid both the $500 per month and the $50,000—you have to select one of the two options. You try re-reading all the documents, but you cannot really decipher the meaning. Nonetheless, you both distinctly remember the promise of both benefits. Did the salesperson mislead you, "lowball" you (chapter 10), or, legally, commit fraud? What you should do is see a lawyer, because these problems occur nearly every day.

The first three of these scenarios pose a different problem than the others. The unique situation is that (a) you do not *know* you are being manipulated; (b) you can learn about being manipulated only by some unique circumstance, the manipulation being difficult to detect on your own; and (c) you would have difficulty providing proof that you have been manipulated. The best line of defense is to be aware of what is happening and to *never* take the actions of others at face value. Unfortunately, always being suspicious of others will make you paranoid; however, we hope that reading this book will make you more aware of tactics and strategies used by some people, sometimes. Awareness is always the first line of defense. The second is knowing that companies hate negative publicity. Sears paid back millions of dollars after its auto repair shops were caught defrauding consumers. The more an individual or group can stir up controversies and publicity over questionable actions, the greater the likelihood that the practice will cease and that the company will be corrected.

The last two examples are cases of outright fraud, in which complaints should be filed.

Puffery Versus Deception

Who are Bartles and James? Who is that posing as "Rosie Rosarita" making Mexican food in her kitchen? Did that young lady really make thousands of cans of refried beans, without a factory? Did that athlete who just ate a Snickers candy bar *really* win a gold medal because s/he ate the candy bar? Does eating a red M&M make you hit a home run, and eating a yellow one make you hit a triple?

"Puffery" is related to deception, but is viewed "outside" deception and is a special category to the Federal Trade Commission and the courts. Richards[30] provides a thorough assessment of the "puffery" versus deception issue, although we still believe that there are questions concerning *who* draws the boundary between mere puffery and outright deception. Puffery is defined here as mere exaggeration that any reasonable adult would understand as a "mere exaggeration."

An Ethical Position for Persuasive Communicators

The first part of our discussion on ethics has focused on the rules and guidelines that professional communicators have developed to insure that all members of the profession will act ethically. In some cases, government agencies like the Federal Communications Commission have been given enforcement powers to make sure that the public is protected from unethical communicators.

How about the individual communicator? Are ethics important to you in your daily life? What can you do to help assure yourself that you are operating ethically, and that those who communicate to you are also operating from ethical foundations? We believe that every individual must develop his/her own set of ethical guidelines, and so have devoted the rest of this chapter to helping students to do that. First, we raise some questions about persuasion that have occurred to many people who study this subject. And then we make some broad suggestions that may be of help to you as you work at developing your own personal set of ethical guidelines.

Questions About Ethics

Persuasion is a field for scientific research, a field similar to those disciplines that study political behavior, mental illness, or juvenile delinquency. Few object to the psychologist who is interested in trying to cure the psychotic, the criminologist working at the prevention of crime, or the historian trying to understand the causes of war. Many people, however, have objected to the study and practice of persuasion. The term itself seems to suggest the manipulation of others, whether by physical force, or by the force of words playing on the emotions. This concern about the power of persuasive communication arose early in recorded history, and philosophers from Aristotle to David Hume to John Stuart Mill have addressed some of the philosophical problems arising from the recognition that persuasion can be a very powerful tool.

The charges against persuasion are difficult to answer simply. We shall attempt to do so by fashioning a series of related questions, and answering them.

1. Can persuasion be used for evil ends? Of course it can, but so can medicine, law, banking, or accounting. No one would argue that we should close all medical schools because they have the potential for being used wrongly. A more rational suggestion is that we keep the medical school, and place some restrictions on the way in which people practice medicine. With regard to persuasion,

our society has argued the same way. The advertiser is allowed to attempt to persuade people to buy his product, but we make him legally responsible for the safety of the product.

2. When we teach about persuasion, do we put power over others in the hands of those we teach? Yes, we do, but we do also when we teach a child how to write, teach a college student how to take a blood sample, or teach a soldier how to use a bayonet. Knowledge is always powerful, but its power to control depends on the exclusivity with which it is held. If only a few knew how to persuade others, persuasion would be a very powerful weapon indeed. When everyone knows how to use persuasion effectively, and knows how to evaluate the persuasive messages that are received, persuasion becomes far more a tool, and less a weapon.

3. Does the use of persuasion lead to manipulation, and, thusly, does it make people into objects? If you mean by "manipulation" the changing of the behavior of others through conscious attempts to change their behavior, persuasion does result in manipulation. Having said that, we might examine the original question a bit more closely. The use of the word "manipulation" has come to have a very negative meaning. If we substituted the word "education" or "socialization" or "rehabilitation" for the term manipulation, no one would worry about the association of persuasion with any of the three concepts. Yet each of them can be defined as conscious attempts to change the behavior of others. Society regards education, socialization, and rehabilitation as positive in nature. We all attempt to control the environment around us. We wouldn't be living organisms if we didn't, and persuasion is but one way we use to fit ourselves into our society.

4. Can we protect people against persuasion? Our answer here has to be: not completely. Unless we bar all communication between people, human beings are always going to attempt to persuade others and are always going to be subject to persuasion by others. Societies can pass laws forbidding certain types of persuasion, as we have done in putting limitations on advertising. Such laws or limitations on persuasion can cover only a very small number of possible communication situations. We believe firmly that a better solution to the use of unethical communication is to teach all people to use persuasion effectively, and to recognize and evaluate persuasion when it is directed toward them. The more information the people in a society have about persuasion and persuasive techniques, the more likely it is that people can increase their resistance to would-be hucksters.

Personal Ethical Responsibilities

Each one of us is constantly working to develop our own ethical position. Below are some suggestions that might help you in that task:

1. Develop a personal set of ethical standards of conduct to help guide your own behavior. We are not advocates for any particular moral code or any specific set of ethical standards. We do believe that as authors, teachers, citizens, and scholars, we do have a personal set of ethical standards. By the time you finish this book, you should be able to identify those standards that we possess, and be able to evaluate them in terms of your own standards. When you engage in persuasive communication it should always be consistent with the set of ethical and moral standards you have developed.

2. Know all you can about persuasion. You do not normally attempt to use an electric drill without finding out where the switch is and what the drill can do. Persuasion is also a tool, and you ought to know what the effects are likely to be if you use this tool.

3. Establish for yourself some criteria for making decisions. Decision making is an important part of the persuasive process, and you ought to understand the ways in which decisions are made. Persuasion is used in communicating decisions about a topic. If the decision you make is a poor one, your persuasive efforts may or may not be successful, but most probably, the long-range effects are not likely to be desirable.

We all act as both source and receiver of persuasive messages. Most of our formal education, however, has gone toward training us to be better sources of communication, while the fact remains that we act as receivers of communication far more than we are able to act as sources of communication. We listen to the radio, read the newspaper, listen to other people, and view the television set many more hours a day than we spend in actually putting out messages. Here are some suggestions to help you predict the effects of particular persuasive messages:

1. Know what your own biases are. We cannot know exactly how we will react to each persuasive message we face, but we can make ourselves aware of some of the types of arguments to which we tend to react favorably or unfavorably.

2. Know your source. You are exposed to newspapers, magazines, television, radio, neighbors, friends, and relatives. It is impossible for you to become an expert on all the problems that face you. You will have to depend on the credibility of people with whom you communicate.

3. Become a collector of information. As you listen to the messages available to you, your predispositions toward listening to one message and refusing to listen to another message may make it difficult for you to make final decisions based on all the available information. If, however, you collect information from all kinds of sources, and of all degrees of reliability, you can include this information in your decision-making process.

FOOTNOTES

1. D.K. Berlo, *The Process of Communication*, (New York: Holt, Rinehart, and Winston, 1960), pp. 40-72.

2. G. Gerbner, "The Interaction Model: Perception and Communication," in J. Ball and F. Byrnes, eds., *Research, Principles and Practices in Visual Communication*, (E. Lansing, Mich.: National Project in Agricultural Communication, 1960), pp. 4-15.

3. E. Schramm, "How Communication Works," in W. Schramm, ed., *The Process and Effects of Mass Communication*, (Urbana, Ill.: University of Illinois Press, 1954), pp. 3-26.

4. B.H. Westley and M.S. McLean, Jr., "A Conceptual Model for Communication Research," *Journalism Quarterly*, vol. 34 (1957), pp. 31-38.

5. C. Shannon and W. Weaver, *The Mathematical Theory of Communication*, (Urbana, Ill.: University of Illinois Press, 1949), pp. 4-6.

6. *The Random House Dictionary of the English Language*, (New York: Random House, 1967), s.v. "persuasion."

7. K. Andersen, *Persuasion Theory and Practice*, (Boston: Allyn & Bacon, 1971), p. 6.

8. T. Scheidel, *Persuasive Speaking*, (Glenview, Ill.: Scott, Foresman and Co., 1967), p. 1.

9. R. Bostrom, *Persuasion*, (Englewood Cliffs, N.J.: Prentice-Hall, Inc., 1983), p. 11.

10. See R.E. Petty and J.F. Cacioppo, *Attitudes and Persuasion: Classic and Contemporary Approaches*, (Dubuque, Iowa: Wm. C. Brown, 1981).

11. See Petty and Cacioppo, *Attitudes and Persuasion: Classic and Contemporary Approaches*.

12. See Petty and Cacioppo, *Attitudes and Persuasion: Classic and Contemporary Approaches*.

13. In truth, the term "propaganda" is not viewed as a negative term in other countries. In some countries, a Department or Division of Propaganda exists which serves to circulate to the public the views of the government, which may or may not be intentionally biased or deceptive material. Further note that if we define propaganda as an ideologically oriented slant or view on materials, our textbook may be viewed as "propaganda" in socialist countries, because our material is

slanted toward capitalism, free enterprise and the accumulation of goods. A book on "persuasion" in socialist countries would actually look like a book on "group discussion" in which members of a political group or caucus (as happens on a kibbutz, or in a factory) meet to make a decision.

14. See Petty and Cacioppo, *Attitudes and Persuasion: Classic and Contemporary Approaches.*

15. See, for instance, R.B. Zajonc, "On the Primacy of Affect," *American Psychologist*, vol. 39 (1984), pp. 117-123.

16. D. Katz, The Functional Approach to the Study of Attitudes. *Public Opinion Quarterly*, vol. 24 (1960), pp. 163-204.

17. Petty and Cacioppo, *Attitudes and Persuasion: Classic and Contemporary Approaches*, p. 8.

18. M.J. Rosenberg and C.I. Hovland, "Cognitive, Affective, and Behavioral Components of Attitudes," in C.I. Hovland and M.J. Rosenberg, eds., *Attitude, Organization and Change*, (New Haven, Conn.: Yale University Press, 1960), pp. 1-14.

19. R. LaPiere, "Attitudes versus Actions," *Social Forces*, vol. 13 (1934), pp. 230-237.

20. D.P. Cushman and R.D. McPhee, eds., Message-Attitude-Behavior Relationship: Theory, Methodology, and Application (New York: Academic Press, 1980); A.W. Wicker, Attitudes versus Actions: The Relationship of Verbal and Overt Behavioral Responses to Attitude Objects. *Journal of Social Issues*, vol. 25 (1969), pp. 41-78.

21. R.W. Weigel and L.S. Newman, "Increasing Attitude-Behavior Correspondence by Broadening the Scope of the Behavioral Measure," *Journal of Personality and Social Psychology*, vol. 33 (1976), pp. 793-802.

22. I. Ajzen and M. Fishbein, "Attitude-Behavior Relations: A Theoretical Analysis and Review of Empirical Research," *Psychological Bulletin*, vol. 84 (1977), pp. 888-918.

23. R.H. Fazio and M.P. Zanna, "Direct Experience and Attitude-Behavior Consistency," in L. Berkowitz, ed., *Advances in Experimental Social Psychology*, vol. 14 (New York: Academic Press, 1981), pp. 161-202.

24. A.R. Davidson and J.J. Jaccard, "Variables That Moderate the Attitude-Behavior Relation: Results of a Longitudinal Survey," *Journal of Personality and Social Psychology*, vol. 37 (1979), pp. 1364-1376.

25. Louis A. Day, *Ethics in Media Communications: Cases and Controversies*, (Belmont, Calif.: Wadsworth, 1991).

26. W.J. Brown, and A. Singhal, "Ethical Dilemmas of Prosocial Television," *Communication Quarterly*, vol. 38 (1990), pp. 268-280.

27. K.S. Johnson-Cartee and G.A. Copeland, *Negative Political Advertising: Coming of Age*, (Hillsdale, N.J.: Erlbaum, 1991).

28. R.P. Adler, G.S. Lesser, L.K. Meringoff, T.S. Robertson, J.R. Rossiter, and S. Ward, *The Effects of Television Advertising on Children* (Lexington, Mass.: Lexington Books, 1980).

29. See, for a brief history, C.U. Larson, *Persuasion: Reception and Responsibility* (5th edition) (Belmont, Calif.: Wadsworth), p. 43-44.

30. J.I. Richards, *Deceptive Advertising: Behavioral Study of a Legal Concept*, (Hillsdale, N.J.: Erlbaum, 1990).

K E Y   T E R M S   A N D   C O N C E P T S

communication model
persuasive communication
information dissemination (campaign)
compliance
propaganda
mass media effects
beliefs
attitudes
affective primacy
ego-defensive function
value-expressive function
knowledge function
utilitarian function
cognitive change
affective change
behavioral change
attitude-behavior problem
ethics
subliminal messages
manipulation
puffery
deception

DEVELOPING ATTITUDES AND BELIEFS

The model of persuasion we discussed in Chapter 1 emphasizes changes in attitudes and beliefs. The fact that we emphasized changes suggests that the parties to persuasive communication situations already have a set of attitudes (or beliefs) before they are exposed to persuasive messages. In truth, attitudes are often shaped very early in life. How do people obtain the attitudes they have? What kinds of beliefs do people have? This chapter looks carefully at these questions. First we will talk, specifically, about how attitudes and beliefs are formed and shaped. Then, we will talk about the psychological motivation to hold together similar or compatible attitudes and beliefs.

LEARNING: CONDITIONING AND MODELING

What are Attitudes? What are Beliefs?

Obviously, not everyone has the same attitudes. Take a simple object, such as Silly Putty. One child may have little direct experience with this doughy plaything, but sees others having fun with it on television. This is called "observational learning," learning attitudes (or behaviors) by observing others. In preschool, the child is excited to play with Silly Putty for the first time and has a wonderful time playing with it with his/her new friends. S/he makes things and can make imprints of the comics from the newspaper. The teacher praises the child's actions, thereby *rewarding* her, and strengthening the attitude. Later, the parents take the child to a store to buy some putty, and the child shows a liking (interest, excitement) not *only* for Silly Putty in the store, but to similar products (like modeling clay) as well. This child learned a positive attitude toward the putty and then *generalized* this liking to other playthings similar in appearance. It is part of human nature to

generalize our likes and dislikes for objects to other objects similar in appearance (size, shape, color, odor, and so forth).

Another child may have a radically different experience with the same plaything. An older sibling may have stuck Silly Putty in the child's ear when s/he was asleep as part of a prank, or the child could have gotten some stuck in her/his hair and felt pain when a parent tried to remove it. The child could have left it on the car's back seat on a hot day, where it melted and s/he was punished. On the first day of preschool, such a child would avoid the Silly Putty, or perhaps sit quietly, experiencing some feelings of uneasiness, apprehension, or dread, while other kids played with the dough. At the store, the child would avoid the product and would shy away from other doughy products.

It is possible for a *single* experience with an object to shape an attitude. A child bitten at an early age by a large dog might need only one such experience to develop highly negative attitudes toward dogs. However, most attitudes are formed after *many* experiences. For example, in "learning experiments" (see below), an attitude toward a name is conditioned after it is *paired* sixteen (or ten or twenty) times with other words for which we have *negative feelings*.

Once we have formed our basic set of attitudes, we use these as a kind of filter that determines how new attitudes are going to be formed. For almost thirty years, this set of attitudes has been called a *frame of reference*. Clearly, some children are reared to have high levels of confidence and self-esteem; they are optimistic, helpful, outgoing, energetic and appear unafraid to take risks. This optimistic and outgoing orientation affects how they view other people (potential friends), whether they'd try something new, seek out being the center of attention, and so on. On the other hand, a number of children are apprehensive, lacking in esteem, do not want to be the center of attention, are suspicious of new people and avoid new things and avoid taking risks. Persuading these people requires different approaches and appeals (see Chapter 6).

Children are engaged in gathering information about the world from the minute they are born. They receive this information from their parents, brothers, sisters, aunts, uncles, friends, neighbors, teachers, and television. They have pleasant and unpleasant experiences, and the child learns to avoid the neighborhood bully or is attracted to a nice kid down the block. Each time the child has an experience, there is a good chance the frame of reference is further developed, reinforced, or modified in some way.

The information we gather is not perceived as a "blooming, buzzing confusion." Our brain operates in such a way that the information we receive is placed into belief structures containing related information. We develop structures about nature, people, education, churches, and governments. By the time we are adults, these structures have become extremely complex. Reference frames are not composed of simple attitudes alone; for every attitude there can be a plethora of beliefs we hold concerning how the world operates. Following Rokeach,[1] we view beliefs as simple propositions or statements that can be preceded by the phrase, "I believe that . . . " All of us have many different beliefs. For example, most of us would agree with "I believe that the world is round," but most of us would not agree with "I believe that voodoo magic is strong and powerful." Yet people who have adopted this latter belief hold it with great conviction and sincerity. We can hold literally thousands of beliefs. In order to better understand the nature of beliefs, we need to talk about basic distinctions made between different beliefs.

First, we can distinguish between beliefs that tell us about the world around us (called *descriptive* beliefs), beliefs that focus on our judgments of what is good and bad (called *evaluative beliefs*), and beliefs concerning how people should behave (called *prescriptive* beliefs). Examples of descriptive beliefs include:

- I believe oranges are round.

- I believe egg shells are delicate.

- I believe the sky is blue.

- I believe we have entered a gang territory, based on this graffiti.

There are many descriptive beliefs dealing with our senses. While many of these beliefs are self-evident, we can test the validity or truthfulness of the descriptive beliefs by testing the roundness of oranges, how much pressure is required to break egg shells, and so on. Many commercials, like the "info-commercial" we see late at night, rely on audience members *describing* what they sense when they experience juice machines, car wax that protects a car from fire, and knives that can cut through metal. These claims deal with the sense of touch, smell, hearing, and so on.

Evaluative beliefs include statements like:

- I believe that my university is a good institution.

- I believe that this diet is a good, safe diet.

- I believe that buying this car will prove to be a wise financial investment.

- I believe this is a good major for getting a job when I graduate.

Evaluative beliefs link buying a product or taking some action with a positive consequence or benefit (or, perhaps, with avoiding a negative consequence or cost). Proof or evidence for holding such a belief does not stem solely from direct observation of what our senses tell us, but rather from evidence accumulated over time (actually losing weight on the diet but not losing energy, hearing from authorities or experts that a car or a major purchase is a good choice). Of course, an important question is "What is the difference between an evaluative belief and an attitude?" The two are related, because the development of an evaluative belief is obviously related to developing an attitude on the same topic. However, it is possible to develop an evaluative belief that is highly "rational," "unemotional," "detached," and possessing no "affective component." For example, a person may say "I have studied consumer reports and I have decided that Quaker State is better for my car, and that Tylenol is a better overall product than the other brands I have studied." This consumer has developed several evaluative beliefs, but few *affective* feelings (such as arousal or excitement) are involved with the beliefs.

Third, there are beliefs *prescribing* what people should do. Prescriptive beliefs commonly are linked to "higher-order" beliefs called *values* that focus on certain important consequences: a World at Peace, Equality, Salvation, a Comfortable Life, a Happy Family Life, and so on. For example, people who emphasize equality between men and women might advocate a prescriptive belief concerning the "modern" role of women in advertising ("I can relate to this ad; her husband should, and is, sharing household duties").[2] On the other hand, a "traditional" person might prescribe behaviors deemed appropriate to that role (such as, "If being a housewife is a full-time job, she should be able to find time to cook"). Because of their different beliefs, "modern" and "traditional" people would react very differently to the roles portrayed in commercials.[3] Prescriptive beliefs deal with what people *should* and *should not* do, and these beliefs run a gamut of roles: male, female, minority member, supporter, sponsor, citizen, and so on.

Second, beliefs can be distinguished from one another on the basis of their origination. Sarbin, Taft and Bailey[4] argue that there are four major sources of beliefs:

1. *Induction.* A person develops a generalized belief based on a summation of past observations. Through repeated and confirmatory experiences a person may state "I believe that red apples are good," "I believe that smoking has a negative effect on my breathing."

2. *Construction.* A person develops a belief concerning how two or more events are related to one another, and this construction may have little or nothing to do with reasoning or logic. Some constructions may be nothing more than conjecture based on limited observations: "I believe people who drive yellow cars are mean and dangerous."

3. *Analogy.* A person develops a belief based on similarities among things or events. If two objects (oranges and tangerines) are both round, and both are surrounded by a certain kind of peel, one may assume that the two are also similar in tastes. One believes a tangerine would taste like an orange, until it is tasted and direct experience tells us otherwise.

4. *Authority.* A person develops and maintains a belief based on the authority of others. A vast majority of beliefs stem from authorities—the world is round, there exists a hole in the ozone, Napoleon was a great leader, Nazis were evil, and so on. These examples reflect only a few of the thousands of authority-related beliefs.

Depending upon who the authority figure is and whether other authority figures provide collaborative support, any number of beliefs based on authorities may be called into question by induction, or direct personal experience. For example, a person may have grown up using a certain automobile wax because the parents claimed it was superior. If this evaluative belief (Car wax J is the best on the market.) is anchored only by the parents' advice, such a belief can be changed easily.

A third way of classifying beliefs is in terms of a "central-peripheral" dimension.[5] Figure 2.1

EXAMPLE OF BELIEF SYSTEM: CENTRAL, AUTHORITY, AND PERIPHERAL BELIEFS

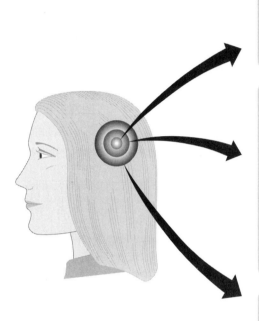

Central Belief

This is our only planet and I believe we must protect it if we (the human race) are to survive, and if we are to maintain a good quality of life.

Authority Beliefs

Give a hoot, don't pollute.
Only you can prevent forest fires.
Recycle: It's in your hands.
Be prepared!
Don't be a litterbug.
Don't play with matches.

Any other beliefs and instructions communicated by fire marshals, scout masters, teachers, the mass media, and parents concerning the environment that can be phrased into "I believe..." statements ("I believe it is wrong to pollute").

Peripheral Beliefs

I believe these cotton clothes, made and dyed without toxins, are more environmentally safe than other clothes I might buy.

I believe these garbage sacks, though plastic, will break down more quickly than the alternative garbage sacks.

illustrates this view of an individual's belief structure. Highly central beliefs, such as: "The world is round"; "Water is heavier than air"; "Democracy is a desirable form of government"; and "I believe what my eyes see" form the core of any individual's belief structure. We acquire our most central or "primitive" beliefs very early in life.

Furthermore, we continue to strengthen these beliefs as we go through life, and continuously validate them from our experiences.

Rokeach[6] suggests that there are two types of central beliefs. For one type, there is complete agreement within the society that the belief is correct. The belief that "rocks fall to the ground when dropped" is an example of a primitive belief everyone within a society would agree upon. The other type of highly central belief is illustrated by expressions such as "I believe in God"; "Black cats bring bad luck"; "I am basically a nice person"; "I believe it is up to us, now, to save this planet from pollution and abuse" (see Figure 2.1). These beliefs are strongly held by individuals, but there may not be consensus among members of a society as to their validity.

A second layer of beliefs illustrated in Figure 2.1 is comprised of those connected with authority. Children learn they can trust some individuals and not others. They learn to put faith in what their parents and teachers tell them. They learn that the president of the United States ought to be believed, but that certain other world leaders are untrustworthy. Our beliefs about authorities lead us to categorize others either as positive or as negative authorities. We place faith in the statements of positive authorities and tend to disbelieve what negative authorities tell us. Authority beliefs are less firmly held than central beliefs, but they help govern to whom we will listen and to respect. Many individuals who hold authority positions (teachers, fire marshals, scout leaders, and so on) communicate a number of messages to us that can be recast as descriptive or evaluative beliefs: "I believe it is good to care about the environment and to not pollute," and "I believe it is good to not cause forest fires." Finally, we can talk about peripheral beliefs. Beliefs such as: "Shampoo Q makes your hair look luxurious"; or "Steak is best when it is cooked rare"; or "CBS has the best news program" are examples of peripheral beliefs. Peripheral beliefs can be divided into two categories: those which are based on central beliefs and those which are not. An example of a centrally based (primitively derived) belief is where an individual holds that the "morning-after pill" is just like abortion and should be banned; the person arrived at that belief from central beliefs concerning the value of life. Many peripheral beliefs concerning the value of life. Many peripheral beliefs are not based on central beliefs. Supposing two very different people adopt the peripheral beliefs in Figure 2.1. The one whose peripheral belief is also centrally based and authority-based will probably be more resistant to change. S/he will probably buy the environmentally safe products for a longer period of time, maybe even paying more for them, than the other person, who adopts the peripheral belief because it is the trendy, "cool," or currently politically correct thing to do.

We construct frames of reference composed of our attitudes and beliefs. These reference frames can be used to make predictions about the effects of persuasion. Beliefs are formed along a set of central-peripheral dimensions, and this organization allows us to make predictions about the probable effects of persuasive messages.

1. The more central the belief, the more resistant individuals will be to changes in the belief. If your persuasive goal demands that the receiver change a central belief, it is very unlikely success will come easily or at all. The difficulty of changing a primitive belief through persuasion is greatly magnified if the belief is one that has consensus within the society.

Beliefs based on authority are also resistant to change, but not to the extent central beliefs are. The individual who believes through long experience that "policemen are always trustworthy" may have that belief weakened if an example of "police brutality" is witnessed. Later, as s/he accumulates more evidence concerning police actions of intolerance, brutality, and so forth, s/he will change this authority belief.

2. Those beliefs derived from central beliefs are more resistant to change than those existing only as peripheral beliefs. To a unionized laborer, the belief "People should buy American-made products" may be linked to patriotism and equality (we Americans are all together in this recession;

we are losing power to other countries in the world). Other individuals may hold the same belief, but the belief of buying American may not be linked to important central beliefs; such a peripheral belief would be easier to change, compared to that of the unionized worker.

3. The more central the belief which is changed, the more widespread will be the changes in the remainder of the individual's belief structure. The central beliefs we hold are connected to many peripheral beliefs. A strong belief in God may lead also to a belief in the Bible as an authority, in ministers as mediators between God and man, in tax exemption for churches, in the desirability of using public funds for church-supported schools, and in the importance of prayer in the public schools. Each of these beliefs may have been derived from the central belief in God (and the value of organized religion).

This principle suggests that a desired change in belief may produce unexpected changes in other beliefs. It is impossible to predict whether this secondary change will be favorable or unfavorable to the communicator's cause. The communicator who is able to effect a change in a receiver's beliefs about the value of compulsory government health insurance may find the receiver has also changed beliefs about the role of physicians in the health care system.

One of the best examples of a change in a central belief occurred (and is still occurring) in what was once the U.S.S.R. Imagine people who lost family members in the Bolshevik Revolution and in World War II, devoting their lives, and making sacrifices in the name of Communism, believing that capitalism was bad. Today, these people have to come to grips with the belief that what was once good (Communism) is now bad and to be discarded, while what was bad (capitalism) is now good and to be embraced. Among older, more devout Communists, such radical belief changes would be resisted at first. Later, when the change in the fundamental, central belief is in place, there

will be a reassessment pervading many other beliefs.

So far, we have characterized the types of beliefs and attitudes that combine to form different "reference frames." Now, we draw attention to how attitudes are learned or "conditioned."

Classic Approaches to Learning

Most people have a common understanding of what is meant by the term "learning." We "learn" to read, to ride a bicycle, and to drive a car. This common sense definition can be extended to a general definition of learning as the process by which some aspect of human behavior is acquired or changed through an individual's encounter with events in the environment. Basic to all theories of learning is the assumption that there is an explainable or predictable relationship between stimuli and responses. A "stimulus" can be defined as any event which can be perceived by the organism. Thus, in a persuasive communication situation, the message serves as a stimulus. The source serves as another stimulus, as does the physical setting for the situation. A "response" can be defined as anything which the receiver does as a result of perceiving a stimulus. The original category scheme we defined in Chapter 1 (changes in affect, cognition, and behavior) covers the kinds of responses in which we might be interested. We will consider three fundamental ways of learning: classical conditioning, instrumental learning, and social learning theory.

Classical Conditioning

This form of learning involves the famous Pavlov's dog situation. Normally, when a hungry dog (the organism) is presented with food, the dog will salivate. The food is called *the unconditioned stimulus* and the salivating is called the *unconditioned response;* they are "un" conditioned because no learning or conditioning has yet taken place, and the food-salivating relationship occurs naturally in the world. However, when a bell or a light is *simultaneously paired* with the presentation of the food, the dog "learns" to salivate when the light (or bell) is presented. In the diagram of this learning format (Figure 2.2), the natural order (uncondi-

tioned stimuli and unconditioned response) is presented along the bottom of panel (a). In the Pavlov studies, a bell (or light) does not produce, naturally, salivation in a dog. However, after the bell (or light) has been repeatedly paired with the presentation of the meat over time, then a dog will learn to salivate when the bell is rung, even when food is not present. The dog is *conditioned* to

FIGURE   2.2

ILLUSTRATION OF CLASSICAL CONDITIONING

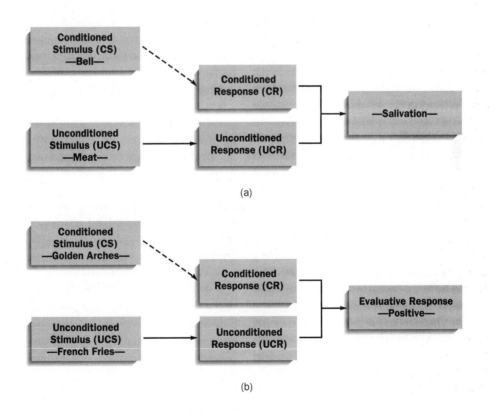

Panel (a) illustrates conditioning of a dog's response to a ringing bell. Panel (b) illustrates the conditioning of a favorable attitude toward golden arches, through a person's love of french fries.

salivate when a bell (or light) is presented. Similarly, some of us enjoy tasty french fries and salivate at the thought of french fries. If the act of eating french fries is consistently paired with a pair of golden arches, then the positive feeling of eating french fries carries over to our liking for the golden arches.

Considerable research evidence supports the operation of classical conditioning. For example, many studies have paired offensive odors with nonsense syllables, Turkish letters, and so forth (stimuli about which we have neutral attitudes), or with names of people. After consistently pairing the two, students tend to dislike the name, or the Turkish character, or whatever. In fact, one study conducted by Berkowitz and Knurek[7] paired either the name of George or the name of Ed to 16 unpleasant adjectives over the course of a study. Later, the students walked down the hall of the psychology building and reported to a "second study," which allegedly involved group discussion. This second experiment was rigged so that two of the group members were called Ed and George. The students who had just been exposed to negative adjectives paired with the name George behaved in a manner friendlier toward Ed than toward George, while the students who were conditioned to dislike the name Ed behaved in a manner friendlier toward George than toward Ed. Classical conditioning, then, can influence our attitudes.

Conditioning principles are also frequently used by persuasive communicators. In 1982, Gorn,[8] in fact, renewed interest in the use of classical conditioning to advertisements by simultaneously pairing music from the movie *Grease* (which students liked at the time) with a pen (toward which students had an initially neutral attitude). According to Gorn, students later showed a more positive attitude toward the type of pen that was linked to the (well-liked) music. Other attempts in classical conditioning have used humor,

as is done with the Phillips light bulb commercials—the light bulb burns out and we hear the cat being sucked into a vacuum cleaner (there are a series of humorous commercials ending in darkness and humor like this one). As we smile (unconditioned response to a joke), the word "Phillips" appears across a black screen—thus, a positive attitude is shaped towards the word Phillips. This company markets a package that is black with familiar Phillips lettering so the positive response might be cued when we are in the store.

Gorn elicited a positive attitude toward the pen after only one pairing or association made between the music and the pen. Other researchers are not so optimistic concerning the effectiveness of a single exposure. Stuart, Shimp, and Engle,[9] for example, used a slide-show format to link a brand of toothpaste with four splendid, pleasant scenes: a mountain waterfall, a sunset over an island, a blue sky with clouds photographed through the mast of a boat, and a sunset over the ocean. Stuart and her colleagues compared "one trial" (the toothpaste was paired to one scene), with "three trials," "ten trials," and "twenty trials." They thought more frequent exposures would result in more positive attitudes. They found, like Gorn, one exposure was effective in producing a more positive attitude, although slightly more positive evaluations occurred with ten and twenty exposures. People indicated greater liking for the toothpaste after it was paired with strikingly beautiful scenes.

While classical conditioning does in fact work to shape or "condition" attitudes, serious limitations arise with its everyday use. First, note that what we mean by "simultaneous pairings" can actually involve one of three presentations: (a) a *forward conditioning* occurs when the conditioned stimulus (the toothpaste) is presented for a few seconds before it is paired with the unconditioned stimulus; (b) a true *simultaneous* pairing occurs when the toothpaste and unconditioned stimulus (scenery) co-occur for exactly the same time frame—starting and ending at the same time; and, (c) a *backward* conditioning occurs when the scenery is presented first, and then presented along with the toothpaste. Stuart and her colleagues argue that the forward conditioning is vastly superior to the other formats. In their study, they presented a slide of the toothpaste for five seconds, followed by five seconds of one of the four pleasant scenes, followed by a five-second photograph of the toothpaste superimposed over the photograph of the pleasant scene. Of course, it is impossible to reproduce this exact sequence in real communication settings. However, the implication is obvious: whenever possible, one should present the new product (the unconditioned stimulus) prior to actually pairing it with the unconditioned stimulus. Watch the sequence of these events next time you view commercials.

Two other limitations should be mentioned. First, classical conditioning largely works for products that are neutral or unfamiliar to the receivers. Most people have a fairly neutral initial response to the word Phillips. Other names, like Bush, Hitler, Cody, Kennedy, are already associated with other attitudes and thoughts, so there would not be any straightforward kind of conditioning using these names. Second, the typical advertising situation relying on classical conditioning does not contain an *information* component. There are a number of products sold using simple associations with jokes, humor, pleasant music from the 1950s and 1960s, and these ads do not have a narrator telling the receiver the facts or evidence concerning the product. The goal is to allow the positive feelings to be transferred to the new product. Interrupting the music-product or humor-product association to mention facts and evidence would cause a whole different type of reaction in the mind of the receiver, and the conditioning effect may not be quite as strong.[10]

Instrumental Learning

In instrumental (also referred to as "operant") learning situations, a stimulus is presented to an organism. When the correct or desired response has been made, some reinforcement or reward is given in order to either fix or strengthen the response. Instrumental learning situations suggest that if the organism makes several incorrect responses not immediately rewarded and then makes a correct response which is rewarded, the probability increases that the subject will repeat the correct response if the same stimulus is presented.

Instrumental learning works because people want to maximize rewards and minimize punishments. If rewards are contingent upon a person's successfully selecting the correct behavior, and if the rewards are indeed valued by the individual, then rewards strengthen the individual's tendency to engage in the behavior. We have all used instrumental learning on others and have had instrumental learning used on us. For example, suppose a fund-raising agency sends several letters urging an individual to donate money to some charity. If the individual eventually does send a contribution, the fund-raisers immediately send a letter of thanks, and perhaps a small token of appreciation such as a pin or a ballpoint pen. As an example of instrumental learning, the follow-up letter and gift are designed to be the reinforcing agent.

Considerable research evidence indicates we can verbally shape the attitudes of others. Since the 1950s, studies have found that experimenters can influence the frequency at which a person engages in a behavior by conditioning the behavior with positive verbal statements (such as, "good"). The study by Insko[11] is an excellent example of this approach. The study was conducted at the University of Hawaii, where there is an annual

Aloha Week Festival. Students were called and interviewed about their attitudes toward establishing a second, springtime Aloha Festival. Generally speaking, most students should have mixed feelings about the second festival since on one hand it would disrupt university operation and distract from the traditional festival. On the other hand, a second festival would be fun. Students who were telephoned were read fourteen statements concerning pros and cons about the springtime festival and were asked to indicate the extent to which they agreed or disagreed with the statements. During this interview phase, whenever students made a statement favoring the Aloha week Festival, the interviewer would reward them by saying "good"; the other students were also rewarded with "good" whenever they expressed an attitude toward the festival which was unfavorable.

If verbal reinforcement can shape one's attitudes, then you'd expect that the pro-springtime-festival students would be more in favor of Aloha Week after the interview, while the others would be less in favor of it. This expectation was exactly what Insko found. A week or so after the telephone survey, Insko distributed a "Local Issues Questionnaire" and one of the items just happened to be about a Springtime Aloha Week Festival. Even a week after being interviewed, students who had been rewarded for making positive statements about the festival indicated more positive attitudes than students rewarded for expressing anti-festival sentiments.

Why does verbal reinforcement work? According to Insko and Cialdini[12] a verbal reward does several things. First, a verbal reward communicates to the student the interviewer's attitude. This communication represents the information conveyed by reinforcement—that "good" informs the student of the interviewer's point of view and allows for agreement or conformity to exist. Second, a verbal reward communicates approval and liking for the student. According to this

second outcome, the more often an interviewer says "good," the better the interviewer-student rapport becomes. Insko and Cialdini argued that verbal responses have an impact on two psychological variables: amount of information and rapport. An interviewer uses "good only" when rewarding the receiver for making the "correct" yes responses, and this verbal conditioning results in high levels of interviewer-receiver rapport, and moderate levels of information. The "good and humph" format is used when the interviewer uses "good" when the receiver responds in a desired fashion, and "humph" when responding in the opposite direction. (Some of you may train your dog or toilet train your child using this format.) This produces high levels of information, and moderate levels of rapport (it is moderate because people do not like to hear "humph"). Finally, the "humph only" format is only moderate in the level of information it conveys, and creates low rapport. Insko and Cialdini argued, and found, that learning was more effective with both the "good only" and "good and humph" formats, while the "humph only" was less effective.[13]

Social Learning Theory

So far we have talked about types of learning that view the receiver (organism) as relatively passive, reacting to attempts to associate products to humor, music, or sex, or waiting for us to provide rewards after behaving in a desired fashion. Such learning situations are important and are relevant to certain contexts; however, humans are capable of "self-regulation," meaning we often reward ourselves, influence ourselves and make plans for the future based on past knowledge and the use of symbols. Smith[14] noted three essential aspects of Bandura's "social learning theory":[15]

1. We are capable of self-reward and self-influence.

2. Environmental punishments and rewards are no more than symbolic representations of costs and benefits that are stored in memory and later used to direct behavior.

3. Our internal and external worlds continuously interact to shape many of our behaviors.

We all learn rules that govern our behavior or gain knowledge about the consequences of our actions. We learn that there is some probability that engaging in behaviors a, b, c, and d will provide rewards, and that engaging in behaviors e, f, g, and h will elicit punishments. This theory also views people as actively choosing to reward themselves, and learning to apply contingencies concerning when and how they will reward themselves. Advertisers, for example, reinforce self-rewards by messages such as "You deserve a break today," "For all you do, this Bud's for you," "You work hard, you deserve to (buy yourself a gold necklace)," "The reward" (the only words on a billboard advertising hard liquor).

Bandura argues that reinforcement is essentially *knowledge of the probable (including imagined) positive or negative consequences of a future behavior*.[16] Bandura further believes reinforcement serves two functions. First, *information* is conveyed in reinforcement such that a person "learns" which behaviors result in favorable outcomes and effects, or in unfavorable outcomes and undesirable effects. There are endless examples of the "information" value of the reinforcement one has received from others. One *knows* not to use swear words in front of the minister, the nuns, the school principal, and so on. A driver believes (based on movies, television, what parents say, what the driver education teacher claimed, and what friends have confided) that being polite to a police officer might pay off better than trying to argue with him/her.

The second function served by reinforcement is *motivational*. A good deal of behavior is not reactive (as in operant learning, when a reward is given *after* we have successfully completed a task); a good deal of behavior is designed toward the fulfillment of future goals or consequences. Future consequences, such as getting accepted into a good law school, or being promoted to vice-president of the company, all require the development and implementation of plans. These future consequences operate as *current motivators*, although the goal we hope to achieve may take months or years to achieve.

As Smith[17] noted, reinforcement stems from three environmental sources:

1. **Direct Experience.** As in the case of *induction* concerning beliefs, or our example with Silly Putty, personal experiences create attitudes. We learn it is not a good idea to melt Silly Putty in the back seat of the car and there is some probability we will be punished.

2. **Role Playing.** A person may also learn attitudes and behavior-attitude relationships by role playing someone else. For example, role playing a person who is dying from cancer or role playing a member of a different race who experiences racism can have a strong impact on both children and adults regarding attitudes toward smoking and equality.

3. **Modeling.** We observe others behaving and we model our behaviors after theirs. Obvious examples of *observational learning* include how to perform some dance or aerobic routines. We see other individuals use a particular product, or engage in a certain action, and they increase status, win gold medals, successfully lose weight, and so forth. Children model the pro-social and anti-social actions of parents, friends and television characters. Modeling is more likely to occur if: (a) the observer focuses his/her *attention* on the model's behavior; (b) the observer *retains* the information

SOME GENERAL PRINCIPLES OF LEARNING

Individuals differ radically in learning. One person may quickly see a stimulus or a message, react quickly and make a prompt decision. Another person may ignore a message for months, and slowly change behaviors. Keeping in mind major individual differences, the following principles should help explain some of the differences receivers make when exposed to the same message.

1.   *Individuals differ in their ability to respond.*

Imagine a message urging people to take a wonderful ten-day vacation to Tahiti. Even though many people may wish to take the trip, it is likely that only a few would have the money, or would be able to take the time.

2.   *Individuals differ in their readiness to respond.*

Most people cannot operate at full efficiency early in the morning. Others have a period immediately after lunch or dinner when they are not very attentive to messages. Do this little experiment in your spare time: Count up how many advertisements your local newspaper contains each day for gyms, spas, and diet centers. When we did this little project we found that the Monday newspaper had the most ads. Why? People are busy as the typical work week progresses, and then they tend to party, attend games, and eat out over the weekend. When feeling guilty, they are *most likely to respond* and join a gym early in the week.

Here are some questions that may prove helpful: (1) Is the receiver paying attention? (2) Are the physical surroundings such that they will not detract from the communicator's message? (3) Has there been any attempt at "preteaching"? The term "preteaching" refers to the messages that may be sent ahead of time to give the receiver the necessary background for an understanding of the source's message. (4) Did we make the message easy to comprehend for a receiver? People will always differ in readiness, but if we can answer "yes" to these questions, persuasion should be easier.

3.   *Individuals differ in their motivation to respond.*

There are a number of motives or drives that help to determine how people will respond to a message. Learning is facilitated when the receiver is made to feel that a message is appealing to a particular motive.

4.   *Reinforcement is helpful in establishing response.*

This is the principle of reward and punishment that has been discussed in the text. To be effective, the reward (or punishment) given has be something that is truly valued by the receiver. People do not all react to the same reward. For some, praise given after completion of a response is sufficient to insure future repetition of the behavior, while money is necessary to influence another. Others are motivated to avoid fear, to gain economically, or to gain esteem. One needs to match appropriate rewards with the appropriate audiences.

5. ***In learning, active participation is better than passive participation.***

This principle is useful whether you are engaged in a traditional persuasive campaign, or are engaged in mutual persuasive attempts with another individual. Pay close attention to advertisements and make a list of commercials that prompt participation in receivers. McDonald's managed to get millions of receivers to repeat the ingredients of a "Big Mac," and later challenged millions to quickly repeat the entire McDonald's menu. Active participation on the part of the individual facilitates learning and recall.

6. ***Meaningful responses are learned more easily than meaningless ones.***

This is another principle that seems obvious, but examples exist to show that communicators sometimes forget to make their demands meaningful to the receiver. In 1966, Medicare became part of the American scene, and everyone over the age of sixty-five who signed up for the program by March 31, 1966, was to be covered under the program. Those who did not sign up by that time would have to wait more than two years. Still, many did not sign up in time. The main emphasis in the messages sent out by the government was that people need sign up by a particular date, but very *little* attention was given to telling receivers just what Medicare would do for them. Without a fuller explanation, people simply understood that the government wanted them to sign up for something, but they did not understand the benefits. Eventually, the deadline had to be extended, and emphasis in the advertisements was changed.

so that it can be used later; (c) the observer is *competent* in engaging in the behaviors or in the sequence of behaviors required to perform the observed behaviors; and, (d) the observer has to be *motivated* to enact the behavior or the sequence of behaviors—there needs to be some end-state or final outcome that is desired.

There are six factors that affect the success of modeling:[18]

1. Receivers are motivated to engage in rewarded behaviors and avoid punished ones. However, since behaviors often have both costs and benefits associated with them, this first rule is phrased as: Observers are more likely to model behavior when there is a greater ratio of positive reinforcements to the negative reinforcements for engaging in the behavior.

BOX 2.2

Principles Concerning the Development of Habits

If ten percent of the population *habitually* bought the same toothpaste, millions of dollars can be made. Hence, the study of habits is important. Six principles to keep in mind:

1. As the number of rewarded repetitions of the response increases, the probability that the response will be made increases. Many campaigns have immediate effects. People become concerned about crime, and join Neighborhood Watch programs. As time passes, however, the response to repeated messages lessens and eventually disappears. Usually, "extinction" takes place when the consequences of learning are no longer elicited by the same message or stimuli; for example, the statement "Pick up your room if you want to go swimming" no longer prompts the child to clean his/her room.

2. The time interval between response and reward must be kept short for effective building of habit patterns. When there is a long delay between the time a desired response is made to a particular stimulus and the time the receiver perceives the reinforcement to the response, the probability that the response will be repeated is lowered.

3. Habit formation is facilitated when stimuli are isolated. The persuasive communicator who has to compete for space in the newspaper or has to sandwich the message in between many other messages on the radio will have a more difficult time in securing desirable responses than if able to present the message in the absence of other messages. We are all faced every day with many, many competing messages. Most of the strong evidence concerning classical conditioning, noted above, comes from laboratory studies, where there is little competition to the receiver's attention. Indeed, people attend "retreats" so they can get away from competing messages and pressures and learn better from workshops.

4. The complexity of the response desired affects the ease of habit formation. Many machines in industries today are complex and difficult to learn. To train workers, corporations make videotapes that break down the operation into smaller units, so that a complex task can be more easily understood and learned. Videos, "simulators," and interactive computer programs can provide sufficient experience and practice with complex materials, so that responses become routine and habitual. If the response is complex, break it down and teach the process over time.

5. Individuals tend to generalize the responses they make. Generalization is a common phenomenon in learning situations. Stimulus generalization is the making of the same response to slightly different stimuli. Response generalization is an analogous phenomenon in which slightly different responses are made to the same stimuli.

Stimulus generalization explains many of the effects seen in persuasive communication. For example, many of the large multinational corporations have established a single trademark. Corporations such as ITT, TransAmerica, and CitiBank have spent hundreds of thousands of dollars attempting to identify and then publicize an appropriate trademark to be attached to all of their products. The intent is that favorable responses about one product will be transferred to any other product bearing the same label.

On the other hand, "copyright infringement" legal disputes occur when one company uses a product, or a company logo, that is perceived to be similar to a larger, more reputable company (or the brand leader). Because we naturally generalize our learned responses, a child may go to a store to look for one product, but become sidetracked by similar products in similar packages. Some companies, like Ralph Lauren with its polo player symbol, have to be vigilant against others using a symbol that is "too similar" in appearance to their logo, or others would be taking advantage of their reputation.

6. Providing information about receiver performance leads to improved performance. This principle is particularly important to the interactive view of persuasion that we have discussed. The acquisition of language and the ability of the individual to develop intrinsic rewards leads to an ability to use information about a performance to correct the performance for subsequent presentations. Thus, if one can systematically inform receivers about the quality of the responses being made, the information can be used to improve future responses.

2. Receivers are more likely to model a person or character who is similar to themselves (as opposed to a dissimilar model, but see Chapter 5) (example: We may buy casual clothes and swimwear worn by models who are the same age as we are).

3. Receivers are more likely to model a person or character who appears to be competent, reliable, and informed about the behavior(s) portrayed (relative to incompetent ones) (example:

We are likely to buy a tape on exercise and weight lifting, or on woodworking from a competent expert in these areas).

4. Receivers are more likely to model a person or character who appears to possess high status (example: We are likely to wear the same type of business suit, read the *Wall Street Journal,* and model the behavior of Gordon Gekko (in the movie *Wall Street*) because we have aspirations of being rich and powerful).

5. Receivers are more likely to model a person or a character who appears to be *consistent* in his/her behavior, as opposed to a person or character who behaves erratically or unpredictably.

6. Receivers are more influenced by *multiple* role models, as opposed to a single role model. Obviously, the success claimed in the early 1990s concerning the "Designated Driver" campaign (see Chapter 14) is largely due to the fact there are many role models who consistently engage in this behavior, with unanimous approval of other characters.

These external sources, however, represent only half the story. As Smith and Bandura[19] note, if receivers never *internalized* the lessons they learned via direct experience, role playing and modeling, they would be forever changing their lives, based on the most recent videotape, movie, book, and so forth. People develop *self-reinforcement* systems that deal with regulating our behavior so that we are satisfied with our activities, self-concept, and self-imposed demands. For example, people who are driven by a sense of ethics and by principles of honesty, fairness, and devotion to friendship are likely to reciprocate favors friends do for them, to help their friends when help is needed, and so forth. Obviously, opportunities would arise in which such a person could cheat, ignore a friend's need, ignore reciprocating a favor, and the like. However, since such persons *anticipate* guilt and self-criticism if they do not behave in accordance with their self-reinforcing system, they (often) decline such behaviors.

A person could develop any number of "self-reinforcement systems." Functionally, such systems parallel the "frame of reference" notion developed in this chapter and the personality and group differences discussed in Chapters 6 and 7. Early work in social learning theory looked at aggression, referred to as a "mass media" effect in Chapter 1. However, we have witnessed a tre-mendous movement toward using all media to promote, *intentionally*, "pro-social" actions on television. Chapter 14 looks at attempts at changing society in a pro-social direction.

So far in this chapter we examined characteristics of beliefs and attitudes, and have covered three major approaches to learning. A number of additional factors must be understood if one wants to become fully versed in persuasion.

THEORIES OF PERSUASION AND ATTITUDE CHANGE

What is a Theory?

We have already used the term "theory," and will continue to use this term throughout this book. But what is meant by the term theory? We use the term "theory" to encompass five elements:[20]

1. A theory is important because it provides an *understanding* concerning *why* receivers are influenced in a particular set of contexts.

2. A theory identifies a set of *relevant* variables critical in persuading others, and tells us which variables are irrelevant in the influence process.

3. A theory integrates and "explains" many empirical findings and parsimoniously summarizes them into a set of propositions.

4. A theory allows us to make predictions concerning how one set of variables will influence a set of outcomes (belief, attitude or behavioral changes).

5. A theory offers guidelines or "scope conditions" to tell us the contexts in which the theory is most likely to be used.

The theories of learning reviewed provide excellent examples of these five elements. First, theories such as social learning assume people want to maximize rewards and minimize costs, and will attend to messages and behaviors enacted by models so they can effectively learn and execute behaviors perceived to lead to desired outcomes.

Second, the theory informs us of the important relevant variables involved in the process: It tells us how reinforcement affects receivers; it tells us where reinforcement comes from; and it tells us which aspects of "models" are relevant and have an effect on modeling. It also *assumes* that people develop self-reinforcement systems. We use "assumes" because we cannot see, directly, a "self-reinforcement system." By conjecture, or indirect evidence, we can tell a person has developed and employs such a system when engaged in goal-directed activity (such as to get a promotion).

Third, a theory integrates and "explains" many empirical findings because each single study relies on the same variables (models who are similar, competent, possessing status, and the like), and scholars try to repeat or "replicate" studies. Social scientists (such as in communication, psychology, sociology, marketing) are a very critical group. If a study is done at an all-male Jesuit school in Indianapolis, we do not accept the conclusions fully until the same research is replicated in other universities, in other cities, with many children, with college students and adults. Once the same results are obtained repeatedly, then they are presumed to be correct.

Fourth, a theory allows us to make predictions concerning how one set of variables will influence outcomes, such as beliefs, attitudes and behavioral changes. In applying social learning theory to encourage children to adopt "pro-social behaviors," we would predict that children would learn and use pro-social activities (that is, act less violently and more cooperatively) if appropriate models were selected, if television programs used consis-

tency in displaying models' cooperative behavior, and if children attended, retained, and perceived themselves as competent in engaging in the behaviors, and perceived the end-state or final outcome to be sufficiently desirable.

Fifth, no *one single* theory of persuasion can be applied across all situations and all contexts. Instead, there are several major theories. Each theory is relevant to certain aspects of our lives, but not to other settings or contexts. Recall what we said about classical conditioning: Classical conditioning is usually *more* effective with forward conditioning, repeated exposures, when presented in isolation, without complex semantic structure or information included, and when the unconditioned stimulus is fairly neutral (see above). These guide our use of this theory in real-life contexts.

Motivational Theories

Some of the most important attitude change theories have been termed "consistency theories." Consistency theories were first propounded in the early 1940s, although the roots for such theories undoubtedly go back much further.[21] Since World War II, various cognitive consistency theories have provided one of the most fruitful areas of study within communication and the behavioral sciences.

The term "cognitive consistency" refers to a number of specific theories which apply to different types of persuasive communication situations. Although the various consistency theories have unique aspects, all the theories are based on the common premise that inconsistency is somehow unpleasant or painful or distasteful, and that the tensions created by this unpleasant state will lead to attempts to reduce the tensions. Festinger refers to consonance and dissonance,[22] Osgood to congruity and incongruity,[23] Abelson and Rosenberg to consistency,[24] and Heider to balance and imbalance.[25] Our discussion will be limited to two of the major theories: Balance and Cognitive Dissonance. A third variation on motivational theories will also be briefly presented: Psychological Reactance.

BALANCE THEORY

When we say we have a theory of "cognitive consistency" we are saying we have a theory about "cognitions" which deals with the "consistency" of those cognitions. "Cognitions" are all the beliefs you might have. These various cognitions can be related to one another in a number of ways. First, two beliefs may simply be unrelated to one another: "The price of snowshoes in Nome went up 25 percent since last year," and "Bus 25 will take you downtown." Second, two beliefs can be consonant or compatible or positively related to one another: "Labor prices went up last year," and "The price of snowshoes went up 25 percent." Finally, two cognitions can be incompatible or contradictory: "University of Southern California will win the Rose Bowl" and "Michigan State University will win the Rose Bowl." We dislike inconsistency and contradiction among our beliefs and are often motivated to resolve discrepancies as they are experienced.

The simplest version of a cognitive consistency theory relevant to persuasion is balance theory.[26] In this perspective three cognitive elements are called a cognitive structure, where elements can have a positive or negative relationship with one another. Various combinations of these structures are in Figure 2.3; where "P" means person, "O" means other and "X" means the topic or issue that Person and Other view, discuss, and so forth. The three elements in the structure can form one of two kinds of relationships: balanced or imbalanced. By balanced we mean that the elements are in a harmonious relationship with one another, where we see the relationships among elements as pleasant, desirable, stable, and ex-pected, and where we do not feel any pressure to change any of the elements in order to make them fit together.

All of the structures on the top row of Figure 2.3 are balanced, and all of the structures in the second row are imbalanced. Structure (a) is balanced—Person (P) likes Other (O), Other likes modern art (X) and Person likes modern art. All the elements are harmonious to one another—Person likes the people who like the same things he likes. Structure (b) is also balanced: Person likes Other and both Person and Other dislike new wave music. Structure (c) is also balanced—Person does not like Other, Other does not like the Republican Party and Person does. Such a relationship is harmonious—Person thinks that people he dislikes dislike the things he likes. Finally, structure (d) is also balanced—Person dislikes Other, Person doesn't like opera and Other does like opera. This structure is balanced because it makes "sense" to us that people we dislike do not share our attitudes—people we dislike like those things we dislike.

Structures e, f, g, and h, are imbalanced and we feel some tension toward making them balanced. In (e), Person doesn't like Other, but both Person and Other enjoy modern art. Person would feel a little out of sorts with this arrangement because he anticipates liking people who like the things he likes, and does not anticipate that his enemies would get pleasure from the same things he gets pleasure from. The more intensely Person hates Other, the more likely Person would be disturbed by the relationships among elements in (e). To make the structure balanced, Person can change his attitude toward modern art or change his attitude toward Other. Which? *One of the most important rules of making structures balanced is that the less important element is usually the one which is changed.* If Person truly hated Other, he would tend to lose some of his liking for modern art.

In the last paragraph we noted two ways in which a structure could be made balanced—

Balanced and Imbalanced Cognitive Structures

Balanced Structures

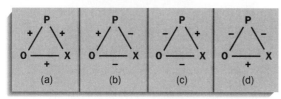

Imbalanced Structures

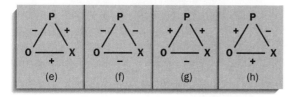

changing the p-x relationship or changing the p-o relationship. Certainly, there are other ways to make a structure balanced. In fact, Heider[27] noted a range of ways in which balance can be achieved. In one study, students were given the following scenario, and were asked for their reactions:

> "Bob thinks Jim is very stupid and a first class bore. One day Bob reads some poetry he likes so well that he takes the trouble to track down the author in order to shake his hand. He then finds that Jim wrote the poems."

Heider noted that 46 percent of the students felt that Bob would upgrade his opinion of Jim; another 29 percent felt that Bob would feel less enthusiastic about the poetry. Still, 19 percent felt they wouldn't resolve the imbalance, but noted

some tension would be felt. Five percent of the students even questioned Jim's authorship of the poetry, and 2 percent felt Bob would make a concession—thinking Jim wrote some good lines and some bad lines. As these numbers indicate, it is typical of people to try to balance a structure when exposed to an unbalanced one.

The remainder of the structures are also imbalanced. In (f), Person dislikes Other and also dislikes opera, and Other also dislikes opera—Person finds himself in the peculiar situation of sharing the same attitude (disliking opera) with his enemies. In (g), Person likes Other and Person likes the Detroit Lions, but Other dislikes the Lions; while in (h) Person likes Other, Other likes the Lions and Person does not.

Considerable research has focused on our reactions to balanced and imbalanced structures; we find balanced ones to be more pleasant, harmonious and memorable and perceive them to be more stable than imbalanced ones. Further, there is considerable evidence that we prefer the structure where all elements are positive—structure (a) in Figure 2.3 is rated highest in preference. This preference for positive relationships between all elements is used by advertisers on a routine basis. That is, advertisers find spokespersons we like for their products thus making the P-O relationship positive (they put you in the structure as P). Then, these spokespersons extol the positive virtues of a particular product (X), thus creating a positive O-X relationship. What is your attitude toward X if balance theory is correct, and the P-O relationship is positive and O-X relationship is positive? A brief look at television commercials or a look through some magazine layouts will indicate the existence of a preponderance of positive P-O and O-X links. If we receivers like celebrity A and celebrity A likes product X, a balanced structure calls upon us to have a positive attitude toward product X.

The second implication of balance theory for persuasion deals with dyadic communication—

BOX 2.3

EXAMPLES OF PRINT ADS AND BALANCE THEORY

Photo A (on the right) illustrates the use of Balanced Structure (a) in Figure 2.3. You (Person) like (+) Oliver Stone, Oliver Stone likes (+) The Gap clothing store, and, to complete the Balanced Structure, you should like (+) The Gap clothing store—providing a balanced (+, +, +) cognitive structure. The two page Photo B (below) shows, to our left, a happy Chris Evert, and, to our right, a number of Matrix Essentials products (for the hair). If you like (+) Chris Evert, and Chris Evert likes (+) Matrix products, you can complete the structure (as we did with photo A) by liking Matrix products, again providing a balanced (+, +, +) cognitive structure.

The Gap, Inc.

Matrix Essentials

The use of Balanced Theory in persuasion is not limited to either the +, +, + structure (structure (a) in Figure 2.3), nor is the theory limited to print advertisements. Two frequently used ad campaigns on television rely on structure (c) in Figure 2.3. They rely on the idea that we like things that people we do not like dislike. For example, you (Person) do *not* like the school principal (−), and the school principal hates (−) Bubble Gum Tape.

To make the structure balanced, you should like (+) Bubble Gum Tape. Another example: People you do not like (weird, uptight people) hate Twister fruit juices ("Juice combinations nature never made, but should have"). To balance out a negative p-o and negative o-x link (See Figure 2.3), you should like Twister juices. That is, you should like things that unlikable people dislike.

since one possible option is for Person to try to persuade Other to like the Lions. Newcomb[28] developed a model of balance very similar to Heider's, where communication was one of the means by which an individual can reduce strain caused by imbalanced structures. Suppose Person and Other were discussing who they would vote for in a presidential campaign, and the structure (a) in Figure 2.3 represented the state of affairs. Little persuasion would occur because Person and Other like each other and both agreed about voting. However, we would see one probable effect their communication would have—communication between the two will probably strengthen the resistance of both individuals to outside communicators who may transmit messages to them about voting for the opponent. Their resistance would increase because both have received new information (in this case, social support) consistent with an already existing belief structure. However, in a number of situations (such as g and h), we find that Person can try to persuade Other to change his mind toward the topic on hand in order to make the structures balanced.

THE THEORY OF COGNITIVE DISSONANCE

As noted above, two cognitions can have an irrelevant relationship with one another or can have a relevant relationship between one another. Relevant relations are of two types: dissonant and consonant. According to Festinger, "two elements are in a dissonant relation if, considering these two alone, the obverse of one element would follow from the other."[29] Suppose, for example, Mike believes "Smoking causes cancer, contributes to emphysema, and harms people around me." However, Mike started smoking when he was in high school and continues to smoke today. The two cognitions ("I smoke," and "Smoking is bad for me") are incompatible with one another and Mike experiences a state of dissonance, one he has to reconcile in some way. How can we reconcile these two cognitions?

Festinger suggested three ways of reducing dissonance.[30] First, Mike can *change one of the elements to make the two cognitions more consonant*. Obviously, dissonance is eliminated when Mike quits smoking. However, some behaviors dealing with habits and addictions are difficult to change. So, the second way of reducing dissonance is to *add additional consonant cognitions*. Mike can read articles in magazines critical of smoking research which point out that thousands of people who smoke do not experience any of the negative consequences claimed by the research. Third, Mike can reduce dissonance by *changing the importance of the cognitions*. Mike believes that he needs his cigarettes to wake up in the morning and to stay awake at his boring job, and that he will gain weight when he quits smoking; therefore, the advantages of continuing to smoke outweigh (in Mike's mind) the advantages of quitting. According to Petty and Cacioppo,[31] Mike will use one of these modes which offers the *least resistance to change*. Changing the behavior and stopping smoking is probably highest in resistance. Further, it may become more and more difficult for smokers to find faults with the growing body of research. So, Mike often uses the option of "change the importance of the cognitions."

We experience dissonance every day, but the dissonance we feel can vary tremendously in *magnitude*. Very high levels of dissonance make us feel distraught, guilty, aroused, upset, threatened and so on. The magnitude by which we experience dissonance is related to the importance of the elements involved, the intensity with which attitudes are held toward the elements, and the number of elements. Typically, the more important elements involve issues pertaining to one's self-concept, or important beliefs about the self: "I am a smoker," "I am not a racist," "I am a good decision maker," and so on. Further, *public commitment* is important because public actions and behaviors are difficult to deny and disclaim—hence, a person who says "I am not racist," but said something racist on a talk show millions of people watched will experience high levels of dissonance (and a need to resolve the inconsistency).

Dissonance and Decision Making Dissonance theory dates to the 1950s and three areas of research have been examined: Dissonance and Decision Making, Counter-attitudinal Advocacy, and Disconfirming an Important Belief. In the 1957 book on dissonance, Festinger began with analyses concerning decisions to buy cars, or to select appliances.[32] In contexts such as these, a consumer can believe "I make good decisions." If this is true, then the belief, "I made the wrong choice when I bought the Edsel" would be undesirable since it would be dissonant to the first one. Hence, shoppers would be motivated to avoid the second belief.

The more the person experienced post-decisional dissonance (doubt about whether they are in fact "good decision makers"), the more the person would feel a need to *psychologically* justify why one car (the Edsel) was the "right, correct choice" relative to the unselected car. Before making a decision, shoppers are described as engaging in "predecisional search" of products to purchase. Postdecision dissonance is aroused, however, when (a) the decision is important to the person, (b) the decision means giving up relatively attractive features of the unchosen object, and (c) the objects one selected from had dissimilar attributes. This latter criterion needs clarification.

A shopper wanting to select between two high-performance cars would experience a certain amount of dissonance when selecting between two very similar objects. However, if the shopper had to select from a high-performance car and a four-wheel-drive vehicle s/he would experience *more* dissonance since what s/he can do with one car cannot be done with the other. Suppose the shopper went out and bought a motorcycle instead. Now, a motorcycle can certainly be more fun than a street car, but the attributes are extremely dissimilar—no place to put the two kids, it is cold, unsafe, and impractical for work or for formal functions. Obviously, the shopper would experience very high levels of dissonance if s/he purchased a motorcycle; there would have to be a good deal of justification given.

In this situation, there are four ways to reduce dissonance:[33]

1. A shopper can try to revoke the decision.

2. A shopper can increase his or her liking for the selected object (you start liking your new car even more, and you selectively expose yourself to information supportive of the decision, or, similarly, decrease your liking for the car you didn't buy).

3. A shopper can increase the "cognitive overlap" between the two cars (you tell yourself that, now that you've thought about it, the two cars are pretty similar after all, so making the decision was not important). Of course, this is harder to do when the shopper brought home the motorcycle.

4. A shopper can add consonant elements to change the ratio of dissonant to consonant ones. As noted above, the shopper can add elements such as, "but with the motorcycle we have solved our parking problem, and we can get through traffic jams. Also, we don't go to formal events that often, and we can have more fun on the weekends . . . "

This "post-decisional dissonance" occurs not only when we buy an object, but also after decisions have been made, such as decisions in betting. After gamblers placed bets, they "rationalized" the betting by becoming more confident in their bet and thinking of themselves as luckier.[34]

This aspect of dissonance theory also gave rise to the idea that, after making a decision, we *selectively expose* ourselves to information supportive of our decision and avoid information indicating we made the wrong decision. Certainly, this happens in many situations—having just paid $20,000 for a car, we'd like to believe (at least for weeks or months) we made the right decision.

The company we bought the car from is likely to send us information supportive of our decision, surveys concerning our satisfaction, and so forth, thus feeding on our desire to believe we made the correct choice. There appears to be a limit to selective exposure and the notion of selective exposure today is not as popular as in the 1950s and 1960s. There is a functional, utilitarian reason to pay attention to all information regarding cars, even after we have bought the Edsel. Negative information about the car we bought is useful in case of recalls, or when there is something that needs to be corrected about the car. Unbiased information is useful in helping us decide how long we want to keep the car, and important in determining a realistic resale value, and so forth. Having positive information about the unselected car is also useful because in a few years we might switch cars. Nonetheless, selective exposure might very well occur for many people for a certain length of time after they make a major purchase; but we no longer conclude that people have strong or consistent needs to expose themselves to only positive information and to avoid negative information after making a decision.[35]

Disconfirming an Important Belief Sometimes beliefs are held with a strong, firm conviction. Such beliefs however, may prove wrong later. If we predicted, "I will get into law school," "I will win a gold medal in the Olympics," "The world will come to an end this weekend," we will experience dissonance if the prediction proves false. In a classic study on cults, Festinger and his colleagues infiltrated a group that predicted an immediate devastating flood.[36] The group further acted publicly on this prediction by selling their homes and property. Local people and the media ridiculed the group, which increased strong feelings between group members. The flood did not occur. What did the members of the group do?

Since they felt so strongly about their religious beliefs, it was difficult for them to change

their views and come to believe that God had abandoned them. Instead, they decided *that their faith was so strong* God had postponed the imminent flooding. However, what proof did they have that *their faith was responsible for God's decision to spare the continent from disaster?* With no real physical proof or evidence that they had caused God to spare the continent, members of this group sought out what we call *social proof* (see Chapter 10)—they tried to recruit more and more people into their cult, the idea being that if hundreds and hundreds of people adopt this belief, it must be correct.

Festinger and others[37] indicate that dissonance is aroused in this area when: (1) the belief is held with strong conviction; (2) there is public commitment to the belief; (3) the belief is of the type that can be "unequivocally disconfirmed;" (4) the belief is in fact unequivocally disconfirmed; and, (5) social support for the changed beliefs must be available to the believer after the disconfirmation. By "unequivocally disconfirmed" we mean that the prediction or the belief is one that can be disconfirmed without argument or dispute—for example, that the world will end, that an athlete will win the gold medal, and so on. Beliefs or predictions like "You will soon travel over water," "There will be an earthquake in California registering over 5.0 on the Richter scale" cannot really be disconfirmed unequivocally, unless more specific information is provided. When will you travel or when will the earthquake take place? Sometime between now and the year 2000? There will be little or no dissonance unless some specific prediction or belief is disconfirmed in public. The fifth rule noted above deals with how group members cope jointly with the disconfirmed belief—that as a group, the members will develop and uniformly accept a new belief.

Counter-attitudinal Advocacy Sometimes people agree to do things that contradict what they believe. For example, as a class assignment, a person may have to defend, write an essay, or debate a point that actually goes against his/her beliefs. Examples of such situations that occur in real life include a worker who defends company policy on seniority, limits on medical coverage, limits on child care leave, or claiming the cost of an operation as "not covered" under the policy holder's health plan (even though you, the insurance agent, believe your client should be covered). These are classic situations for the emergence of dissonance: People possess one belief, but have to communicate, in public, the opposite view.

Research on the topic of "counter-attitudinal advocacy" first elicits students (or workers) to write essays on topics they would normally disagree with—such as advocating the reading of comic books, advocating trips to Communist countries, or even supporting police actions during a riot. If these people were paid $20 to spend an hour or two to write an essay for an experimenter, they might believe that the $20 justifies writing the essay and experience little dissonance. However, what happens if people were asked to spend time writing an essay arguing against their own beliefs and were paid only fifty cents to do so? These people may ask themselves "Why am I doing this for just fifty cents?" These people feel *insufficient justification* (fifty cents is not really sufficient reason or "justification" for arguing against one's beliefs), and need to reduce dissonance by finding some way of reconciling two dissonant beliefs: "I am against the police action," and "I am writing an essay in support of the police action." So, when people in situations such as these ask themselves, "Why am I doing this?" they try to justify writing their counter-attitudinal advocacy essays by changing their beliefs—"The police action really wasn't so bad," or "Actually, there are a lot of good reasons for reading comic books." According to this perspective, the *fewer external justifications (money, rewards) people receive for their behaviors, the greater the dissonance, and the more they are likely to change their beliefs and attitudes.*

This area of counter-attitudinal advocacy has produced volumes of research, and considerable controversy. Why? Because the prediction is counter-intuitive: The *fewer* the incentives offered, the *greater the change in attitudes*. If this is true, we ought to be able to convince workers to write essays against pay raises, give them little incentive to write the essays, and expect them to believe that they should not get pay raises. Obviously, this would never happen. In fact, a good deal of research has contrasted the dissonance-theory approach to counter-attitudinal advocacy, with an incentive view of counter-attitudinal advocacy—which argues that the *more* incentives a person is offered to write the essays, the more motivated the person would be to work hard on the essays, think of convincing reasons, and actually convince themselves to change opinions. As Smith[38] concluded, both of these approaches are true, depending upon the situation at hand. Dissonance is in fact increased and operates when:

1. A person freely agrees to write a counter-attitudinal message on the topic.

2. There are few (or no) *external* rewards or incentives for arguing against one's own beliefs.

3. The person writes a message for a negative source or sponsor. That is, a person writes an essay for the Soviet Embassy, the American tobacco Company, the Ku Klux Klan, and so forth.

4. The person writes a message that may harm someone else. When these conditions apply (You are paid very little to write a message in favor of smoking that the American tobacco industry will use to sell cigarettes to others), you would experience guilt and all the negative feelings associated with dissonance, and you would want to change your opinions so that you could convince yourself smoking really isn't that bad.

On the other hand, probably the most typical scenario involving counter-attitudinal argument involves a sponsor considered positive (newspapers, public television, schools, the company you work for) where others are not going to be harmed by the message (you do not encourage smoking, racism, or encourage others to engage in dangerous activities). In these situations, when people are paid more, they work harder and write persuasive essays with more and stronger arguments.[39]

In sum, dissonance theory is an important theory of human behavior with strong implications for persuasive communication. The theory seems to correctly predict how we react after we make decisions and when an important belief is disconfirmed.

PSYCHOLOGICAL REACTANCE THEORY

Our third example of a motivation theory is called psychological reactance theory. This theory is based on Brehm and Brehm's work demonstrating reactions of arousal, resentment, and anger when a person or an agency threatens to restrict or eliminate a free behavior.[40] Aptly named, the theory deals with situations when individuals "react" to rules, laws, or any other restriction placed on them. Smokers fight for the right to smoke, gun owners for the right to own guns, teenagers rebel when parents interfere too much in their "rights," and rock and roll listeners pay more attention, spend more money, and increase protests when censorship or the banning of recordings is discussed. Psychological reactance is clearly relevant to a wide range of areas involving persuasion. Box 2.4 presents the five basic propositions of the theory.

The term "reverse psychology" is occasionally used to refer to the operation of a psychological reactance, meaning when we forbid our child from playing with the pots and pans, the more the child *wants* to play with pots and pans. However, the authentic term is *psychological reactance*, and its operation is very specific (see Box 2.4). It is critically important to keep in mind that this theory

works *only when the person being influenced wants to engage in a behavior and expects (or expected) that s/he is or was free to do so.* When this situation exists, then the reactance can be manipulated: When the individual believes a loss of freedom will occur, s/he will (a) value the restricted behavior more; (b) want to engage in the behavior; (c) devalue the alternatives they are "stuck with"; and/or (d) resent and/or devalue the source of agency restricting the behavior.

Here are some areas in which this theory is relevant to persuasion and influence:[41]

1. *Censorship.* Recordings censored or banned are more desirable, making the bands more popular, increasing sales and possibly even increasing how much a consumer is willing to pay for a limited or restricted set of recordings.

2. *Limited editions.* When a company such as Fiat or Ferrari makes only 100 limited edition cars, consumers are willing to pay more for the privilege of owning one of the few cars. When there are only six cars in the series left, the belief is that the ability or freedom to buy one will be lost, so some people may act quickly to buy the last one.

3. *The scarcity rule.* We discuss in Chapter 10 the "scarcity rule" as it applies to face-to-face influence. When the sales clerk says, "This is the last blue sweater we have in stock and in this size," you realize that if you don't buy it today, you may lose the opportunity. Similarly, items that look like they may sell out, or when there are shortages in supply, we are likely to buy the Nintendo or Genesis game today or spend more for a hard-to-find Cabbage Patch doll, Tyco Glow in the Dark racing set, and so on.

4. *Reactions to "orders."* A judge who turns to a jury and says "I absolutely forbid you to use the last piece of evidence you heard, because it is inadmissible," creates reactance in the minds of the jury, and they are *more* likely to use the evidence that was forbidden. Similarly, a sign

BOX 2.4

BASIC PROPOSITIONS OF THE THEORY OF PSYCHOLOGICAL REACTANCE

1. *To arouse reactance in people, they must first perceive it is likely that they are no longer free to think or do something that they previously could. Further, more reactance is experienced when people feel there was weak justification for the restriction; less reactance is experienced when better or more justification is provided.* Consider a person smoking in a smoker's section of a restaurant. If the attendant forcefully says, "Put that out cigar! I hate cigar smoke!" the smoker will clearly experience resentment, will *want* to smoke the cigar, and may argue with the attendant or complain to the manager. Alternatively, less reactance is created when an attendant expresses a request, with good reason: "I am sorry to ask this because you are smoking in the smoker's section and you do have the right to smoke. However, those two pregnant women over there complained, and we hate to have any of our patrons complain. Can you resume smoking that after they leave?"

2. *The less important the threatened behavior is to an individual, the less reactance aroused by its elimination.* A person who is a heavy "two-pack-a-day" smoker will experience more reactance than the smoker who smokes only two or three cigarettes a day.

3. *Reactance is aroused in direct proportion to the extent to which the free behavior is limited.* In (1) above, the attendant asked the smoker to resume smoking his/her cigar only after the pregnant women left the area. If the two were to leave in half an hour, there may be little (or no) reactance. However, imagine that the situation was a wedding anniversary celebration lasting hours. The longer the restriction, the more the smoker would experience reactance.

4. *The extent to which reactance is aroused depends upon the similarities of the alternatives to the restricted behavior.* If you cannot smoke cigars or cigarettes, or chew tobacco, and someone also bans chewing gum, you will experience greater reactance than if the ban is only on cigar smoking. In a classic study in reactance theory, Mazis found that when the use of phosphates in laundry detergents was banned, people who had used phosphates *increased* their evaluation of phosphates' cleaning ability, and wanted to use their phosphate products. However, some consumers still could use their old brand product—they could use Tide without phosphates after they could no longer buy Tide with phosphates. But other consumers had to *switch* to new brands completely, and these *switchers* were very unhappy and experienced greater reactance than non-switchers (people who could still use their old brand, just without the phosphates).

5. *People vary tremendously in how quickly and how strongly they react to restrictions.* Some people are quick to assert their rights and demand freedom to act as they see fit, and become assertive even at the prospect of losing a freedom. Others are less assertive, more compliant, more complacent, more likely to be influenced, and experience less reactance. Petty and Cacioppo and Brehm and Brehm argue that people who feel they competently and adequately control their lives and effectively control their social world are less likely to be influenced by messages that produce reactance (such as, "You *must* buy this brand of bread").

For more information on Psychological Reactance Theory, read:
S.S. Brehm, and J.W. Brehm, *Psychological Reactance: A Theory of Freedom and Control* (New York: Academic Press, 1981).
M.B. Mazis, "Antipollution Measures and Psychological Reactance Theory: A Field Experiment," *Journal of Personality and Social Psychology,* vol. 31 (1975), pp. 654-660.
R.E. Petty and J.T. Cacioppo, *Attitudes and Persuasion: Classic and Contemporary Approaches,* (Dubuque, Iowa: Wm. C. Brown, 1981).

that reads Absolutely No Dumping Here may actually prompt some people to litter and dump at the site, relative to no sign or a sign that reads, Please Keep Area Clear. Managers who rebuke a worker by saying things like: "I got you this time! You are late and I got you sneaking in! You are guilty and you will pay!" create a *defensive* reaction in the worker which will make it difficult for the two to communicate and resolve differences; rebuke that threatens a worker's esteem and image increases conflict.[42]

5. *Political reactions.* Laws restricting guns, abortions, smoking, phosphates, saccharine, and any other behavior that people have learned to live with as a "free" or relatively unrestricted behavior will prompt individuals to protest and rally to remove officials from office, and so on.

6. *Romantic involvements.* Called the "Romeo and Juliet effect," scholars have found that the more the parents try to interfere and break up a high-school-aged couple, the more "in love" the couple becomes over time.

This theory is important for two reasons. First, the theory is used every day to prompt consumers to buy a product in limited supply *today* while they still can. Thus, you should be aware when this tactic is being used on you (and why). Second, this theory is useful for understanding why people behave the way they do. Clearly, you see this principle operating on the Home Shopping Network when a "special offer is announced, giving the next two hundred callers a special deal on *both* an emerald pendant and a ruby stickpin. The television screen will show how quickly people are calling in, giving the appearance that many viewers want to "rush" to get in on the special offer, apparently to not lose the freedom they have to cash in on this particular deal.

F O O T N O T E S

1. M. Rokeach, *The Open and Closed Mind* (New York: Basic Books, Inc., 1960). See also: M. Rokeach, *Beliefs, Attitudes and Values* (San Francisco: Jossey-Bass, 1968).
2. T.W. Leigh, A.J. Rethans, and T.R. Whitney, "Role Portrayals of Women in Advertising: Cognitive Responses and Advertising Effectiveness," *Journal of Advertising Research* (October/November, 1987), pp. 54-62.
3. Leigh, Rethans, and Whitney.
4. T.R. Sarbin, R. Taft, and D.E. Bailey, *Clinical Interference and Cognitive Theory* (New York: Holt, Rinehart and Winston, 1960). Also see: K.E. Scheibe, *Beliefs and Values* (New York: Holt, Rinehart and Winston, 1970).
5. Rokeach (Note 1); D. Bem, *Beliefs, Attitudes and Human Affairs* (Belmont, Calif.: Brooks/Cole Publishing Co., 1970).
6. Rokeach (Note 1).
7. L. Berkowitz and A. Knurek, "Label-mediated Hostility Generalization," *Journal of Personality and Social Psychology*, vol. 13 (1969), pp. 200-206.
8. G.J. Gorn, "The Effects of Music in Advertising on Choice Behavior: A Classical Conditioning Approach," *Journal of Marketing,* vol. 46 (1982), pp. 94-101.
9. E.W. Stuart, T.A. Shimp, and R.W. Engle, "Classical Conditioning of Consumer Attitudes: Four Experiments in an Advertising Context," *Journal of Consumer Research*, vol. 14 (1987), pp. 334-349.
10. Stuart, Shimp, and Engle, "Classical Conditioning of Consumer Attitudes."
11. C.A. Insko, "Verbal Reinforcement of Attitude," *Journal of Personality and Social Psychology*, vol. 2 (1965), pp. 621-623.
12. C.A. Insko and R. B. Cialdini, "A Test of Three Interpretations of Attitudinal Verbal Reinforcement," *Journal of Personality and Social Psychology*, vol. 12 (1969), pp. 333-341.
13. For a readable discussion of Insko and Cialdini's "two-factor model of verbal reinforcement," see: R. E. Petty and J.T. Cacioppo, *Attitudes and Persuasion: Classic and Contemporary Approaches* (Dubuque, Iowa: Wm. C. Brown, 1981).
14. See: M.J. Smith, *Persuasion and Human Action* (Belmont, Calif.: Wadsworth, 1982).
15. A. Bandura, *Social Learning Theory* (Morristown, N.J.: General Learning Press, 1971); A. Bandura, *Social Learning Theory* (Englewood Cliffs, N.J.: Prentice-Hall, 1977).

16. Smith, *Persuasion and Human Action*, p. 194; Bandura, A. Bandura, *Social Learning Theory* (Morristown, N.J.: General Learning Press, 1971), p. 3-4, p. 33.
17. Smith, *Persuasion and Human Action*, p. 195-196.
18. Smith, *Persuasion and Human Action*, p. 201-202.
19. Smith, *Persuasion and Human Action*, p. 197-198; Bandura (note 15).
20. The first four elements listed here are from: P. Zimbardo, E.B. Ebbesen, and C. Maslach, *Influencing Attitudes and Changing Behavior* (Reading, Mass.: Addison-Wesley, 1977), p. 53-56. Zimbardo, Ebbesen and Maslach list (p. 55), as a fifth element: A theory allows for the derivation of nonobvious predictions (that is, statements about reality that one would not make on the basis of intuition). However, we are not very interested in deriving nonobvious predictions. Instead, we think it important to keep in mind that theories have guidelines or "scope conditions" that specify their applicability and/or limitation to particular settings; concerning scope conditions, see: W. Crano and M. Brewer, *Principles of Research in Social Psychology* (New York: McGraw-Hill, 1973).
21. For discussion of early work on consistency theories, see W. McGuire, "The Current Status of Cognitive Consistency Theories," in *Cognitive Consistency*, S. Feldman, ed., (New York: Academic Press, 1966), pp. 2-4; R.P. Abelson, E. Aronson, W.J. McGuire, T.M. Newcomb, M.J. Rosenberg, and P.H. Tannenbaum, eds., *Theories of Cognitive Consistency: A Sourcebook* (Chicago, Ill.: Rand McNally, 1968).
22. L. Festinger, *The Theory of Cognitive Dissonance* (New York: Harper and Row, 1957).
23. C.E. Osgood, P. Tannenbaum, and G. Suci, *The Measurement of Meaning* (Urbana, Ill.: The University of Illinois Press, 1957), pp. 189-216; also see: C.E. Osgood and P. Tannenbaum, "The Principle of Congruity in the Prediction of Attitude Change," *Psychological Review*, vol. 62 (1955), pp. 2-55.
24. R.P. Abelson and M.J. Rosenberg, "Symbolic Psycho-logic: A Model of Attitudinal Cognition," *Behavioral Science*, vol. 3 (1958), pp. 1-13.
25. F. Heider, "Attitudes and Cognitive Organization," *Journal of Psychology*, vol. 21 (1946), pp. 107-112. See also F. Heider, *The Psychology of Interpersonal Relations* (New York: John Wiley & Sons, 1958); W.H. Crockett, "Balance, Agreement, and Positivity in the Cognition of Small Social Structures," in L. Berkowitz, ed., *Advances in Experimental Social Psychology*, vol. 15 (1982), pp. 1-57.
26. F. Heider, *The Psychology of Interpersonal Relations*

(New York: John Wiley & Sons, 1958); see also: C.A. Insko, *Theories of Attitude Change* (New York: Appleton-Century-Crofts, 1967).

27. F. Heider, *op. cit.*

28. T. M. Newcomb, "An Approach to the Study of Communicative Acts," *Psychological Review*, vol. 60 (1963), pp. 393-404.

29. L. Festinger, *The Theory of Cognitive Dissonance.*

30. J. Cooper and R.H. Fazio, "A New Look at Dissonance Theory," in L. Berkowitz, ed., *Advances in Experimental Social Psychology*, vol. 17 (1984), pp. 229-266; D. O'Keefe, *Persuasion: Theory and Research* (Newbury Park, Calif.: Sage, 1990); R.E. Petty and J.T. Cacioppo, *Attitudes and Persuasion: Classic and Contemporary Approaches* (Dubuque, Iowa: Wm. C. Brown, 1981); M.J. Smith, *Persuasion and Human Action* (Belmont, Calif.: Wadsworth, 1982); For the latest word on dissonance theory research, see: R.C. Schank and E.J. Langer, eds., *Volume in Honor of R.P. Abelson* (Hillsdale, N.J.: Erlbaum, in press).

31. Petty and Cacioppo, *Attitudes and Persuasion: Classic and Contemporary Approaches.*

32. L. Festinger, *The Theory of Cognitive Dissonance.*

33. Also see Petty and Cacioppo, *Attitudes and Persuasion;* Smith, *Persuasion and Human Action.*

34. See Petty and Cacioppo, *Attitudes and Persuasion.*

35. See Smith, *Persuasion and Human Action;* Petty and Cacioppo, *Attitudes and Persuasion.*

36. See Petty and Cacioppo, *Attitudes and Persuasion;* L. Festinger, H.W. Riecken, and S. Schachter, *When Prophecy Fails* (Minneapolis, Minn.: University of Minnesota Press, 1956).

37. Festinger, *The Theory of Cognitive Dissonance;* Festinger, Riecken, and Schachter, *When Prophecy Fails;* Petty and Cacioppo, *Attitudes and Persuasion.*

38. Smith, *Persuasion and Human Action.*

39. Smith, *Persuasion and Human Action.*

40. S.S. Brehm and J.W. Brehm, *Psychological Reactance: A Theory of Freedom and Control* (New York: Academic Press, 1981); Petty and Cacioppo, *Attitudes and Persuasion.*

41. See Brehm and Brehm, *Psychological Reactance;* Petty and Cacioppo, *Attitudes and Persuasion;* R.B. Cialdini, *Influence: The New Psychology of Modern Persuasion* (New York: Morrow, 1984).

42. D.O. Braaten, M.J. Cody, and K.B. DeTienne, "Account Episodes in Organizations: Remedial Work and Impression Management," *Journal of Management Communication*, vol. 6 (1993), pp. 219-250; M.J. Cody and M.L. McLaughlin, "Interpersonal Accounting" in H. Giles and P. Robinson, eds., *Handbook of Language and Social Psychology* (London: John Wiley, 1990), pp. 227-255; P. Schonbach, *Account Episodes: The Management or Escalation of Conflict* (Cambridge, England: Cambridge University Press, 1990).

K E Y   T E R M S   A N D
C O N C E P T S

attitudes
observational learning
frame of reference
beliefs
descriptive beliefs
evaluative beliefs
prescriptive beliefs
induction-based beliefs
construction-based beliefs
analogy-based beliefs
authority-based beliefs
central beliefs
authority beliefs
peripheral beliefs
learning
stimulus
conditioned/unconditioned stimulus
response
conditioned/unconditioned response
classical conditioning
simultaneous pairing
instrumental (operant) learning
reinforcement
reward
active/passive participation
stimulus generalization
social learning theory
habits
role playing
modeling
self-reinforcement system
theory
variables
cognitive consistency theories
balance theory
cognitive dissonance theory
counter-attitudinal advocacy
psychological reactance theory

MESSAGE LEARNING THEORY AND THEORIES OF SELF-PERSUASION

Throughout the 1940s and 1950s, Carl Hovland at Yale University conducted the first systematic, comprehensive set of research projects on attitude change. The research he and his students conducted had, and continues to have, a major impact on research in persuasion. Underlying this approach to the study of persuasion was the assumption that the more people *learned* and *remembered* from a message, the more they would be *persuaded*. Their approach, labeled the "Message Learning Approach," is reviewed in the first half of this chapter. An alternative view to persuasion is offered by scholars who study "self-persuasion"—how people engage in role playing or respond to a message so that they persuade themselves. One of the most recent models of persuasion is called the "Elaboration Likelihood Model," and this model argues that when the topic of persuasion is personally relevant and significant to the receiver, the receiver will cognitively "elaborate" and react to the message. The receiver is persuaded to the extent that *s/he reacts favorably to a message and generates his/her own arguments in favor of the message conclusion.* Not all persuasion, then, is caused by receivers merely learning the content of a message. Extensive research has focused on both approaches, and both offer considerable insights into the process of persuasion.

MESSAGE LEARNING AND PERSUASION: THE YALE SCHOOL

Issues pertaining to attitude change, public opinion, and propaganda became extremely important when World War II broke out, and scholars realized there was no large body of research concerned with how people are influenced or how they resist influence. Carl Hovland and others at Yale began a research program to investigate many of the important issues in persuasion. They first asked, "How are people persuaded?" To answer this question, they concluded that there were four *underlying processes* that occurred in a sequence (over time). These four processes are listed in the middle column of Figure 3.1.

First, to be effective, a persuasive message must be able to gain the receiver's *attention*. A receiver must be able to notice the advertisement on radio, billboards, television, and so forth, and read or hear what the message argues or claims. Second, a receiver must be able to *comprehend* what the message is saying. Typically, it is assumed that "comprehensibility" of a message deals with the language and the organization of a message. A message that is difficult to comprehend is one filled with legal terminology, technical jargon, slang, complex sentences, statistical terms and evidence, and so on. An easy-to-comprehend message relies on simple words communicated in a well-organized manner. Such messages make it easy for the receiver to learn, and increase the chance that persuasion will occur.

The third process Hovland and his colleagues identified is that of yielding to a persuasive message. Hovland and his colleagues believed a persuasive message was effective if it *raised* a question in the receiver's mind concerning the topic at hand (such as, which car to buy), and provided *incentives* or rewards for adopting the advocated position. A persuasive message, then, may raise a question in the receiver's mind ("So, this time you want a car that is safe, reliable, and economical. It is time to think Ford again . . ."). A message would provide information supporting the claims that the advertised car is safe, reliable, and economical. Such information represents the "rewards" or "incentives" in the message because safety, reliability, and economy are good and important reasons for buying a car. The incentives, of course, can be portrayed in a number of ways—with statistical evidence of graphs, pie charts, and the like, with survey reports of customer satisfaction, or with

Factors, Underlying Processes,
and Persuasion Outcomes, Based on Message Learning Approach

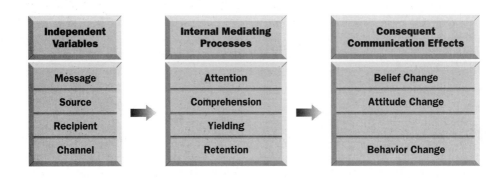

emotional advertisements dramatizing how safe the car is for a driver's infant daughter, or how safe the car is during a lightning storm.

Finally, scholars of the Yale school argue that receivers must *retain* the information in order for persuasion to occur. If receivers do, in fact, attend to a comprehensible message that provides good incentives and rewards, receivers would rehearse mentally the arguments by saying to themselves, "Oh, that car is second in customer satisfaction, it gets forty miles per gallon, and it is only $9,000. That sounds good to me." Persuading receivers is more likely if they remember all the claims that a message contains.

Factors Affecting Persuasion

A considerable amount of research has focused on issues dealing with increasing the amount of long-term learning that occurs with different kinds of messages, and with increasing the amount or type of incentives that prompt a receiver to yield to various messages. Four "independent variables" affect the receiver's level of attending, comprehending, yielding, and retaining information: characteristics of the message itself, characteristics of the source or the speaker of the message, characteristics of the receiver, and characteristics of the channels used in the persuasion attempt (see the left column in Figure 3.1). Each variable is introduced here, although entire chapters are later devoted to many of these topics.

Message Characteristics

There are many components of a message which help make it persuasive, including:

—the language used; is it comprehensible and easy to follow? Is it emotionally arousing, convincing, and memorable?

—the organizational pattern used; is the entire message easy to follow, convincing, and memorable?

—the use of "comparison advertisements;" a "one-sided" message contains the reasons for buying brand X, but a "two-sided" message compares brand X with another, rival, brand. Sometimes, a two-sided message is more convincing.

—the use of logic or the use of emotional appeals. Emotional appeals include appealing to fear, warmth/nostalgia or happiness. Emotional appeals have a strong impact on attitudes toward products. They make for memorable advertising and may impact behavior at some future time.

—the number of arguments employed, and the repetition of arguments; often, persuasion is increased when more arguments are presented (see later in this chapter), and repetition of arguments increases the chance receivers will learn from the message.

—the timing of the presentation of the message. Often, receivers learn more and remember more of a message when it is the first message they hear in a series of messages, compared to messages that are buried in a middle position (but see below).

—the movements of the speaker and the physical layout of visual material (that is, whether the brand name is to the left or right of the photograph) impact on gaining our attention and making a message memorable (See Chapter 9).

Message characteristics such as these have a profound impact on at least one of the four underlying process in persuasion: attention, comprehension, yielding, and retention. For example, humorous appeals on television often gain attention and are easy to comprehend. If the advertisement is truly humorous, the ad should be memo-

rable. However, receivers rarely yield to a humorous appeal to change a habit (smoking, exercise, diet), or to engage in some serious behavior (voting). Humor can be used, however, to prompt receivers to yield to very simple requests: to try a new brand of cookie, chips, beer, and so forth. That is, if receivers have already decided to purchase a product like beer or cookies, humor can be used to prompt them to try a particular brand. Nonetheless, the point to be emphasized here is that scholars in the Message Learning School specifically study characteristics of messages that directly impact at least one (if not all four) of the processes underlying persuasion.

Recall that the Message Learning Model claims the four processes of persuasion operate in a sequence—receivers must first attend and comprehend the message in order to move toward yielding and retaining the message content or conclusion. Eagly[1] demonstrated the importance of this sequence in a study on the comprehensibility of messages. Eagly first prepared a well-organized, easily understood, and persuasive speech arguing that people can function effectively with less sleep per night than is typically believed. Eagly also prepared a second, "medium comprehensibility" version in which the sentences of the speech had been cut up and placed back together in a random order. In a third version, the "low comprehensibility" version, the words of the message had been cut out and placed back together in a random fashion. Obviously, the students who read the "highly comprehensible" version recalled more of the arguments and were persuaded much more than students who read the "low comprehensiblility" version. The students who read the "medium comprehensiblility" version were able to pick out and recall some of the arguments but not as many as the students who read the "highly comprehensible" version, and they were not persuaded by the poorly organized message. Thus, comprehensibility is important both in prompting receivers to learn message arguments and in changing opinions regarding the amount of sleep a person needs.

If a message is in fact persuasive, then receivers should be able to recall many (if not all) of the message arguments (or, at least, the general "substance" or "conclusion" of the message). But, high levels of recall are likely to occur only immediately after hearing the message. As time passes, receivers forget the message content unless the message is reinforced via repetition, or the message is made in some vivid way (see Chapter 8 regarding vividness). Figure 3.2 illustrates the expectations concerning the learning of a message and the decay of that learning over time. Assuming a message is competently made, receivers should be able to recall, immediately after the message, the general substance or conclusion of the message and most of its specific arguments. As time passes (four weeks, six weeks, and more), receivers recall fewer and fewer specific message arguments, but they may still recall the general gist of the conclusion (see Figure 3.2).

There are many nonverbal and structural ways to help make a message easily understood and convincing, and we will devote considerable attention to these topics in Chapters 8 and 9. However, it is obvious any message characteristic increasing the amount of learning over time is one which has an important role in persuading receivers. In this chapter, we will highlight two fundamental areas which are centrally related to the learning model: repetition of the message and the timing of the message delivery.

Message Repetition   A single exposure to any message is unlikely to produce much in the way of a lasting effect. However, exposing receivers to several repetitions of a message can provide two benefits important to persuasion. First, several repetitions provide the receivers with a better opportunity to learn message arguments. Second, receivers tend to like familiar materials (products, faces, symbols and the like).

On the other hand, when receivers have been exposed frequently to a message, they reach a "satiation" point referred to as the "wear-out threshold." At this wear-out point receivers have learned all there is to learn from the message and are bored with it. The fundamental question is: How frequently should the persuader repeat the message (or part of it) so that not only does learning take place, but the message is still appreciated and effective before reaching the wear-out threshold?

Classic research indicates the magic number of repetitions is three.[2] In fact, the typical commercial aimed at children repeats some slogan or brand name three or four times in each commercial. Other projects demonstrate that three to five showings of a commercial an evening provide strong recall of the commercial, although five airings in one hour is clearly irritating. Further, some research indicates there is little gain in learning or in liking of the commercial when there is an increase in repetition from three airings to five airings during a viewing session (such as an entire evening), (but see the second half of this chapter).

Because of its obvious importance in persuasion, considerable information has been obtained from basic research on message repetition, especially concerning ways to extend the wear-out threshold for messages. Here are some general conclusions about repetition and persuasion, the first two dealing with effects of repetition, the rest with ways to extend the wear-out threshold:

1.   Repetition increases consumer learning.

2.   Repetition helps to establish new products or brands in the market.

3.   A group of commercials should not wear out as fast as a single commercial given the same overall frequency of exposure.

4.   Only *good* commercials wear out. A commercial that is ineffective when first shown will radi-

F I G U R E   *3.2*

THE MESSAGE-LEARNING APPROACH SPECIFIES THE UPPER BOUNDS OF PERSISTING ATTITUDE AS A FUNCTION OF THE RETENTION OF EITHER THE SPECIFIC MESSAGE ARGUMENTS OR THE "SUBSTANCE" OF THE MESSAGE.

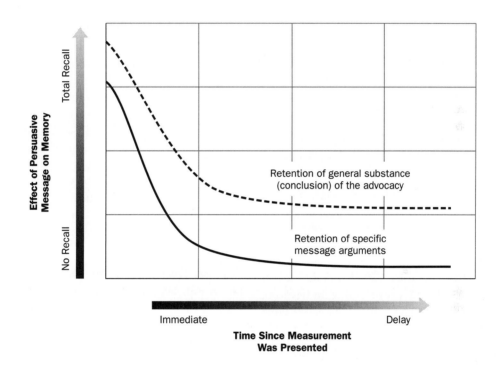

From: R.E. Petty and J.T. Cacioppo, *Attitudes and Persuasion: Classic and Contemporary Approaches.* Copyright © 1981 Wm. C. Brown Communications, Inc., Dubuque, Iowa. All rights reserved. Reprinted by permission.

cally decrease in effectiveness (and in how it is evaluated) as it is more frequently aired. Good commercials actually become more effective as they are shown more frequently, until they reach a wear-out threshold.

5. Commercials wear out faster among those who are heavy TV viewers.

6. If the number of commercials to be produced is limited, one might consider using a subtle approach in the few commercials that can be made in order to lengthen the learning process.

7. Commercials whose single point of humor is a gag or a punch line tend to wear out more quickly than commercials relying on a narrative approach.

8. Commercials for infrequently purchased products have a longer life because there is a natural turnover in the market in terms of receivers who attend to the messages. For example, most receivers who are not in the market for buying a refrigerator typically tune out refrigerator commercials, or "zap" to another channel, or "zip" past a commercial for an irrelevant product.

9. Several commercials are frequently produced on a single creative theme, and the rate that the commercials will wear out does not depend as much on the actual numbers produced and aired as on the viewer perception of how similar or dissimilar they are. For example, an advertising campaign may be made around one or a few basic slogans (most beer and soft drink slogans fit into this category: "Tastes great! Less filling"). Receivers would become bored with any one advertisement that expressed a basic or simple slogan. Thus, to extend the wear-out threshold, a pool or a series of commercials would be made, *each one sufficiently different from the others so that wear-out or boredom of one message does not generalize to the second, third, or fourth version in the campaign.* Something new to look at, process, think about, and learn has to be provided to extend wear-out. If this is not done, commercials that rely on simple slogans would be ineffective within a week (or weeks) of their first airing.

10. The greater the time span between commercial airings, the longer the single commercial can run.

11. Commercials can be removed and later reintroduced, but their second airing will wear out faster than the first. An added bonus, however, occurs when particular advertisers re-run "classic" Christmas or Easter advertisements during the holidays. Since the average person has had happy holidays in the past, such airings can also capitalize on generating positive feelings.

12. Commercials involving viewers have a longer effective life than commercials that simply present a straightforward product story. Thus, commercials that have children recite the contents of a Big Mac, or memorize a menu, or challenge them to some task are commercials that maintain high interest and facilitate learning. Also, advertisements with varied and active backgrounds help to extend wear-out by reducing boredom and by providing more stimuli for the receivers to process.

In sum, repetition increases the receivers' ability to learn the content in the message, up to the point when they reach satiation (when there is nothing new to learn). However, the wear-out threshold can be extended in a number of ways by creating more visually stimulating commercials, by increasing interest and active involvement in the commercial, or by creating a series of messages that repeat the same slogan, but differ in so many other ways that tiring of one of the commercials doesn't extend to tiring of all of the commercials.

Temporal Order of Messages   Should you speak first or last? Should you present your strongest evidence first in order to convince the audience early and get them on your side? Or should you present your strongest evidence last in order to have a strong conclusion? The term "primacy" is used to show that the first speaker, argument, or evidence carries more weight and has a greater impact than later information. The term "recency" means that the last speaker, or argument, or evidence was most influential. Usually, speakers (or evidence) located in the middle of speeches tend to be buried—research on "order effects" seeks to answer the question: Will the information presented first or last be more influential when persuading receivers?

There are three ways of viewing the issue of "primacy" and "recency." Our first model is a direct extension of the message learning model, and was explored in research by Miller and Campbell.[3] First, they noted that when receivers listen to a message once, they will remember much of the message immediately afterwards, and then forget message arguments over time (recall this from Figure 3.2). However, when two messages are presented in a sequence (Message A first, followed by Message B *without a break separating the two speeches*), there is a chance that there will be an added primacy effect because the information which is learned first lasts longer. It could also be the case that receivers become fatigued after hearing one speech and are tired when they hear the second one. It is further possible that receivers are still thinking about the content of Message A when they hear Message B, and this "interference" or distraction results in a reduction in learning from Message B. For a number of reasons, then, when receivers are exposed to two messages in sequential order, with no break or time delay between the two speeches, receivers tend to "learn" more from Message A.

So, when is it likely that a primacy effect will occur, or a recency effect will occur? The top panel in Box 3.1 summarizes Miller and Campbell's work on primacy and recency. Under speaking context (1), receivers are first exposed to Message A and are then exposed immediately to Message B. Some time later (one or two weeks later, for example), a vote is taken. A primacy effect is likely in this context because receivers learn more of the message content from Message A than Message B, and over the time delay, receivers are likely to forget more of Message B's content and remember far more of Message A's content. Thus, receivers will favor Message A.

However, a recency effect is favored if Message A is presented, then Message B is presented, and the vote is taken immediately after Message B. In this speaking context—(2) in Box 3.1—receivers are likely to remember far more information from the message immediately heard, compared to a message they heard a week earlier.

As indicated in the top panel in Box 3.1, neither a recency or a primacy effect can be predicted if no time delay separates the three events (Message A, Message B, Voting), or when time separates each of the three events (speaking context (4) in the box).

The Miller and Campbell model of primacy and recency directly follows from the Message Learning Model in that they were solely concerned with the learning of message content and with the decay of learning occurring over time. A second approach to the study of order effects involves reviewing the literature on when primacy and when recency effects are obtained, and then constructing viable explanations for why the effects emerge. Rosnow and Robinson[4] reviewed literature from all relevant social science research to make their assessment, and Lind[5] more recently focused on the importance of primacy and recency in legal settings. In regards to primacy effects, Rosnow and Robinson offered the first four conditions listed in the bottom panel of Box 3.1— primacy may be expected in any situation in which people are prone to making a "snap" or quick decision. When the issue is controversial, the topic is interesting, materials are familiar, and the issue is seen as relatively unimportant, the receiver's attention level is quite high and then tends to decrease over time. Thus, the receiver attends more, comprehends more and retains more from the beginning of the presentation than from the middle or from the end.

Lind—condition (e) in Box 3.1, under the heading of primacy effect—concluded that in courtroom settings a primacy effect is more likely to occur when a person's character is at stake; that is, does this man look like a wife-beater? A liar? A defrauder? A molester? A good deal of literature in interpersonal relationships indicates we make first impressions of others within a few minutes of

---

B O X 3 . 1

HIGHLIGHTS OF ORDER EFFECTS: PRIMACY OR RECENCY?

Model I: Miller and Campbell

Speaking Context: —Outcome?
(1) Message A, Message B—(time delay)—Vote   —Primacy
(2) Message A—(time delay)—Message B—Vote   —Recency
(3) Message A, Message B—Vote   —Neither
(4) Message A—(time)—Message B—(time)—Vote   —Neither

Model II: Rosnow and Robinson; Lind

Primacy effect likely if:

(a) topic is of interest to the receivers;

(b) materials are familiar to them;

(c) issues are seen as relatively unimportant;

(d) decision is made regarding a particular person's character.

Recency effect likely if:

(a) topic is of low interest to the receivers;

(b) materials are unfamiliar to them;

(c) issues are seen as important; and,

(d) decision deals with general issues, technicalities, not issues pertaining to a particular person's character.

Top panel is adapted from R.E. Petty and J.T. Cacioppo, *Attitudes and Persuasion: Classic and Contemporary Approaches* (Dubuque, Iowa: Wm. C. Brown, 1981), p. 78.
N. Miller and D.T. Campbell, "Recency and Primacy in Persuasion as a Function of the Timing of Speeches and Measurements," *Journal of Abnormal and Social Psychology*, vol. 59 (1959), pp. 1–9.
R.L. Rosnow and E.J. Robinson, *Experiments in Persuasion* (New York: Academic Press, 1967), pp. 99–104.
E.A. Lind, "The Psychology of Courtroom Procedure," in N.L. Kerr and R.M. Bray, eds., *The Psychology of the Courtroom* (New York: Academic Press, 1982), pp. 13–38.

meeting. This "snap" judgment would be reflected in a primacy effect.

A recency effect, however, is likely to occur if the topic is of low interest, materials are unfamiliar, and issues are seen as important. Lind further argued that when the decision deals with general issues, technicalities, and legal precedents, jurors tend to hold back, not knowing how to decide, until all the evidence is in, thus, exhibiting a recency effect. A perfect example of this occurs in legal settings when the lawsuit concerns the infringement of international copyright laws. The average juror is unfamiliar with such a topic, and interest is often very low—until the jurors hear that the lawsuit is for $25 million (or more). They then see the issue as important and decide to pay attention. Since they are unfamiliar with the topic, they do not make the snap or quick judgments that occur in other cases (of criminal law), and they pay attention to the evidence and wait until all the evidence is in before making a decision. Closing statements, then, are extremely important. In fact, the general recommendation to lawyers in situations such as these is to help the jurors form a framework of what is happening, why, and what will happen next, along with the summaries. Why? Because these legal matters require a good deal of time, and a lawyer would not want the jurors to become fatigued, lost, or impatient.

Of course, most of the sequences of messages we hear do not involve long messages but rather short thirty- to sixty-second commercials shown on television. In this situation, there are both "contrast" effects and fatigue effects. By a "contrast" effect we mean that different commercials in a series are contrasted against one another (see Chapter 10 concerning the nature of contrast effects). For example, Aaker, Stayman, and Hagerty[6] studied receivers' reactions to a series of commercials and found that if the first advertisement was irritating, any commercial (humorous, warm, or the like) following it benefitted by comparison, while a humorous ad followed by a warmth ad or a warmth ad followed by a humorous ad prompted better recall and liking for the brand name of the product advertised in the second commercial. The basic notion of a contrast effect is simple: If the first speaker is boring, irritating, or ill-prepared, the second speaker benefits by contrast (conversely, if the first speaker or first commercial is exceptionally witty, funny, and convincing, the second speaker may be at a disadvantage). By "fatigue" effect we simply mean receivers tire of any long stream of commercials that are too similar to one another. For learning to occur, something new must gain the receiver's attention and/or provide something new to process and learn.

SOURCE CHARACTERISTICS

The source of any message makes all the difference in the world. In their original formulation of the Message Learning Model, Hovland and his colleagues argued that the source component has a strong impact on the *incentives* included in the persuasion attempt. That is, receivers are motivated to hold correct beliefs and to behave in a competent, informed manner. Who is better to tell receivers what is correct and competent than people experienced in appropriate areas (such as investments, computers, child rearing, golf, home improvements, and the like)? A speaker who is an expert in the area at hand provides greater incentive for following her/his advice, relative to a nonexpert, or a speaker whose expertise can be questioned.

Hovland and members of the Yale school originally included two components of "source characteristics": the level of expertise of the speaker, and the level of trustworthiness of the speaker. Expertise includes the idea that the speaker is trained in her or his areas of competence. Trustworthiness includes the idea that the speaker is honest, sincere, and truthful. These two source characteristics are *independent* of each other—they can occur simultaneously in some speakers (that is, Speaker A is both expert and trustworthy), or a speaker can be high in one characteristic but low in another. Many politicians can be extremely expert and competent in certain areas (finances, defense systems, and so forth), but may not be perceived as very trustworthy, while others may be honest and sincere (hence, trustworthy), but are not perceived as possessing expertise. Each of these source characteristics plays a vital role in persuasion.

Over the years, communication scholars have examined additional source characteristics, including: the amount of *similarity* between the speaker and the receiver, the perception of another as an *opinion leader* (that is, a person you know who leads your opinions concerning areas in which they are well read), *power* (a person occupies a position in which s/he has authority to influence you), a speaker's level of *attractiveness* and the perception that the speaker is a *celebrity*. Each of these components has a specific role in persuasion, typically in regards to the *yielding* process noted above. However, the latter two components (attractiveness and celebrity endorsement) are currently popular on television because they also affect the *attending* process; receivers are more likely to pay attention to commercials featuring likable, attractive celebrities.

Chapter 5 thoroughly reviews the literature and proposes guidelines for the effects each of the above source characteristics has on persuasion outcomes. As an illustration of the Message Learning Model, however, we want to draw attention to the importance of source characteristics, yielding, and persuasion *over time*. The argument is that source characteristics are primarily important when the receivers *remember* who gave the message. When receivers forget who gave the speech they heard last month, they are influenced only by the arguments they heard. A line of research that provides some fascinating implications for persuasion stemming from the Hovland school is called the "sleeper effect."

The Sleeper Effect A single message from a highly competent source typically prompts receivers to change their opinions so that they agree with the source. However, any single message is likely to have limited effects as receivers begin to forget the message content over time (and possibly, revert to their old, original opinions on the matter). One exception to this rule is the "sleeper effect," a situation in which *more* attitude change is obtained days or weeks after the speech than *immediately* after the speech. The term "sleeper effect" was coined by Hovland and associates when they were doing research on American soldiers' attitudes toward our British allies. One of the movies they showed was called *Battle of Britain*. Immediately after seeing the film, the soldiers indicated on a questionnaire that they were *not* more strongly in favor of aiding the British. However, several weeks later, when asked again, they had shifted their attitudes *more* in favor of aiding the British. Since at least some of the message content was probably forgotten over a time span of weeks, the fact that increased persuasion occurred over time was surprising. How can such an effect occur?

Research into the sleeper effect has occurred in two phases. First, Kelman and Hovland[7] proposed a *cue hypothesis explanation* for the sleeper effect, arguing that there are different *cues* operating in persuasion. Typically, we think of persuasion as a message in which facts, evidence, and arguments are organized and communicated in some fashion, and are linked to the message conclusion. However, there are "cues" to know how to accept or react to the conclusion other than the actual arguments. There are, in fact, two different types of cues that might be linked to the message conclusion. An *augmenting cue* is any cue that causes the receiver to accept a conclusion of the message. Usually, an augmenting cue is some type of source characteristic, such as the beauty of the speaker, her/his power, and so forth. The augmenting cue adds additional incentives for adopting the conclusion.

On the other hand, a *discounting cue* causes a receiver to question or to resist the message conclusion. The discounting cue usually is a characteristic of the source (that is, speaker of questionable honesty, a person who lacks experience, an unlikable person). A discounting cue, however, can be any cue used by receivers to discount the conclusion. Many persuasion encounters occur in which the receiver can question the value, merits, or authenticity of a conclusion—such as propaganda films on driver education, drug abuse, or pro-war films, such as *Battle of Britain*. Indeed, when individuals are *forced*, against their wills, to view films or other persuasive material (like anti-syphilis films in the Navy), receivers are likely to experience *psychological reactance*, and are likely to resist (or rebel against) the message conclusion. A more subtle example of a "discounting cue" can occur when the speaker creates a persuasive message but is compelled to add a "disclaimer" prior to expressing the conclusion. For example, a speaker may say, "Having studied this matter for months, we are seventy-five percent confident the recession is over and that IBM stock will rebound by next January. However, *since not all the facts are in, we advise investors not to take action at this time.*" This disclaimer, not to take action, operates as a "discounting cue"; receivers may believe the evidence presented in the message itself, but agree to keep an open mind about the conclusion.

A sleeper effect occurs when the message arguments and conclusion are remembered over time while the discounting cue is forgotten. That is, the arguments (the statistics, and such) are so impressive and the conclusion so persuasive that receivers would have been persuaded by the message if they had not discounted the message conclusion due to the presence of a discounting cue. However, some weeks later receivers forget that the source of the message was a non-expert, or that they disliked the speaker, or were forced to watch the movie, or that the speaker had strongly disclaimed the message conclusion—they still re-member the arguments and the conclusion. At this point in time, when they recall the persuasiveness of the message but forget the discounting cue, receivers are susceptible to a "sleeper effect." Technically speaking, this explanation is called the "dissociative-cue hypothesis" because it involves the dissociation of the discounting cue from the message conclusion over time.[8]

Kelman and Hovland conducted a classic study to demonstrate when the sleeper effect occurs. They obtained permission from teachers to visit high school classes and conduct the study, in which the students listened to an excerpt of a radio show on juvenile delinquency. The communicator advocated lenient treatment of juvenile delinquents, arguing against things such as reform schools and strict punishments for youths who had committed delinquent acts. The radio show "excerpts" were bogus and were contrived by the experimenters in order to manipulate high and low levels of speaker prestige; a prestigious speaker would be an augmenting cue, a low-prestige speaker, a discounting cue. The prestigious speaker was described as "Judge Howard Elson, presiding judge of the juvenile court of this city, author of several books on delinquency, and well known for his views on the integration of the delinquent into society." Other students, however, heard a message from a "man on the street," who was selected from the radio audience—a person who gave the impression of being obnoxious, self-centered and possessing a shady past and present, a person who was ungrateful for his parents' assistance in getting him out of trouble with juvenile authorities when he was younger, and who had recently been picked up on a charge of drug-peddling.

Students were asked their opinions about lenient treatment of juvenile delinquents twice—once immediately after hearing the radio show, and again three weeks later (called the "delayed postcommunication" assessment). As you'd expect, the high school students demonstrated greater agreement with the message conclusion immediately after hearing the prestigious judge advocate the reasons for lenient treatment. Students who heard the low-prestige, unlikable speaker advocate the same position were not persuaded and resisted the idea of lenient treatment.

However, three weeks later, the students were asked their opinions again. In some of the classes, the experimenter reminded the students of the radio show and the nature of the speaker (they again heard the recording of the two speakers being introduced); these conditions were called the "reinstatement of the speaker groups"). In other classes, the experimenter did not return and the speaker heard three weeks earlier was not mentioned. In these "no reinstatement groups" the instructor merely distributed the questionnaire to the class.

Figure 3.3 illustrates the findings. When the source of the message was highly prestigious and he was re-introduced to the students, attitude change was high—the students favored lenient treatment of juvenile delinquents. However, when there was no reinstatement of the source, a marked decline occurred in student agreement with the message conclusion—as one would expect of three weeks' forgetting the message content. Further, when the low-prestige speaker was re-introduced there was again a marked resistance to his conclusion. However, when the students who heard the low-prestige speaker three weeks earlier were asked their opinions again, without re-instatement of the source, the students expressed more positive agreement with the conclusion, favoring lenient treatment of delinquents, more so than those who heard the reinstatement of the low-prestige speaker. Kelman and Hovland argued that the "sleeper effect" was obtained when the students in the low-prestige speaker/no reinstatement condition were significantly and substantially more in favor of lenient treatment of delinquents than the students in the low-prestige speaker/reinstatement condition (see bottom half of Figure 3.3 for "delayed postcommunication" measurement). Further, the reason for this sleeper effect was due to the fact that the students remembered the message content, which was persuasive, but forgot, over time, the discounting cue (that the speaker was low in prestige).

1. A message must be persuasive on its own merits. If this is not true, then simply removing a discounting cue won't affect attitudes.

2. The discounting cue must severely suppress the amount of immediate attitude change. The receiver must feel that the source cannot be trusted, or, for some other reason, puts up resistance to changing attitudes at the time of hearing the speech.

3. Over time, the discounting cue must be dissociated from the message.

4. The receivers must dissociate the discounting cue from the message *before* they also forget all of the message and message content. That is, after a year or so, there will be no sleeper effect because everything will be forgotten.

RECEIVER EFFECTS

Receiver variables are so important that both Chapters 6 and 7 are devoted to a further examination of this area. Scholars using the Message Learning Approach focused a good deal of effort on how people attended, comprehended, yielded, and retained various persuasive messages. In the earlier years, they raised the question as to whether there was *one* type of receiver (as a personality type) who was generally more easily influenced than others. However, the attempt to find exceptionally susceptible types was abandoned, and scholars progressed toward studying other receivers—especially women (versus men), low self-esteem receivers (versus high self-esteem ones), and highly intelligent (versus less-intelligent ones).

FIGURE 3.3

ATTITUDE CHANGE MEASURED IMMEDIATELY AND THREE WEEKS AFTER THE COMMUNICATION, WITH AND WITHOUT REASSOCIATING THE SOURCES AND THE ADVOCATED POSITION

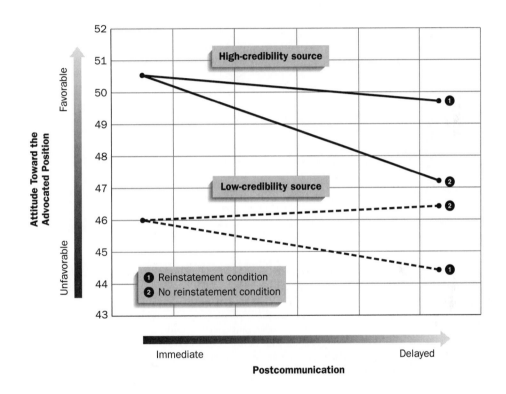

Adapted from: H.C. Kelman and C.I. Hovland, " 'Reinstatement' of the Communicator in Delayed Measurement of Opinion Change," *Journal of Abnormal and Social Psychology*, vol. 48 (1953), pp. 327–335. Copyright by the American Psychological Association. Used with permission.

Receiver variables are grouped into two types: Those based on personality differences (Chapter 6) and those based on demographic differences (Chapter 7). Personality differences include such things as self-esteem, intelligence, anxiety, dogmatism (closed-mindedness), and the like. De-mographic group differences are those dealing with age, gender, social class, and membership groups.

Two aspects of the Message Learning Model must be emphasized here. First, it is important to remember that the Message Learning Model

F I G U R E **3.4**

THE RELATIONSHIP BETWEEN RECEIVER VARIABLES AND PERSUASABILITY

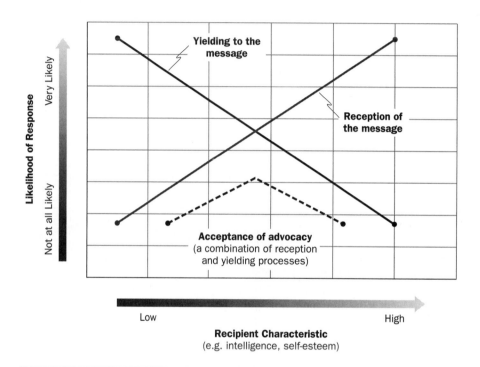

The relationship between receiver variables and persuasability. At the low end of the continuum of the personality variable (that is, low IQ), receivers are likely to yield to the message, but are not fully able to receive and comprehend the message's components; while at the high level of the personality variable, receivers demonstrate a skill at receiving and comprehending the message, but are best able to resist yielding. In these situations, the receivers best able to accept the advocated position are the individuals who are average in the personality variable, and who display an average amount of both acceptance and yielding.

holds that the receiver-persuasion relationship is moderated by the four underlying processes. Considerable energy has been devoted over the years to the creation of messages that get children's *atten-* *tion*, that they easily *comprehend*, that appeal to things children like and are likely to *yield* to (such as popularity, action, success, fun, appealing tastes, and the like), and are *memorable* (retained in memory). As a general rule, persuading *any* receiver group is dependent upon being able to reach the group and gain attention, making the message easily understood, identifying how to prompt the group to yield to the persuader's messages, and increasing the chance receivers will retain the information. Indeed, one of the most important aspects of influencing others is that different people *yield* to different message appeals: anxious individuals desire to decrease anxiety, low self-esteemed individuals desire to rid themselves of worry. Hispanic consumers (as a rule) value family togetherness and value companies that accommodate them and invest in their communities. Strong argument based on irrefutable evidence is required to influence highly intelligent receivers (see Chapters 6 and 7 for more details).

Certain receiver variables are related to the four underlying processes in different ways, sometimes tending to cancel out the effects of persuasion. For example, it is not difficult to create messages for the very young receiver (three to five years of age) that gain his or her attention and prompt yielding (the desire to possess the advertised product). However, this child may not retain much of the information in the advertisement over the course of hours or days. McGuire[10] argued that persuasion is dependent on two processes—the "reception" process dictated by attention, comprehension, and retention, and the "yielding" process. McGuire further maintained that any number of receiver variables may be strongly and positively related to one process, but strongly and negatively related to the other. For example, highly intelligent individuals are better equipped to learn from messages via the reception process, comprehending and retaining the information that is learned. However, part of the nature of higher intelligence is confidence in one's ability to know "good argument" and why and when one should change an opinion; highly intelligent receivers are better able to see through poor arguments, illogic, and the misuse of evidence and to *counterargue*

messages they hear. In general, then, higher intelligence is not consistently related to increased levels of persuasion because such receivers learn more but yield less to messages. On the other hand, receivers with less intelligence should be expected to yield more to a speech (at least one that sounds competently crafted), but are less likely to comprehend, and retain, various arguments supporting the message conclusion.

McGuire's model is presented in Figure 3.4. *Acceptance* of an advocated position in a speech is dependent on receivers' both yielding to a message as well as receiving and comprehending it. At low levels of a receiver variable (low IQ, low self-esteem, and the like), receivers are likely to yield to the message, but are not likely to comprehend fully the message's components. On the other hand, at high levels of the receiver variable (high IQ, high self-esteem), receivers are likely to understand and more fully comprehend the message's components, but also to counterargue. Thus, the receiver at the mid-range of the personality construct (the average IQ, or the person with a moderate level of self-esteem) is often the individual most likely to "accept the advocacy" and be influenced.

The value of McGuire's work on receiver variables and the Message Learning Model is that it explains *why* receivers are influenced the way they are; some by yielding and some by reception processes. The potential persuader has to be aware that both of these processes must be kept in mind when attempting to influence others, and sometimes the effects of one process appear to cancel out another.

Channel Effects

Scholars in the Yale school were the first to champion the idea that the mass media can be used to persuade large groups of receivers. Although the mass media can be used to reach large audiences, it appears that little behavioral change occurs unless there is reinforcement via face-to-face influence. For example, Smokey the Bear's message, "Only you can prevent forest fires," achieved some amount of success over the years because the PSAs (public service announcements) were reinforced by additional messages (to not play with matches) through schools, and through groups such as the Boy Scouts. Matters of changing diets, exercise routines, drug abuse, the role of women (or minorities) in society, and so forth, probably cannot be changed solely on the basis of mass media messages, although such messages are critically important in getting the word out and maintaining awareness. A clear example of this is the "designated driver" campaign in which television shows in America agreed to include in their stories designating a non-drinker to be the driver. The messages were coupled with a plethora of advertisements by alcohol companies calling upon consumers to be responsible. Thus, millions of Americans knew of the appropriateness of designating a driver due to the many messages they heard from multiple sources.

Mass media and face-to-face channels operate differently on receivers due to the four basic processes underlying persuasion. Channel effects are about getting the receiver's attention. Older, more affluent Americans read more magazines and newspapers and are more likely to be critical of television advertisements. Younger children watch incredible amounts of television in the mornings and in the evenings, while teenagers listen to more radio, watch MTV and films, but read very little. Reaching the audience appropriate to a persuader's goal is often a major problem. For example, many anti-drug PSAs failed to reach the targeted audience until put on MTV, videos, and video games.

Another important consideration deals with "channel attributes"—attributes or qualities that are limited to certain types of channels. For example, in an audio/visual-type channel, emotions of warmth (or nostalgia) may be elicited by the scenario of two individuals sharing coffee (or

beer), by their emotional expressions, the colors used, and by the appropriate background music. Obviously, print-only materials manipulate emotions less fully relative to visual and audio presentations. When the potential persuader wants to manipulate emotions, the channel of choice should offer multiple attributes.

However, channel differences (print, audio, and audio-visual) are critically important because of: (a) the impact channels have on the comprehension of messages and (b) the impact channels have on drawing and focusing the receiver's attention to specific aspects of the message. The impact on message comprehension was clearly demonstrated in research by Chaiken and Eagly[11], who had students read what they thought were legal materials involving a labor management dispute. One version of the legal material was written in legal terminology and complex sentences, employing a high level of vocabulary. A second, "easy to comprehend," version was written in simple language with shorter sentences. Some of the students read the material, another group heard an audio version and another group viewed a video tape of a law student discussing the case.

Chaiken and Eagly had students act as "mock jurors" by providing feedback about the message they heard and whether they agreed with the advocated position. Not surprisingly, those who heard the hard-to-comprehend version had a more difficult time following the arguments when they listened/watched the speaker communicate the message, but rated the language as more appropriate, pleasant, and understandable when they were able to *read* the difficult version. Those who were exposed to the difficult-to-comprehend version were persuaded much more by the written channel than students who were exposed to the audio and audio-visual channels. On the other hand, individuals who were exposed to the easy-to-comprehend version were most influenced by the audio-visual presentations and least influenced by the written presentation. The conclusion: Complex material is best presented in written or printed channels so that receivers can best process and learn the message content.

Another Chaiken and Eagly study[12] provides evidence for the conclusion that audio and audio-video presentations draw the receivers' attention to the *source* of the message, while the written or print channel draws attention away from the source and toward the actual *message content*. In this study, a university official was described as new to the University of Toronto, having moved from the University of British Columbia. The university official advocated that the university should change to a trimester schedule, like the one used in British Columbia. Students heard the official speak in what appeared to be an interview about changing the schedule; but prior to expressing this view, the interviewer asked the official, "How do you like being at the University of Toronto, compared to the University of British Columbia?" At this point in time, two versions of the interview segment were made. In one, the official appeared to be likable by stating that he preferred being at the University of Toronto, and he listed a number of positive reasons concerning the city, the students, and so forth. In the "unlikable" version, the official complained about the city, the university, and the quality of the students.

Chaiken and Eagly had students at the University of Toronto either read the interview excerpt, listen to an audio version or watch a videotape of the performance. Afterwards, the students rated (on a questionnaire) the extent to which they changed their opinions to agree with the official concerning the change to a trimester schedule, and they were asked to list their thoughts during the message. The results are presented in Table 3.1. Students changed their opinions to agree more with the likable source, but especially when they heard his voice and saw him on videotape, rather than simply read the script. On the other hand, when the speaker was unlikable, students resisted the influence and did not

change their opinions. However, this resistance was limited to the audiotape and video channels; when they read the written material by an unlikable person, they were still influenced (see the M of 3.43 in Table 3.1 for unlikable source, written version), presumably because of the message content (rather than merely agreeing with a likable person). When Chaiken and Eagly examined the thoughts the students had when exposed to the messages, they found, on the average, students generated only one thought about the speaker when they were reading the written message ("Seems like he plans ahead," "Seems competent," and so forth). However, when exposed to videotaped messages, the students thought more about the communicator, especially when he was likable (see Table 3.1). The conclusion is that different channels draw attention to different aspects of the persuasion encounter—videotape messages naturally draw the receiver's attention toward the source of the message, written messages draw attention toward the content of the message.

Channel effects, then, play an important role in persuasion. The last two studies highlight that if the language of the message is difficult to comprehend, the persuader should avoid using audio and audio-visual presentations, because more learning and persuasion will occur in a written modality. However, if the language is easy to comprehend, then an audio or audio-visual presentation is preferable. Further, a likable personality is more likely to *augment* persuasiveness (recall the augmenting and discounting cues noted above) when the presentation is an audio-visual one. But, if you are unlikable, it is preferable to draw attention away from yourself as the speaker by using written presentations.

SELF-PERSUASION

Having outlined the importance of *learning* message arguments, we now have to admit an

T A B L E	**3.1**

Modality Effects and Influence

| | Communicator Likability | | | | | |
| | Likable | | | Unlikable | | |
Persuasion Outcome	Written	Audiotape	Videotape	Written	Audiotape	Videotape
Opinion change	3.66	4.82	4.87	3.43	1.47	.48
Communicator-oriented thoughts	1.05	1.72	2.12	1.00	1.41	1.44

NOTE: Higher numbers indicate greater opinion change and more communicator-oriented thoughts.
Adapted from: S. Chaiken and A.H. Eagly, "Communication Modality as a Determinant of Persuasion: The Role of Communicator Salience," *Journal of Personality and Social Psychology*, vol. 45 (1983), pp. 241–256. Reprinted by permission of the authors and the American Psychological Association.

important limitation to the Message Learning Model: Sometimes we, as the receivers, do far more than merely remember the arguments a source is communicating. Sometimes we have a strong reaction to speakers and become mentally engaged in what they are saying. When we are involved actively in the speech, debates, or discussion, we can react in two important ways: We can think of the errors, mistakes, and lack of logic being used as we *counterargue* the content of the speaker's message, or we can add our own *supportive thoughts* that build on, extend, or otherwise add to the speaker's message. (Of course, we can also think "neutral thoughts" during the message, but these are clearly not as important as counterarguments and supportive arguments).

This involvement occurs when receivers tune in to watch political debates with friends. Receivers who say things like "He's lying," "That's not the complete truth," "That won't solve anything. We'll all be paying more taxes," are receivers who are counterarguing the speech. Comments made during a debate, such as, "Good idea," "That

would help solve a problem," "That's true! We have to stay by our allies," are listing supporting thoughts as the speaker presents ideas.

What is "self-persuasion?" Self-persuasion occurs when the receivers take an active role in persuading themselves to change their opinions. We've already seen one example of self-persuasion in Chapter 2, when we discussed "counter-attitudinal advocacy." If a positive source (school board, department of education) were interested in your ideas and provided an incentive for you (that is, paid you money) to advocate the position that children should be encouraged to read comic books, you may accept the task. If the incentive was valued (a good sum of money), you may be motivated to work hard on the essay, come up with good persuasive reasons and actually persuade yourself that reading comic books is a good idea. You engage in self-persuasion—you may have been paid by someone else, but during the hours you worked on the assignment, you generated the ideas, thoughts, and rationale for why the conclusion should be adopted.

There are a number of situations in which we persuade ourselves to change an attitude, belief, or behavior. The most thoroughly researched model of self-persuasion is called the "elaboration likelihood model."

Elaboration Likelihood Model

Petty and Cacioppo[13] have devoted considerable effort to develop a comprehensive model of how receivers "elaborate" on the messages they hear. By the term "elaboration" we mean that a receiver engages in *issue-relevant thinking*—the receiver was busy thinking of thoughts regarding the topic at hand, the implications, and consequences. Imagine the following two situations: You are sick in bed with a vicious head cold, and you hear on television that Medicine A resolves twelve cold symptoms and works fast. You ask a friend to buy it for you. You don't even remember what the twelve cold symptoms are, and you do not generate any of your own issue-relevant thoughts regarding the medicine (except to get it to you soon and that you hope it works). On the other hand, imagine you are interested in birth control and the problem of communicable diseases, and you listen to a message on the relative merits of various devices and practices. Chances are, you will have a good number of "issue-relevant thoughts" concerning safety, comfort, effectiveness, costs, maintenance, and the like. There are questions that you'd like to ask, counterarguments will be generated about some devices, and you'd generate supportive thoughts about other devices. You were motivated to *elaborate* on the message you heard on this important topic.

How do we know when people are elaborating on messages? Typically, researchers will have receivers list, on paper, their thoughts immediately after hearing a persuasive message. Another way to tell if people are "counterarguing" a message would be to assess the tension in certain facial muscles (the more tension, the more they are disagreeing with the speaker); however, there are ethical problems with such a procedure. Usually, scholars have receivers list their thoughts, and the generated thoughts can be grouped on the basis of whether they are supportive, opposing or neutral to the speaker's advocated position.

Next, it is important to realize that receivers may vary greatly in how *involved they become with messages and how they elaborate* on message content. There are varying levels of receiver involvement, or manner of cognitive elaboration. Greenwald and Leavitt[14] argue that there are four basic levels at which receivers can become involved with (and react to) messages. At the lowest level is the "preattention" level of processing, when receivers merely hear repeated stimuli, such as music and slogans, while they listen to the radio or watch television. Receivers may like familiar music, and there may be liking for a product with which the music is paired (recall Chapter 2), but receivers do not generate any thought about the music or product at this level, and it is unlikely that there will be much in the way of a lasting, long-term effect. (This is the level at which the term "subliminal" is used in the popular literature.) The second level, "focal attention," is one in which the receiver at least tunes into the channel and attends to the message, typically concerned with the sensory elements of loud, colorful, moving, novel, unexpected or emotionally arousing messages. Emotions may be manipulated, and the receiver may or may not move to the next level of involvement and think about the product or the message.

At the third level of involvement, called "comprehension," the receiver tunes into the channel and attends to the semantic elements of the message (words and language), learning the content of the message. This point of processing was the focus of the Message Learning Model. Finally, a receiver can "elaborate" on the message by generating his/her own arguments concerning the message's arguments or conclusion. Often, self-generated arguments are those in which the receiver thinks about the impact or relevance for his/her future, frequently visually imagining the implications or consequences ("I'd look good in that dress," "But if tuition goes up, I'll have to work this summer, and I'll have to skip summer school").

Figure 3.5 lists the basic seven principles of the Elaboration Likelihood Model. First, it assumes that people are motivated to hold correct attitudes. They want to buy the right medicine, invest in the right stock, vote for the politician who will do the things the voters want done, and so forth. Since receivers want to be correct in their attitudes, they should be motivated to attend and elaborate on a vast number of messages involving taxes, investments, diet and medicine, child rearing, home improvements, and the like. Of course, it is not possible to be well-read and knowledgeable on all of these topics, so receivers have to be selective in attending to and elaborating on various messages. Hence, the second principle states that receivers will be willing to engage in high levels of message elaboration dependent on a variety of *individual* and *situational* factors.

By "individual" we mean that some receivers simply are not able or motivated to engage cognitively with a message or to counterargue its claims. For one, individuals who score lower on IQ tests (compared to the ones who score high on the tests) do not appear to know how to separate "good" argument from "weak" argument, and do not appear to recall as many details from the same message. Further, many parents do not appear very competent at counterarguing the exaggerated claims made in children's advertisements, and the majority spend little time trying to teach children to counterargue such claims. Thus, there are many consumers who are deficient in elaborating intelligently on a number of topics. However, a good deal of research on the Elaboration Likelihood Model has relied on situational factors that affect

FIGURE 3.5

PROPOSITIONS OF THE ELABORATION LIKELIHOOD MODEL

1. People are motivated to hold correct attitudes.

2. Although people want to hold correct attitudes, the amount and nature of issue-relevant elaboration in which they are willing or able to engage for evaluating a message vary with individual and situational factors.

3. Variables can affect the amount and direction of attitude change by (a) serving as persuasive arguments, (b) serving as peripheral cues, and/or (c) affecting the extent or direction of issue and argument elaboration.

4. Variables affecting motivation and/or ability to process a message in a relatively objective manner can do so by either enhancing or reducing argument scrutiny.

5. Variables affecting message processing in a relatively biased manner can produce either a positive (favorable) or negative (unfavorable) bias to the issue-relevant thoughts attempted.

6. As motivation and/or ability to process arguments is decreased, peripheral cues become relatively more important determinants of persuasion. Conversely, as argument scrutiny is increased, peripheral cues become relatively less important determinants of persuasion.

7. Attitude changes that result mostly from processing issue-relevant arguments (central route) will show greater temporal persistence, greater prediction of behavior, and greater resistance to counterpersuasion than attitude changes that result mostly from peripheral cues.

From: R.E. Petty and J.T. Cacioppo, *Communication and Persuasion: Central and Peripheral Routes to Attitude Change*, New York: Springer-Verlag, 1986. Used with permission.

the receiver's motivation or ability to elaborate on a message.

Principle 3 argues that attitude change can stem from three types of factors: The persuasiveness of the arguments employed, a set of peripheral cues that tell the receiver what her/his reaction ought to be, and the amount and type of cognitive elaboration in which the receiver engages. The first of these, the persuasiveness of the arguments employed, assumes certain arguments made regarding a particular message or message conclusion are good, valid, reliable, and convincing. Figure 3.6 provides examples of strong and weak arguments for two topics; one for the claim that the university plans require all graduating seniors to pass a comprehensive examination, and one for a new type of razor, called Edge. As evidenced in these examples, strong arguments are more convincing and persuasive, while weak arguments are not, and can be counterargued more easily.

The fact that strong arguments are more convincing than weak ones is easy to demonstrate; further, when repeated three or five times, weak arguments quickly become *less* and *less* persuasive, while strong arguments remain persuasive. To demonstrate this, Petty and Cacioppo[15] did a study in which community volunteers were involved in a study presumably to assess the sound quality of audio commercials. (They were told this so they wouldn't know that the study was on the issue of message repetition.) The commercials dealt with advocating an increase in the price of the local newspaper—an action all would find objectionable. Some receivers heard arguments judged as strong (that is, the paper plans to use the money to increase news coverage), and some receivers heard weak arguments (that is, the paper plans to use the money in ways similar to those used when it last increased the price). A third group of receivers heard "novel, but weak" arguments favoring the price increase (that is, the

paper plans to use the money to increase advertising space and cut down on excess news coverage). Some of the receivers were exposed to one repetition of a type of argument (weak, strong, or novel), others three times, and others five times.

Figure 3.7 illustrates whether the receivers had a relatively favorable or unfavorable attitude toward the price increase. When exposed to a message only once, receivers indicate little difference in attitude between strong and weak messages. As the message is repeated, receivers show an increase in favorable attitudes only for the strong arguments (from three exposures and then to five exposures). When arguments are weak, there is only a decline in attitude. Why? While the Message Learning Model argued that frequent exposure to messages increased the likelihood that receivers will *learn* the message content, the Elaboration Likelihood Model argues that message repetition allows the receiver a better opportunity to scrutinize the quality of message argument and to elaborate on it. When elaborating on the repeated message, receivers are likely to generate more supportive arguments and fewer counterarguments when arguments are strong, but generate fewer supportive arguments and more counterarguments when arguments are weak.

Finally, novel/weak arguments produced a very negative response with one exposure, but attitudes increased dramatically with three exposures. However, when exposed to the arguments five times, the receivers easily de-valued and counterargued the claim. The Elaboration Model and the Message Learning Model both agree that moderate amounts of exposure (three to five repetitions) are more effective than only one exposure, or seven to ten exposures (per a certain time frame), but they do so for different reasons. The Message Learning Model claims receivers learn from repeated exposure, and a message's effectiveness wears out when there is nothing more to

FIGURE **3.6**

EXAMPLES OF STRONG ARGUMENT
AND WEAK ARGUMENT

*Strong Arguments (Comprehensive Exams for
Seniors):*
1. Prestigious universities have comprehensive exams to maintain academic excellence;

2. Institution of the exams has led to a reversal in the declining scores on standardized achievement tests at other universities;

3. Graduate and professional schools show a preference for undergraduates who have passed comprehensive exams;

4. Average starting salaries are higher for graduates of schools with exams;

5. Schools with the exams attract larger and more well-known corporations to recruit students for jobs;

6. The quality of undergraduate teaching has improved for schools with the exams;

7. University alumni would increase financial support if the exams were instituted, allowing a tuition increase to be avoided;

8. The (fictitious) National Accrediting Board of Higher Education would give the university its highest rating if the exams were instituted.

Strong Arguments (Edge Razors):
1. New advanced honing method creates unsurpassed sharpness;

2. Special chemically formulated coating eliminates nicks and cuts and prevents rusting;

3. Handle is tapered and ribbed to prevent slipping;

4. In direct comparison tests, the Edge blade gave twice as many close shaves as its nearest competitor;

5. Unique angle placement of the blade provides the smoothest shave possible.

Weak Arguments (Comprehensive Exams for Seniors):
1. Adopting the exams would allow the university to be at the forefront of a national trend;

2. Graduate students have complained that since they have to take comprehensives, undergraduates should take them also;

3. By not administering the exams, a tradition dating back to the Greeks was being violated;

4. Parents had written to administrators in support of the plan;

5. The exams would increase student fear and anxiety enough to promote more studying;

6. The exams would help cut costs by eliminating the necessity for other tests that varied with instructor;

7. The exams would allow students to compare their performances with that of students at other schools;
8. Job prospects might be improved.

Weak Arguments (Edge Razors):
1. Floats in water with a minimum of rust;

2. Comes in various sizes, shapes, and colors;

3. Designed with the bathroom in mind;

4. In direct comparison tests, the Edge blade gave no more nicks and cuts than its competition;

5. Can only be used once, but will be memorable.

*Very Weak Arguments (Comprehensive Exams for
Seniors):*
1. Most of the author's friends supported the proposal;

2. The author's major advisor took a comprehensive exam and now has a prestigious academic position;

3. Whatever benefit the exams had for graduate students would also accrue to undergraduates;

4. Requiring graduate students but not undergraduate students to take the exams was analogous to racial discrimination;

5. The risk of failing the exam was a challenge most students would welcome;

6. The difficulty of the exam would prepare one for later competitions in life;

7. The Educational Testing Service would not market the exams unless they had great educational value;

8. If the exams were instituted, the university would become the "American Oxford."

Source: R.E. Petty, S. Harkins, and K. Williams, "The Effects of Group Diffusion of Cognitive Effort on Attitudes: An Information-Processing View," *Journal of Personality and Social Psychology*, vol. 38 (1980), pp. 81-92; However, all studies employing the topic of comprehensive examinations for seniors have employed these arguments; For Edge Razor example: R.E. Petty, J.T. Cacioppo, and D. Schumann, "Central and Peripheral Routes to Advertising Effectiveness: The Moderating Role of Involvement," *Journal of Consumer Research*, vol. 10 (1983), pp. 135-146.

learn. The Elaboration Likelihood Model claims that repeated exposure allows receivers greater access to the message arguments in order to scrutinize their quality and elaborate in either a supportive or counterargumentative manner.

What is meant, then, by "peripheral cues" in Principle 3? Certain "cues" may be used by receivers as guidelines in knowing how to behave, or in knowing how to react to a message. Some of these cues or factors may not be *relevant or important* in regards to the message conclusion. A person may sign a petition or agree to some request (say, to recycle) solely because the individual who canvased their home was a stunningly beautiful person of the opposite sex. The person may not be committed to recycling, or even remember the message content or his/her reaction to it; he or she complied to a request on the basis of a "peripheral cue" (a speaker's beauty). The Elaboration Likelihood Model claims that there are two very different routes to persuasion: a *central* route, which is dependent upon the receiver scrutinizing the quality of messages, and a *peripheral* route, which involves a number of simple rules which govern

whether or not the receiver will follow the advice of the speaker. These rules are based on what are called "heuristic principles."[16]

Sometimes a receiver will not be motivated to scrutinize a message, or will not be able to do so (see below). Instead, the receiver will look for "easy" ways to evaluate a message, called "heuristics." The three most common are the *credibility heuristic*, the *liking heuristic*, and the *consensus heuristic*. The credibility heuristic rests on the fact that we believe the arguments of a person we perceive to be credible. Many individuals do not really want to do their own income taxes, or do not feel competent in negotiating contracts so they follow the simple rule of trusting the advice of credible people. The liking heuristic is based on the fact that we often comply to requests of likable and attractive others. The consensus principle simply states that "if everyone else believes it, it must be true." In Chapter 10 on gaining-compliance, we refer to these three heuristics as the "authority principle," the "liking principle," and the "social proof principle."

There are other simple rules which receivers follow, including the "what is expensive must be good" rule and the "more arguments the better" rule. However, it is important to remember that some receivers are either not motivated to actually tune into and scrutinize a message or don't know how to assess the quality of an argument. These receivers will look for a peripheral cue as a guide.

Principle 4 asserts a number of factors that affect either the motivation or the ability to scrutinize message arguments. Factors influencing motivation include: (1) receiver involvement, (2) need for cognition, and (3) the presence of multiple speakers communicating multiple arguments. Factors influencing ability include: (1) distraction and (2) prior knowledge.[17] Receivers are more motivated to elaborate on a message if they are *personally involved* with the topic at hand. Changes in tuition, taxes, course requirements in

---

FIGURE 3.7

EFFECTS OF MESSAGE REPETITION OF WEAK AND STRONG ARGUMENTS

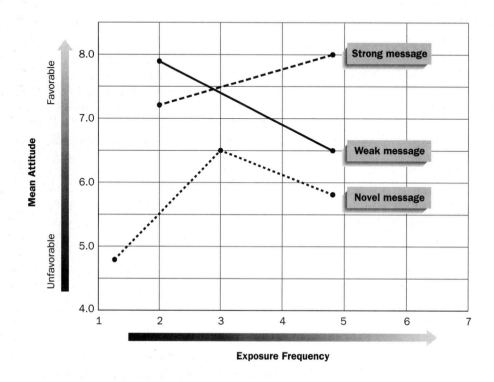

From: J.T. Cacioppo and R.E. Petty, "Persuasiveness of Communications as Affected by Exposure Frequency and Communication Cogency: A Theoretical and Empirical Analysis of Persisting Attitude Change," in J. Leigh and C. Martin, eds., *Current Issues and Research in Advertising* (Ann Arbor: University of Michigan, 1980), p. 112. Reprinted by permission.

your major, and the like, are topics which prompt higher levels of elaboration.

Second, Petty and Cacioppo have developed a scale, called "Need for Cognition," which deals with an individual's tendency to engage in and enjoy thinking about topics.[18] Receivers who score high on "Need for Cognition" are those who attend automatically to the quality of the arguments employed in persuasive messages. Individuals

high on "Need for Cognition" are more likely to elaborate on messages than those who score low on this measure; they are likely to scrutinize argument quality and to generate either counterarguments or supportive arguments.

Third, receivers are more motivated to scrutinize a message claim or conclusion if multiple sources communicate multiple arguments for the claim or the conclusion. Consider the case in which one speaker communicates nine reasons for buying a Ford automobile. It is natural for receivers to devote a certain amount of energy and attention to scrutinizing the nine arguments. However, receivers are likely to pay far more attention and are motivated to scrutinize each of the nine arguments when nine different speakers each communicate one argument. Why? Because we naturally assume each speaker is independent of the other and is communicating his/her own (independent) reason for buying a Ford. This tactic can be seen in some advertisements for automobiles, grocery stores, or movies—several different speakers each point out favorable features of the automobile, the store, or the movie.

Finally, receivers are not *able* to elaborate on messages if they are distracted from paying attention or lack knowledge of the topic. Distraction, such as eating or watching a movie when exposed to messages, means that receivers cannot fully scrutinize argument quality and elaborate on messages. The way distraction affects persuasion is that: (1) strong arguments in a message result in elaboration and the generation of supportive arguments; however, distraction would interfere with the strong arguments-favorable reaction, and distraction thus reduces the level of persuasiveness and (2) weak arguments in a message result in elaboration and the generation of counterarguments, but distraction reduces a receiver's ability to generate counterarguments; thus, distraction increases the persuasiveness of weak arguments (by interfering with receiver's counterarguing).

Principle 4 focuses on scrutinizing arguments in a "relatively objective manner" for the sake of uncovering correct, valid attitudes (Principle 1). Principle 5 focuses on processing messages in a "relatively biased manner," and there are obviously certain topics in which the receiver will be *biased* toward self-righteous or defensive attitudes (as in denying that one has a drinking problem, or denying that one's children are delinquents). "Bi-

ased processing" means that when receivers elaborate on messages, they do so with the motive in mind of supporting certain existing attitudes. When told ahead of time that there will be an attempt to persuade you, you (typically) are motivated to generate the counterarguments to defend yourself from influence. These situations occur in real life when we have dinner at a friend's house and we know ahead of time the friend will try to talk us into joining his church.

Finally, Principles 6 and 7 deal with persuasion effects and outcomes. If you are not motivated to, or not able to, scrutinize message quality, you are likely to comply to a request based on peripheral cues (the heuristics mentioned above), while if motivated and able to focus on message quality, then peripheral cues become less important and quality of argument becomes the primary source of attitude change. Principle 7 asserts that when receivers do follow the "central route" of persuasion, scrutinizing message quality and elaborating on messages, then attitude changes which occur will be more persistent over time, have a greater impact on behaviors, and be more resistant to later attacks.

FACTORS AFFECTING THE INVOLVED AND THE UNINVOLVED RECEIVER

Having overviewed the basic principles of the Elaboration Likelihood Model, we'd like to discuss three classic empirical projects that demonstrate the importance of the model.

Quality of Arguments and the Number of Arguments

Petty and Cacioppo[19] demonstrated the importance of strong versus weak argument in a classic study involving the topic of comprehensive examinations for seniors. The students were asked to respond to a proposal, written by a faculty member who was the chairperson of the "University Committee on Academic Policy." The message called for a change in policy in which all seniors

| T A B L E | 3.2 |

ATTITUDE, FAVORABLE THOUGHTS, AND UNFAVORABLE THOUGHTS AS A FUNCTION OF RECEIVER INVOLVEMENT AND QUALITY OF ARGUMENTS

| | Arguments | | | |
| | Weak | | Strong | |
Measure	*Three*	*Nine*	*Three*	*Nine*
Low Involvement:				
Attitude	4.52	7.71	4.95	8.66
Favorable Thoughts	1.14	1.19	1.48	1.57
Unfavorable Thoughts	1.62	2.14	1.52	1.33
High Involvement:				
Attitude	4.10	1.05	8.32	11.30
Favorable Thoughts	.75	.65	1.82	2.45
Unfavorable Thoughts	3.00	2.70	1.50	.95

The higher the numbers, the more positive the attitude, the greater the number of listed thoughts.
From: R.E. Petty and J.T. Cacioppo, "The Effects of Involvement on Responses to Argument Quantity and Quality: Central and Peripheral Routes to Persuasion," *Journal of Personality and Social Psychology*, vol. 46 (1984), pp. 69–81. Reprinted by permission of the author and the American Psychological Association.

would be required to pass a comprehensive examination. The students' *level of receiver involvement* was manipulated by telling some receivers that the policy was to take effect before they become seniors *(High Involvement),* or would take effect after they graduated *(Low Involvement).*

After the faculty member announced the proposed change, he communicated one of four messages (students heard only one of these messages): three weak arguments in support of the change, three strong arguments in support of the change, nine weak arguments in support of the change, or nine strong arguments in support of the change. Based on our discussion of this model, what do you predict were the responses by receivers with high and low involvement?

Table 3.2 presents the students' attitudes (the higher the number, the more positive the attitude), and the number of thoughts generated. When the students were uninvolved with the topic (they would not have to take the comprehensive examinations themselves), their attitudes were influenced by the *number of the arguments they heard.* When uninvolved, they were influenced by a peripheral cue (merely the number of arguments): M = 7.71 (nine weak arguments); M = 8.66 (nine strong arguments). Further, the students generated more favorable thoughts when exposed to strong arguments, and generated more unfavorable thoughts when exposed to weak arguments, especially nine weak ones: M = 2.14.

When the topic of the persuasion was personally involving and relevant, positive attitudes were shaped by *strong* arguments, especially nine strong arguments (M = 11.30), compared to only three strong arguments (M = 8.32). However, nine weak arguments elicited extremely low ratings (M = 1.05), lower than three weak arguments. The same pattern of responses was obtained for favorable thoughts; most were obtained with nine strong arguments, the least with nine weak arguments. Unfavorable thoughts were obtained when involved students were exposed to weak arguments.

What do the results of this study show us about persuasion and the Elaboration Likelihood Model? First, we see that receiver involvement is related to elaboration and cognitive responses to messages; when receivers were low in involvement, there were relatively few favorable or unfavorable thoughts. When receiver involvement was high, there was more elaboration and more cognitive response, both favorable (with strong argument) and unfavorable (with weak argument). Second, the study demonstrates that involved receivers are primarily influenced by strong arguments. When uninvolved, receivers are influenced by peripheral cues (the sheer number of arguments communicated).

Quality of Arguments and Celebrity Endorsements Petty, Cacioppo and Schumann[20] also completed a project that assessed the role of another peripheral cue and its effect on uninvolved receivers: celebrity endorsements. In this study, students were exposed to magazine (print) advertisements for a new type of razor blade, the Edge razor. Some messages included strong arguments, others included weak arguments (see Figure 3.7 for a list). "Highly involved" students were told they could purchase the razor in their area; "uninvolved" students were told that they could not purchase the razor in their area. Finally, half the students were led to believe that the product was endorsed by professional athletes; the other half by citizens of Bakersfield, California (called a "citizen endorsement").

Table 3.3 illustrates the student attitudes toward buying the Edge razor (high positive numbers reflect a positive attitude, high negative numbers reflect a negative one). When students were low in involvement, they were not motivated to scrutinize message quality and probably did not elaborate on the arguments provided. Instead, their attitude was shaped primarily on the basis of the celebrity endorsement (both when arguments were weak, M = 1.21, and strong, M = 1.85). Thus, when uninvolved with the message, receivers relied on a peripheral cue to tell them how to respond—one of the "heuristics" noted above. When the topic was personally involving, receivers were motivated to scrutinize message quality and gave positive responses when arguments were strong and negative responses when arguments were weak.

Multiple Arguments and Multiple Sources As noted above, receivers are motivated to scrutinize message argument when they are exposed to persuasive situations in which multiple speakers communicate multiple arguments. A very straightforward illustration of this was conducted by Harkins and Petty[21]. Again using the topic of comprehensive examinations as the issue, all students were led to believe they would have to take an examination in their senior year. Failing the examination would mean that they would have to

---

TABLE 3.3

ATTITUDE AS A FUNCTION OF QUALITY OF ARGUMENTS, TYPE OF
ENDORSEMENT, AND RECEIVER INVOLVEMENT

| | Low Involvement | | High Involvement | |
	Weak Arguments	Strong Arguments	Weak Arguments	Strong Arguments
Citizen endorser	−.12	.98	−1.10	1.68
Celebrity endorser	1.21	1.85	−1.36	1.80

From: R.E. Petty, J.T. Cacioppo, and D. Schumann, "Central and Peripheral Routes to Advertising Effectiveness: The Moderating Role of Involvement," *Journal of Consumer Research*, vol. 10 (1983), pp. 135–146. Used with permission.

complete remedial work before receiving degrees. Students would naturally resist the proposed test.

Harkins and Petty constructed four video-tapes of messages in which "other students" had videotaped their arguments for the Faculty Committee on Academic Affairs: (a) one student communicating one argument; (b) one student communicating three different arguments; (c) three different students, each communicating the same basic argument; and, (d) three different students, each communicating a different argument. Only strong, persuasive arguments were employed in this study. To obtain additional comparisons with the multiple speaker-multiple arguments group, two other groups of students were employed in the study. One group was told that some people on the campus had proposed that a comprehensive examination policy should be passed. This group of receivers heard no arguments concerning the proposal—they were simply asked what their reactions were (the attitude control group). The other group was told about the proposal and told that they would hear three stu-

TABLE 3.4

ATTITUDE AND FAVORABLE THOUGHTS AS A FUNCTION OF MULTIPLE SOURCES AND QUALITY OF ARGUMENTS

Experimental Group	Attitude	Favorable Thoughts
Three-person/three-argument	1.88	3.75
Three-person/one-argument	.30	2.20
One-person/three-argument	.04	1.85
One-person/one-argument	.03	1.50
Information control	.12	1.95
Attitude control	−2.38	.70

High positive numbers = positive attitudes, more thoughts. From: S.G. Harkins and R.E. Petty, "Effects of Source Magnification of Cognitive Effort on Attitudes: An Information-Processing View," *Journal of Personality and Social Psychology*, vol. 40 (1981), pp. 401–413. Reprinted by permission of the authors and the American Psychological Association.

dents advocate the examination policy. However, the experimenters gave this group of receivers the questionnaires immediately after reading the instructions, and prior to actually listening to the arguments (information control group).

Table 3.4 presents the students' attitudes and the number of favorable thoughts generated. Basically, the attitude control group had a very negative reaction to the proposed idea, and there were no real differences among five of the groups: three-person/one-argument, one-person/three-argument, one-person/one-argument and information control groups. Only the one group, the three-person/three-argument group, produced a positive change in attitude, and generated a substantial amount of positive thoughts. Thus, as the Elaboration Likelihood Model prescribes, the multiple speaker/multiple arguments context prompted greater attention on message quality, which, when strong arguments are included, produced positive thoughts and a positive attitude.

F O O T N O T E S

1. A.H. Eagly, "Comprehensibility of Persuasive Arguments as a Determinant of Opinion Change," *Journal of Personality and Social Psychology*, vol. 29 (1974), pp. 758–773.

2. G.J. Gorn and M.E. Goldberg, "Children's Responses to Television Commercials," *Journal of Consumer Research*, vol. 6 (1980), pp. 421–424; R. Grass and W.H. Wallace, "Satiation Effects on TV Commercials," *Journal of Advertising Research*, vol. 9 (1969), pp. 3–8; A. Greenberg and C. Suttoni, "Television Commercial Wearout," *Journal of Advertising Research*, vol. 13 (1973), pp. 47–54; H.E. Krugman, "Processes Underlying Exposure to Advertising," *American Psychologist*, vol. 23 (1968), pp. 245–253; R.L. Miller, "Mere Exposure, Psychological Reactance, and Attitude Change," *Public Opinion Quarterly*, vol. 40 (1976), pp. 229–233; M.L. Ray and A.G. Sawyer, "Repetition in Media Models: A Laboratory Technique," *Journal of Marketing Research*, vol.

8 (1971), pp. 20–28; M.L. Ray, A.G. Sawyer, and E.C. Strong, "Frequency Effects Revisited," *Journal of Advertising Research*, vol. 11 (1971), pp. 14–20; D.J. Stang, "Methodological Factors in Mere Exposure Research," *Psychological Bulletin*, vol. 81 (1974), pp. 1014–1025; D.J. Stang, "The Effects of Mere Exposure on Learning and Affect," *Journal of Personality and Social Psychology*, vol. 31 (1975), pp. 7–13.

3. N. Miller and D.T. Campbell, "Recency and Primacy in Persuasion as a Function of the Timing of Speeches and Measurements," *Journal of Abnormal and Social Psychology*, vol. 59 (1959), pp. 1–9.

4. R.L. Rosnow and E.J. Robinson, *Experiments in Persuasion* (New York: Academic Press, 1967), pp. 99–104.

5. E.A. Lind, "The Psychology of Courtroom Procedure," in N.L. Kerr and R.M. Bray, eds., *The Psychology of the Courtroom* (New York: Academic Press, 1982), pp. 13–38.

6. D.A. Aaker, D.M. Stayman, and M.R. Hagerty, "Warmth in Advertising: Measurement, Impact, and Sequence Effects," *Journal of Consumer Research*, vol. 12 (1986), pp. 365–381.

7. H.C. Kelman and C.I. Hovland, " 'Reinstatement' of the Communicator in Delayed Measurement of Opinion Change," *Journal of Abnormal and Social Psychology*, vol. 48 (1953), pp. 327–335.

8. See: R.E. Petty and J.T. Cacioppo, *Attitudes and Persuasion: Classic and Contemporary Approaches* (Dubuque, Iowa: Wm. C. Brown, 1981).

9. See, for instance: C.L. Gruder, T.D. Cook, K.M. Hennigan, B.R. Flay, C. Alessis, and J. Halamaj, "Empirical Tests of the Absolute Sleeper Effect Predicted from the Discounting Cue Hypothesis, *Journal of Personality and Social Psychology*, vol. 36 (1978), pp. 1061–1074.

10. W.J. McGuire, "Personality and Susceptibility to Social Influence," in E.F. Borgatta and W.W. Lambert, eds., *Handbook of Personality Theory and Research* (Chicago: Rand McNally, 1968), pp. 1130–1187.

11. S. Chaiken and A.H. Eagly, "Communication Modality as a Determinant of Message Persuasiveness and Message Comprehensibility," *Journal of Personality and Social Psychology*, vol. 34 (1976), pp. 606–614.

12. S. Chaiken and A.H. Eagly, "Communication Modality as a Determinant of Persuasion: The Role of Communicator Salience," *Journal of Personality and Social Psychology*, vol. 45 (1983), pp. 241–256.

13. R.E. Petty and J.T. Cacioppo, *Communication and Persuasion: Central and Peripheral Routes to Attitude Change* (New York: Springer–Verlag, 1986).

14. A.G. Greenwald, and C. Leavitt, "Audience Involvement in Advertising: Four Levels," *Journal of Consumer Research*, vol. 11 (1984), pp. 581–592.

15. J.T. Cacioppo and R.E. Petty, "Persuasiveness of Communications as Affected by Exposure Frequency and Communication Cogency: A Theoretical and Empirical Analysis of Persisting Attitude Change," in J. Leigh and C. Martin, eds., *Current Issues and Research in Advertising* (Ann Arbor: University of Michigan, 1980).

16. See, for a good summary: D.J. O'Keefe, *Persuasion: Theory and Research* (Newbury Park, Calif.: Sage Publications, 1990).

17. See, for a good summary: D.J. O'Keefe, *Persuasion: Theory and Research* (Newbury Park, Calif.: Sage Publications, 1990); R.E. Petty and J.T. Cacioppo, *Communication and Persuasion: Central and Peripheral Routes to Attitude Change* (New York: Springer-Verlag, 1986).

18. R.E. Petty and J.T. Cacioppo, *Communication and Persuasion: Central and Peripheral Routes to Attitude Change* (New York: Springer-Verlag, 1986).

19. R.E. Petty and J.T. Cacioppo, "The Effects of Involvement on Responses to Argument Quantity and Quality: Central and Peripheral Routes to Persuasion," *Journal of Personality and Social Psychology,* vol. 46 (1984), pp. 69–81.

20. R.E. Petty, J.T. Cacioppo, and D. Schumann, "Central and Peripheral Routes to Advertising Effectiveness: The Moderating Role of Involvement," *Journal of Consumer Research*, vol. 10 (1983), pp. 135–146.

21. S.G. Harkins and R.E. Petty, "Effects of Source Magnification of Cognitive Effort on Attitudes: An Information-Processing View," *Journal of Personality and Social Psychology*, vol. 40 (1981), pp. 401–413.

KEY TERMS AND CONCEPTS

Message Learning Model
emotional appeals
repetition
wear-out threshold
primacy/recency
order effects
contrast effect
fatigue effect
sleeper effect
augmenting/discounting cue
dissociative-cue hypothesis
channel attributes
self-persuasion
Elaboration Likelihood Model
peripheral cues
credibility heuristic
liking heuristic
consensus heuristic

CHAPTER 4

ATTRIBUTION THEORY AND THEORIES OF BELIEF CHANGE

In this chapter we focus on two of the central ways receivers deal cognitively with *information* in persuasion. The first major theory is called "attribution theory" and deals with how individuals go about perceiving the *causes* of behavior. The second type of theory deals with belief change and how individuals evaluate, combine, and/or alter existing beliefs they have; further, the Theory of Reasoned Action is outlined, which deals with how beliefs, attitudes, and norms affect the receiver's *intentions* to *behave* in a particular way.

ATTRIBUTION THEORY

Attribution theory is concerned with causal inferences: How people make *causal inferences,* what type of inferences people make, and the consequences which follow from making certain types of inferences. By "inference" we mean a judgment a person makes concerning perceptions of the world—the inference, for example, as to why a celebrity is endorsing a product, or the inference as to why a product does not perform as effectively as it appeared to do in the television commercial. The relevance of this theory for consumer behavior and persuasion has been reviewed by Mizerski, Golden, and Kernan[1], and by Folkes[2]. We first overview basic approaches to the study of attributions, and then discuss the theory's importance to persuasion, and to consumers' responses to advertising, product performance, and sales.

Attribution Theory: Basic Elements

The basic notion of studying inferences that people make stems from Heider's book *The Psychology of Interpersonal Relations*[3]. First, Heider drew attention to the fact that it was valuable to understand and appreciate the average person's "naive" or commonsense explanations for the surrounding external environment (that is, the world at large). Second, Heider was the first to draw upon the kinds of distinctions people generate when making attributions. For example, people can infer that a product doesn't appear to be performing adequately at home (compared to the advertisement) either due to *personal causes* (they didn't assemble the product correctly), or *external causes* (the product's portrayal on television was exaggerated and deceptive).

A third important element of attribution theory deals with *how* people come to make inferences about the world. Scientists actively create hypotheses, engage in systematic observations, complete statistical analyses to test the hypotheses, and discount any rival or alternative explanation for a relationship. However, the "layperson's" explanations about the world are "naive" in that they do not scientifically or systematically define, conceptualize, test, or evaluate their explanations. (The term "layperson" is applied to the untrained person on the street, who makes causal explanations about the world.) However, Heider was the first to recognize that people (laypersons) do in fact make inferences in a basically logical and analytic manner.

Kelley[4] developed the first elaborate model of attributional processes. Kelley argued that people infer *causality* from the various kinds of *co-variations* they see in the world around them. For example, children infer that a light switch *causes* the light to come on and to go off. Why? Because *every time* the light switch is altered, the light comes on or goes off. Children are much less likely to infer that the use of a telephone *causes* a person to deliver a pizza within a half hour, because (usually) the telephone is used only occasionally for ordering a pizza. The first part of our review focuses on the Kelley model.

KELLEY'S ATTRIBUTION MODEL

Suppose you go to every football game. The fellow on your left is friendly with the group around him and the group has never been drunk or rowdy. Then, after midterms and during the Notre Dame game, he and his friends drink excessively. You probably will think they were celebrating some occasion. You would make a *situational* (also called "external") attribution—the situation causes the behavior, the cause of the behavior was "external" to the individual. The fellow on your right, however, has come to every game in the same inebriated state, regardless of his friends. You are likely to make a *personal* (or "internal") attribution—he loves beer, *he* is the cause of his behavior. Why do we make these attributions (sometimes quickly)? The first fundamental question in attribution theory deals with *how we go about making internal or external attributions.*

Kelley suggests three factors we take into consideration when making attributions of causality: *distinctiveness, consistency,* and *consensus.* Distinctiveness generally refers to whether or not a person's behavior is distinctly different in one situation or task from others. For example, if a worker performs well on all tasks but one, then we are likely to make a dispositional judgment—the one task is too difficult for the worker. On the other hand, low distinctiveness means the worker had trouble on all tasks and we make an internal attribution (the worker is inept). In our example of the drinking student, the more different situations in which you saw the student drinking, the more likely you are to infer that he is the cause of his own behavior (he is a beer lover, or an alcoholic).

Consistency refers to the extent to which the worker's behavior is the same over time. Low consistency means the worker has performed well on one particular machine in the past; hence, difficulty with the machine today cannot be attributed to a fault of the worker—the machine is out of order. Low consistency leads to external attributions. High consistency means the worker has consistently had difficulty running a particular machine over time. In our football example, we are more likely to believe that the student loves beer (which is, of course, the internal attribution) if we see the student drink beer consistently over time.

Consensus deals with the perception of how all of the workers perform with the machine (or whether all of the other spectators are also drinking). High consensus means all the workers have a difficult time operating a particular machine, and we are less likely to believe that one worker who had a difficult time operating the machine was inept (internal attribution). Similarly, if the student drank beer with a large group of other people who drank beer (high consensus) then we are more inclined to say they are all celebrating—not necessarily that the one student is a beer lover or an alcoholic. In this framework, then, we are inclined to make an internal attribution when distinctiveness is low, consistency is high, and consensus is low; or when the student drinks beer in many situations, drinks beer consistently over time, and drinks beer when no one else is drinking beer.

This model is called a "co-variation" model because it compares a person's behavior over time, across situations, and across other people; or compares a product's performance over time, situations, and across related products. After making one (or many) observations about a person or a product, people *infer* that the person is an alcoholic (or, alternatively, is celebrating an event) or that the reason a product appears defective is because the manufacturer is disreputable (or, alternatively, that they failed to assemble the product correctly). The layperson does not make the same type of "systematic" observations about how people and products co-vary as do scientists. The layperson's ability to infer is strongly affected by a number of biases and limitations. It is important to take a look at these biases.

Motivational Biases There are three important types of motivational biases. Two of the more common motivational biases are the self-serving bias and the false consensus bias. A third, the false uniqueness bias, has had less study by persuasion scholars, but clearly is applicable to persuasion

First, consumers have a vested interest in protecting their self concepts and positive feelings of esteem; hence, they are motivated to infer in such a way as to make themselves look good and feel positive, or, at least, to defend themselves from negative information. When products work well, consumers may well congratulate themselves on making smart, well-informed purchases, but when a product does not work well, they frequently blame someone else for the quality of the merchandise. They accept responsibility for the good; assign blame for the bad[5]. The self-serving bias in attributing the cause of success and failure occurs in many situations. Bettman and Weitz[6] also found such a bias existing in annual reports mailed to shareholders. When a company performed well, and profits were high, the firm accepted responsibility for success by claiming that the causes for the success were *internal* (firm-related), *stable* (permanent), and *firm-controlled* reasons (cutbacks, improved efficiency, and so forth). However, when a company performed poorly, and profits were low, the shareholders heard that the causes for the poor performance were *external* to the firm, *unstable* (temporary problems), and *firm-uncontrollable* (riots, hurricanes, or other problems impossible to anticipate ahead of time).

Consumers also prefer to believe that others share the same preferences and consumption patterns as they do. A behavior like eating a particular food item for breakfast seems appropriate and reasonable when one believes millions of others also consume the item; further, the fact that millions share a person's preferences reinforces the person's self-esteem. Smokers, for example, are clearly a minority group and are prone to the false consensus effect. According to Sherman, Presson, Chassin, Corty, and Olshavsky[7], adolescent smokers in the Midwest overestimate how many people smoke in an attempt to justify their own smoking behavior.

Van der Pligt found that "nonconservationists" (those failing to conserve energy, to recycle, and such) justified their irresponsible actions by claiming that most other consumers in the country also waste energy[8]. The term "hedonic relevance" is used to characterize the individual's motivation to believe that others will also share resistance to tuition increases[9], tax increases, or utility increases. When individuals have a vested interest regarding taxes, payments, increases in utility bills, and so forth, they are motivated to think others will also react negatively to the changes.

An additional study on the false consensus effect, by Gilovich, Jennings, and Jennings[10], suggests consumers are more likely to assume that others agree with their preferences if they attribute the behavior to situational causes, rather than to personal or idiosyncratic causes. For example, the incredible amount of "hype" centering around the Super Bowl conveys the message that Sunday is basically a type of national holiday in which individuals consume too much junk food and drink alcohol. Since this is a strong situational pull to engage in these behaviors, it is easy to assume "everyone" is watching the Super Bowl, eating submarine sandwiches and drinking beer. This is a false consensus (millions actually do not watch the Super Bowl). On the other hand, some behaviors are personal and idiosyncratic, such as drinking strawberry soda and avoiding cola drinks, eating peas and ketchup, and liking liver. When the causes of such behaviors are personal and idiosyncratic, consumers are not likely to be susceptible to the false consensus effect (although they may be susceptible to false uniqueness effects; see below). Obviously, advertisers prefer situations in which all consumers might be prone to believing all other consumers are participating in Super Bowl celebrations, Secretary's Day, Grandparents' Day, or Valentine's Day.

Another possible bias is the false uniqueness bias, which infers that one's own behaviors and preferences are more unique and atypical than those of others[11]. Generally speaking, one can equate the "false consensus" bias with a "Popular = Good" heuristic, while a "false uniqueness" bias reflects a "Being Different = Good" heuristic. A consumer bolsters self-esteem by succumbing to the snob appeal employed in some advertising which claims s/he is not just an average person, but is more highly discriminating in tastes, goals, and such, than others.

The Discounting and Augmenting Principles The discounting principle represents one type of belief people hold concerning how causes are related. People are expected to *discount* the effect of an attribution for an action when alternative attributions could account for the behavior. Stated otherwise, the more possible causes there are for a behavior, the *weaker* the viability of any *single* cause. The *augmentation* principle states that an unexpected response will be attributed to something unique about the actor. For example, suppose receivers *expect* a source to advocate a particular position (such as that Ted Kennedy is expected to endorse a liberal position, that Ralph Nader is expected to endorse a pro-environmental position, or that Rush Limbaugh is expected to endorse a conservative position). However, when any of these speakers endorses a position different than expected, receivers are likely to ask themselves *why* the speaker is behaving in such a fashion. As they scan the environment searching for possible causes, they may infer that he changed his mind because strong facts and evidence convinced him to change. If receivers come to believe a biased speaker changed his/her mind be-

cause of the persuasive quality of the facts and evidence, then *they* should also be strongly influenced by the same facts and evidence. Persuasion is enhanced when speakers argue against their own biases and self-interests.

The discounting principle is important in persuasion. The clearest example of this principle stems from reactions to endorsements celebrities make for products. Consider these three examples: (A) Speaker A, a famous athlete, endorses a particular spaghetti sauce because he loves it and claims it is zesty, tasty, and authentic. Speaker A was also paid a million dollars for the endorsement; (B) Speaker B, a famous baseball player and professional league coach, endorses a particular spaghetti sauce because he loves it and claims it is zesty, tasty, and authentic. The sauce is also used in his restaurants, carries his name and photograph, and he makes a profit on sales; (C) Speaker C, a famous movie star and sex symbol, also advertises a particular spaghetti sauce, and, as in the case of Speaker B, the product carries his name and photograph. The claim is made that the product is zesty, tasty, and authentic. You come to understand, however, that Speaker C's friends were impressed with his sauces and talked him into putting the product on the market. Speaker C makes no financial profit from sales; profits are donated to drug abuse programs.

The fundamental attribution question is: *What causes each speaker to endorse each product?* Similarly, we can ask which claim is the more likely to be seen as credible and persuasive? Presumably, all three of the speakers like and eat the sauces they endorse, but the first two speakers were *also* paid to endorse the particular product—there are multiple causes for their behavior. It is easy to question the sincerity of their claim (that the sauce is a zesty, tasty, authentic one) because they were paid to say what they said. However, for the third speaker, we can *discount* the one cause (personal profit), and discounting this one cause

FIGURE 4.1

EFFECTIVENESS OF COMMUNICATORS WHEN ADVOCATING STRONGER OR WEAKER COURTS

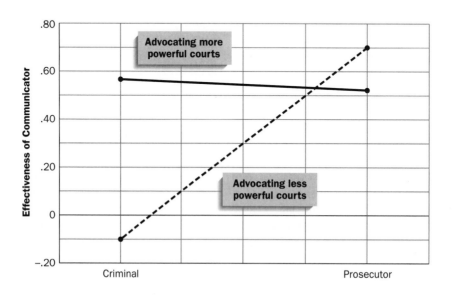

From: E. Walster (Hatfield), E. Aronson, and D. Abrahams, "On Increasing the Persuasiveness of a Low Prestige Communicator," *Journal of Experimental Social Psychology*, vol. 2 (1966), pp. 325–342. Reprinted with permission of the American Psychological Association.

increases the viability and importance of the second cause (the sauce is truly considered to be a zesty, tasty, and authentic sauce).

When speakers advocate a biased position, and/or advocate self-interest or selfishness or appear to possess ulterior motives, receivers are likely to resist influence. However, receivers should be strongly influenced when they believe the speaker is being altruistic or has changed his/her opinion based on facts and evidence. One of the classic studies demonstrating this effect was conducted by Walster (Hatfield), Aronson, and Abra-

hams[12]. High school students enrolled in a course on "Problems in Democracy" read one of four versions of a speech by either a low-prestige speaker ("Joe 'The Shoulder' Napolitano, serving the third year of his twenty-year sentence for smuggling and peddling dope"), or a high-prestige speaker ("G. William Stephans, the New York prosecutor who has sent more criminals to prison than any other prosecutor").

Further, some of the students were led to believe that the speaker advocated that *more power* be awarded to courts, while other students were led to believe that the speaker advocated *less power*. The reasons for advocating increased power included claims that any criminal can beat the rap with a smart lawyer, sentences were too soft to deter crime, and the crime rate would continue to climb until stiffer sentences were given to criminals. The reasons for advocating decreased power included claims that innocent people with badly trained lawyers were often convicted, and that when innocent people go to prison, they come out "as tough as any real convict," and that long sentences given those guilty of crimes produce desperate, not rehabilitated, individuals.

So, half of the students heard a message from Joe "The Shoulder"; half of those heard Joe advocate *more* power to the courts, and the other half heard him advocate *less* power to the courts. Half of the students heard a message from the New York prosecutor, who advocated either less power or more power to the courts. After hearing the messages, students indicated whether they agreed or disagreed with the advocated position, and they rated the credibility of the speakers (see Chapter 5; in this study the prosecutor was rated as more credible).

Figure 4.1 illustrates the extent to which the students were persuaded. When the topic was to *reduce* the power of the courts, the criminal was absolutely unpersuasive. However, when the topic was to increase court power the criminal bolstered his ability to be persuasive by speaking against his self-interest; Joe "The Shoulder" was just as persuasive in advocating powerful courts as the prestigious New York prosecutor. Note that when the prosecutor advocated a position contrary to his own self-interest (when advocating *reduced* court powers), he was slightly more persuasive than when he advocated the expected position (in favor of stronger courts). Although the difference was not significant in this study (the conclusion is that the prosecutor was effective regardless of what he advocated), the effect one expects from attribution theory is present—that speakers generally increase their persuasiveness when they speak against their own biased positions.

The ploy of speaking against one's own biases and self-interest can be used realistically in everyday persuasion. Ex-convicts appear on television and tell how to protect one's home from burglary and from car-jacking, smokers who were models in print ads portraying the right "image" of the smoker later recant and attack the cigarette industry. Individuals leaving the police force admit that there was rampant racism and sexism over the years. Whistle-blowers in industry often are credible speakers. In cases like these, the fact that a person advocates a position contrary to his/her own past biases, and advocates a position void of ulterior motives (in fact, s/he may be punished or become unpopular for his/her actions) increases the persuasive quality of the speech.

The single most important study on attribution theory and speaker persuadability was conducted by Eagly, Wood, and Chaiken, who offered an important twist on the "speak against one's own interest" research: They asked receivers to rate the importance of different *causes* for why the speaker advocated the position being taken[13]. When a politician delivers a speech advocating a plan for eliminating pollution from the city's river, there are three distinct causes for *why* the politician is taking such a stand. First, the politician has made a careful, independent, unbiased assessment of the situation, and the facts and evidence led him/her to conclude that the river needs to be cleaned. Second, the politician is the cause of the behavior—s/he may have a long history of endorsing any and all environmental causes. Third, the politician may be endorsing the cleanup proposal primarily because s/he believes this is what the audience members or voters want to hear.

Clearly, when voters infer the last two causes are strong and viable causes for the politician's behavior, it follows that (a) they do not perceive the politician as being *sincere* and (b) they are not convinced that the cleanup is truly necessary. Voters are most likely to believe that the river does, in fact, need cleaning when facts and evidence indicate that it is necessary to do so and they believe that the speaker is not being biased.

Eagly, Wood, and Chaiken had students read one of many different versions of a scenario describing Jack Reynolds, a mayoral candidate, running for office in a (fictitious) Pacific Northwest city where an aluminum factory was operating. The persuasive message communicated by Jack Reynolds was a pro-environmental stand in which he advocated that the aluminum company should be forced to close down operations and to make radical changes in its methods of waste disposal.

However, Eagly, et al., also manipulated the characteristics of the speaker, the audience, and expectations of the speaker's advocated position. First, we have to define two types of bias:

(1) *Knowledge bias*. A knowledge bias deals with the speaker's previous background, and how this affects the speaker's knowledge and view of the world. For example, in this study, Mr. Reynolds was described as having devoted much time and energy to either pro-environmental issues or to pro-business interests. So, when Mr. Reynolds is introduced as being "pro-environmental" for many years, he is simply *confirming* expectations when he advocates that the aluminum plant should be shut down, the river cleaned, and the plant's disposal system altered. However, when he is introduced as being "pro-business" for many years, he *disconfirms* expectations when he advocates the pro-environmental persuasion message in the mayoral campaign.

(2) *Audience reporting bias*. An audience bias deals with the characteristics of the audience. An audience can be characterized as being well-known for its "pro-environmental" concerns or well-known for its "pro-business" concerns. When Mr. Reynolds advocates a "pro-environ-

mental" position before a "pro-environmental" audience, he is simply *confirming* expectations of what a politician would advocate. When he advocates a "pro-environmental" position before a "pro-business" audience, he is *disconfirming* expectations.

Given this framework, Eagly, et al., had receivers read a number of versions of the scenario prior to Mr. Reynolds' advocating the pro-environment persuasive message:

Confirmed Expectation/Knowledge bias only. These receivers heard that Mr. Reynolds had a history of supporting environmental issues, but they were not provided with any *audience-biasing* information (they were told only that he was speaking in front of a "cross section of the citizens").

Confirmed Expectation/Audience reporting bias only. These receivers heard that Mr. Reynolds was speaking in front of a group well known for its pro-environmental concerns (they were told nothing about Mr. Reynolds' personal history/ knowledge bias).

Confirmed Expectation/Both Knowledge bias and Audience reporting bias. These receivers were told that Mr. Reynolds had a history of support of environmental issues, and that he was speaking to a pro-environmental audience.

Disconfirmed Expectation/Knowledge bias only. These receivers heard that Mr. Reynolds had a history of "pro-business" concerns. Despite this bias Mr. Reynolds was advocating the disconfirming expectation (pro-environment). (These receivers were not told anything about the nature of the audience.)

Disconfirmed Expectation/Audience reporting bias only. These receivers heard that Mr. Reynolds' was speaking to an audience which had a long history of advocating "pro-business" and "pro-industrial growth" concerns (they were told nothing of Mr. Reynolds' personal background); since Mr.

Reynolds was advocating the pro-environmental plan of action, he would be *disconfirming* the expectation that a politician would strategically adapt to an audience.

Disconfirmed Expectation/Both Knowledge bias and Audience reporting bias.

These receivers heard that Mr. Reynolds had a long history of pro-business concerns and that he was speaking to a pro-business audience. Obviously, to argue in favor of a pro-environmental plan in this setting clearly violates expectations.

After reading the scenarios, receivers rated the extent to which they agreed with the pro-environmental arguments made by Mr. Reynolds. They also indicated whether they thought he was unbiased and sincere. Further, the receivers were asked to rate the importance of three causal inferences *why* he was advocating the position he was advocating: the importance of his own background, the importance of the audience opinion, and the importance of the objective facts in the matter. The importance that these three reasons had on the speaker's advocated position was rated on fifteen-point scales (the higher the number, the more important the cause). Table 4.1 presents the summary of the results[14].

Receivers changed their opinions to be more in favor of the pro-environmental advocacy when the speaker disconfirmed expected biases (see Table 4.1, the higher the number, the greater the agreement with the advocated position). This was especially true when Mr. Reynolds advocated the pro-environmental position to a pro-business audience ($M = 4.55$). There was much less opinion change when knowledge or reporting biases were present and he advocated the expected position ($Ms = 2.60$ to 2.87). Further, Mr. Reynolds was perceived to be more sincere and to be unbiased when he disconfirmed expectations and advocated the pro-environmental position in front of a pro-business audience, or when both knowledge and reporting biases were present. He was rated as in-

sincere and as biased when he confirmed expectations and communicated a pro-environmental message in front of a pro-environmental audience, or when both the reporting bias and the knowledge bias were present.

The central reason to devote so much attention to this study deals with the reasons *why* the receivers believed the speaker was advocating the pro-environmental position. When the speaker confirmed expectations and a knowledge bias was present, the importance of his own background was in fact rated as the most important reason for advocating the position ($M = 12.52$). However, when he disconfirmed expectations and advocated the pro-environmental conclusion, the importance of the speaker's background was rated low ($M = 7.97$). Instead, the receivers scanned the environment and rated the importance of the two alternative reasons for why he advocated this position as equally high in importance (importance of audience's opinion, the importance of the facts; both $M = 11.09$).

When the speaker confirmed expectations and advocated a pro-environment course of action to a pro-environmental audience, receivers rated the importance of the audience's opinion as the most important cause of his behavior ($M = 12.10$). However, when he disconfirmed expectations and advocated a pro-environmental message to a pro-business audience, receivers obviously downgraded the importance of the audience's opinions as the cause of his behavior ($M = 5.62$); rather, the single most important cause for taking this action (arguing a position contrary to the opinions of one's audience) was perceived to be the importance of the objective facts in the case ($M = 12.17$). Keep in mind that this is the one situation in which receivers were most influenced in terms of opinion change.

The discounting principle, you will recall, claimed that when any behavior (for example, advocating a pro-environmental message) has a number of plausible causes, the viability of any

4.1

OPINION CHANGE, SOURCE PERCEPTIONS, AND CAUSAL INFERENCES AS A
FUNCTION OF CONFIRMATION OF EXPECTANCY AND TYPE OF ENDORSEMENT

	Confirmed Expectation			Disconfirmed Expectation		
	Knowledge Bias Only	Reporting Bias Only	Both Biases	Knowledge Bias Only	Reporting Bias Only	Both Biases
Opinion Change	2.87	2.60	2.71	3.44	4.55	3.86
Speaker Perceptions:						
Unbiased	−.39	−.69	−.76	.38	.67	.62
Sincere	.01	−.66	−.48	−.22	1.08	.65
Causal Inferences:						
Source's background	12.52	8.03	11.07	7.97	8.14	8.75
Audience's opinion	9.90	12.10	10.82	11.09	5.62	7.57
Importance of facts	12.19	11.10	10.43	11.09	12.17	12.25

NOTE: For each measure, the larger, positive numbers reflect higher levels of opinion change, source unbias, source sincerity, increased importance of the causal inference.

Adapted from: A.H. Eagly, W. Wood, and S. Chaiken, "Causal Inferences About Communicators and Their Effect on Opinion Change," *Journal of Personality and Social Psychology*, vol. 36 (1978), pp. 424–435. Used with permission of the American Psychological Association.

single cause is discounted and weakened. Indeed, when we see that both biases are present and the speaker confirms an expected advocacy, all three possible causes are given fairly equal weights: Importance of speaker's background, $M = 11.07$, Importance of the audience's opinion, $M = 10.82$, and the Importance of the facts, $M = 10.43$. However, when the expectations are disconfirmed and the speaker advocates an environmental message contrary to the opinions of the audience and his own history, the importance of the facts become the single most important cause for explaining behavior ($M = 12.25$), outweighing by far the importance of the speaker's background ($M = 8.75$), or the importance of the audience's opinion ($M = 7.57$).

The value of the Eagly, Wood, and Chaiken study rests in demonstrating that disconfirming expectations and arguing against expected personal and audience biases result in inferring the cause of the speaker's behavior to be facts and evidence, and not other possible causes of behavior. Such underlying causal inferences parallel increases in opinion change and the perceptions that the speaker is sincere and unbiased.

Attribution principles of discounting and augmenting are not limited solely to the credibility of the speaker. It is also possible to apply this theory to the credibility of claims made in advertisements. Nearly all receivers *expect* to hear persuasive messages that consistently extol the virtues of a particular product; we hear that there are six good reasons for buying a watch, and twelve good reasons for buying a clock radio or nose spray. What happens when our expectations are violated and the advertisement claims that the product is superior on only four criteria, and only average on two others? Does the advertisement appear more honest and sincere when it avoids the pitfall of mentioning only the pluses of the product?

Settle and Golden[15] conducted such a study to demonstrate whether complete superiority claim (products are claimed to be superior on all five of the selling attributes), or advertisements that contain disclaimers (claim superiority on three attributions but do not claim superiority on two other attributes) produce more believable and convincing advertisements. They doctored up print advertisements for a number of products (The Mock 1, a 4 dollar ballpoint pen; The Chronomatic, a 16 dollar wristwatch; The Blend-A-Matic, a 24 dollar blender; The Simplex, a 32 dollar camera; and The Digitex, a $40 clock radio). Consistent advertisements were ones in which the product claimed to offer features which were superior to those offered by the brand leader; for example, the Digitex clock radio claimed to offer superior musical tone, accuracy in keeping time, style, quality, length of cord, and a superior-

sounding buzzer for waking up the owner. In the "low consistent" or "disclaimed" advertisements, the superiority claims were made in regard to the first three features, but the product was not claimed to be superior to other brands in regards to the length of the cord and the sound of the buzzer. These two attributes were considered "throw away" attributes because they are relatively less important reasons for buying a clock radio.

Business students read through a magazine containing the various versions of print advertisements, and were asked to rate each of the five product attributes for each of the products in terms of "how important the feature is when deciding to buy this product," and "how confident are you that this feature of the product is superior to that of the leading seller, brand X?" Settle and Golden found that the believability of some product claims and the credibility of the message are increased by disclaiming superiority on some product features. There was a boost in persuasiveness when advertisements claimed superiority on three of the most important product attributes, but admitted the product is only average on relatively unimportant features.

Kamins[16] has continued this line of research in assessing the impact of disclaiming one "weak" or "throw away" feature of a product to enhance the overall credibility of the advertisement. Specifically, Kamins and Assael[17] found one-sided appeals (the message claimed consistent superiority along all product attributes) led to more source derogation (speaker is perceived to be biased, insincere) than when using two-sided messages (claiming superiority for most attributes, but disclaiming drawbacks for other attributes).

Kamins and his colleagues recently argued that the effectiveness of celebrity endorsements can be enhanced by the use of two-sided messages—ones containing both the positive features and the limitations of a product[18]. Generally speaking, celebrities are perceived as likable, but receivers can well ask why they should purchase an endorsed product from a person paid a considerable salary to make the endorsement. By using a two-sided message, however, the celebrity making the claim is perceived to be both likable and believable. In one study, Leonard Nimoy endorsed a home computer system. He pointed out seven positive features of the computer (one-sided), and added the fact that the brand of computer is not a familiar name (two-sided). In another study, a similar manipulation was employed in the advertisement of a business consulting firm. In both cases, the celebrity was rated as both likable and believable if the two-sided approach was employed.

Finally, it is clear that when consumers hear or read testimonials (other consumers' personal evaluations of automobiles, films, and such), consumers discount information that is completely positive[19]. Reading negative information about the product results in stronger, more extreme feelings about the products. As noted by Folkes[20], consumers may perceive that praise is more socially acceptable, expected, and normative.

Negative information is more persuasive and it may be judged as more representative of the communicator's true feelings. Additional projects indicate that negative evaluators are perceived as more discriminating, intelligent, and competent than positive evaluators[21].

The Self-Perception Theory Another application of attribution theory to persuasion situations involves what is referred to as "self-perception theory." According to Daryl Bem[22]: "Individuals come to 'know' their own attitudes, emotions, and other internal states by inferring them from observations of their own overt behavior and/or the circumstances in which this behavior occurs." In our main discussion of attribution theory we discussed how *observers* look at the behavior of others and make causal attributions about people's behavior. Bem claims that we often observe our own behavior as if we were observing someone else and draw causal inferences about our own behavior.

Consider the Super Bowl phenomenon. Millions of viewers who don't usually watch football tune in to see this one game: the Super Bowl. Many of these viewers don't even know much about the game, or about the two teams who are participating in the year's contest. As these people wait in long lines at the supermarket to buy unhealthy snack foods and alcoholic beverages for their Super Bowl celebrations, each can legitimately ask: "Why am I doing this?" As these consumers scan the environment for possible causes for their behavior, the majority undoubtedly conclude that they must like celebrating Super Bowl Sunday; why else would they expend this effort, go off their diets, and devote an entire day *on their own free will* to being at a Super Bowl party? Thus, people observe their own behaviors and infer causes from the way they act; they infer that they *like* the things they do.

"Which comes first—the attitude or the behavior?" Clearly, even before they shop most consumers *know* they like barbecue potato chips, steak, and chili, and they hate liver, onions, and beef tongue. Attitudes plus habit undoubtedly cause behavior buying and eating what one likes. If this is true, then why do we "infer" our attitudes *after we behave?* According to Bem, people infer attitudes after they engage in overt behaviors *only* when "internal cues are weak, ambiguous, or uninterpretable[23]." What he meant by this is that if people don't hold or possess attitudes, haven't given an issue much thought, or are uncertain about their attitude, then they are likely to infer that they must like or approve of a behavior *after* they engage in it.

There are plenty of examples of situations in which people first behave and then, after the fact, "self-perceive" the causes of their behavior. For example, a person at the mall or at the airport may drop change in a collection container for homeless people, and may do so with little thought ("This is a nice thing to do"). He or she may ask afterwards, "Why did I give money away to that charity?" The person makes an internal attribution when s/he says, "Look, I am a generous person, this is a worthwhile cause, and generous people contribute to worthwhile causes." An internal attribution is one in which the person gives to a cause because of personal, internally driven causes. An *external* attribution would be one in which the person gives money because of some situational constraint or an external reward, "Look, see those cute (boys/girls) looking at us over there? I wanted them to think I'm a nice person. I wanted to impress them." In the "internal attribution," the individual looks inwardly for an explanation of behavior while in the "situational attribution," the individual looks for reasons and rewards in the environment.

The importance of self-perception theory for persuasion rests in its application to what is referred to as the Foot-in-the-Door Compliance Technique. The term "foot-in-the-door" refers to a situation in which a solicitor or persuader gets a foot in the door by asking for a small favor first, and then following up with a larger, second request. In this compliance technique, people are first asked to *commit* to some small request, such as signing a petition in favor of helping the disabled, displaying a sign advertising the United Way fund drive, or wearing a pin in their lapel announcing a blood drive. If people agree to this small request, if they make the *internal* attribution ("I am doing this because I am a generous person"), and if agreeing to this first request makes them feel committed to the cause, then people are more likely to agree to a second, larger request.

Scholars agree that self-perception theory is an important element in making the foot-in-the-door technique an effective way to gain compliance from others. However, the simple actions which underlie self-perception theory cannot completely account for all the times in which foot-in-the-door technique works. Chapter 10 devotes attention to various rules or guidelines having a significant effect on the effectiveness of foot-in-the-door technique.

Interpersonal Influence When providing examples of Kelley's model of *distinctiveness, consistency,* and *consensus,* we refered to workers who may or may not work in the same manner as do other workers. Mitchell and Wood[24] demonstrated the importance of attribution theory in research dealing with nurses. First, managers are likely to make an *internal* attribution concerning a worker's performance when distinctiveness is low, consistency is high and consensus is low. A worker is likely to be judged as internally causing problems (that is, is inept or incompetent) if s/he has trouble working *all* of the machines, trouble working machines consistently *over time,* and trouble working machines *other* workers do *not* have trouble working. If a worker is judged as *internally* responsible for errors and makes a serious error (gives an incorrect injection), then the worker is likely to be disciplined.

On the other hand, if consistency is low (the worker competently worked the machine before, but now has trouble), consensus is high (other workers also complain about the machine), and distinctiveness is high (the worker has trouble only with this one machine), then managers are likely to believe that there is some external cause to the problem that needs to be solved, and they will not blame the worker personally. We say more about managerial influence in Chapter 12.

WEINER'S ATTRIBUTION MODEL

Most early research on attribution theory focused attention on the question of when laypeople make an internal, or personal, causal inference versus an external, or dispositional, causal inference. There are other ways to locate the cause of an action. Weiner[25] devoted considerable attention to uncovering relevant reasons people give for behavior. Four of the most common types of causes include:

(1) *Intention*. "I was speeding because I was in a hurry to get home. I was in a high crime area and I was afraid," compared to an unintentional cause: "I didn't mean to spin my wheels and burn rubber when I accelerated. I'm not used to this new car yet."

(2) *Controllability*. "I ran out of gas" is certainly more controllable than "The baseball game let out early because of the rain, and I unexpectedly got stuck in traffic. It was something I couldn't control."

(3) *Stability*. "The traffic was bad, as it always is on Friday afternoons," compared to unstable causes: "I can't believe there was a toxic spill on the road, and the road was closed for an entire day."

(4) *Locus of control*. Internal locus: "I don't want to go to that party," compared to external locus: "My car was hit in the street by a hit-and-run driver and I can't go because I have to wait for the insurance adjuster."

As Folkes noted[26], consumers rely on these dimensions of causes when judging why products do or do not work as expected, and when determining who is to blame for product failures. In terms of locus of control, consumers who believe that companies are responsible for problems (such as that the oil companies manipulate shortages, energy crises, and oil prices) are consumers who strongly believe government should pressure companies for a solution[27]. Alternatively, when consumers believed that the general public is responsible for energy crises and rising oil prices, they believe that the public is obligated to voluntarily conserve energy.

Attribution scholars have also examined the impact of *stability* of the underlying cause. Some states have "lemon laws" which are designed to protect consumers from having consistent problems with their new automobiles over time. Unstable causes for a product's failure might be just a simple problem (a loose fuel injection line caused by transporting the car from the factory), and consumers are less likely to complain or demand a refund if problems are unstable (one-shot problems). However, when consumers infer that the problems they are experiencing are stable (recurring) ones, they have strong emotional reactions, refusing exchanges (why get stuck with the same problems again?), and hold out for refunds.

Each of these links between perceived causes and their consequences is important for the persuasion scholar. It is to the advantage of the company or firm to foster the idea that the company controls and is responsible for product success. (Consumers are happy, praise the company, repeat as customers, and refer others to the company.) When products fail, however, it is critical from the company's point of view that the problem is not perceived to be a problem the company could easily have controlled, or one the company is responsible for. If so, the product failure will prove very costly for the company.

We have outlined two main versions of attribution theory (Kelley's and Weiner's). A speaker's credibility is strongly influenced by the type of causal inference receivers make concerning why the speaker is advocating a particular position. Further, attribution theory is relevant to the issue of making inferences about one's own attitudes. Finally, the types of causes consumers see underlying events (like energy crises, product successes, and product failures) have a significant impact on how consumers react to a firm. The second half of this chapter looks at the question of how individuals combine information in order to take "reasoned" action.

MODELS OF BELIEF CHANGE

Behavior is almost *never* caused by only one or two beliefs or by a single attitude. Behaviors we engage in are shaped by beliefs about behavior and its consequences, our attitudes (likes and dislikes), and the pressure to behave in a *normative* manner (the pressure to behave in ways others expect us to behave). In this part of the chapter, we will look at two major ways in which receivers combine information in order to form attitudes and to make decisions about behavior. The first approach is a general model of persuasion developed by Fishbein and his colleagues over several decades. Actually, Fishbein's work has progressed through three phases[28]. First, he developed a *summative* model of attitudes in the 1960s. Second, he developed a general theory of persuasion called the Theory of Reasoned Action. Third, Fishbein and his colleagues altered their Theory of Reasoned Action in the 1980s by adding a component of "perceived behavioral control"— a component important in increasing the prediction of health behaviors (weight loss, use of contraceptives, and so on). Most research, however, has focused on the Theory of Reasoned Action.

THE THEORY OF REASONED ACTION

There is no doubt that many consumers behave in quite rational ways when engaged in "pre-decisional" searches for products such as automobiles and appliances. Fishbein and Ajzen[29], in fact, are quite specific in noting that consumers are rational animals who "systematically utilize or process the information available to them[30]. Figure 4.2 illustrates the main components of this rational model, the Theory of Reasoned Action. As indicated in this figure, receiver variables such as gender, age, personality, and so forth, have a direct impact on beliefs and how those beliefs are evaluated. We are primarily interested here in components of the theory that predict behavior.

What causes behavior? According to this model, behavior is directly and solely a function of the individual's *behavioral intention* to perform or to not perform the behavior. Does the consumer *intend* to buy a Chrysler or Ford, or some import? Does the voter *intend* to vote for a Democrat, a Republican, or an independent? Intentions to behave in a particular manner do not come into existence in isolation. Instead, intentions are comprised of two components: (1) the individual's *Attitude* toward the behavior (Ab) and (2) the person's *Subjective Norm* (SN). The theory also specifies a mathematical formula for associating Attitude and Subjective Norm (see below). First, however, we need to discuss how this theory views and constructs the *Attitude* and *Subjective Norm* components.

The Attitude Component

The Theory of Reasoned Action is explicit in its treatment of the link between beliefs and attitude. One's attitude is a function of one's *salient beliefs* about the behavior. When consumers are about to buy a car, for example, ask them to list the beliefs they have about buying an automobile and the consequences of buying the automobile. The theory claims that one's *Attitude* toward buying the car is a function of the *strength by which one holds a salient belief* and the *evaluation* of whether the consequence of that belief is highly positive, positive, neutral, negative or highly negative. In fact, the relationship between beliefs and attitudes is given as a *summation* of all relevant beliefs by the evaluation of those beliefs:

FIGURE 4.2

THE THEORY OF REASONED ACTION

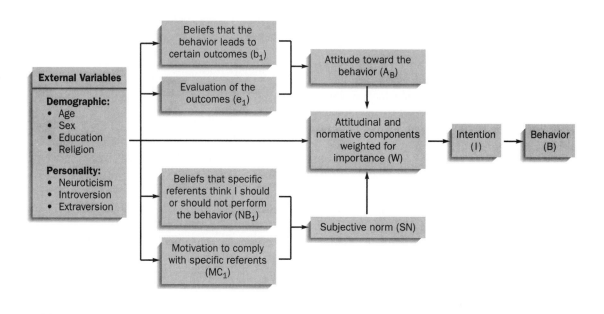

Adapted from M. Fishbein, "A Theory of Reasoned Action: Some Applications and Implications," in H. Howe and M. Page, eds., *Nebraska Symposium on Motivation*, vol. 27 (Lincoln: University of Nebraska Press, 1980), pp. 65–116. Copyright by the University of Nebraska Press. Used with permission.

$$A_B = \sum_{i=1}^{N} b_i e_i$$

Table 4.2 illustrates how this equation is used to calculate consumers' attitudes from beliefs and from their evaluations of those beliefs. Presume that a set of consumers hold only four important beliefs concerning the possible consequences of buying a new car: the car will provide better gas mileage, the car will provide increased prestige, buying the car will reduce the consumer's bank account, and buying the car will increase the consumer's insurance premiums. Each consumer is

asked, first, to rate these possible consequences on a scale of +3 (extremely likely to occur) to −3 (extremely unlikely to occur). Second, each consumer is asked to rate each consequence in terms of how desirable or valuable the consequence is in his or her assessment of the behavior. These evaluations are also rated on a scale of +3 (very positive) to −3 (very negative).

Consumer A in our worked example (see Table 4.2) believes that better gas mileage and less money in the bank will *definitely* (+3) follow as consequences if the new car is purchased. Further, this consumer believes that there is a slight chance

T A B L E	4.2

DETERMINING ATTITUDE (A) FROM b(i) AND e(i)

Consequences of buying new car	(b)		Belief Evaluation (e)		(b)(e)
Consumer A:					
1. better gas mileage	(+3)	×	(+3)	=	+9
2. prestige	(+1)	×	(+3)	=	+3
3. less money in bank	(+3)	×	(−1)	=	−3
4. higher insurance premiums	(+1)	×	(−1)	=	−1
Attitude:					+8

$$A = \sum_{i=1}^{N} b_i e_i = +8$$

Consequences of buying new car	(b)		Belief Evaluation (e)		(b)(e)
Consumer B:					
1. better gas mileage	(+3)	×	(+3)	=	+9
2. prestige	(+1)	×	(+3)	=	+3
3. less money in bank	(+3)	×	(−3)	=	−9
4. higher insurance premiums	(+3)	×	(−3)	=	−9
Attitude:					−6

$$A = \sum_{i=1}^{N} b_i e_i = -6$$

that s/he will gain in prestige from buying the car (+1), and that there is a slight chance that s/he will have to pay higher insurance premiums as a consequence of buying the new car (+1). This consumer places a very high value or evaluation on the first two consequences (better gas mileage, increased prestige), and gave these consequences the highest possible evaluation (+3). However,

s/he indicated that the last two consequences were slightly negative in evaluation (−1).

How do we calculate the overall attitude? As indicated in the equation, for each consequence (i) through the total number of beliefs (N), we multiply the strength of the belief (b) by the evaluation (e) and sum the product of all (b)(e) components. For consumer A, the very strong and

T A B L E   **4.3**

DETERMINING SUBJECTIVE NORM (SN) FROM NORMATIVE BELIEFS (NB) AND
MOTIVATION TO COMPLY (MC)

Important Referents	NBi		MCi		(NBi)(MCi)
Consumer A:					
1. my spouse	(+3)	×	(+3)	=	+9
2. my father	(+1)	×	(+1)	=	+1
3. my neighbor	(−3)	×	(+1)	=	−3
4. my child	(+3)	×	(0)	=	0
Subjective Norm:					+7

$$SN = \sum_{i=1}^{M} (NB)_i (MC)_i = +7$$

Important Referents	NBi		MCi		(NBi)(MCi)
Consumer B:					
1. my spouse	(−3)	×	(+3)	=	−9
2. my father	(+1)	×	(+1)	=	+1
3. my neighbor	(−3)	×	(+1)	=	−3
4. my child	(+3)	×	(0)	=	0
Subjective Norm:					−11

$$SN = \sum_{i=1}^{M} (NB)_i (MC)_i = -11$$

Adapted from a table in R.E. Petty and J.T. Cacioppo, *Attitudes and Persuasion: Classic and Contemporary Approaches.* Copyright © 1981 Wm. C. Brown Communications, Inc., Dubuque, Iowa. All rights reserved. Reprinted by permission.

positive consequences of better gas mileage and prestige provide positive outcomes (+9, +3), while the loss of money in the bank and higher insurance premiums are slightly negative outcomes (−3, −1). When summed, we have a fairly positive attitude (+8).

Consumers, of course, can vary radically from one another in terms of the belief component or the evaluation component. For example, consumer B in our worked example shares the same values as did consumer A for the first two beliefs. However, consumer B indicated s/he would *definitely* have less money in the bank after buying the car, and evaluated this consequence as quite negative (−3). Further, consumer B indicated higher insurance premiums as a *definite* consequence and also rated this consequence as extremely negative. Hence, although the general outcome of improved gas mileage and prestige is positive (+9, +3), the financial consequences produced very negative outcomes (−9, −9). Hence, this consumer has a fairly negative attitude (−6) toward buying a new car.

The Subjective Norm Component

The second component that predicts a person's *Behavioral Intention* is the *Subjective Norm* component. According to the Theory of Reasoned Action, a Subjective Norm consists of two elements: the person's *normative beliefs* and his/her *motivation to comply*. *Normative beliefs* are the opinions formed in response to pressures placed on the individual by others. For example, parents, grandparents, dentist, teacher, and friend may encourage a young person to maintain his/her dental hygiene. Individuals often seek the advice of others in regard to voting, purchasing goods, or choosing a career. When seeking to make a rational or "reasoned" choice, consumers will be influenced by these groups of significant others and friends.

Table 4.3 illustrates how Subjective Norms are constructed. Each referent (influencing party) is rated on a scale of whether that person or group would be supportive of the consumer buying the new car (that is, a +3 indicates that the person or group is very likely or "definitely" in support of buying the new car), or whether the person or group would not be supportive about the new purchase (−3). Each referent is evaluated in terms of the extent to which the consumer is *motivated to comply* with the referent person's opinion or pressure. As in the case of attitudes (see Table 4.2), these elements are multiplied and summed to index the amount and direction of the Subjective Norm which is given by the following equation:

$$SN = \sum_{i=1}^{M} (NB)_i \, (MC)_i$$

In our worked example (see Table 4.3), consumer A indicated that both her/his spouse and his/her child would definitely support the new car purchase. Further, s/he indicated that motivation to comply to the spouse's wishes was high (+3), but that the motivation to comply to the child's wishes was non-existent (0). Further, the consumer believed that there would be slight approval from one's father for buying the car (+1), but that since the neighbor would be jealous, s/he would disapprove (−3). However, the motivation to comply to these two individuals' advice or pressure was rated as slight (+1). The general outcome of these calculations is a Subjective Norm which is fairly positive (+7), due to the spousal and parental support.

Consumer B in our example shares the same perceptions and evaluations for the father, neighbor and child referents, but believes that his/her spouse will disapprove of buying the new car (−3). Hence, given strong negative spousal and neighbor support (−9, −3), and weak parental support (+1), this consumer knows, and predicts, that s/he will elicit disapproval from significant others if the car is purchased (−11).

Behavioral Intentions

Behavioral Intention is given by the following equation:

$$I = (W_1)(A_B) + (W_2)(SN)$$

Intention equals some Weight multiplied by the Attitude plus some Weight multiplied by the Subjective Norm. These weights come from the statistical analyses involved in the research using the model, and the size of these weights vary from one sample of receivers to another (recall that the left part of Figure 4.2 specifies that different receivers will, in fact, rate beliefs, subjective beliefs, and motivation to comply differently). For example, in a classic study assessing behavioral intentions to engage in premarital sex, Fishbein[31] found that, for females, the *Attitude* component was a more powerful determinant of one's intentions to engage in premarital sex than was the *subjective* norm component. The opposite was true for males, however; the *subjective* norm component was significantly stronger in its pull toward intending to have premarital sex than was the *attitude* component. Men, then, were influenced by others' views on premarital sex, while women were guided by their evaluation of consequences stemming from taking action. According to Ajzen[32], the strength of the relationship between *intentions* and *behavior* also varied between males and females. For females, there was a much stronger and highly positive relationship between intention to have premarital sex and actually engaging in the behavior. In our society, it is relatively easy for females to obtain the cooperation from males when the females intend to pursue this goal, relative to a male's ability to find a willing female when his intentions are high.

Nonetheless, if we assume that both consumer A and consumer B in our example placed equal weights on the *attitude* and the *subjective* norm components (we will assign a 1 for each weight), we have the following:

Consumer A's Intention to buy a new car

$$= (1) (Ab) + (1) (SN)$$
$$= (1) (+8) + (1) (+7)$$
$$= +15.$$

Consumer B's Intention to buy a new car

$$= (1) (Ab) + (1) (SN)$$
$$= (1) (-6) + (1) (-11)$$
$$= -17.$$

Clearly, consumer A intends to buy a new car, and probably will do so when the opportunity avails itself; consumer B does *not* intend to buy a new car (at this time).

How Beliefs, Attitudes, Norms, Intentions, and Behaviors are Changed

As O'Keefe noted[33], the Theory of Reasoned Action has been applied effectively to a number of areas in persuasion, including voting[34], consumer purchases[35], family planning[36], seat belt use[37], patronizing restaurants[38], conserving energy[39], and seeking dental care[40]. In all cases, the attitudes combined with subjective norms resulted in predicting behavioral intentions, which are highly correlated with actually performing the targeted behavior[41].

A number of implications for persuasion can be derived from this theory. The first four stem from altering components in the *Attitude* construct:

1. *Change the total number of beliefs to be considered by the consumer.* Obviously, persuaders can increase the number of beliefs which are related to the behavior in question. For example, nearly everyone knows cigarette smoking is linked to lung cancer. Persuasive messages can add additional facts or beliefs concerning smoking, including the fact that smoke contains carbon monoxide, smoking results in low birth weight of babies, that second-hand smoke harms others, and that smoking causes emphysema. The added beliefs should make persuasion easier.

2. *Change the belief strength of receivers' held beliefs.* Despite years of public service announcements and warnings about smoking, many people still question the link between smoking and various health risks; many consumers will rate the likelihood of getting cancer, emphysema, or other diseases as only +1 when responding to questionnaires. Therefore, one way of influencing others is to provide plenty of messages convincing the receivers that *they personally* are susceptible to the diseases and consequences of smoking. Then they cannot deny that there is a +3 chance that the consequences will befall them.

3. *Change the evaluations by which receivers rate the consequences of the beliefs.* Persuaders want to increase the positive evaluations of beliefs which support buying their product, while increasing the negative evaluations of beliefs which oppose the action advocated or desired by the persuader. One can easily emphasize the undesirability of any of the negative consequences associated with smoking, such as asking smokers if they would like to "kiss an ashtray," for example, thus making sure that there are plenty of highly negative evaluations of the various beliefs associated with smoking (so that they will be rated a −3). Also, the positive consequences of quitting may be emphasized (so that they will be rated as +3).

4. *Change the configuration of beliefs in order to make certain beliefs more salient.* According to O'Keefe[42], it is possible to alter the overall belief saliency of a set of beliefs already held by the consumer to increase the chance the consumer will make the decision desired by the persuader. Functionally, in our view, the best way of actually adopting this plan of action is to group beliefs into several types, link the beliefs to an overarching goal or value, and have the consumer decide between two divergent viewpoints. For example, if a consumer had thoroughly studied all aspects of buying a new car, a persuader/salesperson may group together all beliefs concerning safety (for example, how safe the car is in an accident, how it protects children, what the car's record is for repairs, whether air bags afford protection, and how it performs in rain and snow), and then group together all the beliefs dealing with saving money. Ultimately, the persuader wants to raise the fundamental question: Which is more important, safety of one's family members or saving a few dollars?

A persuader can also operate to change the components of the *Subjective Norm.* Some viable ways include:

1. *Increase the number of referent individuals, or salient others who advise the consumer or provide approval or disapproval of the behavior.* To convince a consumer to keep an open mind on buying a car, we can have a number of people encourage new car buying by communicating their approval of the idea.

This approach was employed in the late 1980s as an integral part of the designated driver campaign. Scriptwriters wrote story lines on prime time television shows, depicting popular characters selecting a designated driver who would not drink. Beer advertisements were produced which reinforced responsibility in drinking. The outcome was an increase in the number of significant referents who encouraged responsible behavior.

2. *Change the strength of the normative beliefs.* Consumer B believes (see Table 4.3) that her/his spouse and neighbor both will strongly disapprove of buying a new car (−3), and believes that the father only moderately approves (+1). Obviously, if the spouse were to change his/her views of buying a new car, consumer B would have a much easier time in deciding to buy the car. The same is true if the neighbor changed her/his viewpoint, but the influence on *Subjective Norm* is less (because the motivation to comply is less). Nonetheless, by increasing the number of referents who are supportive, and by decreasing the number of referents who are non-supportive, persuaders can affect the Subjective Norm component.

3. *Change the Motivation to Comply Component.* Although this approach may sound rather devious, it is in fact a viable way of altering a consumer's intent to behave. A persuader can attempt (given our example of consumer B in Table 4.3) to decrease the consumer's felt motivation to comply and satisfy his/her spouse's wishes, while increasing the felt motivation to comply with the father's and child's wishes or concerns. For example, a persuader can claim that the spouse has her/his car, and that the consumer has the right to select his/her own car. Therefore, the consumer should have the freedom, without the spouse's interference, to make the decision (a his car-her car dichotomy).

4. *Change the configuration of supporters (versus distractors) who impact on the consumer's decision.* It may be possible to group together supporters of an action and contrast these supporters with the group of referents who discourage taking the action. A persuader may call into question the motives of those who desire to keep the consumer from buying a new car—the neighbor is simply jealous, or the spouse wants to limit the consumer's freedom. Note, however, that this persuasion ploy sounds much less devious when we apply this type of influence to support, or self-help, groups. Victims of domestic violence, alcoholics who join support groups, and so forth, join a group of similar others who become, usually, a new group of referents for the individual who wants to change; and part of the solution may be to identify the individual's dependency on former intimates, and to decrease one's felt motivation to comply to their requests.

Despite all of these possible ways of influencing others, it is important to keep in mind that the vast majority of approaches employed in advertisements and in information campaigns involve changes in the *Attitude* component, although potential persuaders should not forget about important changes that can be made by altering the *Subjective Norm* component.

Planned Action

Ajzen and colleagues[43] expanded on the basic Theory of Reasoned Action depicted in Figure 4.2 by adding an additional component that affects *Behavioral Intention*, called *Perceived Behavioral Control*. In our Figure 4.2, this new component would be placed immediately below the square labeled "Subjective Norm." *Perceived Behavioral Control* has a direct impact on *Intention*, and, like other elements in this theory (various receiver variables such as demographic variables and personality differences), affects one's perceptions of control; receivers differ substantially from one another by the extent to which they believe they can or cannot control actions in developing a true *Intention* to behave in a certain way, or to later engage in the behavior.

What is meant by *Perceived Behavioral Control?* The term is used to refer to the situation in which the individual claims or perceives that s/he can control relevant behaviors which lead to the action one intends to engage in: to lose weight, to reduce cholesterol levels, to get a 4.0 G.P.A., to quit smoking, to improve one's stamina and body, and so forth. The original theory proposed that individuals have attitudes and that they anticipate expectations from relevant others; but the original theory said very little about the individual's *ability* to actually stay on a diet or quit smoking. Individuals who question their ability to control their appetites, to get to the gymnasium each day, or to actually put down cigarettes for good, are low in perceived control, and will probably not achieve a desired behavior—even if they have developed appropriate attitudes and subjective norms.

For our purposes, the additional component of *Perceived Behavioral Control* is similar to the notion of *Self-efficacy*[44] which we discuss in other chapters. When we discuss fear appeals (see Chapters 6 and 8), we will conclude that it does little good to increase the receiver's level of fear, anxiety, and panic without telling the receiver how to take specific action reducing the fear and the threat, and without telling the receiver that s/he is capable and competent to take the desired action.

THE INFORMATION INTEGRATION THEORY

So far, we have discussed research relying on the *summation* model of combining information. The second model is called the *information integration model,* and relies on a form of *cognitive algebra.* Communication scholars have devoted far less research to this model than to the Fishbein/Ajzen model. We will simply introduce the model and describe its elements. The model has been used in assessing how people combine information when constructing impressions of others, and has been used in consumer research projects.

Anderson[45] argues that any attitude will be the result of several beliefs. Much like the Fishbein/Ajzen model, consumers are expected to evaluate each belief element in two ways: a scale value (*s*), and a weight (*w*). The *s* scale value is identical to the Fishbein/Ajzen evaluation (*e*) component, and represents how favorable or unfavorable the consumer is toward the belief information. The *w* weight component represents how important the information is personally to the consumer; there is a general similarity to the Fishbein/Ajzen component of belief strength (*b*).

The essential differences between the models deal with the assumption of how individuals combine information. The summation model of Fishbein/Ajzen involved multiplying belief strength (*b*) with the evaluation (*e*) component, and then adding together the various outcomes (or products) for n-number of beliefs. Anderson's model is called a *weighted averaging* model, and claims that, for each n-belief relevant to the topic (buying a new car, judging how much you liked another person, and so forth), the consumer multiplies together the weight of importance (*w*) and the scale (*s*), and then averages the outcomes or products into a weighted average. The equation for this operation is as follows:

$$A = \frac{\left[w_o s_o + \sum_{i=1}^{N} w_i s_i \right]}{w_o + \sum_{i=1}^{N} w_i}$$

NOTE: The w_0 and s_0 are the weights and scale values for the consumer's *initial attitude* toward the object or behavior at hand. For example, prior to a political campaign, or prior to searching out a new car, a voter or a consumer may have initial attitudes, and have initial feelings of importance concerning Democrats, Republicans, Fords, Chevrolets, Buicks, and so forth. If the consumer has completely neutral initial attitudes, then w_0 and s_0 are in fact, zero, and the consumer (or voter) is expected to simply multiply all pairs of weights and scales for the beliefs communicated in the persuasive communications and average the elements.

Based on the summary and explication by Petty and Cacioppo[46], we provide a guide to these calculations in Table 4.4. Assume that a consumer is evaluating several new cars to purchase, and, to keep things simple, let's assume that only two criteria are being used in the judgment: type of car, and color. Also assume that the consumer places a greater value (weight) on the type of car than on the color of the car; indeed, s/he places three times as much weight on type of car than on the color. Finally, we will assume that the consumer likes blue twice as much as red, and that s/he likes Fords twice as much as Chevrolets.

When evaluating the first option, a Red Ford, the equation functions as follows:

A = (Weight placed on Color × Scale Value placed on Color) + (Weight placed on Type of Car × Scale Value placed on Type of Car)/ These two elements added together are divided by the sum of the Weights—in this case, there are two Weights (for Color and for Type of Car)

T A B L E   4.4

Hypothetical Weights and Scale Values Assigned to Four Kinds of Cars and the Evaluations Predicted from the Weighted Averaging Model of Attitudes

W	s	s	s	s
COLOR 1	*Red* (+2)	*Red* (+2)	*Blue* (+4)	*Blue* (+4)
MAKE 3	*Ford* (+4)	*Chevy* (+2)	*Ford* (+4)	*Chevy* (+2)
$\dfrac{\Sigma w_i s_i}{\Sigma w_i}$	$\dfrac{(1\times2)+(3\times4)}{1+3}$	$\dfrac{(1\times2)+(3\times2)}{1+3}$	$\dfrac{(1\times4)+(3\times4)}{1+3}$	$\dfrac{(1\times4)+(3\times2)}{1+3}$
	$\dfrac{2+12}{4}$	$\dfrac{2+6}{4}$	$\dfrac{4+12}{4}$	$\dfrac{4+6}{4}$
ATTITUDE = 3.50		2.00	4.00	2.50

NOTE: In this example, the person has weighted the make of the car as three times as important as the color of the car. The person also likes blue twice as much as red and Fords twice as much as Chevys.
SOURCE: R.E. Petty and J.T. Cacioppo, *Attitudes and Persuasions: Classic and Contemporary Approaches*. Copyright © 1981 Wm. C. Brown Communications, Inc., Dubuque, Iowa. All rights reserved. Reprinted by permission.

Or,

$$A = \frac{(+1 \times +2) + (+3 \times +4)}{(1+3)}$$

$$= \frac{(2+12)}{4} = \frac{14}{4} = 3.50.$$

As the remaining three calculations indicate, the Red Chevrolet receives a low evaluation (2.00), as does the Blue Chevy (2.50), while the highest evaluation is for the Blue Ford (4.00); not a surprising outcome, since our assumptions (see above) included a preference (higher *s* values) for Fords, and for the color blue.

The information integration model of attitude is a viable model for explaining how people combine information about others and about objects when evaluating their overall liking for candidates, cars, and the like. As some reviewers have noted[47], there is great curiosity among scholars to find out whether Anderson's *averaging model* is a better or poorer predictor of a person's attitude than the *Attitudinal* component of the Fishbein/Ajzen calculations, based on *summation*. There is currently no answer to the question. Neither of the models may be universally better than the other, although Anderson's averaging model may provide certain advantages when combining lots of different perceptions about others. Nonetheless, the reader should be familiar with both models. The full Theory of Reasoned Action does provide more implications for persuasion relative to the Anderson model, which is limited to calculations of attitudes.

F O O T N O T E S

1. R.W. Mizerski, L.L. Golden, and J.B. Kernan, "The Attribution Process in Consumer Decision Making," *Journal of Consumer Research*, vol. 6 (1979), pp. 123–140.

2. V.S. Folkes, "Recent Attribution Research in Consumer Behavior: A Review and New Directions," *Journal of Consumer Research*, vol. 14 (1988), pp. 548–565.

3. F. Heider, *The Psychology of Interpersonal Relations* (New York: Wiley, 1958).

4. H.H. Kelley, "Attribution Theory in Social Psychology," in David Levin, ed., *Nebraska Symposium on Motivation* (Lincoln, Nebr.: University of Nebraska Press, 1967), pp. 192–238; H.H. Kelley, "The Process of Causal Attribution,"*American Psychologist*, vol. 28 (1973), pp. 107–128.

5. See Folkes (Note 2); also see M. Ross and G.J.O. Fletcher, "Attribution and Social Perception," in Gardner Lindzey and Elliot Aronson, eds., *Handbook of Social Psychology*, vol. 2 (New York: Random House, 1985), pp. 73–122.

6. J.R. Bettman and B.A. Weitz, "Attributions in the Boardroom: Causal Reasoning in Corporate Annual Reports," *Administrative Science Quarterly*, vol. 28 (1983), pp. 165–183.

7. S.J. Sherman, C.C. Presson, L. Chassin, E. Corty, and R. Olshavsky, "The False Consensus Effect in Estimates of Smoking Prevalence: Underlying Mechanisms," *Personality and Social Psychology Bulletin*, vol. 9 (1983), pp. 197–207.

8. J. Van der Pligt, "Attributions, False Consensus and Valence: Two Field Studies," *Journal of Personality and Social Psychology*, vol. 46 (1984), pp. 57–68.

9. W.D. Crano, "Assumed Consensus of Attitudes: The Effect of Vested Interest," *Personality and Social Psychology Bulletin*, vol. 9 (1983), pp. 597–608.

10. T. Gilovich, D. Jennings, and S. Jennings, "Causal Focus and Estimates of Consensus: An Examination of the False Consensus Effect," *Journal of Personality and Social Psychology*, vol. 45 (1983), pp. 550–559.

11. Concerning the false uniqueness bias, see Folkes (Note 2), and M. Ross and G.J.O. Fletcher, "Attribution and Social Perception," in Gardner Lindzey and Elliot Aronson, eds., *Handbook of Social Psychology*, vol. 2, (New York: Random House, 1985), pp. 73–122.

12. E. Walster (Hatfield), E. Aronson, and D. Abrahams, "On Increasing the Persuasiveness of a Low Prestige Communicator," *Journal of Experimental Social Psychology*, vol. 2 (1966), pp. 325–342.

13. A.H. Eagly, W. Wood, and S. Chaiken, "Causal Inferences About Communicators and Their Effect on Opinion Change," *Journal of Personality and Social Psychology*, vol. 36 (1978), pp. 424–435.

14. For brevity's sake, we provide here only a general overview of the full details that were obtained in the Eagly, Wood, and Chaiken study. See original study for additional factors dealing with the perceptions of the source, and for additional details.

15. R.B. Settle and L.L. Golden, "Attribution Theory and Advertiser Credibility," *Journal of Marketing Research*, vol. 11 (1974), pp. 181–185.

16. M.A. Kamins, M.J. Brand, S.A. Hoeke, and J.C. Moe, "Two-Sided versus One-Sided Celebrity Endorsements: The Impact on Advertising Effectiveness and Credibility," *Journal of Advertising*, vol. 18 (1989), pp. 4–10; M.A. Kamins, "Celebrity and Noncelebrity Advertising," *Journal of Advertising Research*, June/July (1989), pp. 34–42.

17. M.A. Kamins and H. Assael, "Two-Sided Versus One-Sided Appeals: A Cognitive Perspective on Argumentation, Source Derogation, and the Effect of Disconfirming Trial on Belief Change," *Journal of Marketing Research*, vol. 24 (1987), pp. 29–39.

18. M.A. Kamins (Note 16).

19. R.W. Mizerski, "An Attribution Explanation of the Disproportionate Influence of Unfavorable Information," *Journal of Consumer Research*, vol. 9 (1982), pp. 301–310.

20. V.S. Folkes (Note 2).

21. T.M. Amabile, "Brilliant But Cruel: Perceptions of Negative Evaluators," *Journal of Experimental Social Psychology*, vol. 19 (1983), pp. 563–579.

22. D.J. Bem, "Self-Perception Theory," in L. Berkowitz, ed., *Advances in Experimental Social Psychology* (New York: Academic Press, 1972), p. 2.

23. D.J. Bem, "An Experimental Analysis of Self-Persuasion," *Journal of Experimental Social Psychology*, vol. 1 (1965), p. 200.

24. T.R. Mitchell, S.G. Green, and R. Wood, "An

Attributional Model of Leadership and the Poor Performing Subordinate," in L.L. Cummings and B.M. Staw, eds., *Research in Organizational Behavior,* vol. 3 (Greenwich, Conn.: Aijai Press, 1981), pp. 151–198; R.E. Wood and T.R. Mitchell, "Manager Behavior in a Social Context: The Impact of Impression Management on Attributions and Disciplinary Actions," *Organizational Behavior and Human Performance,* vol. 28 (1981), pp. 356–378.

25. B. Weiner, *An Attributional Theory of Motivation and Emotion* (New York: Springer-Verlag, 1986).

26. V.S. Folkes (Note 2).

27. R. Belk and J. Painter, "Effects of Causal Attributions on Pollution and Litter Control Attitudes," in F. Kelly Shuptrine and P. Reingen, eds., *Non-profit Marketing: Conceptual and Empirical Research* (Arizona State University, Tempe, Ariz.: Bureau of Business and Economics Research, 1983), pp. 22–25; R. Belk and R. Semenik, "Preferred Solutions to the Energy Crisis as a Function of Causal Attributions," *Journal of Consumer Research,* vol. 8 (1981), pp. 306–312.

28. M. Fishbein, "A Theory of Reasoned Action: Some Applications and Implications," in H. Howe and M. Page, eds., *Nebraska Symposium on Motivation,* vol. 27 (Lincoln: University of Nebraska Press, 1980), pp. 65–116; M. Fishbein, and I. Ajzen, *Belief, Attitude, Intention, and Behavior: An Introduction to Theory and Research* (Reading, Mass.: Addison-Wesley, 1981).

29. Fishbein and Ajzen (Note 30).

30. R.E. Petty and J.T. Cacioppo, *Attitudes and Persuasion: Classic and Contemporary Approaches* (Dubuque, Iowa: Wm. C. Brown, 1981), p. 193.

31. M. Fishbein, *Sexual Behavior And Propositional Control.* Paper presented at the meetings of the Psychonomic Society, 1966; cited in Petty and Cacioppo (Note 32), and in C. Ajzen, "From Intentions to Actions: A Theory of Planned Behavior," in J. Kuhl and J. Beckman, eds., *Action Control: From Cognition to Behavior* (Berlin: Springer-Verlag, 1985), pp. 11–39.

32. C. Ajzen (Note 33).

33. D.J. O'Keefe, *Persuasion: Theory and Research* (Newbury Park, Calif: Sage Publications, 1990).

34. C.H. Bowman and M. Fishbein, "Understanding Public Reaction to Energy Proposals: An Application of the Fishbein Model," *Journal of Applied Social Psychology,* vol. 8 (1978), pp. 319–340; M. Fishbein and I. Ajzen, "Attitudes and Voting Behavior: An Application of the Theory of Reasoned Action," in G.M. Stephenson and J.M. Davis, eds., *Progress in Applied Social Psychology* (New York: Wiley, 1981), pp. 253–313; M. Fishbein, I. Ajzen, and R. Hinkle, "Predicting and

Understanding Voting in American Elections: Effects of External Variables," in I. Ajzen and M. Fishbein, eds., *Understanding Attitudes and Predicting Social Behavior* (Englewood Cliffs, N.J.: Prentice-Hall, 1980), pp. 173–195.

35. M. Fishbein and I. Ajzen, "Predicting and Understanding Consumer Behavior: Attitude-Behavior Correspondence," in I. Ajzen and M. Fishbein, eds., *Understanding Attitudes and Predicting Social Behavior* (Englewood Cliffs, N.J.: Prentice-Hall, 1980), pp. 148–172; P.R. Warshaw, "A New Model for Predicting Behavioral Intentions: An Alternative to Fishbein," *Journal of Marketing Research,* vol. 17 (1980), pp. 153–172.

36. M. Fishbein, J.J. Jaccard, A.R. Davidson, I. Ajzen, and B. Loken, "Predicting and Understanding Family Planning Behaviors: Beliefs, Attitudes, and Intentions," in I. Ajzen and M.A. Fishbein, eds., *Understanding Attitudes and Predicting Social Behavior* (Englewood Cliffs, N.J.: Prentice-Hall, 1980), pp. 130–147.

37. R.J. Budd, D. North, and C. Spencer, "Understanding Seat-Belt Use: A Test of Bentler and Speckart's Extension of the 'Theory of Reasoned Action,'" *European Journal of Social Psychology,* vol. 14 (1984), pp. 69–78.

38. D. Brinberg and J. Durand, "Eating at Fast-Food Restaurants: An Analysis Using Two Behavioral Intention Models," *Journal of Applied Social Psychology,* vol. 13 (1983), pp. 459–472.

39. C. Seligman, D. Hall, and J. Finegan, "Predicting Home Energy Consumption: An Application of the Fishbein-Ajzen Model," in R.P. Bagozzi and A.M. Tybout, eds., *Advances in Consumer Research* (Ann Arbor, Mich.: Association for Consumer Research, 1983), pp. 625–643.

40. J. Hoogstraten, W. de Haan, and G. ter Horst, "Stimulating the Demand for Dental Care: An Application of Ajzen and Fishbein's Theory of Reasoned Action," *European Journal of Social Psychology,* vol. 15 (1985), pp. 401–414.

41. See review by B.H. Sheppard, J. Hartwick, and P.R. Warshaw, "The Theory of Reasoned Action: A Meta-Analysis of Past Research with Recommendations for Modifications and Future Research," *Journal of Consumer Research,* vol. 15 (1988), pp. 325–343.

42. D.J. O'Keefe (Note 35), p. 89–90.

43. I. Ajzen, "From Intentions to Actions: A Theory of Planned Behavior," in J. Kuhl and J. Beckman, eds., *Action Control: From Cognition to Behavior* (Berlin: Springer-Verlag, 1985), pp. 11–39; I. Ajzen, "Attitudes, Traits, and Actions: Dispositional Prediction of Behavior in Personality and Social Psychology," in L. Berkow-

itz, ed., *Advances in Experimental Social Psychology* (New York: Academic Press, 1987), pp. 1–63; I. Ajzen, "Attitude Structure and Behavior," in A.R. Pratkanis, S.J. Breckler, and A.G. Greenwald, eds., *Attitude Structure and Function* (Hillsdale, N.J.: Lawrence Erlbaum, 1989), pp. 241–274; I. Ajzen and T.J. Madden, "Prediction of Goal-Directed Behavior: Attitudes, Intentions, and Perceived Behavioral Control," *Journal of Experimental Social Psychology*, vol. 22 (1986), pp. 453–474; D.E. Schifter and I. Ajzen, "Intention, Perceived Control, and Weight Loss: An Application of the Theory of Planned Behavior," *Journal of Personality and Social Psychology*, vol. 49 (1985), pp. 843–851.
44. A. Bandura, "Self-efficacy: Toward a Unifying Theory of Behavioral Change," *Psychological Review*, vol. 84 (1977), pp. 191–215; A. Bandura, "Self-efficacy Mechanism in Human Agency," *American Psychologist*, vol. 37 (1982), pp. 122–147; A. Bandura, *Social Foundations of Thought and Action: A Social Cognitive Theory* (Englewood Cliffs, N.J.: Prentice-Hall, 1986).
45. N.H. Anderson, "Integration Theory and Attitude Change," *Psychological Review*, vol. 78 (1971), pp. 171–206; N.H. Anderson, *Foundations of Information Integration Theory* (New York: Academic Press, 1981).
46. Petty and Cacioppo (Note 32).
47. See: O'Keefe (Note 35); Petty and Cacioppo (Note 32).

discounting principle
augmenting principle
knowledge bias
audience reporting bias
confirmed expectations
disconfirmed expectations
disclaimer
self-perception
Foot-in-the-Door technique
Weiner's attribution model
intention
controllability
stability
locus of control
Theory of Reasoned Action
behavioral intention
attitude component
subjective norm component
perceived behavioral control
self-efficacy
Information Integration Theory

KEY TERMS AND CONCEPTS

attribution theory
inference
layperson
situational (external) attribution
personal (internal) attribution
Kelley's attribution model
high/low distinctiveness
high/low consistency
high/low consensus
co-variation model
motivational biases
self-serving bias
false consensus bias
false uniqueness bias
hedonic relevance

PART

t w o

COMPONENTS OF PERSUASION

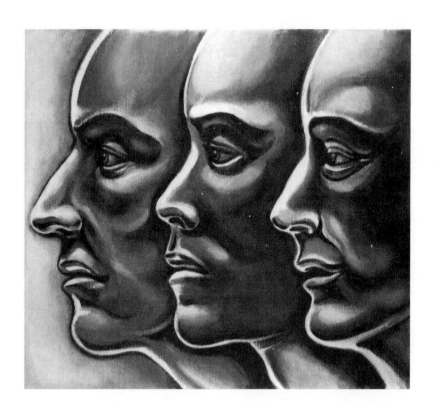

SOURCE CHARACTERISTICS

The Influence of the Communicator

The belief that some communicators are better at persuasion than others is not a new idea. Aristotle[1] regarded the speaker as important in persuasion as the message. His observations: Persuasion is achieved by the speaker's personal character when the speech is so spoken as to make us think him/her credible. We believe good speakers more readily than others. Centuries later Quintillian, a Roman rhetorician, said the ideal communicator is "A good man, speaking well."[2] Since the times of Aristotle and Quintillian, many scholars have been concerned with identifying the factors that lead to speaker effectiveness.

This chapter reviews some of the major ways in which the *source* of the message influences receivers. Traditionally, communication scholars have devoted considerable attention to "source credibility"—the perception that a speaker is credible and believable. Terms such as "trustworthy," "expert," "dynamic," and "sociable" are used to describe various characteristics of speakers, which influence the persuasion process. In the first part of the chapter, we begin with a discussion of credibility research, and then we discuss the importance of three additional characteristics: physical attractiveness, celebrity endorsements, and opinion leadership. The second part of this chapter focuses on the role of *power* in persuasion.

Source Credibility: The General Case

Imagine that a speech is prepared calling for a balanced budget amendment to the U. S. Constitution. A speaker is selected, and the message is audiotaped. Researchers then assemble two audiences with members chosen randomly from a large city. After the two audiences are assembled in two different auditoriums, the researchers give the audience members a test to find out their attitudes toward taxes, a balanced budget amendment, and other relevant topics. The investigators determine that there are no apparent differences between the two audiences. Then the researchers ask the audiences to listen to the taped speech. Both groups hear exactly the same tape. For one group, however, the investigators announce that the speaker is a nationally famous economist and expert on taxation. The second group is told that the speaker is a college student.

Later, the investigators ask the members of both audiences to again record their attitudes toward the amendment. The group that thought it had listened to the economist and tax expert changed its attitudes more in favor of the topic than had the audience that thought it was listening to a student speaker. Since both groups heard exactly the same tape, and since the groups were similar in their original attitudes, the only conclusion that can be drawn is that differences between the two groups are due to a difference in the perceived credibility between the two sources. This hypothetical example represents the basic paradigm under which much credibility research has been conducted. The experimenter holds the message constant, uses equivalent audiences, and then systematically varies the characteristics of the communicator to find out what factors attributable to the source are persuasive.

What is it that caused the one audience to change attitudes more than the second audience? Obviously, when the topic at hand deals with taxes and budgets, receivers are likely to defer to the advice of an *expert*. However, there is no law that states that experts are *always* more influential on all topics. Communication scholars Cronkhite and Liska[3] advocate a "functional" approach to the study of credibility, and argue that receivers "use different criteria and use their criteria differently depending upon the functions a source is expected to perform in a specific topic-situation."[4]

Other scholars use the term "contingency approach" to speaker characteristics by saying that specific source characteristics (for example, expertise, beauty) may be effective in certain specific situations, but not necessarily in others.[5] For example, receivers want to look beautiful, so they accept the advice of sexy and beautiful models when selecting perfume, cosmetics, shampoo, and the like. On the other hand, when deciding to invest $10,000 in stocks, most people would defer to the advice of an experienced and trustworthy stockbroker, and his/her beauty may be of minor importance. Part of understanding the process of persuasion is to know when particular speakers are likely to be effective for particular topics, and receivers—knowing how to match up speaker, topic, and audience characteristics.

Credibility is defined as a *set of perceptions* about sources held by receivers. Since credibility is defined as the *perceptions*, two constraints must be kept in mind. First, we can be certain that receivers believe someone is credible only by asking them. A person who is highly credible to some people may not be perceived as highly credible by others; just witness political campaigns. Large-scale political polls are taken weekly, and tell us how various candidates are perceived by Latinos, blue-collar workers, college-educated groups, and so on. The second constraint deals with the fact that public images and perceptions are often *fabricated*—we are often led to believe that a person is an expert, or is honest and sincere, when he or she is not.

The two main perceptions that determine credibility involve beliefs about the speaker's *trustworthiness* and the speaker's level of *expertise* or competence. These two sets of beliefs were first advocated by Holvand, Janis, and Kelley[6], and confirmed by other researchers. McCroskey[7] later obtained several perceptions he labeled "authoritativeness" (which is similar to expertise/competence), and "character" (which is similar to trustworthiness). Perhaps the most thorough examination of source credibility was conducted by Berlo, Lemert, and, Mertz[8], whose analyses indicated that there were three independent dimensions or factors which people used in judging the credibility of various kinds of sources. They termed the first factor a *safety* factor—a factor similar to the trustworthiness factor discussed by Hovland, Janis, and Kelley. A second factor was labeled a *qualification* factor, which is identical to the expertness factor (that is, the speaker is perceived to be *qualified* to speak on a particular topic). The third factor was labeled as *dynamism*. The third factor seemed less important than the first two in many persuasion situations, but has a definite role in politics, and in areas in which perceived power, strength, and energy are important.

More recently, McCroskey, Jensen, and Valencia argued that we should consider additional factors: composure, sociability, and extroversion.[9] Their description of these factors suggests a similarity between extroversion and dynamism, but composure and sociability seem quite different from expertise and trustworthiness. We first examine the two most common characteristics, expertise and trustworthiness, and then discuss these other, more personal, characteristics. Indeed, the two main criteria (expertise and trustworthiness) parallel what Eagly, Wood, and Chaiken[10] refer to as the two most basic types of communicator biases: knowledge bias and reporting bias. A knowledge bias refers to the belief that a source possesses a greater knowledge of the content area than do the receivers, while a "reporting bias" refers to the belief receivers have concerning a communicator's willingness to communicate facts and arguments accurately.

Expertise

A source who is perceived to possess high levels of expertise by receivers is described as trained, experienced, skillful, informed, authoritative, able, and intelligent. There are many studies that demonstrate the importance of expertise in influencing receivers. Bochner and Insko,[11] for example, prepared messages that students told they could function adequately on fewer hours of sleep each night. A number of persuasive speeches were created—some advocated that people could function without any sleep, while others told students they needed one hour a night, two hours a night, three hours a night, and so on up to eight hours a night. Half of the receivers were told that the message they were reading was written by a Nobel Prize-winning physiologist (high expertise), and the other half of the receivers were told that the message was written by the director of the YMCA. Afterwards, they were asked: how many hours do you believe people need to sleep each night? Receivers changed their opinions to agree with the expert, agreeing with the expert's advice (at least until the expert advocated zero hours; see results later in chapter). In order to be correct in our beliefs, and to be knowledgeable, we accept the advice and recommendation of experts.

The fact that experts persuade is obvious. Less obvious is the answer to the question: When is expertise important to persuasion, as opposed to some other characteristic of the speaker? Keeping in mind the Cronkhite and Liska[12] notion that different sources are important in different persuasion areas, we offer three areas in which expertise seems naturally important. First, Weitz[13], in a review of the literature on personal sales, concluded that salespersons should emphasize expertise when: (a) the salesperson is recruiting new customers; (b) the salesperson does, indeed, possess a high level of knowledge; and, (c) the customer is engaged in a complex purchasing task. Why? A salesperson needs to emphasize training and expertise early, if s/he is to prompt customers to switch from one company or vendor to another. Further, if the customer is involved in complex purchasing tasks, the salesperson needs to emphasize expertise to appear *more* expert than the client so that the client will *depend* on the salesperson's higher level of training and experience.

These "complex purchasing tasks" may involve buying a computer system, a communications system, or an investment package. Television advertisements for such products focus on a company's ability to solve a client's present needs, as well as solve any potential problems. We are told to buy AT&T, Prudential, Met Life, IBM, and so forth because of the experience these companies can offer, and we are told they can help us solve problems in the future.

An area in which expertise is critical deals with the teaching of skills. Receivers may desire to learn how to play better golf, repair their homes, repair motors and the like; and consumers tune in to informative television shows and buy videotapes and publications from sources they believe are competent in improving such skills.

Issues of similarity may affect situations where expertise is emphasized. Imagine watching a series of shows on Public Television in which an expert cook from New Orleans teaches individuals how to prepare Cajun cooking. You buy the correct ingredients and follow directions carefully. You *believe* you are preparing authentic Cajun cooking. You eat the food and realize that you do not *like the taste* of this kind of food—perhaps you do not like the spices involved or some ingredients.

This example highlights a difference between *beliefs* held about the world at large and *personal preferences, tastes, values, and feelings.* When receivers want to know about the world at large—to learn something beyond their own personal experiences—they often seek out the advice of people who are better informed. Thus, we should emphasize expertise when the topic of persuasion deals with beliefs about the world at large—issues such as: What is the correct pH level for shampoo? Is stock X a good investment over a ten-year period? Will there be a good market for communication majors in four years?

On the other hand are matters of personal preference, tastes, likes, and dislikes. Some people like spicy food, others don't. Receivers do not need experts to tell them about the things they already like. When it comes to Tex-Mex food, North China food, a brand of soft drink, the look that a particular lipstick provides, the softness of one's hand, face or hair after using a product, the odor of a particular perfume, and so forth, receivers probably pay relatively little attention to experts and pay more attention to the advice of friends, people they trust, similar others, or celebrities.

Simply being an expert does not guarantee that the speaker will be successful. Recall what was said earlier about *strong* and *weak* arguments. When a speaker is described to an audience as an expert, members of the audience *expect* the expert to possess and communicate facts and evidence. If s/he communicates weak arguments, or presents only opinions, failing to provide evidence, receivers are *not* persuaded. Employing the topic of comprehensive exams for seniors (see Chapter 3), Heesacker, Petty, and Cacioppo[14] had some students hear a message containing either strong or weak arguments from one of two sources: an expert (the Carnegie Commission on Higher Education, chaired by a professor of education at Princeton University) or a non-expert (a journalism student in high school). The expert was significantly more persuasive in changing the opinions of students—but primarily when the expert included *strong arguments* in the speech. Indeed, some of the receivers were *less* persuaded by the expert when *weak* arguments were used than when non-experts used the same arguments. Similarly, Norman[15] describes a study where a speaker was introduced as an expert (a professor who had co-authored a book on sleep behavior). In half of the speeches the communicator provided six specific pieces of evidence bearing on the topic of sleep behavior; the other half of the speeches contained no evidence, only the speaker's opinion. Receivers were persuaded only when the expert

employed arguments. The conclusion: To be persuasive, experts should act "expert-like" and present facts and evidence.

How much change in beliefs does the persuader want to achieve? Research confirms the idea that the more change one desires, the more one should emphasize expertise. Recall the Bochner and Insko study mentioned earlier. They created different versions of a speech, advocating eight hours per night to zero hours per night. Since most people believe that a person requires eight hours of sleep, the eight-hours-a-night version would not be discrepant from the receivers' beliefs. On the other hand, when the speaker concluded that people only need two, one, or zero hours of sleep per night, the message would be highly discrepant from the receiver's beliefs.

Figure 5.1 illustrates the amount of sleep receivers said that people need each night after they heard the speeches in the Bochner and Insko study. When the speakers argued positions that were not discrepant from the receivers' point of view (eight, seven, six, five, or four hours of sleep, per night), both the expert and the non-expert received the same amount of belief change (see Figure 5.1). However, the expert speaker was significantly more influential when arguing the more highly discrepant conclusion that receivers needed only two or one hours per night. Both speakers were equally ineffective when arguing the extreme position of zero hours of sleep. Higher levels of expertise are important when asking for higher amounts of change.

We also need to mention the impact of heritage. Aronson and Golden[16] had sixth graders hear a message that argued that arithmetic courses were important. Some of the students thought the message was from an engineer (high expertise), others from a dishwasher (low expertise). Further, some were led to believe the speech was by an African-American, others by a Caucasian. As a general rule, the engineer was more persuasive than the dishwasher. However, race and prejudice were important.

FIGURE 5.1

BELIEF CHANGE AS A FUNCTION OF DISCREPANCY FOR THE HIGH EXPERT SPEAKER [NOBEL PRIZE WINNER (DASHED LINE)] AND THE LOW EXPERT SPEAKER [YMCA DIRECTOR (SOLID LINE)]

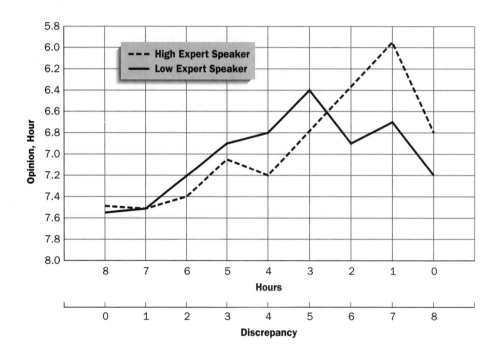

From: S. Bochner and C.A. Insko, "Communicator Discrepancy, Source Credibility, and Opinion Change," *Journal of Personality and Social Psychology,* vol. 4 (1966), pp. 614–621. Reprinted by permission of authors and American Psychological Association.

Those sixth graders who were judged by the researchers to be prejudiced were *less* influenced by the African-American engineer than by the Caucasian engineer. On the other hand, sixth graders who were judged as low in prejudice were *more* influenced by the African-American engineer than by the Caucasian engineer. Presumably, the latter group assigned greater credibility to the African-American under the belief that he must be very competent to have overcome racial prejudice to become an engineer.

CONTRASTING EXPERTISE WITH COMMUNICATOR SIMILARITY

Sometimes, there is a problem with being an expert. When receivers come to believe the expert knows substantially more about a topic than they do, the expert can appear to be very dissimilar, different, and distant from the receiver. Sometimes receivers comply with requests from sources who are *similar* to themselves—people who have the same problem, the same concerns, who are the same age, and who have the same interests and preferences. When does similarity influence receivers?

One of the classic studies on similarity effects was conducted by Brock[17], in a paint store. After a customer had selected the paint s/he was going to buy, a salesperson introduced himself as a college student who worked parttime at the paint store and who could give the customer some advice. The salesperson claimed that two weeks earlier he had finished a job using two types of paint. He told the customer that he had used the same amount of paint as the customer was planning to buy (similar), or he told the customer that he had used twenty times the amount of paint as the customer was planning to buy (dissimilar). The "dissimilar" salesclerk was considered an "expert" because he had considerable experience in painting. Since the salesclerk had also compared brands of paints, he recommended a paint which was either more expensive or less expensive than the one the purchaser was planning to buy. Would the customers take the advice of the similar clerk, or the dissimilar clerk who had more experience?

The results indicated that people followed the advice of the similar communicator: 64 percent of the people complied with the request of the similar clerk versus 39 percent for the dissimilar clerk. Further, in the "similar condition," 73 percent of the customers complied when the communicator recommended the less-expensive paint; 55 percent did so for the higher-priced paint.

Bersheid[18] and others[19] have also demonstrated that similarity increases compliance. Why? One of the reasons why similarity is effective stems from the outcome of Festinger's[20] social comparison process. We naturally compare our abilities, skills, and attitudes with people who are similar to ourselves in age, gender, and other variables relevant to our self-concept (for example, our occupation or ethnicity). (See Chapter 7.) It is common for people to compare test scores, and other abilities and skills, with others. We compare ourselves to people who are similar because such a comparison provides a realistic idea of our own abilities and skills. A jogger, for example, may be interested in knowing how fast world record holders run, but probably judges his/her ability as "excellent," "good," "average," or "poor" relative to others in his/her own age bracket and gender.

Studies by Suls, Gastorf, and Lawhon[21], Wheeler, Koestner, and Driver[22], and Miller[23] represent some of the research done on social comparison processes. Suls, et al., gave high school students a creativity test and, when returning the scores, gave the students a selection of different group averages so they could compare scores. Overwhelmingly, students opted to compare scores first to the same sex-same age group, followed by the same age-different sex group. That is, female high school students first compared their scores to other high school females, and then compared the scores to high school males.

Festinger extends this comparison process to areas beyond test scores in abilities and skills, to include attitudes and opinions. Since we are motivated to hold "correct" ideas and make "smart" decisions, we look around for proof or evidence about the *correct* decision we should make. For some topics, we do not have empirical proof that one brand of paint is absolutely better than others, or we do not have proof that voting for Proposition A will solve a community problem and *not* raise taxes. In situations such as these, we pay attention to what others say and do: We pay attention to what other people do who are similar in age, income, gender, or occupation.

The "proof" concerning the correct or appropriate action to take becomes "social proof" in that the power of the majority, or people "just like us," can persuade us to take a particular action when we lack scientific evidence or verifiable proof about what to do.[24] Exactly such a tactic was used by college newspapers during the Vietnam War. College students had mixed feelings about this war and were uncertain about the credibility of the nation's leaders. Campus newspapers would print the results of polls showing age breakdowns that revealed that other eighteen- to twenty-year-olds were increasingly against the war in Vietnam. What should be your attitude if 70 percent of the people in your age/gender group believe something, and you are uncertain about it?

Simmons, Berkowitz, and Moyer[25] reviewed the literature on similarity vs. dissimilarity and concluded that: "Attitude change toward the position advocated by the source depends on the extent to which interpersonal similarities or dissimilarities are perceived as having instrumental value for the receiver." What we mean by "instrumental value," in part, is that we can rely on similar individuals to help us with our needs, and to provide information for decision making.

Consider the Brock study again. A customer wants to buy two gallons of paint in order to paint a bathroom. The customer wants to buy a good paint that will cover the walls well—not a cheap paint. On the other hand, the customer does not want to spend too much money. When the salesclerk states that he just completed an identical painting job and he has some advice for the customer, the advice seems relevant to the decision being made by the customer (it has "instrumental value"). So, the customer accepts the advice. But imagine what happens when the salesclerk tells the customer that he had just used forty gallons of paint on a recent job. Many customers undoubtedly would think something like, "Well, that's fine for you, but hardly relevant to a weekend painter who wants to put up two gallons in a bathroom." The experience of the "expert" in this case is rejected by the consumer as being irrelevant or unhelpful.

Earlier when we talked about expertise, we touched on beliefs about the world at large and matters of personal preferences, tastes, values, and feelings. In their classic study, Goethals and Nelson[26] argued that when a *belief* is at issue, agreement from another person who is *dissimilar* should increase one's confidence in adopting the belief because a dissimilar person may be expected to have different sources of information and evidence. But, when issues deal with *values, personal preference, and personal issues*, agreement with a *similar* person would be more influential.

To validate their approach, Goethals and Nelson had groups of high school students view a videotape involving two alleged applicants to the university. These observers were asked either to indicate the extent to which each student would be more academically successful at the university (Belief Condition) or to indicate the extent to which they liked the applicants (Value Condition). After the observers made their estimates, they were given an evaluation of the two applicants written by someone who had supposedly participated in the study previously. Half of the students were led to believe that the evaluation they would be receiving came from a person who was similar to themselves in judging others; the other half were led to believe that the evaluator judged others differently than they did. The evaluations that the students received also *agreed* with their own evaluations. After reading the other evaluator's comments, the students were asked again to indicate their estimates of success/liking and the level of confidence they had in making the estimates. The results show that when the students decided which of the two applicants would do better in college, *confidence* in their beliefs was enhanced more by *dissimilar agreers* than by *similar agreers;* similar agreers were more influential in raising confidence in estimates of *likability* of the applicants than were dissimilar agreers.

That similarity or "peer appeal" is successful at changing attitudes concerning personal preferences was demonstrated in an interesting study by Cantor, Alfonso, and Zillman,[27] who explored the impact of three source characteristics on attitudes toward birth control devices: (1) age similarity (a twenty-one year old peer versus a thirty-nine year old nonpeer); (2) level of medical expertise (the source was either a medical student or nurse versus a music student or music teacher); and, (3) level of personal experience (the speaker was described as either having used an IUD or as knowing a friend who used one). The results showed that receivers who heard the same-age peer indicated they were more likely to use an IUD than receivers who heard the same message from an older speaker. Receivers who heard the woman who personally used the IUD rated it higher in effectiveness than other receivers.

In regard to personal selling, Weitz[28] concluded that similarity should be emphasized when (1) the salesperson and the customer may be expected to have future interactions together over years; (2) the salesperson is actually similar to the client, and (3) the customer is engaged in simple, low-risk purchase decisions, or is engaged in purchase decisions that involve social risks. The first of these states the obvious: Salesclerks should create rapport with a person who is likely to be a repeat customer. By "low-risk" purchase decisions we mean that the client isn't spending much money or/and the product is not complex or difficult to work with. By "social risks" we mean contexts in which a person may be embarrassed because s/he may not behave in a socially correct manner (such as, wearing the appropriate attire for an event, or bringing the right kind of gift). Similar others can reduce uncertainty about such issues.

O'Keefe[29] on the subject of similarity maintains that "simple generalizations will not do." Advisedly, we will conclude this topic with a few germane particulars: (1) Similarity is likely to be useful if it satisfies some personal need or concern of the receiver. (2) The similarity between receiver and speaker should be relevant in some important way to the persuasion topic.[30] (3) Similarity is important in producing the desired persuasive effects if the similarity increases liking for the speaker and/or trust. (4) Similarity can entail infinite variables, including attitude, occupa-

tion, speech dialects, and ethnicity.[31] (5) Different kinds of similarities are not equally effective in producing persuasive outcomes; but similarity in *attitudes* produces consistently increased persuasiveness.

Sharing the same preferences, attitudes, and tastes with someone, we may *generalize* those preferences and attitudes into new experiences. For example, if we meet someone who shares a passion, say, for world travel, and we *like* the person and find that we share interests and attitudes, we would tend to follow this person's advice ("If you liked Florence, you really need to go to Venice.") We tend to believe these recommendations because we generalize all the agreements, similarities, and commonalities from related areas to new topics and issues.

Employing *both* expertise and similarity to bolster persuasion, Woodside and Davenport[32] conducted a study in a stereo store manipulating both variables. The salesclerks introduced customers to a head-and-capstan-cleaning kit for tape decks as the customers were purchasing tapes. The clerks manipulated similarity by stating that they owned the same tapes and enjoyed the same type of music as did the customer, or by stating that they preferred a different kind of music. Then, the clerks demonstrated expertise (or lack of it) in knowing how to use the device:

EXPERT: "Here is a device we have on special that will clean the dirt and tape oxide from the guides, the head, and especially the drive wheels for your tape player. You just put a few drops of this cleaner on these two pads, stick it in just like a tape, let it run for about ten seconds while you wiggle this (points to head of cleaning bar). It will keep the music clear and keep the tapes from tearing up by winding up inside the player. It's only $1.98. Would you like one?"

NONEXPERT: "Here is a thing we have on special that they tell me will keep your tape player clean. I don't really know how it works, but you can read the directions right here on the package

---

T A B L E   **5.1**

COMPARISONS OF EXPERT AND SIMILARITY MANIPULATIONS IN PERSONAL SALES RESEARCH

	Brock Study		
	Similar Salesperson	*Dissimilar Salesperson*	*Total*
Lower-priced paint	73 percent	45 percent	59 percent
Higher-priced paint	55 percent	32 percent	43 percent
Totals	64 percent	39 percent	

	Woodside and Davenport Study	
	Purchase	*No Purchase*
Expert salesperson		
Similar	80 percent	20 percent
Dissimilar	53.3 percent	46.7 percent
Nonexpert salesperson		
Similar	30 percent	70 percent
Dissimilar	13.3 percent	86.7 percent
Control group	13.3 percent	86.7 percent

	Woodside and Davenport Study, Comparing Expert and Nonexpert Salespersons	
	Purchase	*No Purchase*
Expert	66.7 percent	33.3 percent
Nonexpert	21.6 percent	77.4 percent

	Woodside and Davenport Study, Comparing Similar and Dissimilar Salespersons	
	Purchase	*No Purchase*
Similar	55 percent	45 percent
Dissimilar	33.3 percent	66.7 percent

SOURCES: T.C. Brock, "Communicator-Recipient Similarity and Decision Change," *Journal of Personality and Social Psychology*, vol. 1 (1965), pp. 650–655; A.G. Woodside and J.W. Davenport, "The Effect of Salesman Similarity and Expertise on Consumer Purchasing Behavior," *Journal of Marketing Research*, vol. 11 (1974), pp. 198–202.

as to how to use it and what it does. I never have used one, and really don't know anything about playing tapes except how to listen to them, but this thing is supposed to help the tape player a lot. It's only $1.98. Would you like one?"

Table 5.1 presents the full results of the study (along with Brock's results). Who was effective in selling the device? Experts were more effective (66.7 percent of the time) than nonexperts (21.6 percent of the time). Also, clerks who showed similar musical interests were more effective (55 percent of the time) than non-similar clerks (33.3 percent of the time). However, when the clerk employed both tactics, sales jumped to 80 percent.

TRUSTWORTHINESS

Receivers who perceive a speaker to be trustworthy describe the speaker as kind, congenial, friendly, warm, agreeable, pleasant, gentle, unselfish, just, forgiving, fair, hospitable, ethical, honest, sincere, and principled. Untrustworthy speakers are ones who deceive, manipulate, cheat, and persuade others in order to increase personal gain. Petty and Cacioppo[33] note that when the topic of persuasion becomes more personal, trust becomes more important. Indeed, we see a good deal of trustworthiness in commercials for health products. Safe, trusting, kind, and honest people confide their solutions for pain, muscle aches, hemorrhoids, and many other personal problems. Of course, we are also more likely to vote for a trustworthy candidate, and to buy from a trustworthy salesperson.

Recall from our discussion of attribution theory in Chapter 4 that speakers who are low in trustworthiness are expected to be biased reporters and to slant information. Thus, studies by Hatfield, Aronson, and Abrahams[34] and others (for instance, studies by Arnold and McCroskey, and Eagly, Wood, and Chaiken)[35] demonstrate that speakers who speak against their own (apparent) interests (or contrary to the expected bias) can sig-

nificantly increase their perceived credibility. There are many daily examples of this technique.

"Reformed" speakers, who no longer use drugs, no longer commit crimes, or who have left gangs, and so forth, appear frequently on television shows, and seem to have credibility with viewers. Pratkanis and Aronson[36] further list a number of situations in which apparent "reformed" individuals increase their perceived credibility and persuasiveness: Patrick Reynolds, who inherited $2.5 million from the R.J. Reynolds Tobacco Company, founded by his grandfather, speaks out against the smoking establishment and actually encourages ex-smokers (or their survivors) to file lawsuits against the industry; J. Robert Oppenheimer worked for years to develop nuclear power, but later cautioned against further development; and Admiral Zumwalt, former naval commander, later campaigned against a number of military developments. People who speak against their expected biases and personal interests increase their credibility.

Another way to make up for initially low levels of credibility is to have it appear that the message was "overheard." Studies by Walster and Festinger and by Brock and Becker[37] indicate that when receivers "overhear" some "fact" (for example, a change in the tuition fees), they are influenced by this "overheard" message more than when they are told the information directly. Reasons why overheard messages are effective include:

1. The overheard communicator arouses less defensiveness and counterargument on the part of the typical receiver.

2. Listeners are especially influenced by communications they were not supposed to hear.

3. Fewer ulterior motives are attributed to the speaker when the message is overheard; and fewer ulterior motives means that the speaker's trustworthiness is less questioned.

PERSONAL CHARACTERISTICS

Additional source credibility factors include "composure," "dynamism," and "sociableness." The perception of composure deals with the extent to which the speaker is relaxed, comfortable, poised, and calm. Composure is important in making first impressions and is therefore very important in interview contexts and public speaking situations. Speakers who are tense and nervous are not persuasive.

"Dynamism" or "extroversion" is a concept based on the image of a speaker as being powerful, strong, potent, active, energetic, healthy, and outgoing. Most Americans prefer to listen to a "conversational style" speaker (like Johnny Carson or Jay Leno), as opposed to "dynamic style" speakers, like the ones we see on late-night advertisements. However, dynamism is an important perception that must be monitored in national politics. When President Reagan made speech errors and lacked fluency in his first debate with Walter Mondale in the 1984 campaign, many voters thought that Reagan looked old, tired, and lacking in energy. Voters prefer strong, energetic, healthy, and potent candidates.

When speakers need to appear strong, they will be filmed in such a way as to show activity, as being outgoing and extroverted. The speaker walks quickly, jogs or exercises, employs sweeping hand gestures, walks tall (or is filmed with shorter people), and speaks quickly and confidently. Politicians are not the only ones who use these ploys. In the early 1980s there was some doubt as to whether the federal government would make a sizable loan to the Chrysler Corporation. Chrysler President Lee Iacocca made several commercials portraying strength and confidence. The goal was to show him as strong, powerful, and able to change a major American corporation. See Figure 5.2 for a contrasting example.

"Sociableness" is the third personal characteristic identified in the studies investigating

PICTURE IS WORTH 1,000 VOTES. DEMOCRATIC PRESIDENTIAL CANDIDATE DUKAKIS EMPLOYS A PRO-MILITARY PHOTO OPPORTUNITY TO BOLSTER AN IMAGE OF STRENGTH. DID IT WORK?

AP/Wide World Photos, Inc.

source credibility. Some speakers are friendly, nice, helpful, likable, and deferent. This is quite a different perception than dynamism or composure. The friendly approach is important in making compliance requests (see Chapter 10) and in making personal sales and in waiting on clients. Cialdini[38] described the actions of a waiter named Vincent, who was renowned for raking in tips. So strategic were Vincent's actions that it would appear he read every important book on persuasion and applied them to his advantage in gaining tips:

1. When waiting on a family, he was charming, effervescent, even clownlike in talking to both

parents and children. Providing more than crayons (toys and puzzles) to the children was also an advantage, providing the children with things to do, and the parents a chance to relax.

2. With a young couple, he was formal and talked exclusively to the man, to whom he might even appear intimidating. Proposing expensive items and champagne would help to impress the fellow's date—and consequently increase Vincent's tip.

3. With an older couple Vincent would remain formal, but he dropped his superior attitude in order to show respect, even bowing, leaning toward the clients, using a hushed tone of voice, and he would monitor their table frequently.

4. When a person ate alone, Vincent acted in a friendly way. He would be cordial, warm, and converse with the patron. He made the lone diner feel comfortable as a guest in his dining room.

5. Vincent, however, made a real killing on tips when he could manipulate large parties. When it was time for members of the group to order, Vincent would take the first order (usually a woman's), and then react in a negative manner. He would hesitate, frown, look worried, and look over his shoulder to see if the manager was watching. He would lean toward the patron, acting like a conspirator, and say that whatever the woman ordered "wasn't very good tonight"; then he would recommend an entree that was slightly less expensive. The patrons would be very impressed by this bogus trick to make them like him. After gaining their trust, Vincent would recommend a number of choice wines that would complement the meal—and Vincent was an expert in wines. Virtually without exception, the patrons would trust Vincent with the wine list, and Vincent made sure that no wine glass was left empty of the most expensive wines he could talk the party into trying. Thus, Vincent increased the amount of money he made from tips.

The Physically Attractive Speaker

There is considerable evidence that good-looking people are perceived to be more likable, friendly, interesting, and poised, to be more likely to be successful, to make more money, and so forth.[39] The most impressive study was conducted by Chaiken[40], who trained students to deliver a persuasive speech. Their practice performances were videotaped, and the students' speech fluency, eye contact, smiling, and vocal confidence were evaluated. Then, the students (that is, "solicitors") approached targets on the campus and delivered the persuasive message. They asked the students to sign a petition banning the serving of meat at lunch and breakfast; they argued that Americans eat too much red meat and students should be offered a healthier choice. The targets were given a "student opinion" questionnaire asking their opinions on a number of matters, including the issue of banning meat, and were asked to sign a petition. A group of judges ranked all solicitors in attractiveness. The question is: Did good-looking solicitors get more people to comply and sign the petition than less attractive solicitors?

Table 5.2 presents the two outcomes from the study: Attractive solicitors got more people to sign the petition, and female targets were more likely to sign the petitions than male targets. When the solicitor was unattractive, petition signing was 24 percent to 38 percent and averaged about 32 percent. There were no major differences between male and female targets. However, when the solicitors were attractive, petition signing averaged about 41 percent (53 percent when approached by a good-looking male, 47 percent by a good-looking female). In regard to "target agreement" (see Table 5.2), the smaller numbers indicate more agreement that meat should be banned, and the smallest numbers were for females who were approached by attractive solicitors. Second, females, as a general rule, complied more often than males. This should not be taken as evidence that

T A B L E	**5.2**

PHYSICAL ATTRACTIVENESS AND INFLUENCE

A. Receiver Agreement and Petition Signing as a Function of Communicator Attractiveness, Solicitor Sex and Target Sex*

Field Data:	Attractive Solicitor				Unattractive Solicitor			
	M-MT	*M-FT*	*F-MT*	*F-FT*	*M-MT*	*M-FT*	*F-MT*	*F-FT*
Petition Signing:	29%	53%	35%	47%	35%	38%	24%	29%
Target Agreement:	4.59	3.32	4.24	3.53	4.91	4.00	4.53	4.03

Laboratory Data:

Attractive solicitors were more fluent, and were likely to speak more quickly (higher rate of speech) than less-attractive solicitors. Also, attractive solicitors expressed greater optimism (rated self as better in sales, as more attractive, interesting, more likely to make more money).

B. Attractive criminals receive lighter sentences, except when they use their beauty to commit the crime. **

Type of Offense			*Mean Sentence Assigned (in years)*
	Attractive Criminal	*Unattractive Criminal*	*Control Group*
Swindle	5.45	4.35	4.35
Burglary	2.80	5.20	5.10

* Table adapted from: S. Chaiken, "Communicator Physical Attractiveness and Persuasion," *Journal of Personality and Social Psychology*, vol. 37 (1979), pp. 1387–1397.
** Table adapted from: H. Sigall and N. Ostrove, "Beautiful but Dangerous: Effects of Offender Attractiveness and Nature of Crime on Juridic Judgment," *Journal of Personality and Social Psychology*, vol. 31 (1975), pp. 410–414.

women are more gullible than men, since there is considerable evidence that females would be less involved with this particular topic. Men eat more red meat than do women, and men would be more resistant to signing the petition.

Why are attractive people more successful in a situation such as this? First, our society emphasizes beauty and reinforces stereotypes about good-looking people as being taller, more successful, more popular, and having higher incomes—possessing the positive qualities. Consequently, we admire and respect good-looking people; we want to be like them and we want them to like us. Second, good-looking individuals have more self-confidence, are more optimistic, are more fluent, and speak more quickly than less attractive speakers. These variables help the attractive individual perform better.

While the beauty stereotype often helps in soliciting and in selling, the stereotype can either help or hurt the beautiful person in other settings. For one, the beauty bias is quite consistently reported in legal settings; there are a number of reports that indicate that good-looking drunk drivers and criminals receive a lighter sentence by jurors than less attractive drunk drivers. Why? Because of the stereotype that "beauty is good," people believe that after being caught and found guilty, the good-looking individual will change his/her behavior and behave better in the future. However, if the criminal uses his/her good looks to commit the crime, then jurors are *not* very charitable and believe that society must be protected from the beautiful person who went bad.

For example, Sigall and Ostrove[41] had students read different legal summaries, and indicate how long they thought the criminal should be sentenced. Some read of a burglary case in which a woman broke into a home and stole several thousand dollars; others read about a woman who swindled men out of several thousand dollars. A control group of students did not receive any photograph of the women, but other students received either a photograph of an attractive woman or of an unattractive one. The results (panel B in Table 5.2) indicated that, for burglary, a good-looking woman received the benefit of doubt and a lighter sentence (only 2.80 years in jail) relative to the unattractive woman; or to the sentence of the neutral (control) group. However, when the crime was swindling men out of money, and beauty is used to commit the crime, jurors gave a harsher sentence to the attractive swindler (see Table 5.2).

Second, the beauty bias apparently helps men in organizations, but not women. Heilman[42] conducted a series of studies indicating that handsome men are perceived to have more leadership qualities than beautiful women. Beautiful women are still hired for employment, and may make more money than less attractive women, but our society (still) maintains a bias that glamorous women are perceived by people in the business world as lacking in leadership capabilities, relative

to the handsome male. While attempts are made to promote the role of women in society in general (see Chapter 14), the reader should be aware of this bias.

Can the beautiful speaker prompt us to change our opinions and beliefs about highly involving and important topics? Or, are the effects of beauty limited only to face-to-face contexts involving relatively unimportant issues? Actually, we are not quite certain how important beauty is to complex purchasing decisions, political and social issues, or to the purchase of expensive items. Maddux and Rogers[43] found that attractive people were better liked than less attractive people, but were not perceived any differently with regards to sincerity or honesty. Experts, however, were more persuasive than attractive speakers. In the Norman[44] study, a speaker, expert in sleep behavior, was effective only when s/he employed evidence and arguments. However, an attractive speaker was effective in eliciting a modest, but significant, amount of belief change regardless of the absence or presence of strong argument. The expert + evidence produced the most change, followed by both groups exposed to the attractive speaker (attractive + evidence, attractive − evidence), while the expert speaker who failed to communicate any evidence was the least effective. So, receivers expectations are important. To be an expert with no evidence is poor strategy, but how important or lasting is the "moderate" belief change obtained by the attractive speaker?

Puckett, Petty, Cacioppo, and Fisher[45] found that both attractiveness and quality of argument were important. Employing the topic of comprehensive examinations for seniors, college students read persuasive messages either attributed to a "socially attractive" speaker (one who was good looking, had a good family background, and had prestigious hobbies), or a "socially unattractive" speaker. When both beauty and background were manipulated to portray a person with good character, attractiveness and quality of argument interacted, as can be seen in Figure 5.3. When the source was attractive, the students were persuaded by the strong argument, but they reduced agreement with the source when the attractive source made weak arguments.

This latter finding contradicts some studies in persuasion; however, part of the stereotype of the "beautiful person" includes "air head," and it seems obvious that a pretty face that advances a poor, weak argument is going to fail in the persuasion process. What the Puckett, et al., results show is that when sources are attractive, we take the time to read and think about what they are saying. Being good looking, or socially desirable, increases persuasion when the good-looking speaker has something important to say. Indeed, students in this study rated the attractive source as more positive in intelligence, likability, and so on, *only* when the speaker employed strong argument; otherwise, receivers are very critical of attractive speakers who employ weak argument. Since television today is cluttered with a plethora of commercials on many channels, it is undoubtedly important to employ an attractive speaker in order to gain attention. However, the attractive speaker has to have something worth saying for persuasion to take place.

FIGURE 5.3

ATTITUDE TOWARD COMPREHENSIVE EXAMINATIONS AS A FUNCTION OF SOURCE ATTRACTIVENESS AND QUALITY OF ARGUMENT

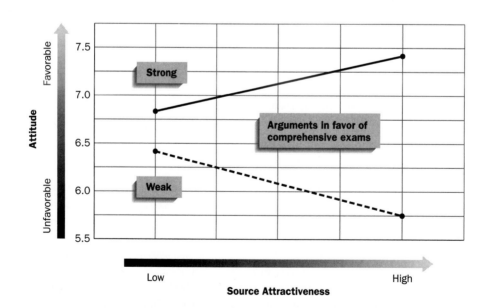

From: R.E. Petty and J.T. Cacioppo, *Communication and Persuasion: Central and Peripheral Routes to Attitude Change* (New York: Springer-Verlag, 1986). Reprinted by permission of Springer-Verlag.

Celebrity Endorsements

The number of celebrities who endorse products rose so dramatically over the 1980s that it is tempting to say that celebrity endorsements are effective. Indeed, one can now hire celebrities to "mingle" with you and claim to be an old friend of yours (see Figure 5.4).

It is hard to say precisely if celebrity endorsements are worth the money—sometimes they work, sometimes they do not. One advertising company was quoted as saying celebrities are effective in only 20 percent of the attempts. Another major company in Chicago (who gave us the "Where's the Beef?" ad in the 1980s) refused to employ celebrities, relying almost exclusively on humorous appeals that use the "guy on the street." Why? Failures are very common. Bill Cosby was successful in selling Jell-O, but failed when trying to endorse stocks and investments for E.F. Hutton. John Wayne was successful in endorsing a bank, but failed to sell antacid tablets.

When are celebrities effective? There does not appear to be any *one* situation that best captures celebrity effectiveness. Keeping in mind the "functional" approach of Cronkhite and Liska again, we can offer three contexts that are important. First, it would appear that there are people who have developed a very strong attachment and admiration for certain celebrities—Vanna White, Elvis Presley, Cindy Crawford, Mel Gibson, Madonna, Janet Jackson and a few others. Their followers will buy a wide array of products endorsed by these individuals: cologne, games, clothes, and so on—and it doesn't appear to matter if the product is relevant in any way to the celebrity's fame. The *cause* of the selling rests in the fact that the receivers identify with the celebrity personalities.

Second, children appear to be strongly influenced by celebrities who are currently "in." Research indicates that children are more likely to be influenced than older receivers, who may question the logic of buying a product simply because an athlete or celebrity was paid to endorse it.[46] Younger children are strongly influenced by the fact that others around them are excited by a celebrity ("Michael Jackson! It's Michael Jackson!"), without really understanding why the person is perceived as a celebrity. Older children may identify with a sports character or an athlete because they want to grow up to possess the celebrity's skills or abilities. It can be assumed that younger receivers will generally be influenced by whoever is currently the "in" celebrity.

A third approach is championed by Kahle and Homer[47] and by Kamins[48]. Kahle and Homer argued that receivers will follow the recommendations of celebrities if doing so helps the receivers adapt to their environment. Will my life be better if I buy and use this product? Will my skin be softer? My hair more lustrous? My running faster?

Kahle and Homer proposed a *match-up* hypothesis which states that effectiveness is increased if there is a good match between the public image of the celebrity and the message about the product and its attributes. Strong match-ups occurred when Dorothy Hamill advertised Short and Sassy hair products, Joe Namath endorsed Brut, Karl Malden endorsed American Express, Lorne Greene (Ben Cartwright on "Bonanza") endorsed Alpo dog food (he was a dog breeder), and basketball stars pitched athletic shoes. Weak match-ups occurred when Arnold Palmer endorsed Pennzoil (it kept the tractor running back on the golf course in Pennsylvania). Poor match-ups are represented by Ed McMahon and Alpo dog food, and Roger Staubach and Rolaids.

As a general rule of thumb, good match-ups are likely to be more effective than other combinations. The Kahle and Homer experiment demonstrated this. They took a sample of celebrities and identified them (from survey data) as being attractive and likable (Jaclyn Smith), attractive and unlikable (Bo Derek), unattractive and likable (Jean Stapleton), and unattractive and unlikable

FIGURE 5.4

TRADING FAME AND FORTUNES

There's no business like celebrity brokering. A mention on a broker's A list may be as much an assurance of stardom as receiving an Oscar, and just as lucrative. A handful of self-styled celebrity brokers in Britain and in America now buy and sell top performers and personalities for corporate clients.

While most celebrities have agents to organize their professional work, brokers peddle them around a worldwide market in which large companies invest heavily to secure well-known promoters. Personal appearances, product endorsements and speech-making at company beanos are the usual fare. Many celebrities earn more from these than from their main professional activities.

One London broker, Celebrity Productions, handles a dozen bookings a week. Its A-list celebrities cost from $20,000 for a newsreader or successful comedian to around $100,000 for an Engelbert Humperdinck. The celebrity is yours for between two hours and a whole day. Lesser personalities, including most sportsmen, are on the B and C lists: there, prices start at around $8,000. Lower down the pile are the after-dinner speakers—business types and professional raconteurs who command $4,500 a time.

Show business appearances are not confined to the annual sales conference or corporate video. One growth area is "mingling." A hard night's mingling, being introduced as the company chairman's oldest friend, earns a celebrity around $4,000.

From: *The Economist*, August 11, 1990. (Scope Features)

(Billy Jean King). Various print advertisements were made, with each of these celebrities endorsing an Edge razor.

Which of these celebrities offers relevant advice on getting a close shave? The idea is that if physically attractive celebrities like Robert Redford, Jaclyn Smith, Bo Derek, and John Travolta trust the Edge razor blade on their beautiful body parts, then we will also receive a safe-but-close shave from this razor. Kahle and Homer found that the participants were more likely to recall seeing the Edge advertisement, were more inclined to intend to buy the product, and recalled more of the arguments that were listed in the advertisement when the celebrities were attractive. Kamins and his colleagues have also obtained support for the match-up relationship for other celebrities and for "attractiveness-related products." For example, Tom Selleck (attractive celebrity) was more effective than Telly Savalas (unattractive celebrity) when endorsing a luxury car, but was not more effective in endorsing a home computer.

Opinion Leadership Research

At a dinner, people are ordering their meals, and Helena proposes a particular kind of wine. Everyone readily agrees with Helena's suggestion. One of the conversational topics at dinner is the economy, and Steve talks about proposals before the U.S. Senate. He advocates two of the proposals as ones that would help the economy, and the rest of the dinner party agrees. Later, when talking about automobiles, George has good things to say about a particular car, and Steve agrees to test drive one.

All participants in the party are equals; no one has a higher status. Further, not one of them is *trained* in wines, taxation, or auto mechanics. Yet, each person successfully persuades the others on particular topics. The relevant term in situations such as these is "opinion leadership." The term applies to situations in which one emerges as a leader of opinions among members within a peer group. Members of the dinner party know that Helena is interested in wines, has read wine magazines, has toured wine districts, and has built up a knowledge base on the topic. Since she is more informed on this topic than her friends, they defer to her opinions and she "leads" their opinions. The same is true for Steve (who is interested in tax law and tax incentives), and George (who keeps well informed on automobiles).

The pioneering study pointing to the importance of opinion leadership was made by Katz and Lazarsfeld.[49] They examined the effects of the mass media on the attitudes and behavior of those who listened to radio and television or read the daily newspaper. Their initial conclusion, after presenting a message over one of the mass media and then measuring the effects of the message, was that there seemed to be little change in audience attitudes; but when they went back to the same group some weeks later assessing attitudes again, they found that there had been significant change. In looking for an explanation for the unexpected later shifts, they suggested that these individuals changed their attitudes only after they had talked to others in whom they had confidence. Katz and Lazarsfeld referred to the people conferred with as "opinion leaders."

Opinion leadership has been studied (1) in looking at the diffusion and adoption of new farming practices and methods in the United States and in foreign countries, (2) in examining the adoption of new drugs by physicians, and (3) in trying to understand the adoption of educational innovations. Obviously, opinion leadership research offers important advice on the study of source characteristics and persuasion.

The most general way of describing opinion leaders is that they tend to serve as models for group members. There seem to be few characteristics that all opinion leaders possess, but there are some factors that are useful in predicting opinion leadership. Rogers has summarized the characteristics of opinion leaders across a wide variety of situations and cultures.[50] We have selected those factors which are most clearly related to the persuasive communication situation, and discuss those characteristics in detail. Opinion leaders tend to be better informed in those areas about which they are consulted. They are better informed about information transmitted by the mass media, particularly the subjects in which they are influential. Berelson and his associates were concerned with an election study and the determination of opinion leaders in a political situation. They reported that leaders were more interested in the election, were better informed about it, held stronger opinions about it, and were more concerned about the election than nonleaders.[51]

One of the major factors that seems to emerge from the research is the amount of communication that is associated with being an opinion leader. Opinion leaders talk to more people than nonleaders. They know more people. They read more, listen more, and view more. They have more than one circle of acquaintances, although they may be opinion leaders in only one circle.

Opinion leaders tend to have more formal education than the people who consult them. They have a higher social status than the people to whom they give advice. They tend to have more empathy than the individuals to whom they offer opinions. Opinion leaders do not seem to possess any of these specific characteristics to an extraordinary degree. They cannot be compared on any characteristic with the population as a whole, but only with the group they serve as opinion leader.

Opinion leaders vary, depending on the topic under consideration. The opinion leader for the political arena is not likely to be the opinion leader for the latest in sports, nor perhaps for the latest in stock market activities. Opinion leaders in the fashion industry, music industry, or movie business are individuals perceived to possess information, contacts, intuition, and knowledge that allow them to predict trends, and to be persuasive with their followers.

Improving the Effectiveness of the Communicator

We have already discussed a number of ways in which a person who has little credibility might increase effectiveness. For example, based on attribution theory (Chapter 4), a speaker may speak against his/her own (apparent) interest, or admit one negative feature about a product when praising six or seven positive attributes about a product. Several other tactics might be employed:

1. If you have low levels of credibility, do not begin persuasion by being introduced to the audience. Receivers are not likely to give a neutral speaker low ratings, and will give a speaker the benefit of doubt. Research by Greenberg and Miller[52] indicates that the effects of low credibility are minimized if the speaker is introduced after speaking.

2. Learn to speak proficiently, employing appropriate language and non-verbal communication.

3. "Flog the dead horse," meaning find some basis of commonality or similarity with the audience. Weiss[53] first coined the term and used the tactic in persuasion research. However, the tactic has to be used in such a way so that it is not obviously ingratiating.

4. Effectively use the media. Research by Eagly and Chaiken[54] indicates that when a speaker stands (or is filmed) in front of the audience, audience members naturally think more thoughts about the speaker. When the message is written, audience members think more thoughts about the message arguments rather than about the speaker. Thus, if the speaker is handsome, likable or credible, a live performance or a videotaped performance is useful because audience members will think more speaker-related thoughts. On the other hand, if your initial levels of credibility are low, (or the audience believes you to be too young, unattractive or unlikable), then using media (such as photographs, slides) should help the speaker become more persuasive—if s/he has quality arguments that can be used to influence the audience.

POWER

Credibility is a set of perceptions receivers hold of speakers. Power is a somewhat different view of source characteristics. In power relationships, for example, a person has *authority* to tell a receiver to take a particular action, and the receiver feels obligated to comply. Individuals in a power relationship also have the ability to use *rewards* and *punishments* when influencing others, while in most situations a credible source cannot pay, promote or punish receivers. In this section, we define and describe six fundamental bases of power; they are important in characterizing influence

T A B L E	5.3

EFFECTS OF USING DIFFERENT TYPES OF SOCIAL INFLUENCE IN TERMS OF
MOVING CLOSER TO THE AGENT (+), MOVING AWAY FROM THE AGENT (0), OR
MOVING AGAINST THE AGENT (−)

Source of Influence Employed by Agent	*Effects on B*			
	Public Behavior	*Private Beliefs*	*Interaction with Agent*	*Identification with Agent*
Information	+	+	0(?)	?
Referent	+	+	+	+
Expert	+	+	0	0
Legitimate	+	+	0	0
Reward	+	0	+	0
Coercion	+	−	−	−

Adapted from B.H. Raven and A.W. Kruglanski, *"Conflict and Power,"* in P. Swingle, ed., *The Structure of Conflict* New York: Academic, 1970), pp. 69–109. Reprinted by permission.

situations, including bargaining contexts (Chapter 11), and organizational contexts (Chapter 12).

Theoretical Bases of Power

According to Raven, there are six basic types of social influence: informational, referent, expert, legitimate, reward, and coercive.[55] Each can have a number of effects on a receiver—including whether the receiver would publicly change a behavior, privately adopt the beliefs of the speaker, have more positive interactions with the speaker, and increase or decrease identification with the receiver. Table 5.3 summarizes these relationships.

Informational Influence. A speaker may attempt to influence receivers by the use of information not previously available to the receivers, or to employ logic or argument that receivers have not thought of. Suppose you go to a new college or start to work for a new company. When people tell you where there are good places to eat, where to park to avoid theft, or how to get off the campus and out of city easily, they are employing informational influence. Informational influence includes attempts at influencing others based on the content of the message, a message including facts, evidence, testimony, or logical argument.

Informational influence very often leads to both a change in overt behavior (you park in parking lot X) and in private beliefs (you believe your car is safer there). However, as Raven and his colleagues note, effective information must be related to the target's value structure and cognitive system. For example, a person may refuse to take advice and park in the safer lot because it is far away—the risk is taken to save walking time.

Referent Influence. Referent influence stems from the fact that the receiver identifies with the source, or influence agent. Generally speaking, what we mean is that the receiver seeks to be "one" with the speaker, identifies with the speaker, admires the speaker, emulates the speaker, and uses the speaker as a role model. Presumably, individuals who buy any product endorsed by a celebrity do so out of a sense of identification with the celebrity.

The term "referent" is used to parallel the sociological use of the term "referent group," a group to which a person belongs (or wishes to belong) as a means of identifying him/herself. Referent group identification, much like the same-age, same-sex comparisons we noted above, has a strong impact on behavior. Receivers who want to grow up to be like their favorite football or basketball stars, movie star, corporate raider, and so on will adopt the behaviors and practices these heroes have adopted. In work environments, leaders in organizations and in the military have a strong following from many of their subordinates.

When a person is attracted to another, and perceives similarity between them, he or she may comply with a request. Referent influence is, like source credibility, a quality that is perceived from the receiver's perspective (he or she would like to grow up to be just like Joe Montana, Martin Luther King, Diane Sawyer, Connie Chung, Michael Jordan, Arsenio Hall, and so on). We generally call any appeal to similarity or to mutual attraction an instance of referent influence. Referent power leads to a change in both public behaviors and in private beliefs. It also leads to positive interactions with the agent, and, of course, with increased identification with the agent.

Expert Influence. Following from the work on credibility, we say that a speaker has expert influence on power over the receiver if the receiver believes that the source has superior knowledge and ability. Individuals who are gifted at computer work, who have a masterful command of the En-glish language, or who are excellent musicians are perceived to be experts in these particular domains. As Table 5.3 indicates, expert influence often leads to changes both in public behavior and in private adoption of beliefs. However, there are no specific predictions about future interactions and to identification with the expert, for several reasons: Sometimes we do like an expert and seek out that expert; at other times an expert would be seen as intimidating, and we would not seek future interactions.

Legitimate Influence. On occasion, people ask us to do things, and because the speakers have a right to make the request we feel obligated to comply. In an organization, a supervisor has the right to tell people to work at a particular rate, to be prompt, to be safe, and so forth. In our daily lives, we feel that we have a right to peace and quiet in our own homes, free of barking dogs, loud stereos, and phone solicitors who call late at night. However, legitimate influence is the most problematic of all the theoretical forms of influence because what we see as rights and obligations depends, in part, on how we were socialized.

For example, most people would feel that the loud barking of a neighbor's dog infringes on their rights. Such a person would try to persuade the neighbor to do something about the dog. He might, however, fail to talk to the neighbor, but would rather take action directly by calling authorities to complain, killing the dog, or opening the neighbor's gate and letting the dog out. At the other extreme, some people believe that an individual has the right to do whatever s/he desires on their own property, and that others have no business interfering. This person would take no action. Rights and obligations in a community setting are strongly affected by how the individual is socialized.

Legitimate influence can be effective in influencing others and in reducing conflict if both parties share the same perspective concerning legitimacy. Legitimate influence can lead to changes in public behavior and in private beliefs (see Table 5.3).

Reward and Coercive Influences. If an agent can control the rewards and punishments the target receives, then the agent may use rewards or coercion to effect changes. Any student who has received money for good grades and has had privileges revoked for breaking house rules knows parents use reward and coercive tactics in order to shape behavior. Rewards and punishments can include physical materials (money, candy) as well as intangible ones (love, affection, disapproval). The use of rewards leads the target to change public behavior. Further, sources who reward their receivers often promote more positive interactions between the target and the agent. However, when we perform a behavior just for the M & M's or bonuses, we do not necessarily change our private beliefs. Further, agents who reward targets do not necessarily increase the extent the target identifies with them. Coercive power can lead to a change in public behavior. However, we identify less with, avoid interacting with, and learn to dislike the beliefs of agents who use threats and punishments.

In sum, there are six theoretical methods for influencing others. Each of these may effectively produce a change in public behavior. However, the methods of influence may vary considerably in how they affect private beliefs and relational outcomes. We must note that each of these methods of influence differs in the range of contexts to which it may apply—perhaps the least used is referent, because it requires knowing who the receiver identifies with, but informational influence is used frequently.

F O O T N O T E S

1.   W.R. Roberts, "Rhetorica," in W.D. Ross, ed., *The Works of Aristotle*, vol. 2 (New York: Oxford University Press), p. 7.

2.   Quintillian, *Institutes of Oratory*, trans. by J.S. Watson (London, 1856), XII, ii., 1.

3.   G. Cronkhite and J. Liska, "The Judgment of Communicatant Acceptability," in M.E. Roloff and G.R. Miller, eds., *Persuasion: New Directions in Theory and Research* (Beverly Hills: Sage, 1980), pp. 101–139; G. Cronkhite and J. Liska, "A Critique of Factor Analytic Approaches to the Study of Credibility," *Communication Monographs*, vol. 43 (1976), pp. 91–107.

4.   Cronkhite and Liska, "A Critique of Factor Analytic Approaches to the Study of Credibility," p. 105.

5.   B. Weitz, "Effectiveness in Sales Interactions: A Contingency Framework," *Journal of Marketing*, vol. 45 (1981), pp. 85–103.

6.   C.I. Hovland, I.L. Janis, and H.H. Kelley, *Communication and Persuasion* (New Haven, Conn.: Yale University Press, 1953), pp. 19–53.

7.   J.C. McCroskey, *An Introduction to Rhetorical Communication* (Englewood Cliffs, N.J.: Prentice-Hall, 1968), pp. 60–61.

8.   D.K. Berlo, J.B. Lemert, and R.J. Mertz, "Dimensions for Evaluating the Acceptability of Message Sources" (Research Monograph, Department of Communication, Michigan State University, 1966).

9.   J.C. McCroskey, T. Jensen, and C. Valencia, "Measurement of the Credibility of Peers and Spouses" (Paper presented at the International Communication Association Convention, Montreal, 1973).

10.   A.H. Eagly, W. Wood, and S. Chaiken, "Causal Inferences about Communicators and their Effect on Opinion Change," *Journal of Personality and Social Psychology*, vol. 36 (1978), pp. 424–435.

11.   S. Bochner and C.A. Insko, "Communicator Discrepancy, Source Credibility, and Opinion Change," *Journal of Personality and Social Psychology*, vol. 4 (1966), pp. 614–621.

12.   Cronkhite and Liska (Note 3).

13.   Weitz, "Effectiveness in Sales Interaction: A Contingency Framework."

14.   M. Heesacker, R.E. Petty, and J.T. Cacioppo, "Field Dependence and Attitude Change: Source Credibility can alter Persuasion by Affecting Message-Relevant Thinking," *Journal of Personality*, vol. 51 (1983), pp. 653–666; also see: R.E. Petty and J.T. Cacioppo, *Communication and Persuasion: Central and Peripheral Routes to Attitude Change* (New York: Springer-Verlag, 1986).

15.   R. Norman, "When What is Said is Important: A Comparison of Expert and Attractive Sources," *Journal of Experimental and Social Psychology*, vol. 12 (1976), pp. 294–300.

16. E. Aronson and B. Golden, "The Effect of Relevant and Irrelevant Aspects of Communicator Credibility on Opinion Change," *Journal of Personality*, vol. 30 (1962), pp. 135–146.

17. T.C. Brock, "Communicator-Recipient Similarity and Decision Change," *Journal of Personality and Social Psychology*, vol. 1 (1965), pp. 650–654.

18. E. Berscheid, "Opinion Change and Communicator-Communicatee Similarity and Dissimilarity," *Journal of Personality and Social Psychology*, vol. 4 (1966), pp. 670–680.

19. H.W. Simmons, N.N. Berkowitz, and R.J. Moyer, "Similarity, Credibility, and Attitude Change: A Review and a Theory," *Psychological Bulletin*, vol. 77 (1970), pp. 1–16.

20. L. Festinger, "A Theory of Social Comparisons," *Human Relations*, vol. 7 (1954), pp. 117–140.

21. J.M. Suls, J. Gastorf, and J. Lawhon, "Social Comparison Choices for Evaluating a Sex- and Age-Related Ability," *Personality and Social Psychology Bulletin*, vol. 4 (1978), pp. 102–105.

22. L. Wheeler, R. Koestner, and R.E. Driver, "Related Attributes in the Choice of Comparison Others," *Journal of Experimental Social Psychology*, vol. 18 (1982), pp. 489–500.

23. C.T. Miller, "The Role of Performance-Related Similarity in Social Comparison of Abilities: A Test of the Related Attributes Hypothesis," *Journal of Experimental Social Psychology*, vol. 18 (1982), pp. 513–523.

24. R. Cialdini, *Influence* (New York: Morrow, 1984).

25. Simons, Berkowitz, and Moyer, "Similarity, Credibility, and Attitude Change: A Review and a Theory," p. 12.

26. G.R. Goethals and R.E. Nelson, "Similarity in the Influence Process: The Belief-Value Distinction," *Journal of Personality and Social Psychology*, vol. 25 (1973), pp. 117–122.

27. J. Canton, H. Alfonso, and D. Zillman, "The Persuasive Effectiveness of the Peer Appeal and a Communicator's First-Hand Experience," *Communication Research*, vol. 3 (1975), pp. 293–310.

28. Weitz, "Effectiveness in Sales Interactions: A Contingency Framework."

29. D.J. O'Keefe, *Persuasion: Theory and Research* (Newbury Park, Calif.: Sage, 1990).

30. Note that in Chapter 10 we discuss "ingratiation" tactics that are used in getting others to like the speaker. Ingratiation tactics often involve trying to find commonalities and similarities between individuals in order to create friendship, and the ingratiator may not actually be selling or persuading the receiver while pointing out similarities—but may do so at a later date.

31. D.J. O'Keefe, *Persuasion: Theory and Research*.

32. A.G. Woodside and J.W. Davenport, "The Effect of Salesman Similarity and Expertise on Consumer Purchasing Behavior," *Journal of Marketing Research*, vol. 11 (1974), pp. 198–202.

33. R.E. Petty and J.T. Cacioppo, *Attitudes and Persuasion: Classic and Contemporary Approaches* (Dubuque, Iowa: Wm. C. Brown, 1981).

34. E. Walster, E. Aronson, and D. Abrahams, "On Increasing the Persuasiveness of a Low Prestige Communicator," *Journal of Experimental Social Psychology*, vol. 2 (1966), pp. 325–342.

35. W.E. Arnold and J.C. McCroskey, "The Credibility of Reluctant Testimony," *Central States Speech Journal*, vol. 18 (1967), pp. 97–103; A.H. Eagly, W. Wood, and S. Chaiken, "An Attribution Analysis of Persuasion," in J.H. Harvey, W. Ickes, and R.F. Kidd, eds., *New Directions in Attribution Theory* (Hillsdale, N.J.: Erlbaum, 1981), pp. 37–62; also see: D.J. O'Keefe, *Persuasion: Theory and Research*.

36. A. Pratkanis and E. Aronson, *Age of Propaganda: The Everyday Use and Abuse of Persuasion* (New York: Freeman, 1991).

37. E. Walster and L. Festinger, "The Effectiveness of 'Overhead' Persuasive Communications," *Journal of Abnormal and Social Psychology*, vol. 65 (1962), pp. 395–402; T.C. Brock and L.A. Becker, "Ineffectiveness of 'Overhead' Counterpropaganda," *Journal of Personality and Social Psychology*, vol. 2 (1965), pp. 654–660.

38. R. Cialdini, *Influence*.

39. See: E. Berscheid and E. Walster, "Physical Attractiveness," in L. Berkowitz, ed., *Advances in Experimental Social Psychology*, vol. 7 (New York: Academic Press, 1974), pp. 157–215; see for recent review: D. Canary and M. Cody, *Interpersonal Communication: A Goals Approach* (New York: St. Martin's Press, 1994).

40. S. Chaiken, "Communicator Physical Attractiveness and Persuasion," *Journal of Personality and Social Psychology*, vol. 37 (1979), pp. 1387–1397.

41. H. Sigall and N. Ostrove, "Beautiful but Dangerous: Effects of Offender Attractiveness and Nature of Crime on Juridic Judgment," *Journal of Personality and Social Psychology*, vol. 31 (1975), pp. 410–414.

42. M. Heilman and L. Saruwatari, "When Beauty is Beastly," *Organizational Behavior and Human Performance*, vol. 23 (1979), pp. 360–372; M. Heilman and M. Stopeck, "Being Attractive, Advantage or Disadvantage? Performance-based Evaluations and Recommended Personnel Actions as a Function of Appearance, Sex and Job Type," *Organizational Behavior and Human Decision Processes*, vol. 35 (1985), pp. 202–215; M. Heilman and M. Stopeck, "Attractiveness and Corporate Success: Different Causal Attributions for Males and Females," *Journal of Applied Psychology*, vol. 70 (1985), pp. 379–388.

43. J. Maddux and R. Rogers, "Effects of Source Expertise, Physical Attractiveness, and Supporting Arguments on Persuasion; A Case of Brains over Beauty," *Journal of Personality and Social Psychology*, vol. 39 (1980), pp. 235–244.

44. Norman, "When What is Said is Important."

45. J. Puckett, R.E. Petty, J.T. Cacioppo, and D. Fisher, "The Relative Impact of Age and Attractiveness Stereotypes on Persuasion," *Journal of Gerontology*, vol. 38 (1983), pp. 340–343; Petty and Cacioppo, *Communication and Persuasion.*

46. See, for instance: C. Atkin and M. Block, "Effectiveness of Celebrity Endorsers," *Journal of Advertising Research*, vol. 23 (1983), pp. 57–62.

47. L.R. Kahle and P.M. Homer, "Physical Attractiveness of the Celebrity Endorser: A Social Adaptation Perspective," *Journal of Consumer Research*, vol. 11 (1985), pp. 954–961.

48. M.A. Kamins, "An Investigation into the 'Match-Up' Hypothesis in Celebrity Advertising: When Beauty May be Only Skin Deep," *Journal of Advertising*, vol. 19 (1990), pp. 4–13; M.A. Kamins, J.J. Brand, S.A. Hoeke, and J.C. Moe, "Two-sided versus One-sided Celebrity Endorsements: The Impact on Advertising Effectiveness and Credibility," *Journal of Advertising*, vol. 18 (1989), pp. 4–10.

49. E. Katz and P.F. Lazarsfeld, *Personal Influence* (New York: Free Press of Glencoe, 1955).

50. E.M. Rogers, *Modernization Among Peasants: The Impact of Communication*, (New York: Holt, Rinehart and Winston, 1969), p. 227.

51. B. Berelson, P.F. Lazarsfeld, and W.N. McPhee, *Voting: A Study of Opinion Formation During a Presidential Campaign*, (Chicago: University of Chicago Press, 1954).

52. B.S. Greenberg and G.R. Miller, "The Effects of Low Credible Sources Message Acceptance," *Speech Monographs*, vol. 33 (1966), pp. 135–136.

53. W. Weiss, "Opinion Congruence with a Negative Source on One Issue as a Factor of Influencing Agreement on Another Issue," *Journal of Abnormal and Social Psychology*, vol. 54 (1957), pp. 180–187.

54. S. Chaiken and A.H. Eagly, "Communication Modality as a Determinant of Message Persuasiveness and Message Comprehensibility," *Journal of Personality and Social Psychology*, vol. 34 (1976), pp. 605–614; S. Chaiken and A.H. Eagly, "Communication Modality as a Determinant of Persuasion: The Role of Communicator Salience," *Journal of Personality and Social Psychology*, vol. 45 (1983), pp. 241–256.

55. J. French and B. Raven, "The Bases of Social Power," in D. Cartwright and A. Zander, eds., *Group Dynamics* (2nd ed.) (Evanston: Row, Peterson, 1962), pp. 607–623; B.H. Raven, "Interpersonal Influence and Social Power," in B.H. Raven and Jeffrey Z. Rubin, *Social Psychology* (New York: John Wiley and Sons, 1983), pp. 399–443; B.H. Raven, "French and Raven 30 Years Later: Power/Interaction and Interpersonal Influence" (Paper presented at the 24th International Congress of Psychology, Sydney, Australia, August, 1988).

KEY TERMS AND CONCEPTS

credibility
expertise
trustworthiness
knowledge bias
reporting bias
communicator similarity
social comparison process
peer appeal
overheard messages
composure
dynamism
extroversion
sociableness
physical attractiveness
celebrity endorsements
match-up hypothesis
opinion leadership
power
informational influence
referent influence
expert influence
legitimate influence
reward influence
coercive influence

CHAPTER 6

SUCCESSFUL PERSUASION: PREDICTING INDIVIDUAL RESPONSE

OUTLINE

Know your receivers. Adapt to your audience. Appeal to the interests of your listeners. One of the most undeniable truths concerning social influence is that speakers must adapt to the interests and needs of an audience in order to be effective. It is also a fact that audience members are often radically different from one another. A message that proves effective to viewers of "Love Connection" fails miserably at influencing viewers tuned to "60 Minutes" or "20/20." A speech that goes over well to high school students bombs with an audience identified as "important local civic leaders." What are the *important* differences between these audiences?

Audience analysis can tell you about many of the identifiable characteristics of an audience. Sometimes, audience analysis is very easy. If you talk to members of a group called MENSA, you will be talking to a group of individuals who have particularly high IQs. It is an obvious, salient characteristic of the group. A group of campus leaders will tend to be intelligent, concerned with achievement, and they are likely to possess high levels of self-esteem. Knowing these facts, how do you go about preparing an effective message?

There is a long history underlying how persuasion scholars have examined *individual differences* in people's reactions to persuasion. In the 1950s scholars investigated the question of whether or not there is one type of person who is generally easy to persuade.[1] There isn't. In 1970, some scholars proclaimed ". . . one of the most consistent and reliable findings in the field of persuasion" is that females are more easily influenced than males.[2] False. In truth, the search for some magical *one* type of easily-persuaded receiver has given way to the assessment of receivers on the basis of multiple *personality* characteristics, as well as *social* and *demographic* characteristics.

Because the operation of "receiver" variables is so important, we have devoted two chapters to the area. Here, we focus on the individual response—the psychology of individual differences.

Included are a number of personality variables called "self-esteem," "intelligence," "anxiety," "dogmatism," "authoritarianism," and "self-monitoring." We then outline the "theory of social judgment" and discuss research focused on the "ego-involved receiver." The following chapter discusses how persuaders attempt to influence groups, including children, mature receivers, women, and various ethnic and social groups.

PERSONALITY VARIABLES

This is the age of Psychological Man. Newspapers carry columns about human behavior, songs try to interpret our behavior, and a number of popular magazines are devoted to the analysis of human behavior. Business and government spend large sums training their personnel in management methods based on psychology. Thus, it is not surprising to find studies indicating that psychological differences between individuals are important in determining the effects of persuasive messages.

The English language contains approximately 18,000 words to help differentiate between people. Some of these words refer to physical differences between individuals, words such as tall, bald, heavy, young, and well-dressed. Others refer to an individual's affective orientation toward some person, such as interested, attentive, angry, fearful, sad, loving, and jealous. Finally, some refer to firmly structured, persisting, cognitively oriented differences in the ways people face the world. We call these structured differences "personality," and use the structures to make predictions about behavior. Of all the terms that characterize humans, which are most important to the area of persuasion? This chapter highlights some of the personality-persuasion relationships, starting with one of primary importance throughout the life-cycle: self-esteem.

Self-Esteem

A person displaying high self-esteem typically appears to be confident, optimistic, and competent. This person displays few feelings of inadequacy, does not feel socially inhibited, and does not exhibit a high degree of anxiety. People with high self-esteem face the world with good impressions of themselves. In contrast, individuals with low self-esteem admit to being anxious in decision-making situations, tend to be pessimistic, may not appear competent, and may not feel confident in social situations. Such individuals are always consulting others before making decisions or taking a position on a topic.

Self-esteem is the liking and respect one has for oneself. Self-esteem, self-regard, self-worth, and self-acceptance are terms often used interchangeably. Another way of viewing self-esteem is to assess a person's perception of the "ideal self" and his or her true, current "self" today. If there is a large discrepancy between current self and ideal self, the person has low self-esteem.

There are several different measures of self-esteem,[3] typically:

1. I feel that I'm a person of worth, at least on an equal basis with others;

2. I feel that I have a number of good qualities;

3. I take a positive attitude toward myself;

4. I'm a lot of fun to be with;

5. Things usually don't bother me;

6. Things are all mixed up in my life;

7. I often wish I were someone else;

8. I can't be depended on;

9. I'm not as nice looking as most people;

10. I get upset easily at home.

Respondents are asked to indicate whether they strongly agree or strongly disagree with each statement (or to indicate whether the statement sounds "like me," or "unlike me").[4] If they agree strongly with each of the first five (positive self-regard) statements, and strongly disagree with the last five (negative self-regard), the respondents possess high self-esteem. We say that a person's score on a questionnaire such as this represents a person's *chronic* or normal level of esteem.

On the other hand, the term *acute* self-esteem is used to refer to situations in which we fail to achieve some important goal, or we experience a major setback (such as, dismally low scores on an SAT, GRE, or LSAT, or a rejection to a job application). Our confidence is shaken by such events, and a series of important setbacks such as these *may* reduce our normal self-esteem. Many high-self-esteem individuals have a number of different *sources* from which esteem is derived— family, friends, romantic partner(s), previous achievements, and so forth. It would take more than one or two setbacks to permanently reduce a highly self-esteemed individual's chronic level of esteem (but it does happen).

High self-esteem is not a view of self that is created or maintained easily. Parents of children with high self-esteem raise them in an atmosphere of acceptance and encouragement; they set clear and well-articulated rules and goals for the children, set positive examples for the children to emulate, and provide high levels of quality stimulation and interaction.[5] Later, in high school, these individuals display less shyness and less depression, while seeking out more extracurricular activities and displaying more confidence and assertiveness.

The fact that high- and low-self-esteemed individuals radically differ in general *styles* of interacting with the environment prompted Cohen[6] to argue that the two differ fundamentally in "ego defenses." Cohen argued that receivers with high self-esteem maintain a high level of self-esteem by using *avoidance defenses*, while low-self-esteemed individuals typically rely on *expressive* defenses. A high-self-esteemed individual will often avoid unfavorable information about the self—preferring to find some excuse for the information's bias. For example, if a high-self-esteemed person participated in a group project that failed to produce a quality product, the individual would blame other group members for not doing their jobs, for being incompetent, or for failing to take the advice of the high-esteem individual. Self-esteem is maintained, in part, because the high-self-esteem individual protects his/her level of esteem by keeping the self away from bad news and failure.

On the other hand, low-esteem individuals pay close attention to what others do and expect, seeking advice, support and identification from others around them. People with chronic low levels of self-esteem lack confidence in their own abilities to make a decision and are anxious about making such decisions. When behaving and when making decisions, low-self-esteemed individuals not only attend to advice from others, they also want approval from others for having made the "correct" decision.

Cohen reviewed studies in which high- or low-self-esteemed individuals were placed in groups that were to give feedback concerning how to complete a task. Half the time, the expectations were easy to follow, and the task easy to achieve. Half the time, the expectations were extremely difficult to follow and the task virtually impossible. Participants were asked, "How important to you is the group's expectations?" High-esteem individuals rated the group's expectations as important only when the expectations were easy to achieve (when the group's expectations would reinforce the view "I am successful"). But the high-self-esteem individuals basically ignored group pressure when the task was difficult to achieve. The results "suggest that persons of high self-esteem better protect themselves against unfavorable evaluation by becoming unresponsive to the expectations communicated by their group when an unfavorable comparison with others would be likely."[7] After sizing up the situation and realizing that the experiment itself wasn't going to reaffirm their positive self-feelings, high-esteem individuals appeared to psychologically withdraw from the event and from the pressure of the group. High self-esteem is maintained.

On the other hand, low-esteem individuals rated group expectations as *more* important when the task was difficult to achieve and failure was imminent than when the task was easy to achieve and success likely. Why? Low-esteem individuals desired very much to have the approval of others, and continued to work harder and harder to achieve a goal that wasn't going to be achieved. Low levels of self-esteem are maintained, in fact, because the individual works so hard to appease others at an unrealistic expectation that will result in failure.

A number of projects in self-esteem and persuasion suggest the following conclusions regarding the general relationship between influence and esteem:[8]

1. High-self-esteemed individuals try to influence others more often than low-self-esteemed individuals;

2. High-self-esteemed individuals are more resistant to influence than are low-self-esteemed individuals; and,

3. Receivers react differently to persuasive appeals.

Obviously, high-self-esteemed individuals are interested in maintaining their level of self-esteem and are well-practiced at protecting this important aspect of their self-evaluation. Thus, informing the high-self-esteemed individual of negative information or information that contradicts a positive view of self will be discounted very easily. It appears to be the case that high-self-esteemed individuals might comply to requests for easy-to-achieve tasks which help to maintain positive esteem. Many diet companies, spas, gyms, and clothing companies do, in fact, appeal to how one can *continue* to look good, and feel good, about oneself by using a particular product, one that is not difficult to learn, nor is very costly.

On the other hand, low-self-esteemed individuals are *generally* more easily influenced than others. However, the low-self-esteemed individual is also much more interested in deriving approval from others and is more compliant to *immediate external pressures*. Advertisements reflecting deflated self-esteem include the famous "ring around the collar." In these ads, a person is blamed for a failure, a significant loved one shows disapproval, as well as the rest of the family, the people who live next door, and the family dog. The person buys a product in the belief that it will secure the approval of loved ones, and bolster his/her level of self-esteem.

SELF-ESTEEM AND SAFETY/HEALTH MESSAGES

Despite the three general rules of thumb listed above, research on health care messages provides a different view of the esteem-influence relationship: Low-esteem receivers are often *less* affected than moderate- or high-self-esteemed individuals when it comes to coping with threats to their health. Why? Low-self-esteemed individuals are poorly adapted to *coping* with the threatening messages about health; they withdraw from such messages, pay less attention when threatening messages are presented, and become fatigued when watching such messages. Note that low-self-esteemed individuals do not *deny* the presence of some threat (being in a car accident or having a heart attack); rather, low-self-esteemed individuals feel inadequate at actually coping with the threat, and are afraid they will not know how to take an appropriate action to resolve the threat.

Indeed, the term "self-efficacy" is used (see section on fear appeals in Chapter 8) to denote a person's perceived ability to resolve a problem or to achieve a goal. High "self-efficacy" means that a person believes s/he has the ability to change a behavior (that is, to stop smoking). Low-self-esteemed individuals, as a group, do not believe that they can effectively break a smoking habit.

Leventhal and Dabbs[9] and Leventhal and Trembly[10] conducted a series of studies which demonstrated that high-self-esteemed individuals were more active copers and thought of more ways to achieve *protective action*, while individuals with low self-esteem were more passive when confronted with health threats and fear appeals. Leventhal and Trembly had receivers watch one of two films: A five-minute *danger anticipation* film in which receivers watched contrived automobile accidents with crash dummies, at 10, 20, 30, and 40 miles per hour, shown at normal and fast speeds; and an *inhibition fear* film that showed wreckage and victims of four different accidents. The color scenes showed demolished cars and close-ups of mutilated bodies and bloody wounds—with moans of the victims audible.

Besides studying the two types of films, Leventhal and Trembly also examined the *intensity of the material*, which involved manipulating the projected image size and the receiver's distance from the screen. Low intensity meant that the individual viewed the movie on a $3 \times 2\frac{1}{2}$-foot screen from a distance of 20 feet. *High* intensity messages were viewed on a screen 13×10 feet, and the receiver sat 12 feet away from the message. After viewing these films, receivers completed a questionnaire concerning their reactions to the films. Four basic types of reactions were assessed by the authors: *proactive action, preventive aggression, bad thoughts, and deactivation responses*. Proactive action is the category of receivers' thoughts on how they plan ahead and take action to prevent automobile accidents. Preventive aggression is receivers' thoughts concerning how they might force other people to become better drivers (such as, in forcing or ordering others to use their seat belts). Bad thoughts include the thoughts receivers have when thinking about terrible or dangerous things that might happen to people in accidents (that is, dwelling on the negative). Finally, deactivation responses are the statements made by receivers indicating a desire to not deal with the problem, a wish or desire to avoid even thinking about being in an accident.

Leventhal and Trembly found that regardless of the film watched, or the intensity of the viewing, low-self-esteemed individuals characteristically showed more passive reactions and reported less ability to cope with the external environment. Specifically, these receivers indicated less ability to *concentrate* on the messages, more *impotency* at taking action, were *withdrawn* from the situation and less *active* in thinking about driving safety. Even more dramatic results were obtained based on intensity of the presentation and receivers' thoughts about protection and prevention, and bad thoughts and deactivation. These results are illustrated in Figure 6.1.

High-self-esteemed receivers indicated substantially more ability to think about protecting themselves from the threat of an accident than all other receivers. Even in the control group (who completed the questionnaire *before* seeing the film), high-esteem individuals thought about how not to be in an accident—and thus increased such plans and thoughts when exposed to intense messages (see panel A). Medium-level-esteem receivers thought little about protection until prompted to do so by the high-intensity messages. However, low-esteem individuals exposed to intense messages generated extremely few thoughts about protection; generating the most thoughts about deactivation their preference was to not think about the problem.

When asked if drivers should be *forced* to be safe, we see that high-self-esteemed individuals agreed with prevention aggression, and did so

across conditions. Both high- and moderate-esteem receivers strongly advocated prevention aggression when exposed to the high-intensity messages. The opposite was true for low-self-esteemed receivers—who thought little about prevention aggression in both the control groups and in response to the high-intensity message—only advocating forcing others to drive more carefully when exposed to the films at low intensity (panel B). For both *bad thoughts* and *deactivation* high- and moderate-self-esteemed receivers responded in identical ways—few thoughts in the control group, increasing to high levels in the intense exposure; high levels of deactivation in the control group, and decreasing to very low levels of deactivation at the high-intensity levels (see Figure 6.1, panels C and D).

However, when low-esteem individuals were exposed to highly intense messages, they thought fewer thoughts about negative situations befalling them, and were substantially more inclined to be "deactive," that is, they did not want to think about being in an accident. In sum, low-self-esteemed individuals are poor copers when it comes to responding to threats to health; they do not rate themselves as potent, they prefer to withdraw, and they indicate difficulty in concentrating on the message. When exposed to intense messages, low-esteem individuals coped less adequately than high- and moderate-esteem individuals and had fewer thoughts about protection and prevention.

Another classic study on self-esteem, by Nisbett and Gordon,[11] also indicated that low-self-esteemed receivers do not deal well with messages that attack health beliefs and habits. Students were exposed to messages about medical topics ("Some Dangerous Effects of X-Rays" and "Some Dangers of Excessive Tooth Brushing"). Some messages contained "unsubstantiated attacks" on health beliefs—meaning that the "persuasive messages" contained only a sentence stating a medical association's alleged views on the topics. The other half of the messages contained

FIGURE **6.1**

ATTITUDE REACTIONS, BAD THOUGHTS, AND DEACTIVATION OF HIGH-, MEDIUM- AND LOW-ESTEEM RECEIVERS

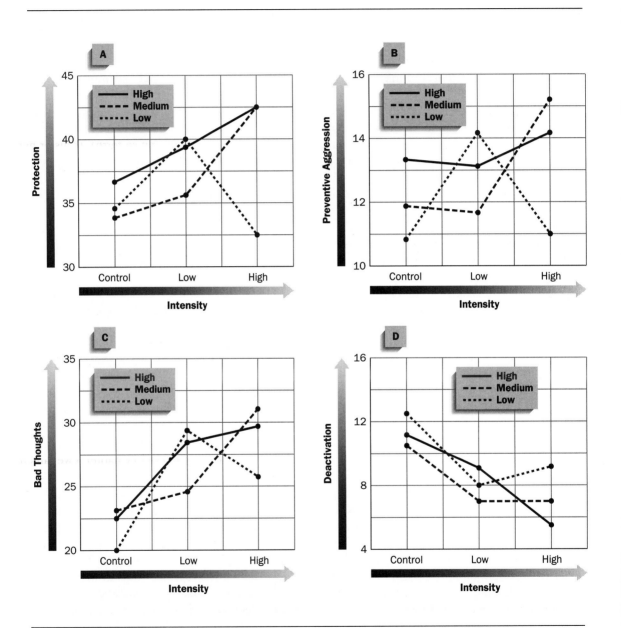

From: H. Leventhal and G. Trembly, "Negative Emotions and Persuasion," *Journal of Personality,* vol. 36 (1968), pp. 154–168. Reprinted by permission of authors and American Psychological Association.

"substantiated attacks," which were 650-word messages that presented material in a logical fashion and appeared to be well-grounded in scientific fact. After being exposed to the written messages, respondents completed a questionnaire dealing with a series of fifteen-point scales asking agreement with various issues—the higher the number, the greater the agreement.

Figure 6.2 shows dramatic results bearing on self-esteem and persuasion. The lowest scorers in self-esteem (the students who scored in the 53 to 94 range, listed at the bottom left of the graphs), were *not* persuaded by either the substantiated message or by the unsubstantiated message attributed to a medical association. As panel A indicates, the receivers who were influenced by the unsubstantiated message were the moderate-self-esteemed receivers. Why? Because the low-self-esteemed individuals presumably withdrew and became inactive, while high-self-esteemed individuals successfully counterargued the unsubstantiated claim—after all, why change a health belief without evidence or facts? As panel B indicates, however, when the receivers read a 650-word message of scientific evidence supporting the change in health belief, both the moderate- and high-self-esteemed receivers changed beliefs, leaving only the low-esteem group inactive and unchanged.

In sum, when it comes to threats concerning one's health and safety, there is little evidence that *low*-self-esteemed individuals are more easily persuaded than high- or moderate-self-esteemed individuals; rather, the opposite is true. High-self-esteemed individuals, who are motivated to maintain continued high, positive self-feelings, are persuaded to adopt safe behaviors and health beliefs when high-intensity messages and/or scientific evidence and facts are employed in the messages. They change their driving habits and health beliefs when sufficiently motivated to do so. However, low-self-esteemed individuals have great difficulty coping with the prospect of altering habits or health concerns.

How, then, do we change the health beliefs of those lowest in self-esteem? In Chapter 8 we discuss in more detail the fact that fear appeals, by themselves, can rarely alter behaviors. Many messages have to be employed over time in order to inform the receiver that a threat is, in fact, real (that he or she is vulnerable to illness, accidents, and so forth), that an effective remedy exists, and that the receiver does have the ability to change a behavior or habit. A low-self-esteemed individual must learn to envision him/herself as capable of successfully engaging a coping response (safe driving, stop smoking, and so forth). If his or her levels of "self-efficacy" cannot be changed, then it is extremely unlikely he or she will change health/safety habits.

Intelligence

Many readers probably think that less-intelligent receivers are more easily persuaded than more-intelligent receivers. However, there is no consistent relationship between intelligence and susceptibility. Some studies have found better-educated and brighter receivers are easier to persuade because they attend, comprehend, and remember more than the less-educated.[12] Other studies found no relationship between intelligence and persuadability.[13] How can such results be explained? Recall in Chapter 3 we talked about McGuire's model of persuasion; underlying persuasion is a specific set of processes of attention, comprehension, retention, and yielding. According to McGuire[14], higher-IQ receivers are more likely to attend, comprehend, and retain message content and arguments, but because they are more intelligent, such receivers are more likely to counterargue and find fault with many messages. Thus, according to McGuire, there may not be any consistent evidence linking IQ to persuasiveness; increased counterargument would cancel out any increases in the high-IQ receiver's

F I G U R E **6.2**

SELF-ESTEEM AND INFLUENCEABILITY FOR UNSUBSTANTIATED ATTACKS (PANEL A) AND FOR SUBSTANTIATED ATTACKS (PANEL B)

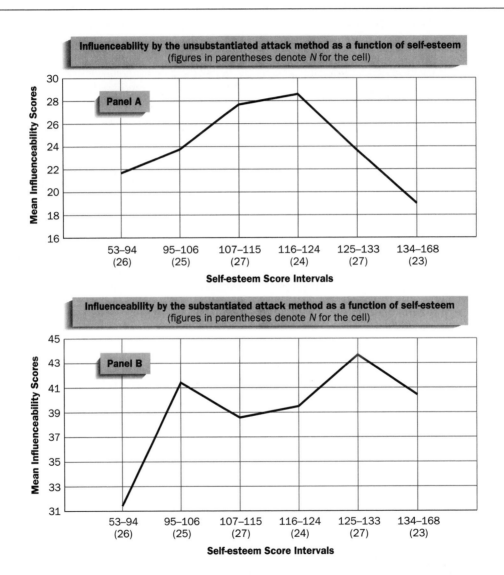

From: R.E. Nisbett and A. Gordon, "Self-Esteem and Susceptibility to Social Influence," *Journal of Personality and Social Psychology,* vol. 5 (1967), pp. 268–276. Reprinted by permission of authors and American Psychological Association.

ability to comprehend and retain more message content.

However, many scholars believe that high-IQ receivers might be strongly influenced only by *strong argument and evidence,* while effectively counterarguing messages containing weak argument. Indeed, Hovland, Janis, and Kelley[15] argued this claim in the early 1960s as a way of accounting for the fact that the more-educated/higher-IQ soldiers who watched the propaganda film *Why We Fight* were more persuaded by the film than the less-educated/lower-IQ soldiers. Earlier studies[16] had demonstrated that the most-intelligent receivers were the least influenced by weak arguments concerning various ethnic, political, and religious groups. Further, Carment, Miles, and Cervin[17] concluded that intelligent + extroverted individuals were more persuasive in face-to-face settings (talking first and most), and were less persuaded by others, relative to the intelligent + introverted individuals, or the less-intelligent individuals who were either introverted or extroverted.

The single most impressive study demonstrating the relationship between mutuality of argument and IQ was conducted by Eagly and Warren.[18] Students' IQ scores were obtained and the students were later exposed to a six-minute tape-recorded message that argued that people brushed their teeth too frequently. Half of the messages employed five strong arguments. Half the messages did not contain any specific facts or arguments; they merely espoused the speaker's unsubstantiated opinions and advice about the topic. These versions were called the "arguments omitted" version. To illustrate what we mean by quality of argument in this situation, we reproduce one of the five arguments:[19]

> The first point is that damage to the gums often results from brushing the teeth as often as many people do. You have probably noticed that brushing the teeth often causes the gums to bleed. Such bleeding obviously indicates some degree of physical injury to the gums. These injuries increase the likelihood of infection. In fact, an article in a medical journal recently concluded that 79 percent of serious gum infections result from accidental injury to the gums inflicted during toothbrushing. Furthermore, repeated injuries of the gums caused by constant toothbrushing can produce mouth cancer. A recent study showed that people with mouth cancer brush their teeth 1.4 times as often as the average person. The danger of cancer is there even though each of the injuries to the gums is only very slight.

After listening to the message, the receivers indicated (1) the extent to which they changed their opinions in order to adopt the speaker's recommendation; (2) the "best recommendation" they believed one should hold about the frequency of brushing; and, (3) the perceived convincingness of the message. The students were also asked to list the arguments they recalled from the message, as well as any of the specific facts from the message. Table 6.1 presents the results—the higher the numbers, the more the receiver agreed with the speaker, rated the speech as convincing and recalled more arguments and facts.

The lowest-IQ group (scoring the lowest third on the IQ inventory) was equally persuaded by the message with arguments omitted as when the arguments were included (see numbers 1.68, 1.67; 3.14 and 3.30 for "best recommendation"). The low-IQ group did rate the arguments-included message as more convincing than the arguments-omitted message. The higher-IQ group rated the arguments-omitted message as substantially less convincing, and high-IQ receivers also recalled more of the arguments and facts; they were not persuaded to change their opinions and to adopt the recommended advice when exposed to the arguments-omitted message. Indeed, the arguments-omitted message produce hardly any change at all on the high-IQ group. High-IQ

MEAN PERSUASION OUTCOMES AS A FUNCTION OF INTELLIGENCE AND ARGUMENTS

Panel A
Mean persuasion as a function of intelligence and arguments

Intelligence Level	Dependent Variable	Arguments Condition	
		Arguments Included	Arguments Omitted
High	Agreement change	2.03	0.46
	Best recommendation	3.24	2.32
	Convincingness	5.51	2.08
Medium	Agreement change	1.56	0.87
	Best recommendation	3.64	2.15
	Convincingness	4.22	1.88
Low	Agreement change	1.68	1.67
	Best recommendation	3.14	3.30
	Convincingness	5.18	3.01

NOTE: *Higher numbers indicate greater persuasion. Agreement change means are differences on the 7-point agreement scale. The best recommendation scale ranged from 1 to 6, and convincingness ratings from 1 to 7.*

Panel B
Mean knowledge of message content as a function of intelligence and arguments

Intelligence Level	Dependent Variable	Arguments condition	
		Arguments Included	Arguments Omitted
High	Arguments	3.88	1.38
	Facts	9.14	4.50
Medium	Arguments	2.50	0.84
	Facts	7.49	3.89
Low	Arguments	1.91	0.32
	Facts	6.31	2.93

NOTE: *Higher numbers indicate greater knowledge with maximum possible range of scores 0–5 on arguments and 0–12 on facts.*
From: A.H. Eagly and R. Warren, "Intelligence, Comprehension and Opinion Change," *Journal of Personality*, vol. 44 (1976), pp. 226–242. Reprinted by permission of authors and American Psychological Association.

receivers also recalled more facts and arguments than did less-intelligent receivers.

The conclusion is obvious: High-IQ receivers pay greater attention than low-IQ receivers to the quality of arguments in messages—they are persuaded only when convincing argument is present in the message, and they recall far more arguments and facts.

Anxiety

One of the factors making up a personality structure is the degree of anxiety exhibited in various situations. Anxiety may be displayed by feelings of tension, apprehension, uncertainty, or panic in everyday encounters with situations and events. The research suggests that people who experience relatively high anxiety levels about decisions are less susceptible to persuasion.

Nunnally and Bobren[20] have shown that persons with high anxiety tend to exhibit low interest in persuasive messages regardless of the message form. Janis and Feshbach[21] and Haefner[22] worked with strong and weak fear appeals in a series of messages and showed that when strong fear appeals are used and the receivers are highly anxious, less persuasion occurs. When weak fear appeals are used, the difference between people high and low in anxiety tends to disappear, but there is still some indication of defensive reactions to the message.

What, then, can be said about persuasion and completely normal levels of anxiety? As mentioned in Chapter 3, regarding McGuire's[23] model of persuasion, if the receiver is already anxious about a topic, increasing anxiety by using fear often results in poor persuasive results; too much anxiety and fear simply make the receiver defensive. On the other hand, if the person has no anxiety at all concerning the issue or topic, some amount of fear or induced levels of anxiety *may*

prompt the receiver to take action, or to change an attitude or behavior.

Also, comprehension levels work differently when one attempts to manipulate complex and simple messages.[24] Complex, difficult-to-understand messages (that is, legal instructions) result in less attitude change when accompanied by high fear because the receiver must contend with both the processing of the material as well as coping with the anxiety about the message.

Petty and Cacioppo[25] conclude that three conditions must be met if anxiety-arousal or fear-arousal is going to be effective. First, a message should provide strong arguments for the possibility that the receiver will suffer some extremely negative consequence unless some action is taken (for example, update one's tetanus shot, get a chest x-ray, or stop smoking). Second, the argument must be made that possible negative consequences are very likely to occur if the recommendations are not followed. Third, the persuasive message must provide strong assurances that if the receiver adopts specific recommendations, he or she can effectively eliminate the negative consequences.

This latter point is important in several ways. First, people who are already anxious about an issue, for example, their health, may take action if they possess specific instructions or knowledge concerning how to reduce anxiety. For instance, Leventhal, Singer, and Jones[26] conducted a study which presented either high or low fear appeals concerning tetanus—recommending that students get a tetanus shot. Further, half of the students received a map which told them very specifically how to go about getting a tetanus shot on the college campus. The results indicated that the fear messages prompted the receivers to worry and to *intend* getting inoculated, but the high-versus-low fear appeal message manipulation was unrelated to actually getting a tetanus shot. However, those individuals who received the specific information and map got more inoculations than students who did not receive this information.

In sum, an effective persuader has to monitor anxiety levels carefully. Too much anxiety will prove ineffective, as receivers become defensive. On the other hand, if anxiety levels are too low, there may be little incentive for receivers to change attitudes or behaviors. Generally speaking, it is practical to provide anxious individuals specific information on how to reduce anxiety, and to provide them with reassurances concerning the effectiveness of ways to reduce anxiety.

Dogmatism

Milton Rokeach and his associates introduced a personality characteristic they refer to as "open-mindedness."[27] They use the terms "closed-minded" and "dogmatic" as synonymous, and suggest that these terms refer to the ways in which individuals tend to approach people, ideas, beliefs, and messages. Dogmatism has been shown to be a pervasive personality trait affecting many aspects of an individual's behavior. Ask yourself if you strongly agree or strongly disagree with statements like:[28]

Most people just don't give a damn for others;

In this complicated world of ours the only way we can know what's going on is to rely on leaders or experts who can be trusted;

The highest form of government is a democracy, and the highest form of democracy is a government run by those who are most intelligent;

Of all the different philosophies which exist in this world, there is probably only one which is correct;

There are two kinds of people in this world—those who are for the truth and those who are against the truth;

Most of the ideas that get printed nowadays are not worth the paper they are printed on.

Individuals who strongly agree with these and similar statements are more dogmatic than individuals who are neutral or who strongly disagree with the statements. The statements themselves show insight into what we mean by the term "dogmatic." The first one taps into a negative view of human nature: people cannot be trusted. The second two tap into the belief that power and control should be given over to trusted, intelligent leaders or experts. The following two statements tap into the categorical thought processes: there is only *one* true philosophy in the world, or only one way of doing things. Finally, the last statements simply reflect the belief that new ideas are worthless. Dogmatic individuals believe that old ways, and traditional and basic values, are preferred over new ideas.

Kirscht and Dillehay[29] argue that the ". . . highly dogmatic person defends himself against anxiety by reliance on authority and sharp, categorical rejection of beliefs not consonant with his/her established values." Dogmatics are fundamentally anxious individuals, and they reduce anxiety by trusting a few leaders and by vigorously (dogmatically) adhering to traditional values, beliefs, stereotypes, and time-tested habits.

Another mode used by the dogmatic person to reduce anxiety is to place great emphasis on order. If all things are placed in their right and correct order, and life is reduced to routines, then a dogmatic character need not worry about change or performance. The need for order and for reducing anxiety is displayed among students, since it appears that dogmatic students prefer large lecture classes (compared to discussion-oriented classes) and prefer objective multiple-choice exams rather than the more-ambiguous essay format.[30]

Although this character is a bit dated, Archie Bunker on the classic situation-comedy "All in the

Family" perfectly characterizes the dogmatic character. He believes what the president says without question, doesn't like new ideas, doesn't like change; he doesn't like the *current* state of the world and he thinks of others not as people (like the Jeffersons), but as members of the stereotypes they represent. This character also shows how such a person lives with discrepancies between beliefs and actions. Archie talked about the importance of the family, but rarely did anything with the family, such as going on picnics, trips, vacations, church, and so on. In one episode, Edith successfully persuaded Archie to go on a family picnic because she appealed to his sense of what a "family" is, and what a "family" is supposed to do.

Dogmatic individuals exhibit five aspects of social behavior relevant to persuasion and influence: (1) stereotypical, categorical thinking and resistance to change; (2) difficulty in integrating information into coherent, holistic belief structures; (3) rejection of new ideas; (4) discounting of logical argument; and, (5) dependence on authority.

The first aspect has been thoroughly investigated.[31] Once the dogmatic individual makes a decision, jumps to a conclusion, or forms a first impression, it is hard to convince the dogmatic individual to change his/her opinion. Even in a group discussion, in fact, a dogmatic individual is likely to adhere stubbornly to original beliefs, withdraw from the group discussion and become isolated—unless an authority figure is used to persuade the dogmatic individual otherwise. A dogmatic person might judge someone as "deviant," "radical," "a threat to tradition," "sick," or "emotionally disturbed" because he/she *thought* the person was a homosexual. Having made this judgment, the dogmatic may later hear that the person wasn't really homosexual, but will still remain suspicious and continue to dislike the person.

This difference between the dogmatic and non-dogmatic individuals is important in a variety of situations: hiring individuals for employment, being on a jury and deciding a person's fate, trusting a salesperson, forming impressions of candidates to vote for, or making first impressions when dating. The dogmatic's first impression of the individual, as one who is "good" or "bad," has lasting effects.

To illustrate the second aspect, the dogmatic's opposite is the open-minded individual, who tends to be able to bring various belief structures together for purposes of comparison. There is little discrepancy in the beliefs held by such an individual. He/she tends to have an optimistic outlook about the way in which the world is put together, will not hold that authorities are absolute determiners of policies, does not believe that decisions made today will hold forever, and tends to view information along a very broad time perspective. The open-minded individual does not compartmentalize beliefs. Open-minded people are more willing to be exposed to controversial materials and are also more expressive about material that might be contrary to their own attitudes.

Relative to the third aspect, the evidence suggests that the open-minded individual is able to relate new ideas to existing reference frames and is able to more easily make adjustments in those frames (open-minded receivers are more creative). Thus, a persuasive message which suggests changes away from the status quo or argues for sweeping changes in the social order ought to be more successful with receivers who are open-minded than with those who are closed-minded. As mentioned previously, the highly dogmatic person holds beliefs and is unwilling to alter those beliefs. However, the highly dogmatic person is especially unwilling to change to a "new" belief or way of doing things. For example, it is inconsistent to believe that smoking causes lung cancer and still continue to smoke. A dogmatic individual might hear new information about a number of negative consequences of smoking, yet dismiss them all as "rhetoric," believing instead the *one* fact that since his/her father didn't experience adverse effects from smoking, neither will he or she. In contrast, we would expect more attitude change from the same message directed toward open-minded receivers (who would be more motivated to integrate the information together, and to assign credibility to the new information).

Because of a combination of the three differences just described between high and low dogmatics, it appears that the highly dogmatic individual differs from the low dogmatic in a number of face-to-face persuasion situations. Druckman found that highly dogmatic individuals are less flexible in bargaining situations than low dogmatics,[32] and Boster and his colleagues found that dogmatics are more likely to use verbal aggression on others—ordering, telling, and commanding others.[33] They do not appear to be open for discussion; rather, they want to find the one true and absolute solution and to end the interaction.

Finally, there is clear evidence that the highly dogmatic individual is heavily dependent on authority figures, discounts the importance of logic, and basically confuses the quality of argument with the authority of the speakers. If an authority whom the dogmatic individual believes in supports a particular position, the dogmatic individual tends to believe that position as well. In a study by Bettinghaus, Miller, and Steinfatt,[34] receivers were asked to judge the logical validity of syllogisms. Some syllogisms had been presented as coming from a source valued positively by the receiver, and some were attributed to negative sources. The results showed that the highly dogmatic subjects made more errors when the syllogisms were attributed to a negative source than to a positive source. The result did not hold true for the individuals classified as "low dogmatic." The more-open-minded individuals tended to evaluate the messages on their own merits, rather than on the recommendations of trusted authorities. In another study, Powell showed that closed-minded individuals had difficulties in separating the ideas

presented in a message from the authorities who supported or rejected the ideas.[35]

Authoritarianism

During World War II and the years that followed, psychologists focused interest on questions such as: Is it possible that there are fascists and people prone to idolizing authorities here in America, as there were in Germany and Italy? How does such a personality come about? What is the nature of the "authoritarian" personality? How many are there? How are they persuaded? Adorno and his colleagues began this research[36], and there are a number of recent books on the topic.[37] Consider the following statements—do you strongly agree or strongly disagree with each one?[38]

Sex crimes, such as rape and attacks on children, deserve more than mere imprisonment; such criminals ought to be publicly whipped, or worse;

What youths need most is strict discipline, rugged determination, and the will to work and fight for family and country;

There is hardly anything lower than a person who does not feel great love, gratitude, and respect for his or her parents;

Every person should have complete faith in some supernatural power whose decisions he obeys without question;

Young people sometimes get rebellious ideas, but as they grow up they ought to get over them and settle down;

Obedience and respect for authority are the most important virtues children should learn;

Homosexuals are hardly better than criminals and ought to be severely punished.

The highly authoritarian individual would more than likely agree with each statement. The highly authoritarian person, like the dogmatic, believes that there is one true way to do something, and believes that a person should do what a leader tells him or her to do.

However, dogmatic and authoritarian individuals differ in how *much* emphasis they place on following leaders; the authoritarian individual is more certain and confident that a person is obligated to follow the directives of trusted authorities. Further, the authoritarian adopts a disciplinary orientation toward child-rearing, believing parents should be strict with their children, and that children should obey, without question, authority figures (parents, police, teachers). Early research indicated that authoritarian parents were strict, creating another generation of authoritarian youngsters who went to school, kept their lockers clean, were modestly popular, were known for their honesty and politeness, and received slightly above-average grades. However, Altemeyer reviewed the literature on parental authoritarianism, child-rearing practices, and children's authoritarianism, and concluded that the evidence for parents' passing down to their children authoritarian tendencies is not as strong today as it may have once been.[39]

Nonetheless, three of the most important differences between dogmatics and authoritarians include: (a) unquestioning obedience to authority; (b) the use of out-groups as "scapegoats" for societal problems, coupled with a belief in a "conspiracy" among political enemies; and, (c) intolerance for out-groups and "deviants."

Basically, people possessing an authoritarian personality tend to be highly reliant on the moral authority of their own reference group, tend to adhere somewhat rigidly to middle-class values, and become preoccupied with the relative power and status of other people, as well as with their own power and status. Such people tend to make absolute judgments regarding the values they hold, and to see the world as black or white. They are not easily swayed by messages that seem to contradict the beliefs they have or the authorities they rely on, despite the judgments of others that the message is rational and logical. Furthermore, the highly authoritarian personality tends to identify with individuals in groups that appear to have power. The authoritarian personality tends to have the same beliefs as the leaders of those groups, and may reject and act prejudiced and hostile toward individuals in other groups.

An analysis of individuals who seem to have highly authoritarian personalities would suggest that their reaction to persuasion will depend on their reactions to factors other than the merits of the ideas presented. Rohrer and Sherif,[40] for example, examined the reactions of individuals to messages about blacks. They report that while individuals who are not high on the authoritarian scales tended to be persuaded by the ideas in the messages they read, the high authoritarians tended to be persuaded by the authorities presented in the messages. This was true for the high authoritarians regardless of whether the message they read was pro-black or anti-black. The controlling factor seemed to be the dependence of high authoritarians on the infallibility of the authority figures cited in the messages. The high authoritarian, then, seems to be highly reliant on the authority dimension of the belief structure, and links beliefs about authorities to peripheral beliefs.

Harvey and Beverly[41] found that high authoritarians changed opinions in the direction of the position advocated by a high status source significantly more so than did low authoritarians. However, high authoritarians could not recall the arguments in the speech with the same degree of accuracy as could the low authoritarians. Again, the results indicate that high authoritarians emphasize *who* is speaking, not *what* is said.

The authors of the book *The Authoritarian Personality* suggest that prejudice can be explained, in part, as a reaction against an "out-group." For high authoritarians, complete confidence and total trust is placed only in members of the groups to which they belong. Other groups are rejected, and rejected in such ways that negative actions are taken against members of the out-groups. It is common, in fact, for the authorities trusted by the authoritarian individuals to sanction certain "out-group" feelings and hostility by blaming various groups for social problems. Groups of homosexuals, African-American rioters, Hispanic migrant workers, Puerto Rican, Jamaican, or Vietnamese refugees, and Japanese executives are explicitly blamed for the decay in a strong America. Once these out-groups are blamed for causing problems, it is easy for the authoritarian personality to seek ways of punishing them.

Authoritarians hand out *more* severe punishments to "out-group" members in our legal system who are identified as either different in terms of ethnicity or values, or who are identified as "sex offenders." Hence, rapists receive longer prison sentences by high authoritarians (compared to low authoritarians), but high authoritarians give *lighter* sentences to police (authority figures) who were charged with police brutality.[42] Authoritarians require less evidence to convict someone (especially in murder cases), and give harsher sentences than low authoritarians.[43] There also is evidence that authoritarians reinforce each other during jury deliberations by becoming even harsher when they realize that other authoritarian jurors also prefer harsh sentences (that is, groups of authoritarians give harsher sentences than juries with a mix of low and high authoritarians). This jury bias is reversed, however, if the defendant is an authority (police officer) or if the defendant claims to have "followed orders."[44] Authoritarians are also less offended when the government violates the rights of the individual (illegal wiretaps, and so forth) while low authoritarianism would emphasize the importance of constitutional rights.[45]

As in the case of the dogmatic receiver, the importance of authoritarianism in persuasion to-day may rest in the area of politics or voting. However, persuasion and legal experts are also very much interested in the legal implications of the authoritarian character. To open-minded legal experts, it is disheartening that some authoritarians would give away constitutional rights to privacy and free speech so that the government would work more efficiently (as in Mussolini's Italy and Hitler's Germany). Conversely, the extremely low authoritarians (the "anti-authority" individuals) might give lighter sentences in any number of cases involving constitutional rights, the rights of the defendant, or they may question the authority of police or other authorities who are witnesses. Fortunately, it does appear that extra-legal biases might be reduced when lawyers emphasize the fact that the evidence is reliable and strong, and/or legal instructions specify the precise limits on sentencing that are allowed for a given crime.[46]

Need for Achievement

McClelland and his associates[47] have been working for years to clarify a personality variable they refer to as "need for achievement" or "n-achievement." McClelland measures n-achievement by having people write short essays about pictures of individuals working and talking with other people. Essays are scored for the number of "achievement" themes in the subject's description of the situation.[48] The replies an individual makes indicate rank on the n-achievement scale.

McClelland's work has been extended in many different directions. Recently, Atkinson and his colleagues[49] have examined the need for achievement in organizations. Persons with a high need for achievement typically seek out more-challenging jobs, desire to accept responsibility for decision-making, and want to receive feedback to improve their performance. Steers and Spencer[50] found persons with a need for achievement performed better when their jobs were rich in responsibility, variety, feedback, and autonomy, while people low in need for achievement did not improve in performance as job richness increased.

Individuals who possess a high need for achievement in our society tend to be entrepreneurs, always trying to improve themselves by their own personal efforts. Lower socio-economic class families tend to produce more individuals who score low on n-achievement, but so do families from the upper classes. High n-achievement is a characteristic of middle-class parents and middle-class children. This does not mean that other individuals will not exhibit high n-achievement, but the trait is found more frequently among the middle class, who aspire to achieve more and to possibly gain access to the next rung on the ladder of success and social class.

The relationship between the n-achievement variable and persuasability seems to lie in the nature of the topics chosen for persuasion and the appeals used in the message. Message topics that seem to promise, in specific terms, how the receiver can advance in personal status, economic condition, or power have a special appeal for the receiver scoring high in n-achievement. On the other hand, we might expect that topics proposing that the receiver give up something for the benefit of society might not be successful with the person who is very high in n-achievement.

Regrettably, we do not know much about n-achievement and use of radio and television, although it is easy to imagine that those high-need achievers subscribe to daily newspapers and probably a number of magazines relevant to their occupations and aspiring social class status. Compatible with the theory of n-achievement is the idea that these receivers would be watching a substantial number of news shows like "60 Minutes," "20/20," and "48 Hours." Indeed, a number of achievement-oriented advertisements (how to buy stocks, use a computer, increase profits, and

own a cellular phone) are shown during these programs (along with the evening news), because high n-achievement people are likely to be viewing them in contrast to game shows and situation comedies.

Self-Monitoring

The "Self-Monitoring" construct is an individual difference variable that separates persons into two types: high self-monitors and low self-monitors. The high self-monitor is pragmatic and behaves strategically and appropriately in order to obtain desired outcomes, regulating public expressions and monitoring self-presentations for the sake of creating and maintaining desired public appearances. The low self-monitoring individual behaves in accordance with his/her own attitudes, feelings and values. The low self-monitor desires to be "true to oneself," and behaves in public according to his or her beliefs about the self. The high self-monitor wants to make a desirable public image for all the different audiences s/he wants to impress. The high self-monitor is a "social chameleon" and adapts strategically to audiences.[51]

Are these statements true or false of how you view yourself?

I have considered being an entertainer.

I'm not always the person I appear to be.

I may deceive people by being friendly when I really dislike them.

I guess I put on a show to impress or entertain others.

I can make impromptu speeches even on topics about which I have almost no information.

A person who is a *high* self-monitor would indicate that these statements are true of him or her, while a *low* self-monitor would say these statements are false. These statements tap only one aspect of the self-monitoring construct: *Acting ability*. Besides being good actors, high self-monitoring individuals are also more *extroverted* and *other-directed* (that is, they pay attention to what others are doing around them).

There are several key areas of behavior that differentiate high and low self-monitors, the eighth bearing directly on the issue of persuasion:

1. When interacting with others, high self-monitors focus on reading and interpreting what is occurring around them, and they do so in order to aid them in choosing how to make their own self-presentations during an encounter. They are also likely to attend to information useful for making (a) inferences concerning others' intentions, and, (b) predictions about what others will do. Low self-monitors, however, behave in ways compatible with their notions of their "true self," and accept people at face value.

2. High self-monitors display high levels of acting ability, flexibility, and adaptability; they are skilled "impression managers." High self-monitors have learned to provide presentations of the self appropriate for situations in which they find themselves. Doing so, however, means that high self-monitors rarely communicate information or self-disclosures about their private beliefs, feelings, and intentions. Low self-monitors, however, present themselves in public in ways that reflect their true, authentic attitudes, values, and beliefs.

3. During conversations, high self-monitors are more highly motivated to work on ensuring that the conversation is smooth and flowing, prompting other conversationalists to talk about themselves, conveying an immediate sense of closeness or intimacy (saying "we," "us," "our," and "ours"), using humor, reciprocating self-disclosures, and employing other skills in order to "lubricate" a smooth-flowing conversation.[52]

4. High and low self-monitors differ radically in the types of situations and goals that they engage in. High self-monitors typically select specific friends for particular activities, and usually only for those selected activities. For example, high self-monitors have certain friends with whom they play golf, and these may be different from their tennis partners or the people they go out dancing with. Low self-monitors, however, share a wide range of activities with the same group of friends; a "best" friend is a person they have many activities with, or, sometimes, a group of acquaintances do almost all of their leisure activities together.

When asked to list people for leisure activities, low self-monitors indicate that they engage in activities with the people they like. High self-monitors prefer to engage in activities with experts, thereby comparing themselves with experts and improving on skills.

5. When selecting casual friends and close friends, low self-monitors prefer other low self-monitors. High self-monitors prefer to have low self-monitors as casual friends, and other high self-monitors as close friends. Presumably, high self-monitors feel more comfortable with other people who understand them and who prefer a life of diversity. However, since friendships are intimately linked to specific activities, it is easier for the high self-monitor to replace friends to play tennis with or dance with. As the high self-monitor improves in skills and gains on better players, he or she "trades up" to better experts.

7. When selecting dates, high self-monitoring males spend more time studying, and place greater emphasis on, a potential date's physical characteristics; in fact, when given the choice, the high self-monitoring male would select a date with a beautiful woman, even after she was described

TABLE 6.2

PRICE WILLING TO PAY FOR PRODUCTS BY HIGH AND LOW SELF-MONITORING CONSUMERS

Type of Advertisement	Self-Monitoring	
	High	Low
Canadian Club		
Image-oriented	$9.75	$7.50
Quality-product	8.24	8.64
Barclay		
Image-oriented	.89	.74
Quality-product	.89	.94
Irish Mocha Mint		
Image-oriented	3.43	2.97
Quality-product	3.28	3.50

Range for Canadian Club was $5 to $15; range for Barclay was $0.50 to $1.50; range for Irish Mocha Mint was $2 to $5.

SOURCE: M. Snyder and K.G. DeBono, "Appeals to Image and Claims About Quality: Understanding the Psychology of Advertising," *Journal of Personality and Social Psychology*, vol. 49 (1985), pp. 586–597. Used with permission.

as "moody, withdrawn, and self-centered."[53] Low self-monitoring men focus more attention on the potential date's psychological characteristics rather than on her physical attributes. High self-monitors date exclusively for briefer periods of time (relative to low self-monitors), date more different people per year, have sex with more people in a year, and have more one-night stands than do low self-monitors. The relatively low level of "commitment" on the part of the high self-mon-itoring individual means that it is easier for him/her to de-escalate or terminate one relationship, while starting new ones at his/her leisure.[54] Low self-monitors adopt a committed orientation in dating relationships.

8. Given that high self-monitors are preoccupied with public images, it is not surprising that high self-monitors are suckers for "image advertising." Part of the personality involves attending to public behaviors, public images, and engaging in appropriate public behaviors; thus, high self-monitors tune in, attend to, and are persuaded by adver-tisements that convey images of fun, status, excitement, glamour, or sex appeal. Low self-monitors are, generally speaking, influenced by claims about the *quality* of the product, or by being a "good buy" for the money. For instance, 59 percent of low self-monitors indicated that they believed generic products were just as good as name-brand products, while only 42 percent of the high self-monitors expressed such a belief.[55]

Snyder and DeBono[56] conducted a series of studies dealing with self-monitoring and advertising, supporting the claim that highs are influenced by image-advertising, while low self-monitoring people are influenced by appeals focusing on the quality of the product. Students scoring high or low in self-monitoring were presented with a series of print advertisements. The *image-oriented* version of a product (say, Canadian Club) displayed the bottle of Canadian Club resting on a set of house blueprints, and the words said: "You're not just moving in, you're moving up." In the *product-quality* claim, the ad claimed: "When it comes to great taste, everyone draws the same conclusion." Image-oriented and product-quality claims were made for two other products as well: Barclay cigarettes and Irish Mocha Mint coffee).

Snyder and DeBono found that low self-mon-itoring individuals would pay far less for products when they were advertised on the basis of image. As indicated in Table 6.2, the low self-monitors were willing to spend money for quality. Snyder and DeBono also expected that high self-monitors would be willing to pay more when the image-oriented advertisement was employed, compared to the quality advertisement. This expectation was not confirmed for the Barclay ad (see Table 6.2). However, high self-monitors were willing to pay more when the other image-oriented advertisements were employed, especially the Canadian Club product (image-oriented, $9.75; quality-product, $8.24).

How do you persuade high self-monitors? Appeal to image—images of glamour, success, sex, and so forth. How do you persuade low self-monitors? Quality and good value.

SOCIAL JUDGMENT THEORY AND THE EGO-INVOLVED RECEIVER

Imagine the following incident: You have to give a persuasive speech in your speech class, and you decide to pick a topic you believe to be safe. You give a speech in which you argue that the state should not change the current drinking age. After all, you argue, eighteen-year-olds are old enough to fight in a war, vote, and pay taxes, and should therefore be treated as adults and allowed to drink alcohol. You conclude that alcoholic beverages should continue to be available, in limited quantities, to eighteen- to twenty-one-year-olds—"this is America, and they have their rights, too." Since the class includes many college-age students, you think that you selected a safe topic. However, almost immediately at the end of your speech, a person stands up to announce that she is co-chairperson of the local chapter of MADD (Mothers Against Drunk Driving), and states that her daughter was hit by a drunk teenage driver five years ago. She further discloses she has led

sign-carrying protesters through the grounds at the State Capitol, has personally lobbied with the governor, and helped to establish two chapters of M.A.D.D. in her part of the state. Finally, she turns to announce that she vehemently disagrees with "everything" you just said. "When it comes to alcoholic beverages, too many youths are immature."

Needless to say, you are not particularly pleased about this occurrence. After all, you felt that you were arguing a fairly neutral position. Chances are, the person from the class was *ego-involved* concerning this particular issue.

Sherif, Sherif, and Nebergall's[57] theory of ego-involvement is a classic theory of attitude change. The theory is also called "social judgment theory" or "assimilation-contrast theory." According to this theory, a person's attitude on a topic can be measured by using a *reference scale*. This scale includes a representative set of statements concerning attitudes on a topic, where the statements can be ordered from extremely favorable to extremely unfavorable. Figure 6.3 provides an example of a reference scale used in research on the use of alcohol and its potential for being banned in Oklahoma.

Respondents are asked to place an "X" through statements they find unacceptable, to put a circle around statements they find acceptable, and to underline the one statement that best reflects their own attitude. The first step identifies the latitude of rejection, and the second step identifies the latitude of acceptance.[58] (If any statements are left blank, they are referred to as the latitude of noncommitment.)

The theory holds that the latitudes of rejection and acceptance, and one's chosen statement, tell us a good deal about the receiver. First, if a person had an extremely wide latitude of rejection (say, rejecting all statements C to I in Figure 6.3) and had a narrow latitude of acceptance (only statement A was included as an acceptable position), then we call the person ego-involved. This

EXAMPLE OF REFERENCE SCALE USED IN RESEARCH ON EGO INVOLVEMENT

A. Since alcohol is the curse of mankind, the sale and use of alcohol, including light beer, should be completely abolished.

B. Since alcohol is the main cause of corruption in public life, of lawlessness, and immoral acts, its sale and use should be prohibited.

C. Since it is hard to stop at a reasonable moderation point in the use of alcohol, it is safer to discourage its use.

D. Alcohol should not be sold or used except as a remedy for snake bites, cramps, colds, fainting, and other aches and pains.

E. The arguments in favor and against the sale and use of alcohol are nearly equal.

F. The sale of alcohol should be so regulated that it is available in limited quantities for special occasions.

G. The sale and use of alcohol should be permitted with proper state controls, so that the revenue from taxation may be used for the betterment of schools, highways, and other state institutions.

H. Since prohibition is a major cause of corruption in public life, of lawlessness, immoral acts, and juvenile delinquency, the sale and use of alcohol should be legalized.

I. It has become evident that man cannot get along without alcohol; therefore, there should be no restriction whatsoever on its sale and use.

Source: C.I. Hovland, O.J. Harvey and M. Sherif, "Assimilation and Contrast Effects in Reactions to Communication and Attitude Change," *Journal of Abnormal and Social Psychology*, vol. 55 (1957), pp. 244–252. Used with permission.

person finds all counterattitudinal positions unacceptable, also finds neutrality unacceptable, and feels that only a limited selection of statements can be tolerated. Such people feel strongly about the topic, have set ideas, and are closed-minded

when it comes to new ideas on the matter. In fact, the anti-alcohol student in your speech class may very well have such an attitude. On the other hand, a person who rejects only statements H and I and finds statements A to E acceptable is less ego-involved, more open to discussion, and is easier to persuade.

Second, according to this theory a person's own position represents an anchor or a reference point which the person uses when perceiving all statements and messages he or she receives on the topic. In fact, this theory argues that when we compare messages we receive to the reference point, we distort the placement of the messages in systematic ways. For example, a person is said to assimilate a message by perceiving it closer to his or her anchor than is actually the case. Contrast effects occur when a person perceives a message as further from his/her anchor than is the case. Generally speaking, the more ego-involved a person becomes, the greater the likelihood that assimilation and/or contrast effects will occur.

There are two major ways in which attention to ego-involvement is useful to persuaders. First, there is considerable evidence that politicians *purposefully* employ ambiguity in their messages so that they appear to be attractive to more of the electorate. That is, politicians who are liked, generally speaking, can maintain an ambiguous, middle-of-the-road campaign so that more and more potential voters will assimilate their positions. Granberg,[59] in fact, lists several specific examples of the operation of the principle of ambiguity:

1. When Bill Brock, the ... Republican national chairman, ran for the Senate in 1970, his billboards read, "Bill Brock Believes." His speeches were about as informative, and before long, he was being attacked for running an empty, issueless campaign. So he promised he would spell out his message more fully before election day. And he kept that promise. With three weeks left in the campaign, the billboards

blossomed with a new slogan: "Bill Brock Believes What We Believe."[60]

2. Carter and Ford are hardly charismatic figures, but experience has taught politicians that it is unwise to sharpen the issues too much. Nixon said almost nothing in 1972 and got a landslide over McGovern, who tried to be specific; so did Stevenson and Goldwater—they got clobbered, too. Our system puts a premium on ambiguity.[61]

The second implication of the work on ego-involvement is that it is extremely difficult to persuade the ego-involved person. As Sereno and Bodaken[62] noted, one needs to prompt the ego-involved person to engage in a good deal of attitudinal restructuring in order for persuasion to occur. Initially, the persuader needs to get the ego-involved person to reduce his/her latitude of rejection and to expand his/her latitude of non-commitment. Then, the person needs to expand his or her latitude of acceptance. No single message can achieve all of these changes, which is not surprising, if one considers how it is that the ego-involved person became ego-involved. According to Miller[63] a minimum of four variables serve as the cause of ego-involvement:

1. The issue has to be perceived as important, and as having important consequences. Protecting the environment, fighting communism, ending racism, eliminating child abuse, reducing accidents caused by drunk drivers, fighting for equal rights, ending abortions, keeping abortions legal, and purging the country of undesirables are some of the issues on which people become ego-involved.

2. The individual has social support from others. People with similar interests join groups, hold rallies, read publications, and generally contact and socialize with friends who agree with their views on the issue at hand. In our opinion, the creation of ego-involvement is further reinforced when individuals in these groups experience conflict with an opposing group and the hostility and animosity breed a "we" versus "they" competition and rivalry, thus creating and maintaining a polarization of attitudes.

3. An individual rehearses or practices at supporting arguments for the issue at hand.

4. The individual is *publicly committed* to the cause in the sense that s/he has distributed literature, walked picket lines, written letters, signed petitions, and let the public know her/his stand on the issue. If the individual has convinced friends and family members to join the movement, we expect increased commitment to the cause.

It is difficult to study ego-involvement on a college campus because students vary considerably in attitudes and are not in universal agreement on any single ego-involving topic. It is also difficult to manipulate ego-involvement in a laboratory context. Instead, the clearest examples of people displaying ego-involvement are "intact" groups who meet weekly or monthly in the pursuit of some goal (change the laws on alcohol use, environmental protection, taxes, and so on). The persuader should realize that such receivers are likely to assimilate or contrast a message, and that changing their views is a very difficult task.

F O O T N O T E S

1. C.I. Hovland and I.L. Janis, eds., *Personality and Persuasability* (New Haven, Conn.: Yale University Press, 1959).

2. M. Karlins and H.I. Abelson, *Persuasion: How Opinions and Attitudes are Changed*, 2nd ed. (New York: Springer-Verlag, 1970), p. 89.

3. J.P. Robinson and P.R. Shaver, *Measures of Social and Psychological Attitudes*, rev. ed. (Ann Arbor, Mich.: Institute for Social Research, 1991).

4. Example items are from two popularly used inventories: S. Coopersmith, *The Antecedents of Self-Esteem* (San Francisco, Calif.: W.H. Freeman and Associates, 1967); M. Rosenberg, *Society and the Adolescent Self-Image*

(Princeton, N.J.: Princeton University Press, 1965).

5. See Coopersmith, *The Antecedents of Self-Esteem.* Concerning high school students, see: Rosenberg, *Society and the Adolescent Self-Image.* For more recent material on self-esteem and children, see: M.V. Covington, *Making the Grade: A Self-Worth Perspective on Motivation and School Reform* (Cambridge, England: Cambridge University Press, 1992).

6. A.R. Cohen, "Some Implications of Self-Esteem for Social Influence," in C.I. Hovland and I.L. Janis, eds., *Personality and Persuasability* (New Haven, Conn.: Yale University Press, 1959), pp. 102–120.

7. Cohen, "Some Implications of Self-Esteem for Social Influence," p. 114.

8. F.J. DiVesta and J.C. Merwin, "The Effects of Need-Oriented Communications on Attitude Change: *Journal of Abnormal and Social Psychology,* vol. 60 (1960), pp. 80–85; I.L. Janis, "Personality Correlates of Susceptibility to Persuasion," *Journal of Personality,* vol. 22 (1954), pp. 504–518; G.R. Miller and M. Burgoon, *New Techniques of Persuasion* (New York: Harper and Row, 1973), pp. 21–23.

9. J.M. Dabbs, "Self-Esteem, Communicator Characteristics, and Attitude Change," *Journal of Abnormal and Social Psychology,* vol. 69 (1964), pp. 173–181; J.M. Dabbs and H. Leventhal, "Effects of Varying the Recommendations in a Fear-arousing Communication," *Journal of Personality and Social Psychology,* vol. 4 (1966), pp. 525–531. Also see: H. Leventhal, "Findings and Theory in the Study of Fear Communications," in L. Berkowitz, ed., *Advances in Experimental Social Psychology,* vol. 5, (New York: Academic Press, 1970), pp. 119–186.

10. H. Leventhal and G. Trembly, "Negative Emotions and Persuasion," *Journal of Personality and Social Psychology,* vol. 36 (1968), pp. 154–168.

11. R.E. Nisbett and A. Gordon, "Self-Esteem and Susceptibility to Social Influence," *Journal of Personality and Social Psychology,* vol. 5 (1967), pp. 268–279.

12. I.L. Janis and D. Rife, "Persuasability and Emotional Disorder," in I.L. Janis and C.I. Hovland, eds., *Personality and Persuasability* (New Haven, Conn.: Yale University Press, 1959), pp. 121–137; C.I. Hovland, A.A. Lumsdaine, and F.D. Sheffield, *Experiments on Mass Communication,* (Princeton, N.J.: Princeton University Press, 1949).

13. L. Wheeless, "The Effects of Comprehension Loss on Persuasion," *Speech Monographs,* vol. 39 (1971), pp. 327–330.

14. W.J. McGuire, "Personality and Attitude Change: An Information-processing Theory," in A.G. Green-

wald, T.C. Brock, and T.M. Ostrom, eds., *Psychological Foundations of Attitudes,* (New York: Academic, 1968), pp. 171–196.

15. C.I. Hovland, I.L. Janis, and H. Kelley, *Communication and Persuasion* (New Haven, Conn.: Yale University Press, 1953).

16. H. Wegrocki, "The Effect of Prestige Suggestibility on Emotional Attitudes," *Journal of Social Psychology,* vol. 5 (1934), pp. 384–394; cited in C.I. Hovland and G. Lindzey, eds., *Handbook of Social Psychology,* vol. 2 (Cambridge, Mass.: Addison-Wesley, 1954); also cited in M. Karlins and H.I. Abelson, *Persuasion: How Opinions and Attitudes are Changed.*

17. D. Carment, C. Miles, and V. Cervin, "Persuasiveness and Persuasability as Related to Intelligence and Extraversion," *British Journal of Social and Clinical Psychology,* vol. 4 (1965), pp. 1–7.

18. A.H. Eagly and R. Warren, "Intelligence, Comprehension, and Opinion Change," *Journal of Personality,* vol. 44 (1976), pp. 226–242.

19. Eagly and Warren, "Intelligence, Comprehension, and Opinion Change," p. 231.

20. J.C. Nunnally and H.M. Bobren, "Variables Governing the Willingness to Receive Communications on Mental Health," *Journal of Personality,* vol. 27 (1959), pp. 275–90.

21. I.L. Janis and F. Feshbach, "Effects of Fear-arousing Communications," *Journal of Abnormal and Social Psychology,* vol. 49 (1954), pp. 211–18.

22. D.P. Haefner, "Some Effects of Guilt-arousing and Fear-arousing Persuasive Communications on Opinion Change," (Ph.D. dissertation, University of Rochester, 1956).

23. W.J. McGuire, "The Nature of Attitudes and Attitude Change," in G. Lindzey and E. Aronson, eds., *The Handbook of Social Psychology,* vol. 3., (Reading, Mass.: Addison-Wesley, 1969), pp. 136–314.

24. S. Millman, "The Relationship between Anxiety, Learning, and Opinion Change" (Unpublished doctoral dissertation, Department of Psychology, 1965); S. Millman, "Anxiety, Comprehension, and Susceptibility to Social Influence," *Journal of Personality and Social Psychology,* vol. 9 (1968), pp. 251–256.

25. R.E. Petty and J.T. Cacioppo, *Attitudes and Persuasion: Classic and Contemporary Approaches,* (Dubuque, Iowa: Wm. C. Brown, 1981).

26. H. Leventhal, R. Singer, and S. Jones, "Effects of Fear and Specificity of Recommendation upon Attitudes and Behavior," *Journal of Personality and Social Psychology,* vol. 2 (1965), pp. 20–29.

27. M. Rokeach, *The Open and Closed Mind* (New York: Basic Books, 1960).

28. Example items are from Robinson and Shaver, *Measures of Social Psychological Attitudes;* specifically: V. Troldahl and F. Powell, Short Dogmatism Scale, *Social Forces,* vol. 44 (1965), pp. 211–214.

29. J.P. Kirscht and R.C. Dillehay, *Dimensions of Authoritarianism: A Review of Research and Theory,* Lexington, Ky.: University of Kentucky Press, 1967), p. 46.

30. Kirscht and Dillehay, *Dimensions of Authoritarianism.*

31. See: Rokeach, *The Open and Closed Mind;* R. Vacchiano, P. Strauss, and L. Hockman, "The Open and Closed Mind: A Review of Dogmatism," *Psychological Bulletin,* vol. 71, no. 4 (1969), p. 261.

32. D. Druckman, "Dogmatism, Prenegotiation Experience, and Simulated Group Representation As Determinants of Dyadic Behavior in Bargaining Situations," *Journal of Personality and Social Psychology,* vol. 6 (1967), pp. 279–290.

33. F.J. Boster, and J.B. Stiff, "Compliance-Gaining Message Selection Behavior," *Human Communication Research,* vol. 10 (1984), pp. 539–556; D.L. Williams and F.J. Boster, "The Effects of Beneficial Situational Characteristics, Negativism and Dogmatism on Compliance-Gaining Message Strategy Selection." (Paper presented to the International Communication Association convention, Minneapolis, Minnesota, 1981).

34. E.P. Bettinghaus, T. Steinfatt, and G. Miller, "Source Evaluation, Syllogistic Content, and Judgments of Logical Validity by High- and Low-Dogmatic Persons," *Journal of Personality and Social Psychology,* vol. 16, (1970), pp. 238–44.

35. F.A. Powell, "Open- and Closed-Mindedness and the Ability to Differentiate Source and Message," *Journal of Abnormal and Social Psychology,* vol. 65 (1962), pp. 61–4.

36. T.W. Adorno and others, *The Authoritarian Personality,* (New York: Harper and Row, 1950).

37. B. Altemeyer, *Right-Wing Authoritarianism* (Manitoba, Canada: University of Manitoba, 1981).

38. Altemeyer, *Right-Wing Authoritarianism,* p. 18.

39. Altemeyer, *Right-Wing Authoritarianism.*

40. J.H. Rohrer and M. Sherif, *Social Psychology at the Crossroads,* (New York: Harper and Row, Publishers, 1951).

41. O.J. Harvey and G.D. Beverly, "Some Personality Correlates of Concept Change through Role Playing," *Journal of Abnormal and Social Psychology,* vol. 63 (1961), pp. 125–30.

42. I.H. Paul, "Impressions of Personality, Authoritarianism, and the Fait Accompli Effect," *Journal of Abnormal and Social Psychology,* vol. 53 (1956), pp. 338–44.

43. W. Weiss, "Emotional Arousal and Attitude Change," *Psychological Review,* vol. 6 (1960), pp. 267–80.

44. Altemeyer, *Right-Wing Authoritarianism;* concerning the "scapegoat theory," also see D. Bar-Tal, C.F. Graumann, A.W. Kruglanski, and W. Stroebe, eds., *Stereotyping and Prejudice: Changing Conceptions* (New York: Springer-Verlag, 1989).

45. R. Bray and A. Noble, "Authoritarianism and Decisions of Mock Juries: Evidence of Jury Bias and Group Polarization," *Journal of Personality and Social Psychology,* vol. 36 (1978), pp. 1424–30; V.P. Hans and N. Vidmar, "Jury Selection," in N.L. Kerr and R.M. Bray, eds., *The Psychology of the Courtroom* (New York: Academic Press, 1982), pp. 39–82.

46. V.L. Hamilton "Obedience and Responsibility: A Jury Simulation," *Journal of Personality and Social Psychology,* vol. 36 (1978), pp. 126–46; Hans and Vidmar (Note 45).

47. Altemeyer, *Right-Wing Authoritarianism.*

48. M.F. Kaplan and L.E. Miller, "Reducing the Effects of Juror Bias," *Journal of Personality and Social Psychology,* vol. 36 (1978), pp. 1443–55; M.F. Kaplan, "Cognitive Processes in the Individual Juror," in N.L. Kerr and R.M. Bray, eds., *The Psychology of the Courtroom* (New York: Academic Press, 1982), pp. 197–220; also consult: S.M. Kassin and L.S. Wrightsman, eds., *The Psychology of Evidence and Trial Procedure* (Newbury Park, Calif.: Sage, 1985).

49. For a review of n-achievement, see: D. McClelland and others, *The Achievement Motive* (New York: Appleton-Century-Crofts, 1953), and D. McClelland, *The Achieving Society* (Princeton, N.J.: D. VanNostrand Co., 1961).

50. T.G. Harris, "Achieving Man: A Conversation with David C. McClelland," *Psychology Today,* vol. 4, no. 8 (January 1971), p. 36.

51. See: J.W. Atkinson, *Motives in Fantasy, Action and Society* (Princeton, N.J.: VanNostrand, 1958). Also see: J.D. Andrews, "The Achievement Motive and Advancement in Two Types of Organizations," *Journal of Personality and Social Psychology,* vol. 6 (1967), pp. 163–168; R.M. Steers, "Effects of Need for Achievement on the Job Performance-Job Attitude Relationship, *Journal of Applied Psychology,* vol. 60, (1975), pp. 678–82; R.M. Steers, "Task-Goal Attributes, N Achievement, and Supervisory Performance," *Organizational Behavior and Human Performance,* vol. 13 (1975), pp. 392–403.

52. R.M. Steers and D.G. Spencer, "The Role of Achievement Motivation in Job Design," *Journal of Applied Psychology*, vol. 62 (1977), pp. 472–79. Quote from page 476.

53. See, in particular: M. Snyder and K.G. DeBono, "Appeals to Image and Claims About Quality: Understanding the Psychology of Advertising," *Journal of Personality and Social Psychology*, vol. 49 (1985), pp. 586–597. Concerning background on this personality construct, and a recent review, see: S.W. Smith, M.J. Cody, S. LoVette, and D.J. Canary, "Self-Monitoring, Gender, and Compliance-Gaining Goals," in M.J. Cody and M.L. McLaughlin, eds., *The Psychology of Tactical Communication* (Clevedon, England: Multilingual Matters, Ltd., 1990), pp. 91–135; D.J. Canary and M.J. Cody, *Interpersonal Communication: A Goals Approach* (New York: St. Martin's Press, 1994), chapter 12; M. Snyder, *Public Appearances, Private Realities: The Psychology of Self-Monitoring* (New York: Freeman, 1987).

54. Snyder, *Public Appearances, Private Realities*.

55. Snyder, *Public Appearances, Private Realities*.

56. Snyder, *Public Appearances, Private Realities*. Also, Smith, Cody, LoVette, and Canary, "Self-Monitoring, Gender, and Compliance-Gaining Goals."

57. Snyder, *Public Appearances, Private Realities*.

58. Snyder and DeBono, "Appeals to Image and Claims About Quality."

59. C.W. Sherif, M. Sherif, and R. Nebergall, *Attitude and Attitude Change: The Social Judgement-Involvement Approach*, (Philadelphia: W.B. Saunders, 1965).

60. See: C. Hovland, O.J. Harvey, and M. Sherif, "Assimilation and Contrast Effects in Reaction to Communication and Attitude Change," *Journal of Abnormal and Social Psychology*, vol. 55 (1957), pp. 242–252.

61. D. Granberg, "Social Judgment Theory," in M. Burgoon, ed., *Communication Yearbook 6* (Beverly Hills: Sage, 1982), pp. 304–29.

62. D. Broder, "Brock and Good Choice," *Columbia Daily Tribune*, February 2, 1977, p. 6; cited in Granberg.

63. TRB, "Gracious Interval," *The New Republic*, November 13, 1976.

64. K.K. Sereno and E.M. Bodaken, "Ego-Involvement and Attitude Change: Toward a Reconceptualization of Persuasive Effect," *Speech Monographs*, vol. 39 (1972), pp. 151–58.

65. N. Miller, "Involvement and Dogmatism as Inhibitors of Attitude Change," *Journal of Experimental Social Psychology*, vol. 1 (1965), pp. 121–32.

KEY TERMS AND CONCEPTS

individual differences
demographic characteristics
personality
self-esteem
chronic/normal self-esteem
acute/situational self-esteem
avoidance defenses
expressive defenses
self-efficacy
intelligence
anxiety
fear appeal
dogmatism
open-mindedness
authoritarianism
need for achievement
self-monitoring
social judgment theory
ego-involvement
latitude of rejection
latitude of acceptance
latitude of noncommitment
assimilation effect
contrast effect

SUCCESSFUL PERSUASION: PREDICTING GROUP RESPONSES

O U T L I N E

Every four years, the United States holds a presidential election. During the political conventions, and throughout the campaign, newspapers, magazines, radio commentators, and television news pundits spend many hours trying to predict which candidates are likely to win the election. There are millions of voters in the United States, and it is impossible to ask each and every person how he or she is likely to vote. What does the political analyst do to improve the chances of making a correct prediction? The political analyst makes a single assumption: People who are alike in important ways tend to vote alike.

In every election we hear references to the "women's vote," the "black vote," and the "labor vote." These references are all based on the assumption that people who belong to a particular ethnic, religious, racial, or socioeconomic group are likely to be responsive to persuasive messages perceived to appeal to that group. This chapter investigates the assumption there is a relationship between persuasion and those characteristics which individuals possess as a result of their membership in particular groups. First, we will discuss some of the reasons why groups are important in persuasion. We will then turn attention to five groups that have received considerable attention by researchers over the years: Hispanic Americans, children, aging Americans, women, and members of differing social classes.

WHY GROUPS?

Perhaps the first question we should ask is whether there is any basis at all for assuming that people who are members of a group behave in ways similar to other members of the group. While there are often exceptions to the rule, scholars believe many people who share the same group affiliation (Roman Catholic, Republican, and so forth) will share similar values, attitudes, and concerns.

Why are members of a group likely to behave uniformly? There are many answers to that question. For example, recall from the last chapter that Miller[1] identified four causes that help make a person become "ego-involved" on a particular topic. Miller identified the four causes from speculating about why groups such as the Women's Christian Temperance Union (which fought to ban alcohol sales) hold strong, uniform, and resistant attitudes about alcohol. Members of such groups tend to be both quite dogmatic and quite ego-involved on the topic of alcohol abuse. The four most obvious reasons why members become so involved include: (a) the individual in such a group believes the issue at hand is a salient, important matter; (b) the individual has considerable social support for his/her beliefs and attitudes; (c) the individual has thought of arguments and counterarguments for the matter; and, (d) the individual is committed to the cause, having perhaps attended rallies, signed petitions, had friends sign petitions, written letters to newspapers and elected officials, and placed signs in visible areas of the car and home. *Commitment* to a cause or to a purpose alters how the individual thinks about the cause or purpose (see Chapters 2 and 10).

There are three other important reasons that have a strong impact on increasing "with-in" group feelings of uniformity and similarity. First, people who share religious, ethnic, and even social-class similarities are raised to adhere to similar *values* of liberty, equality, world peace, a comfortable life, and so on, and they further realize that different groups of people do not share the same values as they do. Second, if an individual identifies with a particular group, that individual is likely to use that group as a "reference group," a group to which the individual compares and relates his or her attitudes and beliefs. Third, sometimes the strongest pull toward uniformity stems from direct pressure placed on the individual to conform to the group. We saw an example of this in our story in Chapter 1, about the family that joined the KKK, experienced intense pressure to adhere to a strict code of beliefs and behaviors, and then experienced threats and violence when attempting to leave the group. Another example of real-life peer influence to conform to a group's expectations can be found in Box 7.1; a "soul patrol" places considerable pressure on other African-Americans to ensure that they stay sufficiently "black." (Comparable essays could be written about other groups.)

Most of the research in this area that we will review deals with group *values* and with *social comparisons* and group pressure. We will review each of these two approaches, briefly, and then illustrate by focusing on groups in legal settings.

Groups and Values

A "value," for Milton Rokeach,

> ... refers to a single belief of a very specific kind. It concerns a desirable mode of behavior or end-state that has a transcendental quality to it, guiding actions, attitudes, judgments, and comparisons across specific objects and situations and beyond immediate goals to more ultimate goals.[2]

With this definition, Rokeach meant to distinguish an attitude, which he described as an organization of several beliefs, from a value, which is a single belief a person holds for a long period of time and which guides behaviors across a wide range of situations. A value is more general and "overarching" and can subsume a number of attitudes. We discussed in Chapter 1, for example, "value-expressive" attitudes are attitudes that have a bearing on some larger goal—such as ecology, world peace, salvation, and so forth. We may possess only one or two dozen values, but

there are thousands of specific attitudes we could hold. Further, a value also represents a *standard* of behavior prescribing how we ought to behave if we desire to achieve some end-goal (salvation, improved ecology), while an attitude reflects our *preference* or predisposition to behave in a certain way. It is also important to note that values occupy a more central position than attitudes within one's personality makeup and cognitive system, and therefore often determine the attitudes one holds.

Rokeach's extensive work on values stemmed from the fact that there are two general kinds of values—values dealing with the *end-states* we hope to achieve, called *terminal* values, and values we use to guide our behavior in a day-to-day, week-to-week time frame, called *instrumental* values. Table 7.1 lists these values. The values presented in the table are in alphabetical order. Terminal values we work toward achieving throughout our lives include *salvation, family security, pleasure, an exciting life, equality, self-respect,* and so forth. Instrumental values, that deal with how we should behave at any given time, include being *responsible, logical, courageous, capable, cheerful, imaginative, polite,* and so forth. Of course, the two lists of values overlap, because instrumental values are used in order to achieve end-goals or terminal goals.

In Rokeach's work, people were given the two lists and asked to arrange or to rank-order the values in "order of importance to *you*, as guiding principles in *your* life."[3] We then study how members of various groups emphasize different values, or guiding principles.

Rokeach found members of various groups differed significantly in the values they indicate as important. African Americans, for example, placed far greater emphasis on the value of *equality* than did the general population. Indeed, while both African Americans and Caucasians ranked *a world at peace* as the most important (terminal) value, African Americans indicated *equality* was the second most important value, while Caucasians placed equality eleventh out of eighteen terminal values. Further, people who rank equality high in impor-

A "SOUL PATROL" COLORS HOW BLACKS SEEK IDENTITY

AP/Wide World
Photos, Inc.

Washington—If you're black, prove it.

That's the challenge issued by the "Soul Patrol," an invisible force that lurks in the minds of many black Americans, defining what black is and what it isn't.

It's a code of behavior that measures blacks against a yardstick of racial conformity. Anything declared "white" is off limits to blacks. Participate in too much "white" behavior and access to the black world will be cut off.

The patrol divides and confuses blacks, leaving many wondering whether they're "black enough" or if there's a way they can be even blacker.

To some, the Soul Patrol is a good way of preserving black identity.

Continued

"You got to be black first," said veteran civil rights activist Hosea Williams. "Stay with black people. Do your black thing."

But to others, including John Blake, the reporter at *The Atlanta Journal-Constitution* who coined the phrase, the rules go too far.

"The Soul Patrol isn't content with picking your friends," he wrote this spring in an op-ed piece. "They want to tell you how to think, where to live, whom to love, how to do your job."

The Soul Patrol has numerous rules, open to loose interpretation.

If you have more white friends than the patrol thinks you should, you're an "Oreo"—black outside, white inside, like the cookie.

If you marry or date someone of another race, you're a "sellout," or a "wannabe," as in "wanna be white."

If you divulge "secrets" that are common knowledge among blacks, or if you don't automatically side with blacks, you're an "Uncle Tom."

These rules can create a dilemma.

"They can leave you in the position of not being accepted by either whites or blacks," Blake wrote. "Who wants to endure that?"

The Soul Patrol polices all arenas, from public figures in show business and politics—including last year's confirmation battle over Supreme Court nominee Clarence Thomas—to the most private aspects of everyday life.

Blacks are aware of these rules. Those who don't subscribe to them are not considered "down" with, or into, blackness.

"If you're in the Wall Street district, if a black guy comes up wearing a suit, he's supposed to speak to you, and you're supposed to speak to him," said Antoinette Hightower, 31, of Orange, N.J., who works on Wall Street for an insurance company.

"Proper speech is looked upon like you're trying to deny your race," said Jacqueline Brytt, 28, a military officer in Woodbridge, Va. "It can be looked at as a negative. When I'm talking to my black friends, I use black dialect."

Brytt says some blacks have rejected her because of her friendships with whites. But she concedes she subscribes to the Soul Patrol philosophy when she sees blacks wearing blue or green contact lenses.

"I'd say, 'What's up with the lenses?' " she said. "It's important for us to have a little of that, to keep us in touch with ourselves."

Sometimes, blacks are victimized for not participating in "black" behavior.

"If you don't play basketball, you're not a brother. That's understood," said Russell Pittman, 30, a Ft. Lauderdale, Fla., teacher. "And if you don't live in what we call the 'hood, you're a sellout, you don't want to be around your own people."

Civil rights activist Williams argues that this philosophy prevents blacks from being swallowed up by white society.

"You got to let that white stuff alone," he said. "It's disbanding our culture, taking on their culture and their ways."

Others disagree.

"If we tried to enforce a black orthodoxy, then we would fall into the white folks' trap. They would love for us to all think alike," said Roger Wilkins, professor of history at George Mason University in Virginia.

Wilkins encountered these attitudes as an assistant U.S. attorney general in the Justice Department in the 1960s, when black nationalists called for a separate culture and clashed with advocates of integration.

"There were those who said, 'He wasn't born poor, so he isn't authentically black,' " Wilkins said. "There were others who said, 'How can they be black if they're in the government?"

Black journalists, too, are targets. They pick up the "sellout" label "for writing about problems in the black community," Blake noted.

Many blacks encounter the Soul Patrol philosophy in childhood, when the academically inclined often are bluntly told by black classmates that being studious makes them "white."

"That gets interpreted as, if you're smart, you're white, you're assimilated," said Chicago psychologist Samellah Abdullah. "There is a demand on peers to be like the group."

The Soul Patrol thrives on long-standing divisions between fair-skinned blacks and darker blacks.

Fair blacks, it says, are favored by white society and must be reminded of their blackness, while darker blacks have not been readily accepted and therefore should not embrace it.

Today, the Soul Patrol flourishes among "gangsta" rappers who define blackness through the underbelly of the inner city; those without intimate knowledge of poverty, crime or violence are not black enough.

But it also extends into worlds where blacks have achieved fame.

Actress Whoopi Goldberg was condemned by some blacks as a sellout during the 1980s because she enjoyed success in Hollywood's white Establishment and wore blue contact lenses. The pressure dissipated after she won NAACP awards.

Continued

Andrew Young, former U.N. ambassador and former Atlanta mayor, was booed at the 1984 Democratic National Convention when he favored presidential nominee Walter Mondale over Jesse Jackson.

The issue surfaced last year when some thought Thomas, a political conservative, was too "white" to replace liberal Thurgood Marshall on the Supreme Court.

Anita Hill, who accused Thomas of sexual harassment, also faced pressure because she was considered to have "tattled" to whites about a fellow black.

The late Rev. Ralph David Abernathy drew heat for stating, in his autobiography, that Martin Luther King Jr. had extramarital relationships. Some said Abernathy would be robbed of his "rightful place in history" if he didn't retract what he'd written. They also suggested white editors influenced him. Abernathy stood firm.

From: *The Los Angeles Times*, September 20, 1992. Reprinted by permission of The Associated Press.

---

tance are also more likely to join groups that work toward equality, and to participate in demonstrations and rallies supporting equality. As a general rule, African Americans can be expected to vote in ways that promote equality.

Our society also instills different values in men and women.[4] Men indicated that *a comfortable life, being imaginative, an exciting life, a sense of accomplishment, freedom, pleasure, social recognition, ambition, capability*, and *being logical* were more important to them than did women, while women indicated that *a world at peace, happiness, inner harmony, salvation, self-respect, wisdom, cheerfulness, cleanliness, forgiveness*, and *loving* were more important to them than did men. Some of these values are reflected in the actions men and women take as receivers (see Gender and Persuasion, p. 199).

Oddly, research projects on values by Rokeach and by Kahle[5] have remarkably little to say about major ethnic groups in America, a point which may account for why misleading stereotypes and poor marketing strategies continue to

be implemented on some groups, such as the Hispanic-American receiver (see below).

Reference Groups and Social Comparisons

The term "reference group" is used to describe any group to which people relate their attitudes and beliefs. Reference groups serve two major functions. One function is to help determine appropriate behavior for an individual by setting group standards or norms of behavior (as we discussed in Chapter 5). The second function of reference groups is to serve as a standard or checkpoint for making decisions about persuasive messages.

Kelley suggested that the use of a reference group as a standard or checkpoint is really a "comparison function." He argued: "A group functions as a comparison reference group for an individual to the extent that the behavior, attitudes, circumstances, or other characteristics of its members

TABLE	7.1

LIST OF HUMAN VALUES, TERMINAL AND INSTRUMENTAL

Terminal Value	*Instrumental Value*
A comfortable life (a prosperous life)	Ambitious (hard-working, aspiring)
An exciting life (a stimulating, active life)	Broad-minded (open-minded)
A sense of accomplishment (lasting contribution)	Capable (competent, effective)
A world at peace (free of war and conflict)	Cheerful (lighthearted, joyful)
A world of beauty (beauty of nature and the arts)	Clean (neat, tidy)
Equality (brotherhood, equal opportunity for all)	Courageous (standing up for your beliefs)
Family security (taking care of loved ones)	Forgiving (willing to pardon others)
Freedom (independence, free choice)	Helpful (working for the welfare of others)
Happiness (contentedness)	Honest (sincere, truthful)
Inner harmony (freedom from inner conflict)	Imaginative (daring, creative)
Mature love (sexual and spiritual intimacy)	Independent (self-reliant, self-sufficient)
National security (protection from attack)	Intellectual (intelligent, reflective)
Pleasure (an enjoyable, leisurely life)	Logical (consistent, rational)
Salvation (saved, eternal life)	Loving (affectionate, tender)
Self-respect (self-esteem)	Obedient (dutiful, respectful)
Social recognition (respect, admiration)	Polite (courteous, well-mannered)
True friendship (close companionship)	Responsible (dependable, reliable)
Wisdom (a mature, understanding life)	Self-controlled (restrained, self-focused, disciplined)

Adapted with the permission of The Free Press, a division of Macmillan, Inc., from *The Nature of Human Values* by Milton Rokeach. Copyright © 1973 by The Free Press.

represent standards or comparison points which he uses in making judgments and evaluations."[6] Newcomb further noted that there can also be *positive* reference groups and *negative* reference groups.[7] A positive reference group is a group with which the individual identifies, or aspires to join. A negative reference group is a group the individual no longer wishes to associate with (such as the KKK, in the earlier example), or opposes.

For example, if a student were a pre-med student and aspired to become a doctor and join the ranks of the American Medical Association, we could predict that s/he would probably be against health care reform or any governmental regulation of the fees doctors charge for services. On the other hand, if the student were in another area of study, say social work, s/he might believe that "all doctors charge too much," and the student might favor health care reform. When this student hears that his/her negative reference group (doctors, or the "medical establishment") is against a bill in Congress to control medical costs, the student will favor the legislation that members of the negative reference group support.

We are interested in reference groups because they are so influential in persuasion, especially in politics. Positive reference groups (the National Rifle Association, the Association of Police Chiefs, and the like) may endorse candidates when voters are concerned about crime and law and order. Likewise, in a more personal setting, we might persuade the children to eat their vegetables, go to bed early, and to get plenty of exercise so that they can grow up to be like Michael Jordan, or other athletes and Olympic stars. Negative reference groups are employed politically when a group of voters, known to dislike certain people who represent particular ideologies of, say, either liberalism or conservatism (like Jesse Jackson, Ted Kennedy, or Pat Buchanan), are told that one or more of these people are strong advocates of a proposed law, thereby increasing the group's opposition to the proposed legislation.

Reference groups are of particular importance according to the theory of social comparisons, which we briefly overviewed in Chapter 5. Leon Festinger[8] proposed the theory of social comparisons formally as follows:

"We start out by assuming the existence of a motivation to know that one's opinions are correct and to know precisely what one is and is not capable of doing. From this motivation . . . we have made the following derivations about the conditions under which a social comparison process arises and about the nature of this social comparison process.

1. This social process arises when the evaluation of opinions or abilities is not feasible by testing directly in the environment.

2. Under such circumstances persons evaluate their opinions and abilities by comparison with others.

3. This comparison leads to pressures toward uniformity.

4. There is a tendency to stop comparing oneself with others who are very divergent. This tendency increases if others are perceived as different from oneself in relevant dimensions.

5. Factors such as importance, relevance, and attraction to a group which affect the strength of the original motivation will affect the strength of the pressure towards uniformity.

This work suggests that people gain information useful to them toward understanding, realistically, how adequate their performance is (or how "correct" their opinions are) given a relevant comparison basis.

Obviously, the implication of this theory is that Hispanic males, Hispanic females, African-Americans, young females, young males, and so forth, will often compare themselves to similar others. As the recent work by Suls and Wills[9] indicates, there are several extensions of social comparison processes relevant to our chapter. First, as Wills[10] notes, the social comparison processes need not be limited to a "reality check" on one's abilities and on the "correctness" of one's opinions, but social comparison processes can also be used to *enhance one's view of the self.* For example, when our self-esteem is reduced, or when our sense of well-being is threatened, we will purposefully engage in a *downward comparison* to compare ourselves with those who are less fortunate. Luhtanen and Crocker[11] further offer that individuals who identify with members of a group can similarly enhance "collective esteem" by comparing their group with a group lower in achievement and success (for example, "Well, at least we Cubans here, in Miami, have proved our worth"). Bolstering the collective esteem, however, often calls upon receivers to maximize the contrasts between their group and the less-fortunate one, a task that obviously increases "we-they," "winner-loser" perceptions.

Second, Miller, Gross, and Holtz[12] maintain that we do not always have the ability or the inclination to seek out information concerning how members of our reference group feel about a particular topic. Instead, we can *project* an attitude onto the group and hold it as our own. The term "assumed similarity" is used to refer to the situation in which we basically assume (project, without evidence) what the group's attitude on a particular topic is likely to be, and adopt it as our own. Miller, et al., admit that the actual social comparison process probably has a greater effect on uniformity of attitudes, and on attitude certainty, than on psychologically projecting attitudes on the reference group. However, sometimes group members may initially react to an issue and hold an attitude believed to be endorsed and held "correct" by the reference group, until the supporting evidence can be processed and the real social comparison can take place. (The reader might care to ponder the social comparison process in the context of the Mike Tyson rape case of 1992.)

The last two sections of this chapter focus on why we should be studying groups. We study groups because there is often considerable pressure, and psychological need, to rely on the group as a means of identification, and as a means of comparing one's abilities or comparing the "correctness" of one's attitudes with a relevant referent group. Now we draw attention to an issue directly related to persuasion: influence in the jury.

Groups and Jury Duty

A variety of studies suggest that people who make up the group influence its processes and outcomes. For example, textbooks in small-group communication suggest that authoritarians, or dogmatics, are firm, demanding, directive, and adhere strictly to norms and roles when they are leaders. When such personalities are in subordinate positions, they tend to be submissive and compliant. In law trials, whether juror characteristics affect processes and outcomes is critically important, since defendants are presumably judged *fairly* by a panel of peers. Is there bias, and, if so, what can be done about it?

Trial lawyers develop ideas as to what to expect from particular types of (potential) jurors. Simon[13] has explored the trial-procedure literature and identified this rather extensive list of possible biases that (some) lawyers may have adopted:

Age and Sex

1. A young juror is more likely to return a verdict favorable to the plaintiff than to the defendant.

2. An older juror is more likely to be sympathetic to the plaintiff than to the defendant in civil, personal-injury cases.

3. A juror whose age closely approximates the age of the client, lawyer, or witness is more likely to give a favorable verdict.

4. A woman juror is more likely to be emotional and sympathetic and to return a verdict favorable to the plaintiff.

5. A male juror is more likely to return a verdict favorable to the plaintiff if she is an attractive female.

6. A female juror is more likely to return a verdict favorable to the plaintiff if he is an attractive male.

7. A woman juror is more likely to be intolerant of the complaints of her own sex and thus return a verdict unfavorable to a party of her own sex.

Socioeconomic Characteristics

1. A juror belonging to the same fraternal organizations, union, or political party as the client or witness is more likely to return a verdict favorable to that party.

2. A juror belonging to the same occupation or profession as the client will be more likely to give a favorable verdict.

3. A juror belonging to an occupation or profession traditionally antagonistic to the occupation or profession of the client or witness is more likely to return an unfavorable verdict.

4. A juror who has or had extensive dealings with the public in matters of law enforcement and investigation is more likely to give a decision favorable to the defendant.

5. A juror whose occupation is that of a bellboy or taxi driver is more likely to be defendant-prone in a criminal case. They see so much of the frailties of human nature that they are not easily shocked.

6. A juror with a small income is more likely to be sympathetic with the poorer party.

Personality Types

1. An intelligent, courageous juror is more desired by parties who feel they have a good case while a weak-minded juror is more desired by parties who feel they have a doubtful case and are dependent upon emotional, sympathetic appeals.

2. A juror who adheres to defiant political or moral values is more likely to use nonlegal sources as his or her basis for arriving at a verdict. Hence, such people are less predictable, among other things.

3. A juror who claims strong opinions on any topic is more likely to be dogmatic and less able to bring various facts together for comparison purposes.

Many of these specific beliefs can be grouped into a small set of biases: *social class*, with older or richer jurors seen as being more conservative than younger and poorer ones; *similarity*, with jurors who are similar to either the plaintiff or defendant seen as being more lenient toward the similar other; *sex roles*, with women seen as being more emotional, socially oriented, and as displaying, in some situations, greater sympathy than men; *susceptibility to stereotypes* (for instance, the idea that men are suckers for good-looking women, women are saps for good-looking men, and so on); and *personalities* (for instance, the idea that dogmatic, authoritarian, or "harsh" persons convict more frequently than egalitarians, liberals, or independent-minded persons.

Do such biases actually operate in real juries? In reality, not much of *consistent and strong* evidence exists to indicate that these biases influence juror's decisions. For example, Simon[14] found trial manuals asserting that a juror's occupation was a very important piece of evidence for predicting bias; yet surveys of jury work have failed to conclude that higher-status occupations lead to more conservative judgments (as predicted). However, bias is sometimes evident: one study (cited in Simon) found higher-status jurors were more likely to convict than lower-status jurors (thus protecting society and property). Another study found Democrats awarded more money (eight percent above average) in personal-injury cases than Republicans (two percent below the average), indicating that Democrats are more willing to protect the victim and help the "little guy" than Republicans.[15]

Hastie, Penrod, and Pennington[16] in a study of jury work in felony cases found juror characteristics such as demographics, personality, and general attitudes are only *weakly* related to verdict decisions. In their view, some jurors' world knowledge concerning events and individuals involved in the facts of the case *may* affect verdict decisions. An upper-class juror, for example, may not have a framework for evaluating what are normal weekend activities in an urban ghetto, or may envision only stereotypes of such events and activities. To the lower-class juror, the fact that the defendant kept a weapon in his car may seem normal, while the same fact might suggest to the upper-class juror that the defendant was looking for trouble. An accumulation of inferences and judgments such as these may result in upper- and lower-class jurors reaching different conclusions. As a general rule, the individual characteristics of jurors are weakly related to verdicts. Instead, juror characteristics are more strongly related to participation in deliberations, since jurors with higher incomes, better jobs, and more years of education will participate more in jury deliberations and will be more persuasive.[17]

We should all be offended by juror bias for

the obvious reason that an injustice is committed each time a group of jurors is more (or less) lenient on a particular defendant solely on the basis of gender, sex, race, or occupation. Fortunately, research has focused on ways to reduce biases. Baumeister and Darley, Kaplan and Miller, and Ugwuegbu[18] have each demonstrated that when lawyers emphasize the *strength, quality,* and *reliability of evidence,* jurors are less likely to display biases.

DEMOGRAPHIC GROUPS

Every individual belongs to many groups. There are some kinds of group membership in which the individual has little or no control. These are *demographic groups,* or *involuntary groups,* and these are indicated by such variables as age, sex, ethnic origin, and occupation. People cannot control how old they are or what color they are born. We might argue that being born at a particular time in history, or of parents of a particular race, ought not to make any difference in individual beliefs and attitudes. The evidence suggests, however, that these demographic groupings *do* make a difference, since individuals sharing demographic characteristics may also have increased interaction with one another.

The second type of membership group is one that people join voluntarily. These are *voluntary groups* and may be such associations as religious groups, social groups, and political groups.

In examining demographic characteristics, we should remember that they can serve only as general guides. Predicting the characteristics of a particular audience or individual from a knowledge of their demographic characteristics is helpful as long as the persuasive communicator realizes predictions may not apply to any one member of the audience.

Focus on Hispanic Americans

Consider these myths and failures in persuasion:[19]

Myth/Mistake 1: There exists a group called the Hispanic community. These people have very similar backgrounds, and to capture their attention one need only use the Spanish language in advertising, adapt messages slightly, and a whole new population can be tapped.

Myth/Mistake 2: Hispanics are, for the most part, low-income, uneducated, blue-collar workers, who are mostly recently arrived illegal aliens not yet assimilated into mainstream American society.

Myth/Mistake 3: A Christmas advertisement illustrating beer served with tacos and enchiladas; the Spanish-speaking receivers were offended. Another beer ad showed a male with his arm around a girl, a beer in one hand and a taco in another. Such an ad was even more offensive.

The first two myths/mistakes are wrong because the four Hispanic communities in the U.S. include Mexicans living in California, Texas, Colorado, New Mexico and other areas of the Southwest; Cubans, most of whom migrated to Miami as political refugees; Puerto Ricans, who have migrated to New York, primarily, and to other urban areas, largely for economic reasons; and Central Americans who, escaping political instability, revolution and economic hardship, have moved into the Southwestern states. These groups share a common language, but because Cuban and other dialects are quite different, and because certain linguistic phrases are different, some companies (Campbell soups and Anheuser-Busch) resort to employing different voice-overs when using the same visual components in different areas of the United States. Both Campbell soups and Anheuser-Busch entered the Hispanic market in the early 1980s, and in order to compete with Goya (a major food supplier in this market),

Campbell alters its recipes to include ingredients from respective native lands (Cuba, Puerto Rico). Campbell realizes how significant this market is in the U.S., and understands that members of this group are impressed by an American company accommodating their needs and preferences.[20]

Both Valencia and Rosa[21] provide examples of dialectical mistakes made in translations attempting to target Hispanic consumers in America. A proud people (see below), native dialects are very important to the Hispanic receiver. So much so that Bartles and James (a wine-cooler company owned by Gallo) ran a series of five advertisements in Spanish-language media that began with the first promising, "If you try Bartles and James, I'll learn Spanish." Progressively, Frank Bartles learned to speak Spanish over the course of the five advertisements, although with a strong Anglo accent. We do not know if such an amusing ad convinced Hispanic receivers to switch to wine coolers from beer and soft drinks (which are popular in this market), but this advertising strategy is, in our opinion, a good one.

Besides a basic common language, what do the four groups have in common? Do *not* assume, as do some, that they share common *traditions* and music. Mexican mariachi music, for example, is basically foreign to Puerto Ricans. Most of the groups vote Democrat, but Cubans are likely to vote Republican, and typically adopt more conservative political views. What are some commonalities of the groups? Typically (but not always) Catholic, they hold family values sacred, emphasize taking care of each other, including extended family and ailing family members. Family reunions are important, as is spending holidays together, celebrating *Quinceñera*, the fifteen-year-old daughter's "coming out" dance party, and making traditional meals together. (Kodak gained popularity by running an ad showing an extended Hispanic family preparing for a *Quinceñera*.[22]) The ad featuring beer with tacos and enchiladas, and the one selling beer with tacos and sex are offensive, in part, because Christmas is a time when one is supposed to be on one's best behavior. A preferred, and more realistic, scene would have portrayed a family together making homemade tamales for the holidays, or having a formal dinner.

Also, consider the impact of a group that characteristically contains large families. Ford bolstered its image in the community by emphasizing family cars and station wagons.[23] Contests that offer *two* free tickets are worthless, because two tickets are hardly adequate when six or more individuals are likely to attend a function. Colgate, on the other hand, ran a contest and offered buyers a chance to win one free trip to Puerto Rico, a contest enabling a family member to return home to visit. Engardio[24] claims that the contest increased sales of Palmolive dishwashing soap by 50 percent. A consumer for a large family also has a direct impact on how much is spent at stores, as well as what is purchased. Hispanic Americans spend more than non-Hispanics at supermarkets; in fact, Hispanic Americans make up 54 percent of San Antonio, Texas, but account for 65 percent of the supermarket sales. Engardio[25] claims that Hispanic Americans spend 26 percent more in grocery stores each week and 36 percent more at fast food restaurants than other San Antonio customers. Presumably, Hispanic Americans buy big supplies for big families, especially snacks, soft drinks, soap and beer. Pizza companies and fried chicken outlets now routinely advertise in Spanish, emphasizing families, and offer special deals to sell large quantities (two for the price of one). On the other hand, it has been reported that advertisements concerning "cheap" rates for long-distance phone calls to family members was offensive to many Hispanic consumers, because one should not be cheap when family is concerned.

Another common characteristic is pride. As a people, Hispanics demand respect and recognition for their culture and for their heritage. Rosa[26] reports that in 1987, 73 percent of Hispanic Americans considered themselves "Hispanic" first

(compared to 46 percent who said the same in 1981; obviously, there has been a surge in Hispanic pride). Proud people are offended by phoney sentiments and by ads which appear to be giving only lip-service. As Rosa pointed out, 60 percent of the Hispanics purchase products made by companies that sponsor Hispanic events and festivals, or show an interest in the Hispanic community. Goya foods, for example, sponsored a baseball league in New York's Central Park on its way to becoming the largest Hispanic-owned firm in the country. Astor[27] also noted that Anheuser-Busch sponsored Miami's March 8th *Calle Ocho Festival,* a festival attracting over 300,000 individuals. Astor also reported that Anheuser-Busch offers scholarships to students. Domino's offers a "deliciOSO" pre-sweetened powdered soft drink designed by a Spanish chemist for Spanish tastes in San Antonio and Miami. The symbol is a bear (*oso* in Spanish), which appears in parades and supermarkets. The point is that Hispanic Americans pay keen attention to community involvement when making purchasing decisions. Other companies have followed: Frito-Lay started a program to build playgrounds in Hispanic communities, J.C. Penney started in 1989 to offer a *Quinceñera* catalogue specializing in dresses for the young teenagers' "coming out" party; and Pepsi also started sponsoring community events in 1989.[28]

Pride and hard work also account for the increasing number of Hispanics buying a Mercedes and designer clothes. Myth/mistake 2 is incorrect because of the incredible growth witnessed in the upward mobility among Hispanic Americans. In some communities (Miami) the typical Hispanic home generates income comparable to others in the community. Pomice and Arrarte[29] note that a number of publications now compete for the growing middle- and upper-middle-class Hispanic consumer, including *Imagen* (for upwardly mobile Puerto Rican women on the East Coast) and *Miami Mensual,* which claims the average subscriber's income is over $58,000 a year. Traditionally, individuals who identify themselves as "Hispanic" indicate that they tend to buy prestige items.[30] Pride can also be used as a positive emotional appeal when a slogan such as Chrysler's pro-American, "America's not going to be pushed around anymore," is converted into "We Espinozas aren't going to be pushed around anymore!" and used in Spanish-language media.

Another common characteristic is loyalty. Hispanic-Americans tend to be brand loyal to products that they trust from companies that sponsor or support the Hispanic community. This is important when one considers the purchasing power of the large families in the Hispanic community. Engardio,[31] in fact, implied that after the Palmolive campaign boosted sales, Palmolive's market share remained high, at 35 percent, relative to Palmolive's general market share of 17 percent. Rosa[32] noted that Hispanic Americans claim 61 percent of the market where "popular name brands I use most often today are going to be the same brands I will be using next year."

Finally, Hispanic families are very traditional in the assignment of roles. Women usually do the shopping, and males pay the bills. One ad, for a telephone company, showed a woman washing up in the kitchen and telling the husband, "Run downstairs and phone Maria. Tell her we'll be a little late." Typically, a woman wouldn't *order* the husband to do something, and Valencia[33] further noted that the ad fell on deaf ears, since it is normal to be late (he claims), and that one would not call to announce being late.

Although a similar analysis of success and failure can be provided to show persuasion among other groups (that is, Chinese, Vietnamese, Romanian, Serbian), we decided to emphasize Hispanic Americans for two reasons: First, this group of receivers is one of the largest groups in the U.S., and one of the most rapidly growing groups. Some data suggest Hispanics will represent the *majority* of voters and consumers in many counties in the U.S. in the next several decades. Second, this

group of receivers exemplifies perfectly what the would-be persuader needs to attend to when thinking of persuading groups—a general "group" exists that contains certain relevant differences (Cubans, Mexicans, Puerto Ricans) pertaining to music and traditions, but at the same time there are overarching, fundamental similarities between the group members: (1) emphasis on the correct use of native language; (2) importance of family and family roles; (3) pride in the culture and its achievements; and, (4) loyalty to well-trusted, tried, and/or prestige brand names. A fifth ingredient is one we want to emphasize with this group—the importance of a *reciprocal relationship* between a company and the Hispanic-American community. There is a tradition for individuals in this group to remain loyal to a company which gives something back to the community, which accommodates the tastes of its members, and which sponsors events and provides scholarships.

Children and Persuasion

Probably no one is more susceptible to persuasion than the three- to seven-year-old. Members in this age group often do not even know what a commercial is, when it begins and when it ends, but they are extremely susceptible to "celebrity endorsements" by their real or cartoon idols.[34] It is a marketing expert's dream come true: millions of individuals not able to cognitively defend themselves from sophisticated commercial appeals are tuned into the same TV shows and programs; advertisers do not have to work hard to locate the receivers. Billions of dollars are spent to sell to this group, and billions of dollars in profits are made. By the time children are in the fifth grade, however, 99 percent of them understand the purpose of a commercial, few are uncritically accepting of the message's content (for example, 66 percent of sixth graders claim that a product in real life is not as good as one shown on television),[35] and few rely solely on television as a source of information about clothes, toys, and so on, as they begin to read magazines and experience social and peer pressure.

Since children in the three-to-seven age group are so susceptible to persuasion, several steps were taken in the last several decades to safeguard this particular group of receivers.[36] First, program personalities or program characters (live or animated) were prohibited from endorsing a product during a show or during any time slot adjacent to the show. Thus, it does not appear to the three-year-old viewer that his/her favorite character on *The Flintstones* walks into the bathroom and swallows pills. Flintstones Vitamins (and Flintstones cereal) must be advertised on shows other than *The Flintstones*.

Why? One obvious reason is that having the popular character endorse a product on a child's favorite program takes advantage of the child; such a rule stems from the fact that consumers must be aware when they are being influenced and must have the ability to defend themselves from influence—each person must be able to say "no" to a persuasion attempt (recall Chapter 1). Thus, if a child does not know when the commercial starts and stops, or cannot identify its function (to persuade the receiver to buy an item), then some means must be found to protect the child, or to help the child understand when the influence (the ad) is occurring during his/her entertainment program.

Toward this goal, a second rule was imposed, requiring television programs to employ a "separator device" that is inserted before a program stops and a series of commercials airs. This separator device is usually a blank or an animated screen that claims (on both video and audio channels), "We will be back after these messages." This device must remain on the screen for at least five seconds, but not more than ten seconds. Further, the device is also used after the series of commercials when returning to the program, exclaiming (on both video and audio channels), "And now back to the show" or something similar to this. Why? We adults habitually look away from a significant portion of advertisements, but some children may be "glued" to the television screen in a transfixed state and must be informed when a break from the television show occurs and that what follows is a commercial.

Scholars in this area have developed a series of guidelines for the use of advertising aimed at children. Meringoff and Lesser[37] present a discussion of some of these guidelines (also see Chapter 1). Some specific guidelines include:[38]

■ **1.** Provide audio disclosure when a product requires assembly.

■ **2.** Provide audio or video disclosure as to a product's method of operation and source of power.

■ **3.** Provide simultaneous audio and video disclosures when items, such as batteries needed to operate a product as demonstrated in the advertising, are not included.

■ **4.** Avoid competitive/comparative/superiority claims about toys and other durable products.

(This last guideline is designed to protect a child's self-concept because a child will usually possess only one bicycle and if advertisers claim that bicycle X is superior to other bicycles, many young people may feel hurt or inferior. Also, since children have not cognitively matured yet, we cannot assume that they understand concepts such as comparison advertising.)

Rules specific to toys include:[39]

■ **1.** To present the toy on its actual merits as a plaything. (The ad shall neither exaggerate nor distort play value.)

■ **2.** To limit any view of a toy or demonstration of its performance to that which a child is reasonably capable of reproducing.

■ **3.** To employ the complete and authentic sound(s) of the toy.

■ **4.** To confine the use of generic stock film footage, real-life counterparts of toys, fantasy and animation (in none of which either a child or a toy appears) to the first one-third of the commercial.

■ **5.** To disclose clearly the original purchase (by video, with audio disclosure where necessary for clarification) in the body of the commercial and in the closing five seconds.

According to Meringoff and Lesser,[40] music, sound effects, volume level, tempo, and other audio techniques should be used with restraint and discretion. It is also recommended that caution be taken in the use of particular video techniques involving camera angles, special lenses, special lighting, and dazzling visual effects. All of these techniques give the child ideas about the toy's operation that encourage distorted and exaggerated perception.

The guidelines we have discussed so far are not *rules* in that they are not enforced in the media. Rather, these guidelines are used as a general set of ethical considerations to protect the more naive and impressionable three- to seven-year-olds. They are only suggested guidelines, and are not completely effective when used. Research, for example, indicates that when no separator devices are used about 50 percent of the four-year-olds recognize it when a commercial is shown to them. When a separator device is used, the figure jumps to 75-77 percent—25 percent of the four-year-olds still do not recognize that they are watching a commercial.

Several volumes are required to address all of the issues relevant to children and persuasion researched in the last ten years. Briefly, we summarize research on how children are persuaded:[41]

■ **1.** Children are susceptible to celebrity or authority endorsements. At young ages they are generally prone to adopt the views of authority figures, and they imitate authority figures. Young children desiring to achieve cognitive mastery over their immediate environment are excited when they correctly recognize a celebrity and learn about the products that go along with the celebrity; and children learn over the years that certain characters are good, likable, and trustworthy (for example, Ronald McDonald, Burger King, Fred Flintstone). Research indicates that if the children in the audience like and identify with the source they will want the product. Celebrity or authority endorsements prompt 57 percent to over 70 percent of the children to want the product.

■ **2.** Younger children (three- to five-years-old) seem to be more susceptible to blatant claims (for example, drinking a milk shake will make you grow up to be strong) than older children. But older children (fifth graders) seem more susceptible to social status appeals (for example, buying a product will gain the buyer more friends and increase his or her status) than younger children (second grade).

■ **3.** Simplified wording and use of more than one modality for some messages can increase children's learning from advertisements. Children do not understand what the term "assembly required" means, and so it is common today for advertisements to report verbally, "Your parents have to put it together." Also, disclosures such as "batteries required" should appear on the screen as well as be communicated verbally on the audio channel. Use of both modalities should increase the chance children will notice and remember the disclosure.

■ **4.** There are fundamental differences in how toys and food are advertised. These differences probably reflect what advertisers have found in successfully selling to children, and possibly reflect how advertisers target products for particular audiences. Advertisements for toys, for example, depict small groups of white children playing with the products, whereas advertisements for food products (candy, cereal, fast food restaurants) show larger and more ethnicly diverse groups of children having fun eating. The main appeals in selling food are humor and fun. Advertisements for toys appeal to affiliation, fun, power, or being grown up. Both toy and food advertisements, however, involve frequent repetition of the name of the product (often over three times in thirty seconds), and 50 percent of commercials in both categories use jingles and slogans.

COGNITIVE DEFENSES

If children are so susceptible to influence and manipulation, should there not be laws or ways to protect them? The Federal Trade Commission, in fact, flirted with the idea of limiting advertising aimed at children in 1978, but ultimately declined to do so.[42] In the age of deregulation, people in power did not want to impose restrictions on the broadcasting industry, opening the floodgate for adopting different rules for different people (that is, one set of rules for children, another set of rules for aging Americans, and so forth). Since television offers so much in terms of information, education, entertainment and the like, parents were encouraged to view TV with children and to "instruct" children on how to resist influence. Doing so encourages a child to become an "adult" consumer, who knows how to tell "puffery" from deception (see Chapter 1).

Placing responsibility solely in the hands of parents, however, does not appear to be effective in keeping children from being manipulated; and the task of co-viewing all or most of a child's shows is impossible. Nonetheless, Carlson and Grossbart[43] review the attempt to instill consumer knowledge in children, arguing that mothers and fathers differ fundamentally in parent-child interactions, in five parental styles. An *authoritarian* parent believes that children have few rights.

These parents are strict, firm, value conformity, foster dependence, exclude influences from outside the family, and place few requirements on a child's early maturing. They are not very warm, do not encourage verbalization or communication, and are fairly anxious. A *rigid controlling* parent is similar to an authoritarian, except that the rigid controlling parent is less anxious, talks more with the child and intends for the child to mature early, relative to the authoritarian parent.

Permissive parents are not restrictive, not at all anxious, and are very warm. Permissives do not favor early maturing, encourage verbal expression, are very nurturing and encourage communication and the pursuit of information from outside the family. These parents score lower than authoritarians, rigid controllers and authoritative mothers in firm enforcement of rules and in conformity. *Authoritative* parents desire their children to mature early and they score high on warmth, nurturance, restrictiveness, firm enforcement, and on encouraging the child's verbalization. Such parents intend to create a warm, restrictive environment in which a child quickly matures. Finally, *neglecting* parents are low in warmth, restrictiveness, and anxiety. They do not foster responsibility or early maturing; they do not encourage verbalization, and do not enforce rules.

How different parental styles are related to consumer socialization and behaviors is summarized in Table 7.2. The authoritative parent is most concerned with children's advertising and is more likely than others to talk about all of the goals being employed in children's commercials (to inform and to persuade), and has a less positive attitude toward commercials. The authoritative parent is also more restrictive of consumption and rates relatively low in materialism. Also, such a parent is much more likely to co-view programs with the child, like the permissive parent; however, the permissive parent appears to instill a positive attitude toward consumption. Both the neglecting parent and the authoritarian parent have

SUMMARY OF DIFFERENCES BETWEEN PARENTAL STYLES

	V	An	P	R	Av	N
General parenting dispositions						
Warmth		Lower	Higher	Lower	Higher	Lowest
Restrictiveness		Higher	Lowest	Higher	Highest	Lower
Anxious emotional involvement		Highest	Lower	Lowest	Lower	Lower
Consumer socialization tendencies and orientations						
Parent-child communication		Lower than all but N	Higher than An & N	Higher than An	Higher than An & N	Lower than P & An
Total goals		Lower than all but N	Higher than An & N	Higher than An	Higher than all but P	Lower than all but An
Restriction of consumption		Higher than P & N	Lower than An & Av		Higher than P	Lower than An
Mediation of the media		Lower than R & Av	Lower than Av and higher than N	Higher than An & N	Higher than all but R	Lower than all but An
Co-viewing		Lower than Av		Lower than Av	Higher than all but P	Lower than Av
Concern about children's advertising		Lower than Av	Lower than Av		Higher than all but R	Lower than Av
Consumer socialization tendencies and orientations						
Attitudes toward advertising		More positive than Av		Less positive than N	Less positive than An & N	More positive than R & Av
Mother's consumer behavior and values						
Friends as information		Lower than AV			Higher than An	
Consumer guidebooks as information sources		Lower than R & Av		Higher than An	Higher than An & N	Lower than Av
Economic motivation for consumption		Lower than Av	Higher than N	Higher than N	Higher than all but P	Lower than all but An
Social motivation for consumption			Lower than N			Higher than P
Favor government control		Higher than R		Lower than An & N		Higher than R
Mother's characteristics						
Mother's education		Lower	Higher	Higher	Higher	Higher

* V = Variable; An = Authoritarian; P = Permissive; R = Rigid Controlling; Av = Authoritative; N = Neglecting
FROM: L. Carlson and S. Grossbart, "Parental Style and Consumer Socialization of Children," *Journal of Consumer Research* (vol. 15, 1988), pp. 77–94. Used with permission.

relatively positive attitudes toward children's commercials, and both favor more government control over the industry, but perhaps for different reasons. The less-educated mother in the authoritarian families may not be very competent in distinguishing puffery from manipulation, or know how to train the child, while the neglecting parent may not be motivated to spend the time or energy in instilling an informed consumer orientation in the child. The authoritarian style also appears to be more *dependent* on commercials, since they rarely use friends or consumer guides to help improve shopping skills. Finally, the rigid controlling parent seeks to control what the child watches, has a fairly negative attitude toward commercials, and encourages studying consumer guides before purchasing products.

The question we raised was whether parents were motivated to and competent at instilling in their children defenses against advertising. It would appear that authoritative parents (17 percent of the parents surveyed) and rigid controlling parents (24 percent of the parents surveyed) may be so motivated and competent. On the other hand, permissive parents (24 percent of the survey) may simply instill a positive attitude toward media, advertisements and consumption. Clearly, however, the authoritarian parents (18 percent of the survey) and neglecting ones (17 percent of the survey) are not motivated to co-view, and are either unable or unmotivated to train children.

Another study of consumer socialization concerns training children to defend themselves against advertising. According to Brucks, Armstrong, and Goldberg,[44] children need four skills for learning cognitive defenses. The child must (1) realize that the advertiser and the viewer have different perspectives and interests (minimally, the child must realize that a commercial is more than just a shorter cartoon segment—that the advertiser is motivated by profit, not to help the child gain a friend, gain status, and such); (2) realize that the advertiser *intends* to persuade the

child to buy a product; (3) realize that all persuasive messages are inherently *biased;* and, (4) realize that biased messages must be viewed, examined, or interpreted differently than informational, educational, or entertainment-oriented messages.

Thus Brucks, Armstrong, and Goldberg[45] argued that children at the age of thirteen or older ought to be able to counterargue advertising messages and to do so automatically, while children eight to twelve years of age are knowledgeable about how to counterargue advertisements, but are often "overwhelmed" when viewing sophisticated advertisements and need to be *prompted* in order to counterargue messages. However, children seven years of age and younger may not be able to adequately counterargue messages even when prompted to do so, because they have not input enough information concerning proof, evidence and the like, and do not comprehend how camera angles and such are used to make "puffery" advertisements.

Brucks, Armstrong, and Goldberg studied nine- to ten-year-olds, who should be old enough to be trained in defenses. High levels of "advertising knowledge" were achieved by showing and discussing two films that demonstrated advertising methods at enhancing a product's attractiveness (or hiding its deficiencies). The films prompted children to question the credibility of celebrities, the giving away of "dinky" free prizes, the implication that a product will produce excitement, good looks, or love. The films exposed the practice of flashing obscure disclaimers at the end of a commercial, and technical tricks such as close-ups, editing for excitement, dramatic sound effects, special sets, camera filters, and attractive lighting. However, possessing *knowledge* is not sufficient to prompt children to use the knowledge each time they view commercials. Brucks, et al., used a *prompting cue* by having some of the students fill out a brief five-question quiz prior to watching commercials. The questions were designed to remind the children of the knowledge

F I G U R E	7.1

EFFECTS OF KNOWLEDGE OF ADVERTISING AND CUE ON ADVERTISING COUNTERARGUMENTS

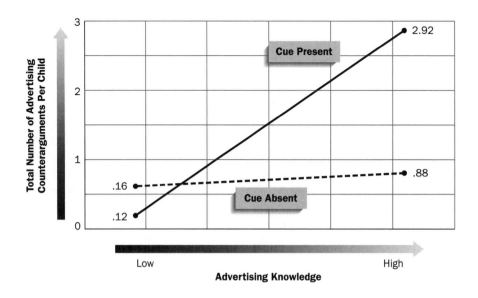

From: M. Brucks, G.M. Armstrong, and M.E. Goldberg, "Children's Use of Cognitive Defenses Against Television Advertising: A Cognitive Response Approach," *Journal of Consumer Research* (vol. 14, 1988), pp. 471–482. Used with permission.

gained from the film—commercials make products look larger, work better, more fun and exciting, and so forth. Brucks, Armstrong, and Goldberg had half of the students (the high knowledge group) watch the *knowledge* films, while the other half (the low knowledge group) watched a film unrelated to advertising. Several days later, all children watched a series of commercials containing some questionable advertising tactics (dinky giveaways, louder sounds, and so forth). The commercials included ads for a doll, a robot, fruit candy, and a drink. Immediately before viewing the commercials, some of the students completed the quiz, which prompted or cued the students to

view the commercial more suspiciously. The researchers, therefore, were examining how students viewed the commercials in four "conditions": high knowledge + cue present, high knowledge + cue absent, low knowledge + cue present, and low knowledge + cue absent.

After viewing the commercials, the children wrote out their reactions to the ads on a piece of paper, and these reactions were coded by the researchers for the amount of "counterarguments" the children generated. The students also rated the ads on perceived deceptiveness and listed the number of deceptive techniques spotted. Figure 7.1 shows the number of counterarguments listed by the students. When information level was low, there was little counterarguing. However, when advertising knowledge was high, the presence of a prompting *cue* resulted in a sizeable increase in the children's ability to list counterarguments. Children need both *knowledge* and a *prompting cue* that triggers or primes the use of knowledge in order to counterargue.

However, the results of the study concerning identification of deception was more straightforward. Children who had viewed the training movies were simply more able to list the sophisticated (and deceptive) tactics used on them. Untrained children were not able to spot the tricks used in the commercials. Prompting or priming the youths had no impact on increasing the number of cues they spotted.

In sum, children who are nine or ten years old can be trained to spot deception and can adequately counterargue a commercial's claims when both knowledge is present and there is a cue that triggers or primes the young person to cognitively defend the self. However, how many parents are able to aid their children is still an open issue, as is how to improve the skills of a younger receiver.

Aging Americans

By some reports, the number of "elderly Americans" (those who have reached and surpassed "normal" retirement age) will soon account for 15 to 20 percent of the population of the United States.[46] As a group, aging Americans spend a good deal of time being exposed to the media. But, unlike children (who, as a group, watch very similar entertainment shows), aging Americans are "segmented" into watching different shows, programs, movies, and print media in order to learn, gain companionship, relax, or to be entertained. Also, while children are impressionable and acquire new attitudes and beliefs, research indicates aging Americans become *less* susceptible to influence as they age. Krosnick and Alwin,[47] for instance, argue

persuasively in favor of an *impressionable years hypothesis*—people develop a number of their attitudes and orientations toward politics, consumption, and the like relatively early in life. Our way of viewing the world becomes relatively fixed sometime between eighteen and twenty-five years of age. As we age, we tend to use the same view of "liberalism," "conservatism," and so on, for decades.

Also, unlike children who have no money of their own and must depend on parents to provide the goods advertised to them, aging Americans have a good deal of expendable income, and these consumers buy qualitatively different things than younger receivers. While millions of dollars are spent trying to convince young children to switch soft drink brands, perfumes, jeans, and so forth, the aging Americans quietly spend millions of dollars on comfortable, safe automobiles, eating out, investments, trips and the like. Indeed, claims are now made that there are more aging Americans than teenagers, that no group of receivers has a higher per-capita income than the fifty-five- to sixty-four-year-old group, and that even after retirement, the over-sixty-four group makes a trivial $500 less per year than the average household in America.[48]

IDENTIFYING AND RESEARCHING THE GROUP

Until the mid-1980s, media portrayals of the elderly were typically quite negative. Often, they were portrayed as feeble, or crotchety, and rarely as sage-like, and studies suggested that the elderly receiver's self-concept became more negative after heavy exposures to such ageist biases.[49] By the late 1980s, much of this view changed (see Box 7.2).[50] Greco[51] surveyed advertising practitioners concerning the use of elderly spokespersons and found that 63 percent indicated that there had been, by 1988, a concerted effort to include the elderly in advertisements during the previous five years. Also, 74 percent indicated that elderly spokespersons were effective in persuading

BOX 7.2

The New Wrinkle in Casting

Turn on the TV, sit back and watch a few commercials. Chances are, you'll soon see a couple of old guys sitting on a porch humorously spinning their entrepreneurial tales, a grandfather triumphantly treating his family to an inexpensive yet satisfying meal, or a venerable old celebrity assuring you of a product's quality. Could these old people possibly represent a period in life Shakespeare described as "poor, full of grief as age, wretched in both?"

Whether or not these advertising oldsters are true to life, in TV commercials, wretchedness and old age are mutually exclusive. Indeed, today's advertisers use positive images of older people to sell everything from investment banking services to fast food. Even though the aged do not rival the Pepsi Generation's historic popularity, the advertising community is starting to realize the potential of older people to attract a general market.

Advertisers' strategies have been influenced by recent changes in American attitudes toward aging. According to the Television Information Office's recent study, *Television Looks at Aging*, "In the past few years, television has moved toward more realistic and sensitive portrayals of aging." Vanishing from TV is the stereotypical image of the old person as helpless, ailing, and dependent. Instead, actors like John Forsythe and Joan Collins have created characters who are over forty and nonetheless rich, powerful, and sexy. Television still doesn't include enough older characters, says the study, but more programs are portraying older in a positive light.

Essentially TV is reflecting the demographic and sociological changes taking place in America at large. By the turn of the century, seniors will be the fastest growing segment of the American public. They are living and working longer, while maintaining positions of financial and political power. As a result, says Helene Brooks, executive editor of *Fifty Plus* magazine, "All the negative associations of aging are diminishing. Instead, young people are beginning to recognize that older people have a wealth of knowledge and experience to offer."

Advertisers have profited from the "graying of America" and the concomitant changes in attitudes towards the aged. "Just look at the enormous success from changing attitudes garnered by using Clara Peller in their commercials," says Brooks. "The old lady who says 'Where's the beef?' has a lot more spunk and innate wisdom than many young people I know. No wonder young and old alike fell in love with those commercials."

There is nothing new about the actual appearance of old people in TV commercials. For years, older actors have touted the quality of products that were targeted to older audiences, such as laxatives, antacids, denture supplies, arthritis pain relievers, and hair coloring. They have also consistently appeared in multigenerational advertisements for "family products." Nynex's current TV campaign, for instance, consists of commercials that focus on different age groups. In one, family members search all over their house for the Nynex Yellow Pages, only to find them under a snoozing grandfather's rocking chair.

Advertisers have also traditionally linked older actors with heritage campaigns, equating the age of the spokesman to the long existence of the product. Pepperidge Farm, for example, combines an endearing old man with the line "Pepperidge Farm Remembers." The consumer is led to believe that the old man has "witnessed" the fact that over the years Pepperidge Farm has consistently provided the consumer with quality products.

TV campaigns focusing on a product's "old fashioned taste" comprise still another example of commercials where older actors have consistently appeared. No campaign better epitomizes this kind of advertising than that of Ogilvy & Mather for Country Time Lemonade. Since 1976, Harry Holcombe, a distinguished-looking older actor who embodies both kindness and credibility, has helped General Foods take the largest share of the powdered drink market. In effect, says one account executive at O & M, "Harry Holcombe *is* Country Time." Dressed in twenties garb and expounding on "the good old days," he makes consumers believe that Country Time differs little from the lemonade he enjoyed as a child.

"We live in a time when people are yearning for extended family and older, believable role models," says Helene Brooks. Advertisers are clearly capitalizing on this nostalgia and sprinkling more TV commercials with older faces.

According to Peter Schweitzer, senior vice president and management director on the Kodak film account, "We deliberately chose older people because of their current appeal. Adulation for the youth generation and the values it represents is dying out. Old age is once again something to be proud of."

Not only do older people in TV commercials evoke the values of the past, they also represent authority and wisdom. Advertisers currently use actors like Karl Malden, John Houseman and Burt Lancaster to this end. Certainly these actors' celebrity status gives their endorsement of a product that much more clout, but it is their age that underscores their credibility.

From: *Madison Avenue*, October 1985, p. 66.

audiences to switch products, 67 percent indicated that such spokespersons enhanced credibility, and 68 percent said that using elderly spokespersons helped gain awareness of new products. Table 7.3 presents a list of the products for which advertisers would recommend using elderly spokespersons; these include such "big ticket" items as vacations, investments, and health packages—things for which individuals with financial resources, time, and ability can spend money. Other products dealing with fashion, changes in image (cosmetics and the like), electronic devices and matters of trends presumably would not fit into the category of recommended usage.

Although we refer to aging Americans as a "group," older receivers do in fact differ substantially from one another. Lazer[52] argued that there are, in fact, four distinct groups: young-old (55 to 64), middle-old (65 to 74), senior (75 to 85) and very old (85+). Who is "old"? People usually employ the term "old" to describe a person who is from 10 to 20 years older than they are. However, most research employs a criterion of 55 or older, 65 or older, or receivers who have retired (many now wait until age 70 to retire). Several significant projects have focused on identifying different *types* or *segments* of aging Americans suggesting how they can be reached and the appeals to be used. We will discuss three types of studies here.

Rubin and Rubin[53] concluded that older receivers use the media for one of four general reasons: *to be informed, to be entertained, for companionship*, and *to relax*. The *companionship* viewer is often a female or a person who lives alone and watches a number of game shows, daytime serials, and dramas. This type of viewer is more likely to tune into television during early afternoon hours through prime time, and until late at night. Viewers who rated *information* as an important reason for watching television watch more news and talk shows, since they desire to learn about people and events in the world at large. Informed viewers

TABLE	7.3

RECOMMENDED USE OF THE ELDERLY IN ADS AIMED AT AN ELDERLY AUDIENCE BY PRODUCT CLASS

Product Class	Recommend Elderly Spokesperson	Not Recommend Elderly Spokesperson
Health and medicines	92%	1%
Travel and vacations	83	6
Financial services	80	7
Insurance	80	11
Rental property	72	14
Hotels	71	13
Food	66	10
Newspapers and magazines	65	8
Real estate	61	18
Diet aids (weight control)	58	26
Cameras	51	35
Household cleaners	48	19
Household appliances/ tools	48	21
Jewelry	48	29
Clothing	47	35
Cosmetics	44	39
Cars and trucks	41	44
Electronics and communications	35	41
Sporting goods	33	39
Shampoo	33	44

From: A.J. Greco, "The Elderly as Communicators: Perceptions, of Advertising Practitioners," *Journal of Advertising Research*, vol. 28 (1988), pp. 39–46. Used with permission.

watch television much differently than do the companionship viewers (perhaps watching the Discovery Channel and other channels devoted to travel, adventure, and learning about the world). *Entertainment* viewers watch a lot of television, including game shows, adventure programs, comedies, musical productions, and so on. This group is very selective in viewing, and can easily defect to watch other, more informative or interesting shows. *Relaxation* viewers watch television to relax, preferring general comedies and situation comedies.

This information about different types of receivers is important for two reasons. First, it tells us that not all aging Americans share the same interests in viewing, and that their qualitatively different needs of the media are being met. Companionship viewers, for example, who are generally alone, and probably make purchasing decisions without the advice of others, are probably less-knowledgeable consumers (relative to the informed viewer), and may be somewhat dependent on television commercials for input. Second, information such as this suggests how different appeals can be employed to influence members of different groups—how selling cruises to exotic places depends on knowing what the audience members are seeking. Such advertisements can emphasize meeting others (to the companionship viewer), learning about the world (to the informed viewer), food, dances and gambling on board (to the entertainment viewer) and rest and a break from the world of cares (to the relaxation viewer).

Davis and French[54] assessed how receivers are oriented toward advertising, and they identified three segments of aging (60+) female receivers. (This and the study that follows limited research and discussion to females because females substantially outnumber males in this population.) 25 percent of their sample were labeled *engaged* receivers, 41 percent were labeled *autonomous*, and 34 percent were labeled *receptive*. The engaged receivers were women who actively and

fully participated in society, were skeptical of advertising, and relied on friends before making purchasing decisions. They were "information seekers" and often discounted advertisements, although they might be more influenced by ads emphasizing quality products and containing facts, evidence, and statistics (relative to "image" advertising and messages containing testimonials). Engaged women read more newspapers and magazines and watched more news programs than other groups. They scored high on a measure of "cosmopolitanism" dealing with interests in other cultures and they received personal satisfaction from reading fashion magazines and using cosmetics; they were interested in educational television and were health conscious. These women were more innovative (willing to try new things) relative to the other two groups, but were quite cynical about corporations ("Big businesses are out to protect themselves") and were suspicious of warranties. This group is remarkably similar to the "informed" receivers identified by Rubin and Rubin.

On the other extreme, *receptive* receivers believed that advertising helped them to make informed choices, and they did not consult with friends about brands or products. These receivers scored lowest in "cosmopolitan" orientations, but were open to innovation, liked public television, and were quite concerned with nutrition. These receivers were more optimistic about life in general, and were more positive in attitudes toward advertisements and their credibility. They were heavy consumers of comedy shows, suggesting a parallel to Rubin and Rubin's entertainment type of receiver.

Autonomous receivers did not seek out the advice of friends regarding brands and products and were neutral about the value of information from advertising in making purchasing decisions. They were suspicious of advertising and of competitive advertisements, but also did not seek out advice or assistance from friends. Rather, they apparently rely heavily on personal experience as a source of information concerning what to buy. This group views the least TV and reads the least in newspapers. They scored low in innovativeness and indicated low interest in public television.

A similar study was conducted by Day, Davis, Dove, and French,[55] who found two general types of receivers: *self-sufficient* and *persuadable*. Self-sufficient receivers (compared to the persuadables) were more self-confident, more independent, more outgoing, more influential in dealing with others, more traditional; they were more likely (relative to persuadables) to read a book, go shopping, attend events such as concerts and sporting events, dine out and entertain at home, while the persuadables were more likely to stay home.

Day and her colleagues also argued that there are two different types of self-sufficient receivers and persuadable receivers. Self-sufficient receivers could be either *active integrated* or *disengaged integrated*. The term "active integrated" refers to active individuals who are self-perceived *opinion leaders* who give rather than request information from others, who are affluent, confident, opinionated, well educated, nurturing, achievement-oriented, and politically conservative. Disengaged integrated women, however, possess self-confidence, but not the income and social-class connections and background to compare to their active integrated counterparts. The disengaged integrated entertain in their homes, are quite content with life, and routinely keep abreast of world events. The active integrated receiver (compared to the disengaged integrated) was likely to be *more* self-confident, *more* "in control," *more* influential in dealing with others, *more* nationalistic, *more* conservative and traditional, *more* secure with her financial status, and more likely to go shopping and entertain at home, than the disengaged integrated who is more likely to drink cocktails and wine, read a book, and eat breakfast out.

Day and her colleagues also found that the persuadables were represented by two groups:

passive dependent and *defended constricted*. The term "passive dependent" was used because these elderly receivers show a resignation to life that approaches apathy. These individuals have not worked outside the home and are only moderately satisfied with life. New social contacts are minimal, and their homes and family members are the center of attention. The "defended constricted" receivers are very sociable and outgoing, seek acceptance, and have the financial means to satisfy desires; but they lack self-confidence, avoid taking risks and seek assurances from others. As a group, they are threatened by aging and are preoccupied with health and/or the continuation of activities previously enjoyed.

There are many parallels between these various projects on elderly receivers.[56] For example, there exists a higher income, highly confident, active group of receivers who seek to be informed and are suspicious of advertising (*informed, active integrated*, and *engaged*). The *disengaged integrated* receivers have more subdued lives and fewer financial resources. (They are typically *entertainment* viewers who also read the *TV Guide*, and listen to AM country and western music). How to appeal to both these groups of self-sufficient individuals? According to Day and her colleagues, messages should be directed at their "internal locus of control," portraying these people as self-confident, independent, and outgoing. Also, since at least some of these receivers (the fully *engaged* receivers, and the affluent receivers) seriously question the credibility of advertising, it would appear effective for ads to contain strong, convincing arguments concerning the quality of the products (or candidates) being advertised.

The *passive dependent* receivers are emotionally dependent and quite withdrawn from public life and watch indiscriminant television possibly for the sake of companionship. The *defended constricted* receivers, however, are more selective in viewing patterns and are less apathetic, possibly using television for the purposes of being informed or to relax. By definition, these persuadables are somewhat similar to the receptives noted in Davis and French in that both tend to characterize emotional receivers, dependent receivers and ones generally "open" to influence. Day and her colleagues argue that advertisements should show these individuals engaged in familiar activities in and around the home. Further, the passive dependent receivers closely parallel the stereotype of the aging American, who possesses insecurities and lacks social contact. This lack of social support among immediate friends and associates, and the need to reduce anxiety should be ingredients in effective persuasion.

All of the projects on identifying the aging receiver indicated that the more affluent receiver is in fact more suspicious and less trusting of advertisements, and less dependent on the advertisements as sources of information concerning purchases. A recent project that addressed the issue of affluence directly was conducted by Burnett,[57] who compared the life-styles and media attitudes of affluent ($30,000+ a year retired individuals/couples), and "moderates" ($15,000-$24,999 a year). The more-affluent elderly indicated agreement with the statement that advertising insulted their intelligence, while the less affluent indicated that information in advertising was useful for making buying decisions, and that television was a primary source of information.

The implications suggest that the more affluent elderly individual is likely to be critical and negative of the television advertisement. To be effective with this group, advertisements have to be made to a new, higher standard; facts and evidence should be prominent, quality emphasized; and it is probably wise to employ a two-sided message. Two-sided messages were not rated less credible by the more affluent, and two-sided messages are preferable if the receiver is likely to be exposed to opposing messages (see Chapter 8)—which will undoubtedly be true for the more af-

fluent receiver who will also rely on magazines and printed materials for information. Another strategy would be to mail written reports to interested receivers, who can call a toll-free number to further their "information search" on the particular purchase. On the other hand, the less affluent elderly receiver is more likely to regard television commercials as useful; for these receivers, an emphasis on a need fulfilled through purchasing or owning the advertised product should be included.

Gender and Persuasion

Karlins and Abelson concluded, over twenty years ago, that "one of the most consistent and reliable findings in the field of persuasion" is that females are more easily influenced than males.[58] This conclusion is false. Eagly's[59] extensive review of the literature indicated that the context in which the persuasion took place compromised the study. Eagly found little evidence in support of greater susceptibility in *persuasion* studies, and in *conformity* studies *not* involving *group* pressure, and that the trend toward female influenceability " . . . in these settings can be readily explained by researcher's tendency to choose experimental materials somewhat biased against the interests and expertise of women."

However, in group pressure settings, females conformed more than did men. Eagly explored three explanations for why women might conform more than men: (a) sex roles prescribe differences in yielding, with the female role implying submissiveness to influence; (b) the superior verbal ability of females predisposes them to be influenced; and, (c) females' greater concern with interpersonal aspects of situations, in particular with maintaining social harmony, predisposes them to be influenced. She concluded only the latter explanation, that females desire to have harmonious relationships (or to at least avoid conflict)—a tendency strongly affected by their values (see above). Hence, there are two major concerns one should keep in mind when dealing with gender: Is this a topic biased in favor or against men or women? Is there likely to be pressure on audience members such that conformity is important in order to reduce conflict?

There is strong evidence that many traditional roles are changing. For example, in the Eagly review cited above it was noted that 32 percent of the studies published before 1970 indicated females were more persuadable than males, while only 8 percent of the studies published after 1970 indicated such a trend. A good deal of this difference can be attributed to the fact that much of the early research was caused by a *cross-sex influence* effect. As Ward, Seccombe, Bendel, and Carter[60] recently noted, most of the research through the 1950s to the 1970s (the decades in which females were claimed to be more persuadable than males) employed male speakers as communicators. This means that male receivers heard a same-sex speaker while the female receivers heard a cross-sex speaker. Receivers very often behave differently with a speaker who is of a different gender than their own; with an opposite-sex speaker many other variables affect "persuasion" besides agreeing with the logic and evidence of the speaker. What differences are there? For one, there are interpersonal attraction motives which would argue that it is far easier to be compliant in the face of an opposite-sex speaker, and much easier to resist persuasion and to counterargue a speaker of the same sex. Further, it may be "normal" to agree routinely with an opposite-sex partner, not only because we would like opposite-sex partners to like us, but also because we do not want to be perceived as argumentative to such a person. Normal conversations, in fact, contain many statements geared to not contradict or argue a point another speaker makes; otherwise, there would be few smooth-flowing conversations.

Ward and his colleagues are quite succinct in noting when a speaker is likely to obtain this "cross-sex effect":

1.   The persuasive messages must be presented by communicators who are physically present rather than presented through more-remote channels of communication such as written messages or audio tape recordings; and,

2.   The experimental procedure must establish a context in which receivers believe that their opinions may become known to the communicators. If receivers believe that their opinions will remain privately held (for example, in marketing, or when an election is held weeks later), then there will be no "normative" pressure to express agreement with a cross-sex speaker.

These scholars had a male and a female speaker deliver a twenty-five minute persuasive speech (against aspects of Reagan's "New Federalism" and how federal money should be spent) live to both male and female receivers. Females who heard a male speak changed a number of their attitudes, but the changes did not persist over the course of weeks—indicating that females engaged in "agreeing responses" to the male speaker on the day he spoke. (Indeed, there was greater *persistence* in changed opinions over a two-month period when female receivers heard the speech by a female speaker, not the male speaker.)

However, Ward and his colleagues did not find male receivers to be substantially more influenced by the female speaker than by the male speaker (except for the issue of poverty; female speakers prompted male receivers to change opinions on how poverty should be treated). This general limit on the credibility of female speakers was explained in terms of expectations we have concerning the *status roles* females do not yet possess in our country. Males still occupy most of the higher-status roles, and thus are assigned greater access to knowledge and information on matters of government, taxes, and the like. Nonetheless, we cannot conclude that women, as receivers, are more persuaded than males; rather, in a typical study like Ward, et al., there is a tendency to express agreement with an opposite-sex speaker when the speaker is present, but these "agreement responses" are not lasting.

Throughout the 1980s scholars had been preoccupied with the fact that not all women (or men) are inherently equal or equivalent simply because they share the same biological sex organs. Bem[61] feels that perhaps it is best to not relies on *biological* sex, but to rely instead on psychological sexuality. She employed the term "androgynous personality" to refer to two different scores an individual received when completing the "androgynous" (derived from the Greek words for male "andro," and the female "gyne") questionnaire. Not to be confused with the word "gynandrous" (which means a person of doubtful sex), an "androgynous" person has qualities of both masculinity and femininity. Receivers complete an androgynous questionnaire, and receive a score on "masculinity," and a second score on "femininity." A male who scores high on masculinity and low on femininity is referred to as a "traditional sex-typed male," and a female who scores high on femininity and low on masculinity is referred to as a "traditional sex-typed female." Males and females who score high on both masculinity and femininity are referred to as "androgynous" individuals who rely instead on psychological sexuality.

A number of studies have investigated the impact of androgyny on persuadibility. Montgomery and Burgoon[62] provided students with Bem's measure and classified individuals into four groups: traditionally sex-typed males and females androgynous males and females. The students later received a written message, attributed to an independent educational consulting firm, which argued that admission to the university should be restricted to juniors and seniors. The authors found that sex-typed females were persuaded most, followed by androgynous females and androgynous males, while traditionally sex-typed males (high masculinity and low femininity) were least persuaded. In a later study, Montgomery and Burgoon[63] similarly found that the androgynous measure was a better predictor of persuasion than biological sex.

Advertisers would similarly argue that the general category of "women" is too broad and one needs to take into consideration age (or life status) and career expectations.[64] Research indicates women at home with preschool children experience little power and freedom and it is for them that the words "Calgon, take me away" ring true. On the other hand, less than 28 percent of the women in America are stay-at-homes, with another 13 percent planning to work at some time, 37 percent simply want a job to make money to supplement family income, another 22 to 30 percent want a job to make money to supplement family income, and another 22 to 30 percent (or more, today) are career-oriented workers. Simply studying the working woman versus the housewife provides substantial differences in persuasibility. Not surprisingly, advertisements appealing to the woman as a "career partner" are more persuasive to the working woman than the "homemaker's helper."

Differences in consumer behavior are also pervasive. Housewives are more likely to claim that serving nutritious meals and gaining praise for cooking is important, while working women rate shopping as a disliked chore and rate ease of preparation and ease of cleaning as important. Both housewives and career women rate novelty and variety as important in meal preparation, and both considered expense as an important consideration when purchasing food. It is not surprising, then, that frozen food companies offering products such as Lean Cuisine have profited so well over the last decade by offering what 30 to 50 percent of women (not to mention men) are looking for:

variety, ease of preparation, quality taste, and fewer calories.

Finally, Leigh, Rethans, and Whitney[65] recently argued that women differ substantially in terms of their acceptance of "traditional" roles ("If being a housewife is a full-time job, she should be able to find time to cook") and "modern" roles ("I can relate to this ad, her husband is sharing household duties"). There are certainly a number of commercials depicting women in limited roles or in forced traditional roles. For example, Robitussin's "Dr. Mom" advertisement shows all family members (except the mother) helpless in fighting cold symptoms. Such an ad may reinforce a receiver's accepted role and is not perceived as insulting. To another receiver, who adopts a modern role, such an ad is offensive because it forces her into a role she resists (such a person would also resist shopping, so the makers of Robitussin are not going to change this advertising campaign yet). The affluent women have already decided that most of the women's roles in ads show women in a negative way and are condescending. According to Leigh and his colleagues, wider, more-respectable roles for women need to be portrayed in ads, but the ads and the products need to be matched to the "traditional versus modern" concept respective of whether women in the target market are "traditional" or "modern."

Social Class, Education, Occupation, and Income

Although these four variables are frequently separated in research studies, they tend to be highly correlated. A person's level of education tends to determine occupation, which is highly related to income level, and in turn, to social class. Knowing that these relationships *are* interrelated suggests that we can make use of one of the variables as a standard against which to make at least *some* estimate of the others. Social class is the variable about which we have the most evidence, and a number of different studies indicate important differences in attitudes and beliefs between various social classes.

The term "social class" is a label for a series of categories into which people can be placed. Generally, social classes are labeled as lower, middle, and upper, with many researchers further subdividing each class into two or three additional subcategories. Thus, one can talk about the *Upper Americans* (upper-upper class representing 0.3 percent of Americans, lower-upper 1.2 percent, and upper-middle 12.5 percent), the *Middle Americans* (middle class 32 percent, and working class 38 percent), and *Lower Americans* (working poor 9 percent to 12 percent and lower-lower 7 percent).[66]

Different Americans can be characterized according to values and interests. The working American is interested more in local events than the Upper American, who is likely to be interested in national and world events. The working American attends more closely to local news items and to local sports heroes than the Upper American. Further, the working American appears to be particularly interested in family matters and places greater emphasis on family and on the extended family. A working-class individual relies on family for a number of purposes—help getting jobs, advice, help getting through crises. One study even found that only 12 percent of the Upper Americans lived within a mile of a close relative, while 45 to 55 percent of the working class lived close to relatives.[67]

Laborers in America also place greater emphasis on the needs of other laborers. Coleman,[68] for example, noted that American laborers were the last to buy foreign cars during the oil shortages of the 1970s. Even three years after the first oil price shock only 10 percent of the working Americans had purchased a fuel-economy foreign car, as compared to 40 percent of the Upper Americans. In terms of vacationing, laborers in America strongly prefer to stay in America. Typical working-class Americans vacation at home or vacation within a few hours of home. If they travel far to vacation, it usually means they will stay with relatives. Further, even when blue-collar workers were making significant advances in pay raises some years ago, they did not expect to change their status significantly. Rather, extra money was spent on improving the position of all family members—improved schools, better brand-name products for school clothes, and so on.

The most obvious recommendation when dealing with social class involves adjusting the persuasive message to make it suitable to the values of the receivers. Working-class Americans are more susceptible to claims concerning how one can achieve improvements for one's family and to appeals to patriotism. Further, they are likely to be suspicious of claims concerning how they can benefit greatly from a course of action—their expectations of achievement are likely to be limited to practical and short-term gains.[69] On the other hand, Upper Americans are likely to be persuaded by appeals concerning achievement, larger gains, more international or cosmopolitan interests, appeals to different reference groups (exclusive clubs to which they belong) and appeals of a personal nature.

F O O T N O T E S

1. N. Miller, "Involvement and Dogmatism as Inhibitors of Attitude Change," *Journal of Experimental Social Psychology*, vol. 1 (1965), pp. 121-132.

2. M. Rokeach, *The Nature of Human Values* (New York: Free Press, 1973), p. 18.

3. M. Rokeach, *The Nature of Human Values*, p. 27.

4. M. Rokeach, *The Nature of Human Values*.

5. L.R. Kahle, ed., *Social Values and Social Change* (New York: Praeger, 1983).

6. H.H. Kelley, "Two Functions of Reference Groups," in H. Prohansky and B. Seidenberg, eds., *Basic Studies in Social Psychology* (New York: Holt, Rinehart and Winston, 1965), pp. 210-214.

7. T.M. Newcomb, "Attitude Development as a Function of Reference Groups," in H. Prohansky and

B. Seidenberg, eds., *Basic Studies in Social Psychology* (New York: Holt, Rinehart and Winston, 1965), pp. 215-225.

8. L. Festinger, "A Theory of Social Comparison Processes," *Human Relations*, vol. 7 (1954), pp. 117-140; L. Festinger, "Motivation Leading to Social Behavior," in M.R. Jones, ed., *Nebraska Symposium on Motivation* (vol. 2, 1954), pp. 191-218. Quote is from page 217. Also see: L. Wheeler, "A Brief History of Social Comparison Theory," in J. Suls and T.A. Wills, eds., *Social Comparison: Contemporary Theory and Research* (Hillsdale, N.J.: Erlbaum, 1991), pp. 3-21.

9. J. Suls and T.A. Wills, eds., *Social Comparison: Contemporary Theory and Research* (Hillsdale, N.J.: Erlbaum, 1991).

10. T.A. Wills, "Similarity and Self-Esteem in Downward Comparison," in J. Suls and T.A. Wills, eds., *Social Comparison: Contemporary Theory and Research* (Hillsdale, N.J.: Erlbaum, 1991), pp. 51-78.

11. Luhtanen and J. Crocker, "Self-Esteem and Intergroup Comparisons: Toward a Theory of Collective Self-Esteem," in J. Suls and T.A. Wills, eds., *Social Comparison: Contemporary Theory and Research* (Hillsdale, N.J.: Erlbaum, 1991), pp. 211-236.

12. N. Miller, S. Gross, and R. Holtz, "Social Projection and Attitudinal Certainty," in J. Suls and T.A. Wills, eds., *Social Comparison: Contemporary Theory and Research* (Hillsdale, N.J.: Erlbaum, 1991), pp. 177-210.

13. R.J. Simon, *The Jury and the Defense of Insanity* (Boston, Mass.: Little, Brown, 1967). See also R. James, "Status and Competence of Jurors," *The American Journal of Sociology*, vol. 64 (1959), pp. 563-570.

14. Simon, *The Jury*, pp. 33-35.

15. Simon, *The Jury*.

16. R. Hastie, S.D. Penrod, and N. Pennington, *Inside the Jury* (Cambridge, Mass.: Harvard University Press, 1983).

17. Hastie, Penrod, and Pennington, *Inside the Jury*.

18. R.F. Baumeister and J.M. Darley, "Reducing the Biasing Effect of Perpetrator Attractiveness in Jury Simulation," *Personality and Social Psychology Bulletin*, vol. 8 (1982), pp. 286-292. M.F. Kaplan and L.E. Miller, "Reducing the Effects of Juror Bias," *Journal of Personality and Social Psychology*, vol. 36 (1978), pp. 1443-1455. D.C.E. Ugwuegbu, "Racial and Evidential Factors in Juror Attribution of Legal Responsibility," *Journal of Experimental Social Psychology*, vol. 15 (1979), pp. 133-146.

19. G.M. Rosa, "Tapping the Hispanic Market: Myths and Misconceptions," *Credit Magazine* (November/December, 1990), pp. 12-15; H. Valencia, "Point of

View: Avoiding Hispanic Market Blunders," *Journal of Advertising Research*, vol. 23 (1984), pp. 19-20; D. Kimoto-Burns, "Dispelling Hispanic Myths for the Communication Researcher," in D. Porter and L. Samovar, *Cross Cultural Communication: A Reader* (in production).

20. Rosa, "Tapping the Hispanic Market: Myths and Misconceptions"; Valencia, "Point of View: Avoiding Hispanic Market Blunders"; D. Kimoto-Burns, "Dispelling Hispanic Myths for the Communication Researcher," in L.A. Samovar and R.E. Porter, *Cross Cultural Communication: A Reader* (7th edition) (in production). Belmont, CA.: Wadsworth.

21. Valencia, "Point of View: Avoiding Hispanic Market Blunders"; Rosa, "Tapping the Hispanic Market: Myths and Misconceptions."

22. P. Engardio, "Fast Times on Avenida Madison," *Business Week* (June 6, 1988), pp. 62-65.

23. Engardio, "Fast Times on Avenida Madison."

24. Engardio, "Fast Times on Avenida Madison."

25. Engardio, "Fast Times on Avenida Madison."

26. Rosa, "Tapping the Hispanic Market: Myths and Misconceptions."

27. D. Astor, "The Hispanic Market: An In-Depth Profile," *Marketing Communications* (July 1981), pp. 15-19.

28. J. Schwartz, "Frito Parks," *American Demographics* (February, 1989), pp. 44-45; A.E. Gross, "Hispanic Portfolio: J.C. Penney Shows Its Style" *Adweek* (September 25, 1989), p. 11; A.E. Gross, "Pepsi Builds a Dream House," *Adweek* (September 25, 1989), p. 14.

29. E. Pomice and A.M. Arrarte, "It's a Whole Nuevo Mundo Out There," *U.S. News & World Report* (May 15, 1989), pp. 45-46.

30. R. Deshpande, W.D. Hoyer, and N. Donthu, "The Intensity of Ethnic Affiliation: A Study of the Sociology of Hispanic Consumption," *Journal of Consumer Research*, vol. 13 (1986), pp. 214-220.

31. Engardio, "Fast Times on Avenida Madison."

32. Rosa, "Tapping the Hispanic Market: Myths and Misconceptions."

33. Valencia, "Point of View: Avoiding Hispanic Market Blunders."

34. L.K. Meringoff and G.S. Lesser, "Children's Ability to Distinguish Television Commercials from Program Material," in R.P. Alder, G.S. Lesser, L.K. Meringoff, T.S. Robertson, J.R. Rossiter, and S. Ward, eds., *The Effects of Television Advertising on Children* (Lexington, Mass.: Lexington Books, 1980), pp. 29-42.

35. S. Ward, D.B. Wackman, and E. Wartella, *How Children Learn to Buy* (Beverly Hills: Sage, 1977).

36. Meringoff and Lesser, "Children's Ability to Distinguish Television Commercials."

37. L.K. Meringoff and G.S. Lesser, "The Influence of Format and Audiovisual Techniques on Children's Perceptions of Commercial Messages," in R.P. Adler, G.S. Lesser, L.K. Meringoff, T.S. Robertson, J.R. Rossiter, and S. Ward, eds., *The Effects of Television Advertising on Children* (Lexington, Mass.: Lexington Books, 1980), pp. 43-59.

38. Meringoff and Lesser, "The Influence of Format and Audiovisual Techniques," p. 44.

39. Meringoff and Lesser, "The Influence of Format and Audiovisual Techniques," p. 44.

40. Meringoff and Lesser, "The Influence of Format and Audiovisual Techniques," p. 45.

41. R.P. Adler, G.S. Lesser, L.K. Meringoff, T.S. Robertson, J.R. Rossiter, and S. Ward, *The Effects of Television Advertising on Children* (Lexington, Mass.: Lexington Books, 1980); C. Atkin and G. Heald, "The Content of Children's Toy and Food Commercials," *Journal of Communication*, vol. 27 (1977), pp. 107-144; J. Bryant and D.R. Anderson, eds., *Children's Understanding of Television* (New York: Academic, 1983); B. Reeves and B.S. Greenberg, "Children's Perception of Television Characters," *Human Communication Research*, vol. 3 (1977), pp. 113-127; S. Ward, D.B. Wackman, and E. Wartella, *How Children Learn to Buy* (Beverly Hills: Sage, 1977).

42. D. Kunkel and D. Roberts, "Young Minds and Marketplace Values: Issues in Children's Television Advertising," *Journal of Social Issues*, vol. 47 (1991), pp. 57-72.

43. L. Carlson and S. Grossbart, "Parental Style and Consumer Socialization of Children," *Journal of Consumer Research*, vol. 15 (1988), pp. 77-94.

44. M. Brucks, G.M. Armstrong, and M.E. Goldberg, "Children's Use of Cognitive Defenses Against Television Advertising: A Cognitive Response Approach," *Journal of Consumer Research*, vol. 14 (1988), pp. 471-482.

45. Brucks, Armstrong, and Goldberg, "Children's Use of Cognitive Defenses Against Television Advertising: A Cognitive Response Approach."

46. Concerning some of these statistics, see: J.J. Burnett, "Examining the Media Habits of the Affluent Elderly," *Journal of Advertising Research*, October/November (1991), pp. 33-41; E. Day, B. Davis, R. Dove and W. French, "Reaching the Senior Citizen Market(s)," *Journal of Advertising Research*, vol. 27 (1988), pp. 23-30.

47. J.A. Krosnick and D.F. Alwin, "Aging and Susceptibility to Attitude Change," *Journal of Personality and Social Psychology*, vol. 57 (1989), pp. 416-425.

48. B. Gunnerson, "There's Gold in Seniors," *Target Marketing* (October 1986), pp. 19-21; Day, Davis, Dove and French, "Reaching the Senior Citizen Market(s)"; J.R. Lumpkin and T.A. Festervand, "Purchase Information Sources of the Elderly," *Journal of Advertising Research*, vol. 27 (1988), pp. 31-41.

49. J. Pfefferman and J. Robinson, "A Content Analysis of Elderly Characters on Family-Oriented Situation Comedies," (unpublished paper, Communication Arts and Sciences Department, University of Southern California); B.B. Hess, "Stereotypes of the Aged," *Journal of Communication*, vol. 24 (1974), pp. 76-85; F. Korzenny and K. Neuendorf, "Television Viewing and Self-Concept of the Elderly," *Journal of Communication*, winter (1980), pp. 71-81; E.S. Schreiber and D.A. Boyd, "How the Elderly Perceive Television Commercials," *Journal of Communication*, winter (1980), pp. 61-70; L.E. Swayne and A.J. Greco, "The Portrayal of Older Americans in Television Commercials," *Journal of Advertising*, vol. 16 (1987), pp. 47-54.

50. A.J. Greco, "The Elderly as Communicators: Perceptions of Advertising Practitioners," *Journal of Advertising Research*, vol. 28 (1988), pp. 39-46; A.C. Ursic, J.L. Ursic, and V.L. Ursic, "A Longitudinal Study of the Use of the Elderly in Magazine Advertising," *Journal of Communication Research*, vol. 13 (1986), pp. 131-133.

51. Greco, "The Elderly as Communicators."

52. W. Lazer, "Inside the Mature Market," *American Demographics*, vol. 7 (1985), pp. 23-25, 48, 49.

53. A.M. Rubin and R.B. Rubin, "Older Persons' TV Viewing Patterns and Motivations," *Communication Research*, vol. 9 (1982), pp. 287-313.

54. B. Davis and W. French, "Exploring Advertising Usage Segments Among the Aged," *Journal of Advertising Research*, vol. 29 (1989), pp. 22-29; also see J.R. Lumpkin and T.A. Festervand, "Purchase Information Sources of the Elderly," *Journal of Advertising Research*, vol. 27 (1988), pp. 31-41; B.L. Neugarten, W.J. Crotty, and S.S. Tobin, eds., *Personality in Middle and Late Life* (New York: Atherton, 1964).

55. E. Day, B. Davis, R. Dove and W. French, "Reaching the Senior Citizen Market(s)," *Journal of Advertising Research*, vol. 27 (1988), pp. 23-30.

56. Day, et. al., op. cit.

57. J.J. Burnett, "Examining the Media Habits of the Affluent Elderly," *Journal of Advertising Research* (October/November, 1991), pp. 33-41.

58. M. Karlins and H.I. Abelson, *Persuasion: How Opinions and Attitudes are Changed* 2nd ed. (New York: Springer-Verlag, 1970), p. 89.

59. A.H. Eagly, "Sex Differences in Influenceability," *Psychological Bulletin*, vol. 85 (1978), pp. 86-116.

60. D.A. Ward, K. Seccombe, R. Bendel, and L.F. Carter, "Cross-Sex Context as a Factor in Persuasibility Sex Differences," *Social Psychology Quarterly*, vol. 48 (1985), pp. 269-276.

61. S.L. Bem, "Androgyny vs. Tight Little Lives of Fluffy Women and Chesty Men," *Psychology Today*, vol. 9 (1975), pp. 58-62.

62. C.L. Montgomery and M. Burgoon, "An Experimental Study of the Interactive Effects of Sex and Androgyny on Attitude Change," *Communication Monographs*, vol. 47 (1983), pp. 56-67.

63. C.L. Montgomery and M. Burgoon, "The Effects of Androgyny and Message Expectations on Resistance to Persuasive Communication," *Communication Monographs*, vol. 47 (1983), pp. 56-67.

64. See B. Barak and B. Stern, "Women's Age in Advertising: An Examination of Two Consumer Age Profiles," *Journal of Advertising Research*, vol. 25 (1986), pp. 38-47; T.E. Barry, M.C. Gilly, and L.E. Doran, "Advertising to Women with Different Career Orientations," *Journal of Advertising Research*, vol. 25 (1985), pp. 26-35; R. Bartos, *The Moving Target* (New York: The Free Press, 1982); D. Bellante and A.C. Foster, "Working Wives and Expenditure on Services," *Journal of Consumer Research*, vol. 11 (1984), pp. 700-707; R.W. Jackson, S.W. McDaniel, and C.P. Rao, "Food Shopping and Preparation: Psychographic Differences of Working Wives and Housewives," *Journal of Consumer Research*, vol. 12 (1985), pp. 110-113; J.A. Lesser and M.A. Hughes, "The Generalizability of Psychographic Market Segments Across Geographic Locations," *Journal of Marketing*, vol. 50 (1986), pp. 18-27; V.A. Zeithaml, "The New Demographics and Market Fragmentation," *Journal of Marketing*, vol. 49 (1985), pp. 64-75.

65. T.W. Leigh, A.J. Rethans, and T.R. Whitney, "Role Portrayals of Women in Advertising: Cognitive Responses and Advertising Effectiveness," *Journal of Advertising Research* (October/November 1987), pp. 54-62.

66. R.P. Coleman, "The Continuing Significance of Social Class to Marketing," *Journal of Consumer Research*, vol. 10 (1983), pp. 265-280; K. Auletta, *The Underclass* (New York: Random House, 1982); R.P. Coleman and L.P. Rainwater, with K.A. McClelland, *Social Standing in America: New Dimensions of Class* (New York: Basic Books, 1978).

67. Coleman, "The Continuing Significance."

68. Coleman, "The Continuing Significance."

69. In fact, work from even twenty years ago suggests that receivers in the lower classes were susceptible to messages that told them how to achieve the next higher class, but not to social classes two or more levels above the receivers' current level. See J. F. Short and F. Strodtbeck, *Group Process and Gang Delinquency* (Chicago: University of Chicago Press, 1965).

K E Y   T E R M S   A N D
C O N C E P T S

value
terminal/instrumental values
reference group
positive/negative reference group

social comparison
assumed similarity
demographic groups
involuntary/voluntary groups
celebrity/authority endorsement
cognitive defenses
impressionable years hypothesis
cross-sex influence effect
androgynous personality
social class

STRUCTURING MESSAGES AND APPEALS

Persuasive communicators always start with an idea. The idea usually has to be put into *words*, and the words have to be organized into sentences and paragraphs. Opening comments and concluding statements must be written, and a decision has to be made about the use of photographs, slides, or diagrams. A decision concerning how best to present statistics and evidence has to be made—and such supporting material has to be presented in a nonconfusing, easily understood, and persuasive manner. Another decision has to be made concerning the type of appeal to use in the message. This chapter addresses these structuring elements to use in persuasion. Six topics will be addressed: use of language variables, use of visual stimuli, message organization, order effects, message sidedness, and message appeals.

USE OF LANGUAGE VARIABLES

Communication depends upon the use of symbols which have shared meanings for sources and receivers. Words are symbols that convey meaning to others. However, there are different kinds of "meanings," and words can be used in many different ways to communicate a message. First, we need to talk about two types of meanings: denotative and connotative. We will then talk about two types of persuasive speech: speech using intense language and powerful speech.

Denotative and Connotative Meanings

The first type of meaning we assign to a word is its denotative meaning, or that meaning which serves as a link between word and referent, the object to which the word refers. Denotative meaning is sometimes referred to as "dictionary meaning," since it refers to or references the definition that a language community has determined for the word. Persuasive communicators usually assume that receivers will use the same denotative meanings for words as they themselves do; but words vary on a number of important criteria, as we will soon see.

The second type of meaning acquired is connotative meaning, which reflects the attitudes people develop toward words. Certain words can bring a smile to our face and alter our feelings because they have been associated frequently with positive experiences such as a summer vacation area, holidays, or even McDonald's restaurants (or so the commercials claim). Many mature consumers today, for example, grew up eating Fritos, Oscar Mayer bologna, or Planters peanuts with their parents at baseball games. Commercials attempt to cash in on such nostalgic feelings when they employ "warmth" appeals about such familiar products.

Connotative meaning becomes important to persuasion because such meanings are more variable than are denotative, and cannot be easily predicted. Some children were raised in a very loving home, while others were raised in homes where their parents maintained strict discipline, punished them and maybe even spanked them. All of the children may develop the same denotative meanings for the words "mother" and "father," but different connotative meanings are likely to develop. Furthermore, we would expect the children to react differently to a persuasive message suggesting that the child do something "because your mother and father think it best," or appealing to parental love.

We cannot help developing meanings towards the stimuli (words, symbols, nonverbal actions) we encounter; we naturally try to make sense of the words we hear (to define them), and we habitually associate positive or negative feelings with various words and symbols—some more intensely than others. Thus, meaning becomes a critical part of our concern in persuasion. The persuader needs to take into consideration certain issues relevant to both types of meaning.

ISSUES IN DENOTATIVE MEANING

A potential persuasion failure may occur if the persuader fails to elicit an intended or desirable response from the receiver. That is, the receiver may not have the same meaning for the term used in a message as did the source. Consider:

1. **Abstractness** S.I. Hayakawa[1] and other semanticists point to abstract language as a problem in communication. The more abstract a term is, the less likely it is to elicit similar meanings from a group of receivers. Look at Figure 8.1. The terms on the left are relatively specific in meaning. There can be differences in meaning between receivers even with relatively concrete terms, but the probability is that the range of meanings will be narrower with concrete terms than with abstract terms. Most people will have approximately the same meaning for the term "book," although one individual may be thinking of a paperback while another thinks of a hardcover book. Nevertheless, the differences in meaning are not likely to be serious. If the communicator refers to a "teaching aid," however, the receiver may be thinking of a book, film, or picture, or even a teacher.

When abstract terms are used, the persuader has to provide more examples and what are called "operational definitions" in order for the intended meaning to be adopted by receivers. Abstractness, however, can be desired by some persuaders in certain circumstances. Eisenberg[2], for example, argues that managers may employ "strategic ambiguity" so that workers can "read in" and interpret what they think the manager is saying. Political campaigns also provide plenty of examples in which abstract terms are employed. Few people could argue against "family values" (a 1992 campaign slogan), and voters can rally around an abstract, all-American concept (the family).

2. **Technological Terms** Technology has been growing at a phenomenal rate, and there is a ten-

---

FIGURE **8.1**

EXAMPLES OF ABSTRACT WORDS

Less Abstract	More Abstract
Cat	Feline
Mother	Relative
Cow	Cattle
Bees	Insects
Teacher	Educator
Book	Teaching aid
Contraception	Family planning
Littering	Polluting
War	Border adjustment

---

dency for words to move from ordinary to more specialized meanings for the scientist or engineer. Similarly, words that were part of a technological vocabulary sometimes become part of the common language, but with slightly different meanings. Newspapers, magazines and talk shows rarely provide definitions of terms such as "bits," "bytes," "RAM," "controllers," "processors," and the like. If persuaders and advertisers intend to influence receivers successfully, it may be necessary to provide both definitions and exemplary illustrations of what the speaker means by these terms.

Even some of the scientific terminology of persuasion research makes its way into popular language—sometimes accurately, sometimes not. Terms such as "sampling error," "statistically significant difference," "deception in advertising," "subliminal messages," and the like are employed, although rarely defined precisely. For example, the term "subliminal messages" has been used so frequently and in so many different ways by the media that many students believe that "subliminal messages" are any messages that involve sex in advertising, or include any influence attempt that relies on hidden messages or messages that receivers are not aware of. Actually, the term refers to a message that is beneath ("sub") our ability to detect ("limits")—messages that are flashed on a screen for extremely brief durations so that a "message" is "implanted" in our subconscious. There is little evidence that this type of message directly affects our behavior[3], but it does influence our ability to relax, or to be aroused generally[4] (also see the section on Visual Stimuli, page 219). Nonetheless, a persuasive speaker has to be careful with the use of technological terms, perhaps defining how s/he uses these terms, or providing concrete examples (see solutions below).

3. *Euphemisms* One of the major problems in language use has arisen from the attempts by speakers and writers to make language pleasant to receivers. This results in the use of euphemisms that do not have precise meaning and that may produce wide variations of response.

Some expressions may be offensive, so a euphemism is employed—a word or phrase that means essentially the same thing, but is less likely to offend. Terms such as "waste" could be used for kill, "to rock" for partying heavily, "going to powder one's nose" for going to the bathroom, "passed on" refers to a death; "passing gas" and other expressions sound considerably nicer than other options. Virtually all politically correct terms are employed to avoid offending people (that is, hearing or learning impaired, versus "disabled").

4. *Legalese* Closely related to the problem of using language drawn from technology is the problem of using language drawn from law. Lawyers have, over the centuries, developed precise meanings for words within the law. Those same words, however, may have quite different meanings to the layperson.

Since legal terminology is difficult to understand completely, attempts have been made since the 1970s to rewrite the judges' instructions to the jury so that confusion is reduced. Also, some car lease agreements, tax forms, and the like have been simplified in order to make their language more understandable and less confusing.

If there is a high probability that the words or terms in a speech will be misunderstood, the communicator must use one or more of the following methods to increase the likelihood of a desired response:

1. *Relearning* For those words or concepts that have a specific object, person or event as a referent, the receiver can be led through a relearning process. The source can use scale models, visual aids, or other nonverbal clues to assist in demonstrating a complicated process or object.

In the 1960s the terms "progressive" and "liberal" were largely popular terms, linked to the New Frontier and The Great Society of the Kennedy and Johnson administrations, and associated with actions dealing with equal housing opportunities and equality. Over the next several decades, however, the term "liberal" has been (successfully) associated with "quotas," "big spending," "giveaway" programs, and "incompetence" in international diplomacy. Voters have relearned the meaning of "liberal" in regard to both its denotative meaning and connotative meaning.

2. *Classification* In one of the most frequently used types of definition, a source places an unfamiliar term or phrase within a category of other similar objects and then specifies the term's position within this category. For example, the phrase "clear-cutting" might be defined as "a method of lumbering where all the trees in an area are cut down, rather than just selected trees." The source has placed the term "clear-cutting" as one member of a class called "lumbering," and then specified just how clear-cutting differs from other kinds of lumbering.

3. *Negation* A variation of definition by classification is termed "definition by negation." The procedure is for the source to define a term by telling the receiver what is *not* being referred to. For example, a source may refer to "drug users" in talking to a college audience. That term could cover many different activities. The source may define the term by telling the audience, "I am not talking about the use of marijuana, alcohol, tobacco, or legitimate prescription drugs, but only about hard drugs such as heroin or crack." The source has defined the term by eliminating some possible interpretations.

4. *Operational definition* Here, the communicator specifies a set of operations, which, if performed, will identify the term being defined. For example, the term "socialized medicine" might be defined operationally as "payment of all medical bills by an agency of the federal government."

The operational definition is a very useful tool. An example relevant to a topic discussed later in this chapter is "fear appeal." The term "fear appeal" can mean many different things to many different readers—fear of pain, fear of financial loss, fear of victimization, of death, and so on. An operational definition of "fear appeals" tells the receiver exactly what is meant by the persuader. Table 8.1, for example, shows us one operational definition of "fear appeals" employed by Janis and Feshbach[5]. High school freshmen heard one of three versions of a fifteen-minute illustrated speech on oral hygiene practices—one "low" fear, one "moderate" fear, and one "high" fear. The authors wanted to communicate to other researchers who read their article precisely what they meant by each type of fear appeal. As the table indicates, "high" fear included a total of 71 references to pain, infection and the like, compared to 49 "moderate" fear and 18 "low" fear references. We discuss the results of this study at the end of the chapter.

T A B L E 8.1

AN EXAMPLE OF AN OPERATIONAL DEFINITION OF "FEAR APPEALS"

Type of Reference	Form 1 (Strong Appeal)	Form 2 (Moderate Appeal)	Form 3 (Minimal Appeal)
Pain from toothaches	11	1	0
Cancer, paralysis, blindness, or other secondary diseases	6	0	0
Having teeth pulled, cavities drilled, or other painful dental work	9	1	0
Having cavities filled or having to go to the dentist	0	5	1
Mouth infections: sore, swollen, inflamed gums	18	16	2
Ugly or discolored teeth	4	2	0
"Decayed" teeth	14	12	6
"Cavities"	9	12	9
Total references to unfavorable consequences	71	49	18

From: I.L. Janis and S. Feshbach, "Effects of Fear-Arousing Communications," *Journal of Abnormal and Social Psychology*, vol. 48 (1953), pp. 78–92. Reprinted by permission of authors and American Psychological Association.

ISSUES IN CONNOTATIVE MEANING

We defined connotative meanings as the attitudinal meanings people develop for words over years. Charles Osgood and his associates devised ways of measuring connotative meanings.[6] They

BOX 8.1

LANGUAGE INTENSITY: BRADAC, BOWERS, AND COURTRIGHT'S AXIOMS

1. Cognitive stress is inversely related to the language intensity of sources.

2. Language intensity is directly related to receivers' attributions of internality of sources.

3. Obscenity is inversely related to the amount of attitude change produced by messages (at least when the source is male).

4. Obscenity is related to reduced ratings of source competence (after the speech is delivered).

5. Language intensity of a nonobscene type in messages delivered to receivers who initially disagree with the speaker is related to reduced ratings of speaker competence.

6. For highly aroused receivers, language intensity is related to reduced amounts of attitude change.

7. Language intensity and initial receiver agreement with the advocated position interact in such a way that if receivers initially agree with the conclusion, language intensity operates to reinforce the attitude, increase intensity of the attitude or can prompt action; but attitude change is reduced when the receivers initially disagree with the conclusion.

8. Language intensity and initial source credibility interact in the production of attitude change in such a way that intensity enhances the effect of credible sources, but inhibits attitude change if the source is low in credibility.

9. The relationship between initial source credibility, intensity, and attitude change is strengthened when receivers are high in need for approval.

10. Language intensity and "maleness" interact in the production of attitude change in such a way that intensity of a nonobscene type enhances the effect of male, but inhibits the effect of female, sources.

11. Language intensity and active participation in persuasion are positively related to attitude change.

12. If receivers initially agree with the advocated position, language intensity increases perceptions of speaker-receiver similarity; if receivers initially disagree with the advocated position, language intensity decreases perceived similarity.

Adapted from: J.J. Bradac, J.W. Bowers, and J.A. Courtright, "Lexical Variations in Intensity, Immediacy, and Diversity: An Axiomatic Theory and Causal Model," in R.N. St. Clair and H. Giles, eds., *The Social and Psychological Contexts of Language* (Hillsdale, N.J.: Lawrence Erlbaum Associates, 1980), pp. 193-223. Used with permission.

employed the semantic differential scaling technique to measure the intensity of reaction individuals have toward words and concepts. When receivers were asked about the feelings they have toward words, the answers were frequently given in terms of descriptive adjectives. For example, asked how they feel about "government," many might answer "bureaucratic," "slow," "weak," and "cold." Osgood assembled a large number of pairs of polar adjectives, such as pleasant-unpleasant, smooth-rough, active-passive, low-high, good-bad, clean-dirty, and happy-sad. Each adjective is placed at the end of a seven-point scale, and individuals are asked to indicate how they feel about particular concepts—such as "Bill Clinton," "Democratic Party," "Republican Party," and other concepts. Osgood and his colleagues found that there are three major dimensions of connotative meaning:

1 The *evaluative* dimension, in which receivers express the degree of favorableness or unfavorableness they feel toward the word. Evaluative scales include good-bad, valuable-worthless, fair-unfair, honest-dishonest, and so on.

2 An *activity* dimension is one which expresses the perceptions of a receiver toward the amount of movement or activity in an object or event. Activity scales include active-passive, fast-slow, vibrant-still, dynamic-static, and varied-repetitive.

3 The *potency* dimension, which represents the feelings of strength and weakness that are perceived by an individual. Potency scales include serious-humorous, potent-impotent, strong-weak, heavy-light, and hard-soft.

These dimensions of connotative meaning seem to be stable for a number of concepts and even for a number of different languages (Kumata,[7] Suci,[8] Triandis and Osgood,[9] Ware and Morris[10]). This stability does not mean that people have the same connotative meanings for words,

but that they tend to use the same dimensions to judge words. You may feel the words "roast pork" are positive, but your Muslim or Jewish friends might judge them highly unfavorable—both are using the evaluative dimension in their judgments, but they have different evaluations along that dimension.

We illustrate some of the ways in which the connotative aspects of meaning may profoundly affect persuasive communication.

Language Intensity

Many studies have examined the impact of intense language on persuasion. For example, McEwen and Greenberg[11] did a study which suggested that credibility was affected by the use of intense language. Speakers using highly intense language were perceived as more credible than those who did not. Burgoon and Stewart[12] suggest that there may also be a sex difference. Male speakers were more effective than female communicators when using high-intensity language. Miller and Lobe[13] suggest that the nature of the receivers' involvement is related to the use of intense language. Audiences neutral to a topic are more influenced by highly opinionated language, while audiences whose members are already involved are less likely to be influenced. Burgoon and King[14] manipulated intensity of language in communication situations where active and passive participation was used. They found intense language was useful in situations which had active participation built in.

Bradac, Bowers, and Courtright[15] reviewed studies associated with language and communication in an attempt to isolate or identify those language variables most closely associated with communication. Box 8.1 presents their axioms, relating intensity to various causes and persuasive outcomes.[16] By definition, language intensity reflects the degree to which a speaker's attitude toward the topic deviates from neutrality.[17] Highly intense language is emotional, and uses evaluative terms (connotative meanings). Messages containing very negative emotional intensity include words like: *very bad, murder, blunder, pervert, prostitute, lethal, fatal, devastating, condemn, despise;* and very positive emotional intensity messages include: *superior, brilliant, laudable, best of all, wonderful,* and *stupendous.*

The first axiom simply states that when a would-be persuader is experiencing stress (as when a criminal lies to police, or lies on a witness stand), the highly stressed speaker is *not* likely to employ intense language. It is the confident speaker who is more likely to use intense language. Indeed, the second axiom states that the use of intense language is directly related to the receiver's perceptions that the speaker is internally motivated (personally responsible for her/his actions, and personally motivated, compared to externally motivated speakers who believe that fate, chance and powerful others are responsible for changes).

Does it help to use "gutter" language? A study by Bostrom and his colleagues[18] suggest that the answer is "no." The use of obscenity lowered the receiver's appraisals of a speaker's credibility, and it also lowered the overall effect of a speech. However, there may be times when the use of obscenity has a positive effect. For example, in the Bostrom, et al., study, male receivers who heard obscene messages delivered by females tended to react positively toward the speaker. Besides this one "titillation" effect, the use of obscenity in persuasive messages designed for general audiences is probably unwise (axioms 3 and 4).

Other axioms indicate that intensity aids in persuasion if (a) the speaker already has credibility—in fact, a low credible source who uses intense language is likely to reduce his/her persuasiveness (s/he would look biased and emotional);

and, (b) the speaker is a male (although we expect the importance of "maleness" to decline in the future).

Language intensity is also important when members of the audience initially agree with the speaker's conclusion; thus, intense language operates to reinforce the existing attitude, or can prompt the audience member to increase commitment to the cause, or take action. On the other hand, if a receiver initially disagrees with the speaker's position, the use of intense language is likely to prompt the audience member to become defensive and to strengthen the receiver's desire to oppose the speaker's proposition. Imagine a pro-choice (or pro-life) advocate watching a videotape circulated by the opposition. As the opposition's video employs more and more intense language, the receiver is likely to become defensive and argumentative.

Receivers increase the perceived similarity with the speaker if they initially agree with his/her position and the speaker employs intense language (alternatively, receivers perceive increased *dissimilarity* if they initially disagree with the speaker, and the speaker is intense). Intensity is also useful in persuasion if the encounter involves active participation, requiring the receivers to become involved, rather than to merely sit and listen to a speech (axiom 11). Finally, language intensity is also useful if the audience members are already aroused—as they are at a revival meeting, a convention, immediately after a crisis, riot, war, or other significant rallying point.

Powerful and Powerless Style Speech

A line of research very similar to that of "language intensity" is called the "powerful versus powerless" style of speech. Intensity, as just described, may be altered on the basis of the adjectives, adverbs, and nouns that are used in the message. According to O'Barr and his colleagues[19], power-

| T A B L E 8.2 |

COMPARISON OF LINGUISTIC FEATURES OF COURT TESTIMONY BY POWERFUL AND POWERLESS STYLE SPEECHES, BY MALE AND FEMALE WITNESSES

	Female Witness		Male Witness	
	Powerless	*Powerful*	*Powerless*	*Powerful*
Style features				
Intensifiers	34	0	30	0
Hedges	22	2	21	2
Questioning forms	5	2	6	2
Gestures	3	1	3	1
Use of "sir" by witness to lawyer (polite form)	3	0	4	0
Hesitation forms				
uh, eh, ah, um	45	10	21	15
you know	12	0	12	0
other	20	4	21	4
One-word answers	3	15	3	15

Adapted from: B. Erickson, E.A. Lind, B.C. Johnson, and W.M. O'Barr, "Speech Style and Impression Formation in a Court Setting: The Effects of Powerful and Powerless Speech," *Journal of Experimental Social Psychology*, vol. 14 (1978), pp. 266–279. Used with permission of authors and Academic Press.

less style speech is strongly affected by a number of linguistic elements. For example, Table 8.2 presents the "operational definition" for powerful and powerless style speeches employed in a study on the credibility of witness testimonies. *Intensifiers, hedges, questioning forms*, and *hesitation forms* display powerlessness and uncertainty (see Table 8.2). *Gestures* are included as part of powerless style speech, consistent with the idea that certain hand gestures that communicate "over there" and "like this" also show uncertainty or powerlessness (although some scholars would not agree with this—see Chapter 9). The use of "sir" is also included as powerless, because weak, submissive individuals engage in what some call "hyperpolite"

behaviors in the face of a superior (the lawyer doing the questioning).

Research on powerful speech provides two conclusions concerning powerful/powerless styles and persuasion. First, as a general rule, *speakers receive higher ratings of credibility when they employ powerful style speech*. Further, certain components listed in Table 8.2 hurt credibility more than others do. Bradac and Mulac[20], for example, found that hesitations and questioning forms strongly affected powerless speech, much more than did polite terms and intensifiers. Hosman and Wright[21] found that credibility and attraction increased when messages contained low levels of both hedges and hesitations; but it appears that high

TABLE 8.3

CREDIBILITY RATINGS AS A FUNCTION OF POWERFUL AND POWERLESS STYLE
SPEECH, SEX OF WITNESS, SEX OF RECEIVER, AND PRESENTATIONAL FORMAT
(TAPED VERSUS TRANSCRIBED)

Credibility Ratings	Male Witness		Female Witness	
	Powerful Style	Powerless Style	Powerful Style	Powerless Style
Taped Presentations				
Male receivers	+4.37	−2.01	− .27	−2.48
Female receivers	+3.32	−1.45	+4.23	−5.95
Transcribed Presentations				
Male receivers	+4.92	−2.69	− .73	−2.84
Female receivers	+1.66	+4.07	+6.94	−8.50

Adapted from: B. Erickson, E.A. Lind, B.C. Johnson, and W.M. O'Barr, "Speech Style and Impression Formation in a Court Setting: The Effects of Powerful and Powerless Speech," *Journal of Experimental Social Psychology*, vol. 14 (1978), pp. 266–279. Used with permission of authors and Academic Press.

levels of either hedges or hesitations can reduce a speaker's ratings. Nonetheless, powerless style speech (containing hedges, hesitations, and questioning forms) is generally related to reduced ratings of speaker effectiveness.

A second type of finding indicates that receivers evaluate speech style on the basis of the sex of the speaker. For example, in the Erickson, et al., study[22] of courtroom testimony, results indicated that men rated male witnesses low in credibility if the male witness used powerless style speech, and that women rated female witnesses low in credibility if the female witness employed powerless style speech. That is, people do not want members of their own gender to appear powerless, weak, and hesitant; they rate members of their own sex much higher in credibility if they use powerful style speech, and they rate members of their own sex very low in credibility if they use powerless speech.

Another aspect of this study is important. Erickson and her colleagues had some of the students *read* and evaluate the witnesses' testimony (involving an accident between an automobile and an ambulance), but the other students watched a taped presentation of the testimony. Recall that at the end of Chapter 5 we discussed the fact that there are "channel differences" in that live or videotape presentations naturally draw attention to the speaker, while print or written presentations draw attention to argument and evidence. Print presentations also highlight and draw attention to the language employed in the message. In Table 8.3, female receivers rated female witnesses lower in credibility when they watched the female witness use powerless speech, relative to the powerful speech; but when they read the transcript, female receivers rated females using powerless speech even more harshly, and the powerful speaker more highly. A similar pattern can be seen for male receivers responding to male witnesses.[23]

Three conclusions are warranted: As a general rule, speakers should employ powerful style speech in order to bolster credibility. However, it also appears true that people do not like to see members of their own gender (or perhaps any relevant reference group) appear weak and powerless. This second conclusion has important implications in a number of situations. If you are a lawyer, for example, and you confront eight (or more) females on a 12-person jury, and you have three female witnesses, you obviously want to devote more time and effort to "eyewitness preparation" so that the witnesses are prepared to deliver confident, powerful messages. Third, the importance of powerful speech styles is increased when the channel of presentation is a written or printed format.

VISUAL STIMULI

Salience and Novelty

In 1992, *Vogue* magazine published its 100th anniversary issue. It was 526 pages long, packed (or "cluttered") with a photograph on nearly every page. How many of these photographs really caught the receiver's attention and prompted the receiver to focus on the product? Cluttered channels are everywhere—hundreds of commercials on TV, hundreds of billboards on the freeways, hundreds of photos in magazines. Clearly, if the message is lost in this clutter, there is little hope of influencing others. What catches your eye? Of course, beauty, colors, and emotional appeals (like sex, humor, or warmth) help get your attention;

but what if virtually *all* of the competing photographs contain beautiful people, colors, and emotional appeals?

One useful way of viewing the visual materials that you might include in your persuasion efforts is called "salience" by Fiske and Taylor[24]. Salience is the property of stimuli in context—what surrounds the object? Is the figure or object emphasized by being in the front of the photograph? Does the photograph pique our interest because something is unusual or unexpected in the advertisement? Figure 8.2 presents examples. The first uses the approach of having one object in the visual field, which is significantly and conspicuously different from the others. A young model poses with women significantly older than herself. In the second, both humor and novelty are used to draw immediate attention to the ad. Both advertisements capture the receiver's interest, and prompt the question: What is happening here? Further, this type of salience also reinforces a particular view of the focal point. In the first, the young model appears to be younger, more attractive, sexier, and more vital when surrounded by stern elderly ladies. In the second photograph, attention is immediately drawn to the strange combination of an alien with an American Express card.

Photographs 3 and 4 present a very different view of salience—here, characters are engaged in unexpected, novel activities. The first reinforces the action-orientation of the LA Gear advertisement—don't stay inside at a drab party when you can have uninhibited fun, be active! The second reinforces the mysticism and earthy feelings of a gypsy life-style.

Photographs involving salience are more likely to gain our attention than non-salient photographs. Also, salience can have a significant impact on perceptions of the attributes or qualities of the focal object (younger, sexier, in our examples). Salience may *not* be consistently related to recall of a specific ad, but it can reinforce beliefs or feelings one has for a product.

(1)

(Kenar, Inc.)

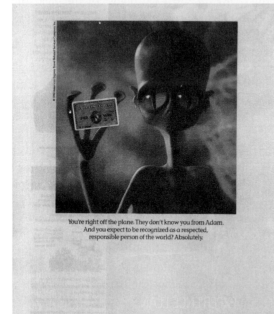

(2)

(1992 American Express Travel Related Services Co., Inc.)

(3)

(L.A. Gear, Inc.)

(4)

(April, 1992 *Vogue;* Conde Nast Publications, Inc.)

Vividness

Nisbett and Ross[25] define vividness as "information that is likely to attract and hold our attention and to excite the imagination to the extent that it is (a) emotionally interesting; (b) concrete and imagery-provoking; and (c) proximate in a sensory, temporal, or spatial way." The opposite of "vividness" is "pallid," meaning weak, tepid, boring, bland, unemotional. There are many different operational definitions for the concept of vividness. First, some strikingly beautiful faces are extremely vivid, making the photograph emotionally arousing. Second, colors may be used "vividly," colors of blue, paprika, kelly green and the like get our attention, and as we look at the photograph, we feel relaxed, content, or perhaps aroused. Motorcycles and automobiles are sometimes filmed in this way, with a person in a shiny red (or black) outfit speeding along a mountainside on a matching motorcycle. The photographs are stunning and captivating.

Another example portrays a suntanned blond person relaxing in the glow of a yellow-pink-orange sunset on a deserted beach, wearing khaki clothes, watching a blue-green sea with a lone white-and-yellow sailboat coming into port, slowly sipping on a (yellow) beer in a bottle. Artistic photographs such as these relax the receiver, arouse feelings and emotions, and (sometimes) prompt some amount of cognitive elaboration ("I wish I were there!").

Although Nesbitt and Ross provided their definition of vividness in 1980, their studies on "graphic evidence," and on "heinousness of the crime" parallel the emotional nature of persuasive material dating back to the 1950s. Although we have placed vividness under the framework of "visual stimuli," *words* can generate vivid mental images.

For example, Reyes, Thompson, and Bower[26] investigated the impact of vivid or colorful language in testimonies concerning a drunk-driving case. In the vivid version, the accused was described as having knocked over a bowl of guacamole dip which splattered over a white shag carpet, before getting into his bright orange Volkswagen and driving off. In a pallid version, the accused was described as knocking into a table and knocking a bowl to the ground before getting into his car and driving away. The vividly portrayed description was more fully recalled 24 hours later—receivers create a mental image of the event and can recall components of this image later. Since a trial might last weeks, and some time might pass before receivers/jurors enter a deliberation room, producing memorable messages is extremely important.

Vivid messages (a) gain and hold receivers' attention; (b) enhance the ability for receivers to construct mental images of the portrayed event; (c) promote recognition and recall of the described event; (d) are more emotionally arousing; and, (e) have more of an impact (than pallid information) in persuasion. Simply making a message vivid does not necessarily make it persuasive.[27] To do so, five considerations need to be kept in mind. First, vividness is not a "yes/no" or "high/low" variable. There are degrees by which messages arouse emotions and degrees by which messages provoke images in the receivers' minds. Vividness probably helps in persuasion if at least some minimal level of emotional response is successfully manipulated, or a certain amount of interest is piqued.

Second, to be persuasive, vivid messages must prompt receivers to engage in *cognitive elaboration*, which means that when exposed to the message, the receiver can easily process the material because s/he possesses a framework for evaluating the content.[28] For example, a former astronaut may vividly describe mobility in zero-gravity to a junior high school audience, yet the audience may not be able to relate to or elaborate on the material cognitively.

Third, the emotional response receivers experience should be the one the persuasive communicator desires. For example, a commercial for special coffees that shows a loving couple sharing a cup of coffee may make some viewers feel warm, happy, and contented, while making those recently divorced or widowed feel sad and depressed or angry.

Fourth, a vivid message is unlikely to be effective if it does not satisfy one's needs. If one isn't involved with fast cars, alcohol, or pursuing an exciting night life, a receiver may pay brief attention to such vivid advertisements; even if such a person once raced motorcycles years ago and does in fact have a framework for evaluating the information, he or she has no interest in buying a motorcycle and the advertisement will have little effect.

Fifth, we have to admit that certain topics (gang violence, victimization of the elderly, AIDS, child abuse, rape) are emotionally arousing topics. It is possible that a fifteen-minute speech on such topics will arouse emotions, even if pallid visual aids are involved. Further, people vary considerably in their ability to form clear mental images of events, and some people might generate their own highly vivid ideas about the topic.

Combining Words and Photos/Illustrations

A message can be reinforced if photographs are employed correctly. Lutz and Lutz[29], for example, found that a Yellow Pages ad integrating both the brand and product names into a picture was recalled later better than an advertisement where the written form of the brand name appeared separate from the depiction of the product. Rossiter and Percy[30] found that receivers have more positive attitudes toward a brand name product when the picture is large and the print is small. Mitchell and Olson[31] found that advertisements for a soft facial tissue received highest ratings when a picture of a fluffy kitten was employed in the advertisement (as compared to rival pictures of pleasant scenes).

Research on print advertisements generally indicates that a verbal-only ad does not capture the receivers' attention in the same way as does the picture + verbal message ad, and that the picture + verbal message ad is more easily and fully recalled than the verbal-only advertisement. Further, Edell and Staelin[32] reasoned that receivers probably respond to verbal print advertisements and pictorial print advertisements differently. A pictorial ad is more attention-getting, pleasant, and easier to process than a verbal-only ad, but the verbal-only ad can convey far more information. Also Edell and Staelin reasoned that a large dominant pictorial advertisement with a reinforcing message (or "framed" picture) could be effective in gaining attention, creating a favorable attitude, and prompting greater recall of the brand name. By "framed" picture advertisement, Edell and Staelin mean one in which the verbal message is relevant to the picture of the brand-named product, usually placed in one of the margins of the page. For example, the words "tough," "strong," or "absorbent" are used with the brand name (for example, Brawny) along with a photograph (a giant lumberjack's shadow cast over a schoolyard).

However, it is also possible that the picture advertisement has little to do with the verbal component. In some advertisements the verbal component is "unframed" in that it does not reinforce the message being sent in the visual channel. For example, a photograph taking up 75 percent of the space on a page shows young, healthy, college-aged students playing in the snow. At the bottom of the page are the words "Now, 10% less tar" or "One free pack in every carton." In advertisements such as these, receivers will place much greater attention on the visual presentation, which could *distract* the receivers from generating thoughts about the advertisement. Edell and Staelin found that receivers responded more favorably to the visual advertisement that was framed than to the unframed versions. Receivers listed relatively few favorable or unfavorable thoughts when exposed to the visual-unframed advertisements. Also, receivers recalled fewer of the brand names after having viewed the unframed versions. Thus, it appears that picture + relevant claim produces a more desirable outcome, compared to picture + irrelevant claim.

If this is true, then, why would advertisers *ever* employ a large-photograph advertisement with a small-print claim that is irrelevant to the content of the photograph? Scan the photograph in Figure 8.3. As you scan it, you focus attention on the smiling face, the eyeglasses, the placement of the cigarette boxes, and you then read "Designed with Taste," and "Today's Slims. Why pay more?" But these smaller, somewhat hidden, verbal claims are irrelevant to the visual material (happy face), so you discount the verbal or semantic content and refocus on the visual array in the photograph. Since cigarette (and now liquor) companies are required by law to label their product as unhealthy, the large visual + small irrelevant-print advertisement functions to draw attention away from the words—including the surgeon general's warning. It is probably the case that cigarette companies rely on repeatedly pairing or matching their product (cigarettes) with positive activities such as surfing, swimming, skiing, flirting, and so forth, so that receivers will ultimately develop positive attitudes (recall Chapter 2).

Janiszewski[33] points out that if a large photograph is employed with a brand name appearing elsewhere on the page, the location of the material prompts different kinds of cognitive processing. Look at the versions of a perfume ad in Figure 8.4. Do you like any one of these better than the others?

Janiszewski had different receivers view various versions of this ad (they did not see all of them) and later had them rate the brand name (Shalimar). He found that placement of the "attended" visual information (the photograph of the woman's face is the central or "attended" visual information in this ad) along with the placement of the brand name and the slogan ("I am Shali-

FIGURE   8.3

EXAMPLE OF "UNFRAMED" PICTURE ADVERTISEMENT

(The American Tobacco Co. 1991)

mar." Gabrielle Lazure) strongly affected liking for the brand name. His reasoning is based on the fact that the left and right hemispheres of the brain process information differently:

> The matching activation hypothesis predicts that the greater activation of the right (left) hemisphere during the processing of attended pictorial (verbal) information could enhance the processing of additional material represented within the left (right) hemisphere, pro-

FIGURE 8.4

THE IMPORTANCE OF VISUAL ORGANIZATION OF PHOTOGRAPHS IN PERSUASION

Source: C. Janiszewski, "The Influence of Print Advertisement Organization on Affect Toward a Brand Name," *Journal of Consumer Research*, vol. 17 (1990), pp. 53–65. (Courtesy of Guerlain, Inc. and J. Walter Thompson, New York.)

vided the material in the opposing hemisphere can be processed by that hemisphere. Brand names often consist of simple words that can be processed with equal efficiency by either hemisphere. Therefore, placing a brand name to the right of the attended pictorial information should send it to the less activated left hemisphere, where it will receive a greater degree of subconscious processing than if sent to the right hemisphere. Likewise, placing a brand name to the left of unattended verbal information should send it to the less activated right hemisphere, where it will receive a greater degree of subconscious processing than if sent to the left hemisphere. In each case, increasing the amount of subconscious processing should increase affect toward the brand name. Thus, a brand name should be liked more when placed to the right of the pictorial information or to the left of the verbal information.[34]

What does all this mean? Since brand names are short and brief, they do not require much effort to process. As we focus on the "attended" visual information and scan the entire page, we can process other materials in the field of vision (although we are not aware that we are processing other information). When the photograph is on the left side of the page (Photographs C and D), the brand name will still be processed if it is noticed. Of these photographs, the brand name is more likely to be noticed and processed if it is located adjacent to the model's face. In fact, Janiszewski found that receivers who viewed Photograph C rated the brand name higher in liking (M = 20.3) than those who viewed Photograph D (M = 16.8); they also rated the brand name higher than those who viewed Photograph A (the same arrangement, but reversing the left and right hemisphere processing; M = 17.9).

The second aspect of this line of research deals with the placement of a brand name adjacent to other verbal material. Placing a brand name to the left of attended verbal material should send the brand name to the less-activated right hemisphere, where it should receive more processing than if sent to the left hemisphere. Receivers who viewed Photograph B did, in fact, rate the brand name high in liking (brand name is left and adjacent to the slogan—the attended verbal content; M=21.0), and these receivers rated the brand name higher than did those who viewed either Photograph D (same arrangement, but different hemispheres are involved), or Photograph A (same hemispheric processing, but the brand name is adjacent to the face, not to the slogan).

These conclusions concerning print advertisements are limited only to those contexts where simple words are placed in a visual stimulus (billboard, magazine photograph, slide presentation). The issue of subconscious processing of information is not relevant when longer words or sentences, or facts, are employed.

Message Organization

There is ample evidence to support the statement that some kind of organization is essential in a speech or an article. There are a number of studies which compare organized messages with disorganized messages in terms of their relative effectiveness.[35] Apparently receivers can *comprehend* a message that is not well organized, but they are not *persuaded* by a message lacking organization. McCroskey and Mehrley[36] also found that speakers were rated low in credibility if the speech was disorganized. Presenting a message in an organized fashion, then, is important in regard to producing attitude change and in building credibility.

But, just how does one organize a message? Communication scholars have identified and researched several basic forms of organization:

1. *Space pattern* In this pattern, the source organizes material in terms of geography or space. For example, in talking about the necessity for further increases in the efforts of the federal government to help solve our population problems, the communicator might make an outline dividing the topic into sections that would cover the major areas in the United States.

Such a basic outline might have five major sections:

I. Problems in the Eastern states
II. Problems in the Midwestern states
III. Problems in the Southern states
IV. Problems in the Far West
V. Problems in Alaska and Hawaii

In each section of the message, the source would then proceed to discuss some of the specific problems associated with each area, and how federal effort might help alleviate the problems. Our example is simple, but the same plan can be used for more complicated material.

2. *Time order* In this familiar pattern, the persuasive communicator outlines a sequence of events leading up to the problem as an historical background against which the proposed solution is judged.

An editorial writer, arguing for the development of a mass transportation system as a way of alleviating the energy crisis, might organize materials as:

I. The use of multipassenger vehicles—trolleys and buses—in the nineteenth and twentieth centuries.
II. The development of the automobile in the twentieth century.
III. The decline of mass transportation between 1945 and 1980.
IV. The necessity for redevelopment of mass transportation in the 1990s.

A time order is useful when some problem has a clear history.

3. *Deductive order* In this organization, the communicator proceeds from a set of general statements to specific proposals or suggestions.

In practice, the writer of an editorial might outline a number of areas on which general agreement is expected. Then the message is concluded by calling for some action that seems to follow logically from the earlier agreements.

Note that in a deductive arrangement, the communicator engages in persuasion at each step of the way. The source has to get audience agreement on each of the major statements before asking for agreement on the final statement. The use of a deductive arrangement is based on the assumption that by agreeing to a series of more general statements, the receiver will find it easy to agree to a more specific proposition as the concluding statement.

4. *Inductive order* An inductive arrangement attempts to let the reader or listener "reason with" the communicator. The communicator presents a number of specific examples and waits until the end of the message before drawing a conclusion.

The following sentence outline illustrates an inductive arrangement.

I. Pittfield has a public swimming pool and a low juvenile delinquency rate.
II. Omio has a new pool, and its juvenile delinquency has dropped drastically.
III. Sunfield had two people killed in drag racing accidents, built a new pool, and has had few problems since.
IV. Therefore, if New Berlin were to build a pool, it could also reduce its delinquency problems.

This example represents an inductive pattern of organization, with an explicit drawing of the conclusion. At times, the communicator will give the audience a number of examples, but will allow the audience to draw the conclusion for themselves. This can be referred to as an implicit conclusion. For example, a political speaker may refer to the poor record the incumbent has generated, but never say the incumbent should be turned out of office. Obviously, there is a danger in using an implicit conclusion. The audience will probably draw a conclusion, but may not draw the conclusion intended by the speaker. The best advice is to use the implicit method of organization only in those situations where the conclusion to be drawn is completely obvious to the audience.

5. *Psychological organization* Monroe and Ehninger suggest that organization be based on what they term the "motivated sequence," a succession of steps that would lead a receiver through the same steps that the receiver might employ in making a decision.[37]

They suggested that such a process would have five steps:

   I. Attention
  II. Need
 III. Satisfaction
 IV. Visualization
  V. Action

The "motivated sequence" is a popular way of approaching the task of preparing a speech. First suggested by Monroe in the mid-1930s, it has served literally millions of speakers as an organizing principle in message preparation. Imagine that the speaker wishes to convince an audience of the necessity for a program of tax credits to stimulate the economy. In the attention step, the source might point to the tremendous increase in unemployment and economic strife that is occurring. In the need step, the speaker points out that businesses could not currently hire more people without the benefit of some tax relief. In the satisfaction step, the speaker might point out that a three-year limited tax credit for business investments has been tried in the past and has helped

to bolster the economy, also pointing out that other countries routinely provide businesses with tax credits in order to rebuild and to make the businesses more competitive. In the visualization step, the communicator outlines exactly how the plan would work. And, finally, the speaker will outline exactly what actions the audience might take to bring the tax credit legislation into effect.

6. *Problem-solution structure* In this structure, the communicator first details the nature of the problem, and then proceeds to discuss the steps that ought to be taken to solve the problem.

An example outline might be as follows:

   I. We have had a number of riots in our community.
  II. These riots are apparently located in areas where most individuals have low incomes and few opportunities for normal recreational activities.
 III. When teenagers and young adults cannot participate in ordinary recreational activities, they are likely to make trouble.
 IV. Perhaps we can solve some of our problems by passing a bond issue for a new park and a new swimming pool within the low-income area of the city, with free access for all residents.

Again, the problem-solution pattern of organization is one used frequently in persuasive communication, since many persuasive speeches suggest changes in attitude or action based on the existence of a specific problem.

7. *The Toulmin pattern* An increasingly popular pattern of message organization is based on an analysis of the way in which people actually make decisions. Stephen Toulmin, a British philosopher, suggested in his book *The Uses of Argument*[38] that people make decisions in everyday life based on a fairly limited number of argumentative patterns. Since his initial formulation, several people have extended his work into more elaborate schemes of argumentative analysis and message organization (Ehninger and Brockriede,[39] Windes and Hastings,[40] and Bettinghaus[41]).

In Figure 8.5 the Toulmin pattern is shown in a basic form, utilizing only three of its six elements. By evidence, we mean any data, observations, personal opinions, case histories, or other information relevant to the issue under consideration. The claim is the statement that the communicator wishes people to believe, or the action that is desired. The warrant is the link between evidence and claim—a statement showing why people ought to accept the source's conclusions. In the simple argument below, each of these elements is present.

> The federal deficit in the United States has risen almost to the $200 billion-a-year level (evidence). During the next fiscal year, we absolutely must cut federal spending by at least $75 billion (claim), because the high deficits will lead us into a renewal of inflation and another recession (warrant).

Obviously, one could take these three simple statements and expand them into a lengthy speech by adding more evidence, extending the claim into a specific plan, and adding support for the warrant so that the connection between the claim and evidence will become clear.

Toulmin would argue that his pattern of argument is valuable because it represents the way in which people actually think. We change our beliefs because someone asks us to, and in the asking gives both evidence and a reason for the change.

The Toulmin method of message organization allows even very complex arguments to be analyzed and placed into an effective message form. Figure 8.6 illustrates a complex message which makes use of all six elements that Toulmin identified. This model introduces three additional elements that need definition. By a "qualifier" we mean the use of some adjective that softens or

FIGURE 8.5

BASIC TOULMIN MODEL

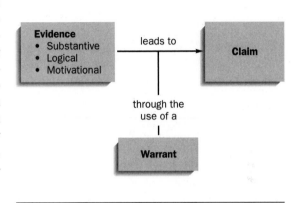

modifies the claim. In the preceding sample we could add a qualifier to the claim by saying, "We must cut government spending by approximately $75 billion a year." Adding a qualifier may make it easier for a receiver to accept the claim. A *reservation* sets out any limitations that the source wishes to place on the claim, conditions under which the claim should or should not be accepted. Using the same example, we could add a reservation by rewriting: "We must cut government spending by approximately $75 billion a year, unless we find that Russia has once again begun to increase the size of their defense budget." By adding the last clause, the source suggests that certain conditions may make it impossible to accept the claim. Finally, the element of *support* adds materials to further justify the use of the warrant in linking evidence and claim. Again, using our example of inflation, the phrase, " . . . since federal deficits allow too much money to be put into circulation," would be support for the warrant. Warrants can be supported by historical data, statistical materials, or analogies from other situations.

A COMPLEX MODEL

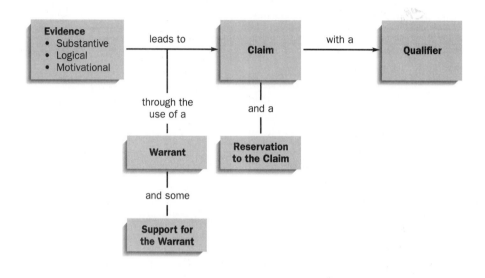

Now let us use that same argument, expanded to incorporate all of the Toulmin elements:

The federal deficit in the United States has risen almost to the $200 billion-a-year level. (evidence) The balance of payments deficit between the United States and our trading partners will account for at least $50 billion of that amount. (evidence) Because of these facts, we must cut spending by the federal government by at least $75 billion a year, (claim) unless we find that Russia has once again begun to increase the size of their defense budget and that we might fall behind Russia in defense preparations. (reservation to the claim) Such a cut in spending is necessary because huge federal deficits lead to higher interest rates (support for warrant) and thus to a renewal of inflation and another recession. (warrant)

This message looks more complicated and now consists of the six elements that Toulmin identifies. You can take this message and diagram it in exactly the same form illustrated in Figure 8.6. Furthermore, the source could expand this short message into a much longer speech either by using a series of similar arguments, or by adding even more evidence in support of the claim.

ONE-SIDED VERSUS TWO-SIDED MESSAGES

In almost all persuasive communication situations, there are those in opposition as well as those in favor of a proposed change. Also, there are arguments that can be used to support either side of a proposition. Should we pass a certain capital gains tax? Should we give a tax credit to first-time home buyers in order to help the economy? There are reasons *for* and reasons *against* many issues like these.

Communication research has investigated the effects of one-sided and two-sided messages. In a series of studies, materials presenting the opposite side of an issue were introduced along with materials from the side supporting the thesis of the message. The first study was carried out during World War II by Hovland, Lumsdaine, and Sheffield.[42] They used two messages supporting the United States in the war against Japan. One message was a straight presentation of materials arguing for the proposition with no mention of materials existing in support of the other side. The other message presented one side but specifically mentioned arguments from the other side. The two-sided message stressed only the side on which most of the material had been presented.

The study concluded that the one-sided presentation was more persuasive for men with lower educational attainment. For men with some high school education, the two-sided presentation was more effective. The one-sided presentation was slightly more effective for men who originally were in favor of the view expressed in the message, apparently serving as a reinforcing stimulus in this case.

A second study conducted by Lumsdaine and Janis[43] added another major finding to the literature in this area. They found that receivers who were in initial agreement with the position advocated in the message were more persuaded by the one-sided message, while those people who were initially opposed to the intent of the original message were more persuaded by the two-sided message. So, one might argue that if the persuasive communicator knows that the audience is in favor of the message, there is no need to spend time and money on opposing arguments.

Finally, Kamins[45] and his colleagues argue that one way to make celebrity endorsements more believable is to employ two-sided messages. Their basic argument is that receivers know that a celebrity is paid to recommend a particular product, so when a celebrity has only positive things to say about the product, receivers are not necessarily convinced of the endorsement's believability. Kamins' studies indicate that when a celebrity (such as Leonard Nimoy) endorses a product and mixes both good features and a negative feature (for example, the computer company is not known or a leader in the field), the speaker appears more believable, credible, and more likable.

The studies considering the effect of message sidedness all suggest that this variable tends to interact with another set of variables. Commitment, level of education, and prior information all interact with message sidedness. The research can be summarized by saying:

1. Two-sided messages seem to be preferable for audiences with higher educational levels, although the obtained differences are not supported in all studies.

2. Two-sided messages seem to be preferable when the audience initially disagrees with the communicator's position.

3. Two-sided messages seem to be preferable when there is a possibility that the audience will be exposed to messages opposing the source's position.

4. One-sided messages are more effective when the receiver is already in agreement with the source, provided that the receiver is not likely to be exposed to later opposing messages.

5. Two-sided messages are more effective when the celebrity endorses a product, producing high levels of liking and believability.

6. Prior attitude and commitment may interact with sidedness, tending to cover up the potential effects of message sidedness.

MESSAGE APPEALS

As a general rule, the mere presentation of data and statistics is not sufficient to change a receiver's attitude or behavior. Some *incentive* or *appeal* must be used to elicit the receiver to change—brands of toothpaste, their vote, to get a dental check-up, and so on. Of course, we have already discussed certain types of appeals throughout earlier chapters. Most of these have been *reward appeals*—messages implying a benefit that a receiver will obtain from adopting the recommended advice. Now, let us talk about *emotional appeals* in persuasion.

The term "emotional appeals" used to conjure up images of fear and intimidation. Employed, in times past, to prompt votes against communist sympathizers, or votes against change, negative connotations have been associated with the term. However, fear is only one emotion. Also, there has been a tremendous growth in the use of emotional appeals in all channels—television, radio, billboards, and in print. Consider four reasons why emotional messages are useful today:[46]

1. Emotional messages grab attention. In cluttered channels we are likely to tune into the radio we hear, actually look at the billboard, and/or watch a commercial (as opposed to changing channels) when a positive emotion is used (humor, warmth, sex).

2. When we experience emotional responses to an advertisement, it is possible that we do not counterargue the verbal message. For example, if humor is used well, and we laugh or smile, most of us will naturally think favorable thoughts afterwards.[47]

3. By their very nature, emotional appeals are more likely than "logical" ones to be vividly portrayed, memorable, and image-provoking.

4. By repeatedly pairing an emotion with a particular product or brand name over time, it may become difficult for competitors to attack the company/product on those grounds. For example, McDonald's corporation traditionally paired itself, and its Golden Arches, with fun—Happy Meals, playgrounds, clowns, birthday parties, dating, flirting, and so on. It is hard for competitors to say, "McDonald's isn't fun." Rather, rival companies started their own kids' clubs, and offered other incentives to a younger audience. In the early 1990s, McDonald's dropped prices to become more competitive during a recession, although, by the 1980s many children were hooked on the restaurant because they were convinced it was fun to eat there.

Although people experience a wide variety of feelings, we will highlight here the importance of three basic emotions.

Fear Appeals

Janis and Feshbach[48] showed three different types of fear appeals to high school students (recall Table 8.1). As you would expect, high-fear-appeal messages were effective in getting the students to worry and become anxious about tooth decay. However, the results also indicated that the *lower* levels of fear were more effective in changing attitudes toward tooth brushing than high levels of fear. Janis and Feshbach argued that high levels of fear produce an avoidance reaction, which negated the effects of the persuasive message.

Several different models of fear appeal research have been offered during the past forty years. The first of these was Janis'[49] *drive model*. Janis argued that when fear is manipulated in receivers, they will be motivated to reduce the unpleasant (drive) state. However, high levels of fear can either make the receiver *more* susceptible to persuasion, or *less* susceptible. Why? If only fear is used, the individuals will find *any* method of reducing the unpleasant feeling—changing how they brush their teeth, going to the dentist. But, taking the recommended action is only half the story. Some people who experience high levels of fear try to reduce the unpleasant experience by denying that the message can be true or authentic—even that the scenes they viewed are bogus; many high school students respond in this way when they see high-fear appeals in driver education courses. Other high-fear receivers become susceptible to counterargument or counterpersuasion. For example, smokers who have been aroused by a fear appeal can buy any number of magazines or books that tell them that there is no proven link between cigarettes and cancer—these receivers want to believe this propaganda.

Leventhal[50] argued that Janis' drive model was too simplistic, and argued that scholars need to study two *parallel processes:* emotional reactions to a threat, and attempts to cope with the fear of that threat. His "Parallel Response Model" was based on the notion that a fear appeal message prompts the receiver to initiate a *danger control process,* enabling the person to cope with the threat (such as, the person realizes that s/he needs to change his/her diet). A second process, a *fear control process,* serves the function of reducing the individual's immediate feelings of anxiety, arousal, worry, and perhaps even panic. The process of controlling danger is often adaptive, as when the individual buys the correct groceries for a diet and joins a gym. Danger control leads to what is referred to as "protection motivation." However, attempts to reduce fear do not always result in adaptive, positive action. For example, behaviors such as the bulimia/anorexia complex may cause weight loss and (temporarily) reduce emotional worries and concerns about being overweight, but are not adaptive.

Rogers[51] built upon the earlier work of Leventhal and proposed a third generation of fear appeal research. Figure 8.7 presents the essence of this "Protection Motivation" theory. One important observation has to be pointed out right away: Some of the most recent work focuses attention on *protection motivation* (getting the receiver to increase motivation to take protective, constructive action), rather than on simple *fear/arousal* manipulations. This is because fear manipulations by themselves are not very useful in shaping receivers' behaviors. On the far left of the figure are all the sources of information that deal with health, behavioral patterns, the need to take protection, and so forth. We have a good deal to say about these sources of information in both Chapters 13 and 14, and these involve "designated driver" campaigns that go beyond public service announcements, "drive responsibly" commercials, shows, commercials and classroom activities that focus on dietary improvements, changing lifestyles and so forth. The far right of the figure lists desired outcomes—from a single act to repeated, multiple acts that are more difficult to change.

Our interest, however, deals with the factors that impact on protection motivation (the middle part of this model). Maladaptive behaviors (that is, obesity, excessive drinking) are affected by both *intrinsic rewards* (pleasure of eating and drinking), and *extrinsic rewards* (friendship with drinking buddies, approval from parents, grandparents, spouses who cook for the obese individual). These rewards keep the individual involved in habitual, repetitive maladaptive responses until such time as s/he becomes aware of the high probability that s/he is in fact *vulnerable* to *severe negative consequences* (that is, the first heart attack, collapsing running up stairs). According to the Rogers' model, fear/arousal messages can impact a receiver's perceptions of vulnerability and severity. The receiver's appraisal of being in a threatened position, and the motivation to take protective action, are a result of adding together all of the intrinsic and extrinsic rewards minus the perceived severity of and vulnerability to the illness, disease,

FIGURE 8.7

SCHEMA OF PROTECTION MOTIVATION THEORY

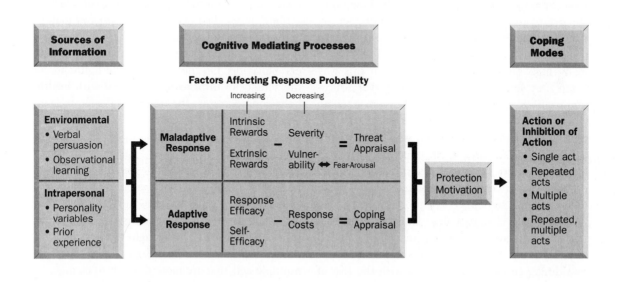

From: R. Rogers, "Cognitive and Physiological Processes in Fear Appeals and Attitude Change: A Revised Theory of Protection Motivation," in J.T. Cacioppo and R.E. Petty, eds., *Social Psychophysiology* (New York: Guilford Press, 1983), pp. 153-176. Used with permission.

harmful practice, and so on. In part, then, a receiver is likely to take positive action if drinking/eating buddies stop rewarding the receiver (indeed, they can start discouraging the individual), and the receiver can no longer ignore his/her vulnerability to an illness or problem that s/he has to admit is severe.

However, the issue now becomes one of the receiver taking an appropriate coping appraisal—to change a life-style rather than to continue to engage in bulimia, smoking, unsafe sex, and so forth. Thus, it is important for persuasion experts to also pay attention to the coping appraisal aspect of protection motivation. To be effective, persuasion campaigns must inform and reinforce the belief that the receiver can effectively change the

behavior and that the benefits will outweigh the costs. Adaptive responses involve *response efficacy* (that getting an inoculation, a nicotine patch, eating fruits and vegetables, and so forth are effective responses), as well as *self-efficacy* (that the receiver's belief in his/her own ability to change can affect the life-style in question). Recall our discussion in Chapter 6 concerning people who have higher self-esteem as more likely to perceive themselves as able to change a health behavior. These types of receivers have higher "self-efficacy." However, coping appraisal is also influenced by the costs associated with changing a life-style—the inconvenience, expense, unpleasantness, difficulty, complexity, side effects, and disruption of daily life may prompt the receiver to decline to take an appropriate coping appraisal. Despite the substantial negative consequences of continuing to smoke cigarettes, for example, some smokers simply refuse to change because they expect that they will gain weight after they stop. Vanity becomes more important than longevity, good health, or less pain later in life.

There are a number of reviews concerning fear appeals, by Boster and Mongeau, by Leventhal, by McAlister, by Rogers, and by Sternthal and Craig.[52] Each of these indicates that fear is useful in prompting worry and anxiety, but fear has to be used in combination with a number of other elements in order to produce a desired response. Consider advertisements for alcohol- or drug-addiction clinics. Different advertisements are employed over months, each making different claims:

(1) Messages evoking fear of negative consequences of continued abuse are vividly portrayed. Such messages work on the severity/vulnerability aspect in Figure 8.7.

(2) Messages emphasizing that the treatment is effective and has a "high success rate." Such messages work on the response efficacy aspect in Figure 8.7.

(3) Messages emphasizing the low cost involved in seeking treatment—most insurance plans cover the cost, and the treatment involves only 10 days and a "couple of two-day follow-ups." Such messages operate to reduce the response cost in Figure 8.7.

(4) Messages emphasizing that the abuser's loved ones want him/her to get treatment. The loved ones are shown discouraging the maladaptive response (reducing extrinsic rewards), and are shown reinforcing and encouraging the individual to adopt the coping response (again, altering response costs and possibly attempting to increase self-efficacy—"I know you can do it . . . ").

(5) A few of the messages emphasize that one should not be embarrassed to admit that s/he is a substance abuser—other characters are shown talking, nonchalantly, about drunk-driving antics, running over mail boxes, and the like. Such messages also work on the response cost aspect in Figure 8.7—the cost of admitting one's problem, the embarrassment, and so forth.

Humor Appeals

Many persuasion textbooks will argue that humor is not useful in persuading receivers. In one way, this is true—simply being humorous does not mean that receivers will be persuaded to buy objects or services they do not need or want. However, if this is true, why is it that 20 to 44 percent of the commercials on TV each night use humor? Why is it that humor is used so frequently on radio or on billboards?

Box 8.2 presents some general rules of thumb concerning the use of humor in advertising and general persuasion. Some of the guidelines are supported by research that indicates males are more easily influenced by humor (like slapstick or visual humor) and that humor promotes positive affect and less counterarguing.[53] We will briefly characterize and give examples of the Madden and Weinberger guidelines.[54]

Perhaps the most widespread use of humor in television, radio, and billboards is where a positive mood is created using simply copy or a mere phrase, for the purpose of promoting *brand switching*. Since humor cannot be expected to change a person's beliefs, values, or habits, it is used to prompt receivers into trying a new product or brand. If you kept a journal of the types of appeals you see, you would note that humor is frequently used for cookies and crackers (the Keebler elves), and for a large number of "consumable goods." Many people eat out for lunch, and again humor

---

B O X   8 . 2

Rules of Thumb Concerning the Use of Humor in Advertising

---

1.   Humor aids in awareness and attention-getting, which are objectives best achieved via humor.

2.   Humor may aid name recall and recall of simple print copy. Humor may aid retention of a simple statement or expression (that is, "Where's the beef?" "the lonely Maytag repairman"). Humorous ads may be recalled more often than serious ads. However, humor may harm recall of complex copy.

3.   Changing attitude or altering habits is not aided by humor. However, humor may aid in the persuasion process by promoting brand switching. Humor also creates a positive mood that enhances persuasion, and can distract receivers away from counterarguing.

4.   Source credibility is not aided by humor. However, humor may increase source liking.

5.   Humor is generally not very effective in bringing about action/sales.

6.   Advertisers who work on creating the ads (in comparison to the account executives) are more positive on the use of humor to fulfill all of the above objectives.

7.   Radio, TV, and billboards are the best media for humor, while direct mail and newspapers are least suited.

8.   Consumer nondurables and business services are best suited to humor, while corporate advertising and industrial products are least suited.

9.   Humor should be related to the product or its use or function.

10.   Humor should not be used with sensitive goods or services.

11.   Audiences that are younger, better-educated, upscale, male, and professionals are best suited to humor. Older, less-educated, and downscale groups are least suited to humor appeals.

Adapted from: T.J. Madden and M.G. Weinberger, "Humor in Advertising: A Practitioner View," *Journal of Advertising Research*, vol. 24 (1984), pp. 23-29. Also see: B. Sternthal and C. S. Craig, "Humor in Advertising," *Journal of Marketing*, vol. 37 (1973), pp. 12-18.

is used to prompt a switch to a new restaurant or to a different type of pizza.

However, brand switching does not completely account for all the humor we see. Another general category of humorous messages involves products generally not bought very often. Maytag, Toro, and a number of other companies use humor to reinforce a particular message: Toro lawnmowers always start right away, so teenagers can't get out of mowing the lawn; Maytag reinforces the idea that its repairmen are lonely because the appliances never break down. The strategy underlying this type of approach is to keep the brand name in the receiver's mind, and to have a positive attitude toward that brand name. Later, when the receiver needs to buy appliances or lawnmowers, s/he will be inclined to investigate one of these products.

Warmth Appeals

The term "warmth" can be applied to a number of messages that appeal to kindness, nostalgia, pride, togetherness, and so on. These appeals significantly increased through the 1980s, starting with telephone commercials of old friends keeping in touch to the popular advertisement about a Vietnam veteran who played basketball on his prosthetic legs. Unlike humor, there are few guidelines for when warmth is effective and when it is not.

Warmth in ads is used in interpersonal settings with individuals showing affection and bonding, or engaged in family reunions and remembering nostalgic times—settings for special coffees, Kodak film, beer, wine, and the like. The warmth appeal is used in commercials in which people recall eating particular foods (such as, Planters peanuts) with parents, old friends, and the like. Presumably, the target audience includes those just out of college and rearing children, to retired people. Figure 8.8 presents an example of

FIGURE 8.8

EXAMPLE OF THE USE OF "WARMTH" APPEALS

REALITY IS THE BEST FANTASY OF ALL.

Liz claiborne

(Liz Claiborne, Inc.)

the warmth appeal. Babies and families are popular approaches.

Aaker, Stayman, and Hagerty[55] argue that warmth appeals strongly affect such physiological measures as galvanic skin response. Further, feelings of warmth can change quickly; it does not appear that a sequence of "warm" commercials sustains warm feelings for very long (unlike some movies and videos). For example, a McDonald's warmth advertisement involving a family reunion was more successful in maintaining sustained feelings of warmth than a Kodak ad they had studied. Aaker, et al., also found that an ideal *sequence* in advertising was for a warmth advertisement to immediately follow a humorous commercial. Presumably, a humorous commercial prompts a positive mood and receivers are more open to the manipulation of feelings of warmth. We have to admit, though, that the opposite sequence (warmth then humor) was not a *bad* sequence, but the results clearly supported the fact that two advertisements of the same type (humor followed by humor; warmth followed by warmth) were *not* as effective as the humor-then-warmth sequence. Indeed, today you will see commercials that employ a sequence within a sixty-second spot— warmth ending with a brief cute, funny scene (an elephant trainer hugging her elephant) that can increase our liking for the ad and the likelihood that we will "tune in" when we see the ad on television. Finally, Aaker, et al., argued that warmth was related to liking of the ad, to recall of seeing the ad, and (sometimes) with higher ratings of intent to buy the product.

F O O T N O T E S

1. S.I. Hayakawa, *Language in Thought and Action* (Cambridge, Mass.: The MIT Press, 1965).
2. E. Eisenberg, "Ambiguity as Strategy in Organizational Communication," *Communication Monographs*, vol. 51 (1984), pp. 25-30.
3. See A. Pratkanis and E. Aronson, *Age of Propaganda: The Everyday Use and Abuse of Persuasion* (New York: Freeman, 1991).
4. R. Robles, R. Smith, C.S. Carver, and A.R. Wellens, "Influence of Subliminal Visual Images on the Experience of Anxiety," *Personality and Social Psychology Bulletin*, vol. 13 (1987), pp. 399-410.
5. I. Janis and S. Feshbach, "Effects of Fear-Arousing Communications," *Journal of Abnormal and Social Psychology*, vol. 47 (1953), pp. 78-92.

6. C. Osgood, P. Tannenbaum, and G. Suci, *The Measurement of Meaning* (Urbana, Ill.: University of Illinois Press, 1957). See also J. Snider and C. Osgood, eds., *Semantic Differential Technique* (Chicago: Aldine, 1969).
7. H. Kumata, "A Factor Analytic Investigation of the Generality of Semantic Structures Across Two Selected Cultures" (Ph.D. dissertation, University of Illinois, 1957).
8. G.J. Suci, "A Comparison of Semantic Structures in American Southwest Culture Groups," *Journal of Abnormal and Social Psychology*, vol. 61 (1960), pp. 25-30.
9. H.C. Triandis and C.E. Osgood, "A Comparative Factorial Analysis of Semantic Structures in Monolingual Greek and American College Students," *Journal of Abnormal and Social Psychology*, vol. 57 (1958), pp. 187-196.
10. C.E. Osgood, R.E. Ware, and C. Morris, "Analysis of the Connotative Meanings of a Variety of Human Values as Expressed by American College Students," *Journal of Abnormal and Social Psychology*, vol. 62 (1961), pp. 62-73.
11. W.J. McEwen and B.S. Greenberg, "The Effects of Message Intensity on Receiver Evaluation of Source, Message, and Topic," *Journal of Communication*, vol. 13 (1963), pp. 94-105.
12. M. Burgoon and D. Stewart, "Empirical Investigations of Language Intensity: I. The Effects of Sex of Source, Receiver, and Language Intensity on Attitude Change," *Human Communication Research*, vol. 1 (1975), pp. 244-248.
13. G.R. Miller and J. Lobe, "Opinionated Language, Open- and Closed-Mindedness and Response to Persuasive Communications," *Journal of Communication*, vol. 17 (1967), pp. 333-341.
14. M. Burgoon and L. King, "The Mediation of Resistance to Persuasion Strategies by Language Variables and Active-Passive Participation," *Human Communication Research*, vol. 1 (1974), pp. 30-41.
15. J. Bradac, J. Bowers, and J. Courtright, "Three Language Variables in Communication Research: Intensity, Immediacy, and Diversity," *Human Communication Research*, vol. 7 (1979), pp. 257-269; J. Bradac, J. Bowers, and J. Courtright, "Lexical Variations in Intensity, Immediacy, and Diversity: An Axiomatic Theory and Causal Model," in R.N. St. Clair and H. Giles, eds., *The Social and Psychological Contexts of Language* (Hillsdale, N.J.: Erlbaum, 1980), pp. 193-223.
16. Bradac, Bowers, and Courtright present 13 axioms in their review, but inconsistent evidence is cited for

one of the axioms, and we have discarded it from our summary.

17. Bradac, Bowers, and Courtright, "Lexical Variations," p. 196.

18. R. Bostrom, J. Baseheart, and C. Rossiter, "The Effects of Three Types of Profane Language in Persuasive Messages," *Journal of Communication*, vol. 23 (1973), pp. 461-475.

19. B. Erickson, E.A. Lind, B.C. Johnson, and W.M. O'Barr, "Speech Style and Impression Formation in a Court Setting: The Effects of 'Powerful' and 'Powerless' Speech," vol. 14 (1978), pp. 266-279; W.M. O'Barr, *Linguistic Evidence: Language, Power and Strategy in the Courtroom* (New York: Academic Press, 1982).

20. J. Bradac and A. Mulac, "A Molecular View of Powerful and Powerless Speech Styles: Attributional Consequences of Specific Language Features and Communicator Intentions," *Communication Monographs*, vol. 51 (1984), pp. 307-319.

21. L.A. Hosman and J.W. Wright, "The Effects of Hedges and Hesitations on Impression Formation in a Simulated Courtroom Context," *Western Journal of Speech Communication*, vol. 51 (1987), pp. 173-188.

22. Erickson, Lind, Johnson, and O'Barr, "Speech Style and Impression Formation."

23. We have carefully reproduced the numbers in Table 8.3 and there is no error—although observant readers would have noted that when reading the transcript version, female receivers perceived the male witness employing *powerless* speech higher in credibility than the male witness employing *powerful* speech. One possibility for this is that the transcript version of a powerful (one-word answers, few hesitations, etc.) male speaker may have prompted some female receivers to think that the male sounded too confident, too self-assured, too prepared, too slick, and too rehearsed—thereby lowering their evaluations of his credibility.

24. S.T. Fiske and S.E. Taylor, *Social Cognition* (Reading, Mass.: Addison-Wesley, 1984).

25. R.E. Nisbett and L. Ross, *Human Inference: Strategies and Shortcomings of Social Judgment* (Englewood Cliffs, N.J.: Prentice-Hall, 1980), p. 45; also see Fiske and Taylor.

26. R.M. Reyes, W.C. Thompson, and G.H. Bower, "Judgmental Biases Resulting from Differing Availabilities of Arguments," *Journal of Personality and Social Psychology*, vol. 39 (1980), pp. 2-12.

27. See Fiske and Taylor, J. Kisielius and B. Sternthal, "Detecting and Explaining the Vividness Effects in Attitudinal Judgments," *Journal of Marketing Research*, vol. 21 (1984), pp. 54-64; J. Kisielius and B. Sternthal, "Examining the Vividness Controversy: An Availability-Valence Interpretation," *Journal of Consumer Research*, vol. 12 (1986), pp. 418-431.

28. See Kisielius and Sternthal, "Examining the Vividness Controversy."

29. K.A. Lutz and R.J. Lutz, "Effects of Interactive Imagery on Learning: Applications to Advertising," *Journal of Applied Psychology*, vol. 62 (1977), pp. 493-498.

30. J.R. Rossiter and L. Percy, "A Visual and Verbal Loop Theory of the Classical Effect of Advertising on Product Attitude," (Paper, Department of Advertising, University of Pennsylvania, 1978).

31. A.A. Mitchell and J.C. Olson, "Are Product Attribute Beliefs the Only Mediator of Advertising Effects on Brand Attitudes?" *Journal of Marketing Research*, vol. 18 (1981), pp. 318-332.

32. J.A. Edell and R. Staelin, "The Information Processing of Pictures in Print Advertisements," *Journal of Consumer Research*, vol. 10 (1983), pp. 45-61; also see T.L. Childers and M.J. Houston, "Conditions for a Picture Superiority Effect on Consumer Memory," *Journal of Consumer Research*, vol. 11 (1984), pp. 643-654.

33. C. Janiszewski, "The Influence of Print Advertisement Organization on Affect Toward a Brand Name," *Journal of Consumer Research*, vol. 17 (1990), pp. 53-65.

34. Janiszewski, "The Influence of Print Advertisement Organization," pp. 54-55.

35. See: C. Petrie, "Information Speaking: A Summary and Bibliography of Related Research," *Speech Monographs*, vol. 30 (1963), pp. 79-91; K.C. Beighley, "The Effect of Four Speech Variables on Comprehension," *Speech Monographs*, vol. 19, (1952), pp. 249-258; K.C. Beighley, "A Summary of Experimental Studies Dealing with the Effect of Organization and Skill of Speakers on Comprehension," *Journal of Communication*, vol. 2 (1952), pp. 58-65; A.H. Eagly, "Comprehensibility of Persuasive Arguments as a Determinant of Opinion Change," *Journal of Personality and Social Psychology*, 1974, 29. pp. 758-773; E. Thompson, "An Experimental Investigation of the Relative Effectiveness of Organizational Structure in Oral Communication," *Southern Speech Communication Journal*, vol. 26 (1960), pp. 59-69; D. Darnell, "The Relation Between Sentence Order and Comprehension," *Speech Monographs*, vol. 30 (1963), pp. 97-100; G. Kissler and K. Lloyd, "Effect of Sentence Interrelation and Scrambling on the Recall of Factual Information," *Journal of Educational Psychology*, vol. 63 (1973), pp. 187-190; R. Sencer, "The

Investigation of the Effects of Incorrect Grammar on Attitude and Comprehension in Written English Message," (Ph.D. dissertation, Michigan State University, 1965); R. Whitman and J. Timmis, "The Influence of Verbal Organizational Structure and Verbal Organizing Skills on Select Messages of Learning," *Human Communication Research*, vol. 1. (1975), pp. 293-301; C. Petrie and S. Carrel, "The Relationship of Motivation, Listening Capability, Initial Information, and Verbal Organizational Ability to Lecture Comprehension and Retention," *Communication Monographs*, vol. 43 (1976), pp. 246-259; C. Spicer and R. Bassett, "The Effect of Organization on Learning from a Message," *Southern Speech Communication Journal*, vol. 41 (1976), pp. 290-299.

36. J. McCroskey and S. Mehrley, "The Effects of Disorganization and Nonfluency on Attitude Change and Source Credibility," *Speech Monographs*, vol. 36 (1969), pp. 13-21.

37. A.H. Monroe and D. Ehninger, *Principles of Speech Communication*, 7th brief ed. (Glenview, Ill.: Scott, Foresman and Co., 1975), pp. 243-265.

38. S. Toulmin, *The Uses Argument* (New York: Cambridge University Press, 1958).

39. D. Ehninger and W. Brockriede, *Decision by Debate* (New York: Dodd, Mead and Co., 1963).

40. R. Windes and A. Hastings, *Argumentation and Advocacy* (New York: Random House, 1965).

41. E. Bettinghaus, *The Nature of Proof* (New York: Bobbs-Merrill, 1972), pp. 123-141.

42. C.I. Hovland, A.A. Lumsdaine, and F.D. Sheffield, *Experiments in Mass Communication: Studies in Social Psychology in World War II*, vol. 3, (Princeton, N.J.: Princeton University Press, 1949), pp. 201-227.

43. A. Lumsdaine and I. Janis, "Resistance to 'Counterpropaganda' Produced by One-sided and Two-sided Propaganda Presentations," *Public Opinion Quarterly*, vol. 17 (1953), pp. 311-318.

44. D. Hilyard, "One-sided versus Two-sided Messages: An Experiment in Counterconditioning," (Ph.D. dissertation, Michigan State University, 1965).

45. M.A. Kamins, M.J. Brand, S.A. Hoeke, and J.C. Moe, "Two-Sided versus One-Sided Celebrity Endorsements: The Impact on Advertising Effectiveness and Credibility," *Journal of Advertising*, vol. 18 (1989), pp. 4-10; M.A. Kamins, "Celebrity and Noncelebrity Advertising," *Journal of Advertising Research*, June/July (1989), pp. 34-42.

46. R. Batra and M.L. Ray, "Advertising Situations: The Implications of Differential Involvement and Accompanying Affect Responses," in R.J. Harris, ed., *Information Processing Research in Advertising* (Hillsdale, N.J.: Erlbaum, 1983), pp. 127-152; M.L. Ray and R. Batra, "Emotion and Persuasion in Advertising: What We Do and Don't Know About Affect," *Advances in Consumer Research*, vol. 10 (1983), pp. 543-548.

47. See, for instance, H.B. Lammers, L. Leibowitz, G.E. Seymour, and J.E. Hennessey, "Humor and Cognitive Responses to Advertising Stimuli: A Trace Consolidation Approach," *Journal of Business Research*, vol. 11 (1983), pp. 173-185.

48. Janis and Feshbach, "Effects of Fear-Arousing Communications."

49. I.L. Janis, "Effects of Fear Arousal on Attitude Change: Recent Developments in Theory and Experimental Research," in L. Berkowitz, ed., *Advances in Experimental Social Psychology*, vol. 3 (New York: Academic Press, 1967), pp. 166-224.

50. H. Leventhal, "Findings and Theory in the Study of Fear Communications," in L. Berkowitz, ed., *Advances in Experimental Social Psychology*, vol. 5 (New York: Academic Press, 1970), pp. 119-186.

51. R.W. Rogers, "Cognitive and Physiological Processes in Fear Appeals and Attitude Change: A Revised Theory of Protection Motivation," in J.T. Cacioppo and R.E. Petty, eds., *Social Psychophysiology: A Sourcebook* (New York: Guilford Press, 1983), pp. 153-176.

52. F. Boster and P. Mongeau, "Fear-Arousing Persuasive Message," in R.N. Bostrom, ed., *Communication Yearbook 8* (Newbury Park, Calif.: Sage, 1984), pp. 330-375; H. Leventhal, "Findings and Theory in the Study of Fear Communications"; A. McAlister, "Antismoking Campaigns: Progress in Developing Effective Communications," in R.E. Rice and W.J. Paisley, eds., *Public Communication Campaigns* (Newbury Park, Calif.: Sage, 1981), pp. 91-104; Rogers, "Cognitive and Psychological Processes in Fear Appeals and Attitude Change"; B. Sternthal and C. Craig, "Fear Appeals: Revisited and Revised," *Journal of Consumer Research*, vol. 7 (1974), pp. 22-34.

53. Lammers, Leibowitz, Seymour, and Hennessey, "Humor and Cognitive Responses to Advertising Stimuli"; Also see: P.E. McGhee and J.H. Goldstein, eds., *Handbook of Humor Research* (New York: Springer-Verlag, 1983).

54. T.J. Madden and M.G. Weinberger, "Humor in Advertising: A Practitioner View," *Journal of Advertising Research*, vol. 24 (1984), pp. 23-29.

55. D.A. Aaker, D.M. Stayman, and M.R. Hagerty, "Warmth in Advertising: Measurement, Impact and Sequence Effects," *Journal of Consumer Research*, vol. 12 (1986), pp. 356-381.

KEY TERMS AND CONCEPTS

denotative meaning
connotative meaning
abstractness
technological terms
euphemisms
legalese
relearning
classification
negation
operational definition
semantic differential scale
language intensity
powerful/powerless speech style

visual salience
vividness
cognitive elaboration
space pattern
time order
deductive order
inductive order
psychological organization
problem-solution structure
Toulmin pattern
data/claim/warrant
order effects
primacy/recency
one-sided/two-sided messages
emotional appeals
fear, warmth, humor appeals
protection motivation
intrinsic/extrinsic rewards
self-efficacy

NONVERBAL COMMUNICATION AND SPEAKER CREDIBILITY

We all use nonverbal code systems, but most of us receive little information about them through formal education. In part, this neglect stems from the fact that until recently there were few scholars studying nonverbal systems. However, in the last twenty years we have witnessed a virtual explosion in the number and variety of research studies concerned with nonverbal communication. This chapter focuses on three areas. First, we will discuss what is included in the nonverbal code system and present an overview of the terms used to define its various features. Second, we will discuss which nonverbal behaviors are linked to credibility and persuasiveness, as well as to a speaker's level of power and status. Third, we will discuss research on honesty and deception—can you tell when someone is lying to you? There are many topics in nonverbal communication that we cannot detail here. However, the interested reader can find a more complete picture in Burgoon, Buller, and Woodall's[1] *Nonverbal Communication: The Unspoken Dialogue*, Knapp and Hall's[2] *Nonverbal Communication in Human Interaction*, and Leather's[3] *Successful Nonverbal Communication: Principles and Applications*.

THE NONVERBAL CODE SYSTEM

Gestural Codes

All of us use gestures to accompany our speech. We point, smile, shrug our shoulders, turn one way or the other, or shake our fist at someone. How should we classify such behavior? There are a number of options, ranging from Birdwhistell's system that includes a muscle-by-muscle examination of a person's gestures,[4] to the nineteenth-century elocutionists' attempts at tying certain gestures to particular words in the language. A most useful analysis is provided by Ekman and Friesen,[5] who suggest that our gestures can be divided into five categories:

1. **Emblems.** Emblems are gestures that can be translated directly into the verbal code system. Emblems may accompany a verbal message or be used alone; however, their meaning can be understood without verbal accompaniment. If you are a fully socialized American, you should be able to recognize and use the following emblems[6]: hitchhiking; shrug of uncertainty; fighting; money; suicide; a woman's nice figure; something stinks; okay; I don't know; he's crazy; shame on you!; stop; go away; come here; do you have a cigarette?; I'm hot; a close shave; tastes good; I'm smart; how could I be so dumb!; counting; and various insults.

Some emblems change in frequency of occurrence because of popularity and the times. The emblems for peace and black power, for example, went out of fashion in the early 1970s. It is important to understand that any system of emblems is influenced by culture, and what an emblem signifies in one culture may mean nothing in another (or worse, something different). Scholars have begun to document the common emblems of other cultures so that fewer instances of miscommunication may emerge and today's travelers can be made aware of subtle nuances. For example, Kendon,[7] and Morris, et al.,[8] note that some gestures are so offensive that they are made illegal—only to evolve into more subtle variations. Hence, the "Italian salute" was altered on Malta to appear to be a gesture similar to what we refer to below as a self-adaptor—the left arm is held straight, with the hand clenched in a fist, while the right arm rubs the inside of the left elbow.

Table 9.1 summarizes some of the most commonly understood American emblems, according to Johnson, Ekman, and Friesen.[9] You should be able to perform and recognize the hand gestures listed there. Emblems, however, are hand gestures carrying meaning to members of any *culture*

T A B L E	9.1

Common American Emblems

Message Type	Encoded Message Meaning	Decoded Message Meaning
Interpersonal Directions (commands)	Sit down beside me	Sit down beside me
	Be silent, hush	Be silent, hush
	Come here	Come here
	I can't hear you	I can't hear you
	Wait—hold it	Wait—hold it
	I warn you	I warn you
	Get lost	*Get lost or get out or go away
	Be calm	Be calm
	Follow me	*Follow me or this way
	Time to go	*Time to go or what time is it?
	Stop	*Stop or halt
	Go the other way	*Go the other way or no, not that way
	I want to smoke and got a cigarette?	*I want to smoke or got a cigarette?
	Look!	*Look, or I see something or look over there
	Go away	Go away or rejection or get out of here
	Take it away	*Take it away or go away or get out of here
	Go this way	*Go this way or over there or that way
	Go ahead	*Go ahead or go on by
	Hurry and quickly	*Quickly or hurry or come here quickly
	What time is it?	*What time is it? or time to go
	Stay here	*Stay here or down here
Own physical state	I'm hot and it's hot	*I'm hot or hard work or a close shave
	Hard work	*Hard work or I'm hot or a close shave
	A close shave	*A close shave or I'm hot or hard work
	It's cold and I'm cold	*It's cold or I'm cold
	I'm full of food	I'm full of food
	I've got a headache	I've got a headache
	I've got a toothache	I've got a toothache
	I've got an earache	I've got an earache
	Tastes good	Tastes good
	I am smart	I am smart
	How could I be so dumb?	How could I be so dumb?
Insults	F*** you (finger)	*Screw you or up yours or f*** you
	F*** you (arm)	*F*** you or up yours or screw you
	The hell with you and rejection	*The hell with you or rejection
	He's crazy and he's stupid	*He's crazy or he's stupid
	Shame on you	Shame on you

Message Type	Encoded Message Meaning	Decoded Message Meaning
Replies	OK (fingers)	OK
	No (head) and I disagree	*No or I disagree
	I don't know	I don't know
	Meaning	Meaning
	Yes and I agree and I like it	*Yes or I agree or I like it
	Absolutely no	*Absolutely no or no way
	I dislike it	*I dislike it or no way
	I promise	*I promise or cross my heart
	Absolutely yes	Absolutely yes
	Hard to think this and thinking	*Hard to think about this or puzzlement or thinking
	I doubt it	I doubt it
Own Affect	I'm angry	I'm angry
	I'm disgusted and something stinks	*Something stinks
	I'm sad	*I'm sad or I'm ashamed
	I'm surprised	I'm surprised
	Whoopee!	Whoopee! or hooray!
Greetings and Departures	Good-bye	Good-bye
	Hello	Hello
Physical Appearance of Person	Woman and nice figure	*Woman or nice figure
Classified	You (finger point)	You
	Me (own chest)	Me
	Hitchhiking	Hitchhiking
	Counting	Counting
	Gossip	*Gossip or talk-talk-talk
	Fighting	Fighting
	Peace and victory	*Peace or victory
	Good luck	Good luck
	Money	Money
	It's far away	*It's far away or over there
Unclassified	Suicide (gun)	*Suicide or shoot myself
	Finished	*It's finished or that's enough

* Either decoded message was accepted, although the first message was given more often than the second.

Adapted from H.G. Johnson, P. Ekman, and W.V. Friesen, "Communicative Body Movements: American Emblems," *Semiotica*, vol. 15 (1975), pp. 335–353.

TABLE 9.2

EXAMPLES OF SUBCULTURE EMBLEMS: GANG AFFILIATION

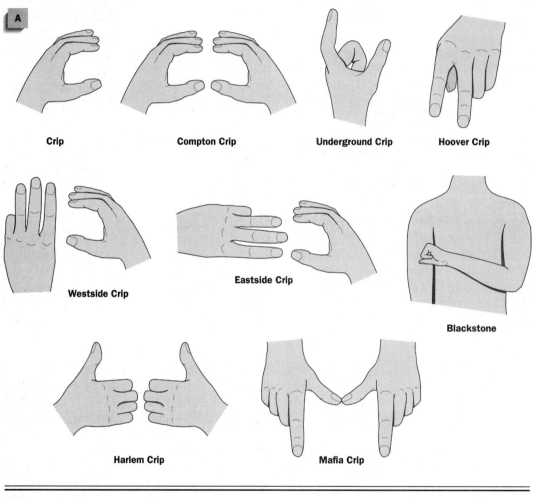

A

Crip   Compton Crip   Underground Crip   Hoover Crip

Westside Crip   Eastside Crip

Blackstone

Harlem Crip   Mafia Crip

B

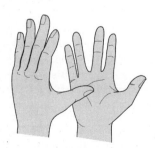

Gang I.D. #1   Gang I.D. #2   Gang I.D. #3

or *subculture*. In most urban settings today, gang members communicate a number of messages to one another by "flashing" hand signals. Table 9.2 (panel A) includes some emblems members would flash to show gang affiliation in Los Angeles according to Jackson and McBride.[10] Panel B includes a few of the signals used by Chicago gangs to signify gang affiliation, according to Sgt. Jerry Simandle.[11] Subculture emblems can change rapidly, and if you are not a member of the particular group, you can communicate inappropriate and even dated messages.

2. *Illustrators*. Illustrators are body movements that accompany speech and help illustrate the point the speaker is making. The gesture of holding one's hands apart when telling someone the size of a just-caught fish is an example of an illustrator. Movements emphasizing a word, pointing to an object when talking about the object, or indicating some action are all illustrators. A subset of illustrators includes, according to Ekman and Friesen, *deictic* movements (pointing to objects, places, or events), *rhythmic* movements (depicting the timing or rhythm of an event), and *pictographs* (showing the shape of what is referenced verbally). Sometimes it is useful to distinguish between illustrators and expansive illustrators—sweeping gestures outside the area of the shoulder and hip area (that is, movement away from the torso). People use more illustrators when excited or enthusiastic, and again, cultures differ in how much illustrating is typical or normal.

Woodall and Folger[12] videotaped conversations which demonstrated the importance of illustrators in persuasion—for example, "Really, I can't keep up with him, he just sits there and shovels it in" was accompanied either with (1) no hand gestures, (2) an *emphasizing* gesture (such as

rhythmic motion like pounding or pointing), or (3) an *emblematic* gesture, which is related semantically to the utterance (in our example, with a sweeping motion of the speaker's hand toward the mouth). The emblematic gesture is *semantically* related to the utterance because the nonverbal gesture transcribes to the words "shovel it in." Observers viewed different versions of the videotapes and were later asked to recall the conversations. Utterances communicated with emblematic gestures were better recalled. Thus, hand gestures may be used strategically to highlight parts of a message that the persuader wants emphasized—and hand gestures best able to secure receiver recall are those closely linked to the words the speaker is communicating.

Hand gestures also serve to *punctuate* speech and to *elicit* receiver *responses*. According to Knapp and Hall,[13] punctuation gestures coincide with voice stress (as when the speaker is emotionally aroused), and are used to organize the stream of speech into units. Politicians will commonly "wave off" a question or a complaint, "point" or "jab" when on the attack, or use "open hand" movements when welcoming or accepting approval or support from others. Since television news programs prefer to show drama and conflict, many of the "sound bites" we see on the evening news involve excerpts of speeches or interviews which show the politician punctuating or gesturing emphatically. Bull[14] also found that politicians commonly use punctuating gestures along with rhetorical devices in order to evoke or to curtail applause from an audience.

3. *Regulators*. Regulators are gestures and facial movements that help control the flow of communication in an interaction. They are used by the source and the receiver to indicate the way in

Table 9.2 on the opposite page from: R.K. Jackson and W.D. McBride, *Understanding Street Gangs* (Panel A, used by permission of authors and Copperhouse Publishing Company, Placerville, CA., 1990)
From: J. Simandle, "Gang Identifiers and Things to Remember." (Panel B, mimeo, Midwest Gang Investigators Association, Chicago, Ill., 1991)

which the conversation is to continue, or to change the nature of the conversation. Such gestures include head nods, certain hand movements, and eye movements. They may tell the speaker that receivers are interested, want further information, or want the speaker to repeat a statement. Used by the source, they may indicate that the source is nearly done, wants to elaborate on a point, or wants to continue speaking after finishing a point.

4. *Adaptors*. Adaptors are employed to satisfy physical or emotional needs and often include rubbing, biting, or scratching. One of your friends may play with her hair when anxious, while another rubs a particular spot on his forehead, and another friend rubs her chin. Obviously, an adaptor does not carry meaning in the same way an emblem does, and you may need to get to know a person in order to know whether a particular adapting behavior reflects anxiety, arousal, deep concentration, or some other state. In general, however, frequent adapting reduces a speaker's effectiveness. Sources are often quite unaware of their own adapting behaviors (unless they receive feedback from others), but they learn to read the adaptors of others without difficulty. Adaptors are commonly divided into two types: *self* (including facial or head, and body) and *object* (playing with objects such as rubber bands, paper clips, or a set of keys).

5. *Affect displays*. Affect displays are facial expressions indicating the state of our emotions. Frowns, smiles, grins, and hand movements may all be used to communicate our affective states. People vary considerably in their ability to communicate emotions. Some people appear to "withhold" emotional expressions (like the receptionist Marilyn on the television show *Northern Exposure*), while other people appear to communicate a wide range of emotions quite readily. Emotional expressions, especially happiness, are communicated in virtually all commercials.

According to Ekman and Friesen[15] there are six basic emotional expressions: surprise, fear, disgust, anger, happiness, and sadness. All other emotional expressions are "affect blends": blends of anger and disgust (showing *contempt* for someone), anger and happiness (showing *smugness*), happiness and surprise (showing *excitement* at a party), and so forth. Display rules are the unwritten rules governing when, and with what intensity, we display emotional expressions in public. Cultural display rules are the guidelines one's culture dictates concerning appropriateness of emotions. It is important to realize that some emotional expressions communicated in public in America (in interviews, advertisements, and political spots), would be inappropriate in other cultures. For example, Chinese job interviewees rarely display frowns or negative emotional expressions, even when revealing negative verbal content[16]. Nurses, physicians, airline assistants, priests (and anyone who counsels others), gamblers, teachers, lawyers, detectives, salespersons, police officers, and bill collectors need to be effective in communicating certain expressions (even looking neutral or unemotional when, in fact, they are experiencing strong emotions).

Former President Ronald Reagan was known as the Great Communicator because of his (acting) ability to express emotions. Table 9.3 illustrates examples of the expressions for happiness/reassurance, fear/evasion, and anger/threat. In a study of receiver reactions, McHugo and colleagues[17] first had Dartmouth students complete a questionnaire concerning initial attitudes toward Reagan. Then the students watched a videotape of Reagan's emotional expressions while their heart rates, skin response, and other physiological reactions were recorded. Later the students completed a self-report questionnaire concerning their emotional reactions.

First, McHugo, et al., found that the students' emotional feelings were directly and profoundly

TABLE **_9.3_**

STILL FRAMES FROM VIDEOTAPE
EXCERPTS SHOWING PRESIDENT
REAGAN DISPLAYING (FROM TOP,
COUNTERCLOCKWISE) HAPPINESS/
REASSURANCE, FEAR/EVASION, AND
ANGER/THREAT

From: J. McHugo, J.T. Lanzette, D.G. Sullivan, R.D. Masters, and B.G. Englis, "Emotional Reactions to a Political Leader's Expressive Displays," *Journal of Personality and Social Psychology*, vol. 49 (1985), pp. 1513–1529. (Courtesy of Gregory McHugo)

affected by Reagan's emotional expressions. This was true *regardless* of their initial attitudes toward Reagan, and was strongest when the students viewed the *silent* videotapes (when the facial expressions were the only stimuli to which the students were exposed). Second, the study found that answers on the last questionnaire (where the students presumably indicated the emotions they *thought* they were experiencing) were strongly influenced by initial attitudes—those who had indicated they did not like Reagan reported more negative reactions and were less responsive to the differences among the displays. This result can be explained in terms of cognitive consistency theories—initial attitudes and reactions would be made consistent with one another, and the receiver would deny, ignore, or discredit the brief physiological, emotional reaction to the speech just heard.

Communication scholars have witnessed a movement toward candidate style variables as a primary reason for voting, and a movement away from party affiliation and issue voting. Voters want to vote for sincere, trustworthy, competent communicators. Accurately communicated facial expressions can play a major role in campaigns because facial expressions inform viewers about the emotional state of the communicator, display the communication skills of the candidate, and evoke distinct reactions. Further, it is tempting to argue that facial expressions are even more important early in a campaign, when voters are undecided, and have not yet developed strong initial attitudes toward the candidate.

PARALINGUISTIC CODES

Many expressions (women's movement, abortion rights, pro-choice, gay rights) can be said sneeringly, encouragingly, deprecatingly, humorously, defiantly, or sadly, all depending on the tone of voice used. The study of those nonverbal cues that surround the verbal code system is called *paralinguistics*. Trager[18] suggested that the study of paralinguistics involves at least two major elements.

1. *Voice qualities*. Voice qualities include such things as speech rate, rhythm pattern, pitch, precision of articulation, and control of utterances by the lips, tongue, and other articulators. Such voice qualities convey meaning as they accompany words and statements. The high-pressure salesman who spits out his message at a very rapid rate conveys a sense of importance and urgency. Thus, rate becomes a paralinguistic characteristic of the message.

2. *Vocalizations*. Vocalizations include sounds that do not have specific meanings but which can indicate emotions when accompanying verbal messages. Vocal characteristics such as swallowing, coughing, heavy breathing, sneezing, yawning, and sighing may indicate importance, nervousness, or other emotional states of the speaker or listener. *Vocal segregates* are interjections such as *uh*, *uh-huh*, or *ah*, within the message. They may signal the source to continue, or to stop for a question, or they may tell the listener that the source has more to say, or is almost finished. By using *vocal qualifiers* we indicate intensity in a message by speaking loudly or softly, indicate emotion by using extremely high pitch, or convey importance by speaking slowly and precisely.

In addition to paralinguistic elements, attention has focused on *speech disturbances*. Many speech disturbances result in a loss of persuasiveness, and are related to deception. As reviewed in Harper, Wiens, and Matarazzo[19], it is important to distinguish between *ah* and *non-ah* speech disturbances because the two types of disturbances serve different functions. *Ah* disfluencies include the *ah*, *er*, *umm* sounds a speaker makes while presenting a speech. *Non-ah* disturbances include:

omissions—which occur during speech production when words or parts of words are omitted. For example: *It was East( ) Sunday. They were really hap( ) about the picnic.*

stutter—which occurs when the speaker repeats a sound. For example: *Sh-she was mean to me. Bu-but I still love her.*

word/phrase repetitions—which occur when a word or even a whole phrase is repeated. For example: *Then we-then we-then we went for a drive.*

tongue slip—which occurs when a speaker makes an incorrect substitution of syllables. For example: A speaker says *darn bore or rage wait* for *barn door and wage rate.*

sentence correction—occurs when a correction in a word choice is made by a speaker while she or he speaks. (This disfluency is different from grammatical error [below] because in the grammatical error disfluency the speaker continues to speak as if he or she were unaware of the disfluency.) For example: *Third World War (ah), I meant Third World Nations. . .*

grammatical error—occurs when a grammatical error is made during the speech. For example, the speaker mixes present and past tense or mixes plural and singular.

There is evidence that *non-ah* disturbances are related to anxiety, while the use of *ah* may indicate several different variables: The speaker may be answering an ambiguous question, the speaker wants to *hold* the conversational floor, or the speaker may have difficulty (cognitively speaking) in answering a question. *Ah* and *non-ah* speech errors play different roles in persuasion. Finally, longer *response latencies* (periods of silence that occur before the speaker holds the floor) reflect increased mental concentration as well as anxiety[20].

The reader now has been provided with the major features of the nonverbal code system and sufficient terminology to describe specific behaviors. The remainder of the chapter links behaviors to persuasion.

BEHAVIORS ASSOCIATED WITH PERSUASIVENESS

A number of studies group nonverbal behaviors together on the basis of what the behaviors communicate. While a number of typologies exist, and different researchers have used different labels, we shall discuss three categories of behaviors relevant to persuasion[21]. First, cues associated with *extroversion* reflect the speaker's level of animation and/or enthusiasm for the topic. These behaviors include forceful, rhythmic gestures or illustrators, high eye-contact rates, higher vocal volume, faster speaking rates, more affirmative head nodding, more facial activity, and greater variety of intonation. Second, a number of behaviors reflect *affiliation* (liking and attraction) that communicates the speaker's attitude toward the audience. Behaviors included in this category are increased gesturing, forward leaning, increased head nodding, closer proximity, and increased smiling, touching, and eye contact. Third, behaviors reflecting the speaker's level of *relaxation* (or, conversely, anxiety) include relaxed posture (asymmetry of arm/leg positions, side-ways lean, backward reclining of the body, and relaxed hand and neck positions), anxiety cues (adaptors, vocal nervousness), and fluency of speech.

As a general rule, persuasiveness increases as the speaker engages in behaviors indicative of extroversion and affiliation while exhibiting few anxiety-related behaviors. More specific conclusions can be made after examining the impact on persuasiveness and speaker evaluations of: body movements, eye contact, distance and touching, speech fluency, speech rate, and vocal qualities.

Body movements

Mehrabian and Williams conducted a series of studies to see what behaviors people exhibit when told to be persuasive.[22] For example, students were told to be either very persuasive, moderately persuasive, or neutral. The subjects were allowed time to prepare and deliver speeches to an audience while being videotaped through a one-way mirror. Mehrabian and Williams found that as intention to persuade increased, speakers were more likely to increase eye contact and do affirmative head nodding, to illustrate or gesture more frequently, to increase facial activity, and to speak more loudly and more quickly. Mehrabian and

---

NONVERBAL CORRELATES OF TRUSTWORTHINESS AND DYNAMISM

To build the perception of *trustworthiness*, the speaker should maintain a high eye-contact rate, nod frequently, smile, display open arms and hands, and employ other behaviors associated with affiliation. The speaker should also avoid exhibiting anxiety-related behaviors, and use a conversational style of delivery.

To build the perception of *dynamism*, the speaker should illustrate expansively, move energetically, speak relatively loudly, speak relatively quickly, display greater facial activity and greater intonation. The speaker should also use few nonfluencies, a "dynamic" style of delivery, a range of inflections, and a varying rate and pitch of speech.

Williams also had observers view the videotaped presentations and rate them on levels of persuasiveness. The speaker was perceived as more persuasive when he/she maintained eye contact, engaged in more illustrating, used fewer adaptors, spoke more quickly with greater volume and fluency, and engaged in more facial activity.

LaCrosse similarly found that in counseling interactions, individuals were perceived as more persuasive when they maintained more eye contact, smiled more, exhibited more affirmative head nods, gestured frequently, and directly faced the listener.[23] Maslow, Yoselson, and London paid an actor to deliver a speech in a confident, doubtful, or neutral manner.[24] Not only did confidence increase persuasiveness, but the "confident" speaker used more forceful and rhythmic gestures, maintained more eye contact, and exhibited a more relaxed posture. During the "doubtful" speech, the speaker engaged in more object and body adaptors, maintained less eye contact, and sat in a tense, upright position.

The above studies indicate that gestures dealing with both affiliation and extroversion are related to perceived persuasiveness. There are also studies indicating that the same cues elicit favorable evaluations in interviews.[25] Generally, these studies note the following:

High levels of eye contact, high energy levels, desirable paralinguistic cues (a low number of speech disturbances, fluent speech, and high modality), and frequent head and hand movements produce higher ratings of effectiveness in job interviews;

Individuals who exhibit energy and involvement in the interview are liked better, and are judged as more competent, qualified, likely to be successful, and motivated;

High nonverbal responsiveness (using vocal cues, facial expressiveness, increased nodding, gaze, and gesturing) led to enhanced ratings of a counselor's expertise, trustworthiness, and attractiveness;

Interviewers who are enthusiastic (versus unenthusiastic) use high amounts of eye contact, smiling, and gesturing, and are perceived to be more job satisfied, approachable, interested, enthusiastic, considerate, and intelligent.

Although many of these behaviors are related to affiliation, there is little doubt that cues associated with extroversion, such as high energy level, expansive gestures, and level of enthusiasm, are related to enhanced evaluations and higher perceived credibility—both in public speaking and in interview contexts.

Listeners have distinct preferences concerning levels of social relaxation and, in general, do not care to be distracted by anxiety cues. Use of a large number of adaptors results in lower ratings of liking and speaker effectiveness. Persuasiveness is also influenced by body tension; females were considered more persuasive when they were slightly tense or slightly relaxed, while males were more persuasive when they were slightly relaxed.[26] The "very relaxed" position produced ratings very low in perceived persuasiveness. Further, listeners prefer a speaker to sit directly in front of them, at least in a dyadic setting.[27]

The preceding literature provides two conclusions concerning bodily movements and speaker effectiveness. First, a number of nonverbal behaviors are consistently related to enhanced performance ratings in both public speaking and interview contexts: maintaining eye contact, nodding, smiling, illustrating, avoiding too much relaxation, and refraining from use of distracting adaptors. Second, there are additional behaviors indicative of extroversion (high energy level, level of enthusiasm, sweeping or expansive illustrating) and affiliation (forward lean, direct body orientation, open hand movements) that are related to improved evaluations in certain contexts.

In a face-to-face or dyadic context, affiliative cues can and often do help in persuasion (as in getting more tips, selling more encyclopedias, or getting people to sign a petition), while in formal contexts persuasiveness can be enhanced by greater extroversion and animation and by less af-

filiation. Studies have found that forward leaning and relaxed hand gestures often are unrelated to effectiveness in formal employment interviews, while verbal output, speech fluency, body composure, eye-contact rate, posture, and appearance are more important. Too much emphasis on affiliative gestures in such a formal context may result in the speaker being perceived as failing to exhibit sufficient seriousness.[28] Thus, we recommend that readers maintain eye contact, nod, smile, illustrate, display few anxiety cues, and adapt other behaviors for the particular context.

Eye-Contact Rate

A number of studies clearly demonstrate that eye-contact rate is linked to perceived sincerity, trustworthiness, friendliness, and qualification, although not necessarily to dynamism, potency, or dominance.[29] For example, one study found that speakers who averaged 63 percent eye-contact rates were judged as more sincere than speakers who averaged 20 percent. Another had a speaker deliver a speech three times, each time manipulating eye-contact rates: 0 percent, 50 percent, and 90 percent. The results indicated that higher eye-contact rates led to improved ratings on Berlo, Lemert, and Mertz's honesty and qualification factors of credibility, but the perception of dynamism was unaffected by eye-contact rate. In interview contexts, eye-contact rates were found to be related to perceptions of friendliness—but not to perceptions of dominance, potency, or confidence. When a person maintains a high rate of eye contact, we feel trusting and safe, and believe he/she is friendly and sincere.

Burgoon, et al., noted that in any interaction, normal rates of eye contact range from 29 percent to 70 percent.[30] Studies indicate rates of 20 percent to 40 percent are detrimental to persuasiveness, while much more persuasion occurs when eye-contact rates range from 60 percent to 90 percent.

Distance and Touching

Increased proximity is associated with intimacy, liking, arousal, and attraction.[31] Similarly, touch is often discussed as one of the most powerful relational messages. Often touch elicits liking from recipients and is linked to warmth, friendliness, and love.[32] One might expect that proximity and touch may influence perceptions of social attractiveness and thus enhance persuasiveness. However, there is no simple relationship between proximity and persuasiveness.

First, Mehrabian and Williams found that decreased distance was associated with increased persuasiveness. However, Albert and Dabbs found that attitude change was obtained as distance *increased*.[33] That is, speakers obtained more attitude change when speaking 14 feet away from an audience than at four feet or one to two feet. The more reasonable explanation for these results is that closer approaches (especially at one foot) make people defensive and resistant. More recently Ellsworth and Langer, Kleinke, and others have argued that a brief touch during a compliance request elicits arousal and a sense of interpersonal involvement.[34] Staring also elicits arousal, but the arousal that occurs when a stranger touches or stares at you may indicate either stress or attraction. Thus, there are only certain circumstances in which increased proximity or touching will enhance persuasiveness.

Two models have been proposed about distance or proximity in persuasion. Patterson proposed a model focusing on the amount of effort or expense involved in complying.[35] According to Patterson, when a stranger approaches you or even touches you, you experience arousal, which can be linked to stress or reflect involvement and attraction. In this situation, if you were asked to comply

with a request that required little effort or expense (loaning a dime) you would probably comply because of the high involvement. On the other hand, if the request were for some cost or effort on your part, then having a person stand too close will make it harder to concentrate. Thus, if persuasion involves effort, being too close may make the receiver defensive.

Burgoon's model focuses attention on normative expectations and the general attractiveness of the speaker.[36] First, all receivers have expectations about how close or far away people should stand from them. You may expect that your neighbor will stand three and a half feet from you. Now, if you liked your neighbor and she moved *closer* than you expected, you would experience heightened arousal and she would become more persuasive. If you disliked the neighbor and she moved closer than you expected, you would experience stress, and neither comprehension nor persuasion would increase. Both of these models have their merits and should be kept in mind when you try to be persuasive or watch others trying to be persuasive.

How a person is approached and touched also makes a difference. Crusco and Wetzel[37] examined how (female) servers in a restaurant returned change to customers, and examined the impact this had on tipping behavior. In the "fleeting touch" approach, the server twice touched the diner's palm with her fingers for one-half second as she returned the change, in what was apparently an "accidental touch." In the "shoulder touch" approach, the server placed her hand on the diner's shoulder for one to one and a half seconds. In the "no touch" approach, the server simply returned the change on the table in a change tray. In each case, no eye contact was made, and the server said "Here's your change." The "fleeting touch" elicited the highest rates of tipping (16.7 percent), followed by the "shoulder touch" (14.4 percent), and the "no touch" approach (12.2 percent).

TABLE	9.4

THE IMPACT OF TWO TYPES OF SPEECH NONFLUENCIES ON SPEAKER CREDIBILITY

	Frequency of Nonfluency				
	0	*25*	*50*	*75*	*100*
Ratings of the Speaker's Competence:					
Vocalized Pauses:	22.81	18.94	15.94	16.31	15.56
Repetitions:	21.91	15.31	14.13	13.44	10.75
Ratings of the Speaker's Dynamism:					
Vocalized Pauses:	22.44	21.81	20.06	18.56	21.19
Repetitions:	22.38	17.44	15.00	17.31	13.81
Ratings of the Speaker's Trustworthiness:					
Vocalized Pauses:	18.38	20.00	15.75	18.00	16.44
Repetitions:	18.31	17.69	19.94	17.50	15.25

From: G.R. Miller and M.A. Hewgill, "The Effects of Variations in Nonfluencies in Audience Ratings of Source Credibility," *Quarterly Journal of Speech*, vol. 50 (1964), pp. 36–44. Copyright by the Speech Communication Association, © 1964.

Speech Fluencies and Delivery Style

Frequent nonfluencies in a speech can reduce the speaker's credibility. A classic study by Miller and Hewgill[38] demonstrated this very clearly. Miller and Hewgill took a flawless persuasive speech containing 1,054 words and constructed a number of versions by varying the frequency of two types of nonfluencies: *repetitions* and *vocalized pauses*. A repetition was defined as a repetition of an utterance (example: "For Newman/Newman, it was . . . "). A vocalized pause—also called a "filled pause"—is a pause during a speech that is filled with an "ah" (example: "For ah Newman it was . . . "). Speeches were constructed containing either 0, 25, 50, 75, or 100 instances of either vocalized pauses or repetitions. Receivers heard the speech and rated the speaker in terms of competence, trustworthiness, and dynamism. The results are presented in Table 9.4; the higher the numbers, the higher the evaluations of the speaker's competence, trustworthiness, and dynamism.

The results indicated that repetitions dramatically reduced the speaker's ratings of competence and dynamism and had a small impact on ratings of trustworthiness. The fact that ratings of speaker's competence dropped from 21.91 (fluent speech) to 15.31 when only 25 repetitions were used shows the importance of fluency on credibility. Competence ratings dropped again when the rate of repetitions increased to 100. Ratings of dynamism also dropped from the flawless version (22.38) to versions containing 25 to 75 repetitions (ratings of 15-17), and then dropped again for very high levels of repetitions. Repetitions were weakly associated with ratings of trustworthiness, showing receivers were more tolerant of the vocalized pause.

These results are simple to explain. As listeners, we believe if a person is competent and speaking in an area of expertise, the speaker should neither be anxious nor have a difficult time thinking about what to say. Thus, too many nonfluencies lower ratings of competence. Also, a dynamic person is expected to be extroverted, active, potent, and charismatic—displaying frequent anxiety-related disturbances is simply incompatible with the expectation of an extroverted speaker. Finally, trustworthiness ratings are only slightly affected by speech nonfluencies because we can still feel safe with a speaker even if he or she stutters or has frequent "ah" speech errors. How many of us question the sincerity of a stutterer or think that a person with frequent "ah" nonfluencies has a hidden or ulterior motive? One variable that is related to trustworthiness is the speaker's style of delivery.

Pearce and others indicate that the speaker's style of delivery influences a wide range of perceptions of the speaker. Pearce and Conklin,[39] for example, hired an actor to record a message using a dynamic style of delivery and a conversational style of delivery. Conversational delivery involved a relatively smaller range of inflections, a greater consistency of rate and pitch, less volume, and generally lower pitch levels than dynamic delivery. When the speeches were played back to students, the researchers found that the conversational-style speaker was perceived as more trustworthy, friendly and pleasant, while the dynamic speaker was rated more dynamic. The students felt that the conversational-style speaker was a more ideal speaker—judged as attractive, educated, professional, honest, person-oriented,

self-assured, and assertive. Pearce and Brommel[40] found that these two delivery styles were significantly related to the credibility factors of evaluation, dynamism, and trustworthiness (but not to competence).

The Pearce studies indicate that people have a distinct stereotype of the calm conversational-style speaker and the more active, dynamic speaker, and that the conversational-style speaker is preferred. Neither of these results is surprising. Television reinforces the stereotypes as well as the preference. Johnny Carson and Jay Leno are popular conversational-style speakers. However, we are also bombarded by 30-second advertisements of hyperactive salespersons selling everything from used vacuums to new Veg-o-matics. The preference for the conversational style is obvious—conversational-style speakers are more pleasing to hear and more likely to be trusted.

The Pearce studies found style of delivery not related to perceived competence. Are there vocal qualities related to competence? According to Scherer, London, and Wolf's "voice of confidence" study, the answer to this question is "yes."[41] Scherer, et al., hired an actor to record a message using both a confident and a doubtful voice. The confident voice was louder, faster, and contained fewer and shorter pauses than the doubtful voice. Results indicated that the confident voice was perceived as more fluent and expressive than the doubtful voice. The confident speaker was also perceived as more enthusiastic, forceful, active, dominant, self-assured, and competent. It would appear that varying pitch and rate (as in the Pearce studies) has less to do with competency ratings than do increased rate, loudness, and lack of pauses.

Speech Rate

Most researchers who study speech rates argue that there exists a range of rates listeners find acceptable. Once a speaker speaks slower or faster than the lower and upper thresholds, respectively, some less than desirable consequence may occur. Normal speech rates vary from 120 to 195 words per minute (wpm); research has employed rates of 102-111 wpm as slow, 140 wpm as moderate, and 191 wpm as fast. The results of research on rate of speech provide us with three general conclusions.

First, only at extremely fast speech rates does comprehension of material decline. Foulke and Sticht reviewed literature on speed of speaking and comprehension and report that the majority of studies found no significant relationship between the two.[42] When studies did find a significant relationship, faster rates resulted in lowered comprehension. Fairbanks, Guttman, and Miron demonstrate this nicely.[43] In this study, the researchers used *compressed speech* methods to alter speech rate, keeping the words on the tape recording as intelligible as when originally recorded, but removing brief segments of silence from the recording. Even at 282 wpm (twice the normal rate) listeners could still comprehend 90 percent of the message. At 353 wpm the listeners could comprehend only about 50 percent of what was said. Orr similarly found that retention of material did not decline until speed of delivery reached 275-300 wpm.[44] Since normal speech rates vary from 120-195 wpm and radio announcers range from 140-191 wpm, it is obvious that increased rate has a negative effect on comprehension only at *extremely* fast rates. According to Street and others, speakers who have extremely fast rates may be perceived equally competent as speakers who use moderate to moderately fast rates, but ratings of social desirability tend to decrease at extremely fast rates.[45]

The second conclusion is that speakers are considered more competent and socially attractive when speech rates are at moderate to relatively fast levels than at slow levels. In Street's studies, subjects listened to a person describe his summer activities at a slow rate, a moderate rate, or a fast

rate. Listeners found the moderate-paced and fast-paced speakers to be more competent and socially attractive than the slow speaker. These effects translate directly into increased persuasiveness. In a study by Miller, Maruyama, Beaber, and Valone, various speeches were made at slow, moderate, or fast speeds.[46] Results indicated that as speed of delivery increased, listeners were persuaded more and rated the speaker as more intelligent, knowledgeable, and possessing greater objectivity. Employing different topics and different speech rates, Apple, Streeter, and Krauss found that slower speakers were judged as less truthful, fluent, and persuasive than moderate to fast speakers.[47] Clearly, speakers who want to be persuasive must avoid the slower end of the speech-rate continuum.

Third, a person's preference for speech rates is partially influenced by his or her own rate of speech. The Orr study above indicated that people prefer a speed of delivery one and one-half times their normal rate of delivery. In several studies the listener's own speech rate was obtained by recording the listener reading a statement as "naturally" as possible. Speakers were rated highest in competence and social attractiveness when the speaker's rates were similar to and up to 50 words per minute faster than the listener's. Ratings decreased as the speaker's rate exceeded 75 words per minute faster than the listener's own rate. Thus, if a campaign encompasses areas where people typically speak slowly, adjustments in recorded messages may be beneficial.

Voice Qualities

One variable often related to success is voice quality. There is evidence that we possess vocal stereotypes and that we use characteristics of the voice to make decisions about others. Addington, for example, has explored seven voice characteristics: thin, breathy, flat, tense, throaty, nasal, and orotund (orotund means that the voice possesses a deep resonating quality).[48] In one study, Addington explored the personality traits associated with vocal characteristics. The results can be summarized as follows:

Nasality—Increased nasality by both sexes resulted in the perception of a wide array of socially-undesirable characteristics, including reduced intelligence, immaturity, being boorish and boring.

Breathiness—Increased breathiness on the part of males resulted in the speaker's being perceived as younger and more artistic. Increased breathiness on the part of females resulted in the speaker's being perceived as more feminine, pretty, petite, effervescent, high strung, and shallow.

Thinness—Increased thinness of voice for males was not associated with any of the forty characteristics assessed. Increased thinness on the part of females was associated with immaturity, sensitivity, and a sense of humor.

Flatness—Increased flatness by both males and females resulted in perceptions of being more masculine, sluggish, colder, and withdrawn.

Tenseness—Increased tenseness by males led to their being perceived as older and more unyielding. Increased tenseness by females led to the perception of their being more emotional, feminine, high strung, and less intelligent.

Throatiness—Increased throatiness by males led to the perception of their being older, more realistic, sophisticated, mature, and well adjusted. Increased throatiness by females led to the perception of reduced intelligence, and their being more masculine, lazier, boorish, unemotional, ugly, sickly, careless, inartistic, naive, humble, neurotic, quiet, uninteresting, and apathetic.

Orotund—Increased orotundity by males led listeners to believe that the speakers were more energetic, healthy, artistic, sophisticated, proud,

interesting, and enthusiastic. Increased orotundity by females affected perceptions of increased liveliness, gregariousness, and aesthetic sensitivity, being proud, and humorless.

Addington also found that orotundity is strongly related to perceptions of competence and dynamism (but not to trustworthiness), while throatiness, tenseness, and nasality led to low ratings on all three of the credibility factors. More recently, Apple, Streeter, and Krauss found that speakers with higher pitch were perceived as less truthful, less emphatic, more nervous, and less "potent" than speakers who had lower pitch.[49] Diehl and McDonald found that both nasal and breathy voices can reduce comprehension, while harsher-sounding voices appear to be unrelated to comprehension.[50] These studies indicate that people form distinct impressions of others from vocal characteristics and, generally, do not like the throaty, tense, or nasal voice.

To summarize:

1. To be persuasive, a speaker should engage in more eye contact, smiling, affirmative head nodding, gestures, fewer adaptors, and should not be too relaxed while standing directly in front of his or her audience. Vocally, one should speak quickly and loudly with few brief pauses and have few nonfluencies.

2. Cues associated with affiliation facilitate communication when employed by an interviewer. Cues of affiliation can enhance persuasion in dyadic contexts. In more formal or task-oriented contexts, cues associated with extroversion (such as verbal output, fluency, body composure, and confident voice) are more important than cues of affiliation.

3. The perception of trustworthiness can be enhanced by increasing eye contact, adopting a more conversational style of delivery, and avoiding a higher-pitched voice. Generally, the perception of competence and dynamism can be enhanced by a

confident voice, speaking more quickly, using an orotund voice, avoiding cues related to anxiety, and displaying cues associated with extroversion. The perception of dynamism can be enhanced by a dynamic style of delivery.

4. Increased proximity may enhance persuasion if a request requires little thought or effort by the receiver, if a request is legitimate and politely stated, and if the person making the request is attractive.

A General Model of Credibility and Persuasiveness

Many past studies were limited in that the typical study examined the impact of only one or two behaviors at a time. One study would examine the influence of different eye-contact rates and another would examine the influence of speech nonfluencies. However, it is obvious that *many* variables jointly affect credibility and persuasiveness, and receivers are likely to be influenced by an entire set of nonverbal/vocalic behaviors. More recent communication research attempts to study multiple factors.

One such study was conducted by Burgoon, Birk, and Pfau.[51] Sixty students were videotaped while giving persuasive speeches and the researchers coded each speech on twenty-two specific nonverbal behaviors. The behaviors reflected one of five general types of cues: *vocalic pleasantness* (fluency, voice quality, pitch variety), *kinesic/proxemic immediacy* (eye contact, body lean/close interpersonal distance, smiling/facial pleasantness), *vocalic potency cues* (tempo variety, amplitude/loudness, tempo, fundamental frequency pitch), *kinesic dominance cues* (facial expressiveness, illustrators), and *kinesic arousal cues* (self-adaptors, object-adaptors, body tension, and random trunk/limb movement). Other students viewed the speeches and rated the perceived persuasiveness of the speech and the speaker's credibility. Bur-

goon and her colleagues examined five aspects of speaker credibility: *competence, dynamism, character* (similar to "trustworthiness"), *composure* (the degree to which the speaker was poised and relaxed), and *sociability* (the degree to which the speaker is likable).

Table 9.5 illustrates the relationships between specific nonverbal behaviors and credibility. Although the figure looks complex, it is quite easy to read. First, note that only nine of the behaviors listed on the left side of the figure were significantly related to credibility: fluency, pitch variety, eye contact, smiling/facial pleasantness, facial expressiveness, illustrators, object adaptors, body tension, and random trunk/limb movement. Each of these nine behaviors is connected to numbers in the center of the figure. These numbers are correlations, and the higher the number, the stronger the relationship is between the behavior and ratings of credibility. Fluency/pauses/response latencies, for example, are linked to four numbers at the top of the figure—they are the correlations between fluency and four ratings: competence, composure, sociability, and ratings of persuasiveness.

As the figure indicates, ratings of a speaker's *character* were significantly affected by four variables. Speakers were rated higher when they varied pitch and maintained high levels of eye contact, smiling/facial pleasantness and facial expressiveness. Ratings of *competence* were higher when speakers were fluent, varied pitch, smiled and used expressive facial portrayals. Ratings of *composure* were higher when speakers were fluent, smiled and used facial pleasantness. Ratings of *sociability/likability* were affected by eight variables: fluency, pitch variety, eye contact, smiling, facial expressiveness, illustrators, body tension, and trunk/limb movement. Dynamism, in this study, was not related to any of the twenty-two variables.

All five aspects of credibility (character, competence, composure, sociability, and dynamism) were strongly related to *persuasion*. Seven of the

SIGNIFICANT RELATIONSHIPS BETWEEN NONVERBAL BEHAVIORS AND CREDIBILITY AND RATINGS OF PERSUASIVENESS

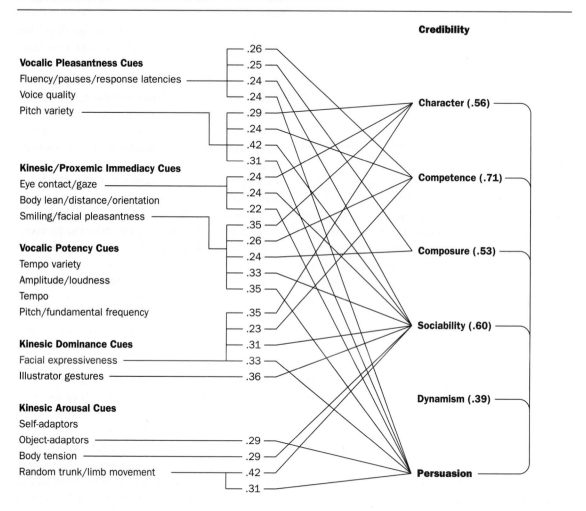

From: J. Burgoon, T. Birk, and M. Pfau, "Nonverbal Behaviors, Persuasion, and Credibility," *Human Communication Research*, vol. 17 (1990), pp. 140–169. Used with permission.

nonverbal behaviors were significantly related to persuasion: fluency, pitch variety, eye contact, smiling/facial pleasantness, facial expressiveness, trunk/limb movement, and object-adaptors. The latter variable was *negatively* associated with persuasiveness; the more a speaker engaged in object adaptors, the *less* persuasive the speaker was judged to be.

Interactional Patterns: The Importance of Communication Accommodation

The research discussed so far in this chapter examines how the speaker's behavior increases or decreases credibility. However, a number of persuasion settings involve a speaker interacting in a face-to-face situation in which *both* speaker and receiver *mutually influence each other's behavior*. We referred to it as an interactive model of persuasion in Chapter 1 (and compared it to a "linear model" in which all of the influence begins with the source). In sales encounters, doctor-patient encounters, mediation sessions, or therapy sessions, we often see two communicators become *more* and *more* similar as they talk. Howard Giles, and others, have developed a theory of *communication accommodation* that explains why this happens.[52]

Communication accommodation theory assumes that we adjust our nonverbal/vocal behaviors in order to accommodate other speakers. Although we are not aware that we are altering our behaviors, a number of speech, vocalic, and nonverbal behaviors are involved in the accommodation, including: dialects (for example, British or Australian accents), utterance length, speech rate, speech volume, speech hesitations, response latency (length of silence that occurs between speakers' turns), gestures, head nodding, facial affect, posture, and eye contact. When we interact interpersonally with others, our behavior can either *converge* toward the communication characteristic of our partner—or it can *diverge* away from

those characteristics. We often *converge* (a) when we want their approval; (b) when we want to be efficient; and (c) when we desire a shared identity with another person or with a group. Members of gangs or social groups (fraternities, sororities, country club groups) often exhibit some convergence in nonverbal behaviors as the members communicate. On the other hand, when we communicate with someone we do not like, or we fear, or who is stigmatized, our behavior *diverges* from the partner. We might speak more loudly, slowly, and gesture more emphatically than the partner as we show, nonverbally, that we are very different.

Although there are many examples of communication accommodation theory in interpersonal settings, we introduce the topic here because the phenomenon is also important in persuasion settings. Giles, Mulac, Bradac, and Johnson[53] argue that the salesclerk is more likely to *converge* toward the behaviors of the customer, and that effectiveness in selling (and perhaps in having customers return for more business) is partially related to accommodation.

POWER, STATUS, AND DOMINANCE

Receivers are strongly influenced when they perceive that the speaker possesses power, status, or dominance. Before a person speaks, you assess whether or not the person appears likable, successful, fashionable, well-groomed, or mature. Public image is extremely important for people in elected offices, and for their spouses and family members. One variable affecting perceptions of status and power is height. Studies reviewed by Gillis[54] indicate that (in American culture) taller individuals are assumed to have higher-status jobs, while shorter people are assumed to have occupations of less status. Presumably, males earn an extra $400 an inch during their peak earning years.

Two other variables relevant to the image of power, status, and dominance are *clothing* and *artifacts*. Obviously, quality clothing, "power suits," and the like make a strong statement concerning both interest in appearance and in ability to purchase the "correct" clothing. We won't say much that is specific about dress, since the precise cut of jackets and skirts, and color schemes change each year. By "artifacts" we mean that individuals acquire objects that signify power and status—watches, automobiles, jewelry, and so forth are used to inform others immediately of one's rank.

There is an increasing body of research concerning how people of power, status, and dominance behave differently than their lower-status counterparts in regard to the use of territory, space and tactility, body movement and gaze behavior, speaking turns and interruptions, and the use of time (see Burgoon, Buller, and Woodall,[55] Knapp and Hall,[56] and Leathers[57] for fuller details). We briefly list some of these conclusions:

Territory, space, and tactility

—People who possess power, own, control, and have more access to more territory and to territory of higher quality. For example, people who possess power often occupy relatively large offices on top floors with windows that provide scenic views;

—People who possess power often insist on greater privacy and use gatekeepers, barriers, and partitions in order to maintain privacy;

—People who possess power and status have the ability to intrude on the space of others by rapidly and deliberately entering subordinates' space, while subordinates obviously enter the power-person's space cautiously. People who possess power and status are also less likely to yield space to others when others approach them;

—People who possess power and status are given more personal space during conversations and take up more space than those of lesser status. People who possess little power and status are more likely to adhere strictly to *norms* concerning the maintenance of interpersonal distance (as well as touching others). However, people of power can move close to subordinates, they are free to touch others, and free to take up as much of the space as they like;

—People who possess power and status are likely to stand or sit in more-central positions;

—People who possess power and status are free to adopt either a direct or indirect body orientation during conversations, while people who possess less power are obliged to maintain a deferent, direct (face-to-face) body orientation. According to Burgoon, et al.,[58] indirect body orientation, along with eye-gaze aversion, increases psychological distance—the power person displays distance and superiority over the subordinate;

—People who possess power and status are more likely to initiate touch. It is extremely inappropriate for a low-status person to touch a superior; superiors establish the frequency, intensity, and intimacy of touch during encounters. People who possess power and status are more likely than their low-status counterparts to use touch and pointing as a way to intrude on others and to continue to dominate the encounter.

Body Movement and Gaze Behavior

—People with power and status are more likely to maintain extended periods of eye contact with subordinates, who show deference by looking down or away.

—Smiling when the eyebrows are raised displays deference, submission, and possibly appeasement; however, raised eye brows and no smile communicates dominance (see Henley[59] and Burgoon, et al.).[60]

—Power and strength are communicated by gesturing, walking, talking, and standing as would a dynamic speaker. Sweeping, frequent gestures, the use of emblems and pointing gestures, and a confident, active, rapid gait all help to communicate that the individual is strong, dynamic, and powerful. Individuals at the lowest levels of power, however, move less, more timidly, and often are "closed off" by shrinking into their chairs and crossing arms and legs when in the presence of someone substantially higher in power.

—People of power and status are also free to deviate from norms concerning posture. People of higher rank are free to adopt greater postural relaxation, to slump in chairs, put feet on desks, and to lean one way or the other. Of course, lower-status individuals would probably be ostracized for behaving in similar ways in front of the superiors.

—People of lower ranks, who possess less power, communicate more expressively, facially, when in the presence of higher-status individuals; while people who possess power may or may not communicate expressively when in the presence of lower-status individuals.

Speaking Turns and Interruptions

—A louder, deeper voice communicates greater size and physical strength. In America, voices perceived as conveying the image of power and status display lower pitch, greater loudness, moderately fast tempo, clearer articulation and enunciation, more intonation, and no accent (see Burgoon, et al.);[61]

—Dominant people talk more frequently, for longer durations, and interrupt others more often than those of lower status. When two speakers start talking simultaneously, the less powerful person usually concedes the speaking turn to the more powerful person. When silences occur, subordinates often wait for the superior to break the silence.

Use of Time

—People in power positions make people wait, do not feel obligated to apologize for making people wait, and are more likely than subordinates to plan several events or meetings to occur at the same time; thus, several subordinates must vie for time with the superior.

This section of the chapter has overviewed information about how powerful, high status, and dominant communicators differ from those with less power. Much of the research in this area comes from organizational communication settings and from research on the *perceptions* of power, based on nonverbal behaviors (such as vocal patterns).

CUES TO DECEPTION: IDENTIFYING THE DISHONEST COMMUNICATOR

Since Watergate, researchers have focused considerable attention on a very specific question concerning nonverbal communication and persuasion: can people tell when a politician, defendant, witness, bargaining opponent, job applicant, or the like, is engaging in deceit? Obviously, if we think a person is lying to us, it is unlikely that he or she will persuade us. There are a number of physiological means by which one can detect deception, but these require electronic surveillance.[62] Our interest, of course, rests in the question of whether people can detect deception without the aid of sophisticated machinery.

We all have a stereotype of the "liar," but does this stereotype help in detecting deception? The stereotype suggests that the liar avoids eye contact, smiles less, engages in more postural shifts, longer response latencies, slower speech rates, increased speech errors, higher pitch, and more speech hesitations.[63] In sum, liars are considered to be less affiliative, less extroverted, and

TABLE 9.6

BEHAVIORS ASSOCIATED WITH DECEPTION

Behaviors	Number of Studies	Relationship with Deception
Facial channel		
Pupil dilation	5	+
Gaze	18	0
Blinking	8	+
Smiling	16	0
Head movements	10	0
Body channel		
Gestures	12	0
Shrugs	4	+
Adaptors	14	+
Foot/leg movements	9	0
Postural shifts	11	0
Speech channel		
Response latency	15	0
Response length	17	+
Speech rate	12	0
Immediacy	2	+
Leveling	4	+
Speech errors	12	+
Speech hesitations	11	+
Pitch	4	+
Negative statements	5	+
Irrelevant statements	6	+
Self-references	4	0

Adapted from: B.M. DePaulo, J.I. Stone, and G.D. Lassiter, "Deceiving and Detecting Deceit," in B.R. Schlenker, ed., *The Self and Social Life* (New York: McGraw-Hill, 1985), pp. 323–370. Used with permission.
A (+) denotes that the behavior is consistently related to deception. A (0) means that the behavior is not consistently related to deception.

more anxious than truth tellers. Possessing a stereotype of the liar does not enable people to detect deception accurately. Generally, people who are untrained in nonverbal communication are moderately accurate at detecting deception by friends and lovers, because they know their idiosyncratic behaviors.[64] However, we want to know which cues allow deception to be detected with greater accuracy and *why* some cues are helpful and others are not.

The single most important contribution to research on deception is the idea that speakers try to control some of their nonverbal behaviors when lying.[65] Ekman and Friesen argue that there are areas of the body that we monitor more closely and use more extensively when communicating. The area of the face is both the most expressive part of our body and the easiest to control. It is high in "sending capacity." On the other hand, adaptors, leg/foot movements, random hand-to-face movements, and so on, go unmonitored, are rarely (if ever) used for intentional communication, and are low in sending capacity. The Ekman and Friesen hypothesis states simply that channels high in sending capacity are less likely to reveal deception. The body should leak more deception cues than the face. (We use the term "leakage" to denote behaviors that reveal our true feelings without our control.) In fact, one study found that when liars had rehearsed their lies, the liars intentionally attempted to maintain eye contact.[66] In another study, liars *increased* eye contact and glanced more frequently at an interviewer who was an "expert."[67] People can rise to the occasion and control some features of the face; the typical study indicates that eye contact is not a reliable source of leakage.

The sending capacity hypothesis has recently been extended to include the audio channel, under the notion that while we may monitor the words we speak, we do not monitor paralinguistic behaviors and *cannot* control voice stress. DePaulo, Stone, and Lassiter[68] identified which cues were reliably associated with deception, across a series of studies. The results are summarized in Table 9.6. The results indicate that the speech-body-face hierarchy is valid: eight out of eleven vocal cues were significantly related to deception, two out of five body cues were related to deception, and two out of five facial cues were associated with deception. Therefore, the face is a very poor place to look to find out if a communicator is being dishonest. The results indicate that liars (compared to truth tellers) blink their eyes more, have dilated pupils, shrug more, have shorter messages, less "immediacy," more leveling terms, more speech errors, higher-pitched voices, more speech hesitations, and more irrelevant and negative statements.

Why do liars behave differently than truth tellers? Scholars have proposed different *underlying* reasons for why differences occur in behavior.

The most comprehensive model of deception behaviors was proposed by Buller and Burgoon.[69] These scholars argue there are two different types of communication behaviors important to the study of deception. The first, *strategic behavior,* deals with intentional behaviors and plans the liar might have concerning how to lie effectively. The second, *nonstrategic leakage,* deals with behaviors that cannot be controlled or manipulated by the liar—what we call real "leakage" of the fact that the person is not being honest. Table 9.7 presents a summary of their general model of communication during deception, based on the Buller and Burgoon theory.

There are four components to the *strategic communication* aspect of the model: *uncertainty and vagueness; nonimmediacy, reticence and withdrawal; disassociation;* and *image- and relationship-protecting behavior.* By "uncertainty and vagueness," we mean that the liar engages in brief messages, and communicates few specific, concrete, or relevant details. One reason for uncertainty and vagueness is that liars simply cannot generate longer answers with concrete and specific detail. However, there

is a strategic reason to not be too specific about details—if one makes up a story and includes the time of day, other people who were involved, and so forth, the liar runs the risk of communicating details that would not hold up to thorough examination later. By "nonimmediacy, reticence, and withdrawal," we mean that the person attempts to create psychological distance between him/herself and the message being communicated. A liar who employs this tactic would seem disinterested in the topic, alienated from the interaction, or answer by leaning away, gazing less, while pausing more frequently and taking more time to answer (longer latencies). "Nonimmediacy, reticence, and withdrawal" include both verbal and nonverbal means used to distance oneself from others, to disaffiliate, and to close off scrutiny or probing communication.

By "disassociation" Buller and Burgoon include a number of linguistic behaviors used to distance oneself from responsibility for one's own statements and actions, and to imply dependence on the actions of others. Behaviors indicative of disassociation include fewer references to the self (fewer "I," "me," and "we" references) and more references to the others ("my professor," "they," "the tourists," and so forth). Engaging in disassociation is a clever ploy if the liar believes that s/he may be interrogated about the details of the lie later.

Finally, "image- and relationship-protecting behaviors" are the verbal and nonverbal behaviors used to make the speaker appear sincere and trustworthy, and to monitor a positive self-presentation. Increases in nodding and smiling are part of the image-protecting function important in some deception contexts.

"Nonstrategic leakage" behaviors are behaviors that "leak out" beyond our control; indeed, we are unlikely to be aware of the behaviors while communicating. Arousal and nervousness cues reflect fear of being detected. Most of us have been punished for lying in the past and we experience

| T A B L E | 9.7 |

A GENERAL THEORY OF THE DETERMINANTS OF COMMUNICATION DURING DECEPTION

Specific Nonverbal and Verbal Behavior

I. Strategic Communication

A. Uncertainty and Vagueness — fewer different words, lower confidence reactions, fewer factual assertions, fewer references to self-experiences, fewer references to the past, more leveling terms ("all," "never"), more irrelevant information, shorter responses, fewer past-tense verbs, less conditional language (males only), greater lexical diversity, more frequent hand shrugs, fewer absolute verbs

B. Nonimmediacy, Reticence and Withdrawal — fewer total words, shorter responses, more probing questions from receivers, verbal nonimmediacy, more pausing, longer response latencies, less gaze, more one-sided gazing, less forward lean, greater distance

C. Disassociation — fewer self-references, fewer self-interest statements, more other-references, verbal nonimmediacy

D. Image- and Relationship-Protecting Behavior — nodding, smiling, refraining from interruptions, suppression of leakage cues

II. Nonstrategic Leakage

A. Arousal and Nervousness — more blinking, greater pupil dilation or instability, more self- and object-manipulations, higher pitch, vocal nervousness, more speech errors and hesitations, more word repetitions, shorter responses, longer response latencies, less gesturing, stiff, restrained trunk and limb positions, more leg, foot, head, and posture shifts, more body blocks, abortive flight movements, fewer facial changes, more bodily activity

B. Negative Affect — micromomentary facial expressions of displeasure and discomfort, less positive feedback (nodding, smiling), reduced gaze, less-pleasant vocal tone, fewer group references, more disparaging remarks, more negative statements

C. Incompetent Communication Performance — a pattern of more speech errors, hesitations, word repetitions, postural rigidity, random nervous movements, and halting, brief messages; faster or slower speaking tempo; channel discrepancies and dissynchrony; exaggerated performances; lack of spontaneity; departure from normal behavior

From: D. Buller and J. Burgoon, "Deception," in J. Wiemann and J. Daley, eds., *Strategic Communication* (Hillsdale, N.J.: Erlbaum, in press). Used with permission.

a good deal of fear, anxiety, or apprehension when lying. Frequent blinking, greater pupil dilation, more adaptors, higher pitch, vocal nervousness, speech errors, and similar behaviors are indicative of arousal and nervousness.

"*Negative affect*" behaviors reflect our negative feelings during deception—a brief look of sadness, less-pleasant vocal tone, more negative statements indicate that the liar has "leaked" true feelings of dislike or unpleasantness when lying. Finally, some communicators may display "*incompetent communication performance.*" Some people may be anxious or worried about a lie performance, and they may over-rehearse the lie, and the lie sounds too rehearsed, prepared, or exaggerated. A full list of the major ways in which communicators fail to make a competent performance can be found in Table 9.7.

Subtle Cues to Deception

All the deception behaviors discussed so far are fairly obvious when watching individuals communicate in person or on videotape. Observers can see individuals engage in adaptors, gesture, nod, or smile. However, sometimes it is not easy to see cues to deception. Two of the more-subtle ways to detect deception require training in facial muscles, or require equipment to study behavior in detailed, slow-motion action. People who are lying cannot completely control their facial configurations. Study the photographs in Table 9.8. Do all four photographs show a woman who is truly feeling happiness?

Actually, only photograph C depicts a woman who is truly happy. You can tell because of two important muscles—the eye muscles (called orbicularis oculi) show "happy looking eyes," and the zygomatic major muscles pull the corners of the mouth upwards (a true smile). Both photographs A and D show some elements of disgust. According to Ekman, Friesen, and O'Sullivan,[70]

disgust is revealed by actions of three different muscles that raise the upper lip. What is wrong with the last photograph? If you detected a hint of sadness, you are correct. A different muscle is pulling the lip corners down on the left side of the picture. The woman is trying to look happy and smile, but some element of sadness creeps into the facial scene.

Are such subtle behaviors important to communication scholars? Yes, definitely. Politicians, salesclerks, international negotiators, even spouses, may smile at us and communicate messages that appear, at face value, to reflect happiness. It is critically important when a therapist has to decide whether or not to believe a mental patient who says s/he is happy and would not try to commit suicide again.

A second less obvious clue to deception is called "channel discrepancy." When communicators send their messages, there exist different messages—from the words communicated (verbal channel), the sound of the communication (tone of voice), and the appearance of the face and body (visual channel). If a person is videotaped while lying, a coder can view the videotape several times, coding whether or not each channel was communicating a positive, neutral, or negative emotion. Truth tellers are significantly more likely to be communicating *consistent* emotions across all these channels. Liars, however, are more likely to communicate a message with some amount of discrepancy—their words and face may communicate positiveness, but their tone of voice may show negativity and tension.[71]

Types of Lies and the People Who Tell Them

One of the most common questions asked by students is: Aren't some people better than others at lying? The answer to this question is "yes" although there is no simple relationship between traits of persons and quality of performance in

TABLE **9.8**

WHICH IS THE "FELT" HAPPY SMILE?

(A)

(C)

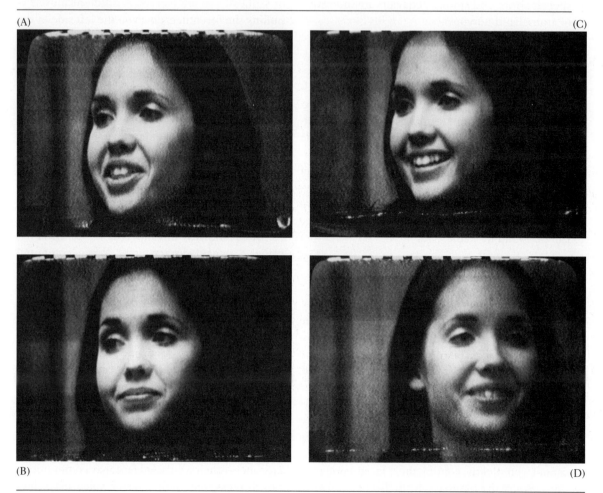

(B)

(D)

From: P. Ekman, W.V. Friesen, and M. O'Sullivan, "Smiles When Lying," *Journal of Personality and Social Psychology*, 1988, vol. 54, pp. 414–420. (Copyright Paul Ekman, 1988)

deceit. A brief overview of different types of lies is called for:

1. Amount of preparation.[72] Some studies allow liars time to prepare and rehearse the lie, while other studies entrap liars into telling lies when the liar did not know that the particular line of questioning was going to surface (spontaneous lies). There is evidence that when liars are prepared to lie, they exhibit short response latencies, engage in less postural shifting and fewer gestures, and provide brief messages that lack spontaneity (the messages *seem* prepared, or rehearsed). Spontaneous lies, however, require the liar to create a message and transmit it off the top of his head—thus, spontaneous lies contain more pauses and nonfluencies, and lack specific detail. In terms of the general rules noted above, being prepared to lie decreases the liar's level of uncertainty, whereas spontaneous lies increase the level of uncertainty.

2. Length of lie/narrative responses.[73] Some lies may be relatively easy to tell because they are relatively short; a "yes" or "no" lie undoubtedly reduces the extent to which liars leak clues to deception via speech errors and pauses. However, if a person had to lie for a full minute, or to list activities occurring during a fictitious event, he/she could not create many specific details, and may speak for a briefer period of time than truth tellers. Liars also leak the fact that they are uncertain by employing more "leveling" or "generalizing" terms, such as "the usual stuff," "stuff like that," "you know," and so on. There is evidence that when liars feel required to give more narrative responses, they sit in very rigid positions. This may be explained by the fact that the more one concentrates, the more he freezes his body movement. In terms of the general rules noted above, longer or narrative lies increase the speaker's level of uncertainty.

3. Motivation to lie convincingly.[74] Some studies induce people to lie convincingly by promising them payment or some type of reward for a quality performance. In the Exline, Thibaut, Hickey, and Gumpert study, liars were implicated in cheating, and successful lying (denying wrongdoing) meant they would not be reported to the Dean's Office. In other studies, the only incentive to lie convincingly was some extra credit to be given for class participation. Highly motivated liars blink less, engage in less head nodding, fewer adaptors, fewer postural shifts, and higher pitch. In terms of

the general rules noted above, high motivation increases arousal and the desire not to be detected (thus, liars try to control more behaviors).

Several personality types have been found to be successful in deceiving others.

One personality type that has received some attention in nonverbal research is the Machiavellian.[75] A high Machiavellian manipulates others; a low Machiavellian believes that people are good, can be trusted, and that lying is inexcusable. Evidence to date indicates that high Machiavellians are no better at lying to others than their low Machiavellian counterparts when telling a prepared or rehearsed lie, when there is no motivation to lie convincingly.

If sufficiently motivated, high Machiavellians can lie quite effectively. In the Exline, Thibaut, Hickey, and Gumpert study, an elaborate experimental treatment was employed to implicate either the low or high Machiavellian subject in cheating. Later, the experimenter confronted the implicated person. The results indicated that when the experimenter asked if cheating had taken place, high Machiavellians managed to maintain more eye contact than low Machiavellians, and held out longer before confessing. More recently, Geis and Moon entrapped either a low or high Machiavellian in a situation that required the person to deny knowledge of a theft. Observers rated the high Machiavellian liars as more believable than low Machiavellian liars.

A second personality measure related to quality of performance during deception is *self-monitoring*.[76] People who score high on self-monitoring are more knowledgeable about managing their behaviors across a wide range of situations. Low self-monitors, however, prefer to behave in ways that are compatible with their own beliefs and dispositions. Miller, deTurck, and Kalbfleisch[77] note that the person who possesses greater "knowledge of others" (the high self-monitor) is more accurate in detecting deception, and prepares better than

BOX 9.2

EXAMPLES OF LIES: A NIGHT AT THE MOVIES

While the text outlines research findings concerning nonverbal "leakage" of deception, it is easy to find good (and bad) liars in the movies and on television. Older movies often showed people lying very poorly. In an "Our Gang" movie, *Little Sinner*, Spanky goes fishing, and lies about going to church. He shows poor ability to control facial muscles and body movements. Speech errors increase, as do speech disturbances (pauses), and he has a long response latency, and higher pitch. He blinks rapidly, and has expressive eye and brow movement representing fear/nervousness. He shrugs, engages in postural shifts, and fidgets.

In *Psycho* a private detective comes to question Anthony Perkins about a missing woman. Anthony Perkins is very easy-going in the early phases of the scene. But the detective reveals that a woman had, in fact, visited the hotel recently—a fact that contradicts Anthony Perkins' earlier claim. As the questioning becomes more detailed, Perkins becomes visibly more tense and nervous. Nonverbally, he lacks eye contact, increases blinking, nods more frequently, increases chewing (on candy), increases his smiling, and it appears that he smiles asymmetrically (one side of the face is more fully "smiling" than the other). Verbally, he answers quickly, with frequent speech errors, hesitations, and stuttering. It is relatively easy for a receiver/moviegoer to detect the lie.

On the other hand, Scarlett (often characterized as a Machiavellian—see text) lies quite convincingly in a number of scenes in *Gone With the Wind*. She tells a *prepared* or *planned* lie when she dresses up and visits Butler in the jail, hoping to obtain money to save Tara.

The actress Linda Hamilton did an excellent job (in our opinion) as Sara Connor in *Terminator 2* when she tried to convince her therapist that she was "okay" and that the terminator never existed. Her level of motivation to tell a lie convincingly was quite high, and you can tell that the character was highly aroused, trying to control many features of her body, but her tone of voice was flat, unemotional, while she sat in a rigid sitting position, holding her body tightly and stiffly.

Thelma lies poorly in *Thelma and Louise* when she calls her husband from the road to lie about their whereabouts—she has high pitch in her voice, she uses filler statements, "generalizing terms," and her breathing is tense. Since her message to her husband was planned, she could have rehearsed and communicated a "better lie." For example, the character Joel in *Risky Business* does a much better job of communicating a planned lie when his parents return home. He uses a steady, confident speech, his response latencies are short, he smiles, he maintains high levels of eye contact, he is very expressive facially, he uses many hand gestures and head nods; on the other hand, he does shrug, changes posture, uses some generalizing terms, and there is an increase in pitch.

the low-self-monitoring individual by finding out as much as possible about the target of the deceptive message. High self-monitors were less likely to be detected than low self-monitors, especially when allowed to rehearse a lie.

Finally, it appears that extroverted, nonanxious, dominant, and exhibitionistic communicators are more successful at controlling leakage, while introverts and highly anxious individuals display more overall leakage cues (arousal, less-effective performances, more intense emotions).[78] Riggio, Tucker, and Widaman[79] found that communicators judged as high in public self-consciousness (that is, they were worried about being observed) were less effective in lying.

We have discussed the concept of deception detection because it is important in a number of situations—politics, eyewitness or defendant testimony, selling, bargaining, and so forth. Lawyers may want to "read" nonverbal communication effectively in order to estimate possible weaknesses in depositions or courtroom testimony; journalists may want to identify fabrications on the part of politicians; and so on. Individuals trying to detect deception are well advised to *listen* closely to what is being said and to watch what the speaker does with his or her body. However, the reader should also realize that if a person is well prepared and has rehearsed a lie, it might be difficult to detect. One needs to keep in mind the kind of a lie being told as well as the personality of the liar, in order to become an effective lie detector.

F O O T N O T E S

1. J.K. Burgoon, D.B. Buller, and W.G. Woodall, *Nonverbal Communication: The Unspoken Dialogue* (New York: Harper & Row, 1989).

2. M.L. Knapp and J.A. Hall, *Nonverbal Communication in Human Interaction* (New York: Holt, Rinehart and Winston, 1992).

3. D.G. Leather, *Successful Nonverbal Communication: Principles and Applications* (New York: MacMillan, 1992).

4. R.L. Birdwhistell, *Kinesics and Context* (Philadelphia: University of Pennsylvania Press, 1970).

5. P. Ekman and W. Friesen, "The Repertoire of Nonverbal Behavior: Categories, Origins, Usage, and Coding," *Semiotica*, vol. 1 (1969), pp. 49-98.

6. H.G. Johnson, P. Ekman, and W.V. Friesen, "Communicative Body Movements: American Emblems," *Semiotica*, vol. 15 (1975), pp. 335-353.

7. A. Kendon, "Gestures and Speech: How They Interact," in J.W. Wiemann and R.P. Harrison, eds. *Nonverbal Interaction* (Beverly Hills: Sage, 1983), pp. 13-46.

8. D. Morris, P. Collett, P. Marsh, and M. O'Shaughnessy, *Gestures: Their Origins and Distribution* (New York: Stein and Day, 1979). Also consult: M.R. Key, *Nonverbal Communication: A Research Guide and Bibliography* (Metuchen, N.J.: Scarecrow Press, 1977); M.R. Key, *Paralanguage and Kinesics* (Metuchen, N.J.: Scarecrow Press, 1975).

9. H.G. Johnson, P. Ekman, and W.V. Friesen, "Communicative Body Movements: American Emblems, *Semiotica*, vol. 15 (1975), pp. 335-353.

10. R.K. Jackson and W.D. McBride, *Understanding Street Gangs* (Costa Mesa, Calif.: Custom Publishing, 1985).

11. Sgt. Jerry Simandle, "Gang Identifiers and Things to Remember," (mimeo, Midwest Gang Investigators Association, Chicago, Ill. 1991).

12. W.G. Woodall and J.P. Folger, "Encoding Specificity and Nonverbal Cue Context: An Expansion of Episodic Memory Research," *Communication Monographs*, vol. 49 (1981), pp. 39-53; W.G. Woodall and J.P. Folger, "Nonverbal Cue Context and Episodic Memory: On the Availability and Endurance of Nonverbal Behaviors as Retrieval Cues," *Communication Monographs*, vol. 52 (1985), pp. 319-333.

13. Knapp and Hall, *Nonverbal Communication in Human Interaction*.

14. P. Bull, "The Use of Hand Gestures in Political Speeches: Some Case Studies," *Journal of Language and Social Psychology*, vol. 5 (1986), pp. 103-118.

15. P. Ekman and W.V. Friesen, *Unmasking the Face: A Guide to Recognizing Emotions from Facial Expressions* (Consulting Psychologists Press: Palo Alto, Calif. 1984).

16. M.J. Cody, W.S. Lee, and E.Y. Chao, "Telling Lies: Correlates of Deception among Chinese," in J. Forgas and M. Innes, eds., *Recent Advances in Social Psychology: An Interactional Perspective* (Elsevier Science Publishers: North Holland, 1989), pp. 359-368.

17. G.J. McHugo, J.T. Lanzette, D.G. Sullivan, R.D.

Masters, and B.G. Englis, "Emotional Reactions to a Political Leader's Expressive Displays," *Journal of Personality and Social Psychology*, vol. 49 (1985), pp. 1513-1529.

18. G.L. Trager, "Paralanguage: A First Approximation," *Studies in Linguistics*, vol. 13 (1958), pp. 1-12.

19. R.G. Harper, A.N. Wiens, and J.D. Matarazzo, *Nonverbal Communications: The State of the Art* (New York: Wiley, 1978).

20. F. Goldman-Eisler, *Psycholinguistics: Experiments in Spontaneous Speech* (New York: Academic, 1968).

21. For example, Miller and Burgoon refer to *extroversion and involvement*, and *relaxation and positivity*, and Cappella employs the terms *animated, aroused*, and *involved*. See G.R. Miller and J.K. Burgoon, "Factors Affecting Assessments of Eyewitness Credibility," in N.L. Kerr and R.M. Brays, eds., *The Psychology of the Courtroom* (New York: Academic, 1982), pp. 169-194; J.N. Cappella, "Conversational Involvement: Approaching and Avoiding Others," in J.M. Wiemann and R.P. Harrison, eds., *Nonverbal Interaction* (Beverly Hills: Sage, 1983), pp. 113-148.

22. A. Mehrabian and M. Williams, "Nonverbal Concomitants of Perceived and Intended Persuasiveness," *Journal of Personality and Social Psychology*, vol. 13 (1969), pp. 37-58.

23. M.B. LaCrosse, "Nonverbal Behavior and Perceived Counselor Attractiveness and Persuasiveness," *Journal of Counseling Psychology*, vol. 22 (1975), pp. 563-566.

24. C. Maslow, K. Yoselson, and H. London, "Persuasiveness of Confidence Expressed via Language and Body Language," *British Journal of Social and Clinical Psychology*, vol. 10 (1971), pp. 234-240.

25. T.V. McGovern, "The Making of a Job Interviewee: The Effect of Nonverbal Behavior on an Interviewer's Evaluations During a Selection Interview," *Dissertation Abstracts International*, vol. 37 (1977), pp. 4740B-4741B; D.M. Young and E.G. Beier, "The Role of Applicant Nonverbal Communication in the Employment Interview," *Journal of Employment Counseling*, vol. 14 (1977), pp. 154-165; R.J. Forbes and R.P. Jackson, "Nonverbal Behavior and the Outcome of Selection Interviews," *Journal of Occupational Psychology*, vol. 53 (1980), pp. 65-72; see also Patterson, *Nonverbal Behavior;* A.S. Imada and M.D. Hakel, "Influence of Nonverbal Communication and Rater Proximity on Impressions and Decisions in Simulated Employment Interviews," *Journal of Applied Psychology*, vol. 26 (1979), pp. 378-383; P.V. Washburn and M.P. Hakel, "Visual Cues and Verbal Content as Influences in Impressions Formed After Simulated Employment Interviews," *Journal of Applied Psychology*, vol. 58 (1973), pp. 137-141.

26. Mehrabian and Williams, "Nonverbal Concomitants."

27. Mehrabian and Williams, "Nonverbal Concomitants." See also studies concerning effective interviewing.

28. J.G. Holandsworth, Jr., R. Kazelskis, J. Stevens, and M.E. Dressel, "Relative Contributions of Verbal, Articulative, and Nonverbal Communication to Employment Decisions in the Job Interview Setting," *Personnel Psychology*, vol. 32 (1979), pp. 359-367; S.R. Strong, R.G. Taylor, J.C. Bratton, and R.G. Loper, "Nonverbal Behavior and Perceived Counselor Characteristics," *Journal of Counseling Psychology*, vol. 18 (1971), pp. 554-561; see also M.L. Patterson, *Nonverbal Behavior.*

29. J. Wills, "An Empirical Study of the Behavior Characteristics of Sincere and Insincere Speakers" (dissertation, University of Southern California, Los Angeles, 1961); S.A. Beebe, "Eye-Contact: A Nonverbal Determinant of Speaker Credibility," *Speech Teacher*, vol. 23 (1974), pp. 21-25; J.M. Wiemann, "An Experimental Study of Visual Attention in Dyads: The Effects of Four Gaze Conditions on Evaluations by Applicants in Employment Interviewing" (paper presented to the Speech Communication Association Convention, Chicago, 1974).

30. Burgoon, Buller, and Woodall, *The Unspoken Dialogue.*

31. For an excellent review, consult J.K. Burgoon, D.B. Buller, J.L. Hale, and M.A. deTurck, "Relational Messages Associated with Nonverbal Behaviors," *Human Communication Research*, vol. 10 (1984), pp. 351-378.

32. The effects of being touched by strangers is a complicated matter; see R. Heslin and T. Alper, "Touching: A Bonding Gesture," in J.M. Wiemann and R.P. Harrison, eds., *Nonverbal Interaction* (Beverly Hills: Sage, 1983), pp. 47-75.

33. S. Albert and J.M. Dabbs, "Physical Distance and Persuasion," *Journal of Personality and Social Psychology*, vol. 15 (1970), pp. 265-270.

34. P.C. Ellsworth and E.J. Langer, "Staring and Approach: An Interpretation of the State As a Nonspecific Activator," *Journal of Personality and Social Psychology*, vol. 33 (1976), pp. 117-122; C.L. Kleinke, "Compliance to Requests Made By Gazing and Touching Experimenters in Field Studies," *Journal of Experimental Social Psychology*, vol. 13 (1977), pp. 218-223.

35. Patterson, *Nonverbal Behavior;* J.K. Burgoon,

"Nonverbal Violations of Expectations," in J.M. Wiemann and R.P. Harrison, eds., *Nonverbal Interaction* (Beverly Hills: Sage, 1983), pp. 72-112.

36. Burgoon, Buller, and Woodall, *The Unspoken Dialogue;* H.M. Klinger, "The Effects of Verbal Fluency upon the Listener" (dissertation, University of Southern California, 1952).

37. A.H. Crusco and C.G. Wetzel, "The Midas Touch: The Effects of Interpersonal Touch on Restaurant Tipping," *Personality and Social Psychology*, vol. 10 (1984), pp. 512-517.

38. G.R. Miller and M.A. Hewgill, "The Effect of Variations in Nonfluencies on Audience Ratings of Source Credibility," *Quarterly Journal of Speech*, vol. 50 (1964), pp. 36-44.

39. W.B. Pearce and F. Conklin, "Nonverbal Vocalic Communication and Perceptions of a Speaker," *Speech Monographs*, vol. 38 (1971), pp. 235-241.

40. W.B. Pearce and B.J. Brommel, "The Effects of Vocal Variations on Ratings of Source Credibility," *Quarterly Journal of Speech*, vol. 58 (1972), pp. 298-306.

41. K.R. Scherer, H. London, and J.J. Wolf, "The Voice of Confidence: Paralinguistic Cues and Audience Evaluation," *Journal of Research in Personality*, vol. 7 (1973), pp. 31-44.

42. E. Foulke and T.G. Sticht, "A Review of Research on the Intelligibility and Comprehension of Accelerated Speech," *Psychological Bulletin*, vol. 72 (1969), pp. 10-19.

43. G. Fairbanks, N. Guttman, and M. Miron, "Effects of Time Compression Upon the Comprehension of Connected Speech," *Journal of Speech and Hearing Disorders*, vol. 22 (1957), pp. 10-19.

44. D.B. Orr, "Time Compressed Speech—A Perspective," *Journal of Communication*, vol. 18 (1968), pp. 288-292.

45. R.L. Street, Jr., and R.M. Brady, "Speech Rate Acceptance Range as a Function of Evaluation Domain, Listener Speech Rate and Communication Context," *Communication Monographs*, vol. 49 (1982), pp. 290-308; R.L. Street, Jr., R.M. Brady, and W.P. Putnam, "The Influence of Speech Rate Stereotypes and Rate Similarity on Listeners' Evaluations of Speakers," *Journal of Language and Social Psychology*, vol. 2 (1983); pp. 37-56; B.L. Brown, W.J. Strong, and A.C. Rencher, "Perceptions of Personality from Speech: Effects of Manipulations of Acoustical Parameters," *Journal of the Acoustical Society of America*, vol. 54 (1973), pp. 29-35.

46. N. Miller, G. Maruyama, R.J. Beaer, and K. Valone, "Speed of Speech and Persuasion," *Journal of Personality and Social Psychology*, vol. 34 (1976), pp. 615-624.

47. W. Apple, L.A. Streeter, and R.M. Krauss, "Effects of Pitch and Speech Rate on Personal Attributions," *Journal of Personality and Social Psychology*, vol. 37 (1979), pp. 715-727.

48. D.W. Addington, "The Relationship of Selected Vocal Characteristics to Personality Perception," *Speech Monographs*, vol. 39 (1971), pp. 242-247.

49. Apple, Streeter, and Krauss, "Effects of Pitch and Speech Rate."

50. C.F. Diehl and E.T. McDonald, "Effects of Voice Quality on Communication," *Journal of Speech and Hearing Disorders*, vol. 21 (1956), pp. 233-237.

51. J.K. Burgoon, T. Birk, and M. Pfau, "Nonverbal Behaviors, Persuasion, and Credibility," *Human Communication Research*, vol. 17 (1990), pp. 140-169.

52. H. Giles, J. Coupland, and N. Coupland, *Contexts of Accommodation* (Cambridge England: Cambridge University Press, 1991); H. Giles, A. Mulac, J.J. Bradac, and P. Johnson, "Speech Accommodation Theory: The First Decade and Beyond," in M.L. McLaughlin, ed., *Communication Yearbook 10* (Newbury Park, Calif.: Sage, 1987), pp. 13-48.

53. Giles, Mulac, Bradac, and Johnson, "Speech Accommodation Theory: The First Decade and Beyond."

54. J.S. Gillis, *Too Tall, Too Small.* (Champaign, Ill.: Institute for Personality and Ability Testing, Inc., 1982).

55. Burgoon, Buller, and Woodall, *Nonverbal Communication: The Unspoken Dialogue.*

56. Knapp and Hall, *Nonverbal Communication in Human Interaction.*

57. Leather, *Successful Nonverbal Communication: Principles and Applications.*

58. Burgoon, Buller, and Woodall, *Nonverbal Communication: The Unspoken Dialogue.*

59. N.M. Henley, *Body Politics: Power, Sex, and Nonverbal Communication* (Englewood Cliffs, N.J.: Prentice-Hall, 1977).

60. Burgoon, Buller, and Woodall, *Nonverbal Communication: The Unspoken Dialogue.*

61. Burgoon, Buller, and Woodall, *Nonverbal Communication: The Unspoken Dialogue.*

62. For a review of polygraph techniques, consult W.W. Waid and M.T. Orne, "Cognitive, Social, and Personality Processes in the Physiological Detection of Deception," in L. Berkowitz, ed., *Advances in Experimental Social Psychology*, vol. 14 (New York: Academic

Press, 1981), pp. 61-107; A. Gale, ed., *The Polygraph Test: Lies, Truth and Science* (Newbury Park, Calif.: Sage Publications, 1988).

63. J.E. Hocking and D.G. Leather, "Nonverbal Indicators of Deception: A New Theoretical Perspective," *Communication Monographs*, vol. 47 (1980), pp. 119-131; B.M. DePaulo, J.I. Stone, and G.D. Lassiter, "Deceiving and Detecting Deceit," in B.R. Schlenker, ed., *The Self and Social Life* (New York: McGraw-Hill, 1985), pp. 323-370; M. Zuckerman, B.M. DePaulo, and R. Rosenthal, "Verbal and Nonverbal Communication of Deception," in L. Berkowitz, ed., *Advances in Experimental Social Psychology*, vol. 14 (New York: Academic, 1981), pp. 2-60.

64. M.E. Comadena, "Accuracy in Detecting Deception: Intimate and Friendship Relationships," in M. Burgoon, ed., *Communication Yearbook 6* (Beverly Hills: Sage, 1982), pp. 446-472.

65. P. Ekman and W.V. Friesen, "Nonverbal Leakage and Clues to Deception," *Psychiatry*, vol. 32 (1969), pp. 88-106; P. Ekman and W.V. Friesen, "Detecting Deception from the Body or Face," *Journal of Personality and Social Psychology*, vol. 29 (1974), pp. 288-298; Hocking and Leathers, "Nonverbal Indicators of Deception."

66. J.K. Matarazzo, A.N. Wiens, R.H. Jackson, and T.S. Manaugh, "Interviewee Speech Behavior Under Conditions of Endogenously-Present and Exogenously-Induced Motivational States," *Journal of Clinical Psychology*, vol. 26 (1979), pp. 141-148.

67. S.S. Figuta, M.C. Hogrebe, and K.N. Wexley, "Perceptions of Deception: Perceived Expertise in Detecting Deception, Successfulness of Deception and Nonverbal Cues," *Personality and Social Psychology Bulletin*, vol. 6 (1980), pp. 637-643.

68. DePaulo, Stone, and Lassiter, "Deceiving and Detecting Deceit."

69. D.B. Buller and J.K. Burgoon, "Deception," in J. Wiemann and J. Daley, eds., *Strategic Communication* (Hillsdale, N.J.: Erlbaum, in press).

70. P. Ekman, W.V. Friesen, and M. O'Sullivan, "Smile When Lying," *Journal of Personality and Social Psychology*, (1988), pp. 414-420; also see P. Ekman, *Telling Lies: Clues to Deceit in the Marketplace, Politics, and Marriage* (New York: W.W. Norton & Company, 1985).

71. M. Zuckerman and R.E. Driver, "Telling Lies: Verbal and Nonverbal Correlates of Deception," in A.W. Siegman and S. Feldstein, eds., *Multichannel Integrations of Nonverbal Behavior* (Hillsdale, N.J.: Erlbaum, 1985), pp. 129-147.

72. Concerning prepared lies, consult M.J. Cody, P.J. Marston, and M. Foster, "Paralinguistic and Verbal Leakage of Deception as a Function of Attempted Control and Timing of Questions," in R.M. Bostrom, ed., *Communication Yearbook 7* (Beverly Hills: Sage, 1984), pp. 464-490; J.O. Greene, H.D. O'Hair, M.J. Cody, and C. Yen, "Planning and Control of Behavior During Deception," *Human Communication Research*, vol. 11 (1985), pp. 335-364; G.R. Miller, M.A. deTurck, and P.J. Kalbfleisch, "Self-Monitoring, Rehearsal, and Deceptive Communication," *Human Communication Research*, vol. 10 (1983), pp. 97-118; H.D. O'Hair, M.J. Cody, and M.L. McLaughlin, "Prepared Lies, Spontaneous Lies, Machiavellianism, and Nonverbal Communication," *Human Communication Research*, vol. 7 (1981), pp. 325-339.

73. Concerning longer or narrative lies, consult R.E. Kraut, "Verbal and Nonverbal Cues in the Perception of Lying," *Journal of Personality and Social Psychology*, vol. 36 (1978), pp. 380-391; Cody, Marston, and Foster, "Paralinguistic and Verbal Leakage"; Zuckerman, DePaulo, and Rosenthal, "Verbal and Nonverbal Communication of Deception."

74. R.V. Exline, H. Thibaut, C.B. Hickey, and P. Gumpert, "Visual Interaction in Relation to Machiavellianism and an Unethical Act," in R. Christie and F.L. Geis, eds., *Studies in Machiavellianism* (New York: Academic, 1970), pp. 53-73; Zuckerman, DePaulo, and Rosenthal, "Verbal and Nonverbal Communication of Deception."

75. R. Christie and F.L. Geis, eds., *Studies in Machiavellianism* (New York: Academic, 1979); O'Hair, Cody, and McLaughlin, "Prepared Lies, Spontaneous Lies"; Knapp, Hart, and Dennis, "An Exploration of Deception"; F.L. Geis and T.H. Moon, "Machiavellianism and Deception," *Journal of Personality and Social Psychology*, vol. 41 (1981), pp. 766-775.

76. M. Snyder, "Self-Monitoring and Expressive Behavior," *Journal of Personality and Social Psychology*, vol. 30 (1974), pp. 526-537.

77. Miller, deTurck, and Kalbfleisch, "Self-Monitoring."

78. A. Mehrabian, *Nonverbal Communication* (Chicago: Aldine, 1972); R.E. Riggio and H.S. Friedman, "Individual Differences and Cues to Deception," *Journal of Personality and Social Psychology*, vol. 45, (1983), pp. 899-915; R.E. Riggio, J. Tucker, and D. Throckmorton, "Social Skills and Deception Ability," *Personality and Social Psychology Bulletin*, vol. 13 (1987), pp. 568-577.

79. R.E. Riggio, J. Tucker, and K.F. Widaman, "Verbal and Nonverbal Cues as Mediators of Deception Ability," *Journal of Nonverbal Behavior*, vol. 11 (1987), pp. 126-145.

KEY TERMS AND CONCEPTS

nonverbal code system
emblems
illustrators
regulators
adaptors
affect displays
paralinguistic codes
voice qualities
vocalizations
vocal segregates
speech disturbances/nonfluencies

extroversion
affiliation
relaxation
response latency
orotund
communication accommodation theory
artifacts
territory
space
tactility
immediacy/nonimmediacy
deception
leakage behaviors
channel discrepancy
reticence
disassociation
Machiavellian personality

PART

three

CONTEXTS FOR PERSUASION

PERSUASION IN INTERPERSONAL RELATIONSHIPS

Many persuasion situations involve interpersonal relationships, and, in the last twenty years, considerable attention has been focused on face-to-face persuasion. In this chapter we discuss the methods used to gain compliance from others in common everyday situations. Recall that we made a distinction between *compliance* and *persuasion* in Chapter 1. This chapter deals with why people *comply* to requests—why they say, *yes, I will buy raffle tickets, give blood, donate time to recycling, teach Sunday School,* and so forth. Our emphasis is on the *effectiveness* of messages designed to increase compliance from others. How do solicitors, charity organizations and businesses employ (and exploit) basic psychological principles in their campaigns to prompt people to agree with requests?

Since we want to emphasize effectiveness in common *persuasion* settings, we will not address issues concerning how individuals influence one another in a number of interpersonal situations, and recommend instead interpersonal books by Canary and Cody,[1] Dillard,[2] and Knapp and Vangelisti[3] to the interested reader. This chapter focuses solely on the *effectiveness* of compliance requests.

SOCIAL INFLUENCE: WHY PEOPLE AGREE TO REQUESTS

According to Cialdini,[4] there are several fundamental reasons why individuals agree to comply to requests. Cialdini devotes attention to six psychological principles of influence: commitment, reciprocity, liking, social proof, scarcity, and authority. A number of these principles have given rise to specific tactics of influence called "Foot-in-the-Door," "Door-in-the-Face," "the Lowball Technique," "Ingratiation," and others. Such tactics are used on people every day, and the reader should become familiar both with *why* each tactic is effective, as well as guidelines for its use. Let's begin with a discussion of "anchoring and contrast effects."

Anchoring and Contrast Effects

In this study, an employee is leaving her place of work, and the staff takes up a collection to buy her a gift. A sign-up sheet asking for money is given to some staff, but they are unaware of how much others are contributing. These people give, on the average, 70 to 80 cents each. However, other staff members see a list in which it appears that others are contributing 25 cents each. People who see this list contribute 32 cents. Another group of workers see a list on which it appears that others are contributing 75 cents each. People who see this list give 63 cents, on the average. People adjusted the amount they contributed based on what they thought *others* were giving.

Blake, Rosenbaum, and Duryea[5] conducted this study in the 1950s; today, the clever use of the principles of anchoring and contrast is common. Two essential elements are employed. First, an *adaptation level* is created which provides the individual (the "target" of the compliance request) with a *standard* level (a normal, typical, or expected amount) to which he/she adapts or becomes adjusted. Standards often apply to the price of clothes (people who haven't shopped in a while are surprised at prices, while those who shop each week become adjusted to current prices), prices of homes, the beauty of others, the temperature, the amount of violence on television or in the news, and so on.

Second, after the adaptation level is established, a new object, person, or event is introduced against which this standard is compared; a *contrast effect* results when the target is displaced away from the adaptation level. In the Blake, et al., study, people gave 70 to 80 cents when they did not know what others were giving. The standard concerning the normal or typical was not established; possibly some believed that a dollar was normal, others believed that 50 cents was normal. However, when they believed that others were giving 25 cents, they declined to give a relatively "large" contribution and they tended to match what others were contributing.

Here is a list of a few examples of the anchoring and contrast approach:

After looking at $800 St. John knit dresses, a $200 dress appears to be a "good" buy. Similarly, after looking at $200 and $300 pairs of shoes, a pair that is "on sale" for $110 appears to be a bargain.

After examining pool tables, buyers are more likely to buy a higher quality, more expensive pool table if they are first shown the most expensive pool tables first, and become anchored at the high end of quality; when they are shown the least expensive/poor quality first, shoppers tend to settle on the least expensive tables (see Cialdini[6]).

People who experience the thrill of winning lots of money in a lottery afterwards consider everyday events like a picnic in the park to be boring (Brickman, Coates, and Janoff-Bulman[7]).

People who have been watching television shows (movies, photographs) of beautiful people rate potential dates as *less* attractive (in comparison to their current adaptation level). Conversely, if people have been watching films or photographs of unattractive people, or burn victims, the potential date is rated as *more* attractive (Kenrick and Gutierres[8]).

People place more tip money in a bartender's tip jar when the jar is "seeded" with $1- and $5-bills, rather than with mere coins.

This anchoring and contrast approach works best when the target of the influence is (a) not aware that s/he is being influenced, and (b) not knowledgeable about the area in question. Clearly, if you knew that the bartender's tip jar

was intentionally rigged or that the salesclerk intentionally took you to the most expensive items in order to create the contrast effect, you might take the option of saying "no" to this attempt at persuasion. Further, if you are knowledgeable about just how much the clothes (or other items) cost to make, or their value elsewhere, say, at discount centers or outlets, then you can resist this attempt to influence you.

Commitment

When we have become publicly committed to a course of action (buying a car, agreeing to help a neighbor, to support the Heart Fund of America, and so forth), our thinking about our relationship with the course of action changes. Even the act of betting on a horse prompts the gambler to increase, mentally, the perceived chances of winning—after placing the bet, he tries to "justify" the bet (see Knox and Inkster[9]). Three aspects of the commitment process will be reviewed. First, the persuasion industry's first common technique for gaining compliance: the Foot-in-the-Door. Second, studies on the impact of *how requests are made*. Third, the Lowball Technique, introduced in the 1970s.

THE FOOT-IN-THE-DOOR TECHNIQUE

In the mid-1960s, Freedman and Fraser[10] tested the notion that if a person agreed to comply first with a small, simple request, then the individual would be more likely to comply later with a larger second request. Specifically, they had a male experimenter contact housewives in their homes in the Palo Alto area in California, where he introduced himself either as a member of the "Community Committee on Traffic Safety" or the "Keep California Beautiful Committee." Half the women were asked to display a small sign in the front windows of their homes; the other half were asked to sign a petition advocating certain legislation. Both of these requests might be considered "small" since they did not involve much cost or effort on the part of the housewives. After two weeks passed, a different experimenter, representing "Citizens for Safe Driving," asked if the housewives would be willing to place a very large sign reading "Drive Carefully" in their front yards. The experimenter showed each housewife a photograph of the sign—it was so large it appeared to obscure much of the front of the house, and it was poorly lettered. Freedman and Fraser found that only 22 percent of the housewives in a control group (who were never asked to fulfill a "small" first request) would agree to the sign. However, 55 percent of the housewives who had previously agreed to putting signs in their windows, agreed to have the larger signs put in their yards.

Since this first empirical study on the Foot-in-the-Door tactic, much attention has focused on its value; and two issues are important: First, why does it work? Second, how can we increase the Foot-in-the-Door effect? Most theorists believe that the Foot-in-the-Door effect is mediated by self-perception processes. Specifically, Freedman and Fraser noted:

> What may occur is a change in the person's feelings about getting involved or about taking action. Once he has agreed to a request, his attitude may change. He may become, in his own eyes, the kind of person who does this sort of thing, who agrees to requests made by strangers, who takes action on things he believes in, who cooperates with good causes.

Several years later, Bem[11] similarly noted that "individuals come to 'know' their own attitudes, emotions, and other internal states partially by inferring them from observations of their own behavior and/or the situation in which this behavior occurs." What does this mean? When the housewives were first approached they may have known in some abstract way that safe driving was important—but they may never have given the issue much thought. When the first request was made, then, they agreed because they had few objections; it didn't cost too much to comply, and they may have been vaguely in agreement with the cause. Later, when asked if they would be willing to put up the large sign, they thought about their behavior and realized that they must have been in favor of good causes (safe driving/keeping California beautiful), since they publicly advertised the fact. Hence, after attributing to themselves the attitude that they favored pro-social issues, it seemed logical to accept the ugly sign.

Several reviews, by DeJong[12] and by Dillard, Hunter, and Burgoon,[13] and Beaman, Cole, Preston, Klentz, and Steblay[14] indicate that the Foot-in-the-Door tactic does not always work. Further, it is clear that the self-perception explanation can not explain all the results obtained. Table 10.1 presents the main set of studies reviewed by DeJong (see DeJong[15] for the citations of the studies listed in Table 10.1). We include this table so that the reader will have a more-comprehensive view of the kind of research done in this area.

Table 10.1 is easy to read and interpret. First, the study reviewed is listed in the left column. The second column, under the heading of "First Request," lists the first requests used in each study. These were the small requests designed to increase the chance that people would become committed to the cause. They are the Foot-in-the-Door requests. The "Second Request" is the larger request, and if the Foot-in-the-Door requests prompted the target to feel greater commitment, then more of the people ought to have complied to this second request. The fourth column presents the results in terms of the percentage of individuals who agreed to the second request. The (C) in this column stands for the control group. These are people who were never asked any version of a smaller, Foot-in-the-Door request. They were only asked the larger request, or the "second" one made of people in the ex-

T A B L E   10.1

SUMMARY OF RESEARCH ON THE FOOT-IN-THE-DOOR TECHNIQUE

Study	First Request	Second Request	Results *	Concl.
Baer, Goldman & Juhnke (1977)	(1) Give the time to experimenter (2) Same as (1); later misinformation given to different experimenter	Correct misinformation given to experimenter by another elevator passenger	(1) 70 (2) 35 (C) 33	FITD No FITD
Baron (1973)	(1) Accept leaflet on the dangers of pollution (2) Sign antipollution petition, get two friends to sign, and mail in	Agree to put 3 foot x 5 foot antipollution sign in front yard	(1) 50b (2) ? (C) 20	FITD No FITD
Cann (1976)	(1) Agree to receive a questionnaire on recycling in the mail and fill it out	Volunteer time for a neighborhood cleanup project	(1) 26 (C) 26	No FITD
Cann, Sherman & Elkes (1975, Study 2)	(1) Answer three questions on driving habits; no delay between the two requests (2) Same as (1); 7–10-day delay between requests	Agree to accept 15 pamphlets on traffic safety and distribute to neighbors	(1) 78 (2) 70 (C) 50	FITD No FITD
Cann, Sherman & Elkes (1975, Study 2)	(1) Answer three questions on driving habits; no delay between the two requests	Agree to accept 15 pamphlets on traffic safety and distribute to neighbors	(1) 72 (C) 45	No FITD
Cialdini & Ascani (1976)	(1) Take and display small card advertising blood drive	Agree to donate blood the next day	(1) 32 (C) 32	No FITD
Cialdini, Cacioppo, Basset & Miller (1978, Study 2)	(1) Agree to display a United Way window poster	Agree to pick up a United Way poster packet at dormitory lobby	(1) 70c (C) 70	No FITD
Crano & Sivacek (Note 1, Study 1)	(1) Answer 10 questions about beverages	Agree to answer 30 questions on driving habits	(1) 66 (C) 31	FITD

Study	*First Request*	*Second Request*	*Results* *	*Concl.*
Crano & Sivacek (Note 1, Study 2)	(1) Answer 10 questions on household products	Agree to answer 45 questions on the mass media	(1) 56 (C) 32	No FITD
DeJong (Note 2)	(1) Agree to sign a petition for pro-disabled legislation; learn they were one of many to sign (2) Same as (1); learn they were the first to sign	Notify a second experimenter that he dropped a quarter	(1) 64 (2) 28 (C) 32	FITD No FITD
DeJong & Funder (1977, Study 1)	(1) Answer 15 questions on the quality of life in the local community	Agree to answer 50 questions on highway safety	(1) 46 (C) 56	No FITD
DeJong & Funder (1977, Study 2)	(1) Answer 15 questions on the quality of life in the local community; receive letter acknowledging participation	Agree to answer 50 questions on highway safety	(1) 66 (C) 56	No FITD
DeJong and Musilli (Note 3)	(1) Agree to participate in a 5-minute survey on parking facilities for compact cars; experimenter appeared physically normal (2) Agree to participate in a 5-minute survey on parking facilities for disabled drivers; experimenter appeared physically normal	Agree to participate in a 30-minute telephone survey on highway laws and driving hazards	(1) 55 (2) 53 (C) 40	FITD No FITD
Dutton & Lennox (1974)	(1) Give money to a white panhandler	Agree to donate time to various activities as part of an inter-racial Brotherhood Week	(1) 54.8d (C) 46.2	No FITD
Fish & Kaplan (1974)	(1) Write a short essay on ways of fighting poverty	Volunteer time and services to a welfare agency	(1) 36 (C) 33	No FITD
Freedman & Fraser (1966, Study 1)	(1) Answer eight questions on household soaps (2) Agree to be in survey on household soaps	Agree to allow six-man survey team to enter home and spend 2 hours classifying all household products	(1) 53 (2) 33 (C) 22	FITD No FITD

Study	First Request	Second Request	Results *	Concl.
Harris (1972, Study 1)	(1) Give directions (2) Give the time	Give the experimenter a dime	(1) 39 (2) 44 (C) 22	No FITD FITD
Harris (1972, Study 2)	(1) Write a letter to a minority high school student, indicating willingness to answer questions about the university and student life	Sign class list to volunteer time to a university publicity campaign	(1) 18 (2) 9	FITD
Harris, Liguori & Stack (1973, Study 3)	(1) Allow name to be sent to local congressman as supporter of organizations' programs	Agree to donate money or cookies to a fund-raising baked-cookie sale	(1) 30 (C) 25	No FITD
Harris & Samerotte (1976, Study 1)	(1) Watch experimenter's possessions; a theft attempt is later thwarted by the subject (2) Same as (1); the second request is made by a different experimenter	Give money to experimenter to permit the purchase of food	(1) 20e (2) 40 (C) 35	No FITD FITD
Harris & Samerotte (1976, Study 2)	(1) Watch experimenter's possessions; a theft attempt is later thwarted by the subjects (2) Same as (1); the second request is made by a different experimenter (3) Watch experimenter's possessions; no theft attempt is made (4) Same as (3); the second request is made by a different experimenter	Give money to experimenter to permit photocopying of an article	(1) 14 (2) 29 (3) 50 (4) 21 (C) 29	No FITD No FITD No FITD No FITD
Lowman (1973)	(1) Answer four questions on recycling and container use	Agree to participate in a glass and metal trash recycling program	(1) 85 (C) 68	FITD
Miller & Suls (1977)	(1) Give directions that are difficult to explain (2) Give directions that are simple to explain	Help a male experimenter pick up dropped groceries	(1) 74 (2) 64 (C) 32	No FITD FITD

Study	*First Request*	*Second Request*	*Results* *	*Concl.*
Pliner, Hart, Kohl & Sari (1974)	(1) Wear pin to advertise a fund drive (2) Wear pin and persuade member of family to do so	Contribute money to the fund	(1) 74 (2) 81 (C) 46	FITD FITD
Reingen & Kernan (1977)	(1) Agree to participate in a 5-question survey on household products	Agree to participate in a 20-question survey on household products	(1) 75 (C) 58	No FITD
Seligman, Bush & Kirsch (1976)	(1) Answer 5 questions on the energy crisis and inflation (2) Answer 20 questions (3) Answer 30 questions (4) Answer 45 questions	Agree to answer 55 more questions for the same survey	(1) 38 (2) 35 (3) 74 (4) 74 (C) 31	No FITD No FITD FITD FITD
Seligman, Miller, Goldberg, Gelberd, Clark & Bush (1976)	(1) Listen to a 2-minute pro-McGovern speech; agree to display a small campaign sign (2) Agree to display a small campaign sign only (3) Listen to a 2-minute speech on fire prevention, agree to display a small fire prevention sign (4) Agree to display a small fire prevention sign only	Agree to display a McGovern poster in front window	(1) 38 (2) 23 (3) 30 (4) 31 (C) 16	FITD No FITD No FITD No FITD
Snyder & Cunningham (1975)	(1) Agree to answer 8 questions on household paper products or on traffic safety	Agree to answer 30 questions for the other organizations	(1) 52 (C) 33	No FITD
Tipton & Browning (1972)	(1) Help an elderly woman pick up dropped groceries	Help a young woman in a wheelchair up over a curb	(1) Of (C) 36	No FITD
Uranowitz (1975)	(1) Watch experimenter's shopping bags while he retrieves a dollar bill (2) Watch experimenter's shopping bags while he retrieves his wallet	Notify a second experimenter that she dropped her package	(1) 80 (2) 45 (C) 35	FITD No FITD

Study	First Request	Second Request	Results *	Concl.
Zuckerman, Lazzaro & Waldgeir (in press)	(1) Agree to participate in a 5-minute survey on traffic safety	Agree to participate in a 20-minute survey on household products	(1) 64 (C) 45	No FITD

Table is from: W. DeJong, "An Examination of Self-perception Mediation of the Foot-in-the-Door Effect," *Journal of Personality and Social Psychology*, vol. 37 (1979), pp. 461–488.

perimental groups. If the Foot-in-the-Door technique was effective, then the percentage of people complying with the second request should be substantially higher than the percentage of people who were in the control group. The last column indicates whether or not the researcher concluded that the FITD (Foot-in-the-Door) effect was statistically reliable, or not ("No FITD").

For example, look at the summary of the study by Cann, Sherman, and Elkes[16] (Study 1). The control group was asked one question (the "Second Request"): "Do you agree to accept fifteen pamphlets on traffic safety and distribute them to your neighbors?" Half of the people who were approached verbally agreed to help (C = 50 percent). One group of people, however, was asked to answer three questions on driving habits first. Once they agreed to help the interviewer by answering these questions, they were asked if they would accept the fifteen pamphlets to distribute to others. This group, labeled "(1)," complied in large number with the request: compliance was 78 percent. The researchers concluded that this was a significant FITD effect. Another group of individuals was first asked to help by answering three questions, and they agreed to do so. However, the interviewer called them back on the phone seven to ten days later, and asked them if they would distribute the pamphlets. Compliance still appeared high (70 percent), showing a drop of

8 percent from the other Foot-in-the-Door group over the course of time. However, although there was a 20 percent difference between this group and the control group, the researchers considered this difference to be not statistically reliable ("No FITD").

A good deal of research has been devoted to the Foot-in-the-Door technique and we have developed a set of guidelines regarding this approach:

1. The first request must be unambiguously smaller than the second request, it must induce compliance, and it must be of sufficient magnitude to commit the individual to future compliance.

This guideline argues that the first request must be large enough to get the people to start thinking that they are committed to the cause, but not so large as to be rejected promptly. If self-perception theory explains why people comply with the second request, then getting people to commit to a relatively large first request would undoubtedly increase the probability that they would attribute the cause of their accepting the first request to their own attitudes. In fact, Seligman, Bush, and Kirsch[17] documented such a relationship. They contacted four different groups of students by phone, asking the students if they would participate in a survey concerning people's reactions to the energy crisis and inflation. Each subject was then asked if he or she would help the caller by answering a number of questions for the survey, which would "only take a few minutes." One-fourth of the subjects were asked five yes/no questions (time elapsed: 15 seconds); another one-fourth, 20 yes/no questions (1 minute); another one-fourth were asked 30 yes/no questions (1 minute and 45 seconds), and the final group answered 45 yes/no questions (3 minutes). Two days later, the experimenters called back and said: "We called some of you the other night, but others haven't been called yet. In any case, we would like to complete the survey tonight. Would you be willing to answer 55 questions on the survey?" These researchers found that only 38 percent of the subjects in the first group agreed to the second request; and only 35 percent in the second group. However, 74 percent of the subjects in both the latter groups agreed to the second request—a 15-second or a one-minute interaction was not sufficiently long to create the Foot-in-the-Door effect.

2. The second request cannot be so large that few would comply; further, the second request cannot be so trivial that all people would comply (otherwise, why bother to use the Foot-in-the-Door tactic?).

If the first request is too small, it will not elicit the appropriate self-perceptions (that is, there must be some minimum amount of true "commitment" felt on the part of the target). Further, since it is obvious that people take into consideration the costs involved (that is, time, money, physical or mental effort), then the Foot-in-the-Door tactic would work to increase compliance if the second request were not too costly. An example of this is the Cialdini and Ascani[18] study (see Table 10.1, and below). Students who agreed to put up a poster advertising a blood drive may have felt some amount of commitment to this cause, but to have a needle inserted into one's vein to give blood the next day is a large increase

in commitment (relative to the first request). On the other hand, if the second request involved so little effort that everyone would comply, there would be no need to use a Foot-in-the-Door approach. For example, in the Cialdini, Cacioppo, Basset, and Miller study[19] (see Table 10.1) the second request merely asked college students to walk to another dormitory and pick up a United Way poster, in order to help out a volunteer. So little effort was involved that people complied when asked simply to help (70 percent), or when they—the foot-in-the-door group—were first asked to display a poster (also 70 percent).

3. Different experimenters can be used successfully to elicit the Foot-in-the-Door effect.

If people in the research situation actually make the self-perception that they are generous or charitable persons, then changing experimenters from the first request to the second request should not have any effect on the rates of compliance. Starting with Freedman and Fraser, many studies found that the Foot-in-the-Door effect does have generality.

4. If the targets believed that there were external pressures which led to their compliance on the first request, then they will not perceive their own personal involvement to be the cause of the compliance, and there will be no Foot-in-the-Door effect.

For example, Zuckerman, Lazzaro, and Waldgrier[20] called homemakers and asked if they would participate in a 5-minute telephone survey. One-half were promised a monetary payment, the other half were not. The subjects were told that if they agreed to participate, an interview would be conducted at a later time. After two or three days, the subjects were contacted and asked to participate in a 20-minute interview. Forty-five percent of the control group agreed to participate, 33 percent of the individuals who were promised a monetary incentive agreed, and 64 percent of those who had agreed to a 5-minute interview agreed to participate of their own free will, and without external pressures or rewards.

5. The Foot-in-the-Door effect works best when the source of the request is a legitimate one.

Dillard, et al., concluded that it was important to employ a pro-social appeal or topic in order to make the tactic work. In fact, they argued that the tactic may have very limited utility in business settings—it worked *only* when the causes were pro-social (that is, contributions to Multiple Sclerosis, Heart Fund, United Way, and so forth). The tactic does not work all the time—research suggests that it works in about half of the studies. Perhaps one of the limitations in this line of research is the assumption that any pro-social organization is worthy of support and is "legitimate" in society. Unfortunately, people have negative attitudes toward some of these pro-social organizations, especially following the mismanagement of the national United Way in the early 1990s. Presumably, the Foot-in-the-Door effect works best if the targeted individuals *agree with the researchers that a particular cause is legitimate and worthy of time or money.*

6. The Foot-in-the-Door effect works over time—the consequence of committing oneself to the first request slowly declines in impact over time.

In truth, quite a controversy exists concerning the time frame in which the two requests are made. Dillard, et al., noted that the effectiveness of Foot-in-the-Door was not related in any way with the time delay of the second request, and DeJong noted that time may be less important than whether the target remembers the commitment at the time when the second request is made. In a fairly complex study by Beaman and colleagues,[21] twenty-four various combinations of large/small-sized requests were manipulated, with and without reminders of earlier commitment, and with days elapsed since the first request was made.

The results indicated only one group produced a strong Foot-in-the-Door effect: a large-request group which received a reminder of their commitment four days later.

There are two concerns that have to be balanced in the question of timing. If agreeing to the first request is actually successful in increasing a person's commitment to a cause, these feelings of commitment probably decrease slowly over time unless the target thinks about and/or is reminded of this commitment. On the other hand, there may be a problem if there is no (or a very little) time delay. Although not thoroughly researched, there is probably a limit to the amount of help others will provide per unit of time. Consider the studies by Crano and his colleagues (see Table 10.1). When asked to answer 30 questions on driving habits, 31 percent of the control group complied (Study 1), and when asked to answer 45 questions on the mass media, 32 percent of the control group complied (Study 2). When people were first asked 10 questions about beverages, the FITD technique was successful—66 percent of those who had agreed to answer 10 questions agreed to answer an additional 30 questions, making a total of 40 questions (Study 1). In Study 2, however, the FITD group was first asked to answer 10 questions on household products, and then asked to answer 45 questions on the mass media. Only 56 percent of this group agreed to answer a total of 55 questions—perhaps because 55 questions was imposing on the participants. Also note the project by Tipton and Browning[22] (see Table 10.1). When a young woman was in a wheelchair outside a store struggling to get over a curb, 36 percent of the people walking by offered some type of assistance. However, of those individuals who had just helped an elderly lady pick up dropped groceries inside a store, *none* offered assistance to the young lady in the wheelchair. Is there a limit to how much altruism people show per hour, day, or week?

Ideal circumstances probably involve (a) making a request of a targeted individual that makes the person feel committed to the cause, (b) praising the individual for assistance and/or making the altruistic motives salient, and, (c) allowing a modest time delay before asking for a reasonable amount of additional aid.

7. Compliance can be increased by employing tactics which help to ensure that the target makes the appropriate self-perception.

Any methods we might use to help the target attribute the cause of accepting the first request to his or her own attitudes and preferences can then increase the effectiveness of the technique. As noted above, one way to help get a receiver to do this is to remove external pressures or incentives as possible reasons why the target agreed to the first request. What else can we do? Some theorists have used labeling to help ensure that the target gets the right attribution. That is, say you just gave $2 to the Heart Fund. The solicitor not only thanks you, but tells you, very honestly, "You know, my job would be a lot easier if I met more charitable people like you," and then leaves. Since the solicitor communicated this ready-made attribution after you gave him the money, it seems to you that there's no ulterior motive on his part. Therefore, the compliment rings true. Did you not, in fact, behave in a generous manner? You must, therefore, be generous. Two weeks later, when a solicitor comes to your home collecting for multiple sclerosis, how much do you give him or her? A study that demonstrated this was conducted by Kraut;[23] and a similar one was completed by Paulhus, Shaffer, and Downing.[24]

How Requests are Made

Although the Foot-in-the-Door tactic sounds very simple at first, there are many factors that influence whether or not the tactic works. Research has added considerable information concerning the nature of compliance, and we offer several additional guidelines that can be applied to *any* compliance request—even one-shot requests for help or assistance.

8. *Behavioral* compliance to donating money, time and so forth (compared to verbal compliance—saying, "yes, I'll help later") is probably increased by use of face-to-face contact, as opposed to telephone requests.

Reeves, Macolini, and Martin's[25] study demonstrated that when solicitors asked for help for a worthwhile cause (Good Friends Shelter), compliance techniques were effective only when the solicitors asked for money on-the-spot in malls. When targets were provided envelopes in which to mail in contributions, only one target responded with such a behavioral compliance. Reeves, et al., argued that individuals are motivated to promote a positive public image and will therefore donate money in public, substantially more so than in private.

9. People are more likely to comply with solicitors who are likable, polite, and positive.

This notion is assumed to be operating in the various studies conducted on the Foot-in-the-Door effect, although there could be variability in the studies. Several projects indicate that using positive labels, being friendly, touching, and being positive make a tremendous difference.[26] A study by Howard[27] is particularly interesting. In his study on the "Foot-in-the-Mouth" effect, more cookies were sold for charity when positive greetings were first employed ("Good evening! How are you feeling tonight?"). Typically, such questions prompt affirmative answers ("Fine, thank you"), which are reinforced and encouraged by the solicitor. A positive exchange and positive mood facilitate compliance.

10. Compliance is increased when solicitors/experimenters employ tactics that *block* the target's ability to use any excuses for *not* complying. Two common approaches: Legitimizing paltry contributions, and increasing the commitment and credibility of the solicitor.

Since people commonly say, "I carry no money," "I'm broke," "Sorry, I can't help today," in order to avoid assisting others, it makes sense that linguistic variations on how one asks for money would make a difference in compliance. Reeves, Macolini, and Martin,[28] following Cialdini and Schroeder,[29] examined three ways in which to legitimize a request. One-fourth of the time, solicitors approached individuals door-to-door and asked for contributions for the Good Friends Shelter Group:

> "We're collecting money for the Good Friends Shelter Group, an organization that is planning to open a short-term crisis-intervention facility for adolescents next year. We've already received some contributions and I wonder if you would be willing to help by giving a donation."

One-fourth of the time, the solicitors added "Even a penny will help," in order to legitimize giving pennies and/or small amounts. In another group, the phrase, "even a dollar will help" was added, while in the fourth group a *social legitimization* phrase was included; targets were told that some contributions had already been received ranging from a penny on up. This last variation was included because the phrase, "Even a penny will help," may sound too much like begging or pleading. The idea of the study was to examine whether implying approval of very small contributions elicited more compliance—not whether pleading or begging was useful.

The results of both the Reeves, et al., and the Cialdini and Schroeder studies are presented in Table 10.2. What the numbers mean is that asking for pennies (both the *social legitimization* and the *even-a-penny* appeals) substantially increased the percentage of people who complied (43 to 57 percent, and 65 to 58 percent—see Table 10.2). However, there were no significant differences in the

amount of money donated—people did, in fact, give more pennies!

A question emerges as to why people should give money to just anyone who is soliciting funds. Who is this person asking for aid? If the solicitor appears worthy, dedicated, and committed to the cause, targets are more likely to contribute. Kraut[30] found that contributions increased significantly when the solicitor established credentials for making the face-to-face request; more money was donated when the solicitor had commented that he had volunteered for the last five years to help children stricken with multiple sclerosis.

THE LOWBALL TECHNIQUE

Our students in Texas told us of an evening when one of the alums at their sorority house asked for volunteers to judge a baton-twirling contest on the upcoming Saturday. Ten of the young women promptly volunteered to help. After the dinner, they were told to show up, at 8 a.m., at a high school an hour away. The students went anyway, although some felt duped by the alum (who cleverly failed to reveal the full details when asking for volunteers). The students admitted they had agreed to go of their own free will and felt committed and responsible. Fraternity members at USC reported use of a similar tactic: to meet and have lunch with a prospective transfer student, so as to help out the president of the fraternity house, while in reality the guest's whole family is there for a tour of the campus.

These are some examples of the common ploy called "the lowball technique." It is called "lowball" because salesclerks (especially ones selling cars) "throw a lowball," meaning that they offer an extremely good price (on a car). The customer commits to that price, believing that s/he has a good deal. The salesclerk then removes the good price offer by some means—claiming that the deal proposed does not include tinted windows, special radio, and so forth, or perhaps saying

10.2

Percent of Targets Donating, and Total Amount Donated, as a Function of Type of Request

	Reeves, et al.		Cialdini and Schroeder	
Type of Request:	Percent Comply	Total Amount	Percent Comply	Total Amount
Control	30%	$29.00	32%	$20.74
Even-a-Dollar	37%	$18.00	47%	$19.35
Social Legitimization	43%	$18.66	65%	$28.61
Even-a-Penny	57%	$25.25	58%	$31.30

Adapted from R.A. Reeves, R.M. Macolini, and R.C. Martin, "Legitimizing Paltry Contributions: On-the-spot vs. Mail-in Requests," *Journal of Applied Social Psychology*, vol. 17 (1987), pp. 731–738. Used with permission.

that the sales manager will not approve the "free giveaway" of the radial tires. Once various options are added back into the sales price, the price is merely comparable to the price quotes that the customer may have received elsewhere. By this time, however, the customer is in the sales office, has nearly finished completing various forms, and finds it is hard to leave. The "lowball" tactic is devised to get the target to commit to a decision *before s/he learns the full cost of the compliance,* such as the true cost of the car, the fact the one has to be in Plainview, Texas, at 8 a.m. on Saturday, or that one is "suckered" into spending an afternoon giving a family a tour of the campus.

Cialdini, Cacioppo, Basset, and Miller[31] completed the definitive set of experiments on the lowball technique. In one of these, students at Arizona State University were called in to participate in an experiment, for which they would receive credit in their classes. Half the students were simply asked, "Can you participate on a project on Wednesday or Friday morning at 7 a.m.?" The other half of the students were low balled: they were asked to participate in a study on Wednesday or Friday, but they were not told beforehand that the experiment began at 7 a.m. Only 31 percent of the students in the first, control, group agreed to show up at 7 a.m. However, 56 percent of the lowballed students verbally agreed to come to the study when the 7 a.m. time was not revealed to them. More importantly, only 24 percent of the control group students actually showed up at 7 a.m., while 53 percent of the lowballed students showed up on time. Why? According to Cialdini,[32] those who are lowballed, and who freely agree with the initial request, feel a greater amount of *commitment* and *responsibility* to their obligation to show up on time.

Reciprocity

Cialdini[33] makes a strong case for the importance of reciprocity in society. We teach our children that they should reciprocate gifts, parties, sleepovers, and the like. We scold them for not "taking turns" and for failing to play fairly with one another. We send Christmas cards to people who send them to us. When a friend helps us, we reciprocate the favor. The movie *The Godfather* illustrates how strongly this reciprocity notion works—the fact that a favor needs to be reciprocated in the future is *never* questioned. We have conflict with those who fail to reciprocate favors, requests, assistance, and the like, and we terminate friendships with people who reveal themselves to be moochers, low-lifes, takers, and self-centered.[34]

Reciprocating favors and gifts among friends, or being obligated to repay people in the community for their help and assistance are fundamental aspects of life. However, some companies try to activate the felt obligation of reciprocity in order to boost sales. For example, "free samples" at the mall or at the grocery store may serve the function of allowing shoppers to taste a new product, but "free samples" may also activate the reciprocity principle: This person gave us something, we should reciprocate the favor and buy a little. Free samples, free discounts, two-for-one specials, and extra assistance in the clothing store may prompt shoppers to feel some debt or obligation to buy something. The Amway distributing company, for example, will drop off a "BUG" (a sampler kit containing a large selection of various products) in a person's home for a week to ten days so that the individual can try all the products, "with no obligation." But, in a sense, there can be felt obligation: The person may believe that since the Amway distributor was nice enough to do him or her the favor of dropping off the products, the least s/he can do is to buy something from the distributor when the distributor comes to pick up the sampler kit. In truth, the distributor may not really be engaging in any "special" treatment by leaving the sampler kit with any particular buyer. Indeed, the distributor may have twenty or so different sampler kits out in the community at any given time. This tactic works if the potential buyer *perceives* that s/he is getting special treatment or a special concession.

THE DOOR-IN-THE-FACE TECHNIQUE

A "free" gift activates a reciprocity rule when the target believes, "They did a favor for me, so I will do a favor for them," "Those people at Hickory Farms gave me some free food, so why not buy a little?" However, being a recipient of a free gift is not the only way that the reciprocity rule can be activated. Cialdini and Ascani[35] demonstrated that the reciprocity rule can be activated through a technique called the "Door-in-the-Face." In this approach, a large first request is made and rejected by the target. Then, the solicitor or salesperson makes a smaller request. The target will feel predisposed to agreeing with the second request because s/he feels that if s/he managed to avoid the larger request then s/he should at least be open to the solicitor's second request. When we say "no," and the solicitor concedes and retreats to a smaller request, we (a) feel that we have won something, and (b) feel that if the solicitor can concede we should concede too.

Cialdini and Ascani went to 189 dormitory rooms at Arizona State University, asking students to give blood. They employed one of three types of requests. First, one group of students was informed that the annual university blood drive was taking place, and the students were asked to give blood the following day when the bloodmobile was to be at their dormitory complex. This group was the control group. Cialdini and Ascani used the Foot-in-the-Door technique on a second set of students. The solicitors would knock on students' doors, announce the blood drive, and ask the students to help get the word out by placing a sign on their doors. The solicitor would then place a sign on the door, and ask (without delay) the students to come and give blood the next day. The third group received the Door-in-the-Face approach:

> "We're currently asking students to become involved in our Long-Term Donor Program. Long-term donors are those who pledge to give a unit of blood once every two months for a period of at least three years. This way we can be sure of a continual supply of blood. Would you be willing to enroll in our Long-Term Donor Program?" (After the student declined, the solicitor continued:) "Oh, well, maybe you'd be interested in another program we're asking students to participate in, then." (The solicitor then made the control group request—to give blood once the next day).

The results are reported in Table 10.3. The verbal compliance column presents the percent-

age of students who verbally agreed to come the following day to give blood. The behavioral compliance column presents the percentage of students who actually gave blood the following day. After giving blood, the donors were asked to complete a card that provided their phone numbers so that they could be called to give blood again when the bloodmobile returned to the dormitory complex; the percentage of students completing this card is listed under the heading of "future verbal compliance." Based on what happened in the control group, we see what happens if solicitors simply ask people to give blood: Solicitors knocked on 63 doors and 20 people verbally agreed to give blood the following day (31.7 percent), however, only 7 people actually gave blood (35 percent of those who said that they would give blood), and only 3 promised to come again to give blood.

The results concerning the Foot-in-the-Door group are not encouraging in terms of prompting individuals to give blood. The same number of individuals verbally agreed to give blood as in the control group, but fewer actually showed up to

---

T A B L E 10.3

PERCENTAGE OF VERBAL, BEHAVIORAL, AND FUTURE VERBAL COMPLIANCE WITH REQUESTS TO GIVE BLOOD

Type of Request	Verbal Compliance	Behavioral Compliance	Future Verbal Compliance
Door-in-the-Face	49.2% (31/63)	38.7% (12/31)	84.0% (10/12)
Foot-in-the-Door	31.7% (20/63)	10.0% (2/20)	0.0% (0/ 2)
Control Group	31.7% (20/63)	35.0% (7/20)	43.0% (3/ 7)

Adapted from R.B. Cialdini and K. Ascani, "Test of a Concession Procedure for Inducing Verbal, Behavioral, and Further Compliance with a Request to Give Blood," *Journal of Applied Psychology*, vol. 61 (1976), pp. 295–300. Used with permission of authors and American Psychological Association.

give blood (only 2 out of the 20 who promised to give blood). Possibly, the use of the Foot-in-the-Door technique in this situation made matters worse because students can now say, "Well, I'm helping already by advertising the blood drive, and I am doing more than other people. So, I will skip giving blood," that is, displaying the sign gave the students an excuse for not giving blood. On the other hand, verbal compliance was much greater when the Door-in-the-Face technique was employed (49.2 percent of the students agreed to come and give blood), as was behavioral compliance (38.7 percent of the students who verbally agreed to come actually gave blood), and future verbal compliance (10 out of 12 students agreed to come again and give blood). The Foot-in-the-Door technique was successful in prompting students to give blood, and they apparently felt a good deal of responsibility, given that the students showed up to give blood, and agreed to give again.

Even-Chen, Yinon, and Bizman[36] conducted a study in Israel concerning safe driving, supporting the usefulness of this technique for other pro-social appeals as well. Even-Chen, et al., offered rules for the effective use of this tactic:

1. The original request must be rejected by the target person.

2. The original request should be large enough so that its rejection will be perceived by the target person as irrelevant for making self-attribution.

3. The original request should not evoke resentment, anger or hostility.

4. The second request must be unambiguously smaller than the first.

5. There should be no delay in the timing by which the two requests are made. According to Dillard, et al.,[37] there should be no delay; obviously, the actual manipulation of *reciprocal concessions* is difficult to obtain if the target says "no" to a first request and the solicitor then delays several days before making a second, smaller, request. Rather, the longer the delay, the more likely it is that the target will see the two requests as two separate requests and that a concession is not being offered by the solicitor.

6. The cause involves a pro-social topic, issue, or cause (see the Dillard, et al., review discussed earlier).

7. For maximum effectiveness, it is probably better to have the same solicitor make both requests, as opposed to having different experimenters/solicitors make the two requests. Recall that in the Foot-in-the-Door tactic, two different solicitors/experimenters could be used—the point was that the first request was hopefully successful in increasing the target's feelings of *commitment to the cause or topic*. In the Door-in-the-Face tactic, the reason *why* the target agrees to the second request is because of the reciprocal concession— something that would occur primarily if the person made the two requests, and clearly appeared to be making a concession. Otherwise, the target would merely be hearing two different people making two different sizes of requests—the tactic would work only if the target believed that the two people represented the same agency, and that a concession was being offered.

One of the authors was asked to "sponsor" a table for twelve at the Governor's Ball with $25,000. After declining, the phone solicitor backed down to $1,000 gifts, and then to smaller gifts. The phone solicitor was trained to "work down" an ordered list. Your alumni association will be using this same approach.

THE "THAT'S NOT ALL YOU GET" TECHNIQUE

How many times do you watch television, especially late at night or the Home Shopping Network, and hear the solicitor say, "And what's more, if you act tonight you will also receive X or Y"? The "Sweeten the Pot" or "That's Not All You Get" technique is a significant compliance-gaining ploy. Burger[38] conducted seven experiments at Santa Clara University employing this approach, and offers several insights into why the approach works. At a psychology club bake sale, both cupcakes and cookies were put on sale but no prices were shown. Students who were assigned to the control group were told that one cupcake and two cookies were to be sold together as a package deal for 75 cents. However, the TNA ("That's Not All") students were told that a cupcake was to be sold for 75 cents. After a solicitor from the psychology club made this announcement, s/he was interrupted by another club member who tapped the first on the shoulder, and the two conferred privately for a moment. Then, the first solicitor announced that the 75-cent price also included two cookies. Forty percent of the students in the control group agreed to buy the cupcake/cookies package. However, 73 percent of the students in the TNA group agreed to buy the cupcake/cookies package. Obviously, the package looked to be a better buy when the students first thought that the cupcake alone was to cost 75 cents, and then found out that they could get a cupcake and two cookies for the same price.

The TNA approach involves presenting a product at a certain price, allowing the customer to think about the price, and then improving the deal by adding a product or lowering the price. Why this approach works appears to be a combination of several of the principles we have already discussed. First, the tactic works best if the approach activates the norm of reciprocity. Targets first are told of a certain price, but the solicitor is seen negotiating a new improved price or offer. Targets witness a new deal and believe that they gained by being there at the time the improved deal was announced. Since they believe that they have gained something new, more targets in the TNA group agree to the new package (compared to the control group, who are offered the same deal but without the appearance of a concession).

Second, Burger also argues that altering the *anchor point* (see above) is an important ingredient in the TNA technique. The value of the many objects (cupcakes, cookies, candles, and so forth), which targets may purchase from charity drives is quite vague. However, when a solicitor starts with a high value, the target is prompted to adopt a higher value as an anchor point. To examine this question, Burger asked targets, "What do you believe is an honest amount to charge for the cupcake—high enough to make a profit for the club but not so high that the customers feel cheated?" The targets who had first been told that the price of each cupcake was one dollar thought that, on the average, 51.4 cents was an honest value. On the other hand, another group of targets who had first been told that each cupcake was priced at 75 cents indicated that 44.6 cents was an honest value. The point? By asking initially for a higher price, the solicitors created in the minds of the targets a higher anchor point or reference point for what is a "good, fair" price. Thus, when the price is dropped to 75 cents per cupcake or when cookies are added to sweeten the pot, the 75-cent value appears more reasonable a price (given an anchor of 51.4 cents).

Liking

The liking rule is yet another pervasive tendency in society—we will help, comply, and give assistance to people we like. We like others for many reasons. We like some people because they are attractive and we want attractive people to like us. We also like others because they are similar to ourselves. Another way to increase liking from others is called "ingratiation," in which communication is employed to alter other's feelings toward us.

INGRATIATION

Ingratiation tactics, according to Jones and Wortman,[39] are a "class of strategic devices illicitly designed to influence a particular other concerning the attractiveness of one's personality." They are "illicit" because they are manipulative. We may exaggerate how well a supervisor is doing her job when we talk to her, not because we believe she is doing such a great job, but because we want to ask her for a letter of recommendation next week. Despite our society's rather negative view of ingratiation, we have all used the technique ourselves with someone at some time. In fact, Jones and Wortman feel that we may not even be consciously aware of the fact that we are ingratiating; we may naturally adopt flirting or self-presentation without giving it much thought.

There are four primary ways of trying to get others to like you: complimentary other-enhancement (flattery), selective self-presentations (self-bolstering or bragging), opinion conformity (you tell the person you want to date that you, too, are a Republican), and rendering favors. Generally, there are three variables which influence how frequently we might engage in ingratiation, and these variables are similar to the ones we discussed above in regard to situational influences. We are more likely to use an ingratiation tactic if (a) there are rewards for doing so; (b) there is some probability for success; and, (c) if the form of ingratiation is perceived to be legitimate for the particular context. The latter variable has received the least amount of research attention, but it is obvious that buying a Coke (rendering favors) for a stranger with whom you have never talked is too obvious, blunt, and direct. What is perceived as legitimate may also depend upon the beliefs and behaviors of the target. Schneider and Eustis,[40] for example, found that ingratiators matched the presentational style of the target. When the target engaged in self-presentations, so did the ingratiator; and when the target was a revealing person, the ingratiator also revealed information. The fact that ingratiation tactics are strategically adapted to the audience was most recently demonstrated by Michener, Plazewski, and Baske,[41] who found that when supervisors valued efficiency, ingratiators bolstered the view of themselves as dedicated workers; and when supervisors valued sociability, ingratiators used flattery which pertains to interpersonal factors.

Thirty years of research has focused on issues involving ingratiation, and we recommend the very readable book by Jones and Wortman for the interested reader who would like more details (see footnote 39). We address two issues here: (1) how does ingratiation work? and, (2) to what extent does it work? To address the first issue, we will focus attention on one of the four tactics: flattery.

To use flattery and praise successfully, the ingratiator must control the types of attributions the target makes about why the praise was given. For example, on their third date, Sid praises Sally by saying she is a great cook and a very sensitive person. As Jones and Wortman point out, there are a number of attributions Sally can make:

1. Sid paid the compliment because he wants something from her; she perceives that there is an ulterior motive. Consequence: Sid is not likely to increase Sally's liking for him. The comment may even hurt.

2. Sid is the kind of person who always makes positive comments to others; Sally does not take the praise personally and does not feel that Sid is discerning. Thus, Sid will not increase Sally's liking for him appreciably.

3. Sid paid the compliment because it was normative to do so. Consequence: if the statement is accepted only as a normal type of communication one receives on a date or over dinner, Sid is not likely to increase the amount of liking Sally has for him.

4. Sid did the praising because he was "just being nice to me" or is "trying not to hurt my feelings." Consequence: since Sid is being such a nice boy, Sally will increase her liking for him, but only modestly.

5. Sally concludes that Sid is sincere. Consequence: Sid will elicit increased liking from Sally.

All ingratiators desire to decrease the likelihood that an attribution such as the first will be made, and to increase the chance for one like Sally's last attribution. Here are Jones and Wortman's recommendations:

1. Make the praise credible.

To do so, there are three tactics to employ. In Sid's case, he should try to reduce the perceived dependency on the target person in order to reduce the suspicion that he needs or expects to benefit. The timing of one's praise is obviously important.

Second, Sid can have the praise delivered by a third party. He can avoid the attribution of being manipulative if he can construct the context where someone else tells Sally that Sid said she is sensitive (or a good cook), and he appears not to know that what he said was repeated.

Third, to be credible, Sid must make the praise plausible. Obviously, Sid must select some topic or issue of praise which Sally is likely to find plausible.

2. Praise an attribute about which the target is insecure.

While this rule may seem simple, an ingratiator must be careful in selecting the topic of his or her praise. Suppose you wanted to persuade a supervisor that she was doing a great job in leading people. If she felt confident she was a good leader, she probably wouldn't question the sincerity of the praise and would believe what you said. She might also consider the praise to be a normal kind of communication, and she would only moderately or slightly increase her liking for you. On the other hand, if she were insecure about her leadership, and if she believes the praise, then you have helped to bolster her self-esteem, and she would significantly increase her liking for you. Hence, it pays to offer praise about a topic on which the target is uncertain or insecure.

3. Be discerning.

"If an ingratiator avoids complimenting the target person when the benefit desired from him is salient, picks an attribute to admire about which the target person is insecure, but makes sure that his compliment is plausible he should reduce the probability that the target person will attribute ulterior motivations to him. But, in addition to avoiding the conclusion that he is manipulative and self-seeking, the ingratiator should also try to avoid the attribution that he is complimenting the target person because he is the kind of person who always says complimentary things to everyone."[42]

Several tactics are recommended so that the ingratiator appears to be a discerning individual. First, one can employ both positive and negative comments in a message. An ingratiator may acknowledge some negative attributes of the target which are already known to the target and, simultaneously, praise a behavior about which the target feels insecure. Or, an ingratiator may let the target know he has high standards and is thus discerning. Another tactic is to be neutral or even negative toward the target and then, over time, become more and more friendly toward the target. Research indicates that we tend to like people who are pleasant and friendly, but that we like people even more if they were, at first, cold, distant, and aloof, and later became friendly toward us. There are three main reasons for this: (1) we may feel that something we did or said helped win the negative persons over to our side, and we enjoy being successful; (2) their being cold and aloof made us aroused and anxious, and when they started to like us our anxiety was reduced; and, (3) while we like being liked by positive people, it is even more enjoyable to be liked by a person whom we see as having high standards or who appears discerning.

4. Make sure that the praise is not seen merely as normative.

Targets are not likely to change their attributes or focus attention on the agent if any praise is simply seen as due the target. To receive attention, praise must be different enough to be noticed by a receiver.

5. Avoid the negative effects of praise.

Three negative effects of praise are that: praise may make a person feel awkward by placing him or her in a difficult social situation; praise may imply a low level of expected performance (after all, why did he praise you—did he think you weren't going to do it correctly?); and, praise may lead to apprehension over future evaluations, since praise now suggests that you are being attended to and monitored.

Ingratiation involves some risk because people do not like to feel they have been manipulated. It is very important to hide any ulterior motive if the ingratiation is to be successful. On the other hand, there is no doubt that the use of any of these methods can increase attraction. Can that attraction get us tangible rewards?

Ingratiation Can Open Doors

The classic study by Kipnis and Vanderveer[43] indicates just how helpful ingratiation tactics can be. Four-person work units were created: a superior worker, an average worker, an ingratiator, and a fourth worker who was either a second "average worker" (control group), an inept worker, or a poor-attitude worker. The superior worker worked at a rate faster than the average worker, of course, while the ingratiator worked at an average rate but passed messages along to the supervisor, such as: "Count on me for help—I'll be glad to give it," "I had doubts about having a college student be my supervisor, but you turned out to be real good . . ., and your assistant is nice too." Our interest is in whether ingratiation influenced performance evaluations, promises of pay raises and actual pay raises.

Their study indicates that the superior worker received higher performance evaluations than the average worker, regardless of whether the fourth worker was a control, an inept worker, or a poor attitude worker. Further, the ingratiator received significantly higher evaluations than did the average worker—evaluations which were not significantly different from those of the superior worker. Thus, ingratiation can elicit higher performance evaluations. Ingratiation, however, did not automatically result in an increase in pay raises (in fact, superior workers received more pay raises, and supervisors "bought off" all workers when the supervisors were confronted with poor-attitude workers). However, ingratiators excelled in getting *promises* of pay raises if a coworker was inept. In this situation, with the supervisor confronted with retraining an inept worker and perhaps falling behind in productivity, the supervisor would offer promises to the ingratiator to see if the ingratiator would increase productivity. Ingratiation, then, provides higher performance ratings and can help to open doors.

Social Proof

Sometimes we jaywalk and are not aware of having done so—we simply followed others across the street. Sometimes we applaud at a concert, even though we may not have been aware of *why* we started to applaud (others started to applaud, and we followed). Laughter breaks out in a movie theater and we laugh or smile, even when the joke didn't seem that funny. There are countless situations in which people are influenced not by logic or rationality—but by the actions of others. The social proof rule stems from the fact that when people do not have statistical evidence, physical proof, or knowledge concerning how to act, they are influenced by *social* proof—relying on what other people are doing. Examples are endless:

When examining boxes of computer diskettes, a shopper really can not tell the difference between different brands. As the shopper reads various labels, several different shoppers walk by and buy brand X. Since the shopper has no superior knowledge about the product, he trusts the judgment of other shoppers, and also buys brand X.

A driver sees that several drivers ahead of him/her have turned on their right turn signals, he/she automatically and instinctively turns on his/her right turn signal (thinking that the left lane ahead must be blocked in some way).

Walking toward a movie theater to see a newly released, well-publicized movie, a couple instinctively stops and lines up in a long line, thinking that the long line must be for the recently released popular movie.

At a wedding, a "money tree" is situated on a table. We see others pinning $20 and $100 bills to the tree. We also pin $20 to the tree.

According to Cialdini,[44] there are two important elements involved in the social proof rule. First, we are likely to follow along with what others are doing when we are not fully *aware* of what is happening. An excellent example of this is research on "canned laughter" or "laugh tracks."[45] Although individuals claim that they do not like

canned laughter on television shows they watch, there is a good chance that they are not always aware of its use. Research shows that when individuals watch humor by themselves and hear laughter in their headsets, they smile. However, when a mirror is placed in the room, they become aware of what is happening, and are not influenced by the laughter. As we noted earlier, being aware of what is happening around you is the first step in defending yourself from manipulation.

Second, we are susceptible to social proof when we do not have knowledge about the topic or issue at hand. Keeping the topic of canned laughter in mind, research indicates that people who are "high expressives" and "high laughers" (people who admit that they like to laugh and pay attention to comedy) are less likely to be affected by canned laughter than people who pay very little attention to humor.[46] The fact that knowledge is important should be obvious: A person who watches and records lots of comedy, reads a good deal of humor, and has practiced writing comedy scripts is going to have a well-developed belief system concerning what is "good," "average," and "poor" quality humor. Such a person would judge a television show, movie, or advertisement on the basis of his/her own view of humor—s/he would "know" good humor when she s/he hears it, and would be more resistant to the influence of others.

Our tipping behavior, consumer behavior, and behavior in public can be affected by the people around us. Even our evaluation of the performance of others can be affected by "social proof." During summer school one year at Michigan State University, Hocking, Margreiter, and Hylton[47] had the students in a persuasion course infiltrate a local campus bar on Thursday evenings. On certain nights, these persuasion students provided positive feedback by screaming and yelling enthusiastically. On certain other nights, however, the thirty students provided negative feedback—

they acted bored and sat quietly while the live band was playing.

On the same nights, another group of students, from an introductory course, went to the bar to work on an assignment to observe the nonverbal behavior of couples in public contexts. The instructor of this course required the students to attend the bar on certain nights—some went on the nights that the persuasion students gave positive feedback, others went on the nights of the negative feedback. These students returned to class later with completed code sheets concerning the nonverbal behaviors of couples. When they turned in these sheets, the students were given a questionnaire, which asked them questions about what it was like to participate in empirical research (the university was interested at the time in whether too much research was being conducted, and wanted to know students' opinions regarding their experiences). Hocking, et al., embedded three questions into this questionnaire: How long did you stay at the bar? On a scale of 0 to 10, how good was this band? On a scale of 0 to 10, would you like to see this band again?

Since the students in the introductory course were not aware of what was happening, and since we can expect that *most* of the students were not experts about the quality of bands, the expectation is that the behavior of persuasion students would act as a form of social proof, affecting the freshmen's opinions of the band—if people are screaming approval, the band must be good. The results, presented in Table 10.4, bear out this effect. When positive feedback was presented, students stayed longer in the bar, and rated the band as a better band than those students who attended on nights when negative feedback was provided.

Another good example of the social proof principle can be seen in research on littering. Cialdini, Kallgren, and Reno[48] conducted a series of experiments concerning the frequency by which individuals litter, based on the environment and actions of others. They discuss a *focus model of normative conduct* that basically argues that people scan the environment to see what norms apply to the situation at hand. There are two types of norms that might operate to guide a person's public behavior. First, a *descriptive norm* deals with a person's perceptions about what everyone is doing in a particular setting (that is, "What is the normal thing to do here? What do people do in this situation?"). Second, an *injunctive norm* deals with the perception of what more people approve or disapprove of in the particular situation (that is, "What is the morally correct, appropriate thing to do in this situation?").

If we see that many people have littered parking structures and parking lots, we naturally come to believe that people typically (normatively) litter in this area (descriptive norm). In this particular setting, if we found an advertisement on the window of our car, how likely is it that we would litter by throwing the paper on the ground? Obviously, the more trash and litter around, the more likely we are to add our own to it. However, the injunctive norm operates in the opposite direction—making us believe that we *ought not* litter. Three environmental factors can affect the activation of the injunctive norm:

(1) You enter into an absolutely clean area and you see *one* spot that someone has befouled, ruined, or placed graffiti on. You are offended because you believe that this should not have happened.

(2) You enter an area that is swept clean, yet you observe a person littering in your presence. You are offended because you believe that this person should not litter in the area others clean and show respect for.

(3) You enter an area and witness another person (or group of people) picking up trash and placing

_T A B L E_ **_1 0 . 4_**			

Evaluation of a Rock and Roll Band as a Function of Intra-Audience Feedback

Reactions?	*Negative Feedback*	*Positive Feedback*	*Significant Difference?*
Number of minutes stayed?	127.73	156.25	Yes
Overall quality of band?*	6.73	7.90	Yes
Will see this band again?*	5.96	7.42	Weak

*The possible range was 0 to 10, with higher scores representing more favorable evaluations.
Adapted from: J. E. Hocking, D.G. Margreiter, and C. Hylton, "Intra-audience Effects: A Field Test," *Human Communication Research*, vol. 3 (1977), pp. 243–249. Reprinted with permission.

it into nearby trash bins, prompting you to think that this really is what *ought to* happen when a person sees trash where it doesn't belong.

Further, a *personal norm against littering* may operate in any number of situations. Some individuals are less likely to litter because they grew up committed to environmental causes (see above concerning commitment); perhaps achieving Eagle Scout status, in part because of an interest in the environment, and so on. Such people generally (but not always) litter less than others.

In one of their experiments, adults at an amusement park were handed a leaflet that said, "Don't Miss Tonight's Show," just as they turned a corner and walked down a 60-yard pathway. Here, the experimenters altered the environmental cues by allowing the pathway to be completely clean (0 leaflets visible), or littered—by 1 discarded leaflet, 2 discarded leaflets, 4 discarded leaflets, 8 discarded leaflets or 16 discarded leaflets (all other litter had been removed). When did the

adults toss away their leaflets? As indicated in the top panel in Figure 10.1, 40 percent of the adults littered when there was plenty of other litter around (informing them that there was a descriptive norm, "this is what people do"). Further, when there was little or no littering, the percentage of adults littering was 18 percent (0 trash), 20 percent (2 pieces of trash), and 23 percent (4 pieces of trash). However, look what happened when there was one leaflet on the 60-yard pathway (see Figure 10.1).When there was only one piece of trash, fewer adults littered (10 percent). Seeing a pathway befouled by one piece of trash activated an injunctive ("people should *not* do this"), and people refrained from adding their leaflets to the pathway.

Even more dramatic results occurred in a similar project in a dormitory mailroom. On some occasions, individuals would enter the mailroom and find it clean. At other times, the mailroom was filthy—it was "fully littered" with papers and discarded handbills, along with a hollowed-out watermelon rind heel. However, the experimenters further constructed a third environment—the room was clean, except for one piece of very noticeable trash: the watermelon rind. The experimenters placed in each person's mailbox a public service handbill. How many of the occupants discarded the handbill by littering, given these three environments? As the bottom panel indicates, 10.7 percent of the occupants littered a clean room, and the percent jumped to 26.7 percent when the room was fully littered. However, when a person spied a beautiful room befouled by one watermelon rind, the percentage of litterers dropped to 3.6.

These experiments on littering are excellent examples of the power of the social proof principle. When we are uncertain as to how to behave, we scan the environment to know how to behave. When the descriptive norm is activated, we do what we believe is typical for the situation ("everyone else litters here"). Under very specific situations, however, we scan the environment (clean but for one foul piece of trash, we see someone picking up trash—see Cialdini, et al.), and an injunctive norm is activated ("people should do X and not Y"); and people in public are *less likely* to litter.

Scarcity

The scarcity principle is simply this: *Opportunities to engage in some behavior or to own some object appear to be more valuable when the opportunity is limited or restricted in some way.* There are three ways in which our behavior is shaped by this scarcity principle: the desirability of scarce objects, planned scarcity, and restricted freedom. The first two are easy to describe. First, people are willing to spend more money on "one of a kind" objects that they will own and that no one else can own. Rare baseball cards, first-edition books, coins or stamps with printing errors, and so forth, become increasingly more valuable as their rarity increases.

Given that scarce objects will fetch higher prices, it should not be surprising to see that marketers actually *plan* shortages of certain desirable products so that customers will pay more for the hard-to-find objects. At Christmas, some dolls, video games, race car sets, and many other products are frequently advertised, but a shortage of the items means that more parents are looking for the products than there are products available. Unfortunately, some parents are unaware of this ploy, and promise their children the desirable products, but then cannot find them. Parents are willing to pay more for the object at Christmas. However, if they still cannot find the desired object by Christmas, they will give the child some other toys or objects, but amazingly, there are plenty of the desired products in January and February—and the children remind their parents of their promise to give them the object. Note that simply making any object scarce does not necessarily make it more desirable. For this overall ploy to work effectively, it is important that the person must first desire the object; then when the chance of owning the object is threatened or becomes limited, the desire for the object *increases.*

Recall our discussion of ethics in Chapter 1. We talked about the importance of the receiver's ability to resist influence. When solicitors or salespersons intentionally withhold information or intentionally mislead the receiver into thinking that objects are scarce, we are confronted with a violation of ethical principles. When a salesperson states, "This is the last blue blazer in this style," the implication is that if we do not buy the blazer today (or put it on layaway) we will lose the freedom to buy the object. Yet, how are we to know that the blue blazer is, in truth, the last one in the store? It is easy for any person to exploit the scarcity principle and cheat people. Consider this ploy: A person rebuilds cars, and sells the cars for

SOCIAL PROOF AND LITTERING

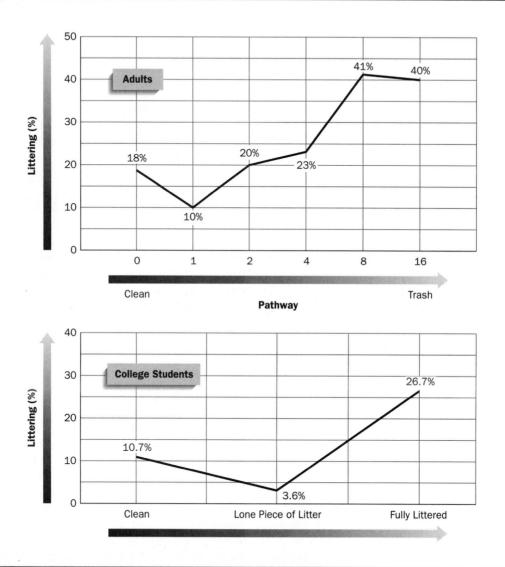

Top Panel: Percent of adults at an amusement park littering when pathway was clean, or containing various pieces of trash; Bottom Panel: Percent of college students littering the mailroom in dormitory complex when mailroom was clean, containing one piece of trash or when fully littered.
From: R.B. Cialdini, C.A. Kallgren, and R.R. Reno, "A Focus Theory of Normative Conduct: A Theoretical Refinement and Reevaluation of the Role of Norms in Human Behavior," in M.P. Zanna, ed., *Advances in Experimental Social Psychology* (New York: Academic Press, 1991), pp. 201-234. Used with permission of authors and Acadmic Press.

a profit. When a potential buyer comes by, the seller already has it arranged for a cousin to show up after the potential buyer has arrived to look at the car. The cousin appears to be another bidder for the car, and if the potential buyer desires to buy the car, the fact that another bidder is present poses a threat to his access to owning the car, and increases both the likelihood of his buying the car, and paying a higher price. Ploys such as these occur with some frequency, and they are unethical because of the deception involved.

A final application of this principle deals with *restricted freedom*. When people have freedom to buy and own guns, lighter fluid, cigarettes, liquor, phosphate-based laundry detergent, disposable diapers, and so forth, and this freedom is threatened, people will fight, take political action, and demand that the freedom be reinstated. They will fight even more vigorously if they believe that their freedom to act is *unjustifiably* threatened. Studies have found that parents can *cause* their children to fall more *in love* with their high school lovers by trying to restrict their teenager's behavior.[49] In another area, voters appeared willing to vote out members of the city council after members of the city council voted unilaterally to ban certain types of laundry soaps.[50]

F O O T N O T E S

1. D.J. Canary and M.J. Cody, *Interpersonal Communication: A Goals Approach* (New York: St. Martin's Press, 1994).

2. J.P. Dillard, ed., *Seeking Compliance: The Production of Interpersonal Influence Messages* (Scottsdale, Ariz.: Gorsuch Scarisbrick, 1990).

3. M.L. Knapp and A.L. Vangelisti, *Interpersonal Communication and Human Relationships* (Boston: Allyn and Bacon, 1992).

4. R.B. Cialdini, *Influence.* (New York: Quill, 1984).

5. R.R. Blake, M. Rosenbaum, and R.A. Duryea, "Gift-buying as a Function of Group Standards," *Human Relations*, vol. 8 (1955), pp. 61-73.

6. Cialdini, *Influence.*

7. P. Brickman, D. Coates, and R. Janoff-Bulman, "Lottery Winners and Accident Victims: Is Happiness Relative?" *Journal of Personality and Social Psychology*, vol. 36 (1978), pp. 917-927.

8. D.T. Kenrick and S.E. Gutierres, "Contrast Effects and Judgments of Physical Attractiveness: When Beauty Becomes a Social Problem," *Journal of Personality and Social Psychology*, vol. 38 (1980), pp. 131-140.

9. R. E. Knox and J.A. Inkster, "Postdecisional Dissonance at Post Time," *Journal of Personality and Social Psychology*, vol. 8 (1968), pp. 319-323.

10. J.L. Freedman and S.C. Fraser, "Compliance Without Pressure: The Foot-in-the-Door Technique," *Journal of Personality and Social Psychology*, vol. 4 (1966), pp. 195-202.

11. D. J. Bem, "Self-perception Theory," in L. Berkowitz, ed., *Advances in Experimental Social Psychology*, vol. 6 (New York: Academic Press, 1972), p. 2.

12. W. DeJong, "An Examination of Self-perception Mediation of the Foot-in-the-Door Effect," *Journal of Personality and Social Psychology*, vol. 37 (1979), pp. 2221-2239.

13. J.P. Dillard, J.E. Hunter, and M.J. Burgoon, "Sequential-request Persuasive Strategies: Meta-analysis of Foot-in-the-Door and Door-in-the-Face," *Human Communication Research*, vol. 10 (1984), pp. 461-488.

14. A.L. Beaman, C.M. Cole, M. Preston, B. Klentz, and N.M. Steblay, "Fifteen Years of Foot-in-the-Door Research: A Meta-Analysis," *Personality and Social Psychology Bulletin*, vol. 9 (1983), pp. 181-196.

15. DeJong, "An Examination of Self-perception Mediation of the Foot-in-the-Door Effect."

16. A.A. Cann, S.J. Sherman, and R. Elkes, "Effects of Initial Request Size and Timing of a Second Request on Compliance: The Foot in the Door and the Door in the Face," *Journal of Personality and Social Psychology*, vol. 32 (1975), pp. 774-782.

17. C. Seligman, M. Bush, and K. Kirsch, "Relationship Between Compliance in the Foot-in-the-Door Paradigm and Size of First Request," *Journal of Personality and Social Psychology*, vol. 33 (1976), pp. 517-520.

18. R.B. Cialdini and K. Ascani, "Test of a Concession Procedure for Inducing Verbal, Behavioral, and Further Compliance with a Request to Give Blood," *Journal of Applied Psychology*, vol. 61 (1976), pp. 295-300.

19. R.B. Cialdini, J.T. Cacioppo, R. Basset, and J.A. Miller, "The Lowball Procedure for Producing Compliance: Commitment Then Cost," *Journal of Personality and Social Psychology*, vol. 36 (1978), pp. 463-476.

20. M. Zuckerman, M. M. Lazzaro, and D. Waldgeir, "Undermining Effects of the Foot-in-the-Door

Technique with Extrinsic Reward," *Journal of Applied Social Psychology*, vol. 9 (1979), pp. 292-296.

21. A.L. Beaman, N.M. Steblay, M. Preston, and B. Klentz, "Compliance as a Function of Elapsed Time Between First and Second Requests," *Journal of Social Psychology*, vol. 128 (1988), pp. 233-243.

22. R.M. Tipton and S. Browning, "Altruism: Reward or Punishment," *Journal of Psychology*, vol. 80 (1972), pp. 319-322.

23. R.E. Kraut, "Effects of Social Labeling on Giving to Charity," *Journal of Experimental and Social Psychology*, vol. 9 (1973), pp. 551-562.

24. D.L. Paulhus, D.R. Shaffer, and L.L. Downing, "Effects of Making Blood Donor Motives Salient Upon Donor Retention: A Field Experiment," *Personality and Social Psychology Bulletin*, vol. 3 (1977), pp. 99-102.

25. R.A. Reeves, R.M. Macolini, and R.C. Martin, "Legitimizing Paltry Contributions: On-the-Spot vs. Mail-in Requests," *Journal of Applied Social Psychology*, vol. 17 (1987), pp. 731-738; also see Kraut, "Effects of Social Labeling," and Paulhus, Shaffer, and Downing, "Effects of Making Blood Donor Motives Salient upon Donor Retention."

26. M. Goldman, O. Kiyohara, and D.A. Pfannensteil, "Interpersonal Touch, Social Labeling, and the Foot-in-the-Door Effect," *Journal of Social Psychology*, vol. 125 (1984), pp. 143-147.

27. D.J. Howard, "The Influence of Verbal Responses to Common Greetings on Compliance Behaviors: The Foot-in-the-Mouth Effect," *Journal of Applied Social Psychology*, vol. 20 (1990), pp. 1185-1196.

28. Reeves, Macolini, and Martin, "Legitimizing Paltry Contributions."

29. R.B. Cialdini and D.A. Schroeder, "Increasing Compliance by Legitimizing Paltry Contributions: When Even a Penny Helps," *Journal of Personality and Social Psychology*, vol. 34 (1976), pp. 599-604.

30. Kraut, "Effects of Social Labeling."

31. Cialdini, Cacioppo, Basset, and Miller, "The Lowball Procedure."

32. Cialdini, *Influence*.

33. Cialdini, *Influence*.

34. D.J. Canary and M.J. Cody, *Interpersonal Communication: A Goals Approach*. (New York: St. Martin's Press).

35. Cialdini and Ascani, "A Test of a Concession Procedure."

36. M. Even-Chen, Y. Yinon, and A. Bizman, "The Door-in-the-Face Technique: Effects of the Size of the Initial Request," *European Journal of Psychology*, vol. 8 (1978), pp. 135-140.

37. Dillard, et. al., "Sequential-Request Persuasive Strategies."

38. J.M. Burger, "Increasing Compliance by Improving the Deal: The That's-Not-All Technique," *Journal of Personality and Social Psychology*, vol. 51 (1986), pp. 277-283.

39. E. E. Jones and C. Wortman, *Ingratiation: An Attributional Approach*, (Morristown, N.J.: General Learning Press, 1973), p. 2.

40. D. J. Schneider and A. C. Eustis, "Effects of Ingratiation Motivation, Target Positiveness and Revealingness on Self-presentation," *Journal of Personality and Social Psychology*, vol. 22 (1972), pp. 149-155.

41. H. A. Michener, J. G. Plazewski, and J. J. Vaske, "Ingratiation Tactics Channeled by Target Values and Threat Capability," *Journal of Personality*, vol. 47 (1979), pp. 35-56.

42. Jones and Wortman, *Ingratiation: An Attributional Approach*, p. 9.

43. D. Kipnis and R. Vanderveer, "Ingratiation and the Use of Power," *Journal of Personality and Social Psychology*, vol. 17 (1971), pp. 280-286.

44. Cialdini, *Influence*.

45. See G.C. Cupchik and H. Leventhal, "Consistency Between Expressive Behavior and the Evaluation of Humorous Stimuli: The Role of Sex and Self-observation," *Journal of Personality and Social Psychology*, vol. 30 (1974), pp. 429-442; H. Leventhal and G.C. Cupchik, "The Informational and Facilitative Effects of an Audience upon Expression and Evaluation of Humorous Stimuli," *Journal of Experimental Social Psychology*, vol. 11 (1975), pp. 363-380; H. Leventhal and G.C. Cupchik, "A Process Model of Humor Judgement," *Journal of Communication*, vol. 26 (1976), pp. 190-204; H. Leventhal and W. Mace, "The Effect of Laughter on Evaluation of a Slapstick Movie," *Journal of Personality*, vol. 38 (1970), pp. 16-30.

46. See citations in footnote 45.

47. J.E. Hocking, D.G. Margreiter, and Cal Hylton, "Intra-audience Effects: A Field Test," *Human Communication Research*, vol. 3 (1977), pp. 243-249.

48. R.B. Cialdini, C.A. Kallgren, and R.R. Reno, "A Focus Theory of Normative Conduct: A Theoretical Refinement and Re-evaluation of the Role of Norms in Human Behavior," in M.P. Zanna, ed., *Advances in Experimental Social Psychology*, vol. 24 (1991), pp. 202-235.

49. R. Driscoll, K.E. Davies, and M.E. Lipetz, "Parental Interference and Romantic Love: The Romeo and Juliet Effect," *Journal of Personality and Social Psychology*, vol. 24 (1972), pp. 1-10.

50. M.B. Mazis, "Antipollution Measures and Psycho-

logical Reactance Theory: A Field Experiment," *Journal of Personality and Social Psychology*, vol. 31 (1975), pp. 654-666.

KEY TERMS AND CONCEPTS

compliance
social influence
anchoring and contrast effects
adaptation level
commitment
Foot-in-the-Door
self-perception process
altruism
social legitimization
lowball
reciprocity
verbal/behavioral compliance
Door-in-the-Face
reciprocal concessions
"That's Not All You Get"
ingratiation
social proof rule
scarcity principle

PERSUASION IN CONFLICT MANAGEMENT

OUTLINE

It is often said that "Conflict is a growth industry."[1] By "conflict" we mean a situation in which two or more individuals or parties have different goals, but must work together in order to achieve their goals. Conflicts involve nations, organizations, families, friends, and strangers. Most of us have had a conflict with family members or roommates about spending money, where to go on vacation, the rights and privileges of staying up late, making noise, using the car, and so on. Persuasion plays an important part in successful conflict management.

The four most common forms of conflict management are negotiation, mediation, arbitration, and litigation. *Negotiation* is a communication situation in which two or more individuals or parties make a series of concessions in order to forge a mutually agreed-upon settlement. In *mediation* a third party "mediates" or "manages" the communication so the disputants can create their own settlement. *Arbitration* typically involves the disputants agreeing to have a neutral third party (a judge, expert, council, and so forth) hear each side and then make a decision to resolve the dispute. Finally, *litigation* means that lawyers, representing the parties, make arguments on behalf of their clients, and then a jury or judge makes a ruling. Of these four forms of conflict management, negotiation is both the most common and the one social scientists have studied most thoroughly. Thus, much of this chapter focuses on how bargainers use persuasive tactics and arguments when involved in the process of negotiating. This chapter also reviews theoretic perspectives on bargaining research and skills for successful conflict management.

DEFINITION AND KEY TERMS

"Bargaining" is used synonymously with "negotiating" in this chapter. While some authors distinguish between the terms, the distinctions are not consistent and the terms are used interchangeably in everyday conversation and in the media.[2] Therefore, *bargaining* or *negotiating* is a communicative process between interdependent parties with differing goals who are attempting to produce a joint decision. Important phrases to note in the definition are: (1) communicative process, (2) interdependent parties, (3) differing goals, and (4) joint decision.

The flow of communication in bargaining is a *process* because each message impacts upon the determination of the final decision. Thomas C. Schelling explains the function of communication in bargaining as: "To discover patterns of individual behavior that make each player's actions predictable to the other; they have to test each other for a shared sense of patterns or regularity, and to exploit . . . impromptu codes for signalling intentions and for responding to each other's signals."[3] That is, once it has been delivered, a bargaining message (verbal or nonverbal) has an immediate effect on negotiations by influencing the perceptions and expectations of the involved parties.

The parties are *interdependent* because neither can obtain its desired outcome without the other. A car salesperson needs a customer and the customer needs the salesperson. If the buyer can achieve the goal of having access to a car by borrowing one from a friend, there would be no interdependence between the car dealer and the buyer and, consequently, no reason to bargain.

By the phrase *"differing goals"* we mean that bargaining occurs in a conflict situation. How the conflict is managed can lead to either cooperative or competitive bargaining. Cooperative bargaining reflects a problem-solving orientation. The parties recognize their areas of disagreement and then work for creative solutions to the problem(s). Cooperative bargaining is called "win-win" or "integrative" bargaining. The integrative bargaining situation can be dealt with through cooperative tactics which facilitate problem solving, such as the promotion of information exchange and brain-storming for alternative solutions.

Competitive, or distributive, bargaining is a win-lose situation. What is won by Party A is lost by Party B.[4] Distributive bargaining occurs when the parties' fundamental interests are in conflict and there is a genuine scarcity of resources. Competition is communicated by withholding information about one's own preferences while attempting to persuade the opponent to modify his or her preferences. Thus, the bargaining messages operate as offensive or defensive strategies designed to secure outcomes.

The final component of the definition is *joint decision*. The parties have determined a way to manage their differing goals and have committed themselves, and their constituents, to act in a prescribed manner. The decision must have mutual consent so that each party has a stake in the outcome, and, consequently, is dedicated to its fulfillment.

Bargaining Structure

While bargaining situations and research methods vary tremendously, a few common terms describe the structure of bargaining.[5] For simplicity, we will use an example of a buyer and seller in an antique shop. They are negotiating over the price of a rolltop desk. The seller needs a minimum of $2,000 to break even on his investment. The buyer is knowledgeable about antiques and knows she can buy a comparable desk for $3,000. The *resistance point* in bargaining is the maximum amount a party will concede. For the seller, $2,000 is his resistance point because any greater concession means an investment loss and he would be better off to wait for another customer. The buyer's resistance point is $3,000. At that price she knows that she can leave the shop and buy a similar desk at or below her resistance point. The difference between the buyer's and seller's resistance points is the *bargaining range*. As long as the

bargaining range includes a common point, a negotiated settlement is possible. However, if the buyer's resistance point was $2,000 and the seller's point was $3,000 then no agreement would be possible because there is no common range between resistance points. In cases where parties cannot reach an agreement and cease bargaining, they are said to return to their *status quo point*.

Even though each bargainer has a resistance point which determines the possible negotiated settlements, each also has an *aspiration level* which is a realistic preferred outcome. The buyer would like to purchase the desk for as little as possible, but realistically she knows that $2,250 is about as low as the seller will go. The seller knows that $2,750 is as much as a buyer is likely to spend. Because each party has an aspiration level which falls within the bargaining range, a settlement that approximates the aspiration levels, but does not violate either resistance point, is possible. The resistance point, status quo point, and aspiration level comprise a bargainer's *utility schedule*. An example of this structure is provided in Box 11.1.

Prisoner's Dilemma

Not all negotiation research employs monetary situations, such as the buyer-seller example. Matrix games that allow bargainers two options, generally, to cooperate or to compete, are used extensively in laboratory research. The most famous of the matrix games is Prisoner's Dilemma. The game situation is presented below.[6]

Two suspects are taken into custody and separated. The district attorney is certain that they are guilty of a specific crime, but s/he does not have adequate evidence to convict them at a trial. S/he points out to each prisoner that each has two alternatives: to confess to the crime that the police are sure they have done, or to not confess. If they both do not confess, then the district attorney states that s/he will book

---

BOX 11.1

STRUCTURE OF BARGAINING

A sale value of $2,000 represents the seller's *resistance point*.	$2,000
	2,100
The buyer's *aspiration level* is a realistic desired purchase	2,200
price of $2,250.	2,250
	2,300
	2,400
	2,500
	2,600
The seller's *aspiration level* is $2,750 and is a realistic retail price.	2,700
	2,750
	2,800
	2,900
The buyer's *resistance point* is $3,000.	3,000

She will go no higher in purchasing the desk.

An antique dealer has a rolltop desk to sell. He needs $2,000 to break even and he would like to receive $2,750. The buyer wants to purchase a rolltop desk. After inquiring in various shops, she knows that $3,000 is the most she should pay. However, she would prefer to pay $2,250. Since the *bargaining range* includes points between the resistance points, a negotiated settlement is possible.

---

them on some very minor trumped-up charge such as petty larceny and illegal possession of a weapon, and they will both receive minor punishment; if they both confess they will be prosecuted, but s/he will recommend less than the most severe sentence; but if one confesses and the other does not, then the confessor will receive lenient treatment for turning state's evidence whereas the latter will get "the book" slapped at him/her.

In terms of years in a penitentiary, the strategic problem might reduce to the situation depicted in Figure 11.1 at right.

FIGURE 11.1

PRISONER'S DILEMMA MATRIX

	Prisoner 2's Choice	
Not Confess	1 year each	10 years for prisoner 1 and 3 months for prisoner 2
Confess	3 months for prisoner 1 and 10 years for prisoner 2	8 years each

This bargaining situation is called *mixed motive* because the bargainers have the option to cooperate or to compete. The cooperative choice is the "not confess" because it has the minimum sentence for an opponent, either one year or three months depending on the opponent's move. The "confess" move is competitive since it gives the opponent either ten or eight years in prison. Also, exploitation of the other prisoner occurs if prisoner 1 confesses and prisoner 2 does not confess.

One reason for the extensive use of the PD game is that it provides researchers a clear and concise bargaining situation from which they can go on to test various bargaining conditions and influences. A very abbreviated list of the topics that have been investigated using the PD game includes: the availability of communication channels, the amount of trust between opponents, demographic characteristics, personality traits, the number of issues to be bargained, and power differences.[7]

This section defines bargaining, identifies key terminology, and explains a common bargaining matrix game. It is important to be familiar with these terms as they are used throughout the chapter.

NEGOTIATION RESEARCH PERSPECTIVES

Perspectives on negotiation research vary according to research goals, methods, and selection of variables. Many of the variables are elements of the bargaining structure. *Structural analyses* examine the distribution of power and studies the relationship between reward strategies, such as promises and bargaining outcomes. *Integrative analyses* have a developmental orientation and examine what happens over time. *Strategic analyses* employ game theory and matrix games to analyze how predetermined utilities and options influence bargainers' decision making. *Process analyses* study the link between concession making and outcomes. *Behavioral analyses* examine bargainers' goals, personality traits, and predispositions.[8]

The preceding analyses identify topical areas of communication, but do not address the philosophical assumptions about the function of communication in negotiation. Putnam and Roloff suggest two approaches for classifying the treatment of communication in negotiation research: *effects* and *key components*.[9]

Effects Models

The effects approach studies how communication affects negotiated outcomes. The effects may be classified as independent, mediating, moderating, or limited.

An *independent effects* model predicts that communication directly impacts the outcome, regardless of any psychological, social, or cultural variable. An example of a hypothesis for an independent effects model is: "Harm arguments produce greater monetary settlements than justifications or responsibility arguments."

The *mediating effects* model predicts causal relationships between psychological, social, and cultural variables and specific communicative behaviors ultimately affecting the negotiated outcome. For example, Bertram I. Spector administered personality profile questionnaires to students who volunteered to role play negotiators in a simulated business bargaining scenario. The results showed that negotiators with different personality profiles employed very different bargaining strategies. Some of the relationships between personality types and bargaining strategy selection are listed below:[10]

1. Highly cooperative bargainers who agreed to share their payoff with the other side were motivated by self-oriented needs for social approval and emotional support rather than outgoing needs for cooperation and friendship.

2. Altruistic bargainers who transferred payoffs that could have been theirs to the opposing side were motivated by defeatist and harm-approaching needs.

3. Bargainers who bluffed and deceived were motivated by needs for play, seduction, cleverness, and exhibitionism.

4. Hostile bargainers who employed elements of coercion were motivated by the mirror-image hostility of their opponents.

In contrast to the mediating effects model, the *moderating effects* model does not assume a direct, causal relationship between personality, social and cultural variables, communicative behavior, and the negotiated outcome. At best, communication is seen as a variable that affects outcomes only under certain conditions. For example, threats and promises are more effective when they are perceived as being credible. In some cultures, language intensity is one way of communicating credibility. A moderating effects model hypothesis would be: "Threats and promises communicated through intense language are more effective within cultures that consider intense language an indicator of credibility."[11]

Finally, the *limited effects* model treats communication as noise or error that contaminates bargaining outcomes. This perspective is used to design laboratory studies, often by mathematicians or game theorists, and commonly employs a strategic analysis perspective. In a typical limited effects study, researchers give participants information about a bargaining situation, their opponent, and the payoff schedule. Participants imagine themselves as bargainers and report to the researchers their proposed strategy. Seldom does any give-and-take negotiation occur, and if it does, it is through writing. The limited effects model offers insight to bargaining inputs, but cannot explain adequately what happens in the negotiation process.

Key Components

Fisher classifies communication research into four perspectives based on treatments of the components of the communication model: sender, receiver, message, channel, and transmission. The perspectives are mechanistic, psychological, interpretive-symbolic, and system-interactional.[12] From the mechanistic perspective, communication is the transmission of a message through a channel. Bargaining research conducted within a mechanistic perspective examines the availability and method of communication between parties. Early research found that face-to-face interactions prompted more cooperative moves than audio, written, or video messages. Bargainers felt that face-to-face communication was more spontaneous, informal, and reciprocal. Audio interactions, however, were described as impersonal and task-oriented.[13] A recent research program directed by speech communication professor Dr. M. Scott Poole at the University of Minnesota investigates how computers and other new technologies (such as video conferencing) impact negotiations. Poole, et al., summarize twenty-eight propositions about media impacts on negotiation (see Box 11.2).[14]

The psychological perspective focuses on communication as information processing. That is, researchers vary the bargaining message as to its accuracy, completeness, ambiguity, and so forth, and then interpret the results for effects upon the orientation and expectations of bargainers. The mechanistic and psychological perspectives are appropriate theoretical frameworks for mediating and moderating effects models.

The interpretive-symbolic perspective is used often by scholars conducting non-laboratory negotiation research. This perspective focuses on the creation of meaning between bargainers. Meaning is jointly constructed within the situational and cultural constraints of the relationship. From an interpretive perspective, labor-management contract negotiations are not isolated com-

---

BOX 11.2

SUMMARY OF PROPOSITIONS OF MEDIA IMPACTS ON NEGOTIATION

Impact	Findings	Is Impact Beneficial or Harmful?
1. Surfaces existing conflicts	text, audio, levels 1,2>ftf	Beneficial, if conflict managed effectively
2. Conflict intensity	text, level 1>ftf	Beneficial within bounds; harmful if too intense
3. Creates "we-they" oppositions	text, audio, video >ftf	Harmful
4. More negative emotional expression	text, level 1>ftf (mixed results)	Beneficial if managed properly; harmful if it polarizes conflict
5. Reduction of status differences	text, audio >ftf (mixed results)	Beneficial
6. Anonymous expression of ideas and opinions	level 1, level 2 permit this	Beneficial
7. Provides time for reflection	text (especially asynchronous) permits this	Beneficial
8. Slows down negotiation	text, level 1,2 >	Beneficial if it leads to reflection; harmful if it frustrates
9. Reduces time spent on listening	text > ftf; video promotes listening	Harmful
10. Physically demanding and tiring	this holds for audio	Harmful
11. Clarifies procedures	level 1, level 2 > ftf	Beneficial
12. Facilitates work on complex tasks	video, level 1,2 ftf > audio (mixed results)	Beneficial
13. Provides a common focus	level 1,2, text, video, audio	Beneficial
14. Enables work on a common document	level 1,2, text permits this	Beneficial

15. Encourages rigid positions	text can do this	Harmful
16. Increases number of ideas considered	level 1,2 > ftf	Beneficial
17. Provides models for generating solutions	level 2 > level 1 ftf	Beneficial
18. Detailed analysis of solutions	asynchronous text may discourage it	Beneficial
19. Commitment to solutions	level 1 > ftf (mixed results)	Beneficial
20. Opinion change	audio > ftf; video > ftf (mixed results)	Beneficial
21. Stronger case wins out	audio > ftf	Beneficial
22. Personal expression	ftf > text, audio, level 1	Beneficial if expression is about needs; harmful if it personalizes conflict
23. Accuracy of impressions	equal for all media	Beneficial
24. Counteracts negative climate	text, audio, level 1,2 > ftf	Beneficial
25. Positive emotional	level 1,2 > ftf	Beneficial
26. Balance participation	video > ftf; level 1, 2, text (mixed results)	Beneficial
27. Perceived to be best by laypersons	ftf > all other media	Beneficial
28. Amount of gain in negotiation	audio > level 1 (mixed results; usually no difference)	Beneficial

Level 1: computer provides technical assistance—vote counting.
Level 2: computer suggests techniques to better structure deliberations.

Source: M.S. Poole, D.L. Shannon, and G. De Sanctis, "Communication on Media and Negotiation Processes," in L.L. Putnam and M.E. Roloff, eds., *Communication and Negotiation* (Newbury Park, Calif.: Sage) pp. 46–66. Reprinted with permission of the authors and Sage Publications, Inc.

munication events. They are influenced by daily organizational practices and the parties' recollection of past contract negotiations. Consequently, the discourse exchanged at the table is more than just offers and counteroffers. Negotiators tell stories, relive dramas, make political statements, and create their own sense of organizational reality. Thus, negotiation facilitates organizational sense-making and shapes an organization's culture.[15]

Finally, the systems-interactional (also called the pragmatic) perspective examines bargaining messages as communicative acts with both relational and content dimensions. Content refers to the information contained in the message. What does the message say? The relational aspect considers how messages are connected to one another. Studies that code messages and then try to identify regularities of behavior exemplify the systems-interactional perspective.

Donohue, Diez, and Hamilton's Cue-Response Negotiation Coding System enables researchers to study both content and relational dimensions[16] (see Box 11.3). The content dimensions of the coding system classify messages as: attacking, defending, and integrating. For example, the content may attack the opponent's position, defend one's own position, or support some or all of the opponent's proposal. Attacking tactics are used to take the offensive by proposing discrediting changes in the opponent's position, or by proposing changes in the negotiator's position in order to undermine the opponent's level of aspiration. Defensive tactics are used to stabilize one's expected outcomes by either rejecting opponent's proposals, or supporting one's position without referring to any proposal of the opponent. Finally, integrating tactics accept opponent's modifications of the negotiator's position. They can reveal weakness or lack of faith in the negotiator's position as well as a willingness to concede in order to improve the proposed solution.

The relational dimension consists of cue and response tactics (hence the name of the system).

Each bargaining utterance is analyzed as a response to the opponent's prior utterance and as a cue to subsequent utterances. Consequently, the relational dimension focuses upon the impact of Party A's utterance on Party B's response, while taking into consideration the fact that Party A is responding to B's previous response.

Let's take a look at a few exchanges in a hypothetical bargaining encounter and see how they would be coded as cue responses.

BUYER: Looking at the price tag on the desk, "Considering the great number of desks in area antique shops, $3,000 is a lot of money for this desk."

[DEFENDING CUE: Substantiation]

SELLER: "Other antique dealers may have desks, but this one is in much better condition and is worth $3,000."

[ATTACKING RESPONSE: Assert Rights/Needs]

[ATTACKING CUE: Assert Proposal/Offer]

BUYER: "Some of the other desks may be in poor condition. . . ."

[INTEGRATING RESPONSE: Proposal Other Support]

"however, this one is not perfect and is not worth $3,000."

[DEFENDING CUE: Substantiation]

SELLER: "What flaws do you see?"

[INTEGRATING RESPONSE: Extension Question]
[DEFENDING CUE: Clarification Request]

Donohue, Diez, and Hamilton used the Cue-Response Negotiation Coding System to analyze labor-management contract negotiations in a major American communications company. They found union bargainers used an attacking strategy

BOX 11.3

CUE-RESPONSE NEGOTIATION CODING SYSTEM

Category Name	Category Definition
Responding Tactics: Attacking	
Deny fault with personal rejection	Challenging, disagreeing with, or rejecting the immediately preceding utterance accompanied with a rationale and personal affront
Topic change	Introduction of a new idea changing the direction of the interaction
Assert rights/needs	Statement that addresses requirements/ expectations consistent with prior subject area, clearly arguing for compliance
Responding Tactics: Defending	
Reject proposal	Challenging, disagreeing with, or rejecting any part of the other's proposal
Reject rationale/utterance	Challenging, disagreeing with, or rejecting the immediately preceding utterance that is not related to the proposal per se
Extension	Extending or continuing the topic in the immediately preceding utterance
Responding Tactics: Integrating	
Proposal other support	Giving agreement, assistance, acceptance, or approval to any part of the other's offer or proposal
Rationale/utterance other support	Giving agreement, assistance, acceptance, or approval to the immediately preceding utterance that is not related to the proposal, per se

Continued

| Extension question | An extension of the prior utterance's topic phrased in the interrogative form |
| Other | Any response not conforming to these category types |

Cueing Tactics: Attacking

Assert proposal/offer	Asking the other to accept specific modifications in the proposal under discussion
Change fault/responsibility	Attributing lack of good faith, incompetence, negligence; derogating something about the other
Decision	Positive structuring of the procedures for discussion

Cueing Tactics: Defending

Substantiation	Providing information or evidence supporting the speaker's own position
Clarification request	Asking for additional information
Deny relevance	Reject suggested structuring of the procedures suggested and/or assert the relevance of the issue/information raised by the other

Cueing Tactics: Integrating

Offer concession	An offer that is less than the speaker's immediately prior offer
Information concession	Offering less information than is requested
Conciliation/flexibility	Proposing flexibility in the speaker's position
Other	Any cue not conforming to these category specifications

From: W.A. Donohue, M.E. Diez, and M. Hamilton, "Coding Naturalistic Negotiation Interaction," *Human Communication Research*, vol. 10, no. 3 (1984), pp. 403-425. Reprinted with permission of the authors and ICA publications.

to respond to management attacks. Managers used integrating tactics in responding to labor attacks and then managers gave defending cues. These results do reflect the bargaining process in a natural setting. Generally, it is the union that is making demands for a change, hence, attacking the status quo. Management responds by either integrating desired changes within the status quo or by defending the system as it currently operates.

Here we show that negotiation research perspectives and philosophical assumptions about communication's role in conflict management interaction are very diverse. The next section breaks down the negotiation process and examines how different strategies and tactics affect negotiated outcomes.

BARGAINING STRATEGIES AND TACTICS

Message strategies and tactics can be thought of as a bargainer's game plan and plays, respectively. Each strategy is made up of specific communicative acts called tactics. The tactics examined below are: negotiation plans, prenegotiation accounts, arguments, threats, promises, commitments, initial bids, and size of concession rates. The importance of knowing the effects of various bargaining messages is twofold. First, bargaining messages reveal the attitude of the parties toward the bargaining. Second, the information exchanged through bargaining tactics discloses a party's utility schedule. Before discussing the research on message strategies and tactics, one needs to become familiar with two forms of bargaining tactics—explicit and tacit.

As the name implies, explicit bargaining messages are those in which the bargainer's intent is stated unequivocally. The message contains no "hidden" meanings. For example, "The rank and file will not ratify a contract without a cost-of-

living clause," is an explicit message. Tacit bargaining messages, however, use subtle nonverbal cues and other behaviors to communicate a bargainer's intentions without explicitly stating them. That is, a bargainer can use vocal intonations or strategic word choice to send a message with an implied meaning. To illustrate this point, consider the following sentence: "We could live with that arrangement." Using the word "could" rather than "will" implies a commitment without explicitly stating one. Thus, the message is tacit. Tacit bargaining messages are often used between chief negotiators when they are being observed by their constituents. The use of these messages allows the bargainers to communicate with each other at one level, but have the message interpreted differently by the constituents. The benefit to the bargainers is that they can be moving toward a settlement while not appearing to be making many concessions, thus, enabling them to appear "tough" to the constituents.

Negotiating Plans and Planning

As people prepare to negotiate they consider their goals and the obstacles to achieving them. Roloff and Jordon provide a thorough discussion of negotiation planning, negotiation goals, and the obstacles for each type of goal.[17] *Negotiation plans* are tactics that emerge from the strategic *negotiation planning* process. Specifically, negotiation plans are the actions that people create to overcome perceived obstacles to goal achievement. Negotiation planning is the process of creating a sequence of actions and anticipating the effects of those actions. Of course, not all actions are planned nor are all planned actions executed. Bargainers are more likely to expend planning effort when the goals are personally important or they anticipate difficulty in achieving their goals. Situational factors such as time pressures also interfere with bargainers' ability to plan. Negotiation planning can be adaptive, interactive, or collaborative. Adaptive planning includes alternative revisions of the plan. The initial plan is not abandoned, rather it is revised to replace the weak components. Adaptive planning may include lowering one's aspiration level, shifting from noncoercive to coercive tactics, and creating time pressures for the opponents. A less competitive adaptive planning process follows a problem-solving format. Negotiators begin with reasonable, yet challenging, commodity goals (discussed below) and work to create a variety of ways for achieving them.

Interactive planning is both an offensive and defensive strategy. This type of planning considers the needs, expectations, and desires of the opponent. Offensively, this allows a bargainer to engage in constructive counterplanning to develop alternatives to anticipated objections to the plan. Defensively, interactive planning enables a bargainer to create obstacles to block the opponent's goal achievement. When bargainers anticipate an opponent's position, they are better able to produce counterarguments. This finding is consistent with earlier persuasion research which found that individuals who create counterarguments prior to receiving a persuasive message are able to resist these influence attempts.

Collaborative planning differs from adaptive and interactive planning because the parties jointly construct the plan. This planning usually addresses only the procedural, rather than substantive, issues. Procedural issues include such items as meeting time and place, number of bargainers on each team, speaking turns, who is empowered to make concessions and agree to offers, and so forth. In formal negotiations, these prenegotiation collaborative planning sessions can aid in establishing a supportive problem-solving orientation which impacts the entire negotiation process.

Negotiation plans are an important factor in the planning process. Because of the complexity of negotiation encounters, bargainers often have multiple goals. Bargainers are concerned with resource gains, building a relationship that facilitates future interactions, and maintaining a positive sense of self. These concerns are classified as commodity, relational, and face goals.

Commodity goals refer to resources such as money, products, or services. Researchers have found that commodity goals with the following characteristics offer the most profitable results. First, the term "goals" should be defined as interests, not singular positions. Interests are the underlying motivation for engaging in negotiations. A manager may want to improve customer service. This interest can be met in a variety of ways: longer hours, better product, extended training, or more employees. Second, goals should be operationalized. If possible, specify a quantifiable range. This range helps to determine the utility schedule. Third, goals should be flexible when considering the type and number of commodities. Usually there are numerous ways of meeting commodity goals, and bargainers seldom know about all available resources prior to negotiation. Fourth, goals should be created to be challenging—goals to which one can remain committed. Bargainers who are not committed to their goals frequently make more concessions and receive lower payoffs. These bargainers lack the motivation necessary to sustain themselves during negotiations. This does not mean that all negotiations are stressful shouting matches; rather, negotiations that best meet the interests of all parties require dedication to working through the decision-making process.

Obstacles to obtaining commodity goals come from: (1) the bargainer's perceptions of the opponent; (2) the bargainer; and (3) pressures of the negotiation context. It is important to remember that negotiation plans are constructed prior to bargaining. Sometimes, the obstacles are assumed and may be based on incorrect perceptions. Preliminary data suggest that negotiators try to overcome opponent's perceived objections by advancing arguments about the legitimacy and value of their product, creating a positive relationship, setting high initial bids and then making concessions, or "logrolling" products together. At this time, scholars have not uncovered the relationship between commodity goal obstacles caused by the bargainer or the negotiation context and discursive tactics to overcome them.[18]

Relational goals are important in conflict situations when a productive relationship must be maintained between disputants: parent-child, husband-wife, employer-employee, and some customer-seller relationships. Relational goals are characterized by an altruistic concern for the relationship, concern for settlements that will work in the future and not just "in the here and now," and the maintenance/restoration of trust. Relational goals are difficult to achieve if bargainers do not like each other, have more attractive alternative relationships available, or perceive that they have little in common. Overcoming these obstacles requires verbal and nonverbal messages of friendliness, cooperative bargaining moves, expressions of similarity, and minimizing the attractiveness of alternative relationships.

Negotiation plans also include tactics to achieve *face goals*. Bargainers may have positive face goals that will maintain or restore positive self-image and opponent-image. Or negotiators can attack the opponent's image as a tactic to get him/her to feel responsible or guilty about negative consequences. Supportive face goals are difficult to obtain when negotiators have high accountability. R. J. Klimoski studied the effects of intragroup forces on intergroup conflict resolution in simulated labor-management negotiations. Accountability was defined as the potential for evaluation by the group. Accountability was manipulated in the following ways. In the no-evaluation condition, participants were told that because of time restrictions they would not meet with their bargaining team again. In the evaluation condition, the participants were told that they would report the bargaining results to their teams, and then the team members would vote as to whether

they would ever want this bargaining representative again. Klimoski found negotiators in the evaluation condition were more resistant to compromise than those in the no-evaluation condition. A concern to "look tough" caused bargainers to use contentious behavior attacking the self-image of the opponent. Thus, negotiator accountability and constituent pressure led to fewer concessions by the negotiator.[19]

Prenegotiation Accounts

Prenegotiation accounts are attempts to manage conflict before it happens. Bies studied the use of accounts in superior-subordinate relationships.[20] He suggests that the effectiveness of an account depends on the timing of delivery, perceived adequacy of the account, and perceived sincerity of the account giver. Bies offers three types of accounts that managers use to de-escalate subordinates' reactions to unfavorable resource allocation: causal, referential, and ideological. *Causal accounts* attempt to mitigate one's responsibility for an unfavorable outcome by placing the blame elsewhere. In car sales, the salesperson often disappears to get approval from the sales manager (whom you seldom see) for the negotiated price. If the sales manager rejects the price and counteroffers, the salesperson may offer a causal account that absolves him/herself from the rejection.

Referential accounts reframe the consequences of an undesirable outcome by referring to social, temporal, or aspirational factors. A bargainer may claim that other social groups have received similar poor outcomes. Temporal references suggest that this is not the time to expect such a favorable outcome. Aspirational references attempt to manipulate the opponent's perception of her/his alternatives.

Ideological accounts appeal to shared values, belief systems, or joint goals. These accounts function normatively to validate a person's decision. Strategically, an ideological account can be used to increase common ground and decrease perceived differences. Ideological accounts are difficult to use because the abstract values are not easily operationalized in contract language; negotiators have multiple value hierarchies, just as they have multiple goals; and espoused values may contradict values-in-practice.

Arguments, Arguing, and Arguers

Argumentation represents a distinguished tradition in the speech communication discipline. From its origins in ancient Greece to contemporary perspectives, argumentation theorists have studied the management of disagreements through human discourse. Since the mid-1980s, communication researchers have shown an interest in using argumentation theory to study conflict management, specifically message and source characteristics.

Message characteristics are studied in two ways. The first line of research uses rhetorical theory and debate pedagogy to define argument as discourse created by a speaker with the intent to persuade a listener to accept a particular course of action or way of thinking. Toulmin's model of argument (Chapter 8) informs much of this research. Researchers analyze negotiation discourse and identify types of claims, reasoning, and evidence. Putnam and colleagues conducted a series of studies of teacher-school board negotiations and found:

1. Argumentative form (types of claim, reasons, qualifiers) changes as issues are dropped, modified, or retained.[21]

2. When the parties had a history of creative problem solving, they used reasoning from analogy, cause, and hypothetical example, rather than "hard data" or "facts" as evidence.[22]

3. Argument selection is determined more by bargaining issue than by bargaining party or bargaining phase.[23]

4. Sub-issues change through shifting types of claims and by adding qualifiers rather than adding more information.[24]

An alternative method of studying bargaining arguments is to study the arguing process rather than argumentative statements. Donohue, et al., suggest negotiations are more like conversations than academic debates because of the emergent nature of argumentation.[25] Conversational argument theorists treat arguments as speech acts that emerge from interaction. "Conversational argument and influence are collaborative activities: influence is not something that a speaker does to an addressee, nor is a line of argument developed from the plan of a single speaker. These speech events are transpersonal structures that persons jointly produce."[26]

Several authors have used conversational argument theory to study linguistic characteristics of bargaining discourse.[27] Representative of this research is Donohue and Diez's study of directive and face saving.[28] Directives are requests for a hearer to do something. By definition, bargaining interaction is full of directives as negotiators attempt to settle a conflict. Directives range from explicit imperatives, "Give me the figures," to tacit hints, "I can't figure this out." Direct imperatives are considered more face threatening than hints. The researchers found the negotiation context influential in shaping directives. More face-threatening directives are used when bargainers have discrepant goals, operate in a less cooperative context, have a substantial relational history, and when the negotiation content is personally involving.

An interesting question that has produced mixed results is: What types of outcomes are produced by different types of arguments? Research findings based on simulated bargaining situations found that responsibility and workability arguments lead to deadlocks on distributive tasks and that "persuasive arguments" are significantly linked to deadlocks in integrative bargaining.[29] Results from actual labor-management negotiations found workability arguments promoted integrative outcomes, as bargainers altered proposals to address feasibility challenges.[30] These contradictory findings are symptomatic of much bargaining argument research. First, researchers operationalize "argument" in different ways. Some authors fail to define the term at all and others define it solely as a competitive tactic. Consequently, finding that arguments promote competitive negotiations is an artifact of the research design. Second, it is difficult to compare across negotiation situations, especially laboratory and real-life negotiations. Students who role-play as buyers or sellers, labor or management, or lawyers, seldom have the experience to know what such a person would really do. Also, deadlocking in laboratory research is void of the consequences in real life. For example, the consequence of the deadlock between railroad labor and management in 1992 was that Congress passed legislation ordering the employees back to work, and the dispute went to mediation. Although few negotiations have such significant consequences, the example illustrates that *real* negotiations have *real* consequences.

Finally, negotiation argumentation is affected by source characteristics. Bargaining messages are created through human invention; and negotiators vary in their ability to construct persuasive discourse. As Ehninger notes, "The worth of any decision, which may emerge from an argumentation exchange, is to a considerable extent dependent upon the good sense and acumen of the individuals who make it."[31] Two concepts are very useful for studying source characteristics: *argumentativeness* and *verbal aggression*.[32]

Argumentativeness is a psychological trait that predisposes a person to recognize controversial issues and to advocate and refute positions. Verbal aggression is the predisposition to attack an opponent's self-concept instead of, or in addition to, his or her position. Onyekwere, Rubin, and Infante suggest that a high degree of argumentativeness contributes to negotiator and mediator competence because people focus on the issues, maintain control of the discussion, and do not resort to personal attacks.[33] Lim reports that rejecting a proposal increases verbal aggressiveness faster than does offering a counterproposal.[34] Studies of family violence also show the value of argumentativeness and the harm of verbal aggression. Abused spouses report being low in argumentativeness and their spouses high in verbal aggression. The inability to argue constructively may cause spouses to become verbally aggressive and violent.[35]

Threats, Promises, and Commitments

Before discussing how these bargaining tactics operate in formulating an overall bargaining strategy and in affecting negotiated settlements, some definitions are necessary. A *threat* communicates one's intent to punish the target if the target fails to concede. A *promise* is a pledge to do, or to not do, something for the target. Most often a promise is thought of as a type of reward. A *commitment* tells the opponent that a bargainer will not move from a stated position so it is up to the opponent to make a move. Threats and commitments are tactics generally used in competitive bargaining strategies, whereas promises can be used in either cooperative or competitive strategies.

The effectiveness of these tactics is influenced by the bargainer's credibility and believability. Tedeschi and Rosenfeld define these terms as follows: "Credibility refers to the truthfulness of the source over the occasions when his or her communications can be checked for accuracy . . . Believability is the target's assessment of how likely it is that the source's present communication is true."[36] Credibility and believability research has focused primarily on the credibility of threats and promises. Three findings are noted below.

First, a person who consistently carries through on his/her threats gains more compliance from the opponent than a bargainer who fails to enforce threats. Consistent performance of promises increases the effectiveness of both promises and threats in gaining compliance. However, the consistent enforcement of threats does not have the same effect on promises. In other words, a person who fulfills promises establishes a level of credibility for delivering threats as well as promises. But a person who establishes credibility for the execution of threats does not gain "carryover credibility" for promises.

Second, the credibility of threats and promises is affected by the status of the source. High-status individuals are perceived to be more credible. Finally, the "cost factor" of a threat or promise impacts upon its credibility. Credibility decreases when a threat or promise is perceived by the opponent (target) to be too costly to the bargainer (source). But when a threat can be enforced with little cost to the source, an opponent is likely to comply.[37]

When threats are used in bargaining they may gain compliance, but generally they increase conflict and tension (see Box 11.4 for an unusual use of threats). Once a threat is made, the opponent must either counter the threat, which exacerbates the conflict, or concede, which signals weakness. Therefore, a threat should be thought of as a "tactic of last resort." In addition to whether or not a threat gains a concession is the issue of how large a concession the threat gains. In other words, the strength of the threatened punishment must also be considered. Tedeschi and Rosenfeld argue that threats will be related to compliance when the threatened punishment is significantly greater to the target than the loss the target will suffer if s/he concedes.[38]

For example, nation A threatens to withhold aid of $300 million to nation B unless nation B concedes its plan to sell weapons to nation C for $100 million. Excluding all contextual and interpersonal consideration, B will comply because the cost of the enforced threat is greater than the benefits of sales to C. Enforcement of the threat means B loses $300 million and gains $100 million for a net cost of $200 million. Conceding to the threat means B loses only the $100 million in weapons sales, but it retains the $300 million in aid, for a net gain of $200 million.

While it is easy to see how threats communicate a competitive strategy, it is not as easy to tell what strategy is communicated through promises. Promises can be viewed as revealing a cooperative strategy when a concession gains the opponent a reward. However, failure to make the necessary concession to gain the promised reward turns the promise into a threat, which is competitive. To illustrate, student A promises to do a study guide for the final if student B prepares a study guide for the midterm. But if student B does not cooperate, then A is implying a threat to not do a final exam study guide.

To determine if a tactic is a threat or a promise, Pruitt suggests that one should take the receiver's point of view.[39] If the receiver believes that noncompliance will result in a loss, then the bargaining message is a threat. But if compliance yields a gain, then the tactic is a promise. Pruitt also notes a special factor unique to promise credibility. The greater the influence of the party receiving the promise over the party making the promise, the greater the likelihood the receiver will make the concession to gain the reward. This is the opposite of threat credibility where greater source influence yields increased opponent compliance.

The way promise credibility operates in this situation is very interesting. Once the necessary concession is made, the receiving party has a legitimate right to the promised reward. If the receiver of the promise has access to legal recourse,

---

BOX 11.4

SUPPORT US OR ELSE

Unions sometimes communciate to external groups in order to increase support for their demands. In light of proposed cuts in state funding, the United Teachers-Los Angeles announced their plans for enlisting civic and business leaders to fight double-digit cuts in teachers' salaries. Their strategy was atypical. Instead of trying to win support through positive persuasive appeals, they threatened to engage a series of competitive tactics if support was not forthcoming.

"The movers and shakers of this city must understand that they will hurt if we hurt," said Helen Bernstein, union president. If civic leaders fail to oppose the cuts, UTLA plans to send letters to corporations, chambers of commerce and real estate firms across the nation warning them of the school funding crisis and discouraging companies and people from moving to Los Angeles. Other "attention-getting strategies" announced by the UTLA include:

■ Having members attend real estate "open houses" to distribute leaflets outlining the district's problems.

■ Notifying mortgage holders and other creditors that teachers will not be able to repay loans if the salary cuts go through.

■ Creating billboards that describe Los Angeles as home to "35,000 unhappy teachers," or "650,000 unserved students."

Excerpted from "Teachers Union President Calls for Removal of Supt. Anton," by Jean Merl, in the August 9, 1992, *Los Angeles Times.*

---

public pressure, and so forth, then s/he has some influence over the source which will help insure reward fulfillment. For an example, let us refer back to the antique seller example. The seller promises that he will repair a broken drawer handle and fill in some nicks in the wood if the buyer will pay $2,500 for the rolltop desk. If the promised repairs are written into the sales agreement, the buyer is more likely to accept the offer. With a written agreement, the buyer has legal recourse, that is, legitimate power, over the seller. Consequently, the promise is more credible.

Commitments are statements which communicate how firmly a party is taking a certain position. Once a commitment is made, then the opponent must act. However, the opponent's reactions to a commitment are dependent upon what type of commitment is made. Walton and McKersie identify three language factors which signal the "firmness" of a commitment. These factors are communicated through language which is final, specific, and states explicit consequences.[40] The following explicit bargaining message leaves little room for reinterpretation:

"We must have a $4-per-hour increase or we will strike." Finality is expressed through "must have." The "$4-per-hour increase" is a specific demand. The explicit consequence is a strike. When firm commitments are made, conflict escalation is possible, because the opponent must either counterattack or concede the point. The firm commitment represents a win-lose issue. Thus, there is no room left for integrative, win-win, bargaining.

Flexible commitments employ ambiguous messages and lead to more accommodations and reciprocal concessions. The ambiguity in the message allows the parties to explore different implications of the commitment. A flexible commitment can be contingent upon future concession by the opponent, so that the bargainer can concede in the future without losing face. Or if a strike occurs, the bargainer can increase his/her demands to adjust for the new costs.

Demands and Concession Rates

"What do I offer?" "What do I accept?" These are two of the most frightening questions facing a bargainer. The opening offer/demand is a difficult decision to make. Not only is the uncertainty in the bargaining situation unnerving, but you realize that this initial bid is a tacit bargaining message that reveals some of your utility schedule. Also, the level of your initial bid and your subsequent concession rate affect the likelihood of reaching a negotiated settlement, as well as the size of the agreement.

One determinant of an opening bid is the bargainer's utility schedule. As discussed earlier in this chapter, the utility schedule defines the resistance points and aspiration level of a bargainer. One reason for making an initial demand that is higher than your aspiration level and then offering concessions is to encourage negotiations that will

result in a negotiated agreement that approximates your aspiration level. By making this level of demand and giving subsequent concessions, the bargainer is protecting his/her aspirations and alternatives. When a bargainer concedes something that had been considered a desirable alternative s/he suffers a position loss.

A second determinant of demand and concession rate is image loss. A bargainer suffers image loss when some other person feels that the bargainer lacks firmness. The other person(s) can be either the opponent or the bargainer's own constituents. A bargainer who is concerned about image loss is likely to exhibit face-saving behaviors such as making higher demands and giving lower concessions to the point of reaching no agreement. This same behavior is found in bargainers who must account for the negotiated outcome to their constituents.

Another example of image loss deals with the level of familiarity between the bargainers. How well you know the other bargainer is the third determinant of demands and concessions. Studies comparing bargaining between strangers and between married couples found that strangers had higher demands, conceded more slowly, and broke off negotiations more frequently than married couples. It is believed that people involved in intimate relationships are less concerned about either position or image loss, and more likely to seek a mutually beneficial solution.

Fourth, time pressure and amount of elapsed bargaining time affect demand and concession rate. It is common to read of contracts being settled just minutes before the start of a strike. Time pressures act to spur negotiators to a settlement because of the costs associated with continued negotiations or an impasse. The increase in likelihood of a settlement is because bargainers may begin to make lower demands and to increase concessions. In light of the costs associated with continued negotiations or an impasse, bargainers will modify their aspiration levels and utility schedules to take account of these new variables.

A final determinant is the opponent's reaction to a party's demand and concessions. This determinant involves the issue of reciprocity of moves. Putnam and Jones found that reciprocity in integrative bargaining resulted in cooperative moves that facilitated agreement. However, when distributive strategies were reciprocated, in the form of one-upmanship, the dyads were caught in a conflictspiral and no agreement was reached. Specifically,a conflict spiral occurs when an attack is followedby an attack, and also when defensive behavior is followed by defensive behavior.

After bargainers have decided what their demand will be and what concessions may be necessary, they need to be aware of the probable effects of these decisions. While the research on the effects of demands and concession rates is not as definitive as that on other types of bargaining research, three general conclusions are presented.[41] Any special conditions to these conclusions are noted.

First, lower initial demands and faster concession rates by one or both parties will increase the likelihood that an agreement will be reached and will decrease the time needed to reach the agreement. This finding is not surprising, since low demands put the bargainers closer to agreement, and fast concessions will move them to a mutually acceptable outcome. This is especially true when both parties reciprocate the opponent's move. However, when reciprocity does not occur, an interesting deviation results. If a bargainer makes a low initial demand and concedes rapidly, there is a decrease in the likelihood of reaching an agreement and an increase in time used if a settlement is reached. The reason for this occurrence is that after the opponent receives a low demand and gets some fast concessions, s/he will exploit the situation. That is, the opponent has been given some concessions, expects more may be

forthcoming, and is going to hold out for that possibility.

A second general conclusion is that large initial demands and smaller concessions will give the bargainer a larger outcome and the opponent a small outcome as long as an agreement is reached. In the cases where agreement is reached it is thought that the large initial demand affected the opponent's impression of the other party's utility schedule, and consequently the opponent modified his/her level of aspiration to accept a smaller gain. A person is likely to modify his/her aspiration level if the negotiations, are over an unfamiliar item or issue.

The third conclusion is drawn from the previous two findings. There is an inverted U-shaped relationship between a party's initial demand and the average outcomes. Too low a demand and either too slow or too fast a concession rate yields low profits since there is little for the party to win. Large demands with slow concessions also will yield low average profits because frequent failures to reach agreements will mitigate the times when a large outcome is won. This is similar to playing the slot machines in Las Vegas. Even though someone occasionally will win a jackpot, most people win little or nothing; therefore, the average payoff is small. A bargainer's "best bet" is with moderate demands and concessions.

Exact quantification of a "high" versus "low" demand or concession rate is impossible. The amount is specific to each bargaining encounter. An opening demand of $75 is very low for a new mountain bike, very high for a child's secondhand tricycle, but about right for a child's secondhand bike.

CONFLICT MANAGEMENT SKILLS

For the last two decades, efforts have been made to divert civil litigation cases from the courtroom to alternative dispute forums. Former Supreme Court Chief Justice Warren Burger urged "increased use of alternative methods such as mediation . . . in divorce, child custody, adoptions, personal injury, landlord and tenant cases, and probate of estates."[42] In addition to negotiation, alternative dispute resolution (ADR) methods include "factfinders without recommending authority; voluntary mediation; mandated mediation; therapeutic mediation; Med-Arb; contractual, final offer, and court-ordered arbitration; mini and summary jury trials. . . . "[43] Some readers may have experienced the impact of the ADR movement. Some major banks now require depositors to waive the option of a legal trial and to use mediation and arbitration to resolve certain disputes. Some hospitals request (but do not require) that incoming patients sign a form whereby they agree not to sue the hospital in court but to use arbitration to settle any dispute. In several states, child-custody cases go through mediation prior to issuance of a final divorce decree. Most medium to large metropolitan areas have community mediation centers. Perhaps most impressive are efforts to teach elementary students mediation skills to deal with playground conflicts. The various forms of mediation and arbitration are extensive topics and a discussion of these procedures is beyond the scope of the chapter.[44] But the following guidelines for bargaining in competitive and cooperative situations should help disputants reach negotiated settlement and avoid other forms of ADR and/or litigation.

Competitive Bargaining

Earlier sections have discussed how competitive behaviors may yield higher profits for one party, but at the expense of the bargaining relationship. Yet some issues are inherently distributive and must be dealt with competitively. Thus, the ques-

tion becomes one of balance. How do negotiators bargain competitively without damaging the relationship? The following suggestions are designed to gain the advantages of competitive bargaining without incurring the disadvantages:[45]

1. *Use competitive tactics to defend basic interests rather than a particular solution.* For example, the antique seller could use competitive tactics to defend his basic interest to not lose money on the desk and to make a reasonable profit.

2. *Send signals of flexibility and concern about the other party's interests in conjunction with competitive displays.* Such maneuvers are designed to make the integrative potential seem large enough to the other party that further attempts at bargaining seem justified. The antique seller could acknowledge that the buyer does not want to overspend on the desk, and that his interest in a fair profit and her interest of a "good buy" can be met.

3. *Insulate competitive behavior from cooperative behavior so that neither undermines the other.* This can be accomplished with the "white hat/black hat" approach. One team member bargains competitively and another team member bargains cooperatively. This strategy functions in the following manner: After black hat has given a series of threats, white hat's cooperative messages are more likely to be reciprocated. The strategy is used also to persuade the opponent to give in now, because party's superior will not be so sympathetic in his/her approach to the negotiations.

4. *Employ deterrent threats rather than compellent threats.* Deterrent threats indicate that the party is opposed to the opponent's favored option, but it does not address other options. Compellent threats require that a particular option be adopted. To illustrate, labor uses a deterrent threat when it rejects management's last wage package and waits to get a better offer in order to avert a strike. But labor uses a compellent threat when it tells man-

agement that the labor's proposed wage package must be adopted in order to avert a strike.

Cooperative Bargaining

In the early 1980s, Professor Roger Fisher and William Ury of the Harvard Negotiation Project published a national best-seller, *Getting to Yes: Negotiating Agreement Without Giving In.*[46] The book focuses upon methods of making bargaining situations cooperative rather than competitive in order to achieve mutually satisfying results. The first four suggestions presented by Fisher and Ury are most appropriate for bargaining situations between parties of relatively equal power. The fifth suggestion is for bargaining with someone with greater power.

First, separate the people from the problem. The bargaining process demands a great deal of psychological and emotional energy. A good interpersonal relationship is important, especially if this is an ongoing bargaining relationship. Fisher and Ury note three communication barriers to effective negotiations. First, the negotiator may fail to address the opponent and instead talk to impress himself/herself or the constituents: "Effective communication is all but impossible if each plays to the gallery," say Fisher and Ury. Second is poor listening skills. A poor negotiator is mentally preparing the next argument rather than attending to the opponent's current message. The final communication problem is misunderstanding or misinterpreting. This is likely when the parties have different native languages, as in international bargaining situations, or if there are many technical terms with which one party is unfamiliar.

Fisher and Ury's second guideline to effective negotiations is to focus on interests rather than positions. To discover each party's underlying interests is a step towards finding creative solutions. Their example of the 1978 Camp David talks be-

tween Israel and Egypt illustrates this point well. Israel had occupied the Egyptian Sinai Peninsula since the 1967 Six Day War. Egypt wanted to regain sovereignty over this land. Restated, Egypt's interest was to control this land that had been a part of Egypt for centuries. Israel's interest was in secured borders. They did not want Egypt to be able to invade at a moment's notice. The agreement worked out at Camp David was for Israel to return the Sinai to Egypt, but a large portion of the peninsula was to be demilitarized. Thus, Israel's interest of security was met as was Egypt's interest in regaining sovereignty over the Sinai.

Another guideline is to invent options for mutual gain. This can be accomplished by employing creative problem solving techniques, searching for many possible solutions, avoiding premature judgments or "fixed pie" assumptions, and working to solve the opponent's problems as well as yours. The fourth guideline is to establish objective criteria to judge possible solutions. Items to be considered in developing this criteria include: precedent, equality, equity, scientific judgment, market value, and professional standards. The use of standards allows the parties to reach an agreement based upon principle rather than pressure.

In situations where you are negotiating with a more powerful opponent, Fisher and Ury suggest that you develop a BATNA—best alternative to a negotiated agreement. Your BATNA is determined by analyzing what is in your best interest and what alternatives you have outside of the negotiation process. The BATNA then becomes the standard against which every proposal is compared. By comparing a proposal with your BATNA, you can determine if the opponent is offering something that meets enough of your interests and should be accepted, or if you are better off leaving the bargaining relationship. In summary, the BATNA protects the less-powerful party from accepting an unfavorable proposal or rejecting a proposal that has potential benefits.

F O O T N O T E S

1. D.M. Kolb, "Women's Work," in D.M. Kolb and J.M. Bartunek, eds., *Hidden Conflict in Organizations,* (Newbury Park, Calif.: Sage, 1992), pp. 63-91.

2. L.L. Putnam and T.S. Jones discuss the interchangeability of *bargaining* and *negotiation* in "Reciprocity in Negotiations: An Analysis of Bargaining Interactions," *Communication Monographs,* vol. 49, (1982), p. 171.

3. Thomas C. Schelling, *The Strategy of Conflict* (Cambridge, Mass.: Harvard University Press, 1980/1960), p. 85.

4. R.E. Walton and R.B. McKersie, *A Behavioral Theory of Labor Negotiations* (New York: McGraw-Hill, 1965), pp. 13-17.

5. J.T. Tedeschi and P. Rosenfeld, "Communication in Bargaining and Negotiation," in M.E. Roloff and G.R. Miller, eds., *Persuasion: New Directions in Theory and Research* (Beverly Hills, Sage, 1980), pp. 227-228.

6. J.Z. Rubin and B.R. Brown, *The Social Psychology of Bargaining and Negotiations* (New York: Academic Press, 1975), p. 20.

7. Rubin and Brown, *The Social Psychology of Bargaining,* pp. 20-32.

8. I.W. Zartman, "Common Elements in the Analysis of the Negotiation Process," *Negotiation Journal,* vol. 4 (1988), pp. 31-43.

9. L.L. Putnam and M.E. Roloff, eds., "Communication Perspectives on Negotiation," in L.L. Putnam and M.E. Roloff, eds., *Communication and Negotiation,* (Newbury Park, Calif.: Sage, 1992), pp. 1-17.

10. B.I. Spector, "Negotiation as a Psychological Process," in W. Zartman, ed., *The Negotiation Process: Theories and Applications* (Beverly Hills, Sage, 1978), pp. 55-56.

11. P. Gibbons, J.J. Bradac, and J.D. Busch, "The Role of Language in Negotiations: Threats and Promises," in L.L. Putnam and M.E. Roloff, *Communication and Negotiation* (Newbury Park, Calif.: Sage, 1992), p. 164.

12. Putnam and Roloff, "Communication Perspectives on Negotiation," pp. 9-10. See also L.L. Putnam and T.S. Jones, "The Role of Communication in Bargaining," *Human Communication Research,* vol. 8, no. 3 (1982).

13. Putnam and Jones, "The Role of Communication," pp. 265-266.

14. M.S. Poole, D.L. Shannon, and G. DeSanctis, "Communication Media and Negotiation Processes," in L.L. Putnam and M.E. Roloff, eds., *Communication and Negotiation* (Newbury Park, Calif.: Sage, 1992), pp. 46-66.

15. H.M. Trice and J.M. Beyer, "Studying Organizational Cultures through Rites and Ceremonials," *Academy of Management Review,* vol. 9 (1984), pp. 653-669.

16. W.A. Donohue, M.E. Diez, and M. Hamilton, "Coding Naturalistic Negotiation Interaction," *Human Communication Research,* vol. 10, no. 3 (1984), pp. 403-425.

17. M.E. Roloff and J.M. Jordan, "Achieving Negotiation Goals," in L.L. Putnam and M.E. Roloff, eds., *Communication and Negotiation* (Newbury Park, Calif.: Sage), pp. 21-45.

18. Roloff and Jordan, "Achieving Negotiation Goals," pp. 25-27.

19. R.J. Klimoski, "The Effects of Intragroup Forces on Intergroup Conflict Resolution," *Organizational Behavior and Human Performance,* vol. 8 (1972), pp. 363-383. See also P.D. Carnevale, D.G. Pruitt, and S.D. Britton, "Looking Tough: The Negotiation under Constituent Surveillance," *Personality and Social Psychology Bulletin,* vol. 5, pp. 118-121.

20. R.J. Bies, "Managing Conflict Before It Happens: The Role of Accounts," in M.A. Rahim, ed., *Managing Conflict: An Interdisciplinary Approach* (Newbury Park, Calif.: Sage, 1992), pp. 83-91.

21. L.L. Putnam and P. Geist, "Argument in Bargaining: An Analysis of the Reasoning Process," *Southern Speech Communication Journal,* vol. 50 (1986), 225-245.

22. Putnam and Geist, "Argument in Bargaining," p. 243.

23. L.L. Putnam, S.R. Wilson, and D.B. Turner, "The Evolution of Policy Arguments in Teachers' Negotiation," *Argumentation,* vol. 4 (1990), pp. 129-152.

24. Putnam and Geist, "Argument in Bargaining," p. 244.

25. W.A. Donohue, M.E. Diez, and R.B. Stahle, "New Directions in Negotiation Research," in R. Bostrom, ed., *Communication Yearbook 7,* (Beverly Hills: Sage, 1983), pp. 249-279.

26. S. Jackson and S. Jacobs, "The Collaborative Production of Proposals in Conversational Argument and Persuasion: A Study in Disagreement Regulation," *Journal of the American Forensic Association,* vol. 18 (1981), p. 79.

27. For a review, see S.R. Wilson, "Face and Facework in Negotiation," in L.L. Putnam and M.E. Roloff, eds., *Communication and Negotiation* (Newbury Park: Calif., Sage, 1992), pp. 176-205.

28. W.A. Donohue and M.E. Diez, "Directive Use in Negotiation Interaction," *Communication Monographs,* vol. 52 (1985), pp. 305-318.

29. M.E. Roloff, F.E. Tutzauer, and W.O. Dailey, "The Role of Argumentation in Distributive and Integrative Bargaining Contexts: Seeking Relative Advantage But at What Cost?," in M.A. Rahim, ed., *Managing Conflict: An Interdisciplinary Approach* (New York: Praeger, 1989), pp. 109-119.

30. L.L. Putnam and S.R. Wilson, "Argumentation and Bargaining Strategies as Discriminators of Integrative Outcomes," in M.A. Rahim, ed., *Managing Conflict: An Interdisciplinary Approach* (New York: Praeger, 1989), pp. 121-141.

31. D. Ehninger, "Argument as Method: Its Nature, Its Limitations and Its Uses," *Speech Monographs*, vol. 37 (1970), p. 106.

32. D.A. Infante and A.S. Rancer, "A Conceptualization and Measure of Argumentativeness," *Journal of Personality Assessment*, vol. 45 (1982), pp. 72-80.

33. E.O. Onyekwere, R.B. Rubin, and D.A. Infante, "Interpersonal Perception and Communication Satisfaction as a Function of Argumentativeness and Ego-Involvement," *Communication Quarterly*, vol. 39 (1991), pp. 35-47.

34. T.S. Lim, "The Influence of Receivers' Resistance on Persuaders' Verbal Aggressiveness," *Communication Quarterly*, vol. 38 (1990), pp. 170-188.

35. D.A. Infante, T.C. Sabourin, J.E. Rudd, and E.A. Shannon, "Verbal Aggression in Violent and Nonviolent Marital Disputes," *Communication Quarterly*, vol. 38 (1990), pp. 161-171; D.A. Infante, T.A. Chandler, and J.E. Rudd, "Test of an Argumentative Skill Deficiency Model of Interspousal Violence," *Communication Monographs*, vol. 56 (1989), pp. 163-177.

36. Tedeschi and Rosenfeld, "Communication in Bargaining," p. 234.

37. D.G. Pruitt, *Negotiation Behavior* (New York: Academic Press, 1981), p. 72.

38. Tedeschi and Rosenfeld, "Communication in Bargaining," p. 236.

39. Pruitt, *Negotiation Behavior*, p. 79.

40. Walton and McKersie, *A Behavioral Theory*, pp. 93-98.

41. J.Z. Rubin and B.R. Brown, *The Social Psychology of Bargaining and Negotiations* (New York: Academic, 1975), p. 20.

42. K. Kressel and D.G. Pruitt, "The Mediation of Social Conflict," *Journal of Social Issues*, vol. 41, no. 2 (1985), pp. 1-10, cited in J.W. (S.) Keltner, *Mediation* (Annandale, Va.: Speech Communication Association, 1987), p. 12.

43. P.S. Adler, "Is ADR a Social Movement?" *Negotiation Journal*, vol. 3, no. 1 (1987), pp. 59-71.

44. For a review of mediation, see Keltner, *Mediation*.

For a review of arbitration, see F. Elkouri and E.A. Elkouri, *How Arbitration Works*, 3rd ed. (Washington, D.C.: Bureau of National Affairs, Inc., 1976).

45. D.G. Pruitt, "Strategic Choice in Negotiation," *American Behavioral Scientist*, vol. 27, no. 2 (1983), p. 190.

46. R. Fisher and W. Ury, *Getting to Yes: Negotiation Agreement Without Giving In* (Boston: Houghton Mifflin, 1981).

K E Y   T E R M S   A N D   C O N C E P T S

conflict
negotiation
mediation
arbitration
litigation
bargaining
cooperative/integrative bargaining
competitive/distributive bargaining
bargaining structure
resistance point
status quo point
bargaining range
aspiration level
utility schedule
Prisoner's Dilemma
mixed motive bargaining
effects model of negotiation
key components model of negotiation
explicit/tacit bargaining messages
negotiation plans and planning
adaptive negotiation planning
interactive negotiation planning
collaborative negotiation planning
prenegotiation accounts
causal accounts
referential accounts
ideological accounts
argumentation
threat
promise
commitment
demand and concession rate

PERSUASION IN THE FORMAL ORGANIZATION

This chapter analyzes some of the tactics persuasive communicators use when working effectively within organizations. We will discuss six relevant topics: managerial influence, supervisor characteristics and supervisor effectiveness, effective behavior change through goal setting and feedback, upward influence and distortion, political strategies, and communication networks and roles.

MANAGERIAL INFLUENCE: PERSUASIVE STRATEGIES USED BY SUPERIORS

While the work on influence discussed earlier in this book applies to organizational settings, two additional issues are important. First, power and status are emphasized in most organizations, and the differences in power affect the tactics people employ in the superior-subordinate relationship. For example, Kipnis, Schmidt, and Wilkinson[1] found that, in organizations which were unionized (thereby giving more power to workers), superiors used more ingratiation tactics, and workers used less rationality ("supporting evidence") and more "blocking" (work slowdowns, forming coalitions) in order to influence superiors. Similarly, Wilkinson and Kipnis[2] found that more powerful organizational units used stronger and more controlling tactics on less powerful units (especially when overcoming resistance). Power differences can, in fact, corrupt the "powerholder," making her/him feel more distant from the people who are influenced, and prompting her/him to devalue those who are controlled.[3]

The second issue is that a good deal of the influence between superior and subordinates is reciprocal in nature—not only do leader behaviors produce changes in subordinate satisfaction and performance, but subordinate behaviors cause

changes in the supervisor's mode of behavior. Studies by Farris and Lim, by Greene, by Herold, and by Lowin and Craig demonstrate the reciprocal nature of influence processes.[4] For many years leader behaviors have been classified as "considerate" (in which case the relationship is characterized by friendship and warmth, mutual trust, rapport, and tolerance) and as "initiating structure" (in which case the supervisor makes overt attempts to organize, define, direct, structure, and lead his or her work unit). Greene[5] studied these types of leader behaviors and found that leader consideration caused greater worker satisfaction, and that workers' high productivity rates caused leaders to be more considerate.

In another study, Richmond, Davis, Saylor, and McCroskey[6] found moderately high correlations between supervisor and subordinate use of various influence tactics, suggesting that when a superior uses a tactic, such use may become sanctioned, and/or that workers model their behavior after the supervisor's. Indeed, the managerial style of individuals at the highest levels of power in the organization has a strong impact on both organizational climate (discussed below as the social/psychological perceptions workers have of their organization), and organizational "culture," which is defined as the history, traditions, and values members of an organization are socialized into adopting.

Influence Tactics

Bachman and his colleagues[7] reported a summary of their findings on the impact of bases of power in organizations:

1. When asked to list reasons for complying with a superior, subordinates listed legitimate power and expert power as the most important. Of lesser importance were referent power and reward

The Effects of Influence Style on Organizational Culture

H-P was started in the 1940s by Bill Hewlett and Dave Packard and has established a corporate culture famed for strong team commitment coupled with a philosophy of innovation through people. The company decided to put the team ethos on the line early in its history, adopting a policy that it would not be "a hire and fire company." This principle was severely tested on a couple of occasions in the 1970s, when declines in business forced the company to adopt the policy of a "nine-day fortnight" whereby staff took a 10 percent pay cut and worked 10 percent fewer hours. Whereas other companies resorted to layoffs, H-P kept its full complement of staff, thus emphasizing that all members of the H-P team shared the same fortune, and that a measure of job security was possible even in unfavorable times.

Being a member of this team, of course, carries a set of obligations. Enthusiasm for work, and an ethos of sharing problems and ideas in an atmosphere of free and open exchange are values which the organization actively encourages. Much of this ethos stems from the day-to-day example set by Hewlett and Packard, the founding heroes who have established a reputation for hands-on management throughout the company. The ethos is also fostered by ritual "beer busts" and "coffee klatches," and by numerous ad hoc meetings that create regular opportunities for informal interaction. Stories, legends, and myths about corporate heroes abound and do much to communicate and sustain the cultural values underlying H-P's success. A new recruit may be treated to a slide presentation which relates how "Bill and Dave" started the company in Bill's garage and used the Hewlett oven for making some of the first products. On another occasion he or she may learn that story when Bill Hewlett visited a plant one Saturday and found the lab stock area locked, he immediately cut the padlock, leaving a note saying, "Don't ever lock this door again. Thanks, Bill." Along with more formal statements of company philosophy, the message soon hits home: at H-P we trust and value you. You're free to be enthusiastic about your job even if it's Saturday, and to innovate and contribute in whatever way you can.

At International Telephone & Telegraph (ITT) under the tough and uncompromising leadership of Harold Geneen we find an example of another kind of corporate culture. The story here is one of success built on a ruthless style of management that converted a medium-sized communications business with sales of $765 million in 1959 into one of the world's largest and most powerful and diversified conglomerates, operating in over ninety countries, with revenues of almost $12 billion in 1978. Under Geneen's twenty-year reign, the company established a reputation as one of the fastest-growing and most profitable American companies—and, following its role in overseas bribery and the downfall of the Allende government in Chile, as one of the most corrupt and controversial.

Geneen's managerial style was simple and straightforward. He sought to keep his staff on top of their work by creating an intensely competitive atmosphere based on confrontation and intimidation. The foundation of his approach rested in his quest for what were known as "unshakable facts." He insisted that all managerial reports, decisions, and business plans be based on irrefutable premises, and developed a complete information system, a network of special task forces, and a method of cross-examination that allowed him to check virtually every statement put forward. Geneen possessed an extraordinary memory and an ability to absorb vast amounts of information in a relatively short time. This made it possible for him to keep his executives on their toes by demonstrating that he knew their situations as well as, if not better than, they did. His interrogation sessions at policy review meetings have become legendary. These meetings, which have been described as "show trials," were held around an enormous table capable of seating over fifty people, each executive being provided with a microphone into which to speak. It is reported that Geneen's approach was to pose a question to a specific executive, or to sit back listening to the reports being offered while specially appointed staff people cross-examined what was being said. As soon as the executive being questioned showed evasiveness or lack of certainty, Geneen would move in to probe the weakness. In complete command of the facts, and equipped with a razor-sharp ability to cut to the center of an issue, he would invariably also cut the floundering executive and his argument to shreds. It is said that these experiences were so grueling that many executives were known to break down and cry under the pressure.

Geneen's approach motivated people through fear. If an executive was making a presentation, there was every incentive to stay up preparing throughout the night to ensure that all possible questions and angles were covered. This intimidating style was set by Geneen from the very beginning of his tenure. For example, it is reported that early in his career with ITT he would call executives at all hours, perhaps in the middle of the night, to inquire about the validity of some fact or obscure point in a written report. The message was clear: ITT executives are expected to be company men and women on top of their jobs at all times. The idea that loyalty to the goals of the organization should take precedence over loyalty to colleagues or other points of reference was established as a key principle.

ITT under Geneen was a successful corporate jungle. High executive performance was undoubtedly achieved, but at considerable cost in terms of staff stress and in terms of the kind of actions that this sometimes produced, such as the company's

Continued

notorious activities in Chile. The pressure on ITT executives was above all to perform and deliver the goods they had promised. Their corporate necks were always on the line. Geneen's approach typifies the managerial style that psychoanalyst Michael Maccoby has characterized as that of the "jungle fighter": the power-hungry manager who experiences life and work as in a jungle where it is eat or be eaten, and where winners destroy losers. The jungle fighter tends to see his peers as accomplices or enemies, and subordinates as objects to be utilized. The "lions" among these fighters are conquerors who, like Geneen, build empires. More foxlike jungle fighters move ahead with more stealth and politicking. Interestingly, the actions of both types help to create the dog-eat-dog world that is implied in their basic philosophy of action.

The "cut and thrust" corporate culture of ITT under Geneen stands poles apart from the successful team atmosphere created at Hewlett-Packard. In these organizations we find very different cultures being created through different styles of corporate leadership. Like it or not, the attitudes and visions of top corporate staff tend to have a significant impact on the ethos and meaning system that pervade the whole organization. At H-P and ITT more successful corporate cultures were produced, though at ITT this was achieved at great private and public cost.

From: G. Morgan, *Images of Organization* (Newbury Park, Calif.: Sage, 1986), pp. 124–126. Reprinted with permission of author, copyright © 1986 by permission of Sage Publications, Inc.

power. Across all organizational units studied, coercive power was rated the least likely reason for complying with a request.

2. Expert and referent power provided the strongest positive correlation with job satisfaction (or with satisfaction with one's supervisor), and did so with consistency across organizations. Coercive power was associated with low job satisfaction. Superior's use of legitimate power and reward power was positively correlated with job satisfaction among insurance agents and production workers (but not among sales personnel and college faculty—for whom knowledge of legitimate rights and obligations, and knowledge of rewards, may stem from many sources other than one's own immediate supervisor).

3. Expert power showed the most consistent relationship with high performance. Referent power was associated with enhanced productivity in branch offices (which included sales and personnel who gave out information to clients) and in production work units (routine production of electrical appliances). However, referent power was unrelated to performance in insurance agencies (when an agent's superior may be a regional manager and with whom contact may be infrequent). The correlations between reward power and performance were predominately positive. Finally, legitimate and coercive power did not have a consistent influence on productivity. Legitimate power was slightly related to increased productivity for insurance salespersons, but had no impact on other types of organizational units. Coercive power was associated with low productivity, or was unrelated to performance.

There are jobs where the worker has considerable autonomy—jobs where one's success is not related to the behavior of the immediate supervisor. When workers are less dependent upon the input of the immediate supervisor, the effects of strategies will be reduced. For example, Richmond, Davis, Saylor, and McCroskey[8] surveyed 201 elementary and secondary school teachers and found that a supervisor's use of influence tactics was either negatively related or unrelated to teacher satisfaction—no influence tactic was positively related to this issue. On the other hand, when teachers attempted to influence students, Richmond and McCroskey[9] found referent and expert power were related to increased learning, reward power was unrelated to learning, and coercive and legitimate power corresponded to poorer learning outcomes—results similar to the results discussed above.

These studies indicate that the role of legitimate influence must be clarified. On one hand, workers rank legitimate influence as the most important reason for complying with a request. On the other hand, legitimate influence is not related to productivity. Part of this discrepancy may rest in the fact that when workers rank legitimate influence as important, they have in mind compliance with specific and single requests that the superior makes—such as rushing an order to the airport or reducing the number of personal phone calls. However, increased productivity reflects a cumulative amount of work produced over a span of time, and many factors influence such a rate—factors beyond a superior's right to make a specific request. If this reasoning is correct, legitimate influence ought to be important primarily when specific decisions are made. Patchen[10] found informational influences were extremely important when major corporations were making decisions, as were expert and legitimate influences. Referent, reward, and coercive influences were rarely mentioned as reasons for making decisions.

The finding that reward power does not have a consistent impact on performance may appear surprising to some readers. However, keep in mind that rewards may be given for many reasons.

Rewards are given not only to superior workers for high productivity, but also as a means to reward ingratiators or to buy the support of people in the work unit when an insecure supervisor is confronted by a hostile worker. Obviously, not all reward influence would be related to productivity.

Recently, increased attention has focused on making rewards and punishments effective. Padsakoff,[11] for example, argued that leaders who administer rewards appropriately (that is, contingent upon performance) "cause increases in performance and satisfaction. Superiors who administer rewards inappropriately (noncontingently), or not at all, are likely to produce many dysfunctional effects, including declining productivity, feelings of inequity, and expressions of negative affects and dissatisfaction among their subordinates." In fact, House[12] argued that a superior's behavior can lead to increased productivity when (a) the rewards under a supervisor's control are valued by subordinates; (b) allocation of the rewards is contingent upon performance; and, (c) the contingency rules for receiving rewards are clearly understood by the subordinates. We would add (d) the organization's rules for allocating rewards must be adhered to consistently over time.

Arvey and Ivancevich[13] provide six propositions relating to effective punishments:

1. Punishment is more effective in organizational contexts if the punishment is delivered immediately after the undesirable response occurs, than if the delivery is delayed.

2. Moderate levels of punishment are more effective than low or high intensity levels. (Low-intensity punishments may be ineffective, and punishments high in severity may cause anxiety, which would inhibit learning and create extremely high levels of job dissatisfaction.)

3. Punishment procedures are more effective where the agent administering the punishment has relatively close and friendly relationships with the employee being punished.

4. Punishment of undesirable behavior is more effective within organizations if: (a) punishment consistently occurs after every undesirable response; (b) punishment is administered consistently by the same managers; and (c) different managers are consistent in their applications of punishment for the same undesirable response.

5. Punishment is more effective when clear reasons are communicated to employees concerning why the punishment occurred, what the contingency is, and what the consequences of repeated behavior will be.

6. To the extent that alternative desirable responses are available to employees and these responses are reinforced, punishment is enhanced.

Kipnis and his associates have furthered our understanding of the choice of influence tactics made by organizational participants.[14] In 1980, Kipnis and associates explored how managers get their way in organizations. The authors asked managers to describe what goals they pursued. The five goals which emerged were: (1) obtain assistance with own job; (2) get others to do their job; (3) obtain benefits; (4) initiate change; and (5) improve (the target's) performance. Kipnis and his associates further argued there were eight dimensions involved in influence: (1) assertiveness, (2) ingratiation, (3) rationality, (4) sanctions, (5) exchange, (6) upward appeals, (7) blocking, and (8) coalitions.

After a series of studies on organizational influence, Kipnis and his associates[15] argued that managers tended to be one of three types: Shotgun, Bystanders, and Tacticians. *Shotgun* managers utilize an above-average amount of each type of tactic (that is, assertiveness, sanctions, ingratiation, and so forth). Shotgun managers may be characterized as wanting to get a great deal from others in the organization. *Bystander* managers use a below-average amount of the tactics and exercise very little influence. Bystander managers lack power in the organization and therefore feel it is useless to try and influence others. Finally, the *tacticians* rely mainly on *reason*, or "rationality," to influence others. Further, tacticians use few other tactics, relying solely on reason. Tacticians get their way by using facts and data in logical arguments, and they project an image of a rational and reasonable manager.

Although Kipnis and associates have been the leaders in researching compliance-gaining in organizations, other scholars have also conducted research in the area. Several other sources for consultation include:[16] Cobb; Freedman; Frost; Krone and Ludlum; Riccillo and Trenholm; Richmond, Davis, Saylor, and McCroskey; Siebold, Cantrill, and Meyers; Stohl and Redding; and Sullivan, Albrecht, and Taylor.

Supervisor Characteristics and Supervisor Effectiveness

For many years organizational communication experts have tried to identify and describe the characteristics of effective supervisors. Redding[17] provided one of the first thorough treatments of the topic. More recently Jablin[18] has reviewed the area in depth. Here are the major reasons why some supervisors are more effective than others:

1. Better supervisors tend to be more "communication minded": they enjoy talking and speaking up in meetings; they are able to explain instructions and policies; they enjoy conversing with subordinates.

2. Better supervisors tend to be willing, empathic listeners; they respond understandingly to so-called "silly" questions from employees; they are approachable; they will listen to suggestions and complaints, with an attitude of fair consideration.

3. Better supervisors tend (with some notable exceptions) to "ask" or "persuade" instead of "telling" or "demanding."

4. Better supervisors tend to be sensitive to the feelings and ego-defense needs of their subordinates; they are careful to reprimand in private rather than in public.

5. Better supervisors tend to be more open in their passing along of information; they are in favor of giving advance notice of impending changes and of examining and explaining the "reasons why" behind policies and regulations.

6. Better supervisors score high in both "consideration" and in "initiation structure." Some studies indicate that high consideration is related to job satisfaction and may be inversely related to performance, since little pressure, motivation, or structure exists if only consideration is high.

These conclusions are offered as general guidelines for effective supervisory behavior. While they are generally true, any particular style of communication or leadership will be more effective in some types of organizations and with some types of workers than with others.

One area of supervisor-subordinate research receiving attention is the degree to which the superior is open (or perceived to be open). There are two dimensions of openness—openness in message sending (the frankness and candidness of disclosures) and openness in message receiving (encouraging frank and candid communications). Klauss and Bass[19] found increased openness consistently led to increased job satisfaction, and that openness led to increased satisfaction with one's communication partner. They also learned that the specific variables associated with satisfaction varied from one type of organization to the next, depending upon their importance in the work environment. In a Navy civilian agency, where rigidity and inflexibility may be typical, workers preferred an informal and open communicator who accurately transmitted messages. In a social service agency, workers need to solve problems and, hence, a person who is a careful listener was rated as a preferable colleague.

The majority of research on openness has focused on two critical aspects: (1) perceptions of organizational climate; and, (2) the effect climate has on satisfaction and performance. An organizational climate is the state of the organization's internal nature, as perceived by its members.[20] According to Redding[21] " . . . the climate of the organization is more crucial than are the communication skills or techniques (taken by themselves) in creating an effective organization." Redding characterized climate as being composed of varying degrees of openness and candor, along with supportiveness, participative decision making, trust, confidence and credibility, and emphasis on high performance goals. Openness, and hence climate, has a very strong impact on a number of organizational variables, as the reviews by Falcione and Kaplan, Hellriegel and Slocum, Jablin, and James and Jones indicate.[22]

In the Hellriegel and Slocum review, for example, thirty-one studies were assessed, and it was concluded that organizational climate is clearly related to job satisfaction in terms of interpersonal relations, group cohesiveness, and task involvement. However, the climate-satisfaction relationship was more consistently observed than a climate-job performance relationship. Why? First, people apparently can adapt to the internal workings of an organization in order to perform effectively in it. Frederickson,[23] for example, found that workers performed better when they perceived the climate consistently as either "rules oriented" (less flexible) or "innovative" (very flexible, emphasizing freedom) than when the climate was perceived to be inconsistent. Inconsistency in the internal workings of an organization leads to increased job stress,[24] and impoverished climates are linked to higher rates of employee turnover.[25] Thus, open superior-subordinate relationships and supportive climates lead to increases in job satisfaction and, usually, to increases in performance. The lowest levels of job performance occur in organizations with inconsistent climates.

Also important to the relationships between climate and either satisfaction or performance is the personality of either the supervisor or the subordinate. Downey, Hellriegel, and Slocum[26] explored the way in which climate interacts with individual personality in influencing job satisfaction and performance. They found: (1) individuals needing social contact and interdependence, who perceived the climate as open and empathic and as encouraging high standards for achievement, were more satisfied with their supervision than those who perceived a closed, bureaucratic, and impersonal climate; (2) individuals who were self-confident and who perceived clearly assigned responsibilities and clear-cut policies were more satisfied with their co-workers than those who perceived the organization as unstructured; and, (3) highly sociable managers who perceived their climate as encouraging, lacking in threats, and humanitarian, performed better than less sociable managers.

Several studies, reviewed by Jablin,[27] explored subordinates' perceptions of their superior's communication behavior and personality. These studies indicate:

1. Superiors who are apprehensive communicators are not particularly liked by subordinates;

2. Subordinate's satisfaction with superiors can be predicted from several dimensions of homophily-heterophily (Homophily means that they are similar to each other—same race, same age, and so forth, heterophily means that they are very different from one another);

3. Authoritarian subordinates are most satisfied when they work for directive superiors;

4. Subordinate satisfaction with immediate supervision is related to subordinate perception of superior's credibility;

5. Confirmation of subordinate's needs for affection and dominance results in greater perceived frequency of interaction between superior and subordinate;

6. Subordinates in small groups, who require high interaction with co-workers and superiors and high interdependence, have negative attitudes toward authoritarian supervisors, whereas subordinates in large work groups, with restricted interaction and highly independent work, have more positive attitudes toward authoritarian supervision; and,

7. Subordinates, regardless of their personality, tend to be most satisfied with superiors high in human relations orientation.

In sum, persuaders who are managers will find their jobs easier in the organization if they do not have to overcome resistance on the part of subordinates, if they do not have to deal with suspicion when sending messages down the hierarchy and if superior and subordinates have a trusting, cooperative relationship. Hence, it is important for the persuader to (a) create the ideal image of being a communication-minded individual who is open, frank, honest, a careful listener and an articulate communicator; and (b) create an open, supportive, trusting, and consistent climate.

Effectively Changing Behavior Through Goal-Setting and Feedback

A common complaint by both supervisors and subordinates is they do not receive sufficient or relevant feedback. This is unfortunate since feedback, according to Jablin,[28] "provides information that denotes the success or failure of policies and objectives, suggests the need for corrective actions and controlling mechanisms, and provides members with knowledge of the other party's sentiments about formal and informal organizational activities." Two issues are of interest: (1) the positive and negative relational consequences of feedback; and (2) how feedback is used to increase performance.

Research has demonstrated that negative feedback has detrimental consequences on the superior-subordinate relationship. As Jablin noted, studies show that positive feedback transmitted to a leader makes him or her more task oriented, while negative feedback increases negative social-emotional behavior; that is, negativity is reciprocated. Further, negative feedback may not have an effect on performance if there are no specific suggestions concerning how the target of the feedback can improve.

More recently, Jablin[29] conducted a number of studies on the impact of communicative responses on the superior-subordinate relationship. He distinguished between five types of messages:

1. Confirmation (a response providing a speaker with both positive content and positive relational feedback);

2. Disagreement (a response providing a speaker with negative content feedback and positive relational feedback);

3. Accedence (a response providing a speaker with positive content feedback and with negative relational feedback);

4. Repudiation (a response providing a speaker with both negative content feedback and negative relational feedback); and,

5. Disconfirmation (a response providing a speaker with irrelevant content feedback and irrelevant relational feedback).

The results of his studies indicated the following:

1. Disconfirming messages were not acceptable in superior-subordinate relationships.

2. Subordinates preferred message responses from superiors that provided positive relational feedback.

3. A substantial degree of reciprocity existed for confirming messages, regardless of the openness of the superior-subordinate relationship.

4. Regardless of perceived openness or closedness of the communication relationship with the superior, subordinates expected the same types of responses from a superior, but evaluated the appropriateness of the responses differently. Subordinates in closed climates were more likely to be defensive than subordinates in open climates, and superiors and subordinates experience greater freedom to communicate in open climates.

5. Subordinates who perceived a closed relationship with their superior were prepared to respond to a superior's message which contained negative relational feedback with a response transmitting negative relational feedback toward the superior; however, this was not true for subordinates perceiving an open climate. That is, subordinates in closed climates were more likely to reciprocate negatively. Subordinates in open climates, however, would find that the use of negative relational feedback would prove costly by potentially ruining a positive and open relationship with their superiors.

Jablin lists a number of additional conclusions concerning the effects of the superior's feedback:

1. Superior's feedback to a subordinate which shows a lack of trust in the subordinate results in subordinate dissatisfaction and aggressive feelings.

2. Superiors perceived as expressive are more likely to provide subordinates with social approval than those superiors perceived as instrumental (task-oriented or directive).

3. In conflict situations, supervisory responses that relate acceptance and encouragement of subordinate disagreement were associated with high subordinate satisfaction.

4. Under low surveillance (infrequent need to report to superior), positive feedback from superior to subordinate leads to greater subordinate compliance than when the subordinate receives no direct feedback, whereas under high surveillance conditions subordinates who receive positive feedback from their superiors comply less than when they receive no direct feedback from their superiors.

5. Positive rewards from a leader are generally associated with subordinate satisfaction, but the relationship between a leader's punitive actions and subordinate satisfaction varies as a function of the nature of the task.

6. Supervisors who frequently criticize their subordinates for poor work are generally rated as less effective than those who criticize less frequently.

7. A supervisor provides positive reinforcement to a subordinate when he or she is positively reinforced by the subordinate's performance and negatively reinforces a subordinate when he or she is negatively reinforced as a result of the subordinate's performance.

These conclusions provide some rules to make feedback more useful and effective.

Further, Locke[30] has proposed a theory of "goal-setting" where productivity can be increased if a manager or persuader follows several rules: set specific and sufficiently challenging goals, select a performance level within the workers' range of abilities, use feedback ("knowledge of results") on a frequent basis to keep workers on track, offer rewards to attain the goal, be a supportive manager, and assign goals which the workers find acceptable.

Kim and Hamner[31] demonstrate that the type of feedback given to workers has a major impact on performance. Kim and Hamner went into four separate production plants of a telephone company and employed a different feedback system in each plant. Hence, there were four groups:

1. Workers in one plant received goal-setting instructions and informal feedback. Each Monday morning, foremen would meet with the workers and reemphasize goals that had not changed and explain any new goals. There was no formal feedback, but workers could receive informal feedback. (control group).

2. Workers at another plant received superior's feedback and praise. Workers received, from the foremen on Mondays, the number of workers who had met the weekly goal. Also, the goals for the current week were set or reemphasized. Then, some time during the week, the foreman would visit each employee and praise him/her on the performance categories in which the goals had been exceeded. The foremen were not allowed to give negative feedback during this session. (This group represented Goals + Superior's Feedback + Praise.)

3. Workers at a third plant received "formal self-feedback." Each Monday morning foremen would meet with employees to set goals or reemphasize goals for the current work week. On Friday of each week, the workers would rate themselves on a set of forms provided. These workers received "formal self-feedback"; no feedback from the superior was given.

4. The fourth and last plant received all of the above types of feedback—Goals + Formal self-feedback + Superior's Feedback + Praise.

Kim and Hamner found that the Goals + Self-feedback + Superior's Feedback + Praise group improved dramatically in cost efficiency over the 90 days, and was safer during the last 30-day period than the control group. The self-feedback group expressed less satisfaction with their present work assignment than did all other groups.

Two conclusions: (1) while it is possible to improve performance merely by implementing a goal-setting program, performance is generally more enhanced when combined with self-feedback, superior's feedback and praise; and, (2) formal self-feedback was not sufficient to provide optimum results.

There are several implications for the information presented here on goal-setting and feedback. When you are beginning a new job, it is likely that supervisors will set performance goals. This goal-setting should be seen as persuasion. Furthermore, the feedback received while attempting to achieve goal(s) has been shown to increase productivity. This feedback is also a form of influence. On the other side of the coin, when you reach a managerial position, it is important to realize the persuasive power of goal-setting and feedback on employees' performances.

Up to this point in the chapter, we have dealt with organizational influence, looking almost exclusively at the ability of superiors to influence subordinates. Now, let's look at how subordinates might influence their bosses.

UPWARD INFLUENCE AND THE DISTORTION OF COMMUNICATION

Upward Influence

According to Goldhaber,[32] upward communication refers to "messages which flow from subordinate to superior. It is usually for the purpose of asking questions, providing feedback, and making suggestions. Upward communication has the effect of improving morale and employee attitude, and therefore upward-directed messages are usually integrative (prosocial) and innovative." Superiors should value and encourage upward communication because: (1) it indicates the receptivity of the environment for downward communication; (2) it

facilitates acceptance of decisions by encouraging subordinate participation in the decision-making process; (3) it provides feedback about subordinate understanding of downward communication; and (4) it encourages submission of valuable ideas. Goldhaber also notes that the most effective way to reinforce upward communication is to listen sympathetically during many day-to-day informal contacts.

Kipnis and his colleagues, Wortman and Linsenmeier, Porter, Allen, and Angle, and Schilit and Locke[33] provide the most relevant literature on upward influence. Wortman and Linsenmeier provide a thorough review of literature on ingratiation, and discuss the possible effects of ingratiation in organizational settings, and Porter, Allen, and Angle offer a number of propositions concerning what types of influence methods different subordinates might use. Porter and associates examined the relationship between upward influence and political activity, arguing that most political activity in organizations involves upward influence. They proposed five methods for upward political influence: positive sanctions, negative sanctions, persuasion (the agent's influence attempt and goal are open), manipulative persuasion (the agent's attempt is open, but the goal is concealed), and manipulation (both the attempt and the goal are concealed).

Wortman and Linsenmeier[34] come to this conclusion about how one might impress a superior:

An ingratiator trying to impress a more powerful other should probably avoid the more obvious tactics. Most types of other-enhancement fall into this category. Directly praising the target person should be avoided, both because it is such an obvious tactic and because it may seem presumptuous. The tactic implies that the subordinate has the capacity to evaluate his superior, that he knows how his superior should behave and how his job can best be done.

Other-enhancement of a superior may be effective, however, if the subordinate compliments the superior on job areas in which the subordinate is recognized as knowledgeable, or on personal qualities that are unrelated to job performance. More subtle other-enhancing strategies, such as positive nonverbal gestures, may also be quite effective, as may other-enhancement if the compliment is conveyed by a third party.

Rendering favors may not be an especially good tactic, since it so often gives rise to the feeling that something is expected in return. Opinion conformity is also risky. . . . [Two studies] . . . have found that when a person's dependence upon another is obvious, he is liked better when he avoids lavish agreement with that person. Strategies such as anticipating the target person's views and expressing them before he has had a chance to do so, or mixing agreement on major issues with disagreement on minor ones would also seem prudent."

The Schilit and Locke[35] study asked for both the subordinate's and the superior's perspective on upward influence, and examined the effects of influence attempts. They found:

1. The typical employee, attempting to have influence on the organization, communicates directly with the superior.

2. Both subordinates and superiors thought that the more common method of influence was to present ideas logically ("rationality").

3. Superiors and subordinates typically recall the same tactics as being used, and, after rationality, listed persistence, using organizational rules, trading job-related benefits (exchange) and going over the supervisor's head as the more common methods. However, although nineteen types of tactics were studied, none of these tactics was, for subordinates, strongly related to success. The tactic, "threatening to resign," was significantly related

to failing to gain compliance. Superiors claimed to be influenced when the subordinate "used them as a platform for presenting ideas." On the other hand, superiors claimed to be very resistant to influence when (a) the subordinate challenged the authority of the supervisor, (b) the subordinate threatened to go over the head of the supervisor, and (c) the subordinate used external pressure.

4. The causes of successful and unsuccessful influence attempts were attributed differently by both superiors and subordinates. The cause of successful influence attempts were attributed to personal qualities by both the superior and the subordinate. Subordinates who were successful felt they were successful because (a) they were competent, (b) they made a positive presentation, (c) the influence attempt contained favorable information, and finally, (d) they had the support of the organization. When superiors claimed to have been influenced, they felt they were influenced because they (a) had favorable relations with the subordinate, or (b) were open-minded.

The results of this study are clear: Subordinates fail to gain compliance when using ultimatums, or when challenging the authority of the superior. They increase the chance of being successful if they convince the superior that they will benefit by complying, and if they emphasize gains over costs for the organization.

Kipnis and Schmidt[36] report on three studies examining the relationship of upward influence to performance evaluation, salary, and stress. They identified four upward influence styles: Shotgun, Ingratiator, Tactician, and Bystander. Figure 12.1 visually portrays the four influence strategy styles. Shotgun workers employed the most tactics (relying on assertiveness, bargaining, higher authority, and coalitions to influence others), while Ingratiators relied on friendliness. Bystanders employed few influence attempts, and Tacticians relied heavily on rationality.

FIGURE **12.1**

USE OF SIX INFLUENCE STRATEGIES BY FOUR TYPES OF INFLUENCERS

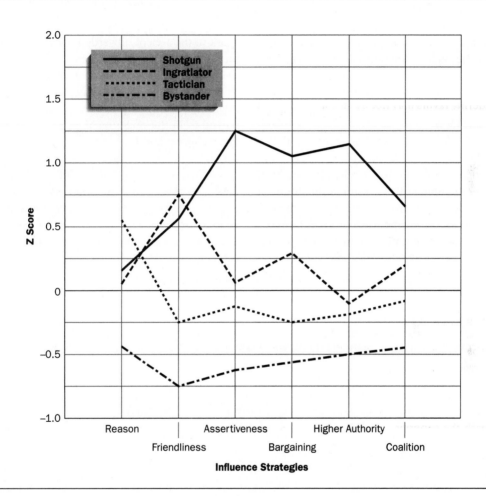

Reprinted from: "Upward-Influence Styles: Relationship with Performance Evaluations, Salary, and Stress," by D. Kipnis, and S.M. Schmidt, *Administrative Science Quarterly*, vol. 33, #4 (1988), pp. 528–542 by permission of *Administrative Science Quarterly*. Copyright © 1988.

Shotgun influencers received less favorable performance evaluations than the other styles. The authors found an interesting sex difference in the style receiving the highest performance evaluations. For men, Tacticians received the highest evaluations. For women, Ingratiators received the highest evaluations in one study, while Bystanders received the highest evaluations in another. The authors reasoned that men and women are socialized to use different influence styles. In other words, women may be *expected* to use an Ingratiator or Bystander style rather than a Tactician style.

In their third study, composed primarily of male CEOs of hospitals, Kipnis and Schmidt found that Tacticians received higher salaries than any of the other three styles (see Table 12.2). Relating influence styles to stress, Shotgun managers reported the highest level of stress, the most job tension, as well as other symptoms of stress such as anger and inability to sleep. Tacticians reported the lowest levels of personal stress and job tension (see Table 12.3).

Kipnis, Schmidt, and Braxton-Brown[37] recently discussed the *metamorphosis* effect. The metamorphosis effect refers to changes occurring to the *agent* of influence as a result of the influence attempt. The use of strong tactics (that is, using a Shotgun style of influence) increases the power-holder's sense of control over the target person. The agent's increased sense of power over the target results in a lower evaluation of the target by the agent.

Upward Distortion

Work in the area of upward distortion is important for at least two reasons. First, to function effectively an organization needs accurate information in order to reduce uncertainty and make appropriate decisions. The more an executive is removed from the operational level, the more messages concerning the status of operations must go through a number of superior-subordinate links. If subordinates want to "look good" to their immediate supervisor, then the information that the executive receives may be incorrect. Thus, if an executive makes a decision to increase sales, erroneously believing that production is high, problems will emerge.

T A B L E   12.1

RELATION BETWEEN SUBORDINATES' UPWARD-INFLUENCE STYLES AND SUPERVISOR'S PERFORMANCE EVALUATIONS

Influence Style	Study 1: Male	Workers Female	Study 2: Male	Supervisors** Female
Shotgun	24.0	32.3	30.1	32.4
Ingratiator	29.4	41.5*	32.7	35.9
Bystander	30.1	30.2	34.7	36.2
Tactician	32.7	31.0	36.0	33.3

* Higher scores denote more favorable evaluations.
** Based on the evaluations of male superiors.

Reprinted from: "Upward-Influence Styles: Relationship with Performance Evaluations, Salary, and Stress," by D. Kipnis, and S.M. Schmidt, *Administrative Science Quarterly*, vol. 33, #4 (1988), pp. 528–542 by permission of *Administrative Science Quarterly*. Copyright © 1988.

TABLE	12.2

AVERAGE ADJUSTED SALARY OF CEOs BY UPWARD-INFLUENCE STYLE

Influence Style	Salary
Shotgun	$57,000
Ingratiator	57,200
Bystander	60,000
Tactician	65,100

Reprinted from: "Upward-Influence Styles: Relationship with Performance Evaluations, Salary, and Stress," by D. Kipnis, and S.M. Schmidt, *Administrative Science Quarterly*, vol. 33, #4 (1988), pp. 528–542 by permission of *Administrative Science Quarterly*. Copyright © 1988.

TABLE	12.3

THE RELATION BETWEEN UPWARD-INFLUENCE STYLES AND JOB TENSION AND STRESS FOR CHIEF EXECUTIVE OFFICERS

Influence Style	Job Tension	Physical Stress	Psychological Stress
Shotgun	44.45	11.25	12.65
Ingratiator	37.55	10.65	10.15
Bystander	35.26	11.00	10.71
Tactician	32.00	8.64	8.55

High scores denote high levels of stress.

Reprinted from: "Upward-Influence Styles: Relationship with Performance Evaluations, Salary, and Stress," by D. Kipnis, and S.M. Schmidt, *Administrative Science Quarterly*, vol. 33, #4 (1988), pp. 528–542 by permission of *Administrative Science Quarterly*. Copyright © 1988.

Second, upward distortion is important because a communicator/persuader in middle management or higher may think that subordinates are more supportive and less resistant to persuasion than is actually the case. It is important, then, to identify sources of either distortion (the transforming of the meaning of a message), or omission (deletion of all or part of the message), and to identify methods for reducing the effects of such problems.[38] In dysfunctional circumstances, people of lower rank will omit critical comments in their communications with higher-ranking personnel who have power over the subordinates' advancement, resulting in a distinct lack of negative feedback at the higher levels of the hierarchy which may further result in incorrect decisions being made by upper management. Box 12.2 highlights the important problems with upward influence.

According to Krivonos,[39] subordinates tend to (a) distort information upward in a manner that pleases their superiors; (b) tell their superiors what they want them to know; (c) tell their superiors what they think they want to hear; and (d) tell their superiors information that reflects favorably on themselves.

Traditional organizational communication literature indicates three variables have a strong impact on upward distortion: trust in the supervisor, the subordinate's perception of how his or her future is controlled by the supervisor, and the subordinate's mobility aspirations. Of these three variables, trust appears to be the more important variable and is most consistently related to upward distortion.[40]

Each of these variables is related to the subordinate's motivations to distort upward messages. If trust is low, you may feel that information may be used against you. Obviously, the other variables reflect the need to maintain a good image.

Some attention has focused on identifying additional variables which influence upward

BOX 12.2

THE HISTORICAL SIGNIFICANCE OF PROBLEMS IN UPWARD COMMUNICATION

In 1756, the Nawab of Calcutta, Siraj-ud-Dowla, led his Indian troops in a surprising uprising against the British East India Company fort and trading post at Calcutta. The attack was successful, and the British surrendered. The Nawab ordered his lieutenants to put the 146 British captives in prison for the night. The only facility available was a small dungeon, about 20 feet by 20 feet with two small windows, which the British had used to lock up an occasional thief caught stealing company property. It was known locally as the "Black Hole."

The Nawab gave the order to lock up the prisoners and promptly went to sleep for the night. All 146 of the British men, women, and children were forced into the small space, ordinarily sufficient for only about 10 prisoners. But orders were orders, and the Nawab's lieutenants carried them out. The crowded prisoners immediately began to fight for air, as claustrophobia seized them in the hot night. Some were trampled. Others went insane. Appeals to the guards, who dared not awaken the Nawab, were not answered.

In the morning, only 23 of the prisoners came out alive.

The Black Hole of Calcutta became a shocking symbol of inhumanity to the British in India, and a rallying cry that led to the eventual defeat of the Nawab by Robert Clive in the battle of Plassey, an historical event that marked the beginning of India as an English colony.

What caused the many deaths in the Black Hole of Calcutta? Watney (cited below) comments that the tragedy began with a "not very intelligent subordinate who . . . obeyed [orders] in too literal a fashion. Later, no one . . . dared to take the responsibility of releasing the prisoners on their own initiative. Tragedies are often caused by such acts of bureaucratic inefficiency."

From: E.M. Rogers and R. Agarwala-Rogers, *Communication in Organizations* (New York: The Free Press, 1976), pp. 86–87; John Watney, *Clive in India* (London: Saxon House, 1974), p. 96.

distortion. Athanassiadas,[41] for example, found that upward distortion was less likely to occur in "autonomous" organizations (ones which give the worker considerable freedom) and more likely to occur in "heteronomous" organizational climates (more restrictive climates). Later, Young[42] found that less distortion occurs if the superior and subordinate are dependent upon each other, rather than when the subordinate is dependent upon the superior.

Level and Johnson[43] noted two factors relevant to reducing the subordinate's use of upward distortion—increasing the trust and openness between superior and subordinate, and increasing the accuracy of downward information. However, if there has not been much openness or trust in the organizational climate in the recent past, it is not simple to build trust quickly. Rogers and Agarwala-Rogers[44] offered three ways for dealing with problems of omission and distortion:

1. Redundancy is the repeating of a message in different forms, over different channels, or over time. For example, if an official has any reason to doubt the accuracy with which messages are relayed, she or he may create two or more reporting channels.

2. Verification is insuring the accuracy of a previous message. When distortion or omission is suspected in a message, an individual may try to use "counterbias" as a means to reduce the effects of distortion. In this case, a superior discounts some of what she or he hears as good or positive information and pays closer attention to (or emphasizes) negative information.

3. Bypassing is elimination of intermediaries in a communication flow. According to Rogers and Agarwala-Rogers, bypassing may be accomplished in one of three ways:

    a. Creating "flat" organizations by reducing the number of hierarchical levels through which messages flow. Here the communication principle that the more links a message must pass through increases the message distortion is applied.

    b. By having high officials directly inspect the operational level.

    c. By using devices such as suggestion boxes or other intermediaries as the bearers of ill tidings.

Unfortunately, all of these methods for dealing with distortion increase the number of messages which are in circulation, and some organizations may already be overloaded with messages and information.

In sum, many of your initial influence attempts in an organization are likely to be aimed upward. Therefore, it is important to understand the "ins and outs" of upward influence. When you become a manager, you need to understand the deleterious effects of distortion and become familiar with how to lessen its occurrence.

POLITICAL STRATEGIES

The term "political strategies" is used to refer to actions taken by employees to accomplish their desired goals. These political strategies often evolve over time, involve communication, and result in increased power for the agent (if successful). Political maneuverings and manipulations are a fact of life in virtually any organization in which people compete for resources, rewards, and recognition.

Pfeffer[45] provides the most cogent discussion of political strategies. We will explain and provide examples of the following strategies: (1) Selective Criteria; (2) Outside Experts; (3) Controlling the Agenda; (4) Coalitions; (5) External Constituencies; (6) Cooptation; and, (7) Informational Influence.

Selective Criteria Think about the entrance requirements for your college. What is the SAT (or ACT) score cutoff? Is there a high school GPA criterion? Did you need to have a foreign language in high school? All of these things are criteria that help determine who will attend your college and who will not. While we normally do not question such criteria, we should ask ourselves, "Who set these criteria?" "What were their motives in setting the criteria as they did?" and "Did they have a specific reason for setting a standard particularly high or low?"

Imagine the following scenario: A full professor, Dr. Einstruck, feels that the quality of students is deteriorating. Einstruck is a very powerful faculty member who, through connections, gains a place on the admissions committee. Through this position, Einstruck persuades the other committee members to institute an extremely high score on the SAT as a prerequisite for admission.

Changing the criteria for the SAT score may seem very rational, but there may have been an enormous amount of political maneuvering to set the scores so high. This is an example, then, of using selective criteria as a political strategy.

Political manipulations concerning "selective criteria" involve many other areas of organizational life besides admitting students. Consider how organizations decide how to assign bonuses and merit. Some workers feel that equality should be a guiding force—all workers should receive an across-the-board pay raise. On the other hand, other workers believe that superior workers (those who are harder working and display more dedication) should be paid higher wages for having helped the organization achieve production standards. Giving an across-the-board pay raise to all workers may not seem fair to the harder-working ones, but giving only merit bonuses to superior workers doesn't appear fair to the average worker. Hence, organizational members need to create guidelines (sometimes involving a compromise) concerning the criteria of who is selected for pay raises.

Outside Experts Imagine you work as an assistant manager of a local AT&T office. You want to institute a change that another manager (at the same level) vehemently opposes. Your boss, manager of the district, says that both of you have six months to bring in evidence for why the change should or should not be implemented. While admiring your graduation ring you suddenly think of an old roommate who is now a management consultant—one who has done well and is renowned in providing excellent business advice. You give your old friend a call and explain the situation. If you hire this person to provide the necessary arguments to get the change implemented, you have used an outside expert as a political strategy.

Controlling the Agenda The person who controls the items discussed at a meeting has the potential to exert tremendous influence. For example, think of a club of which you are a member. Let's say that you are good friends with Sally, the president, who runs the monthly meetings. You tell Sally beforehand that you have an idea for a certain project. Meanwhile, Sally knows that Brad, your archenemy, also wants some time during the meeting to propose a project.

The meeting begins and your club takes care of the usual trivial business. Sally then introduces you to propose your project. Lively discussion follows and your project is approved. Sally then looks at her watch and says, "Well, I know we've all got lots of things to do, so why don't we adjourn for the night." Even if Brad protests, Sally can always say something like, "That's interesting, Brad, why don't we take that up more fully at next month's meeting?" Furthermore, even if Brad does get to discuss his project, it may be less likely to be approved since your project has already gained acceptance. Sally used her power to control the agenda.

Coalitions Coalitions involve individuals (or groups of individuals) joining forces to achieve goals that they would otherwise not have been able to attain. Imagine an organization with three key departments: marketing, production, and accounting. Suppose that the respective power distribution between the departments is as follows: marketing > production > accounting; but marketing < production + accounting. In other words, if production and accounting were to join forces they would be more powerful than marketing. Any time production and accounting are split on votes, marketing will almost certainly get its way. However, if production and accounting pool their voting resources and do something like slice into marketing's budget for the upcoming year, we would say that the two departments formed a coalition to obtain their goals. A downside of coalition formation is that one group may end up owing favors.

External Constituencies Influential friends *outside* the organization can sometimes be as helpful as influential friends *within* the organization. For example, if your university has a School of Law, the alumni (practicing lawyers and judges) are probably very influential in swaying important decisions within the university regarding the School of Law. If the university decided to "retrench" or "downsize" the School of Law (for example, release three faculty members and reduce the library's acquisitions), there would probably be an outcry from the alumni. Since the lawyers and judges may exert their displeasure by curtailing their financial contributions, the administration is more likely to *not* touch the School of Law in times of budget cutbacks. Therefore, by having influential friends *outside* the university, the School of Law has increased its influence *within* the university.

Other examples of potentially powerful external constituencies might be a national labor union for a manufacturing plant, the American Medical Association for a medical clinic, or journalists, lawyers, or politicians who received communication degrees and/or participated in collegiate debates.

At times having a useful external constituency may be even more productive than forming a coalition within the organization. Why? When form-

ing an alliance with groups within your organization, you are likely to make conceptual compromises and are very likely to owe favors in the future. With an external constituency, a group is much less likely to have to compromise their stand or to pay back favors at a later time.

Cooptation Cooptation is a strategy where dissenters are given a voice in the decision-making process (even if it is only a pseudovoice) in order to diminish their ability to protest decisions and/or the decision-making process. Imagine that you are a sectional manager in charge of twelve salespeople in a clothing store. One of your workers, Bob, constantly complains to the other employees about your decisions as biased and whimsical. You have tried to explain that there are many factors which go into your decisions, but Bob still complains. Rather than firing Bob or trying to make his life miserable, you could coopt him by including him in the decision-making process or even by giving him responsibility for making certain decisions such as work schedules for the rest of the employees. By allowing Bob to take part in the decision-making process you may do several things. First, you diminish his ability to justifiably complain about the decisions—he was part of the decision! Second, Bob may actually have some good ideas! If some of his ideas work, great—you win by improving the quality of the department and increasing the satisfaction of the employees. If some of his ideas do not work, great—you may not have to listen to Bob moan and groan all of the time.

Although there are several benefits to cooptation, you should be aware of the potential trade-offs. You *do* have to give someone a certain amount of say in the decision-making process. Also, Bob may take your move as a positive reward for his behavior and start complaining even more. Furthermore, you will have to give Bob access to information you might not otherwise want him to see. Therefore, cooptation may not work well in all situations.

Informational Influence The final strategy we will discuss is using information to influence others. Pfeffer, Feldman, and March[46] have noted that there may be very symbolic ramifications for gathering, processing, and disseminating large amounts of information. For example, recall the example used under the topic of "outside experts" where your boss asked both you and a co-worker to prepare reasons for accepting or rejecting a proposed change. Suppose you compile a 250-page report on the topic suggesting that the best course of action is to accept the change. Meanwhile, your co-worker (who is opposed to the change) has prepared only a lackluster, extemporaneous four-minute oral presentation on why the change should be rejected. Unless your report was absolutely worthless, it is likely that your boss will decide in your favor simply because of the sheer bulk of information you collected. This would be an example of informational influence.

A Case Study of Power Expansion

We have only skimmed the surface of political strategies in organizations. In practice, organization members have to confront the fact that power ploys of a wide variety are always operating at any given time in large-scale organizations. Pfeffer[47] makes a point that is worth noting before we leave the topic. Pfeffer notes that power (or the exercise of power through political strategies) is best used *unobtrusively*. In other words, it is normally preferable to get someone to do something without their even realizing you have persuaded or influenced them.

Most individuals begin work in a company without much power. How individuals go about gaining power is different from one organization to another, depending upon competition, their superior's support for them, and other obstacles or advantages. To highlight *one* way in which individuals might achieve additional power, we will briefly describe the tactics of power expansion employed by a worker at an electronics firm. Izraeli[48] first noted that a middle manager is often in a dilemma: The middle manager is required to achieve certain goals, such as solving worker disputes and increasing or maintaining a certain level of productivity; but a "middle" manager typically has little authority or power to achieve a goal.

Three options are available to a person in this position. First, the middle manager may try to function in a *feudal* mode by becoming dependent on the supervisor, doing the bidding for the supervisor and becoming an extension of the supervisor in order to have authority. Second, the middle manager may try to function in a *bureaucratic* mode by learning a set of rules and rigorously adhering to the rules. Neither of these approaches is likely to be adopted by middle managers who are ambitious and want to be promoted.

A third option is to adopt an *expansionist* mode, in which the middle manager attempts to gain control over organizational resources by seeking alliances with others in the organization. Izraeli details four tactics, used over the course of a year, that helped a middle manager increase his level of power in the organization:

I.   Neutralizing Potential Opposition

The first requirement is for the new middle manager to seek an alliance with the immediate subordinates—the fore(wo)men or the "first line" supervisors. There is some chance that at least one of these people applied for the middle manager's job, and potential jealousy/hard feelings will pose serious problems for the new middle manager who does not reduce such feelings. Individuals in an organization rarely like change, so the new middle manager needs to become familiar with the fore(wo)men, soothe any anxiety, and open lines of communication with these individuals. If successful, the middle manager secures access to information and gains access to the informal communication network.

Workers are going to be suspicious of the new middle manager and of new demands. Some of these workers can be convinced that new quotas on productivity, or new rates and rules, will *benefit* all the workers in the unit—the alternative judgment on the part of the workers (that they work harder and the middle manager takes all the credit) would be devastating to the middle manager's attempt to expand the power base.

Second, the new middle manager is replacing a person who may have held the position for some years. The former middle manager may have had many friends in the work unit. For the new middle manager, these old friends are the greatest threat to an expansionist attempt. One option is to use the "cooptation" strategy discussed above. In the Izraeli analysis, an older worker named Tom continued to work at his own rate, worked as much overtime as possible and reported the overtime directly to the new middle manager's supervisor (blatantly bypassing the line of communication). The new middle manager eventually was successful at characterizing Tom as a troublemaker and sought the assistance of the supervisor to solve these problems with Tom. Life was easier for the new middle manager once Tom's reputation in the organization was tarnished, and Tom was somewhat isolated from others.

II. Strategic Replacements

Workers naturally create little serfdoms and will go to great lengths to control what they can. In the Izraeli example, Queenie presided over quality control, and she blocked the new middle manager's goal of expanding power and increasing productivity. She refused to fully train any other worker, and refused to be hurried in completing quality control checks. She had worked for the company for thirteen years and knew she had the support of the new middle manager's supervisor. Yet, Queenie was disliked by the workers because she slowed production and (so they thought) rejected televisions that were, in fact, error-free.

To increase power, the middle manager had to replace or bypass Queenie's control. The new middle manager could not argue against quality control to his superior. However, he did argue that while Queenie was a valuable employee, she had become an economic liability because of the lack of speed at which quality control checks were being made. A number of discussions focused on the topic of Queenie, with the point made that if she was so competent, she could easily train someone else to do the quality control checks. When the new middle manager's supervisor was also pressured into increasing productivity by the board of directors, the supervisor relented and a second full-time worker was placed on quality control. As months passed, the new middle manager replaced Queenie, with the new worker being promoted to the position of quality controller. The added advantage of replacing Queenie was that workers were happier and could credit the new middle manager.

III. Committing the Uncommitted

Beyond neutralizing potential enemies and replacing people who would block the middle manager's goals, the middle manager needs to seek out the commitment of the remaining workers—to gain their confidence, liking, respect, and to motivate them. Izraeli listed three general influence tactics that can be used: pay raises and bonuses, promises of increases in pay and bonuses, and ingratiation tactics. The new manager was able to secure one-time work bonuses for two of the oldest workers, and identified other merit-worthy workers whom, he told, would receive bonuses when they became available. He joked or otherwise used "personal charm" with younger workers to create a pleasant, happy work climate.

IV. A Winning Coalition

Finally, to expand one's base of power, the motivated middle manager needs to expand his/ her visibility beyond the work unit. The first course of action is to create a positive relationship with his/her superior's immediate superior. Achieving this goal requires different kinds of ingratiation tactics than those employed on subordinates; the middle manager needs to assess the interests, motives, and concerns of the higher status superior and adopt those views as his own (if this can be done credibly and plausibly). A middle manager increases his/her own power and reduces a superior's level of power and control by grooming a relationship with people high in power.

The use of these tactics enables the middle manager to have greater control of the day-by-day operations in the work unit, to be able to accept credit for improved relationships and increased productivity, and to make it difficult for others to neutralize and/or replace him/her in the power hierarchy.

COMMUNICATION NETWORKS AND ROLES

The first few sections of this chapter discussed details of communication between two individuals who are placed in a hierarchical structure. However, much communication relevant to persuasion occurs in informal channels. People "shoot the breeze" discussing politics, satisfactions, dissatisfactions, innovations, and so forth, while eating lunch, at the water cooler, or on the golf course. To study informal channels of communication, scholars study networks—how people are interconnected with one another through communication. A communication network is a picture of who talks to whom. These informal communication patterns are, typically, more likely to emerge spontaneously, to be less structured and less predictable than communication in formal channels. An understanding of the flow of information in the organization is important for any persuader; since we can only briefly present the ideas here, the

reader will find the best discussions of network analysis in Farace, Monge, and Russell, Goldhaber, Rogers and Agarwala-Rogers, and Rogers and Kincaid.[49]

When you were in high school you probably observed that the members of the varsity football team tended to "hang out" together. Also, certain members of the team tended to eat together and do things together after school. The members of the team formed a loose-knit subgroup within the high school. It is possible that the quarterback may have been popular enough to be elected student body president. This person may have been a part-time member of a number of groups, but not a routine or typical member of any one group. If you have made observations such as these, then you have already experienced the dynamics and consequences of networks.

We study networks in order to compare the organizational structure (formal channel) with the actual flow of communication (informal channel), identify specialized roles in the flow of information, and study how the flow of communication impedes or enhances the communication within the organization.

Figure 12.2 presents an example of an organizational network pattern. By observation or by use of questionnaires, we identify who speaks to whom. A communication group is a set of individuals who routinely communicate with one another. There are three groups (or cliques) in Figure 12.2. There are several characteristics about communication groups that persuaders need to note. First, a group may be highly interconnected if all members in the group talk to all other members of the group. Groups 1 and 3 in our figure are highly interconnected. On the other hand, a radial network is one in which an individual interacts directly with others who do not interact with each other.

Rather, they interact with others outside the first small clique. For example, a person is a quarterback, member of the Model U.S. Club, student body president, co-captain of the basketball team

F I G U R E   *12.2*

ILLUSTRATION OF COMMUNICATION NETWORK ROLES

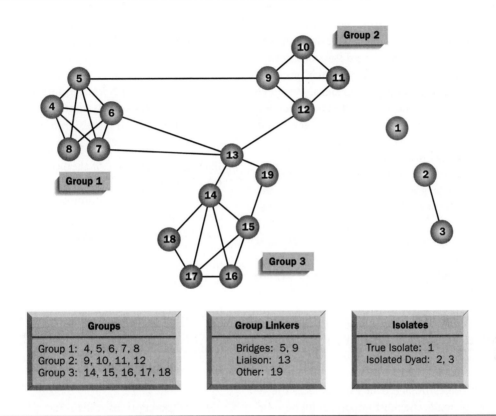

Groups
Group 1: 4, 5, 6, 7, 8
Group 2: 9, 10, 11, 12
Group 3: 14, 15, 16, 17, 18

Group Linkers
Bridges: 5, 9
Liaison: 13
Other: 19

Isolates
True Isolate: 1
Isolated Dyad: 2, 3

From: R.V. Farace, P.R. Monge, and H.M. Russell, *Communicating and Organizing* (Reading, Mass.: Addison-Wesley, 1977). Reprinted with permission of McGraw-Hill, Copyright © 1977.

and an active member of a Christian youth club. This person's personal network extends out to many more people and is called "radial."

Considerable research demonstrates that the distinction between radial and interconnected networks is important. Members of groups which are highly interconnected tend to be very similar to one another, have the same knowledge and opinions, and are, as a consequence, less likely to

be innovative. Individuals in radial networks, however, have access to different types of information; they are more likely to be well informed and generate more innovative ideas.

A second important characteristic of groups is the degree to which they are interconnected with the rest of the organization. All three of the groups in our figure are equally interconnected with other organizational members. However, suppose person 12 left the organization; group 2 would be poorly connected. Further, if a message were transmitted out to organizational members from person 16, the message may not accurately reach group 2.

Bridges are those individuals who help link or "bridge" one group to another. Obviously, a moderately high number of bridges is desirable if one wants a flexible and unrestricted flow of information in the organization. Little research has been done on the characteristics of bridges. Research does, however, indicate that between 45 percent and 75 percent of the members of any organization will be group members and bridges.[50] Persons 5 and 9 are bridges in Figure 12.2.

Isolates are individuals who choose not to talk to others and who are not chosen by others as communication partners. These individuals often become "information sinks" (when they hear something they fail to pass it along), they are less satisfied, they inhibit the flow of information, are less secure, younger, have fewer years of experience, and perceive the organization as less open. Surprisingly, research indicates that in some organizations, the frequency of isolates may range from 27 to 50 percent. Generally speaking, the fewer the isolates, the better the organization functions.

Of the roles depicted in Figure 12.2, the liaison role is clearly the most important for our purpose. Liaisons interact with two or more groups, but are not members of any group themselves. Roughly 5 to 15 percent of members of any organization are liaisons (and as many as 40 percent of the faculty at a university are identified as liaisons). Since the role played by liaisons is so important, considerable research has focused on identifying characteristics.

There are three types of conclusions:[51]

1. Actual differences between liaisons and nonliaisons include:

(a) liaisons have higher agreement between themselves and others they talk to about the identity of their contacts than do nonliaisons;

(b) liaisons are more likely than others in the organization to serve as first sources of information;

(c) liaisons have higher formal status in the organization than do nonliaisons.

(d) liaisons have been organizational members for longer periods of time than have nonliaisons;

(e) the levels of formal education and the ages of liaisons are similar to those of nonliaisons.

2. Liaisons' perception of themselves versus nonliaisons' perceptions of themselves:

(a) liaisons perceive themselves to have greater numbers of communication contacts in the organization;

(b) liaisons perceive themselves to have greater amounts of information with respect to the content dimensions upon which their role is defined;

(c) liaisons perceive the communication system as more "open"—information is seen as more timely, more believable, and more useful;

(d) liaisons perceive themselves to have greater influence in the organization.

3. Others' perceptions of liaisons:

(a) liaisons are perceived by others to have greater numbers of communication contacts in the organization;

(b) liaisons' communication contacts are seen as having a wider range throughout the organization structure;

(c) liaisons are perceived as having more information about the content dimensions on which the network is defined;

(d) liaisons are perceived as having more control over the flow of information in the organization;

(e) liaisons are perceived to have more influence over the "power structure" of the organization;

(f) liaisons are perceived to be more competent at their organizational activities.

Goldhaber[52] adds, from his own research, that liaisons are more gregarious, influential, and satisfied than are isolates, hold higher official positions in the organization, and are integrated with diverse groups which enhance their power.

To the persuader who is inside or outside the organization, knowledge of who are the liaisons and bridges is extremely important in influencing others. If you can persuade the liaisons early in the process, they will help spread the word, help persuade others because they have the contacts, they influence others, and will help reduce resistance.

One of the worst things that could happen to a persuader is to find that the liaisons in the organization are resistant to proposed changes because the liaisons have an automatic coalition already formed. Second, the potential persuader would find it useful to have access to liaisons because they can provide more information about the internal workings of the organization which would help the persuader to better adapt messages to different audiences.

A network role not shown in Figure 12.2, yet related to information flow, is "boundary spanner" or "boundary role person" (BRP). Boundary spanners are those individuals who acquire, process, and pass along information across the boundary between their organization and the external environment. In other words, boundary spanners attempt to keep their organization in close touch with its environment by being linked internally and externally, acquiring and translating important information.[53]

Spekman[54] found that as organizational members' "information requirements increase under conditions of higher perceived environmental uncertainty, the constituent members attribute to the BRP greater power in the decision-making process." Therefore, a boundary spanner has the potential to be very influential, in much the same way as liaisons and bridges. Another way in which communication networks relate to influence in organizations is that simply being in certain networks may be a source of power. In other words, if you regularly communicate with "powerful" people in the organization, you are likely to pick up important information and gain status.

A study by Brass[55] helps explain the importance of being linked to certain networks. Brass studied the networks of men and women in an organization to see if there was a relationship between a person's network activity and his or her perceived influence and promotion. Brass found that while women demonstrated network activity, even being well-connected, they were not sufficiently connected to the "right" network—the dominant networks which included the most powerful people, the networks that could enhance their influence. Brass[56] had earlier examined the relationship between structural position in the communication network and influence in the organization in an article entitled, "Being in the Right Place: A Structural Analysis of Individual Influence in an Organization." The author found that, "Measures of the relative positions of employees within workflow, communication, and friendship networks were strongly related to perceptions of influence . . . and to promotions to the supervisory level."[57] Hence, as the title of Brass's article suggests, being influential may often be a matter of simply "being in the right place."

To fully understand communication networks in organizations, it is important to briefly discuss the differences between formal and informal channels of communication and flexible and inflexible networks. Nearly all organizations will develop both formal and informal channels of communication. In a flexible organization, there is considerable freedom to communicate. There are consequences which follow from allowing increased freedom, and these are five important issues:

First, organizations which exhibit high degrees of flexibility tend to have high levels of knowledge among members. Such flexibility allows for the transmission of information to every member of an organization, rather than only to those people in authority positions. The communicator can often use such channels to avoid material being buried at any given level. There are two disadvantages in working with such an organization. First, there are times when a persuasive communicator might not want information to reach all members of the organization, and that is difficult to prevent when there is high flexibility. Second, the opportunities for distortion of the message are greater when there is a strong grapevine operating. Because the message has not been authorized for transmission, the people who pass it along are frequently not accurate in transmitting the message.

Second, grapevines can be used to sound out the members of an organization. Frequently, individuals in positions of authority will leak information into an informal network as a test. If there seems to be general acceptance of an idea, the message is then placed within the formal system as policy. If the message provokes significant objections while it is in the informal network, the individual releasing the information can deny making the proposal and thus avoid losing credibility or authority. Sometimes, the communicator can reach an individual who is not willing to commit to a proposal, but is willing to leak the proposal.

We should note that this suggestion of "floating a trial balloon" works best in those organizations in which there is a grapevine. In those situations where everyone in the organization has easy access to everyone else, it is easy to check on the accuracy of any new idea with other people in the organization.

Goldhaber[58] makes several points concerning the grapevine. The grapevine is fast, carries much information, travels by cluster (that is, information does not spread out in a chainlike fashion; information spreads in leaps and bounds), and can be very accurate. In fact, Goldhaber argues that the grapevine can be accurate 78 to 90 percent of the time for noncontroversial topics. However, rumors can also spread falsehoods and spread more quickly based on the importance and the ambiguity of the information. Once a rumor begins, it is critically important to convey accurate information to all relevant and affected parties.

Third, organizational flexibility is closely related to the accuracy with which a message is received within an organization. An organization having high flexibility encourages feedback, and individuals within the organization are able to check the accuracy of any persuasive messages transmitted within the organization. On the other hand, an organization having low flexibility but a well-developed grapevine may have a tendency to distort any persuasive messages transmitted within the organization. Feedback is more difficult when a grapevine is being used since accuracy checking is not officially accessible. The informal channel is more likely to make use of oral communication, and thus increase the possibility that a message will be distorted as it passes from person to person. This is a disadvantage because a persuasive message placed by an outside communicator into a channel may become completely distorted, and the source has no opportunity to correct the message.

Fourth, there are few checks on the operation of compliance in an informal channel. When a message ordering some action is transmitted within a formal network, the individual occupying a higher position has the power to urge compliance on those in lower positions. For the message passing through the informal network, however, no such compliance mechanism is present. The message will have to succeed or fail on its own merits. We should note that compliance is also difficult to secure in a highly flexible organization. Such organizations typically encourage communication between members of the organization, and when debate, argument, or suggestions are encouraged, compliance is harder to secure. Persuasion has to depend more on the merits of the issue, and less on the position of the source or the social power the source might possess.

Finally, flexibility may be controlled within an organization. There is no way to determine just how a grapevine is likely to be organized or how it will operate. There may be a grapevine composed of all members of the organization who attend the same church, or who went to school together, or who are in the same car pool. An individual who is in one informal net as a member of a car pool may be in another as a member of the company bowling team. One network may overlap with another solely as a result of this one individual. Predicting exactly who will be in a particular network is difficult, and this may result in the failure of a message to pass through the network.

Most organizations include both formal and informal networks. Which can be used with the most effectiveness is a decision the communicator makes after careful analysis of the situation. Communication flexibility is an important characteristic of any organization. It is closely related to accuracy of information transmission within the organization and to organizational goals. Formal organizations develop rules and norms regarding information transmission within the hierarchy, and frequently develop informal channels that bypass the formal communication networks.

F O O T N O T E S

1. D. Kipnis, S. M. Schmidt, and I. Wilkinson, "Intraorganizational Influence Tactics: Explorations in Getting One's Way," *Journal of Applied Psychology*, vol. 65 (1980), pp. 44-452.

2. I. Wilkinson and D. Kipnis, "Interfirm Use of Power," *Journal of Applied Psychology*, vol. 53, (1978), pp. 315-320.

3. D. Kipnis, The *Powerholders* (Chicago: University of Chicago Press, 1976); D. Kipnis, P. J. Castell, M. Gergen, and D. Mauch, "Metamorphic Effects of Power," *Journal of Applied Psychology*, vol. 61, (1976), pp. 127-135.

4. G. F. Farris and F. G. Lim, "Effects of Performance on Leadership, Cohesiveness, Influence, Satisfaction and Subsequent Performance," *Journal of Applied Psychology*, vol. 53 (1969), pp. 490-497; C. N. Greene, "The Reciprocal Nature of Influence Between Leader and Subordinate," *Journal of Applied Psychology*, vol. 60 (1975), pp. 187-193; D. M. Herold, "Two-way Influence Processes in Leader-Follower Dyads," *Academy of Management Journal*, vol. 20 (1977), pp. 224-237; A. Lowin and J. R. Craig, "The Influence of Level of Performance on Managerial Style: An Experimental Object-Lesson in the Ambiguity of Correlational Data," *Organizational Behavior and Human Performance*, vol. 3 (1968), pp. 440-458.

5. Greene, "The Reciprocal Nature of Influence Between Leader and Subordinate."

6. V. P. Richmond, L. M. Davis, K. Saylor, and J. C. McCroskey, "Power Strategies in Organizations: Communication Techniques and Messages," *Human Communication Research*, vol. 11 (1984), pp. 85-108.

7. J.G. Bachman, D.G. Bowers, and P.M. Marcus, "Bases of Supervisory Power: A Comparative Study in Five Organizational Settings," in A.S. Tannenbaum, ed., *Control in Organizations* (New York: McGraw-Hill, 1968), pp. 229-238.

8. Richmond, Davis, Saylor, and McCroskey, "Power Strategies in Organizations."

9. V. P. Richmond and J. C. McCroskey, "Power in Classroom II: Power and Learning," *Communication Education* (in press); also see: P. Kearney, T. G. Plax, V. P. Richmond, and J. C. McCroskey, "Power in Classroom IV: Alternatives to Discipline," in R. Bostrom, ed., *Communication Yearbook 8* (Beverly Hills: Sage, 1984), pp. 724-746.

10. M. Patchen, "The Locus and Basis of Influence on Organizational Decisions," *Organizational Behavior and Human Performance*, vol. 11 (1974), pp. 195-221.

11. P. M. Padsakoff, "Determinants of a Supervisor's Use of Rewards and Punishments: A Literature Review and Suggestions for Further Research," *Organizational*

Behavior and Human Performance, vol. 29 (1982), p. 58; also: C. N. Greene and P. M. Podsakoff, "Effects of Withdrawal of a Performance-Contingent Reward on Supervisory Influence and Power," *Academy of Management Journal*, vol. 19 (1976), pp. 514-542.

12.   J. J. House, "A Path-Goal Theory of Leader Effectiveness," *Administrative Science Quarterly*, vol. 16 (1971), pp. 19-30; also: R. T. Keller and A. D. Szilagyi, "Employee Reactions to Leader Reward Behavior," *Academy of Management Journal*, vol. 19 (1976), pp. 619-627.

13.   R. D. Arvey and J. M. Ivancevich, "Punishment in Organizations: A Review, Propositions, and Research Suggestions," *Academy of Management Review*, vol. 5 (1980), pp. 123-132; also: H. P. Sims, "Further Thoughts on Punishment in Organizations," *Academy of Management Review*, vol. 5 (1980), pp. 133-138.

14.   Kipnis, Schmidt, and Wilkinson, "Intraorganizational Influence Tactics."

15.   D. Kipnis, S.M. Schmidt, C. Swaffin-Smith, and I. Wilkinson, "Patterns of Managerial Influence: Shotgun Managers, Tacticians, and Bystanders," *Organizational Dynamics*, (Winter 1984), pp. 58-67.

16.   See, for instance, A.T. Cobb, "Informal Influence in the Formal Organization: Perceived Sources of Power Among Work Unit Peers," *Academy of Management Journal*, vol. 23 (1980), pp. 155-161; S.C. Freedman, "Threats, Promises, and Coalitions: A Study of Compliance and Retaliation in a Simulated Organizational Setting," *Journal of Applied Social Psychology*, vol. 11 (1981), pp. 114-136; P.J. Frost, "Power, Politics, and Influence," in F. Jablin, L. Putnam, K. Roberts, and L. Porter, eds., *Handbook of Organizational Communication: An Interdisciplinary Perspective* (Newbury Park, Calif.: Sage, 1987), pp. 503-548; K.J. Krone and J.T. Ludlum, "An Organizational Perspective on Interpersonal Influence," in J.P. Dillard, ed., *Seeking Compliance* (Scottsdale, Ariz.: Gorsuch Scarisbrick, 1990), pp. 123-142; S.C. Riccillo and S. Trenholm, "Predicting Managers' Choice of Influence Mode: The Effects of Interpersonal Trust and Worker Attributions on Managerial Tactics in a Simulated Organizational Setting," *Western Journal of Speech Communication*, vol. 47 (1983), pp. 323-339; D.R. Seibold, J.G. Cantrill, and R. Meyers, "Communication and Interpersonal Influence," in M.L. Knapp and G.R. Miller, eds., *Handbook of Interpersonal Communication* (Newbury Park, Calif.: Sage, 1985), pp. 551-611; C. Stohl and W.C. Redding, "Messages and Message Exchange Processes," in F. Jablin, L. Putnam, K. Roberts, and L. Porter, eds., *Handbook of Organizational Communication: An Interdisciplinary Perspective* (Newbury Park, Calif.: Sage, 1987), pp. 451-502; J.J. Sullivan, T. Albrecht, and S. Taylor, "The Compliance-Gaining Process Between Superiors and Key Subordinates" (paper presented to the annual meeting of the International Communication Association, New Orleans, La, 1987).

17.   W. C. Redding, *Communication Within the Organization*, (New York: Industrial Communications Council, 1972).

18.   F. M. Jablin, "Superior-Subordinate Communication: The State of the Art," *Psychological Bulletin*, vol. 86 (1979), pp. 1201-1222.

19.   R. Klauss and B. M. Bass, *Interpersonal Communication in Organizations* (New York: Academic Press, 1982).

20.   E. M. Rogers and R. Agarwala-Rogers, *Communication in Organizations* (New York: The Free Press, 1976), p. 73.

21.   Redding (Note 17), quoted in G.M. Goldhaber, *Organizational Communication*, 3rd ed. (Dubuque, Iowa: William C. Brown), p. 222.

22.   R. L. Falcione and E. A. Kaplan, "Organizational Climate, Communication and Culture," in R. Bostrom, ed., *Communication Yearbook 8*, (Beverly Hills: Sage, 1984) pp. 285-309; D. Hellriegel and J. W. Slocum, "Organizational Climate: Measures, Research, and Contingencies," *Academy of Management Journal*, vol. 17 (1974), pp. 255-280; F. Jablin, "Organizational Communication Theory and Research: An Overview of Communication Climate and Network Research," in D. Nimmo, ed., *Communication Yearbook 4*, (New Brunswick, N. J.: Transaction, 1980), pp. 327-347; L. R. James and A. P. Jones, "Psychological Climate: Dimensions and Relationships of Individual and Aggregated Work Environment Perceptions," *Organizational Behavior and Group Performance*, vol. 23 (1976), pp. 95-103.

23.   N. Frederickson, "Administrative Performance in Relation to Organizational Climate" (paper presented at the American Psychological Association Convention, San Francisco, September, 1968); N. Frederickson, "Some Effects of Organizational Climates on Administrative Performance" (Research Memorandum RM-66-21, Educational Testing Service, 1966); cited in Hellriegel and Slocum (Note 22).

24.   C. L. Cooper and J. Marshall, "Occupational Sources of Stress: A Review of the Literature Relating to Coronary Heart Disease and Mental Ill Health," *Occupational Psychology*, vol. 49 (1976), pp. 11-48; D. F. Parker, "Organizational Determinants of Job Stress," *Organizational Behavior and Human Performance*, vol. 32 (1983), pp. 160-177; L. R. Smeltzer, "The Relationship

of Communication to Work Stress," (paper presented to the International Communication Association Convention, Boston, Mass., 1982).

25. R. E. Kushell, "How to Reduce Turnover by Creating a Positive Work Climate," *Personnel Journal*, vol. 58 (1979), pp. 551-552.

26. J. K. Downey, D. Hellriegel, and J. W. Slocum, "Congruence Between Individual Needs, Organizational Climate, Job Satisfaction and Performance," *Academy of Management Journal*, vol. 18 (1975), pp. 149-155.

27. Jablin (Note 18).

28. F. M. Jablin, "Superior-Subordinate Communication: The State of the Art," p. 1212.

29. F. M. Jablin, "Message-response and 'Openness' in Superior-Subordinate Communication," in B. D. Ruben, ed., *Communication Yearbook 2*, (New Brunswick, N.J.: Transaction, 1978), pp. 293-309.

30. E. A. Locke, K. N. Shaw, L. M. Saari, and G. P. Latham, "Goal Setting and Task Performance: 1969-1980," *Psychological Bulletin*, vol. 90 (1981), pp. 125-152. Also consult: D. R. Ilgen, C. D. Fisher, and M. S. Taylor, "Consequences of Individual Feedback on Behavior in Organizations," *Journal of Applied Psychology*, vol. 64 (1979), pp. 349-371. The reader interested in feedback should consult: S. J. A. Ashford and L. L. Cummings, "Feedback as an Individual Resource: Personal Strategies at Creating Information," *Organizational Behavior and Human Performance*, vol. 32 (1983), pp. 370-398.

31. J. S. Kim and W. C. Hamner, "Effect of Performance Feedback and Goal Setting on Productivity and Satisfaction in an Organizational Setting," *Journal of Applied Psychology*, vol. 61 (1976), pp. 48-57.

32. G.M. Goldhaber, *Organizational Communication*.

33. C. B. Wortman and J. A. W. Linsenmeier, "Interpersonal Attraction and Techniques of Ingratiation in Organizational Settings," in B. M. Staw and G. R. Salancik, eds., *New Directions in Organizational Behavior* (Chicago, Ill.: St. Clair Press, 1977), pp. 133-178; L. Porter, R. Allen, and H. Angle, "The Politics of Upward Influence in Organizations," in L. L. Cummings and B. M. Staw, eds., *Research in Organizational Behavior*, vol. 3, (Greenwich, Conn.: Aijai Press, 1981), pp. 109-149; W. K. Schilit and E. A. Locke, "A Study of Upward Influence in Organizations," *Administrative Science Quarterly*, vol. 27 (1982), pp. 304-316.

34. Wortman and Linsenmeier (Note 36, pp. 161-162).

35. Schilit and Locke (Note 33).

36. D. Kipnis and S.M. Schmidt, "Upward-Influence Styles: Relationship with Performance Evaluations, Salary, and Stress," *Administrative Science Quarterly*, vol. 33 (1988), pp. 528-542.

37. D. Kipnis, S.M. Schmidt, and G. Braxton-Brown, "The Hidden Costs of Persistence," in M.J. Cody and M.L. McLaughlin, eds., *The Psychology of Tactical Communication* (Clevedon, England: Multilingual Matters, Ltd., 1990), pp. 160-174.

38. Rogers and Agarwala-Rogers, *Communication in Organizations*, p. 93.

39. P. Krivonos, "Distortion of Subordinate to Superior Communication" (paper presented to the International Communication Association Convention, Boston, 1982); see also Goldhaber, *Organizational Communication*.

40. See, for instance, K. H. Roberts and C. A. O'Reilly, "Failures in Upward Communication in Organizations: Three Possible Culprits," *Academy of Management Journal*, vol. 17 (1974), pp. 205-215.

41. J. Athanassiadas, "The Distortion of Upward Communication in Hierarchical Organizations," *Academy of Management Journal*, vol. 16 (1973), pp. 207-226; J. Athanassiadas, "An Investigation of Some Communication Patterns of Female Subordinates in Hierarchical Organizations," *Human Relations*, vol. 27 (1974), pp. 195-209.

42. J. W. Young, "The Subordinate's Exposure of Organizational Vulnerability to the Superior: Sex and Organizational Effects," *Academy of Management Journal*, vol. 21 (1978), pp. 113-122.

43. D. A. Level and L. Johnson, "Accuracy of Information Flows Within the Superior/Subordinate Relationship," *Journal of Business Communication*, vol. 15 (1978), pp. 13-22.

44. Rogers and Agarwala-Rogers, *Communication in Organizations*, pp. 93-94.

45. J. Pfeffer, *Power in Organizations* (Boston: Pitman, 1989).

46. Pfeffer, *Power in Organizations;* M.S. Feldman and J.G. March, "Information in Organizations as Signal and Symbol," *Administrative Science Quarterly*, vol. 26 (1981), pp. 171-186.

47. Pfeffer, *Power in Organizations*.

48. D. Izraeli, "The Middle Manager and the Tactics of Power Expansion: A Case Study," *Sloan Management Review*, vol. 16 (1975), pp. 57-70.

49. R.V. Farace, P.R. Monge, and M.H. Russell, *Communicating and Organizing* (Reading, Mass.: Addison-Wesley, 1977); Goldhaber, *Organizational Communication;* Rogers and Agarwala-Rogers, *Communication in Organizations;* E. Rogers and D. Lawrence Kincaid,

Communication Networks: Toward a New Paradigm for Research (New York: The Free Press, 1981).

50. See, concerning statistics, Goldhaber, *Organizational Communication.*

51. R. V. Farace, P. R. Monge, and M. H. Russell, *Communicating and Organizing,* (Reading, Mass.: Addison-Wesley, 1977).

52. Goldhaber, *Organizational Communication.*

53. M.R. Tushman and T.J. Scanlan, "Boundary Spanning Individuals: Their Role in Information Transfer and Their Antecedents," *Academy of Management Journal,* vol. 24 (1981), pp. 287-305.

54. R.E. Spekman, "Influence and Information: An Exploratory Investigation of the Boundary Role Person's Basis of Power," *Academy of Management Journal,* vol. 22 (1979), pp. 104-117.

55. D.J. Brass, "Men's and Women's Networks: A Study of Interaction Patterns and Influence in an Organization," vol. 28 (1985), pp. 327-343.

56. D.J. Brass, "Being in the Right Place: A Structural Analysis of Individual Influence in an Organization," *Administrative Science Quarterly,* vol. 29, pp. 518-539.

57. Brass, "Being in the Right Place," p. 518.

58. Goldhaber, *Organizational Communication.*

KEY TERMS AND CONCEPTS

organizational structure
superior
subordinate
considerate leader
initiating structure leader
organizational climate
organizational culture
superior openness
locus of control
homophily/heterophily
confirmation messages
disagreement messages
accedence messages
repudiation messages
disconfirmation messages
goal-setting feedback
upward/downward communication
shotgun influence style
ingratiator influence style
tactician influence style
bystander influence style
metamorphosis effect
upward distortion
autonomous organizations
heteronomous organizations
bypassing
political strategies
coalitions
internal/external constituencies
cooptation
communication network
formal/informal channels
communication group (clique)
radial network
bridges
isolates
liaisons
boundary spanner
grapevine
trial balloon

CAMPAIGNING FOR CHANGE

The United States has always been characterized by efforts to *change* the behaviors of its citizens. We want people to eat healthier foods, stop smoking, reduce alcohol consumption, exercise more, or stop abusing drugs. Getting people to change such life-style behaviors is best accomplished through persuasive communication. None of the alternatives has been very successful. In the 1920s, the United States passed the Volstead Act to eliminate alcohol consumption. By all measures, the act was a failure. The great experiment failed after only a few years, and the prohibition laws were repealed. When large numbers of individuals are asked to change ingrained behaviors, persuasive communication, together with changes in the social environment, are used as society's primary instrument of change.

In previous chapters, we have concentrated largely on communication situations involving individuals or small groups of people. Different approaches need to be considered when we become interested in changing the behaviors of very large numbers of people in the society. Getting the attention of the millions of people who smoke cigarettes or use alcohol to excess is a far more difficult task than reaching a few people in your own family or neighborhood.

While persuasive communication can be used with many different topics, we concentrate our attention on *health* issues, and measures designed to produce a healthier population. Paisley[1] suggests that personal health issues always tend to remain high on the public's agenda, while issues such as war or energy can sharply rise and fall.

In recent years, smoking has become an important issue on the public agenda, and its importance is reflected in changes in smoking behavior. More than 50 percent of the adult population in the United States smoked cigarettes in 1964, the year the Surgeon General's first report linking smoking to lung cancer appeared. By 1992, less than 30 percent of the population smoked cigarettes. This major change in behavior is largely the result of federal, state, local, and voluntary agencies' conducting *communication campaigns* designed to effect change. This chapter focuses on the way in which agencies combine all of the aspects we have discussed in prior chapters to change the health-related behaviors of specific target audiences. In contrast, Chapter 14 will be concerned with how agencies employ both educational and entertainment aspects of the media, in order to promote prosocial behaviors and learning.

The chapter has four major sections. First, we look at the determinants of communication campaigns, and identify those characteristics that are associated with successful campaigns. Second, we examine the ways in which communication channels, both mass media and interpersonal channels, can be successfully utilized. Third, we lay out the anatomy of a major persuasive communication campaign. The final section discusses potential successes and failures in persuasive communication campaigns.

Determinants of Successful Campaigns

There are two sets of components one must consider when examining communication campaigns. McGuire[2] characterizes these components as an "input/output matrix." Table 13.1 is an adaptation of McGuire's conceptualization, and it illustrates his approach to identifying and examining the elements of any communication campaign. The *input* components are those independent variables that can be manipulated during a campaign to achieve particular outputs. They are the tools that a group of citizens, or a government official, or any other person or group wishing to serve as a change agent must work with if a campaign is to be successful.

McGuire identifies the five input components and their characteristics as:

TABLE 13.1

ADAPTATION OF MCGUIRE'S "INPUT/OUTPUT MATRIX"

Input Variables	Sources	Messages	Channels	Receivers	Intent
Output Variables					
Exposure					
Attention					
Liking					
Comprehension					
Acquiring Skills					
Changing Attitudes					
Remembering Information					
Retrieving Information					
Deciding to Act					
Behavior Change					
Reinforcing Decisions					
Consolidation of Results					

Adapted from: W.J. McGuire, "Theoretical Foundations of Campaigns," in R.E. Rice and C.E. Atkin, eds., *Public Communication Campaigns*, 2nd ed. (Newbury Park, Calif.: Sage Publications), 1989, p. 21.

1. *Sources*, which may vary in terms of their number, unanimity about the topic, demographic characteristics, attractiveness, credibility, and so forth.

2. *Messages*, which may vary in terms of the appeals used, information presented, message organization, number of repetitions, and similar characteristics.

3. *Channels*, which might vary in terms of the number of channels used, kinds of modalities selected, directness, and context.

4. *Receivers*, which vary in their numbers, demographic characteristics, abilities, life-styles, and personalities.

5. The *intent* of the campaign, which might include such variables as the immediacy of the issue, whether the campaign is designed for prevention or cessation, information only, behavior change, a direct effect, or an immunization effect.

McGuire's model identifies twelve *output* variables that may be important endpoints in a communication campaign, and may help to determine the success or failure of the campaign.

Remember that all of these are measured by examining the reactions of the receivers to the various sources, messages, and channels used:

1. *Exposure* to the campaign. Given very large and diverse populations in most communities, making sure that any message has reached the target audience can be difficult. There are groups in every community that do not watch television or read newspapers, so, if those are the only channels used, exposing a campaign to those audiences will prove difficult.

2. *Attention* to the campaign. All of us are aware of television spots we see, but we cannot remember anything specific about the spot. We have been "exposed" to the message, but are not "attending" to it. It may be necessary to repeat a message many times, or to change the nature of the message to draw attention to the message.

3. *Liking* the message. At times, most of us have become aware of a particular advertisement on television or radio, but only after several repetitions do we decide we "like" the message. To "like" a message does not mean that we necessarily like the product that is being advertised, but only that we find the advertisement itself to be attractive, cute, well done. Although it is sometimes possible to achieve a desired behavior change in response to a disliked message, it is much easier to move from liking the message to liking the product.

4. *Comprehension* of the message is necessary to behavior change. An illustration can be drawn from health campaigns asking people to reduce the amount of fat in their diets. Some of these campaigns ask people to cut down on certain types of fat, but not on others. This is a complex message because most people have never been asked to differentiate between various kinds of fats. Understanding the complexities of a message is more difficult for a receiver than simply attending to a message.

5. *Acquiring skills* is not necessary in all campaigns. If your campaign is to raise the information level of a community about a particular topic, there may be no need to build information about acquiring skills into the campaign. However, if a campaign advocates reducing high-cholesterol foods, it must address strategies for resisting temptation, identifying substitutes, and preparing low-cholesterol foods.

6. *Changing attitudes* is fundamental to communication campaigns. The political campaigner may work hard to ensure that her name and face get exposure in the media, that people appreciate the way in which the campaign is handled, and that the voters understand the issues. If, however, voters do not have favorable attitudes toward the campaigner, she is not likely to win. All through this book, we have emphasized the importance of attitudes as a predisposing condition to behavior in interpersonal communication situations; it is just as important in communication campaigns designed to reach thousands or millions of people.

7. *Remembering* the content of a campaign is important when long-term behavior change is the intent of the communication campaign. Some campaigns are directed toward a single, specific event, such as getting a voter to mark a ballot for a particular candidate. A campaign to get women to have yearly mammograms is quite different. Some women in the audience may not be old enough to need an immediate mammogram. But the campaign wants those to remember the information and to act on it several years in the future. Other women may be old enough, and may actually respond to the campaign by getting mammograms. But the campaign also wants those same women to remember to get mammograms again next year. That calls for messages designed to ensure that the receivers will remember the information for a long time. Such messages will be different than ones designed to elicit behaviors that may be repeated only once.

8. *Retrieving information* is a necessary part of many campaigns. Currently, the American Heart Association is conducting a national campaign designed to get people to reduce their cholesterol levels. If the campaign could concentrate only on the simple message that dietary fat intake is related to cholesterol, and that people should try to reduce their fat intake, the campaign might be fairly easy to structure. But the material to be acquired is actually very complex. The individual targeted in this campaign has to remember that cholesterol contains both low-density cholesterol (LDL) and high-density cholesterol (HDL), to remember that LDL is "bad" cholesterol, and that HDL is "good" cholesterol; and furthermore, must remember which foods to avoid because they have large amounts of saturated fat. Even if a campaign succeeds in getting receivers to understand and remember this information, the campaign may ultimately fail because receivers cannot recall the information when they are in a supermarket. The campaign designs messages to give the receiver some easily remembered "tips."

9. *Deciding to act.* Getting the receiver to internalize the message is a goal of any persuasive communication campaign. Receivers may quickly agree with a message that they should change some behavior, but the action is put on a "some day" basis. They will stop smoking "some day." They will stop eating fatty foods "some day." Workers in health campaigns find that this is one of the most difficult steps to accomplish. There is a lot of evidence that smoking is a disliked activity, even by smokers themselves. In national surveys, 85 percent of current smokers *say* that they want to stop smoking. But when faced with an offer of a cigarette, or even when they see a pack of cigarettes on a desk, they reach for the cigarette, and postpone the decision to change behavior. In many campaigns, getting the target audience member to decide on taking the desired action is the most difficult part of the entire campaign.

10. Overt *behavior change* is the main objective of many communication campaigns. The campaigner wants community members to stop smoking or at least to reduce the number of cigarettes smoked. The emphasis must be placed not just on taking some action, but on taking action in accord with the intent of the communication campaigner. Recent campaigns have attempted to get people to buy foods that have a higher fiber content, and those campaigns have worked hard to get the public aware of foods which are, in fact, high in dietary fiber. Anecdotal evidence derived from asking housewives what they bought and why they bought it suggests that sometimes the actions actually taken were not in accord with the intent of the campaign. They did, indeed, buy cereal, but they did not always buy high-fiber cereal, and they somehow missed the part of the campaign that gave evidence about specific high-fiber cereals. Campaigns must send messages that will help receivers change their behaviors in the desired direction.

11. *Reinforcing a decision* to have a lasting effect is a vital step in any campaign. People may be led to take an action once, but unless their behavior is reinforced, the probability is low that they will take the same action again. Automobile companies are well aware of the importance of this step. Once a buyer has purchased a new car, the dealer follows up that purchase with all kinds of information designed to reinforce the decision in the mind of the buyer. A letter is sent thanking the buyer for making the purchase, and that same letter will contain additional favorable information about the purchase.

12. *Consolidating the results* of a communication campaign is our final output measure. Frequently, a campaign will be conducted in a very intensive manner over a set period of time. Imagine that the intent is to get a thousand women in a community to agree to be screened for breast cancer by having a mammogram. Let us assume the campaign is successful after three months' effort, and one thousand women have a mammogram. The campaigners ought now to evaluate what has happened and see how the results of the campaign can be used in further efforts. Perhaps a number of the women who were screened would agree to help in reaching other women. Perhaps the same group of women can be approached with other health information. The point is that campaigns do not "just stop" in most cases. The period immediately following a campaign can be used to assess a particular effort, and those results can be used to lay the foundation for future efforts.

Any communication campaign can be analyzed in terms of this set of input and output variables. Obviously, the final evaluation of any campaign must be made in terms of whether or not the goals of the campaign are met.

UTILIZING COMMUNICATION CHANNELS EFFECTIVELY

A communication channel may be defined as the "modality" used to transmit a message. Communication campaigns normally involve the use of face-to-face, interpersonal modes of communication and the use of various mass media, such as radio, television, billboards, newspapers, magazines, newsletters, or posters. Both are used in public communication campaigns because they tend to have different effects on the target audience, and thus play different roles within a campaign.

Effective Use of Mass Media Channels. The mass media play a most important role in communication campaigns by getting receivers *exposed* to the campaign, by having receivers *attend* to the campaign, and by *changing attitudes* toward the message. Rice and Atkin[3] have collected accounts and evaluative studies of many different types of communication campaigns, and the role of the mass media we outline above is seen as a central feature in almost all of these campaigns. People *have* stopped smoking as the result of seeing a public service announcement (PSA) on television. People *do* go to the store to buy products after getting fliers in the mail. Voters *do* decide to vote for a candidate as the result of hearing a televised debate. But these reactions are generally shown to be the exception, not the rule. Most studies have shown that complex changes in behavior, such as stopping smoking, occur only when interpersonal, face-to-face communication follows the reception of mass media messages. Look again at Table 13.1. The use of mass media seems to be related to the first six output variables. These variables are generally considered to be easier tasks for a campaign director to accomplish than getting people to remember difficult information, or to perform complex behaviors. It is difficult to generate simple rules to determine exactly how the mass media should be used in any specific situation. Each campaign is likely to be different, because each community is going to be different, the content of the messages will be different, the credibility of sources being used will vary, the target audiences will not be the same from campaign to campaign, and the social situation in which the campaign takes place differs from time to time and place to place. Despite the difficulties of specifying exactly how the mass media should be used in each situation, we can identify five characteristics of the mass media that will help in planning a public communication campaign:

1. *The mass media can reach large numbers of people at reasonable cost.* This is one of the major reasons why the mass media have become such a vital element in public communication campaigns. If one wished to inform every citizen in Rockford, Illinois, or Cedar Rapids, Iowa, about the potential dangers of a batch of contaminated food, using

almost any other channel than the mass media would be prohibitively expensive and very slow. Only through the use of radio, television, and newspapers can there be any chance of reaching the bulk of people in these cities of nearly 100,000. Even with the use of the mass media, there will be people who do not receive the message and who can be reached only by interpersonal contact through established social agencies.

2. *Using the mass media allows for repetition of the message.* This is a very important characteristic of the mass media. The mass media allow one to put an advertisement or public service message on television or radio as many times as a budget will allow. In fact, it is possible to put a message out on different media, and thus maximize the chances that people will be exposed to the message many times. Public health campaigns are a good example of the importance of repetition. A single advertisement about the dangers of smoking is not likely to have much effect on a population. If, however, that advertisement is repeated thirty times on television in a six-week period, shown on ten billboards in the community, broadcast on morning "drive time" radio and run ten times during a six-week period in the daily newspaper, the chances are much greater that the population will be exposed and will pay attention to the message.

3. *The mass media can enhance the importance of a topic.* This effect is vital to successful public communication campaigns. How does this happen? Selnow and Crano[4] point out that the mass media, particularly television, have come to possess a credibility of their own that affects the messages seen on television or read in the newspaper. People have come to expect that important issues *will* appear in the mass media. News shows *will* cover important events and *will not* cover unimportant events. For the viewer, its presence or lack of presence on television may determine how much attention is paid to the topic of a public communication campaign. It is difficult to measure just how important the mass media will be in adding credibility to a topic, but a campaign unable to utilize the mass media is likely to be doomed.

4. *The mass media can add credibility to sources that use the mass media.* Just as important as the credibility the media can lend to a topic is the credibility that the source of a message can acquire through the use of television. Network news anchors like Bernard Shaw, Peter Jennings, and Dan Rather can earn the deep trust of their audience over the years, and can acquire very high credibility as the result. It is not simply appearing on television that makes the difference. The audience members have to come to believe in the trustworthiness of certain media spokespersons. One of the best examples of this phenomenon is the former surgeon general of the United States, Dr. C. Everett Koop. There have been many surgeon generals, and they have appeared from time to time on television. However, they never used the media extensively, and never became highly visible or highly credible as a result of their media usage. Koop became the spokesperson for the entire United States on health matters, and the combination of his personality and his extensive use of the media made him a very credible source for any health-related matter.

5. *The mass media allow for "narrowcasting," that is, reaching small target audiences within the larger community.* Today, there is a mass media outlet that reaches almost every possible segment of a community. Cable television provides from 13 to more than 100 channels in any community. Many of those channels are programmed for, and used by, very small groups of people, people who do not view many other channels. There are channels that provide news about the school system, local government, or that provide educational broadcasts from the local community college. Newspapers may appeal to the whole of a community, but newspapers also target small ethnic groups, church members, age groups, union members, or members of political parties. Newsletters appeal to many different audiences, and are a way of reaching people who do not read other publications. Magazines today are aimed at car owners, motorcycle riders, bird owners, long-distance runners, small boat owners, and several hundred other identifiable, but small, groups of people within the society. The ability of the mass media to contact very small, hard-to-reach populations is another major strength of the media, and an important consideration for the campaigner.

These five characteristics of the mass media are important reasons why the mass media play an important role in public communication campaigns. They are shared by all mass media, although there are differences in the way in which each of the media is best used.

Effective Use of Interpersonal Channels. We indicated that the mass media are most effective in reaching audiences, getting audiences to attend to messages, and in getting audiences to like the messages. In contrast, face-to-face, interpersonal communication is most effective in getting audiences to *learn* complex materials or ideas, *inducing attitude change* toward a topic, and getting people to *change their behaviors* about a topic. Thus, interpersonal channels are essential in achieving the objectives listed in the last half of our input/output matrix.

People have mistakenly thought of mass media and interpersonal channels in an either/or sense—either I make use of the mass media, or I make use of interpersonal channels to accomplish my goal. Looking at our input/output matrix suggests these two types of channels should be viewed as *complementary*. Mass media may be used in the beginning of a campaign to make people aware of the campaign, and to pay attention to the campaign. But if we are to move beyond that point, we will probably need to contact people in-

dividually or in small groups. Interpersonal channels are most effective when they are used to *present complex materials*, to persuade people *to make decisions*, and to *present reinforcing materials*.

1. *Presenting complex materials is most effectively done through personal contact.* That is why teachers are important in the classroom, and why successful communication campaigns try to involve people on a personal basis. The mass media can alert a receiver to become aware that heart disease is enhanced through poor diet, but explaining just what a good diet is can be very complex. Successful campaigns in this area have provided follow-up visits with health care professionals, or established telephone hotlines where further information can be gained, or provided classes for people who are interested in learning more about diet and its relationship to health.

2. *People tend to make decisions after talking to other people.* We see a television program that asks us to donate to the American Cancer Society. We may be favorably inclined to do so. But experience has shown that compliance with the mass media request alone does not occur very often. Rather, people donate after they have been visited by a volunteer in their home. Interpersonal contact is extremely important.

In many effective communication campaigns, interpersonal communication is achieved by making use of already established social groups. Thus, if one is campaigning to reduce smoking among high school students, the follow-up to any mass media campaign might be done by members of the varsity athletic club or volunteers from the local lung association, or the local chapter of the American Cancer Society. If one is putting on a campaign to reduce drunk driving in a community, it may be possible to use members of the local police department to staff a telephone hotline, or to get members of the local chapter of

Mothers Against Drunk Driving to lend their assistance.

While some people may respond directly and immediately to a mass media message, most people tend to *not* make firm decisions until they see or talk to others about making the decision. An effective campaign will provide many opportunities for interpersonal contact with members of the target audience.

3. *Interpersonal channels are the most effective way of presenting reinforcing materials during a campaign.* Many communication campaigns have, as their goal, a long-term change in behavior. Health advocates do not want people to stop smoking for one day or one week, but to stop smoking permanently. If the campaigner is successful in getting people to actually take the desired action, the next most important step is to reinforce, or reward, those individuals who comply. The smoker who decides to stop smoking is very likely to go back to the habit if efforts are not made to reinforce nonsmoking behavior. While the mass media can be used to send reinforcing messages, such efforts are far more effective if they come through interpersonal channels.

The use of different channels is extremely important in planning and running a public communication campaign. Deciding just which mass media channels to concentrate on, how much money to spend on television spots versus radio spots, and when to use the mass media during a campaign is a complex process that may decide the success or failure of the campaign. In similar fashion, finding the best way to involve volunteers in the campaign, and deciding when and how to utilize interpersonal channels is also a complicated set of procedures. Messages must flow through one of these channels in order to reach and impact receivers, and that kind of decision is a vital part of communication campaign planning.

COMMIT: THE ANATOMY OF A PUBLIC COMMUNICATION CAMPAIGN

There are campaigns taking place across the country that serve to illustrate the principles discussed in this chapter. We have selected COMMIT as an example, because it is a very carefully planned campaign designed to make use of many different communication techniques.

What is COMMIT? The letters stand for COMMunity Intervention Trial for Smoking Cessation.[5] It is a four-year campaign, funded by the National Cancer Institute, and conducted in eleven communities (eleven other communities serve as controls) in the United States and Canada. The campaign is specifically directed at reducing the number of heavy smokers in those communities.

Conducting campaigns to improve the health of various populations has become an important part of the public health agenda in the United States. Much research suggests that prevention and cessation campaigns are best conducted on a local level, with existing community agencies and groups heavily involved in conducting the campaign. Prior research also suggests that more positive effects are obtained if local communities feel a sense of "ownership" of the campaign, and do not feel as if the campaign were being "forced" on the community by some outside governmental organization.

The designers of COMMIT based the campaign on the following three principles suggested by prior research:

1. The campaign should be incorporated into already existing educational channels and social structures with the potential to reach large segments of the heavy-smoking population.

2. The campaign should involve community participation at the earliest stages in planning and implementing the proposed program of activities.

3. Campaign strategies should generate peer group influence and social support directed at smoking cessation.

The campaign planners recognized from the start that each of the eleven communities had local laws, customs, and social structures that required local variation. But in order to insure the maximum impact possible, all communities adopted some common strategies that prior research suggested might be effective in each of the communities. There were four elements common to all communities:

a. A broad-based *community board* was established to facilitate, manage, and give local credibility to the campaign.

b. A local office was established, headed by a full-time *field director* who lived in the community.

c. Four *task forces* were established, each one with the responsibility to develop and coordinate a different part of the campaign. Each task force worked under and reported to the community board.

d. A *standardized protocol* was developed mandating a certain number of required activities for each task force, and listing performance standards for each activity.

Each of these elements deserves careful examination. Taken together, they constitute the main campaign strategy, and are an excellent blueprint for many public communication campaigns.

The Community Board

Campaigns that are imposed on a community without the agreement of the political and social leadership of the community are much less likely to succeed than campaigns having the full backing of that leadership. In COMMIT, one of the earliest steps taken was to recruit a broad-based community board. The number of members on the board varied from city to city, depending on the composition of the community. In each case, efforts were made to include representatives from the political leadership, the hospital and medical system, voluntary health organizations (like the American Cancer Society), the media, education, religious groups, and labor and management. Note that the nature of the campaign dictates the nature of community board representation. COMMIT had a goal involving health, thus it was important to involve local health agencies.

Once recruited, the community board was given six guidelines to follow in becoming organized:

1. Develop a set of bylaws for the board and its task forces. It is important to have a set of fairly formal guidelines that everyone is familiar with, and that everyone will follow. Formal bylaws make it easier to avoid jurisdictional disputes.

2. Develop the procedures for working with the field director. A formal procedure to determine how activities are to be carried out is important in setting the agenda for the campaign.

3. Develop plans for staffing the task forces, and determining the scope of authority of the task forces.

4. Help to determine how the required protocol activities can best be implemented in a particular community. This is one of the most crucial tasks for the community board. While prior research may suggest the areas in which a campaign is likely to be effective, only local people, who know the community well, can determine just how an activity can best be implemented in that particular community. In COMMIT this was done through expanded action plans.

5. Recommend optional activities appropriate for the local community. Again, this is an area where a good community board can be of assistance. Maybe there is a local festival where leaflets can be distributed and contacts made with large groups of people. There may be circumstances in a community that will provide the opportunity for special activities that could be very effective.

6. The board can serve to facilitate maximum use of, and help in gaining access to, local resources. Note that we have suggested the selection of a broad-based community board with members who have real influence in the community. Such a group of people can help "unlock" the doors of union halls, churches, public parks, hospital meeting rooms, television and radio stations, and other community resources not readily available to an outside group.

There are many other functions that a good community board can do to aid in the development of strong task forces. The specific function will depend on the nature of the campaign and the community in which the campaign occurs. The principle is that *public communication campaigns work best if there is a strong support group within the community in which the campaign is to be run.*

The Field Director

It is possible to run a communication campaign by committee, and to not have a field director. However, in general, a committee will not be as effective as having one person in charge of the campaign. The ideal situation is where there are many people—from many segments of the community—who work together on the campaign, but where a single director or coordinator manages details, handles jurisdictional disputes, and keeps the campaign on track.

In COMMIT, it was felt that the field director should be an individual drawn from the community, because such a person would be better able to go to work quickly with all segments of the community. However, there are many professionals who are well trained in the conduct of campaigns, and who direct campaigns all across the country. In general, the field director has the responsibilities of serving as a spokesperson to media, staffing task forces, recruiting volunteers, and working with the community board.

The Task Force

While the community board gives overall direction and guidance to the campaign, the task forces are engaged in working with all of the relevant areas identified as important to the success of the campaign. Sometimes these areas are referred to the "campaign channels" for the communication campaign. In COMMIT, prior research on smoking cessation had identified four channels that needed special attention if the campaign were to have a chance of success. A task force was selected to plan and manage the communication efforts that were to take place in each channel. In addition, communities could add task forces if the need was felt to do so. In COMMIT, the four task forces were:

1. *Health Care Providers Task Force* Prior research suggests that physicians, dentists, and other health-care professionals can be very influential in getting people to stop smoking. Thus, a group of people interested in health care and familiar with the local health-care system were recruited into the Health Care Providers Task Force. The task force trained and supported health-care providers in working with people wanting to stop smoking.

2. *Worksites and Organizations Task Force* Many of the heavy smokers in any community smoke on their job, and can be reached with materials and messages through worksites, churches, or social clubs. Thus, a task force designed to find ways of promoting smoke-free policies and enhancing stop-smoking resources in local worksites and other organizations was formed.

3. *Cessation Resources and Services Task Force* Smoking is a habit addicting to many people. Such individuals have real difficulty stopping smoking without the help of professional cessation programs. It was felt that unless the community could identify and publicize the available cessation resources already existing in the community, and determine whether there was a need for more, the overall campaign might fail. Thus, the task force members were drawn from health agencies and voluntary groups in the community that were already offering some cessation services. What the task force did was to coordinate the efforts of these various services, provide continuing education for providers of cessation resources, and help publicize them to the relevant population.

4. *Public Education Task Force* This task force coordinated all of the activities involved in using the mass media, working with youth groups, with civic organizations, and with local governmental groups on the introduction of smoking control policies. This task force was also responsible for publicizing the activities of the other task forces, as well as communitywide stop-smoking activities. This is a very important task force. The local newspaper publisher, television station manager, school superintendent, representative from a local advertising agency, and other individuals highly knowledgeable about local communication channels were asked to serve on this task force. They knew the best ways in which information could be transmitted to the public. Because many of the volunteer health organizations like the American Lung Association also conduct campaigns against smoking, this task force was charged with coordinating with those organizations to obtain maximum impact.

The membership of the task forces and the community board differed in that the task forces were composed of individuals who were experts in their own areas. COMMIT tried to make sure that at least one member of the community board served on each task force, so that there would be coordination between the task forces and the main board. The field director usually tried to attend most task force meetings, as well as all of the community board meetings. In that way, maximum information could flow through all elements of the communication campaign. While there were clear organizational differences across eleven cities, the broad pattern we have described in this section was followed in each city.

The Standardized Protocol

All we mean by a "protocol" is a plan stating what the steps in the campaign are to be, and how and when they are to be implemented. Protocols can be changed if it is determined that conditions in the community have changed; but establishing a protocol at the beginning of the campaign means that we have studied the situation, and are applying all we know to the successful conduct of the campaign. For COMMIT, there were more than forty protocol steps to be implemented over the four years of the campaign.

Remember that a protocol is developed based on what prior research tells us about the community, and about the way in which people react to campaigns of this type. For COMMIT, the four task forces were used as the primary vehicle for the action steps that formed the protocol. Below are just a few of the objectives forming the protocol for two of the task forces:

a. Worksites and Organizations Task Force.

By 1990, promotional materials will have been delivered to 60 percent of targeted worksites in the community.

By 1992, promotional materials will have been delivered to 100 percent of the targeted worksites.

By 1992, a short promotional presentation will have been made to 30 percent of all service organizations in the community.

b. Public Education Task Force.

By 1990, a press kit will have been distributed to all local media with updated local data for smoking behavior in the community.

By 1990, a press conference will have been held to introduce the local Smoking Control Plan to media representatives.

It must be emphasized that a standardized protocol should not be considered a straitjacket for a campaign. As a campaign moves forward, it may be necessary to change a protocol, or to change certain dates. One may think of new ideas that had not occurred when the protocol was developed, or the political situation may change, causing some protocol item to be deleted. The protocol is a set of guidelines to help move a campaign along. It provides a reference point for those connected with a campaign; it represents the best thinking and research that can be brought to bear on a problem at the beginning of a campaign. Experience will moderate or change the protocol, but it serves as an important blueprint for any campaign.

In this section we have briefly presented an account of an important public communication campaign. There are certain elements we recognize in all persuasive communication campaigns. COMMIT is an example of a campaign which made use of what we know about persuasion and about campaigns, maximizing the success of the campaign.

SUCCESSES AND FAILURES IN PRIOR CAMPAIGNS

The reader may get the idea from our presentation in this chapter that achieving behavioral change is simply a matter of following the steps we have outlined, and then waiting for the results to come in. Actual experience in prior communication campaigns, however, has been highly varied. Box 13.1 reports an interesting current campaign. While some campaigns have reported significant behavioral change, many others have not. Rice and Atkin[6] and Flay[7] review many of the health campaigns that have been conducted in the United States and other Western countries, and attempt to draw conclusions as to why some campaigns seem to have succeeded, and others have failed.

In some cases, campaigns have not been systematically organized, nor have they attempted to follow the steps we argue for in this chapter. For example, the American Cancer Society has sponsored an antismoking event known as the Great American Smokeout in most cities in the United States. One day is designated as a day in which all smokers are urged to either stop smoking, or to drastically reduce their consumption of cigarettes. Typically, the mass media have given a lot of time to the Great American Smokeout, schools have put on antismoking programs, hospitals have offered free advice to smokers, supermarkets have display free brochures, and mayors and city councils have passed resolutions urging people to reduce their smoking behaviors. What have the results of this campaign been? There is usually a drop in smoking reported by surveys that have been done immediately after the Smokeout is over. But the decline is almost always of relatively short duration, and smoking prevalence returns to its prior status within a few weeks. Only a few smokers report quitting for weeks or months as the result of the Smokeout.

STATE CAMPAIGN SEEKS TO PERSUADE TEENS TO POSTPONE SEXUAL INVOLVEMENT

In 1992, the State of California began a campaign designed to encourage twelve- to fourteen-year-olds to postpone sexual involvement. Education Now and Babies Later (ENABL) is a multifaceted effort being implemented by the California Department of Health Services, Office of Family Planning. Over a three-year period the state plans to spend $15 million on a direct education curriculum, mass media support, and parental and community involvement. Radio, television, and newspaper advertisements are being designed to help create a social normative support system which says, "If you are not ready for sex, there are a lot of ways to say it."

The Department of Health contracted with Gardner Communications to create ads for the campaign. Gardner is a San Francisco-based agency with an established success record with this age group through its ads for Hacky-Sack bean bags and Frisbee flying disks.

The radio and television ads differ significantly from other ad campaigns directed toward teenagers. For example, anti-drug ads frequently use adults telling kids to "just say no" to drugs—or face the consequences. But the new campaign features messages to teens from teens.

In one spot, a teenager tells her boyfriend, "Just what part of 'no' don't you understand?" In another, a girl says, "You don't have to have sex to have a special relationship." And in a third spot, teenage boys are featured having a discussion about the pressures they feel to have sex and ideas on how to resist those pressures.

The spots are being placed on radio and television in time slots that have been shown to have a high listening or viewing audience of teenagers. For example, "Beverly Hills 90210" has as many as 70 percent of the female teenage audience watching television during its time slot. And target-directed radio spots should reach 90 percent of the twelve- to fourteen-year-olds in California.

In the newspaper portion of the campaign, posters picture two teens sitting together on a bed. Designed to enlist parents as well as teenagers in the drive, the ad reads: "These days, more kids are getting involved in after-school activities. Get involved. Before they do."

Questions:

1. How much effect do you think the campaign will have on teenage sexual behavior?

2. What persuasion principles are being used in this campaign?

3. Are there other persuasive messages that might be more effective?

4. If you were designing this important campaign, what changes would you recommend? Why do you think these changes would help the campaign?

Reprinted with permission of State of California, Department of Health Services.

The results noted in other short-term, but intensive campaigns are similar. Some show short-term effects, but few long-term effects. What does it take to make a campaign potentially successful? We believe that there are at least *five* elements that distinguish successful campaigns from those that are not highly successful:

1. *The campaign must be given sufficient time to succeed.* Behavioral change comes slowly. The Great American Smokeout is run just one day a year. It would be surprising if we could detect significant long-term effects from such a short campaign. COMMIT will run for four years, and the Stanford Five City Multifactor Risk Reduction Project[8] had six years of educational intervention. Although the amount of time is not the only factor that can make a difference, it does seem to be an extremely important factor. People need repeated opportunities and repeat messages. The communication campaign organizer must plan on spending significant periods of time in conducting a campaign.

2. *The campaign must focus on the results desired.* Some campaigns have been run with the intent of raising the general level of knowledge about health, and with the expectation that people will then move toward a healthier life-style. In general, those campaigns show poorer results than campaigns that are focused on changing very specific behaviors.

3. *Campaigns must be well organized to be successful.* COMMIT spent more than a year in each community organizing the details of its campaign before beginning the four years of intervention activities. The Stanford Five City project had almost two years of effort devoted to organizing activities. A campaign that is not well organized has a high risk of failing because poor organization results in some target audiences not being reached at all, and in some being reached inappropriately. The best volunteers may not be recruited, and media efforts may not be well coordinated. The net result of poor organization may well be the failure of a campaign that could have succeeded.

4. *Campaigns must be conducted with intensity to be successful.* Behavior change is difficult to achieve. If you are a heavy smoker, it is not likely that you will stop smoking as the result of seeing a single advertisement in the newspaper. Experience shows that people must be constantly reminded, through several channels, that they are engaging in a behavior that is injurious to their health.

A good health behavior campaign will try to get local television and radio stations to air public service announcements, and to include materials and spokespersons from the campaign on local talk shows. Newspapers will be urged to run stories about the campaign. The campaign will have written materials available for distribution in supermarkets, drug stores, and other places visited by the public. The campaign will ask physicians and other health-care professionals to put materials in their waiting rooms, and to include the information in their visits with patients. To have a chance at success, campaigns must operate with intensity.

5. *Campaigns are best run in the absence of opposition.* If you look at smoking prevalence in the United States over the twentieth century, you see a pattern showing a constantly increasing percentage of smokers until 1964. That was the year that the surgeon general's report linking smoking to lung cancer appeared. The smoking rates took a small dip at that time, but returned to the higher rate very quickly. Then in the late 1960s cigarette ads were banned from television. Anticigarette messages could appear on television, but prosmoking advertisements could not. The rates immediately declined sharply, and have continued to decline ever since.

It is always easier to conduct a communication campaign for a cause that has no organized opposition. Messages do not have to "fight through" opposition to be recognized, understood, and acted upon. When there are opposing messages, people tend to consider both sides, and delay making any choice until they feel that the evidence on one side outweighs the evidence on the other.

Certainly, all of the materials we have discussed in other chapters can contribute to the success or failure of a persuasive communication campaign. The five elements we discuss above, however, are important when one looks at successful and unsuccessful persuasive campaigns.

FOOTNOTES

1. W. Paisley, "Public Communication Campaigns: The American Experience," in R.E. Rice and C.K. Atkin, eds., *Public Communication Campaigns*, 2nd ed. (Newbury Park, Calif.: Sage Publications, 1989), p. 21.
2. W.J. McGuire, "Theoretical Foundations of Campaigns," op. cit., p. 45.
3. Rice and Atkin, *Public Communication Campaigns*.
4. G.W. Selnow and W.D. Crano, *Planning, Implementing, and Evaluating Targeted Communication Programs*, (New York: Quorum Books, 1987), pp. 77-83.
5. The Community Intervention Trial for Smoking Cessation (COMMIT) is made possible by support contracts from the National Cancer Institute. Any description of COMMIT is made possible by the efforts of the investigators and support staff at the eleven research institutions; the Coordinating Center (Information Management Services); the National Cancer Institute; and the community field staff and volunteers.
6. Rice and Atkin, *Public Communication Campaigns*.
7. B. Flay, *Selling the Smokeless Society: Fifty-six Evaluated Mass Media Programs and Campaigns Worldwide*, APHA Public Health Practice Series (Washington, D.C.: American Public Health Association, 1987).
8. J.A. Flora, N. Maccoby, and J.A. Farquhar, "Communication Campaigns to Prevent Cardiovascular Disease: The Stanford Community Studies," in Rice and Atkin, *Public Communication Campaigns*, pp. 233-252.

KEY TERMS AND CONCEPTS

communication campaign
McGuire's input/output matrix
input variables
sources
messages
channels
receivers
intent
output variables
exposure
attention
liking
comprehension
acquiring skills
changing attitudes
remembering
retrieving information
deciding to act
behavior change
reinforcing decision
consolidating results
communication channel
public service announcement (PSA)
narrowcasting
COMMIT campaign
protocol

CHAPTER 14

PERSUASION AND PLANNED SOCIAL CHANGE

Arvind Singhal and Everett M. Rogers

OUTLINE

By Arvind Singhal and Everett M. Rogers

In a recent television soap opera in India, the daughter of an Indian family rejects the husband her parents have chosen for her to marry, and insists on leaving home to pursue a professional career. An audience survey shows many of the young Indian women who identify with their television counterpart are convinced that a working career represents an alternative to marriage at an early age.[1]

In a 1989 episode of "My Two Dads," a popular U.S. television series, the two fathers get drunk and then drive a car, angering their television daughter, who tells them they should have decided which one would be the "designated driver" before they began drinking. Similar messages about the designated driver were included in 76 other television programs as part of a two-month campaign between Thanksgiving and New Year's Day (the heavy drinking season), causing an increase in viewer awareness and use of the designated driver idea.[2] Similar designated driver campaigns were mounted in 1990-1991 and in 1991-1992.

In Mexico, two young rock singers, Tatiana and Johnny, perform "Cuando Estemos Juntos" ("When We Are Together"), whose words argue for teenage sexual abstinence. The song was played an average of fifteen times per day by the average Mexican radio station, over a six-month period. A study showed that this extremely popular song raised consciousness among young Mexican people about the issue.[3]

What all three of these illustrations have in common is use of the mass media as part of an organized communication campaign to persuade individuals to change their attitudes and behavior. The intended result of these communication campaigns is social change, defined as the process by which an alteration occurs in the structure and function of a social system. Such social change can happen at the level of a community, an organization, or a society. Social changes result from many individual-level changes. For instance, if the Ta-tiana and Johnny song in Mexico had an effect in persuading large numbers of Mexican young people not to engage in premarital sex, the presently high rate of teenage pregnancy in Mexico will decrease. If the Harvard Alcohol Project, which includes the "My Two Dads" episode and similar attempts to persuade Americans to designate a driver when they are drinking, reaches its stated goals, the rate of alcohol-related traffic deaths should decrease. Thus we see the relationship between mass persuasion and social change.

PSAS AND SOCIAL CHANGE

In addition to the advertising of commercial products like soaps, toothpaste, cars, and beer, the mass media also carry a type of advertising called PSAs (public service announcements). The content of PSAs consists of unpaid advertisements for various public issues. Examples are drug abuse, AIDS (acquired immune deficiency syndrome) prevention, enrollment in adult literacy classes, and smoking cessation. Well-known examples are such themes as "Take a Bite Out of Crime," "Be Smart, Don't Start," and "Only You Can Prevent Forest Fires."

The Media-Advertising Partnership for a Drug-Free America is a coalition of advertising agencies, television networks, publishers, and so forth that collaborate to use the power of the media to combat drug abuse. Each year the Partnership places about $150 million of public service advertising or radio, television, and print media. Their most famous ad is the "frying egg" PSA ("This Is Your Brain on Drugs"), a hard-hitting message which starkly demonstrates the effects on the brain of taking drugs. This PSA gained great acclaim, but also generated much controversy for its "overly" dramatic content.

PSAs are usually created by advertising agency personnel at no cost for the National Advertising Council, an association of advertising agencies that selects the topics for the PSAs.[4] The time and space for these PSAs is usually provided free by such mass media as radio and television broadcasting stations, networks, and newspapers and magazines. Unfortunately, such free time and space in the media are usually provided when the intended audience is least likely to expose themselves to public service announcements. For example, television PSAs about drug abuse, such as the frying egg ad, are most likely to be broadcast at other than prime time, such as at 3 A.M. when few drug-abusers are viewing television. So its persuasive effects are minimal. Television broadcasters do not promise when a PSA will be broadcast, so a PSA cannot be aimed at a particular audience segment, like stay-at-home housewives, teenagers, working men, and so forth, who watch TV at certain hours.

PSAs on television are typically unable to produce much change in the audience's social behavior.[5] While television particularly attracts children, the elderly, minorities, and low-income audiences, radio is especially popular with teenagers. Newspaper and magazines are consumed more by well-educated and higher-income audiences. If the target audience for a public health campaign consists of teenagers, showing television PSAs at 3 A.M. is an ineffective strategy. PSAs, which are usually created gratis or on a tight budget, can hardly compete for audience attention with other, high-budget commercial advertisements. Anti-smoking and anti-alcohol PSAs are outnumbered by the frequent advertisements for cigarettes, beer, and wine on television, billboards, and in magazines. Commercial advertisements are often more sophisticated, vivid, emotional, and more effective than PSAs. Further, PSAs suffer from "PSA glaze," in which a genre of such advertisements all begin to look similar, and thus have little impact.

Nevertheless, evaluation studies show PSAs can have some intended persuasive effects, especially if they are one part of a multimedia campaign. For example, the Harvard Alcohol Project consisted not only of the seventy-seven different episodes in prime-time television series, but also included a series of PSAs broadcast during the same two-month period each year. At the end of playing the Tatiana and Johnny song, "Cuando Estemos Juntos," radio and television stations often broadcast a PSA announcing the address and telephone number of local family planning clinics for teenagers. This combination of the content of television entertainment shows and PSAs can more effectively influence public awareness, attitudes, and behaviors, than could either type of message alone. The PSA can provide the details of what to do and how to do it. The television entertainment show motivates the change in behavior.

So PSAs are persuasive messages that can contribute toward important social changes if the public service announcements reach the intended audience, if they are carefully designed and created so as to utilize persuasion strategies (such as fear appeals, or providing personal models for the desired behavior), and if they are pretested with the intended audience to ensure they will be effective and not offend sensitivities. For instance, Tatiana and Johnny do a hip-grinding, sexy dance while singing "Cuando Estemos Juntos" on their MTV video, but an audience study indicated that their hip-swinging did not offend teenagers, parents, or priests in Mexico.

THE ENTERTAINMENT-EDUCATION STRATEGY

A needless dichotomy exists in almost all mass media content: Mass media programs must either be entertaining or educational. Educational broadcasts usually require a heavy financial investment, are perceived by audiences as relatively dull, and receive little audience attention. Nor are such programs popular with commercial advertisers. On the other hand, entertainment programs like feature films and television serials generally attract large audiences, and hence are popular with commercial sponsors. Entertainment-educational messages are an emerging genre in the mass media of several nations. This strategy uses the universal appeal of entertainment to persuade individuals to live safer, healthier, and happier lives. The entertainment-education genre offers unique advantages for national governments, broadcasting agencies, commercial sponsors, and for audiences, and has been utilized in the United States to encourage better health, combat drunken driving, and to seek solutions to other social problems.[6]

For Third World countries, education of the public is ordinarily at a high cost, and often a huge and expensive one for a small, poor country.[7] In comparison, the entertainment-education strategy provides an opportunity for an educational message to pay for itself, and often, to yield a profit. Thus, this strategy appears to be a "win-win" situation, in which both the educators' goals and those of commercial media institutions can be met.[8] The entertainment-education strategy is also useful for achieving Third World development and improving the health and quality of life in the United States.

In addition to its practical usefulness, the entertainment-education strategy is of theoretic importance to communication scholars. Several of the previous efforts in Third World countries (for example, family planning television soap operas in Mexico and in India, and the Tatiana and Johnny rock music campaign to promote sexual responsibility among teenagers in Mexico) were based on human communication theories. One such theory is Albert Bandura's social learning theory,[9] which explains how people learn new behaviors by modeling their behavior after other individuals with whom they interact or observe through the mass media. For example, Tatiana and Johnny were character models for the specific behavior (sexual abstinence) that was promoted as socially desira-

ble to listeners/viewers in Mexico. These attractive teenaged singers were asked on television talk shows whether or not they were virgins. So, in addition to singing about sexual abstinence, Tatiana and Johnny provided role models for such behavior. Often an entertainment-education message portrays both positive and negative role models; the positive models are rewarded, and the negative models are punished, thus representing a test of Bandura's social learning theory.

HISTORY OF THE ENTERTAINMENT-EDUCATION COMMUNICATION STRATEGY

The media strategy of entertainment-education has been increasingly applied in creating messages for rock music, television, radio, film, print, theater, and other media. It is quite versatile. The roots of the strategy go back many thousands of years to the origins of oral storytelling, such as Aesop's Fables. But the most important mass media experience in recent decades occurred accidentally in 1969 with the broadcast of the television soap opera "Simplemente María" ("Simple Mary"), in Peru. María was an emigrant to the capital city of Lima, where she worked as a household maid for a wealthy family. She then climbed the socioeconomic ladder of success through her expertise in using a Singer sewing machine. She learned to read and write by attending adult literacy classes, and established a boutique selling elegant clothes that she designed.[10]

"Simplemente María" was successful in attracting very high audience ratings, and the sale of Singer sewing machines increased sharply. So did the number of young girls enrolling in sewing and literacy classes. When "Simplemente María" was broadcast in other Latin American nations, similar audience effects occurred. The Singer

Sewing Machine Company purchased advertising on the broadcasts of "Simplemente María," reaping heavy profits. In appreciation for her contribution to company sales, the Singer company presented a miniature-sized gold sewing machine to the Peruvian actress portraying María, Saby Kamalich.

In the mid-1970s, Miguel Sabido, a brilliant television producer and director in Mexico, showed the lesson taught by "Simplemente María" could be utilized for motivating enrollment in adult literacy classes, the adoption of family planning, encouraging gender equality, and for other educational issues. Sabido's *telenovelas* (literally "television-novels" or soap operas) were audience rating successes for Televisa, the Mexican television network, and evaluation studies showed that these soap operas resulted in widespread behavior changes by audience members. In all, Sabido produced seven entertainment-education soap operas in Mexico from 1975 to 1982, one each year.

Population Communication-International, an organization headquartered in New York City, played an important role in transferring the entertainment-education strategy from the Mexican *telenovelas* of Miguel Sabido (1) to India, where a television soap opera called "Hum Log" ("We People") was broadcast in 1984-85, and (2) to Kenya, where a television soap opera, "Tushauriane" ("Let's Discuss"), and a radio soap opera, "Ushikwapo Shikimana" ("When Given Advice, Take It"), were broadcast from 1987 to 1989.[11] In 1992, a second Sabido-style entertainment-education soap opera, "Hum Raahi" ("Co-Travelers"), promoting the status of women and gender equality, was broadcast in India, earning very high ratings.

The entertainment-education strategy has been widely reinvented and recreated by creative media professionals in several nations: "The Archers," a long-running BBC radio soap opera about improved farming; "Naseberry Street," a Jamaican radio soap opera about family planning; and "Butir-Butir Pasir Di Laut" ("Grains of Sand in the Sea") created by Indonesia's national family planning agency. The strategy can also be applied to comics, books, and other print media. This strategy was utilized in feature films; for example, John Riber created *Consequences*, a 1988 super-hit film in Africa about teenage sexuality in Zimbabwe. Most of these examples were not directly inspired by the work of Miguel Sabido (they represented an independent invention of the basic strategy) although the use of rock music to promote sexual responsibility was patterned after Sabido's approach.

Patrick L. Coleman, deputy director of Johns Hopkins University's Population Communication Services (JHU/PCS), while working in El Salvador as a Peace Corps volunteer in the mid-1970s, viewed one of Miguel Sabido's television soap operas and observed its effects. Later, in 1983, Coleman invited Sabido to present his entertainment-education strategy at a conference sponsored by JHU/PCS in Quito, Ecuador. Since then, Coleman has pioneered in utilizing Sabido's approach in rock music for promoting teenage sexual abstinence and responsible parenthood in Mexico, the Philippines, and Nigeria.

ROCK MUSIC TO PROMOTE SEXUAL RESPONSIBILITY

Early pregnancy is a major social problem in many Third World nations, and especially in Latin America. The main target audience for contraceptive messages—preteens and teenagers—however, is difficult to reach through most mass communication channels. These audiences generally have low media exposure, except to radio, music tapes, records, and in recent years, to MTV (music television).

In 1986, as mentioned previously, a rock music video which promoted sexual abstinence and contraception, entitled "Cuando Estemos Juntos" ("When We Are Together") was launched in Spanish-speaking Latin American countries. A second song, "Detente" ("Wait"), conveyed a similar theme. "Cuando Estemos Juntos" was number one on the pop music charts within six weeks of its release in Mexico, and soon was a top-rated song in eleven other Spanish-speaking Latin American countries.

The unusual popularity of this song resulted from the joint efforts of JHU/PCS communication researchers who conducted formative evaluation research, public health officials, funding from the U.S. Agency for International Development, and the assistance of entertainment industry executives and rock musicians.[12]

The formative evaluation research indicated the common denominator for young people throughout Latin America was rock music. Formative evaluation is a type of research that is conducted while an activity, process, or system is being planned or is ongoing, in order to improve its effectiveness.[13]

JHU/PCS hired FFI (Fuentes y Fomento Intercontinentales), a Mexican marketing and music record company, to produce the two music videos. Audience needs were assessed, and a marketing plan carefully designed. Record companies in Mexico recommended thirty-two composers and writers, each of whom wrote two songs as part of a nationwide contest. Out of the contest entries, six songs were pretested with samples of adolescents to determine their acceptability and content. The lyrics and various attributes of the musical presentation were then tested with focus groups of Mexican teenagers, and this feedback led to finer-tuned changes in the song.

The artists were selected carefully. Several prominent Mexican singers refused to be involved, due to the sensitive nature of the teenage-sex topic. Tatiana, a beautiful sixteen-year-old singer from Mexico, and Johnny, a seventeen-year-old Puerto Rican singer (already popular in Latin America as a graduate of the group called Menudo), agreed to perform "Cuando Estemos Juntos" and "Detente." In "Cuando Estemos Juntos," the teenage singers told their teenage audience not to have sex; they were a much more effective source than having the message emanate from parents or priests. The duet's lyrics included: "You will see that I am right when I say 'no,' even though my heart is burning."

The two songs were released in two phases. A commercial release came first, in 1986, with the premier of the music video of "Cuando Estemos Juntos" on a very popular Mexican television variety show, "Siempre en Domingo," ("Always on Sunday"), which is viewed each Sunday by 150 million Spanish-speaking viewers throughout Latin America.[14] The music was catchy and the video production was of high quality, employing special effects. The sensitive nature of the teenage-sex topic was suitably handled by using life-size male and female dolls in the rock music video. The song was available for sale throughout Latin America in the form of records, audio tapes, and videotapes.

As the commercial release of "Cuando Estemos Juntos" gained success, the second phase, an institutional effort, began. Press conferences were held, news clippings about the artists were provided free to radio and television stations, and Tatiana and Johnny made numerous personal appearances. Keys to the overall success of the project were (1) the high quality of the musical production and (2) the amount of strategic planning and preparation that went into the campaign. An estimated $300,000 and two and a half years of planning were invested in the Mexican music project, plus an additional $100,000 for evaluation research.[15]

Public service announcements on television and radio capitalized on the popularity of the "Cuando Estemos Juntos" music video to promote sexual abstinence among teenagers. Radio and television stations could play the song without paying a broadcast fee if they agreed to accompany the music with an announcement of the address and telephone number of a local family planning clinic that offered contraceptive services to teenagers. This localization helped channel the teenage audiences' knowledge and attitudes into action. An estimated 1 million hours of free radio and television time were thus provided by Latin American broadcasting stations that played and aired discussions about the song.[16] The typical Mexican radio station played "Cuando Estemos Juntos" an average of fifteen times a day for several months during the song's greatest popularity. In comparison, the song on the flip side of "Cuando Estemos Juntos," "Detente" was a more typical hit song, and was played "only" five times per day for several months.

Compared to the results of most communication research on a single message (which typically finds only minimal effects), studies of the effects of entertainment-education messages usually show that they have relatively stronger effects. Why? One main reason is repetition of the message, which provides massive and repeated exposure to audience individuals. Under these conditions, the message is more likely to get through effectively to the intended audience.

As Bradac and others[17] concluded from their extensive review of communication message effects: "The vast majority—probably 99 percent—of the message effects studies reported in the literature have exposed respondents to a single message upon one occasion prior to measuring their attitudes or impressions. Thus whatever generalizations we can offer are largely limited to initial-exposure situations." One of the important qualities of most entertainment-education efforts has been the high degree of repeated exposures to the message. Undoubtedly such repeated exposure to messages is one main reason for the general effectiveness of the entertainment-education strategy.

In Mexico alone, Tatiana's album featuring "Cuando Estemos Juntos" sold over 500,000 cop-

ies. A summative evaluation of the rock music campaign in Mexico showed that the song did more than just sell videos, tapes, and records. Summative evaluation is conducted near the end (or after) an activity, process, or system to form judgments about its effectiveness.[18] The rock music encouraged teenagers to talk more freely about teenage sex, reinforced teenagers who already had decided to use restraint, sensitized younger people to the importance of the topic, and disseminated information about contraception.[19]

Building on the successful experience of Tatiana and Johnny in Latin America, JHU/PCS officials launched similar rock music campaigns in the Philippines (in 1988), and in Nigeria (in 1990). These campaigns were highly successful in influencing audience attitudes and behaviors related to sexual responsibility.[20]

"HUM LOG" AND OTHER SOAP OPERAS IN DEVELOPING NATIONS

"Hum Log" was an attempt to blend the Indian national television system's stated objectives of providing entertainment to its audience, while strengthening the prosocial values of audience individuals. The television series, which combined entertainment and education, was broadcast over eighteen months from 1984 to 1985. "Hum Log" addressed many of the important social and moral issues confronting Indian society: amelioration of women's unequal status, family harmony, family planning, national integration, maintenance of traditional culture, problems of urban life, dowry, and alcoholism (Table 14.1).[21] The 150 episodes were broadcast in Hindi, each lasting twenty-two minutes, two or three times per week. At the close of each episode, a famous Indian film actor, Ashok Kumar, summarized the episode's main points, providing viewers with appropriate guides to action.

TABLE	14.1

EXTENT TO WHICH SOCIALLY DESIRABLE THEMES WERE EMPHASIZED ON "HUM LOG"

Theme and an Example	*Percentage of Subthemes in 149 Episodes (N = 10, 688)*
1. Family harmony (family is close-knit despite individual differences among family members)	38%
2. Status of women (Badki's efforts to fight for the status of women in a women's welfare organization)	26%
3. Character and moral development (Grandfather's commentary on behaviors that are right and wrong)	12%
4. National integration (marriage of a North Indian girl with a South Indian boy)	7%
5. Family planning (Rajjo's determination to undergo a tubectomy after giving birth to her fourth daughter)	6%
6. Health (ill effects of alcohol on Basesar Ram's health)	5%
7. Problems of urbanization (Lalloo's retreat to his village in order to cope with the high cost of urban life)	4%
8. National welfare programs (an eye-donation drive for Inspector Samdar)	2%
TOTAL	100%

NOTE: Each percentage here is the portion of the total number of subthemes (10,668) identified in 149 episodes of "Hum Log." The subthemes identified in each episode could fall under any of the eight mutually exclusive thematic categories. An average "Hum Log" episode had about 70 subthemes that we identified. The intercoder reliability coefficient of three Hindi-speaking coders is .78.
SOURCE: A. Singhal and E.M. Rogers, *India's Information Revolution*, 1989a. Reprinted by permission of the authors and Sage Publications, Inc.

The early broadcasts of "Hum Log" fared poorly in the television ratings. Viewers complained of didactic family planning sermonizing, indifferent acting, and a slowly developing story line. In response, the family planning theme was diluted, and then almost dropped from "Hum Log" after the thirteenth episode. Then such other social themes as the status of women, family harmony, national integration, sustaining indigenous cultures, and improved health, were emphasized in the "Hum Log" episodes.

The soap opera's plot centered around the joys and sorrows of a lower-middle-class extended family, with a parallel story line addressing smug-

T A B L E	14.2

DEGREE OF PARA-SOCIAL INTERACTION BY LETTER-WRITERS TO "HUM LOG"

Indicators of Para-Social Interaction	Percentage of Letters That Indicate Para-Social Interaction
1. Viewer indicates a strong involvement with "Hum Log" characters.	93%
2. Viewer likes and respects Ashok Kumar, who delivers the epilogue at the end of each episode.	83%
3. Viewer compares his or her idea with those of "Hum Log" characters.	65%
4. Viewer perceives a character as a down-to-earth, good person.	43%
5. Viewer talks to his or her favorite character while watching the program.	39%
6. Viewer feels that Ashok Kumar helps him or her to make various decisions, and looks to him for guidance.	39%
7. Viewer adjusts his or her schedule to watch "Hum Log" so as to have a regular relationship with a television character.	30%

SOURCE: A. Singhal and E.M. Rogers, *India's Information Revolution*, 1989a. These data come from a mailed questionnaire that the authors sent to a sample of 500 individuals who wrote letters to Doordarshan, the Indian television network that broadcast "Hum Log." Reprinted by permission of the authors and Sage Publications, Inc.

gling, political corruption, and underworld activities. "Hum Log" rose rapidly in popularity after its first month or two of broadcasts. "Hum Log" commanded audience ratings of 65 to 90 in North India (which is predominantly Hindi-speaking), and between 20 and 45 percent in the main cities of South India, where most television viewers do not speak Hindi. When it ended in December, 1985, after 156 episodes, "Hum Log's" departure was marked by sentimental protests from many viewers.

A tremendous amount of para-social interaction occurred between "Hum Log's" viewers and the characters in the television soap opera. Para-social interaction is the seemingly face-to-face interpersonal relationships between a television viewer and a television performer. Viewers perceive their relationship with a television character as real, as if it were an actual face-to-face encounter. Many "Hum Log" viewers felt that they "knew" the television characters, even though they actually never met (Table 14.2), as indicated by our content analysis of a sample of the 400,000 letters written to the television network by viewers.

A similar phenomenon of para-social interaction occurred in 1992 when Indian television broadcast "Hum Raahi" ("Co-Travelers"), an entertainment-education soap opera promoting gender equality, the status of women, and family planning. "Hum Raahi" achieved 80 percent ratings in North Indian cities, and reached an audience of about 100 million people with its entertainment-education messages. Each episode of "Hum Raahi" closed with an on-the-air slide of a post office box number to which viewers could write with their requests for information, suggestions for the plot, and their likes and dislikes of episodes.

Both "Hum Log" and "Hum Raahi" were directly inspired by Miguel Sabido's entertainment-educational television soap operas in Mexico. Sabido's entertainment-education television soap operas were based on Bandura's social learning theory. Television viewers learned intended behaviors and values from positive and negative models depicted in the television series.

SOCIAL LEARNING THEORY AND PLANNED SOCIAL CHANGE

Television provides its viewers with a variety of observational learning experiences through the role models that it depicts. Incorporation of Bandura's social learning theory in the design of "Hum Log" in India was less rigorous than in Mexico. Did viewers of "Hum Log" model their behavior after that of the television soap opera characters?

Our content analysis of 149 "Hum Log" scripts shows the extent of prosocial and antisocial behaviors performed by the various "Hum Log" characters (see Table 14.1). Prosocial behavior is behavior that is desirable and beneficial to other individuals and/or to society at large. For example, certain television shows in the United States like "Mister Rogers' Neighborhood" teach children to say "please" and "thank you." Antisocial behavior is behavior that is undesirable or detrimental to other individuals and/or to society at large.

Results from our 1987 survey of 1,170 respondents in India show that "Hum Log" viewers learned prosocial models of behavior from generally positive role models, and expressed a strong desire to emulate them in real life. Thirty-seven percent of our respondents believed the grandfather of the "Hum Log" family (a positive role model) to be the best model to copy in real life, and 18 percent of our respondents chose Bhagwanti (a stereotype of the traditional Indian wife/mother, and hence, a generally negative role model for female equality) to emulate. Eleven percent of our respondents believed that Badki (a positive role model for female equality) was the best model to copy in real life and 5 percent chose Chutki (a career-oriented sister of Badki in the "Hum Log" family) to emulate. Only 1 percent of our respondents believed Majhli (a negative female role model) to be the best model to copy, and only 4 percent chose the drunken father, Basesar Ram (a negative male role model), to emulate. The remaining 24 percent of our respondents chose relatively neutral characters as the best models to copy. So our "Hum Log" respondents believed in copying the positive role models in the television program (53 percent in total), rather than imitating the negative role models (a total of 23 percent).

When "Hum Log" was designed, Bhagwanti was conceived as a negative (in the sense of the educational purpose of the soap opera) role model for female quality. She quietly let her drunken husband and overbearing mother-in-law berate her for her inadequate family lineage, her lack of cooking skills, and so forth. However, many "Hum Log" viewers sympathized with Bhagwanti and viewed her as a positive role model of tolerance, compromise, and patience. One seventy-five-year-old woman who wrote to Ashok Kumar said: "Bhagwanti is the epitome of tolerance. She suffers, but quietly. Young Indian women should learn a lesson in patience from Bhagwanti."

Results from our 1987 survey show that 80 percent of the viewers who chose Bhagwanti as a positive role model were women. Seventy-six percent of housewives compared to 7 percent of employed women chose to emulate Bhagwanti. These viewers' perceptions of Bhagwanti's role suggest that "Hum Log"'s modeling effects were mediated by the viewers' prior attitudes and by their occupational experiences and stage-in-life. While Bhagwanti's character was intended to be a negative role model for female equality, viewers identified with her as a positive role model for family harmony (an issue for which she was indeed a positive role model).

In the past, Bandura's social learning theory has been primarily used to demonstrate observational learning (1) by children, (2) in laboratory settings, and (3) with aggression as the dependent variable. Our research on "Hum Log" demonstrates the potential of utilizing Bandura's social learning theory for (1) larger populations, (2) in natural field settings, and (3) with prosocial learning as a dependent variable.[22]

Entertainment Versus Educational Television in the U.S.: A False Dichotomy?

The U.S. mass media generally separate entertainment messages from educational messages. U.S. commercial television networks are large, private, profit-oriented organizations, operating under relatively loose government regulation. They broadcast predominantly entertainment programs because this genre achieves higher audience ratings, and thus maximizes advertising incomes. Popular entertainment programs crowd out educational programs, which are anathema to the three U.S. commercial networks.[23]

On a few occasions, however, the U.S. television networks broadcast programs to raise public consciousness, and to inform the audience about social issues. For example, the immensely popular ABC mini-series, "Roots," and its sequel "Roots: The Next Generation," focused on African American struggles for freedom from slavery and efforts to gain equality with whites in the U.S. Norman Lear's popular CBS television program in the 1970s, "All in the Family," called attention to ethnic prejudice through a highly bigoted character, Archie Bunker. The prosocial objectives of "Roots" and "All in the Family" were secondary byproducts of these television shows that were primarily designed to attract large audiences. Studies of the audience effects of "Roots," "Roots: The Next Generation," and "All in the Family" showed that these American television programs increased audience awareness of racial and ethnic issues.[24] Some already-prejudiced viewers, however, were reinforced in their prejudices.[25]

Numerous organizations (an estimated 200) maintain a presence in Hollywood today in order to try to influence U.S. television producers and scriptwriters to include such issues as gay and lesbian rights, abortion, alcoholism, and the environment in an episode of a television series.[26] Generally, the effects on the U.S. audience of such efforts by these "Hollywood lobbyists" have not been investigated by researchers, but there are now several exceptions.[27] Essentially, the Hollywood lobbyist uses an entertainment-education strategy. Examples of entertaining television programs that were designed through the efforts of Hollywood lobbyists to teach the American viewing public about an educational issue are:

■ A 1990 episode of "MacGyver" that illustrated the poaching of rhino horns in Africa.

■ A decrease in the gratuitous drinking of alcohol by characters on the television series "Dallas."

■ An episode of "Happy Days" in which "The Fonz" (Henry Winkler) secured a library card (Fonz influenced thousands of young Americans to follow suit).

One of the most widely known illustrations of an advocacy group in Hollywood getting a social issue injected into prime-time television occurred in 1972 when Maude, a forty-seven-year-old woman (played by Bea Arthur) in Norman Lear's CBS television series by the same name, realized that she was pregnant. After being indecisive for two episodes (called "Maude's Dilemma"), Maude decided to get an abortion rather than bear an unwanted child. Within minutes of the broadcast, CBS received 373 angry telephone calls, and a public controversy erupted. Pro-life organizations called for a more balanced treatment of the abortion issue, demanding two sequel episodes of "Maude" supporting the right-to-life of unborn babies. This demand was not met. More controversy erupted when the "Maude's Dilemma" episodes were scheduled for rebroadcast the next season (in 1973). Fearing customer backlash, several advertisers withdrew their spots from the "Maude" time slot, and one-fourth of all CBS affiliates, left without advertiser support, refused to carry the two rebroadcasts.

CBS officials debated whether to rerun "Maude's Dilemma." The Population Institute, a successful Hollywood lobbying organization, rallied CBS officials to broadcast the controversial episodes. The "Maude" controversy "tested, as never before, the boundaries of acceptability for program content on prime-time broadcasts."[28]

The next section analyzes several well-known entertainment-education efforts in the U.S. The New York-based Children's Television Workshop pioneered in creating "Sesame Street," an immensely successful entertainment-educational program for preschoolers, broadcast by Public Broadcasting Systems (PBS) stations each weekday.

"SESAME STREET": THE LONGEST STREET IN THE WORLD

Despite decades of public outcry, the quality of children's television in the U.S. has been rather dismal. Most children's programs are mediocre in quality, and several may have harmful effects in conveying violence and other antisocial content.[29] For example, in a highly popular ABC television program, "Beetlejuice," a ghostly central character provides lessons in "grossness." In CBS's "Rude Dog and the Dweebs," a canine hero teaches that it is "cool" to be obnoxious.[30] One clear exception to such U.S. children's television programming is "Sesame Street."

A remarkable illustration of the entertainment-education strategy, "Sesame Street" is one of the most widely watched children's television programs of all time. Since this television series was created in 1969, "Sesame Street" has been viewed by an estimated 12 million young Americans each week, including six million preschoolers.[31] Broadcast in over 100 countries in six continents, "Sesame Street" is "the longest street in the world" (Lesser, 1974).[32]

The idea of creating the Children's Television Workshop (CTW) originated in 1966 when Joan Ganz Cooney, then a television producer, and Lloyd Morrisett, then an executive at the Carnegie Foundation (presently the chairman of CTW's board of trustees, and president of the Markle Foundation), decided to test television's usefulness in teaching young children. Start-up funds of $7 million were obtained from government agencies and private foundations in order to create an autonomous, nonprofit organization,

Children's Television Workshop, that was free from political and economic pressures.[33]

Eighteen months of formative evaluation preceded the first broadcast of "Sesame Street" in 1969. A thorough assessment of preschoolers' needs was conducted in order to construct CTW's educational messages, and entertaining formats with educational appeals were pretested, and often revised, in order to obtain the desired effects. Such intense use of formative evaluation, which continues in current "Sesame Street" productions, is one major reason for "Sesame Street's" audience success.

"Sesame Street's" purpose is to develop the cognitive learning skills of preschool children, teaching them letters, numbers, geometric forms, and such valued prosocial qualities as kindness and cooperation. "Sesame Street" utilizes Piaget's[34] principle of knowledge acquisition: In order to teach something new, relate it to something that an individual already knows. For instance, to teach the shape of the letter Y, a comparison is made with a forked road and with a slingshot. Each item of educational information is repeated several times for enhanced learning. Other techniques are employed to make the child an active participant in the learning process. A variety of entertainment formats are employed to hold children's attention: Muppets, music, animation, action films, special effects, and celebrity visits.[35] Each segment of "Sesame Street" is short (usually less than three minutes), and is designed to be attention-catching and holding.

"Sesame Street" is probably "the most evaluated television program, anywhere in the world."[36] Summative evaluations of U.S. and international productions of "Sesame Street" consistently show that regular viewers score higher in tests of ability in all curriculum areas than do nonviewers.[37] However, there is evidence that learning is greater among children of high- and middle-income families, and that "Sesame Street" may be increasing the information gap.[38]

"Sesame Street" is only one of the entertainment-education television series created by CTW. Others include "3-2-1 Contact," a television series focusing on science and technology, "The Electric Company," designed to enhance students' reading skills, and "Square One TV," geared to enhance children's mathematical ability. "3-2-1 Contact" is broadcast in more than 20 countries (including the U.S.), and "The Electric Company" in some 15 countries.

Entertainment-education television programs such as "Sesame Street" offer tremendous economies of scale in delivering messages to target audiences. For example, the cost of reaching each preschooler in the United States via "Sesame Street" is less than one cent per child per viewing hour.[39]

THE PROFOUND EFFECTS OF "ROOTS"

The immensely popular ABC mini-series, "Roots," and its sequel, "Roots: The Next Generation," focused on African-American people's struggle for freedom from slavery. Based on Alex Haley's best-selling book, "Roots" was broadcast as eight one-and-a-half-hour episodes in 1977. Viewed by an estimated 130 million Americans, "Roots" became one of the most-watched programs in U.S. television history. Seven of "Roots' " eight episodes ranked among the top 10 in all-time television ratings, achieving an audience share between 62 to 71 percent.[40] The tremendous popularity of "Roots" led some to call it the "nightly superbowl" for Americans, and some compared viewers' outpouring of emotions with the television coverage of the John F. Kennedy assassination.

While "Roots" was criticized for its historical inaccuracies and for its stereotyping of some of the characters, over 50 percent of its viewers hailed it as "one of the best" television programs they had ever watched.[41] "Roots'" depiction of the whites' brutal treatment of blacks resulted in its seemingly profound effects on the American audience.[42] Many white viewers expressed feelings of guilt and anger, and expressed sympathy with the cause of African Americans. While whites developed an improved appreciation of black history, "Roots" led many black viewers to rediscover their own genealogy.[43]

The broadcasts of "Roots" raised audience awareness of racial issues. But the effects of "Roots" and its sequel, "Roots: The Next Generation," were found to be highest among viewers who were already sympathetic to the program's content.[44] In fact, some already-prejudiced viewers were reinforced in their racial prejudices.[45]

"Roots" overcame the assumption of most television executives that "quality" television programs dealing with social causes could not achieve high audience ratings.[46] "Roots" addressed a historically relevant and controversial social issue and gained not only high audience ratings, but profoundly affected its viewers' attitudes.

THE GREAT AMERICAN VALUES TEST

On February 27, 1979, a thirty-minute television program called "The Great American Values Test" was broadcast by all three networks' local stations in the Tri-Cities area of eastern Washington state. Initiated by Professors Sandra Ball-Rokeach and Milton Rokeach of Washington State University in collaboration with Dr. Joel Grube of the Economic and Social Research Institute in Dublin, Ireland, the purpose of the television program was to test whether viewers changed their beliefs, attitudes, and behaviors related to certain human values which were discussed in the television program.

Hosted by Ed Asner (former star of the "Lou Grant Show") and Sandy Hill (a former anchor of ABC's "Good Morning America"), "The Great American Values Test" earned spectacular audience ratings (65 percent) in the Tri-Cities area.[47] The first part of the program discussed the nature of human values, and how social scientists measure them. The latter part of the program discussed three basic human values—"freedom," "equality," and "a world of beauty," forcing viewers to examine their commitment to these values, and to evaluate the intrinsic consistency/inconsistency of their value system. For example, Asner told viewers that in a given hierarchy of values, Americans ranked "freedom" as being a very important value, but "equality" as relatively less important (Table 14.3). Did this mean that Americans value their own freedom much more than the freedom of other people? The television program sought to investigate if viewers recognized inconsistencies in their belief systems, if such inconsistency produced dissatisfaction among viewers, and if such dissatisfaction led viewers to reassess and to change their belief systems to resolve the inconsistency.

"The Great American Values Test" included a proenvironment segment in which Asner and Hill pointed out that the value which Americans place on "a world of beauty" conflicts with their desire for material comfort. In a given hierarchy of values, environmentalists valued "a world of beauty" more highly than "a comfortable life."[48] Through such carefully prepared segments, viewers of "The Great American Values Test" were forced to examine their belief systems pertaining to certain human values.

To determine the impact of "The Great American Values Test," pre- and post-viewing data on certain human values (and their related attitudes and behaviors) were gathered from a sample of the television program's viewers and nonviewers. Those who watched the program demonstrated more egalitarian and pro-environment attitudes and behaviors, and ranked "free-

T A B L E	1 4 . 3

Hierarchical Ranking of Values by Americans, Including the Three Values Featured in "the Great American Values Test"

Rank-Order	Value
# 1	Family security
# 2	A world at peace
# 3	Freedom
# 4	Self-respect
# 5	Happiness
# 6	Wisdom
# 7	A sense of accomplishment
# 8	A comfortable life
# 9	True friendship
# 10	Salvation
# 11	Inner harmony
# 12	Equality
# 13	National security
# 14	Mature love
# 15	A world of beauty
# 16	Pleasure
# 17	An exciting life
# 18	Social recognition

SOURCE: S.J. Ball-Rokeach, M. Rokeach, and J.W. Grube, 1984, "The Great American Values Test," *Influencing Behavior and Belief Through Television* (New York: The Free Press), M. Rokeach, 1982. *Rokeach Value Survey* (Palo Alto, Calif.: Consulting Psychologists Press). Adapted with the permission of The Free Press, a division of Macmillan, Inc. Copyright © 1984 by Sandra Bell-Rokeach, Milton Rokeach, and Joel Grube.

dom," "equality," and "a world of beauty" higher in a given hierarchy of values.[49] Viewers (compared to nonviewers) donated four to six times more money to political causes related to the values of "freedom" and "equality" (such behavior was observed several months after the program's broadcast).

"The Great American Values Test" demonstrated that "when done right" even a thirty-minute television program could alter individuals' beliefs, attitudes, and behaviors related to certain socially desirable human values. What if such a program promoted socially undesirable behaviors? The ethical dilemmas in creating such prosocial programs as "The Great American Values Test" are discussed later in this chapter.

The Harvard Alcohol Project: A Designated Driver Campaign

A prestigious U.S. academic institution, Harvard University, lobbied Hollywood television producers to combat drunk driving in the United States. During 1988-1989, representatives of the Harvard School of Public Health worked closely with television network executives, producers, and scriptwriters to incorporate messages in prime-time television programs warning against drinking and driving. Dr. Jay Winsten, director of the Harvard Alcohol Project (HAP) in the Harvard School of Public Health, was inspired by designated driver behavior that he had observed in Sweden: Typically a group of friends selects one of their number to abstain from drinking alcohol so this designated driver can safely drive everyone to their home destinations.[50]

The Harvard Alcohol Project represents the rare case when the effects of a Hollywood lobbyist-type campaign were evaluated. During the 1988-1989 television season, seventy-seven different prime-time programs promoted the designated driver concept by including at least a few lines of dialogue. In some series, an entire show was devoted to the concept. For example, on an episode of "L.A. Law," Michael Kuzak (played by Harry Hamlin) asked a bartender to call his girlfriend "and tell the lady I need a ride home."[51] These dialogues were supplemented by public service announcements (PSAs) that encouraged designated driver behavior. The entire campaign was concentrated in the period between Thanksgiving and New Year's Day, a period of high alcohol consumption. Pre- and post-test data gathered from national samples of the U.S. adult population found (1) increased levels of awareness of the designated driver concept, and (2) somewhat higher levels of designated driver behavior.[52]

What factors contributed to this relative success of the Harvard Alcohol Project? Harvard representatives did not demand that the U.S. television networks drop their extensive advertising of beer and wine. The HAP's purpose was to attack drunk driving, not alcoholism. Further, the Harvard Alcohol Project did not ask for major changes in television program content, but just for certain adjustments which could be easily incorporated in one or more episodes.

How could "Hollywood lobbyists" become more effective in influencing network programming? Montgomery concluded from her research on Hollywood lobbyists that appreciating the constraints and commercial imperatives of the entertainment industry, establishing a local office in Hollywood, gaining personal friendships with television writers and directors, and suggesting episodes or scenes are the most effective strategies for success.[53]

ETHICAL DILEMMAS

Using the persuasive power of the entertainment-education strategy for planned social change presents several ethical dilemmas.[54] Ethics is a branch of philosophy which studies the rightness or wrongness of human conduct. Ethical communication upholds and protects an individual's freedom, equality, dignity, and physical and psychological well-being.

The entertainment-education approach presents at least four ethical dilemmas: (1) the prosocial content dilemma, that is, how to distinguish prosocial from antisocial content; (2) the sociocultural equality dilemma, that is, how to ensure that the prosocial media messages maintain socioeconomic equality among audience members; (3) the unintended effects dilemma, that is, how to respond to the unintended consequences of prosocial media, and (4) the prosocial persuasion dilemma, that is, how to respond to those individuals who argue that it is unethical to use the media as a persuasive tool for planned social change.

1. The prosocial content dilemma asks the ethical question: "Who will decide what is prosocial for whom?" In Third World countries, a national government usually decides what is prosocial. While certain national governments may abuse the media, others use the media more ethically for prosocial purposes. Assurance that the media will be used for prosocial purposes is not any greater in nations where private producers determine media content. Television producers and advertisers usually avoid addressing controversial social and educational issues.[55]

2. The sociocultural equality dilemma addresses the problem of providing an equal media treatment of various social and cultural groups. Sociocultural equality means regarding each social and cultural group with the same value or importance.[56] Ensuring sociocultural equality through prosocial television is problematic, especially in socioculturally diverse countries such as India. While the "Hum Log" television series confronted viewers' traditional beliefs about the status of women in Indian society, the viewers' ethnicity, linguistic background, and gender were found to determine beliefs about gender equality.[57] So television's treatment of all viewers as socioculturally "equal" in India represents an ethical dilemma.

3. The unintended effects dilemma arises when undesirable and unintended consequences result from the diffusion of prosocial messages. Many fear that media messages intended to promote sexual responsibility may encourage sexual promiscuity instead. For example, when the present authors showed the Tatiana and Johnny music videotape in their media effects class, pointing out how successful the rock music campaign was in persuading teenagers to say "no" to sex, a student replied: "I thought it said 'yes' to sex." Indeed, Tatiana and Johnny end their MTV segment with a rather sexy dance, while their words encourage sexual abstinence.

4. The prosocial persuasion dilemma addresses the question: Is it ethical to use the entertainment-education strategy as a persuasive tool for social change? It is virtually impossible to produce "value-free" or "socially innocuous" entertainment programs.[58] The idea that persuasive communication is unethical and therefore should be avoided denies the reality indicated by much past research. Television does persuade people; how much, is debatable. Even if 1 percent of a population is persuaded to change a belief or behavior because of watching a television series, that can be an important change.

However, the unequivocal promotion of persuasive communication to direct social change can also represent an untenable ethical position. When disagreement exists about the "rightness" or "wrongness" of certain media messages, what is considered "prosocial" by one group of people (whether that group represents the majority of the population or the highest court of the land), should not be uncritically promoted on the media. Whether or not it is ethical to use persuasive communication depends on the direction of social change, who decides the prosocial nature of a certain belief or behavior, and what effects the promotion of a certain belief or behavior are likely to have on an audience.

Thus the ethics of using entertainment-education as a persuasive tool for social change is inextricably intertwined with the three other ethical dilemmas that we previously discussed.[59]

F O O T N O T E S

1. A. Singhal, "Entertainment-Education Communication Strategies for Development," (Ph.D. dissertation, Los Angeles, University of Southern California, 1990).

2. W. DeJong and J.A. Winsten, *The Harvard Alcohol Project: A Demonstration Project to Promote the Use of the 'Designated Driver'* (Cambridge, Mass.: Harvard School of Public Health, 1990).

3. D.L Kincaid, R. Jara, P. Coleman, and F. Segura, "Getting the Message: The Communication for Young People Project," Washington, D.C.: U.S. Agency for International Development, AID Evaluation Special Study 56 (1988).

4. D.L. Paletz, R. Pearson, and D.L. Willis, *Politics in Public Service Advertising on TV* (New York: Praeger, 1977).

5. C.A. Atkin, "Mass Media Information Campaign Effectiveness," in R. E. Rice and W. J. Paisley, eds., *Public Communication Campaigns* (Newbury Park, Calif.: Sage, 1981), pp. 265-280.

6. A. Singhal and E.M. Rogers, *India's Information Revolution* (Newbury Park, Calif.: Sage, 1989a).

7. A. Singhal and E.M. Rogers, *India's Information Revolution*, 1989a.

8. E.M. Rogers, S. Aikat, S. Chang, P. Poppe, and P. Sopory, "Proceedings from the Conference on Entertainment-Education for Social Change," (Los Angeles, Calif.: University of Southern California, Annenberg School for Communication, 1989).

9. A. Bandura, *Social Learning Theory* (Englewood Cliffs, N.J.: Prentice-Hall, 1977).

10. E.M. Rogers, S. Aikat, S. Chang, P. Poppe, and P. Sopory, "Proceedings from the Conference on Entertainment-Education for Social Change," 1989.

11. E.M. Rogers, S. Aikat, S. Chang, P. Poppe, and P. Sopory, "Proceedings from the Conference on Entertainment-Education for Social Change," 1989.

12. D.L. Kincaid, R. Jara, P. Coleman, and F. Segura, "Getting the Message," 1988.

13. A. Singhal and E.M. Rogers, *India's Information Revolution*, 1989a.

14. D.L. Kincaid, R. Jara, P. Coleman, and F. Segura, "Getting the Message," 1988, p. 2.

15. E.M. Rogers, S. Aikat, S. Chang, P. Poppe, and P. Sopory, "Proceedings from the Conference on Entertainment-Education for Social Change," 1989.

16. D.L. Kincaid, R. Jara, P. Coleman, and F. Segura, "Getting the Message," 1988.

17. J.J. Bradac, R. Hopper, and J.M. Wiemann, "Message Effects: Retrospect and Prospect," in J. Bradac, ed., *Message Effects in Communication* (Newbury Park, Calif.: Sage, 1989), pp. 294-317.

18. A. Singhal and E.M. Rogers, *India's Information Revolution*, 1989a.

19. D.L. Kincaid, R. Jara, P. Coleman, and F. Segura, "Getting the Message," 1988.

20. D.L. Kincaid, J.G. Rimon, P.T. Piotrow, and P. Coleman, "The Enter-Educate Approach: Using Entertainment to Change Health Behavior," (paper presented at the Population Association of America, Denver, 1992).

21. A. Singhal and E.M. Rogers, *India's Information Revolution*, 1989a.

22. A. Singhal, E.M. Rogers, and W.J. Brown, "Entertainment *Telenovelas* for Development: Lessons Learned about Creation and Implementation," (paper presented at the International Association for Mass Communication Research, Sao Paulo, Brazil, 1992).

23. K.C. Montgomery, *Target: Prime-Time* (New York: Oxford University Press, 1989).

24. N. Vidmar and M. Rokeach, "Archie Bunker's Bigotry: A Study in Selective Perception and Exposure," *Journal of Communication*, vol. 24 (1), (1974), pp. 36-47; E. Tate and S. Surlin, "Agreement with Opinionated TV Characters across Cultures," *Journalism Quarterly*, (1976), pp. 199-203; P. Wander, "On the Meaning of 'Roots,'" *Journal of Communication*, vol. 27 (4) (1977) pp. 64-69; S. Ball-Rokeach, J. Grube, and M. Rokeach, "Roots: The Next Generation—Who Watched and with What Effect?" *Public Opinion Quarterly*, vol. 45 (1981), pp. 58-68.

25. N. Vidmar and M. Rokeach, "Archie Bunker's Bigotry: A Study in Selective Perception and Exposure," 1974.

26. C.L. Shefner and E.M. Rogers, "Hollywood Lobbyists: How Social Causes Get in Network Television," (paper presented at the International Communication Association Conference, Miami, Florida, 1992).

27. K.C. Montgomery, *Target: Prime Time*, 1989.

28. K.C. Montgomery, *Target: Prime-Time*, 1989.

29. E.L. Palmer, *Television and America's Children: A Crisis of Neglect* (New York: Oxford University Press, 1988).

30. H.F. Waters, "Watch What Kids Watch," *Newsweek* (January 8, 1990), pp. 50-51.

31. *Children's Television Workshop*, Corporate Profile, (New York: Children's Television Workshop, 1987), p. 6.

32. G.S. Lesser, *Children and Television: Lessons from "Sesame Street"* (New York: Vintage, 1974).

33. Lesser, *Children and Television*.

34. J. Piaget, *The Origins of Intelligence in Children* (New York: International Universities Press, 1952).

35. *Children's Television Workshop*, International Adaptations of "Sesame Street" (New York: Children's Television Workshop, 1988).

36. A. Tan, *Mass Communication Theories and Research*, 2nd ed. (New York: Macmillan, 1986), p. 288.

37. S.J. Ball and G.A. Bogatz, *The First Year of "Sesame Street": An Evaluation* (Princeton, N.J.: Educational Testing Service, 1970); G.A. Bogatz and S.J. Ball, *The Second Year of "Sesame Street": An Evaluation* (Princeton, N.J.: Educational Testing Service, 1971); *Children's Television Workshop*, 1988.

38. T.D. Cook and others, *Sesame Street Revisited* (New York: Russell Sage Foundation, 1975).

39. G.S. Lesser, *Children and Television*, 1974.

40. K.K. Hur and J.P. Robinson, "The Social Impacts of Roots," *Journalism Quarterly*, vol. 55 (1978), pp. 19-25.

41. Hur and Robinson, "The Social Impacts of Roots," 1978.

42. P. Wander, "On the Meaning of Roots," *Journal of Communication*, vol. 27, no. 4 (1977), pp. 64-69; J. Howard, G. Rothbart, and L. Sloan, "A Response to 'Roots': A National Survey," *Journal of Broadcasting*, vol. 22, no. 3 (1978), pp. 279-287; R.E. Balon, "The Impact of 'Roots' on a Racially Heterogeneous Southern Community," *Journal of Broadcasting*, vol. 22, no. 3 (1978), pp. 299-307.

43. Hur and Robinson, "The Social Impacts of Roots," 1978.

44. Hur and Robinson, "The Social Impacts of Roots," 1978.

45. S. Ball-Rokeach, S. Grube, and M. Rokeach, "Roots: The Next Generation—Who Watched and with What Effect?" 1981.

46. P. Wander, "On the Meaning of Roots," 1977.

47. S.J. Ball-Rokeach, M. Rokeach, and J. W. Grube, "The Great American Values Test," *Psychology Today*, (November 1984), pp. 34-41.

48. S.J. Ball-Rokeach, M. Rokeach, and J.W. Grube, "The Great American Values Test," November 1984a.

49. S.J. Ball-Rokeach, M. Rokeach, and J.W. Grube, "The Great American Values Test," November 1984a.

50. W. DeJong and J.A. Winsten, *The Harvard Alcohol Project: A Demonstration Project to Promote the Use of the 'Designated Driver'* (Cambridge, Mass.: Harvard School of Public Health, 1990).

51. N. Finke, "TV Series Join Crusade to Curb Drunk Driving," *Los Angeles Times,* (November 25, 1988) p. A-11.

52. J.A. Winsten, *The Designated Driver Campaign* (Cambridge, Mass.: Harvard School of Public Health, 1990).

53. K.C. Montgomery, *Target: Prime-Time,* 1989.

54. W.J. Brown and A. Singhal, "Ethical Dilemmas of Pro-Social Television," *Communication Quarterly,* vol. 38 no. 3 (1990), pp. 1-13.

55. K.C. Montgomery, *Target: Prime-Time,* 1989.

56. W.B.Y. Gudykunst and Y.Y. Kim, *Communicating with Strangers* (Reading, Mass.: Addison-Wesley 1984), p. 5.

57. W.J. Brown, "Effects of 'Hum Log,' a Television Soap Opera, on Pro-Social Beliefs in India" (Ph.D. dissertation, Los Angeles, University of Southern California, 1988); W.J. Brown and A. Singhal, "Ethical Dilemmas of Pro-Social Television," *Communication Quarterly,* vol. 38, no. 3 (1990), pp. 1-13.

58. E. Thoman, "Media Education: Agenda for the '90s," *Media Ethics Update,* vol. 2, no. 1 (1989), pp. 8-9.

59. W.J. Brown and A. Singhal, "Ethical Dilemmas of Pro-Social Television," 1990.

K E Y   T E R M S   A N D
C O N C E P T S

social change
public service announcement (PSA)
entertainment-education strategy
para-social interaction
Bandura's social learning theory
role model
prosocial behavior
antisocial behavior
sociocultural equality
"Hum Log" soap opera
"Sesame Street"
"Roots"
Great American Values Test
Harvard Alcohol Project

SUBJECT INDEX